Only This Much

Module I

- Company Secretarial Practice (CSP)
- Drafting, Appearances & Pleadings (DAP)

CS A. N. S. Vijay

Divya Mittal R. Ashwin R. Anand Venkatraman

A Learn Labz Compilation

KNOWLEDGE WORLD
KW Publishers Pvt. Ltd.
New Delhi

in association with

Learn Labz Knowledge Sharing Pvt Ltd
Chennai

2011 FIPBIA BEST PUBLISHERS AWARD (ENGLISH)

KNOWLEDGE WORLD

KW Publishers Pvt Ltd
4676/21, First Floor, Ansari Road, Daryaganj, New Delhi 110002

www.kwpub.com

ISBN 978-93-81904-17-6

With the blessings of my parents and God.

Published by Kalpana Shukla, KW Publishers Pvt Ltd,
4676/21, First Floor, Ansari Road, Daryaganj, New Delhi 110002

Printed and Bound in India

READERS OUR-GURUS
OUR-GUIDING-FORCE
OUR-PARENTS

OTM-DEDICATION

OTM-INSPIRATIONS

Mr.K.S.Anantharaman

Mr.K.Ramesh

Mr.M.R.Venkatesh

Dr.Chandratre

Mr.P.K.Jain

Ms.ShantiBalamurugan

Mr.S.Muralidhar

Mr.R.Giridharan

Mr.V.S.Datey

Mr.K.Vaitheeswaran

Mr.K.S.Ravichandran

Mr.M.Y.Khan

Mr.B.Ravi

OTM-ACKNOWLEDGEMENTS

N.Hariharan
K.S.SenthilRaani
SaiSundar
S.R.Sridhar
Sreevathson
Ramprasad
Alagarsamy
ShwetaBhargav
V.P.Palanichamy
ICSI-SIRC-Officials-Library
M.Sundar
Sajith
N.A.Srinivasan
Senthil
K.V.Hari
KetanThaker
K.SaiKumar
Nagapriya
ShivShankar
SarahArokiasamy
PradeepRamakrishnan
P.L.Manickam
K.ViswanathaReddy
M.Manoharan
N.Sridharan
P.V.Ramesh
R.Prakash
V.Kavitha
T.Balasubramanian
N.Priyadarshini
RajKumar
Baskar

Preface

The great response to our publication of first edition of the book **ONLYTHISMUCH FOR CS PROFESSIONAL PROGRAM** has been very gratifying. The numerous e-mail messages and letters from our readers and the students helped us to perceive their interest. We have also built up a large file of ideas based on the paradigm changes happened in the field of corporate laws since the publication of the first edition.

With more than 70 amendments made in the last year in corporate laws, the Ministry of Corporate Affairs has awakened and introduced a lot of changes and cast more responsibilities on the directors of all the companies and professionals like Company Secretaries, Charted Accountants and Cost Accountants. Enforcing stringent actions against defaulting professionals and also referring these matters to the respective institutes to take disciplinary actions against them, the Ministry of Corporate Affairs has also come out with voluntary guideline on the topics: Corporate Governance, Corporate Social Responsibility, and Sustainability for all companies in India. Even various departments of Government like Department of Public Enterprisers, Department of Telecom and Insurance has come out with various guidelines on these aspects. In addition, SEBI, Tax authorities and RBI have also given their amendments.

With the aid of all these information that we have gathered, including the pragmatic comments mailed by our readers, we have completely revised this book. The new subjects on Financial Management and Taxes are added to the earlier subjects on law in the first edition. Apart from the addition of the revised ICSI study material **2012**, objectives, one words, past exam question papers, the obvious changes in this second edition are the categorized Modules.

We have retained the usual friendly iconic approach of 'Only This Much' to give you a lucid explanation.

We are grateful to Mr.P.L.Manickam, Ms.Neha Agarwal, Ms.B.Prity and Mr.T.V.Rajaram for their contributions to this edition.

While reading the OBJECTIVES at the end of this book, ensure you read it thoroughly as it would also be helpful to answer 5 marks question in exams.

We hope your craving for knowledge and your thirst for passing is well balanced while reading the book. We are waiting for your tit-bits and ideas at onlythismuch@ lawlabz.com as they go a long way in motivating us. We are happy to attend to any of your queries. Do visit http://learnlabz.com for updates.

We are much delighted that **KW Publishers Pvt. Ltd.** has offered to publish the second edition of this book in four modules:

Module 1: **Company Secretarial Practice (CSP) and Drafting, Appearances & Pleadings (DAP)**

Module 2: **Financial Treasury and Forex Management (FTFM) and Corporate Restructuring & Insolvency (CRI)**

Module 3: **Advance Tax Law and Practice (ATLP) and Strategic Management, Alliances & International Trade (SMAIT)**

Module 4: **Due Diligence & Corporate Compliance Management (DDCCM) and Corporate Governance, Business Ethics & Sustainability (CGBES)**

We remain grateful to our readers and wish them the best in their progress.

We hope OnlyThisMuch will provide you a wholesome learning experience!!! This series deconstructs complex law, condenses important ideas so that u read less, understand more and write so much to enjoy laws.

With Best Regards,

A.N.S. VIJAY

ON BEHALF OF AUTHORS

CONTENTS

Company Secretarial Practice (CSP)

Drafting, Appearances & Pleadings (DAP)

Company Secretarial Practice (CSP)

- Drafting, Appearences & Pleadings (DAP)

Every company which is formed and registered under Companies Act shall comply with the requirements of Registrar of Companies (RoC). RoC is a public office where,

↳ A company can be incorporated;

↳ every company has to intimate compliances under Companies Act,1956;

↳ every person can find out details about the company in a prescribed manner.

So, there are lots of physical filing of things to RoC, which shall be made by a Company and now its automated (as electronic filing) by the famous project called MCA-21, a 21st century initiative. Hence under MCA-21, one can incorporate a company just by sitting before a computer and only by sitting before the computer.

In this chapter, we have tried to compile all the e-forms which shall be filed with RoC at all stages along with the mandatory attachments for the same. The whole basis of the subject Company Secretarial Practice lies in how well you can remember the name of the form, attachments which are mandatory and signing authorities. Read this chapter as many times as possible to get a hang of e-forms, thus understanding the whole of Companies Act.

MCA - 21

the 21st century initiative of Ministry of Corporate Affairs

Companies (Amendment) Act, 2006 read with
Company (Director Identification Number) Rules, 2006 read with
Companies (Electronic Filing and Authentication of Documents) rules, 2006 read with
'Scheme for filing of Statutory Documents and other Transactions by Companies in Electronic mode' with relevant amendments in Companies Act, 1956

MCA - 21 project is designed to fully automate all processes related to proactive enforcement and compliance of legal requirement under Companies Act, 1956 by Government of India (Ministry of Corporate Affairs) with Tata Consultancy Services (TCS).

This came into effect from 15th September 2006 for electronic filing of documents with Registrar of Companies (RoC).

↳ Physical filing of documents is discontinued with effect from 15-09-2006 and e-filing is compulsory from that date.

↳ Winding up procedures under Companies Act, not covered.

Filling of e-Form:

You can use 'Prefill' button to fill in the static data automatically like, the **Corporate identity Number (CIN).**

Once the CIN number is given, company details are automatically filled-in by using pre-fill function. CIN has 21 digits,

1st Digit	Listing Status
Next 5 digits	Economic Activity (Industry)
Next 2 digits	State of Registration
Next 4 digits	Year of Incorporation
Next 3 digits	Ownership
Last 6 digits	RoC Registration Number

Check form - Forms have built in facility of check and validation. It can be done offline too. Form can be modified by clicking 'Modify' button.

Pre-scrutiny - After 'check form' is done, it has to be digitally signed and online pre-scrutiny of forms is required to be done before the form is uploaded. It requires the system to be connected online.

DSC (Digital Signature Certificate) ensures that when a digital signature is attached to an electronically generated document, the document becomes locked for editing or alteration. **Digital certificate shall be of class II or class III specification.**

Breaking of big attachments:

The size of e-form cannot exceed 2.5 MB to facilitate filing.

Submission of original papers in physical form in some cases:

It was done away because of E-stamping.

CFC & FRONT OFFICES: Certified Filing Centres (CFC's) are set up by Professionals of ICSI, ICAI & ICAI-Cost for the purposes of enabling e-filing of corporate under Companies Act. While the services available from the MCA Facilitiation Centres (like Virtual & Physical Fron Offices) are FREE, the services provided by CFC's are for payments. The VFO (Virtual Front Office) is what the online e-filing mechanism under www.mca.gov.in/MCA21 whereas the PFO (Physical Front Office) is a facilitator to enable scanning & filing of documents that is set up in Metropolitan cities and will function till 2013.

E-STAMPING

Companies (Electronic Filing and Authentication of Documents) rules, 2006 read with scheme for Filing of statutory Documents and other transactions by Companies in electronic mode (Amendment) Scheme, 2009 enables Collection of stamp duty through MCA portal, thus, Dispensing with the requirement of physical filing. this scheme is optional now and will be made mandatory with effect from 1st January 2010. Currently e-forms 1 regarding incorporation, e-form 5 regarding authorised capital and e-form 44 regarding documents delivered by Foreign company can be electronically stamped.

In case of any other forms/documents where the stamp Duty payable is UPTO Rs.100/-, then E-FILING the scanned copy is sufficient PROVIDED the ORIGINAL is retained for 3 years. However, with regard to e-form 61 when filed for COMPOUNDING of offences u/s. 621A, physical copy shall be filed irrespective of value.

E-PAYMENTS

Accept payments of ANY value for MCA 21 services only in electronic mode:

However, in following cases challan mode for payment is allowed for amount less than Rs. 50,000/-.

- **Payment to 'Investor Education and Protection Fund' through 'Pay Misc. fee' functionality.**
- **Any payment made by user having category as 'Official Liquidator (OL) office.**
- **Any payment made by user having category as 'MCA employee'.**

E-CERTIFICATES BY ROC

The certificates and letters are issued under the Digital Signature of the Registrar of Companies. This has been implemented after taking into consideration Section 5 of the Information Technology Act, 2000 that gives legal recognition to digital signatures.

1. Director Identification Number (DIN) (2007 - December)
2. E - Filing with registrar of Companies (2007 - December)
3. E - forms DIN - 1 and DIN - 2 (2007 - December)
4. Filing of document in physical form in the context of MCA - 21 (2010 - December)
5. Corporate Identification Number (CIN) (2010 - December)
6. What are the key benefits of MCA - 21 Project? (2008 - December)
7. Bring out the salient aspects of the Companies (Director Identification Number) Rules, 2006 leading to the issue of Director Identification Number (DIN) (2010 - June)
8. What are the contents of Form 1A relating to availability or change of name? (2008 - June)

Registration of Digital Signature Certificate [called Role Check]

Only a Director / Manager / Secretary of the Company who's Digital Signature is registered along with DIN / PAN can file e-Forms and also such details can be viewed in "View Signatory Details" link.

Addendum to form already submitted:

Form with the given SRN. Payment of fees is not required while submitting addendum. The system will accept 'addendum' only when status of the form is 'in Progress'.

Status monitoring:

It can be done by tracking the SRN of the relevant form. It can be any of following, Waiting for payment or Transaction cancelled - payment not received or Work in progress or Waiting for user information Approval or Required resubmission or Rejected.

Statutory Provisions Regarding DIN:

A proviso has been inserted to section 253 of Companies Act w.e.f. 1-11-2006 to provide that no company shall appoint or reappoint a person as director, unless DIN has been allotted to him.

Sec 226A → Individual to be appointed as Director must apply for obtaining DIN in form **DIN-1**.

Sec 226B → CG will allot DIN within 1 month in prescribed manner. Sec 266C 4 a person cannot have more than one **DIN**.

Sec 266D → Director to inform DIN to company within one month from receipt of number from CG in form **DIN-2**.

Sec 266E → Intimate DIN to ROC within one week of receipt of information u/s 266D in form DIN-3.

Section 266G → penalty for contravention of above UPTO Rs. 5,000 PLUS Rs. 500 for every day during which the offence continues.

DIN 3 → for Directors appointed before 1st July 2007.

DIN 4 → for change in address or any other particulars.

The DIN-1 application can also be submitted online by the applicant himself using his DSC and has to be digitally signed by the practicing Chartered Accountants, Company Secretaries or Cost Accountants, who shall also verify the particulars of the applicants. Where the DIN 1 is VERIFIED by the professional, the DIN will be approved by the system IMMEDIATELY ONLINE. In other cases the DIN cell will examine the application and same shall be confirmed WITHIN 1 or 2 days. Penal action against the applicant and professional certifying the DIN application in case of FALSE INFORMATION / CERTIFICATION as per provisions of Section 628 of the Act will be taken in addition to action for professional misconduct and revocation of DIN, allotted on false information. The Mandatory fields in the DIN-1 eform are as follows:

- Name of the Applicant
- Father's name of the Applicant
- Date of Birth
- Income Tax Permanent Account Number (PAN) in case of all Indian Nationals
- Passport in case of all Foreign Nationals.

If a person has been allotted DIN, the said DIN shall also be used as DPIN for all purposes under Limited Liability Partnership Act, 2008 and VICE VERSA. If a person has been allotted both DIN and DPIN, his DPIN will stand cancelled and his DIN hereon will be used for both purposes.

Provisional Din:

The provisional DIN number is valid for 60 days from the date on which it was generated.

Search of Documents and obtaining copies:

The public documents filed with ROC are available for online public inspection by way of SEARCH based on CIN and on payment of prescribed fees of Rs.50/- per Company; the documents can be viewed/downloaded for 3 hours from logging in the website or for next 7 days, whichever is earlier. These are:

↳ Incorporation Documents

↳ Charge Documents

↳ Annual Returns and Balance Sheet

↳ Change of Directors

↳ Other Documents.

Forms 20B, 21a, 23aC, mandates DIN for all Directors of the Company.

Enumerate the search facilities in MCA - 21 (2009 - December)

LIST OF E-FORMS

Approval Services (Central Government)

Description	e-Form
Application to Central Government for modification in the matters to be stated in the company's balance sheet or profit and loss account pursuant to Section 211(4)	Form 23AAA
Application for exemption from attaching the annual accounts of the subsidiary companies pursuant to Section 212(8)	Form 23AAB
Application to Central Government for not providing depreciation pursuant to Section 205(2)(c)	Form 23AAC
Form of application to the Central Government for appointment of cost auditor pursuant to Section 233B(2)	Form 23C
Form for filing application for giving loan, providing security or guarantee in connection with a loan pursuant to Section 295	Form 24AB
Form of application to the Central Government for obtaining prior consent for holding of any office or place of profit in the company by certain persons pursuant to Section 314(1B)	Form 24B
Form for filing application for declaration as Nidhi Company with MoA & AoA containing only prescribed objects, details of financial dealings with non-members with Certificate from PCA & Auditors certificate as to compliance of MCA directions, Board Resolution & 2 directors Certificate that it has atleast 500 members on the date of application	Form 63
Form for filing application or documents with Central Government pursuant to Rule 2 of Companies (Application for extension of Time or Exemption u/s. 58A(8)) Rules, 1979 or explanation to qualification of cost audit report u/s. 233B(7)	Form 65
Form of application for approval for declaration of dividend out of reserves pursuant to Section 205A(3) & Rule 2 of Dividend out of reserve rules, 1975	Form
Form of application for removal of disqualification of directors pursuant to Section 274 Companies (Disqualification of Directors u/s. 274(1)(g) of the Companies Act, 1956) Rules, 2003	Form DD-C
Form of application for approval of the Central Government for the appointment of sole selling agents by the company pursuant to Section 294AA & Rule 2 of Companies (Appointment of Sole Agents) Rules, 1976	Form I
Form of application for approval of the Central Government for the appointment of sole buying agent by a company pursuant to Section 294AA & Rule 2 of Companies (Appointment of Sole Agents) Rules, 1976	Form II
Form for filing Cost Audit Report and other documents with CG pursuant to Sections 233B(4), 600(3)(b) and Rule 2(c) & 4 of Cost Audit (Report) Rules, 2001	Form I

Approval Services (Regional Director)

Description	e-Form
Application for confirmation by Regional Director for change of registered office of the company within the state from the jurisdiction of one Registrar to the jurisdiction of another Registrar pursuant to Section 17A	Form 1AD
Form for filing application to Regional Director pursuant to Sections 22, 25, 224(3) (7) & 297 or service of notice u/s. 391-394	Form 24A
Form for filing application for opening branch(s) by a nidhi company	Form 64

Approval Services (Registrar of Companies)

Description	e-Form
Application for approval of the Central Government for change of name or conversion of a public company into a private company pursuant to Section 21 or 31(1)	Form 1B
Form for filing an application with Registrar of Companies pursuant to Sections 166, 210, 394, 560, 621A	Form 61

Change Services

Description	e-Form
Application form for availability or change of a name pursuant to Sections 20 & 21	Form 1A
Application for approval of the Central Government for change of name or conversion of a public company into a private company	Form 1B
Notice of consolidation, sub-division, conversion, re-conversion, redemption, cancellation, re-classification, etc. or increase in share capital or increase in number of members pursuant to Sections 95, 97, 94A(2), 81(4)	Form 5
Notice of situation or change of situation of registered office pursuant to Section 146	Form 18
Particulars of appointment of managing director, directors, manager and secretary and the changes among them or consent of candidate to act as a managing director or director or manager or secretary of a company and/ or undertaking to take and pay for qualification shares pursuant to Sections 303(2), 264(2), 266(1)(a) & 266(1)(b)(iii)	Form 32

Charge Management

Description	e-Form
Particulars for creation or modification of charges (other than those related to debentures) including particulars of modification of charge by asset reconstruction companies in terms of SARFAESI Act, 2002 pursuant to Sections 125, 127, 130, 132 & 135 with 600	Form 8
Particulars for registration of charges for Debenture pursuant to Sections 125, 127, 128, 129, 130, 132, 134, 135 with 600	Form 10
Particulars for satisfaction of charges pursuant to Section 138 with 600	Form 17

Company Registration

Description	e-Form
Application or declaration for incorporation of a company pursuant to Sections 33 (1) & (2)	Form 1
Application form for availability or change of a name	Form 1A
Notice of situation or change of situation of registered office	Form 18
Declaration of compliance with the provisions of section 149(i)(a), (b) and (c) of the Companies Act,1956 pursuant to Section 149(1)(d)	Form 19
Declaration of compliance with the provisions of section 149(2)(b) of the Companies Act,1956 pursuant to Section 149(2)(c)	Form 20
Declaration of the compliance with the provisions of section 149(2A) and (2B) pursuant to Section 149(2A)(ii)	Form 20A
Particulars of appointment of managing director, directors, manager and secretary and the changes among them or consent of candidate to act as a managing director or director or manager or secretary of a company and/ or undertaking to take and pay for qualification shares	Form 32

Compliance Related Filing

Description	e-Form
Statement of amounts credited to investor education and protection fund pursuant to Rule 3 of IEPF (Awareness & Protection of Investors) Rules, 2001	Form 1
Return of allotment pursuant to Section 75(1) and for allotment of shares for consideration otherwise than in cash where agreement or contract is executed in writing	Form 2
Particulars of contract relating to shares allotted as fully or partly paid-up otherwise than in cash pursuant to Section 75(2) and for allotment of shares for consideration otherwise than in cash where NO agreement or contract is executed in writing	Form 3
Statement of amount or rate percent of the commission payable in respect of shares or debentures and the number of shares or debentures for which persons have agreed for a commission to subscribe for absolutely or conditionally pursuant to Section 76(1)	Form 4
Return in respect of buy Back of Shares	Form 4C
Statutory Report pursuant to Section 165	Form 22
Registration of resolution(s) and agreement(s) and postal ballots pursuant to Section 192 & 192A	Form 23
Information by Auditor to Registrar pursuant to Section 224(1A) [Sec 224(1B) also for Public Companies]	Form 23B
Return of appointment of managing director or whole time director or manager pursuant to Section 269(2) & Schedule XIII	Form 25C
Form for submission of documents with Registrar of Companies pursuant to Sections 44, 60, 77A, 488, 497, 509, 516, 551 & 555 read with Company Court Rules 313, 315, 327, 331, 335 & Acceptance of Deposit Rule 10.	Form 62
Report by a public company pursuant to Sections 274(1)(g) & Rule 5 of Companies (Disqualification of Directors u/s. 274(1)(g) of the Companies Act, 1956) Rules, 2003	Form DD-B

Provisions related to Managerial personnel

Description	e-Form
Form of application to the Central Government for increase in the number of directors of the company pursuant to Section 259	Form 24
Form of application to the Central Government for approval of appointment or reappointment and remuneration or increase in remuneration or waiver for excess or over payment to managing or whole-time director(s) or manager and commission or remuneration or expression of opinion to directors pursuant to Sections 198(4), 269, 309(3), 309(5B), 310, 311, 387, 388, 2(24), 4(7), 309(1)(b), 309(4)(a)-(b) & 316(4)	Form 25A
Form of application to Central Government for approval to amendment of provisions relating to managing, whole time or non rotational director with Copies of the proceedings along with board or general meeting resolution and NOC from Bank/FI, if any.	Form 25B
Form of application for removal of disqualification of directors	Form DD-C

Annual filing eForms

Description	e-Form
Form for filing annual return by a company having a share capital with the Registrar	Form 20B

pursuant to Section 159 Particulars of annual return for the company not having share capital pursuant to Section 160	Form 21A
Form for filing balance sheet and other documents with the Registrar pursuant to Section 220	Form 23AC
Form for filing Profit and Loss account and other documents with the Registrar pursuant to Section 220	Form 23ACA
Form for submission of compliance certificate with the Registrar pursuant to Section 383A & Rule 3(2) of Compliance Certificate Rules, 2001	Form 66

Other Forms

Description	e-Form
Form of Return to be filed with RoC pursuant to Section 187C(4)	Form 22B
Notice of address at which books of account are maintained pursuant to Section 209(1)	Form 23AA
Information to be furnished in relation to any offer of a scheme or contract involving the transfer of shares or any class of shares in the transferor company to the transferee Company pursuant to Section 395(4A)(a)(i)	Form 35A
Appointment or cessation of receiver or manager pursuant to Section 137 & 600 with particulars of No. of charges and Court order, as signed by Receiver/Manager along with SRN of Form 36	Form 15
Receivers or Managers abstract of No. of Receipts & Payments pursuant to Section 421, 424 & 600 with Charge ID & Instrument or Court order details, as signed by Receiver/Manager	Form 36
Application by an existing joint stock company or by an existing company (not being a joint stock company) for registration as a public limited or private limited or an unlimited company pursuant to Sections 565, 566, 567 & 568	Form 37
Registration of an existing company as a limited company pursuant to Sections 565(1), 567 (a) & (c) and 568(a)	Form 39
Particulars of persons or directors charged or specified for the purpose of Section 5 (f) & (g)	Form 1AA
Notice of Court or CLB order pursuant to Sections 17(1), 17A, 17(5), 79, 81(2), 81(4), 94A(2), 102(1), 107(3), 111(5), 141, 155, 167, 186, 391(2), 394(1), 397, 398, 445, 466 (under liquidation), 481 (under liquidation or dissolved), 559 & 621A	Form 21
Documents delivered for registration by a foreign company pursuant to Section 592	Form 44
Form of annual return of a foreign company having share capital pursuant to Section 600(3)(b)(i) & Rule 3 of application of Section 159 to Foreign Companies Rules, 1975	Form 1
Return of alteration in the charter, statute or memorandum and articles, address of registered or principal office & directors & secretary of foreign company pursuant to Section 593 (a)/(b)/(c)	Form 49
Form for filing addendum for rectification of defects or incompleteness pursuant to Rule 20A(3) of the Companies (Central Government's) General Rules and Forms, 1956	Form 67

The following are the new e-forms inserted recently:

1. Form 5INV for Statement of Unpaid & Unclaimed amounts pursuant to rule 3 of the Investor Education and Protection Fund (Awareness and Protection of Investors) Rules, 2001
   a. Companies are required to file the form annually within 90 days from the AGM date WITHOUT any filing fee.
   b. The Investor-wise details of unclaimed and unpaid amounts need to be uploaded on the IEPF portal using the excel template WITHIN 14 days of uploading this e-form & UPLOAD confirmation to be given.
   c. Total size of all the excel files uploaded in respect of a particular SRN cannot exceed 40 MB.
2. Form 14 for intimating the Registrar of Firms/ Registrar of Companies of conversion of the firm/ company into limited liability partnership
3. Form 23AC/ACA - XBRL for filing under eXtensible Business Reporting Format
4. Form CSR for reporting of compliances under MCA Voluntary Guidelines on Corporate Social Responsibility
5. Form FTE for closure of defunct companies u/s. 560 of Companies Act, 1956.

MCA has also introduced new facilities like:

1. Free Public Search of Trademark based on 45 classes as per Schedule to Trademarks Act through a link to the concerned website.
2. To verify details based on the Directors Identification Number (DIN) of Directors.

Following are not required to register DSC on MCA portal: [Role Check is NOT required]

- Attorney or pleader or advocate for the purpose of form 1.
- Authorised representative of a foreign Company.
- Charge-holder or assignee. However, recently banks & financial institutions are also mandated to do Role Check.
- Receiver or Manager in case of form 15 and form 36.
- Liquidator
- Person charged in case of form 1AA.
- Person filing form for a Company to be incorporated, for example form 1A, 1, 18, 24A, 32, 37, 39.
- Signatory of a section 25 Company

The email ID is required for the purpose of communication with the company/applicant. It has been made as a mandatory field for the following eforms:

- eForm 1A (email of applicant)
- eForm 18 (email of Indian company)
- eForm 44 (email of Foreign company)
- eForm 8 (email of charge holder)
- eForm 10 (email of charge holder)

E-FORM COMPLIANCE CHART

Every e-form shall be annexed with mandatory attachments, certified by Digital Signature and shall be filed online along with the prescribed fees. While reading the certification part in the table, carefully observe the highlighted "&". When it is written as Director & Secretary as signing authorities, then both of their signatures will be mandatory.

E-FORM	MANDATORY ATTACHMENTS	OPTIONAL ATTACHMENT	CERTIFICATION (signing authority)	PRIOR FILING & stamp duty
1	Memorandum, Articles, Details of Subscribers	No objection certificate in case there is change in promoters (first subscribers to the MoA)	PCS/PCA / Advocate/Attorney / director, manager or secretary of the company	Form 1A, Form 24A (for Sec 25 Co) (stamp duty to be paid). Simultaneously file Form 18 & 32
1A	**Part A:** Availability of Name **Part B:** Change of Name	Copy of board resolution or central government direction. No objection certificate, if any	Applicant or MD or director or manager or secretary of the company	DIN 1
1AA	Copy of Board Resolution		Person charged **&** MD or director or manager or secretary of the company	Form 23 or Z999999999
1AD	Copy of minutes of meeting, Copy of newspaper advertisement & details of prosecution filed against the company and its officers in default, if any.	Investor grievances, if any	MD or director or manager or secretary of the company	Form 23
1B	Minutes of members meeting. If change in name is due to change in main activity, then CA certificate of	Order for condonation of delay, Copy of any approval order, Copy of previous order for change of name.	MD or director or manager or secretary of the company	Form 1A for change of name; Form 23

	turnover from new activity.			
2	List of allottees as per the format & resolution for bonus shares or issue at discount, if any	<u>Note:</u> Same form for Chronological Events falling within 30 days of filing date.	MD or director or manager or secretary of the company & PCS or PCA or PCWA	Form 23, if any
3	Copy of Board Resolution		MD or director or manager or secretary of the company & PCS or PCA or PCWA	(stamp duty to be paid)
4	Contract for payment of commission, resolution for payment & consent of ALL directors of the company		MD or director or manager or secretary of the company	Also quote the Article No. which authorizes to pay commission
4C	Description of securities bought back by the company & Particulars relating to holders of securities before buy back	Special Resolution or Board Resolution	MD or director or manager or secretary of the company	Form 23, if any Form 62 (for filing of Form 4A) Government approval, if debt equity ratio is more than 2:1
5	Articles, if it is amended		MD or director or manager or secretary of the company & PCS or PCA or PCWA	Form 23, if any; SRN of maximum stamp duty paid already, if any or pay stamp duty
8	Instrument evidencing creation or modification of charge & Particulars of other charge holders in case of consortium finance or joint charge		MD or director or manager or secretary of Indian company & Charge Holder or Asset Reconstruction Company or its assignee or authorized representative of foreign company	

10	Copy of resolution authorizing issue of debenture series & Instrument evidencing creation or modification of charge			MD or director or manager or secretary of the company & trustee of debenture holders or charge holder & ARC/assignee & PCS or PCA or PCWA	
17	Letter from Charge holder stating full satisfaction			MD or director or manager or secretary of Indian company or authorized representative of foreign company & charge holder & ARC/assignee & PCS or PCA or PCWA	Charge Identification No. as per form 8/10
18	Board or Special Resolution (for existing companies), as the case may be			MD or director or manager or secretary of the company & PCS or PCA or PCWA	Form 1A (for new companies) Form 23 (for outside the local limits of city, town or village), Form 1AD (for RoC to RoC within state) Form 21 (state to state)
19	Copy of Prospectus	RBI approval	NBFC	Director or Secretary of the company or PCS	(Stamp duty to be paid)
		NHB approval	Housing Finance Company		
		IRDA approval	Insurance Company		
20	Statement in lieu of prospectus (SLoP) as per Schedule III	RBI approval	NBFC	Director or Secretary of the company or PCS	(Stamp duty to be paid)
		NHB approval	Housing Finance Company		
		IRDA approval	Insurance Company		
20A	Copy of Special	This is also for		Director or	(Stamp duty to be

	Resolution or CG approval letter in case of Ordinary Resolution	shifting for other objects to main objects by public company	Secretary of the company or PCS	paid)
20B	Annual Return as per Schedule V as on the date of AGM & approval letter for extension of financial year or AGM, if any.		MD or director or manager or secretary of the company & PCS or PCA or PCWA	As certified by PCS, if listed company Note: List of Shareholders & debenture holders as attachment or CD to RoC
21	Copy of court order of CLB or other authority with Petitioner No. & Order No. Note: Original Court or CLB order shall be filed with RoC		MD or director or manager or secretary of Indian company or authorized representative of foreign company & PCS or PCA or PCWA	Form 61 for compounding of offence. Form 8, 10, 17 [condonation of delay in charges], 18 [u/s. 17(1)], 21 [for condonation of delay in order], 23 [u/s. 102(1)] or any, if applicable, including payment of penalty, if any. Also Form 21 of Transferor Company for Amalgamation
21A	Annexure containing particulars of total amount of indebtedness as on date of AGM & details of present & past members		1 director & MD or director or manager or secretary of the company & PCS or PCA or PCWA	
22	Notice of statutory meeting, Abstract of Receipts & Payments & Details of preliminary expenses	Details of arrears, due on calls from directors & managers, details of commission & brokerage to director or manager for issue or sale of shares or debentures	1 director & MD or director or manager or secretary of the company & statutory auditor of the company	

COMPANY SECRETARIAL PRACTICE

22B	Declaration by person referred to in Section 187C (1) (2) & (3) with Name of Registered owner & beneficial holder or not		MD or director or manager or secretary of the company	Form I & II as per Rules
23	Copy of resolution along with Explanatory Statement u/s. 173, altered Memorandum or Articles & copy of agreement. Also attach the Notice of the Meeting.	**Fill necessary details for object clause amendment with new industrial activity & for voluntary winding up u/s. 484** Note: Same form for Chronological Events falling within 30 days of filing date unless otherwise it is an agreement.	MD or director or manager or secretary or liquidator of the company & PCS or PCA or PCWA	Form 21 (for object clause amendment filing with condonation of delay)
23AA	Copy of board resolution		MD or director or manager or secretary of the company	
23AAA	Copy of board resolution for exemption sought, indicating the specific para of Part II of Schedule VI with reasons & financial year	Recommendation of concerned Administrative Ministry, if any & RBI approval, in case of banking company	MD or director or manager or secretary of the company	Also to state whether similar exemption is given in Tax Audit Report, if not, with reasons
23AAB	Board resolution mentioning the names of subsidiary & their financial year under reference, copy of any previous approval order, documentary proof when	Attach adequate proofs in support of difficulties on account of internal disturbance to avail exemption. Further, irrespective of legal requirement of foreign subsidiary in foreign country, it has to audit its	MD or director or manager or secretary of the company	

	accounting years are different & documentary proof of subsidiary company pending cases or liquidation or non-finalisation of accounts	account to seek exemption		
23AAC	Certificate from Secretary or Director certifying that non-concealment or representation of relevant facts, Undertaking that no public issue or fresh deposits within 18 months, copy of board resolution & shareholding pattern of promoters & their relatives	Copy of concurrence of Administrative Ministry, if any	MD or director or manager or secretary of the company	Form 25A, if any or enter Z999999998
23AC	Copy of balance sheet authenticated u/s. 215 (with Balance Sheet Abstract) with Directors Report, Auditors Report, etc..., Statement of subsidiaries u/s. 212, if any, Statement of fact & reason for non-adoption of balance sheet or default in AGM, if any.	Attach Supplementary or Test Audit Report, if conducted u/s. 619(3)(b)	MD or director or manager or secretary of the company & PCS or PCA or PCWA	Form 66, if applicable & Form 23B for appointment of auditors. Ensure filing of Form DIN 3, Form 32 for all directors
23ACA	Copy of Profit & Loss Account	ITC code of products from	MD or director or manager or	

	duly authenticated u/s. 215 & Statement of subsidiaries, if any	Director General of Commercial Intelligence & Statistics, Kolkata	secretary of the company & PCS or PCA or PCWA	
23B	Copy of intimation received from the Company	**NO provision for re-submission or Addendum**	Statutory Auditor	
23C	Copy of CG order directing Cost Audit, Copy of board resolution & Copy of Certificate from Cost Auditor regarding 224(1B)	Letter to previous auditor informing the change, letter for extension of financial year, etc…	MD or director or manager or secretary of Indian company or authorized representative of foreign company	
24	Copy of board & members resolution for increasing the number of directors, members resolution for amending Articles, Details of present Board & proposed appointee with detailed justification, Minutes of general meeting of company with details of voting, Newspaper clippings as per Section 640B & No default certificate from CS or director	In case of negative covenants, NOC from bank or financial institution	MD or director or manager or secretary of the company	
24A	**<u>For Issue of license u/s. 25:</u>** Memorandum, Articles,		MD or director or manager or secretary of the company	Form 1A for Section 25 Company, Form 23, if any. (stamp duty to be

	Annexure V declaration under Companies Regulation, Declaration by PCS or PCA or Advocate or Attorney, Details of promoters & proposed directors, List of responsible positions of directors in other companies, Grounds of making application. **Kindly note,** in case of registered companies proposed to become Section 25 Company, then Future annual income & expenditure, Asset & Liability statement and financials for last 2 years. **<u>For to enter into contract u/s. 297:</u>** Copy of agreement with particulars of proposed contract, Copy of board resolution & detailed application **<u>For appointment of auditor u/s. 224(3):</u>** Copy of			paid for issue of license u/s.25)

	proceedings of the General Meeting **For removal of Auditor u/s. 224(7):** Copy of ordinary resolution, Copy of Special Notice, Copy of representation of Auditor. **For notice u/s. 391-394:** Complete copy of petition filed with High Court or NCLT **For rectification of name:** Copy of board resolution			
24AB	Copy of resolution indicating terms & conditions of proposal, Declaration that loan is not out of borrowed funds & no defaults are made in repayments & the said funds are not required for working capital atleast for a year, Copy of draft loan agreement, Copy of employees loan scheme, Copy of approved members resolution with explanatory statement, List of		MD or director or manager or secretary of the company & PCS or PCA or PCWA	372A compliance, if any

	directorships & shareholding pattern of both borrowing & lending company. **Declaration** from PCS or Statutory Auditor that the company has not defaulted in fixed deposits, dividend, debentures **&** is regular in filing forms under Companies Act **&** the proposal is in conformity with Section 372A. **Certificate** from PCS or PCA that the company has not defaulted any undisputed dues to CG			
24B	Copy of board resolution proposing appointment, Copy of employee rules or certificate from director/secretary that similar benefits are offered to other employees & Shareholding pattern	Copy of selection committee minutes, Particulars of employees with remuneration of Rs.50,000 or more per month and an undertaking from appointee that he/she will be in exclusive employment of the company and will not hold place of profit in any other company	MD or director or manager or secretary of the company	Form 23
25A	Part A [Profile of the Company] - Managerial Remuneration & Net profit for last	Part C [CG application] – While remunerating in the absence of inadequacy of	MD or director or manager or secretary of the company	

COMPANY SECRETARIAL PRACTICE

	3 years. Part B [Details of proposal] – Copy of Calculation sheet of Effective Capital under Schedule XIII, Copy of remuneration committee/board resolution, NOC from financial institution or declaration from Director/Secretary that there is no default, BIFR scheme, if any, Draft appointment agreement, Newspaper clipping, Visa copy, Professional Education certificate copy, 637B condonation copy, if any. Auditors certificate for compliance of 274 & PCS/PCA certificate for waiver of excess or overpayment.	profits or remuneration in excess of Section 198(1) or 309(3) with separate fees		
25C	Copy of Board Resolution. Certify that Schedule XIII is complied with	Shareholder resolution, if any	MD or director or manager or secretary of the company **&** PCS or PCA or PCWA	Form 23 for registration of agreement/resolution
32	Consent to act as director in case of public company should be verified.	Consent of the appointee, Declaration regarding qualification,	MD or director or manager or secretary of the company **&** PCS or PCA or PCWA	Form 1A (for New Company) & DIN 3, if date of appointment is on or before 30th June

	Evidence of payment of Stamp duty where directors agree to pay for qualification shares.	Evidence of cessation, if any. <u>Note:</u> Same form for Chronological Events falling within 30 days of filing date unless otherwise it is of the same person.		2007
35A	Details of transfer of shares by directors 2 years prior to offer, Statement of valuation, Auditors Certificate of offer, Statement with steps to be taken by transferee company to make the cash available and Statement of valuation of shares			Auditor of transferee shall certify the offer or recommendation is correct
37	Copy of the instrument constituting or regulating the company		MD or director or manager or secretary of the company	Form 1A
39	Part A [List of Equity & Preference shareholders] - pursuant to Section 567 & Schedule V Part B [Shareholders Resolution assenting to registration with limited liability] - pursuant to 565(1) provisio,		2 authorised directors of the company	Form 1A

	(vi) & (vii)			
44	List of persons resident in India as authorized to accept service of documents, Charter, Statutes or memorandum & articles or other instrument defining constitution of the company, Individual Director details with DIN, RBI approval letter & Power of attorney or Board resolution authorizing representatives	Details of Body corporate directors & Secretary	Authorised representative of foreign company	
1	Details of past & present members, debenture holders, directors, managers & secretaries, Verification by MD or Director & director or manager or secretary		Authorised representative of foreign company	
49	Copy of general meeting resolution, **Part A** [alteration in memorandum or articles] – Copy of amended documents, **Part B** [alteration in registered or principal office], **Part C** [alteration in particulars of		Authorised representative of foreign company	

	directors & secretaries] – Director returns.			
61	**In case of arrangement or amalgamation**, Board resolution, Amalgamation scheme, Copy of petition, Affidavit & detailed application. **In case of compounding**, Board resolution, power of attorney (Form 5 – CLB Regulations), Affidavit, General profile, Facts of case, Compliance, Prayer for compounding, & detailed application as per CLB Regulations. **In case of extension or exemption of AGM**, Board resolution, extension within 3 months & reasons for extension or exemption. Its applicable for **extension of financial year** also. **In case of declaring as defunct company,** NIL balance sheet,		MD or director or manager or secretary of Indian company or Authorised Representative of foreign company. In case of compounding by an individual not having DSC, PCS or PCA or PCWA	Form 23

COMPANY SECRETARIAL PRACTICE

	Indemnity bond, Affidavit & detailed application **In case application is filed pursuant to notice from RoC or Competent Authority,** copy of the same			
62	Copy of prospectus authenticated as per Sections 56 & 60 read with Schedule II, Copy of Statement in lieu of prospectus authenticated as per Section 44 read with Schedule IV, Form 4A, Deposit returns Rule 10, Company court rules forms 149, 152-154, 156-159.		MD or director or manager or secretary of the company. In case of Form 149 filing, Liquidator of the company.	Form 23 (stamp duty to be paid for forms 41, 149 & 154)
65	**In case of time extension or exemption of deposits,** detailed application along with Statutory Auditors certificate regarding non-contravention of any other provision of deposits & deposits held by the company are within limits &	Copy of Articles, audited accounts of company for last 3 years & demand draft for application fees	MD or director or manager or secretary of Indian company or authorized representative of foreign company	Cost Audit Report

	details about position of deposits in the company. **In case of cost audit report,** provide information & exemption or reservations & qualification, as given			
66	Compliance Certificate	**NO provision for re-submission or Addendum**	MD or director or manager or secretary of the company	
1 (IEPF)	Copy of challan evidencing the deposit of amount to IEPF		MD or director or manager or secretary of the company & PCS or PCWA or PCA or statutory auditor	Form 1 u/s. 205A (6) & (7)
-	No objection letter from company's lead financial institution & Board resolution supporting company's proposal		MD or director or manager or secretary of the company & PCS or PCA or PCWA	
I	Cost Audit Report as per CARR, 2001		Cost Auditor & MD or director or manager or secretary & a director of Indian company OR Cost Auditor & authorized representative of foreign company	Form 23C
I/II	Copy of proposed agreement for appointment of Sole Selling	Competitors & Company's share in India, Auditor Certificate from SSA	MD or director or manager or secretary of the company	Form 23

	Agent	certifying the expenditure, Interest or Directorship of SSA, inter se relationship with other SSA, break-up of sales during last 3 years, foreign shareholding & profits remitted during last 3 years. If SSA is a firm, then details of partners, investment & profit.		
DD-B	With Name of Directors & DIN		MD or director or manager or secretary of the company	
DD-C	Board Resolution and mention date & ground of disqualification		MD or director or manager or secretary of the company	Date of disqualification to be given
67			MD or director or manager or secretary of Indian company OR authorized representative of foreign company & MD or Director. If relevant form is certified by applicant or subscriber or advocate or attorney or pleader or Charge Holder or Asset Reconstruction Company or its assignee or trustee of debenture holder or receiver or person securing appointment or	Only for forms already filed & 'Pending for user clarification' (PUCL)

			auditor or liquidator or cost auditor or PCS or PCA or PCWA, **then** such person. **AND** by PCS or PCA or PCWA	

In what respect Form No. 25C is required to be filed and in addition to the official of the company who else has to digitally sign it and the purpose thereof? (2008 - June)

At an annual general meeting of a company held of 28th August, 2007, the following items of businesses were transacted:

(i) Adoption of audited balance sheet as on 31st March, 2007 and profit and loss account for the year ended on that date along with directors' and auditors' reports thereon.

(ii) Declaration of dividend on equity shares.

(iii) Re - Appointment of directors retiring by rotation.

(iv) Appointment of statutory auditors.

(v) Increase in authorised share capital of the company.

(vi) Amendment in articles of association of the company

(vii) Increase in the borrowing limits of the Board of directors under section 293(1) (d).

(viii) Shifting of registered office of the company from Kota (Rajasthan) to Jaipur (Rajasthan).

Being the Company Secretary of the company, you were advised by the Managing Director of the company to submit a note on the e - forms required to be filed with Registrar of Companies in respect of the above transactions.

Prepare the note desired by the Managing Director indicating the last date for filing of each e - form.

State the important features of electronic filing of documents under the Companies Act, 1956. Mention against the following e - forms, the subject matter for which these forms are meant:

(i) E - forms - 3

(ii) E - forms - 4C

(iii) E - forms - 24B (2009 - June)

State the matter along with relevant section(s) of the Companies Act, 1956 for which the following E - Forms are required to be filed:

(i) E - Form 1B

(ii) E - Form 20B

(iii) E - Form 23B

(iv) E - Form 25C (2010 - June)

Having understood the basic concepts of MCA and the forms that shall be filed, it is necessary to understand how to use this knowledge while reading further parts of the book. We have followed a different approach in this book. First, you will get to know the type of e-form, why is it required, what are all the attachements and who shall certify the same. After this, during the course of your study whenever you see any reference to your e-form, recollect the aforementioned points or recap again the first chapter to put it in your mind slot. The mandatory attachements to e-forms form the basis of major compliance under Company Secretarial Practice. Hence, while quoting any e-form, always mention the standard points of attachments, certification person etc. Whenever you see the word e-form, it would have been mentioned "comply with E-FORM COMPLIANCE CHART", which is the chart supra. This will solve most of the questions under this subject. Now, hurry back to the list of e-forms and start studying it with more attention!

Most of the concepts dealt under this chapter are either new or important to understand from the exam point of view. Remain updated.

Important Concepts

HAGUE CONVENTION

As per the provisions of Rule 16 of Companies Central Government General Rules & Forms, FOREIGN NATIONALS residing outside India in countries who are SIGNATORIES to the Hague Convention and seeking to REGISTER a company in INDIA, their signatures and addresses on the Memorandum of Association and proof of identity shall be NOTARIZED before the notary of the country of their ORIGIN and duly APOSTILLISED in accordance with the Hague Convention. Thus, the requirement of notarization by Indian Embassy is not required in such cases.

DEFECTIVE FORMS

Regulation 17 of Companies Regulations, 1956 now provides for an amended procedure regarding filing & processing of e-forms or documents under Companies Act, 1956,

1. RoC's will examine the defect in the form & COMMUNICATE to the applicant by e-mail or placing it on website WITHIN 60 days of filing EXCEPT where approval of Central Government or Regional Director or CLB or Court or other authority is involved;
2. Applicant shall RECTIFY the defect or re-submit the form WITHIN 30 days by filing e-form 67;
3. In case of e-forms regarding amendment of Object clause or shifting of Registered office, the time limit shall be 15 days;
4. In case of e-forms filed through Straight Through Process (STP) such as Balance sheet & Annual Returns, RoC can scrutinize at ANY time and may label it as DEFECTIVE, which shall also be rectified within 30 days;
5. On expiry of 15/30 days, RoC shall REJECT the e-form & record it as INVALID & inform the company or applicant accordingly;
6. Now, the company/applicant has the only option to follow a DENOVA process by submitting a FRESH e-form with ADDITIONAL filing fees without prejudice to other liability.

CONFIRMATION OF MINUTES

Honourable Supreme Court has passed a landmark decision in the case of Kerala State Electricity Board v. Hindustan Construction Company Ltd. regarding the confirmation of minutes. The essence of the judgment is as follows,

"The ACCURACY of the minutes and NOT the VALIDITY of the decision is there before the subsequent board meeting. Hence, once a decision is duly taken, it can only be changed by a SUBSTANTIVE resolution properly ADOPTED for such a change. Thus, NON CONFIRMATION of minutes in the subsequent meeting does NOT have any effect on the decision taken at the earlier meeting."

COURTS POWER TO GRANT RELIEF

Power of Court to grant RELIEF in certain cases: [SECTION 633]

- TO Directors / Officer (not being employee / Company)
- WHEN proceedings / apprehends - Negligence, default, breach of duty, misfeasance or breach of trust.
- NO relief shall be given from criminal proceedings

CONDITIONS to be satisfied:

- Show cause notice to ROC & Others.

  Court should be SATISFIED that

  1. Officer is liable.
  2. Officer has acted Honestly & Reasonably.
  3. Officer shall ought fairly to be excused.

CONDONATION OF DELAY & ADDITIONAL FILING FEES

Section 611 read with Schedule X of the Companies Act deals with payment of ADDITIONAL fees (not exceeding 10 times the fees) when document is filed BELATEDLY. If late fee is not paid, the document will not be deemed to have been filed.

Period of Delay	Fixed rate of additional fee
Upto 30 days	Two times of normal fee
More than 30 days and upto 60 days	Four times of normal fee
More than 60 days and upto 90 days	Six times of normal filing fee
More than 90 days	Nine times of normal filing fees

However, it shall be 2% of filing fee per month for delay UPTO 1 year and 2.5% for delay BEYOND one year in case of amendment of authorized capital as filed in e-form 5. Such payment of belated fee for DELAYED filing is WITHOUT prejudiced to any other liability specified in the Act for its filing. Say for instance, directors can be prosecuted even if Annual Return is filed belatedly with a late fee as it is without prejudiced to any other liability. Hence in such cases, it is advisable to file an application to Central Government for condonation of delay u/s. 637B (ie) such application shall be made if any document is not filed within specified time to RoC. However, no condonation application shall be made for filing e-form 25C for appointment of MD/WTD/Manager within Schedule XIII limits, instead additional fees shall be paid.

INVESTOR COMPLAINT FORM

MCA has introduced Investor Complaint Form (an e-form) for redressal of complaints. Separate forms shall be filed for every company and every complaint. Complaints regarding NBFC shall be filed with RBI and complaints regarding listed or plantation companies shall be filed with SEBI. The nature of complaints are classified into following,

1. Shares or dividend
2. Debentures or bond
3. Fixed deposits (non-receipt of amount)
4. Miscellaneous non-receipt
5. Non filing of return of cessation of a director in Form 32
6. Other like complaint of serious nature.

Interestingly, this form also has a CAPTCHA (Completely Automatic Public Turing test to tell Computers & Humans Apart) which requires the user to type letters or digits from a distorted image that appears on the screen to prevent spamming.

Defaulting Companies: Section 610 of the Companies Act, 1956 confers a right to any person to inspect any document kept with RoC such as the financials & returns of the company. Some companies are filing only their event based information with the Registrar of Companies without filing their UPTO date Balance Sheet and Profit & Loss Accounts and Annual Return. Therefore, such companies are DEPRIVING THE RIGHT of the public to inspect these basic documents.

If the Company has defaulted in filing up-to-date Balance Sheet, Profit & Loss Account and Annual Returns, then NO other filing EXCEPT certain event based filings shall be accepted from SUCH companies and also from OTHER companies where the director of SUCH company is a director. Auditors & Company Secretaries of such companies or any other practising professionals like CA/CS/CWA shall NOT issue any certificates TILL such defect is RECTIFIED and ACTION in case of default shall be taken. However, this DOES NOT apply to companies MARKED AS HAVING MANAGEMENT DISPUTE. The permissible filings are:

(a) Filing by Directors of defaulting Companies in respect of such companies:- E-forms 2, 3 *(for allotments)*, 8, 10, 17, (for charges) 5 *(for capital)*, 23 *(for resolutions requiring registration)* & 61 *(for compounding of offences)*.

(b) Filing by Directors of defaulting Companies in respect of Companies having the status of DORMANT COMPANIES:- E-forms 61 *(for compounding of offences)*, DIN-3, 32 *(for directors & secretary)*, 21 *(for orders)* & FTE *(for fast track exit schemes)*.

(c) Filing by Directors of defaulting Companies in respect of Companies having the status as ACTIVE IN PROGRESS companies:- E-forms DIN-3, 32 *(for directors & secretary)*, 2, 3 *(for allotments)*, 5 *(for capital)*, 21 *(for orders)*, 23 *(for resolutions requiring registration)*, 61 *(for compounding of offences)*, 23AC, 23ACA, 66, 20B, 21A *(for financials & returns)*, 23B *(intimation by auditors)* & FTE *(for fast track exit schemes)*.

COMPANIES MARKED AS HAVING MANAGEMENT DISPUTE:

1. Court or CLB directed to maintain STATUS QUO (to maintain the same state of affairs) with respect to forms & status of directors.
2. Where RoC is a party, Court or CLB has granted injunction/stay from taking document into record.
3. Where RoC is neither a party nor intimated, then the liability is on the parties for compliance.

MASTER CIRCULAR ON PROSECUTION OF DIRECTORS & COMPANY SECRETARY OF THE COMPANY

It is noticed that penal actions are also initiated against certain DIRECTORS WHO ARE NOT CHARGE with the responsibility, particularly in following cases: -

(a) Independent directors for Listed companies

(b) Government directors for public sector undertakings

(c) Various Public Sector Financial Institutions, Financial Institutions and Banks having PARTICIPATION IN EQUITY of a Company also nominate Directors to the Board of such companies.

(d) Directors nominated by the Government u/s. 408 of the Companies Act, 1956.

The Registrar of Companies should take extra care in examining the cases where ABOVE Directors are also identified as OFFICER IN DEFAULT. Such directors shall NOT be held liable for any act of omission or commission by the company or by any officer of the company which constitute a breach or VIOLATION of any provision of the Companies Act, 1956, and which occurred WITHOUT HIS KNOWLEDGE/CONSENT/CONNIVANCE attributable through board process. The BOARD PROCESS INCLUDES meeting of any committee of the Board and any information which the Director was authorized to receive as Director of the Board as per the decision of the Board.

POINTS TO BE CONSIDERED:

1. The above SAID violation can be concluded from examining Board Minutes book of the company by the INSPECTING OFFICERS.
2. If a director resigns and the company does not file Form 32 as required in terms of Section 302(2) of the Act, the RoC should enquire into such cases and try to find out whether such director has actually resigned or not. RoC can also get guidance from Regional Directors.
3. In case the status of a director, i.e. whether he is a nominee director or not, is not reflected in the Annual Return or other documents of the company, available with RoC, the same should be CROSS CHECKED with the Annual Report filed by the company.
4. The timing of the commission of offence is also material to identify the director's responsibility; and Form 1AB *(officer in default)* should also be checked in case any person has been charged by the Board under Section 5(f) with the responsibility of complying with some particular provision or in case any director has been specified by the Board under Section 5(g) of the Act (to be MD/WTD/Manager).
5. SPECIAL DIRECTORS appointed by BIFR under section 16 (6)(b) of SICA 1985, shall not incur any obligation or liability for anything done or omitted to be done in GOOD FAITH and in discharge of duties. Hence they shall be EXCLUDED in the list of officers in default.

Further, all Registrar of the Companies (RoC's) are requested to make a prayer before the Hon'ble Court to pass an order u/s. 614A(1) of Companies Act, while deciding the cases for violations and provisions of section 159/220 of the Companies Act, 1956 BY DIRECTING the accused for non-filing of documents within a specific time or for payment of additional filing fee SO THAT action as contemplated under penal provisions of Section 614A(2) of the Companies Act 1956 could be taken against the accused directors of the companies by RoC's.

OFFICERS IN DEFAULT u/s. 209(5), 209(6), 211 and 212 of the Act *[Annual Accounts related]*:

1. It can be MD/WTD/Manager, if any and in addition, the Company Secretary appointed u/s. 383A OR the per-

son who has been CHARGED with work of maintenance and preparation of ANNUAL ACCOUNTS in compliance with aforesaid provisions.

2. Where there is NO MD/WTD/Manager, EVERY DIRECTOR and the Company Secretary.
3. Any other OFFICERS AND EMPLOYEES charged by Managing MD/WTD/Manager or Board with specific responsibility.
4. Directors including Non-Executive Directors, officers and employees NOT CONNECTED with responsibility with the above provisions should NOT be arrayed as delinquent directors.
5. Where prosecution is required to be filed against any Government company, its directors/officers and Member of Parliament and Member of Legislator under the Companies Act, 1956, Registrar of Companies should seek PRIOR AUTHORIZATION of Central Government in terms of Section 621 of the Act.

PRE-CERTIFICATION BY PRACTISING PROFESSIONALS

Some forms require pre-certification by professional e.g. Practising CS, CA or ICWA to ensure its authenticity. In addition to the Digital Signature of the Company Official, a Professional also has to certify the same by affixing the Digital Signature. The e-Form Nos. **DIN-1, 1** (for declaration of dividend out of reserves & for Investor Education Protection Fund) **2, 3, 5, 8, 10, 17, 18, 20B, 21A, 23, 23AC, 23ACA, 24AB, 32** and **61** are required to be pre-certified.

Practicing professionals registered as Members of the professional bodies namely, ICAI, ICSI & ICAI (cost) are now to be responsible *(as mentioned above)* for submitting /certifying documents (to be signed digitally by them) and system would accept most of these document online WITHOUT APPROVAL by RoC or other officers of MCA (ie) taken on record through Straight Through Processing (STP) mode. To ensure the DATA INTEGRITY, there will be CHECKING of such submissions to guard against fraudulent filing. In addition to the PENAL ACTIONS against the companies and their officers in default for furnishing incorrect or false information in the documents as provided under the Companies Act, 1956, ACTION AGAINST SUCH PROFESSIONALS would also be taken on receipt of any complaint, anonymous or otherwise, in the following manner:-

1. Alleged wrong submissions: In such cases, QUICK ENQUIRY will be conducted by the concerned RD who will be assessing prima facie, cases of wrong doing by the professionals AFTER giving an opportunity of being HEARD.
2. This report will be submitted to e-Governance CELL of MCA. The CELL will inform in the concerned Professional Institute to initiate an enquiry *(for misconduct)* and complete the same within a MONTH'S TIME.
3. SIMULTANEOUSLY, the concerned professional shall be DEBARRED *(for 30 days or till final enquiry report form Institute)* and shall NOT be allowed to enter to submit any document on MCA Portal.
4. MCA will take a FINAL DECISION after considering the report so received.

The Members of ICSI, ICAI & ICAI-Cost discharge important economic functions and render services to the public. The CONFIDENCE of the public in the integrity of the members is vital. If any such member brings DISREPUTE to such Institutes, an action under PROFESSIONAL MISCONDUCT can be taken against them. Accordingly, Central Government has directed the following:

1. On information of arrest of such professionals by police or law enforcement agency, the Institutes shall get the details from such agencies (within 3 weeks) and initiate disciplinary action against them.
2. Following correct procedures, the Institutes shall take steps to pursue SUCH matters vigorously and bring them to a conclusion.

3. The Institutes shall continuously MONITOR press reports & take note of matters bring DISREPUTE to the profession and LIST OUT such members in their websites & official journals.

CRITERIA FOR DECLARING PUBLIC FINANCIAL INSTITUTION (PFI) U/S. 4A

1. A Company or Corporation should be established under a Special Act or the Companies Act being Central Act AND registered as Infrastructure Finance Company (IFC) with RBI or as an Housing Finance Company (HFC) with National Housing Bank AND has a NETWORTH of Rs. 1,000 crores.
2. Main business of the Company should be Industrial/Infrastructural Financing. The Company must be in existence for at least 3 years and their financial statement should show that their income from Industrial/Infrastructural financing exceeds 50% of their income.
3. However, relaxation can be given to Central/State Public Sector Undertakings in case of the above.
4. Anyother financial institution applying for declaration as PFI shall also fulfill the aforesaid criteria.

ROC'S & REGIONAL DIRECTORS

Under MCA, there are 6 Regional Directors and about 25 RoC offices. In certain places like Shimla, Jaipur, Nainital, Ranchi, Bilaspur, Cuttack & Patna, there is "Roc-cum-Official Liquidator's" office. The Regional Directors are:

1. Northern Regional Director, Noida
2. North Western Regional Director, Ahmedabad - for Rajasthan, Gujarat, Madhya Pradesh, Chhattisgarh and Dadra & Nagarhaveli.
3. Southern Regional Director, Chennai
4. South Eastern Regional Director, Hyderabad - for Karnataka & Andhra Pradesh.
5. Western Regional Director, Mumbai
6. Eastern & North Eastern Regional Director, Kolkata

XBRL FILING

"Extensible Business Reporting Language" (XBRL) means a standardised language for communication in electronic form to express report or file financial information by the companies under the Act. This method of filing with RoC for financials of a company in e-forms 23AC & 23ACA for Balance Sheet & Profit & Loss is MANDATED for all Companies listed with any Stock Exchange(s) in India and their Indian subsidiaries; Companies with Paid-up capital of Rs.5 crores or above; Companies with Turnover of Rs.100 crores or above.

"Taxonomy" means in XBRL an ELECTRONIC DICTIONARY for reporting the business data as approved by the Central Government in respect of any documents or forms indicated in this Companies (Filing of documents and forms in XBRL) Rules, 2011.

Thus, these are some general points which are very important. Keep it mind and quote it at the appropriate places, if necessary.

This chapter is approached in a unique way.

- First, it lists resolutions for which e-form 23 shall be filled.
- Next, it lists provisions which mandate special resolution in chrono logical order. Kindly learn this list by heart, remember all other acts require only Ordinary resolution.
- The chapter details the Secretarial practice for every item mandating special resolution.

Note: Whenever Special resolution is mandated, please remember it is preceded by a Board meeting which seeks the approving for holding a General meeting where in the Special Resolution is passed. This is followed by filling the e-form 23 along with the attachments as mentioned in the E-FORM COMPLIANCE CHART above.

The second segment of this chapter deals with the items which shall be done only through postal **Ballot** for a listed company. Here again the list of items mandating postal ballot is given and further explained.

The third segment of this chapter items with the items which requires ordinary resolution. Everywhere the relevant legal provision for the same are also explained, It is highly advisable to be thorough with the basic provisions of Companies Act before reading this chapter. You can also refer Only This Much for CS Executive Program for the said purpose.

The last portion of this chapter gives and explains other legal provisions regarding general meeting which are not covered elsewhere.

General Meeting Resolution

NO.	ORDINARY RESOLUTION	SPECIAL RESOLUTION
1	Law dictates cannot be 'concentrated'. If Act prescribes Ordinary Resolution, thenSpecial Resolution cannot be mandated	Law dictates cannot be 'diluted'. If Act prescribes Special Resolution, then Ordinary Resolution will not suffice.
2	Vote cast FOR should be GREATER than Vote cast AGAINST. "For [>] Against"	Vote cast FOR should be NOT LESS THAN 3 times the Vote cast AGAINST
3	E-Form 23 to be filed, if it is u/s. 192.	e-Form 23 is a mandatory requirement u/s. 192
4	Notice need not communicate the intention	Notice shall communicate the intention to pass it as special resolution as per Section 189.
9	Chairman can exercise his right of CASTING VOTE, if AoA authorizes.	Not applicable.

RESOLUTIONS REQUIRING REGISTRATION

According to Section 192, every company must file with the ROC copies of following resolutions and agreements (i.e.) it requires registration.

RESOLUTIONS	AGREEMENTS
1. ALL Special Resolutions 2. Board resolution regarding Managing Director [appointment / re-appointment / amendment / variation in terms] 3. Ordinary resolution u/s. 293(1)-(a), (d) & (e) 4. Ordinary resolution u/s. 294 for appointing SSA 5. Ordinary resolution u/s. 484 for voluntary winding up 6. Resolution binding all members of a class, whether agreed or not by all 7. Resolution agreed by all members but requires, ↳ Special resolution or ↳ Particular majority UNDER the Act or Articles.	1. Agreement regarding Managing Director [appointment / re-appointment/ amendment / variation in terms] 2. Agreement for appointment of Sole Selling Agent (SSA) 3. Agreement binding all members of a class, whether agreed or not by all 4. Agreement agreed by all members but requires, ↳ Particular majority UNDER the Act or Articles.

Procedure for registration:

Step 1	File e-Form 23 WITHIN 30 days to RoC
Step 2	ALONG WITH, Certified True Copy of, [signed by officer of Company] ● Notice & resolution / agreement; ● Explanatory Statement annexed to the Notice
Step 3	Pay requisite filing fee
Step 4	Annex such resolution & agreement with every copy of Articles, if it has the effect of altering Articles.

LIST OF SPECIAL RESOLUTIONS

Whenever special resolution is passed file e-form 23 within 30 days to roC along with copy of notice, extract of resolution, explanatory Statement and filing fees following the procedure given under EFORM ComplianCe CHart.

To alter the object clause [Section 17]
To change the name of the company [Section 21]
To OMIT Limited or Private Limited from the name of the company [Section 25] (i.e.) to change the name of the charitable organization
To alter the Articles [Section 31]
Buy Back of securities exceeding 10% of Paid up equity capital & Free Reserves [Section 77A] Issue of sweat equity [Section 79A]
Issue of further pre-emptive shares [Section 81(1A)]; (i.e.) further issue NOT to be offered as Rights issues; **in this case, where no such special resolution is passed, then ordinary resolution with CG approval may be obtained.**
Conversion of loans or debentures into shares [Section 81(3)]
Creation of Reserve Capital [Section 99]
Reduction of share capital [Section 100]
Approval of variation of rights of shares of special class of shares [Section 106]
To change the registered office outside the local limits of town [Section 146]
To commence new line of business (i.e.) transfer from other objects to Main Objects by a Public company [Section 149]. **in this case, where no such special resolution is passed, then ordinary resolution with CG approval may be obtained.**
To keep the registers at a place outside the registered office [Section 163] and to enable inspection of the same
To authorize the payment of interest out of share capital [Section 208] for ventures not made profitable over a considerable period such as construction contracts
To appoint auditors of Companies in which 25% of Subscribed Capital is held singly/jointly/in combination by CG/SG/Government Company/Public Financial Institution/Insurance Company/ Nationalised banks and Financial Institutions, 51% of its capital is held by SG [Section 224A]. though it is an ordinary business, it requires special resolution.
To request CG for investigation into the affairs of the company and to appoint inspectors [Section 237(a) (i)]
To appoint sole selling agents by company with Paid-up capital of Rs.50 lakhs [Section 294AA]
To fix remuneration of directors , where article requires Special Resolution [Section 309(1)] To pay
commission to non-executive directors [Section 309(4)]
make liability to director or manager unlimited [Section 323]
To make inter-corporate loans and investments [Section 372A]
To apply to the court for winding up [Section 433]
To wind up the company voluntarily [Section 484]

Power of Liquidator to sell company's property for shares [Section 494]
Powers of Liquidator in Voluntary Winding up [Section 512]
Arrangement when binding on company & creditors [Section 517]
Liquidator to exercise power u/s. 546
Disposal of books & papers [Section 550]
Deed of Settlement by Company registered under Part IX of the Act [Section 579]

CHANGE OF OBJECT CLAUSE

MAIN OBJECTS	ANCILLARY OBJECTS	OTHER OBJECTS
Which the Company proposes to carry on Incorporation	Incidental Objects to attain the Main Objects	Which the Company may carry on at a Future Date
For any amendment in Object Clause, Special Resolution to be filed in e-Form 23 within 30 days to RoC		

Commencement of new business by public company

For carrying on any activity mentioned in the other objects clause [ie, commencing a new business by transferring from other objects to main objects] which is not germane to the business in main object clause [sec 149 (2a)], the following to be done:

(Not applicable to Private Companies)

- Special Resolution or where special resolution is not passed. Ordinary Resolution with CG approval may be obtained.
- e-Form 23 within 30 days shall be filed
- Declaration in e-Form 20A to be filed.

Note: Hence, Section 149 is not applicable to a private limited company, it can start a new business just by passing a board resolution.

Note: For the purpose of amending the Situation / Object Clause, any one of the clauses in section 17(1)(a)-(g) should be fulfilled,

1. To carry on business more economically / efficiently;
2. To attain its maintain purpose by new / improved means;
3. To enlarge / change area of operations;
4. To carryon some business advantageously combined;
5. To restrict / abandon objects specified in Memorandum;
6. To sell / dispose, whole / part of undertaking-s of the Company
7. To amalgamate with any other Company

OBJECT CLAUSE - During Incorporation & Amendment

The Object clause determines the BUSINESS of the company. The nature of the company will change based on the object clause. If the Company's main business is finance, housing finance, chit fund, leasing, investments, securities or combination thereof, then NAME of the company should be INDICATIVE of such related financial activities, viz., Chit Fund/ Investment/ Loan, etc.; Further if the object of the company is to carry on the business of Banking, Investing in other entities (NBFC), Insurance or to practice the profession of Architecture, Chartered Accountancy, Cost Accountancy & Company Secretaries, then the concerned Registrar of Companies/LLP shall incorporate the same only on production of **IN-PRINCIPLE APPROVAL / NOC** from the concerned regulator/professional Institutes (RBI, IRDA, Council of Architect, ICAI, ICWAI & ICSI).

Meetings to be Convened	: Board Meeting & General Meeting
Approvals	: Special Resolution / ordinary with CG in some cases
Applicable Section	: Section 17
E - Forms	: 20A, 23 **(postal Ballot for listed companies)**

1. Issue notice of meeting as per Section 286 to every director.
2. Convene a Board Meeting to consider the proposal to amend the Object Clause and for that purpose, ↳ fix the day, date, place and time of EGM; ↳ approve the draft notice and explanatory statement; ↳ authorize any one of the Director or Secretary of the Company to issue the Notice.
3. The minutes of the meeting to be entered into the minutes book within 30 days of the meeting.
4. Issue the Notice by giving such period as required under the Act read with Articles; Issue notice of the general meeting to - Members - Directors - Auditors - Stock Exchanges
5. Hold the General Meeting on appointed date and pass the following Special Resolution. Prepare & sign the Minutes within 30 days of meeting. RESOLVED THAT, subject to such approvals as may be necessary, Clause III of the Memorandum of the company be altered by inserting therein new sub-clauses in Clause III thereof as set out below: ...[here set out the new sub-clauses concerning new businesses] ...
6. File e-Form 23 with prescribed fees within 30 days of the Resolution & file declaration in e-form 20A; follow E-FORM COMPLIANCE CHART for other details.
7. Obtain Registration Certificate from the RoC, as only then the amendment will take effect.

Note:

1. Private company can shift from OTHER OBJECTS to MAIN OBJECTS by passing Board Resolution itself.
2. Public company shall pass Special Resolution or Ordinary resolution with Central Government approval to shift from other objects to main objects.

Draft the specimen resolutions along with requisite explanatory statement, wherever necessary, for transacting the following items of business indicating the kind of meeting at which each resolution is to be passed and the type of resolution required for Alteration of objects clause. (2008 - June)

Change of name shall NOT be allowed to a Company which is defaulting in filing its due Annual Returns or Balance Sheets or which has defaulted in repayment of matured deposits and debentured and/or interest thereon.

The facility of name approval through Straight Through Processing (STP) is available an additional system check for ascertaining the similarity with any registered trademarks or if any two words of such name matches exactly with the name of any other Company name, then such e-form 1A will be transferred to processing in non-STP mode.

To enable processing e-form 1A in STP mode, the application should contain [NOUN-NAME] + [ACTIVITY-BUSINESS] + [LTD/P LTD].

If the name through STP mode is approved by the system upto 11.00 AM on any working day, then the incorporation set of forms like e-forms 1, 18, 32 will be accepted only after 7.00 PM of the same day.

If the name through STP is approved after 11.00 AM, then the incorporation set of forms will be accepted only after 7.00 PM of the any next working day.

In determining whether a proposed name is identical with another, the following shall be DISREGARDED as per Name Availability Guidelines, 2011:

1. The plural version of any of the words appearing in the name;
2. The type and case of letters, spacing between letters and punctuation marks;
3. Joining words together or separating the words, as this does not make a name distinguishable from a name that uses the similar, separated or joined words. Such as Ram Nath Enterprises Pvt. Ltd. will be considered as similar to Ramnath Enterprises Pvt. Ltd.;
4. The use of a different tense or number of the same word, as this does not distinguish one name from another. Such as, Excellent Industries will be similar to Excellence Industries and similarly Teen Murti Exports Pvt. Ltd. will be to Three Murti Exports Pvt. Ltd.;
5. Using different phonetic spellings or spelling variations, as this does not distinguish one name from another. For example, J.K. Industries limited is existing then J and K Industries or Jay Kay Industries or J n K Industries or J & K Industries will not be allowed. Similarly if a name contains numeric character like 3, resemblance shall be checked with 'Three' also;
6. The addition of an internet related designation, such as .COM, .NET, .EDU, .GOV, .ORG, .IN, as this does not make a name distinguishable from another, even where (.) is written as 'dot';
7. The addition of words like New, Modern, Nav, Shri, Sri, Shree, Sree, Om, Jai, Sai, The, etc., as this does not make a name distinguishable from an existing name such as New Bata Shoe Company, Nav Bharat Electronic etc. Similarly, if it is different from the name of the existing company only to the extent of adding the name of the place, the same shall not be allowed. For example, 'Unique Marbles Delhi Limited' cannot be allowed if 'Unique Marbles Limited' is already existing;
8. Such names may be allowed only if no objection from the existing company by way of Board resolution is produced/ submitted;
9. Different combination of the same words, as this does not make a name distinguishable from an existing name, e.g., if there is a company in existence by the name of "Builders and Contractors Limited", the name "Contractors and Builders Limited" should not be allowed;
10. Exact Hindi translation of the name of an existing company in English especially an existing company with a reputation. For example, Hindustan Steel Industries Ltd. will not be allowed if there exists a company with name 'Hindustan Ispat Udyog Limited';

CHANGE OF NAME:

Meetings to be Convened	: 2 Board Meeting & General Meeting
Approvals	: Special Resolution & Central Government
Applicable Section	: Section 21
E- Forms	: 1A, 23, 1B

1. Issue notice of meeting as per Section 286 to every director.
2. Convene the Board Meeting to consider and approve the proposed name and authorise Company Secretary to file e-form 1A to seek availability of name.
3. The minutes of the meeting to be entered into the minutes book within 30 days of the meeting.
4. Company Secretary shall file e-form 1A by paying prescribed fees of Rs.1000/-.
5. On receiving name availability, in consultation with the Chairman fix date, time and venue to hold another Board meeting for transaction following business: To fix the time, date and venue and place of an extra-ordinary general meeting and approve the draft notice (along with explanatory statement under section 173(2) of the Act) for the following purposes: i To change the name of the company (Section 21) and, consequently, to alter the memorandum in respect of the name (Section 16); ii To alter the articles of association in respect of the name (Section 31). This will be applicable if public is converted into private.
6. Issue notice of the general meeting to - Members - Directors - Auditors - Stock Exchanges
7. Hold the General Meeting to pass above resolutions.
8. The minutes of the meeting to be entered into the minutes book, initialed on each page and signed on last page by the Chairman along with the date within 30 days of the meeting. (Section 193) (note: minutes of Board meeting to be entered in minutes book within 30 days but can be signed even after that, usually in the next Board meeting. Whereas in case of general meeting it has to be entered and signed within 30 days)
9. Send altered Memorandum and Articles of Association to stock exchange along with a copy of the proceedings of the general meeting
10. File the following forms with attachments & certifications as per E-FORM COMPLIANCE CHART a. e-form 23 (Special Resolution) b. e-form 1A (Change of Name) c. e-form 1B (CG approval)
11. On approval, ROC will issue new Certificate of Incorporation.
12. Issue general notice in Newspaper and inform all concerned persons including stock exchange
13. Arrange a new common seal and get approved in meeting of BoD.
14. Enter new name in name boards of the company, registers, stationeries, letter heads, etc.

CHANGE OF NAME BY SECTION 25 COMPANY:

Meetings to be Convened	: 2 Board Meeting & General Meeting
Approvals	: Special Resolution & Regional Director
Applicable section	: Section 25
E - Forms	: 1A, 24A

E-Form 24A requesting for a license to be granted u/s 25 to a company which is proposed to be incorporated as a company, with limited liability, but without theaddition to its name of the word 'Limited' or the words 'Private Limited' as thecase may be [Regulation 3].

1. Issue notice of meeting as per Section 286 to every director.
2. Convene the Board Meeting to consider and approve the proposed name and authorise Company Secretary to file e-form 1A to seek availability of name.
3. The minutes of the meeting to be entered into the minutes book within 30 days of the meeting.
4. Company Secretary shall file e-form 1A by paying prescribed fees of Rs.1000/-.
5. On receiving name availability, in consultation with the Chairman fix date, time and venue to hold another Board meeting for transaction following business: To fix the time, date and venue and place of an extra-ordinary general meeting and approve the draft notice (along with explanatory statement under section 173(2) of the Act) for the following purposes: File e-Form 24A to Regional Director requesting for a license to be granted u/s. 25 to a company which is proposed to be incorporated as a company, with limited liability, but without the addition to its name of the word 'Limited' or the words 'Private Limited' as the case may be as per Regulation 3 with documents as per Regulation 4.
6. Issue notice of the general meeting to - Members - Directors - Auditors - Stock Exchanges
7. Hold the General Meeting to pass above resolutions.
8. The minutes of the meeting to be entered into the minutes book, initialed on each page and signed on last page by the Chairman along with the date within 30 days of the meeting. (Section 193)
9. File the following forms with attachments & certifications as per E-FORM COMPLIANCE CHART a. e-form 23 (Special Resolution) b. e-form 1A (Change of Name) c. e-form 24A (CG approval)
10. On approval, ROC will issue new Certificate of Incorporation.

ALTERATION OF ARTICLES OF ASSOCIATION:

POWER TO AMEND ARTICLES, IS SUBJECT TO,

- Consistency with Statute & Laws;
- Consistency with MoA of the Company;
- Increase prospectively the liability of Members ONLY with Written Consent;
- Not to nullify a Contractual Obligation;
- Central Government approval, when Public Co is converted into Private Company.

Type of Meeting	: General Meeting
Approval	: Special Resolution
Applicable Law	: Section 31 of the Act
E - Forms	: 23

1. Hold Board meeting for transaction following business: a. Resolution by simple majority for alteration of Articles. b. To fix the time, date and venue and place of general meeting and approve the draft notice (along with explanatory statement under section 173(2) of the Act) of the general meeting for passing special resolutions for alteration of Articles of Association.
2. Send to stock exchanges the particulars of alteration of Articles of Association.
3. Issue notice of the general meeting to - Members - Directors - Auditors - Stock Exchanges
4. Hold the General Meeting to pass following resolution, RESOLVED THAT, subject to such approvals as may be required, the articles of association of the Company be altered in the manner set out below: *(a)* By inserting in the articles the following new articles [here state the article to be inserted]: *(b)* By deleting in article [number] the words ['words to be deleted']; *(c)* By substituting for the existing article [number] the following article: [here state the article to be inserted]; and *(d)* By deleting in article [number] the words ['words to be deleted'] and substituting therefore the words ['words to be inserted'].
5. Send to stock exchanges the proceedings of the meeting.
6. File with the ROC within 30 days of passing the special resolution and follow E-FORM COMPLIANCE CHART

> Draft specimen resolutions along with necessary explanatory statements, wherever required, for transacting the following items of business indicating the kind of meeting at which each resolution is to be passed and the type of resolution required for alteration of articles by addition / insertion of a new article. (2007 - June)

BUY BACK OF SECURITIES EXCEEDING 10% of Paid up Equity Capital & Free RESERVES:

Type of Meeting : General Meeting

Approval : Special Resolution

Applicable Law : Section 77A of the Act

E - Forms : 23, 4A, 4B, 4C & E-FORM COMPLIANCE CHART

(Postal Ballotfor Listed Companies)

Refer Buy Back under Companies Act as dealt at the end of this part of the book.

Sample Special Resolution for buy-back of securities of Listed Company

RESOLVED THAT

(1)	Pursuant to the provisions of section 77A and 77B and other applicable provisions of the Companies Act, 1956 and SEBI (Buyback of Securities) Regulations, 1998 and Article __ of the Articles of Association of the Company, and also subject to the approval of SEBI, the Company do buyback from the shareholders of the Company fully paid-up Equity Shares of Rs. 10 each constituting up to .... % of the total existing paid-up equity share capital of the Company
(2)	The buyback as aforesaid shall be completed within a period of 12 months from the date hereof from the existing shareholders on a proportionate basis through the tender offer; or through book building or any other method at Board's discretion
(3)	The Board of Directors is authorised to determine the time frame for such buyback and the specific price for the buyback of the equity shares of the Company as aforesaid at a price not exceeding Rs. ___ (Rupees __________ only) per equity share, for which purpose, the Board is authorised to invest a maximum sum of Rs. _________ (Rupees _______________ only) towards buyback as aforesaid, provided that the maximum amount does not exceed 25% of the paid-up capital and free reserves of the Company and the said amount towards funding the buyback be drawn out of free reserves/share premium account of the Company.
(4)	The Board of Directors is authorised to do all such acts, deeds, matters and things including the appointment of Intermediaries incidental to the implementation of the scheme of buyback as also to prefer all applications to the appropriate authorities, parties and the institutions for their requisite approvals as also to initiate all necessary actions for such questions or difficulties whatsoever whichmay arise in the matter and take all such steps and decisions in this regard as it may in its absolutediscretion deem fit, necessary or proper.

EXPLANATORY STATEMENT FOR THE RESOLUTION

The Company wishes to add value for its shareholders by fresh initiatives, including a Share Buyback program. Even after premature redemption of approximately Rs. _____ crores debt in recent months, the Company continues to have a cash surplus of approximately Rs. _____ crores that is deployed in financial investments. Since the Company does not presently envisage any major investments and continues to enjoy heavy cashflows from its present business, it believes that it is in a position to return upto Rs. _____ crores of cash to its shareholders. The Board of Directors has approved the proposal for the buyback at its meeting held on

The buyback as aforesaid can be implemented by the Company as per Companies Act and SEBI Regulations as follows,

- The maximum amount that will be utilised for the buyback of shares would be Rs. __ crores considering the maximum price stated in the resolution.
- Considering all circumstances the Board presently expects the price range for the purpose of buyback between Rs. ___ and Rs. ___ per equity share.
- The Company proposes to buyback its shares upto a maximum of __________ equity shares constituting upto 25% of its issued and paid up equity share capital of the Company.
- The aggregate shareholding of the promoters and of the directors of the promoter companies and of persons who are in control of the Company including directors of the Company as on the date hereof is _______ equity shares constituting ___ % of the issued share capital of the Company.
- Neither the promoters nor the persons in control of the Company intend to tender the shares held by them in the proposed buyback.

ISSUE OF SWEAT EQUITY SHARES

Type of Meeting	: General Meeting
Approval	: Special Resolution
Applicable Law	: Section 79A of the Act
E - Forms	: 23, 3 **(postal ballot for listed company)**

"Sweat equity shares" means equity shares issued by the company to employees or directors at a discount or for consideration other than cash for providing know-how or making available rights in the nature of intellectual property rights or value additions to company.

It is to retain the talent of the work force, now-a-days, companies in IT and ITES sectors are issuing sweat equity shares and ESOP / ESPS. It may be noted that ESOP is an option which may or may not be exercised by the employees by converting them into shares by paying the stipulated amount where as sweat equity shares are equity shares issued at discount or consideration otherwise than cash [Independent valuation to be done].

Sweat Equity Shares. (2007 - December)

Conditions for issuance of sweat equity shares:

1. Shall be authorised by a special resolution specifying the number of shares, current market price, consideration, if any, and the class or classes of directors or employees to whom it is issued;
2. Shall be issued after 1 year of commencement of business;
3. Unlisted companies to follow Unlisted Companies (issue of sweat equity shares) rules, 2003:
   - ↳ Separate resolution in the general meeting shall be obtained in case of grant of shares to identified employees and promoters, during any 1 year, 1% or more of the issued capital (excluding outstanding warrants and conversion).
   - ↳ Shall maintain a separate register entering the details.
   - ↳ Issue of sweat equity shares for more than 15% of paid up capital or of value Rs. 5 Crores, whichever is higher, only with the prior approval of the Central Government.
   - ↳ Sweat equity shares to be issued to employees and directors
   - ↳ Shall be at fair price calculated by an independent valuer;
   - ↳ Shall be locked in for 3 years from the date of allotment.

4. Copy of the valuation report shall be sent with the notice of the general meeting along with justification for the issue.
5. Explanatory statement and Directors report shall contain specified details relating to sweat equity shares.
6. Sweat equity shares issued to managerial personnel for consideration otherwise than cash (which does not take the form of an asset which can be carried to the balance sheet of the company) shall be included while computing the limits of managerial remuneration.
7. Board of Directors shall at AGM place before the shareholders a certificate from the auditors / PCS that sweat equity shares have been allotted in accordance with the resolution.
8. Listed companies to comply with SEBI (Issue of Sweat Equity) Regulations, 2002.
   - The issued sweat equity shares shall be subject to lock-in for 3 years.
   - Each transaction of sweat equity issue shall be voted by separate resolution.
   - Pricing shall be higher of average weekly high & low prices during last 6 months or 2 weeks.
   - Certificate from Auditors that issue is made according to the Regulations shall be placed before shareholders.

PROCEDURE TO ISSUE SWEAT EQUITY SHARES (LISTED COMPANIES):

1. Decide before convening a Board Meeting, the number of shares, their current, market price and consideration , if any and the class or classes of directors or employees to whom such of Sweat Equity Shares are proposed to be issued.
2. Convene a Board Meeting after giving the notice to the directors of your company as per section 286 to consider the proposal of issue of Sweat Equity Shares and to fix up the date, time, place and agenda for the General meeting and pass an special resolution for the same.
3. Issue notices in writing at least 21 days before the date of the meetings for the general meeting with suitable explanatory statement as per schedule to the Regulations
4. The Proposed Special Resolution must specify the number of shares, their current market price and consideration, if any and the class or classes of directors or employees to whom such Sweat equity shares are to be issued.
5. The explanatory statement to the notice and the resolution for approving the issuance of sweat equity should inter alia contain the following the information: ● the total number of shares to be issued as Sweat equity. ● the current market price of the shares of the company.
6. If the Sweat equity shares are to be issued by the listed companies to its promoters as defined in SEBI (Substantial Acquisition of shares and takeovers) Regulation, 1997, obtain the approval of shareholders, ● By ordinary resolution in general meeting. ● also through postal ballot.
7. Hold the general meeting and pass the special resolution for issue of sweat equity shares to employee and directors.
8. File the special resolution with the concerned ROC with explanatory statement in e- form 23 within 30 days and e-form 3, follow E-FORM COMPLIANCE CHART
9. Forward 3 copies of the notice and a copy of the proceedings of the general meeting to the stock exchange within 7 days of issue.

ISSUE OF FURTHER PRE-EMPTIVE SHARES NOT AS RIGHTS ISSUE

Type of Meeting	: General Meeting
Approval	: Special Resolution or Ordinary Resolution with CG approval
Applicable Law	: Section 81(1A) of the Act
E - Forms	: 23 & E-FORM COMPLIANCE CHART

As per Section 81, any public company issuing shares AT ANY TIME

↳ after 2 years from the date of incorporation OR

↳ 1 year from the date of first allotment of securities,

SHALL issue them only to existing holders in proportionate basis (Rights issue) UNLESS issuance to others (Preferential issue) is authorized by "special resolution" OR "ordinary resolution with CG approval".

Preferential Issue: Unlisted companies can make private placement of equities or any other convertible instrument on complying with section 81(1A) read with Unlisted Public Companies (Preferential Allotment) Rules, 2003.

Preferential Allotment MEANS allotment of shares or other instrument convertible into shares INCLUDING hybrid instruments convertible into shares on PREFERENTIAL BASIS made pursuant to Section 81(1A) of the Act.

Conditions for Preferential Allotment:

1. Articles should authorise the issue and allotment with respect to offer or invitation made earlier should have been COMPLETED by filing a complete final prospectus with total capital raised and final closing price after closing of issue with RoC & SEBI, if applicable..
2. The persons to WHOM offer is proposed shall be UPTO 49 (in number) as per Section 67 of the Act. Otherwise, it shall be treated as a PUBLIC OFFER and provisions of SEBI shall apply. Purusuant to this offer, the company shall NOT release any public advertisements or utilise any MEDIA, marketing or distribution channels or use agents to inform the public AT LARGE about such offer.
3. Where warrants are issued on a preferential basis with an option to apply for and get the shares allotted, the issuing company shall determine beforehand the price of the resultant shares.
4. Issue the notice to convene a General meeting. The Explanatory statement to the notice shall contain details like no. of shares, object of issue, class of shareholders to whom it is allotted, intent etc...Further, the Statutory auditors / PCS shall certify that the issue of the said instruments is being made in accordance with the Rules. Such certificate shall be laid before the meeting of the shareholders convened to consider the proposed issue. The Special resolution authorizing the board to make preferential issue shall be passed mentioning the name & description (address, occupation & their father's name) of the proposed allottees and it shall be ACTED UPON within 12 months.
5. The monies payable on subscription shall be received through cheque or demand draft or through banking channels & NOT by cash. The monies so received shall be kept in SEPARATE bank account and shall be utilised ONLY FOR adjustment against allotment of securities OR repayment of moneis where company is UNABLE to allot.
6. On such receipt of money, the company shall ALLOT within 60 days OR REPAY within NEXT 15 days OR REPAID with interest @ 12% p.a after SUCH period.

Preferential Issue / QIP: Listed company making preferential issue or make qualified institutional placement (QIP) [made only to QIB] shall comply with sec 81(1A) and shall comply with Chapter VII or Chapter VIII of SEBI (ICDR) Regulations, 2009 respectively, which includes pricing provisions, lock-in conditions, time within which the resolution as to be acted upon, certification etc…

Kindly note, in case of public company the approval under this section is mandatory for all types of issues such as Sweat equity, ESOP, etc…(i.e.) all such issues which are not in the nature of public issue or rights issue or bonus issue.

Further issue of shares by private limited Company, as may be decided by Board of Directors, UNLESS Articles provides OTHERWISE, as Section 81 is NOT applicable to Private Company.

So, a PRIVATE LIMITED COMPANY need not allot shares WITHIN 60 days of receipt of consideration. However, if the consideration is from a non-resident, FEMA prescribes allotment to be made WITHIN 180 days of receipt. Otherwise, **they can show the sum under SHARE APPLICATION MONEY PENDING ALLOTMENT *(NOT exceeding Issued capital & to the extent is NOT refundable; otherwise it is to shown as a NON-CURRENT liability)* in Balance Sheet for a REASONABLE period of time *(NOT exceeding 7 years, as then it shall be transferred to IEPF)***. Further Schedule VI requires DISCLOSING terms of allotment, period of allotment & REASONS for non-allotment in the NOTES *(for all companies)*. Recently, a provisio is added in Section 68 of Income Tax Act, 1961 *(which comes into effect from 1st April 2013)* which states that any explanation offered by the COMPANY & the resident INVESTOR as regards the nature and source of any sum credited SO shall be deemed to be NOT SATISFACTORY, then it will be treated as an INCOME of the previous year. However, this provisio is NOT applicable to venture funds.

CONVERSION OF LOANS OR DEBENTURES INTO SHARES

Type of Meeting	: General Meeting
Approval	: Special Resolution
Applicable Law	: Section 81(3) of the Act
E - Forms	: 23, 10

For issuance of **debentures** or **loans** raised with a **option** to convert into equity shares at a later date, Sec 81(1) & 81(1A) to be complied with UNLESS:

- terms of issue contains such a term for conversion;
- Authorised by special resolution or issued to / raised from the Government or any institution specified by CG in this behalf; Comply with Public Companies (Terms of Issue of Debentures or raising of Loans with Option to convert such Debentures or Loans into Shares) Rules, 1977 OR approval of CG shall be obtained.

Procedure for Issue of Debentures with Right of Conversion into Shares

1. Draft a debenture trust deed; In case of Public issue, prepare prospectus and file it with SEBI.
2. Convene a Board meeting to approve the proposal and approve the draft notice to call for a General Meeting
3. At a general meeting, pass a special resolution relating to the issue and consequential mortgage of assets. Resolutions will be passed at this stage, if considered necessary, for increasing the authorised capital and amendment of Articles. File e-form 23 and follow E-FORM COMPLIANCE CHART.
4. The trust deed will be placed before the Board and execution thereof under the common seal will be approved. The trust deed will be stamped and signed accordingly. The trust deed and the issue will be registered under the Indian Registration Act.
5. File e-Form 10 with RoC & follow E-FORM COMPLIANCE CHART. The certificate of registration granted by the RoC should be endorsed on every debenture certificate.

Swan Limited was sanctioned a term loan of ₹ 15 Crore by Fantastic Bank Limited with a stipulation of conversion of loan into equity. The company could not repay the loan as stipulated. As per one of the conditions of sanction, the bank now wants to exercise the right of conversion of ₹ 5 crore loan into equity. State the procedure for the same. (2009 -December)

CONVERSION OF LOANS OR DEBENTURES INTO SHARES

Type of Meeting : General Meeting

Approval : Special Resolution

Applicable Law : Section 99

E - Forms : 23

Reserve Capital is a reserve liability. This will arise if the company has NOT called up the balance portion of capital which is known as UNCALLED CAPITAL. Such uncalled capital is an ASSET of the company which can be used as security to raise loans. This capital can be converted into RESERVE CAPITAL by passing a special resolution. In that event, such capital can be called only during WINDING up of the company.

REDUCTION & VARIATION OF CAPITAL

Type of Meeting : General Meeting

Approval : Special Resolution

Applicable Law : Section 100 to 107

E - Forms : 23, 21 & EFORM COMPLIANCE CHART

Form : Company (Court) Rules

Refer the detailed procedure in the chapter Reduction & Variation.

1. State the resolution & procedure for variation in the member's rights. (2007 - June) (2008 - December)
2. Draft the specimen resolutions along with requisite explanatory statement, wherever necessary, for transacting the following items of business indicating the kind of meeting at which each resolution is to be passed and the type of resolution required for reduction of share capital of the company from ` 20 Crore to 15 Crore. (2008 - December)
3. Variation of members rights is hanging like Damocles' sword (the sword that was suspended by a hair over the head to make one realize how active the person should be) on the members in the present liberalized global economy." Do you agree with this statement in India context? Support your answer with reasons. (2010 - December) As an equity holder, one has to keep their eyes & ears open, as company has the right to vary shareholders right to give more voting right to a particular class of holders, excluding others.

SITUATION CLAUSE

↳ Memorandum will mention only the STATE in which the Registered Office of the Company is situated.

↳ e-Form 18 (in every case) is filed for change of address of the company with police jurisdiction within 30 days to RoC.

↳ As per Sec 146, company should have a registered office at the time of commencement of business or within 30 days of incorporation whichever is earlier.

Within CITY	**Within STATE [City to City]**	**Within STATE [RoC to RoC]**	**Within INDIA [State to State]**
Board Resolution	Special Resolution	Special Resolution and Regional Director (RD)	Special Resolution and Company Law Board approval

Within STATE [RoC to RoC]	**Within INDIA [State to State]**
↳ Apply in e-Form 1AD along with prescribed fees to RD; ↳ RD to confirm within 4 weeks of application by way of order; ↳ File such order with RoC within 2 months; ↳ RoC to issue Fresh Certificate of Registration within 1 month of filing.	↳ Registered post Notice to ↳ creditors with 'amount due' ↳ proposed change of address ↳ proposed petition to CLB. ↳ An advertisement is published in 2 newspapers [Regional & Nation-wide]. ↳ File petition with CLB after 1 month of advertisement but within 2 months of Regd Post Notice. ↳ File e-form 21 with RoC

1. Draft the specimen resolutions along with requisite explanatory statement, wherever necessary, for transacting the following items of business indicating the kind of meeting at which each resolution is to be passed and the type of resolution required for Shifting registered office within the same city. (2007 - December)
2. You are the Company Secretary of All time Favourites Limited a listed company, and the Managing Director of your company wants to know the procedure for shifting of registered office from Mumbai to Pune. Prepare a note for him. (2009 - December). This is from RoC to RoC; as Mumbai & Pune have different RoC, though both fall under Maharashtra; similarly Chennai & Coimbatore has different RoC's, though both fall under Tamilnadu.
3. Decent Dealing Limited wants to shift it registered office from 21, Sadashiv Peth, Pune to 16, Nagindas Master Road, Mumbai. State the procedure to carry out this intention of the Board considering the fact that the State of Maharashtra has two Registrars of Companies one at Pune and other at Mumbai (2007 - December)
4. Aman Limited has resolved at its annual general meeting to shift its registered office from Mumbai to some other place in the State of Maharashtra, which falls in the jurisdiction of other Registrar of Companies. In terms of Section 17A, Aman Limited filed e - Form 1AD with Regional Director along with enabling fee and the following documents:
   (i) Certified copy of minutes of the annual general meeting; and
   (ii) Certified copy of newspaper advertisement.

After scrutiny of the filed form, the Regional Director rejected the request of Aman Limited. In terms of provisions of 17A, what remedy is available to Aman Limited? (Clue: Regional director approval is not obtained)

SHIFTING REGISTERED OFFICE FROM ONE STATE TO ANOTHER:

Type of Meeting : General Meeting

Approval : Special Resolution + Central Government

Applicable Law : Section 17, 18, 19, 146

E - Forms : 18, 23 **(Postal Ballot for listed companies)**

Earlier, when the companies is shifting its Registered office from one state to another, it was required an approval from Company Law Board. Recently, this power is shifted to Central Government, which in turn has delegated the same to RoC. MCA is in the process of evolving the procedure to grant the approvals. Finally, RoC will issue the Registration Certificate within 1 month and the change of registered office shall be effective from the date of issue of registration certificate.

MAINTAINING REGISTER NOT AT REGISTERED OFFICE & INSPECTION

Type of Meeting : General Meeting

Approval : Special Resolution + CLB

Applicable Law : Section 163 & Articles

E - Forms : 23

Register of Members & Debenture holders and their Index can be maintained at ANY OTHER PLACE within city where Registered Office is situated, if such place is approved by Special Resolution and ADVANCE intimation shall be given to RoC. This is to enable SUB-CONTRACTING with Registrar & Share Transfer Agents (RTA). Further, a member or debenture holder is entitled to inspect SUCH registers & indexes at Registered office of the company, hence enable it for inspection at least 2 hours in a day at the Registered office by providing an inspection time in ARTICLES. It was held that a member is entitled to get a list of registered shareholders too apart from extracts.

Model letter giving the intimation of proposed resolution regarding change of place of keeping Register of Members

ABC Limited

Registered office: ...

Date: ……………..

The Registrar of Companies

Dear Sir,

Subject: Notice under clause *(iii)* of the proviso to section 163(1)

We enclose a certified true copy of the notice of general meeting scheduled to be held on ... At that meeting it is proposed to pass a special resolution under the proviso to section 163(1) of the Companies Act, 1956 for keeping the Register of Members, Index of Members, Register of Debenture holders, Index of Debenture Holders and Copies of all Annual Returns together with the copies of certificates and documents required to be annexed thereto under sections 160 and 161, at ………, instead of at the registered office of the company.

Yours faithfully,

For ABC Limited

Company Secretary

PAYMENT OF INTEREST OUT OF CAPITAL:

Type of Meeting	: General Meeting
Approval	: Special Resolution + CG
Applicable Law	: Section 208
E - Forms	: 23

When Dividend is PAID OUT of Paid-up Capital, it is said to be **INTEREST** OUT OF Capital. It is only for,

↳ Ventures which CANNOT be made profitable for a lengthy period;

WHEN ?

Yes, it is only in the case of projects with huge investment which in turn takes time to generate income.

1. The Company may pay INTEREST on the Paid-up Capital AND
2. CHARGE the same to INTEREST as part of Construction Cost,
3. When, shares are issued for the purpose of raising money to defray the expenses of the construction of any work or building, or the provision of any plant.

PROVISIONS

The interest can be paid out of Capital, SUBJECT TO,

1. Articles Authorisation or Special Resolution;
2. Previous Approval of Central Government;
3. Inquiry by Central Government at the expense of the Company;
4. Security for payment of costs of Inquiry, if any;
5. The Period shall NOT exceed the close of the half-year next after the half-year during which the work or building has been actually completed;
6. The Rate of Interest shall NOT exceed 12%

APPOINTMENT/REMOVAL OF AUDITORS OF PRESCRIBED COMPANIES:

Type of Meeting	: General Meeting
Approval	: Special Resolution + Special Notice
Applicable Law	: Section 224A
E - Forms	: 23

Ordinary Business at AGM requires special resolution with special notice only when, If Company is having 25% or more of Subscribed Capital held by,

↳ Public Financial Institution or Government Company or Central or State Government;

↳ Financial Institution under State Act WHERE State Government holds 51% or More;

↳ Nationalized Banks or Insurance Company doing General Insurance business.

Kindly note, the said shareholding shall be determined as on the date of Annual General Meeting. In case of change in shareholding after issue of notice by making it above 25%, then meeting shall either be ADJOURNED or OMIT the item regarding appointment of auditors. In case of OMITTING the said item, auditor shall be appointed by Central Government.

1. Members who intend to appoint/remove Auditors in a company where 25% of subscribed capital is held by prescribed institutions shall give atleast 14 clear days notice before General Meeting to the company.
2. Company shall send notice to auditors immediately and then to members or has an option to publish Advertisement atleast 7 clear days before meeting.
3. In case of removal, Company shall receive REPRESENTATION from auditors which shall be circulated to members or READ at meeting or seek CG permission to NOT to circulate, if it is to secure needless publicity for defamatory matters.
4. Convene the General Meeting and pass the Special Resolution for appointment/removal of the said auditors.
5. File e-form 23 as per EFORM COMPLIANCE CHART.

CENTRAL GOVERNMENT TO ORDER INVESTIGATION:

Type of Meeting : General Meeting

Approval : Special Resolution + Special Notice

Applicable Law : Section 237(a)

E - Forms : 23

Central Government sHall order investigation into the affairs of the company and appoint inspectors on passing of Special Resolution by shareholders. It is the obligation cast upon the CG to order investigation of the company.

APPOINTMENT OF SOLE SELLING AGENT:

Type of Meeting : General Meeting

Approval : Special Resolution + Special Notice

Applicable Law : Section 294, 294A & 294AA read with Companies (Appointment of Sole Agents) Rules, 1975

E - Forms : 23, I & II

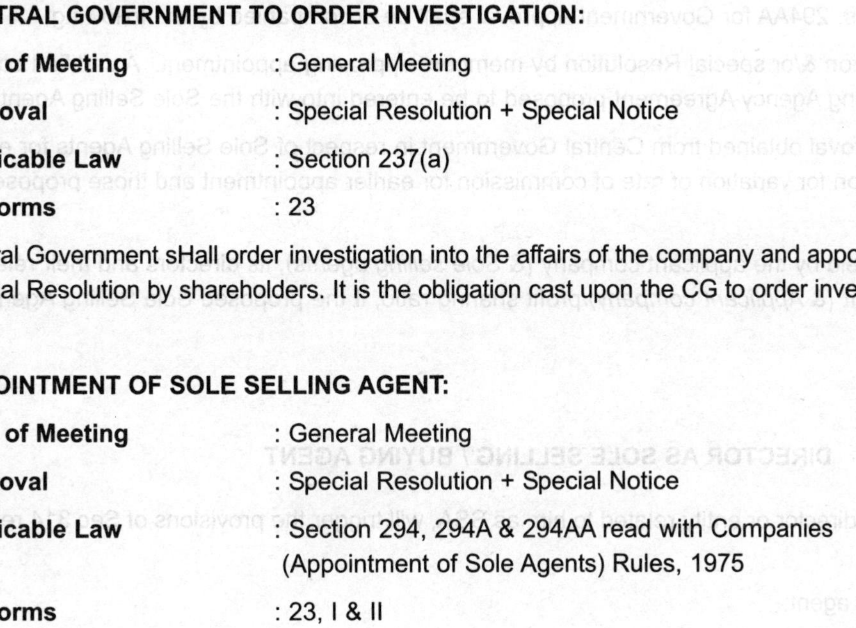

Paid-up Capital (PC) Limits	Approval Sought for Appointment
LESS THAN 50 lakhs	Ordinary Resolution (NOT prior)
50 lakhs or more	**Special Resolution + Central Government Approval (Not Prior)**
Substantial Interest on the Date of Appointment (need NOT be on approval)	Prior approval of Central Government mandatory (PCG)

Substantial Interest = lower of 5% or 5 lakhs on paid-up capital; To determine substantial interest of the following, club the respective holdings,

If individual, its = Individual + Relatives' Interests; If Firm, its = Partners + Relatives' Interests;

If Body Corporate (BC), its = BC + Director (s) + Relatives' Interest.

Substantial Interests, to be identified, irrespective of the Paid-up Capital; If the Paid-up capital is less than 50 lakhs, but the concern to be appointed as SSA is having a Substantial Interests, then Ordinary Resolution + PCG is required.

An application submitted u/s. 294AA for Government approval shall be accompanied by the following:

- A copy of Board resolution &/or special Resolution by members approving appointment. A certified copy of the Marketing/Sole Selling Agency Agreement proposed to be entered into with the Sole Selling Agent.
- A copy of previous approval obtained from Central Government in respect of Sole Selling Agents for earlier period, if any. Justification for variation of rate of commission for earlier appointment and those proposed *(in case of reappointment)*.
- Percentage of shares held by the applicant company *(& Sole selling agents)*, its directors and their relatives in the Sole Selling Agent *(& Applicant company)*/profit sharing ratio, if the proposed Sole Selling Agent is a partnership firm.

DIRECTOR AS SOLE SELLING / BUYING AGENT

Note that appointment of a director or entity related to him as SSA, will trigger the provisions of Sec 314 regarding office of profit.

Appointment of sole selling agent:

1. Hold the Board meeting a. To decide the whether sole selling agent is required and in which areas they are required b. To select and appoint sole selling agents c. To approve the notice of the general meeting for approving the appointment of sole selling agent.
2. Issue notice of general meeting atleast 21 days before the date of meeting to members, directors, auditors and stock exchange.

3. Hold the general meeting and pass the following resolutions appointing the sole selling agent. Special resolution is required for appointment of sole selling agent if the paid up capital is more than 50 lakhs. **When NO substantial interest in involved** RESOLVED as Special Resolution and subject to the approval of Central Government, the Board approves the appointment of LABZ as sole selling agent for the sale of …… in the territory of …… for a period of 3 years with effect from ……, on the terms and conditions set out in the draft agreement to be entered into between the Company and LABZ or with such modifications as may be mutually agreed to by the Board and LABZ. RESOLVED FURTHER THAT Mr.A, Company Secretary of the company is authorized to file application for Central Government approval in e-form i. **When substantial interest in involved** RESOLVED as Special Resolution and having obtained the approval of Central Government through e-form ii, the Board approves the appointment of LABZ as sole selling agent for the sale of …… in the territory of …… for a period of 3 years with effect from ……, on the terms and conditions set out in the draft agreement to be entered into between the Company and LABZ or with such modifications as may be mutually agreed to by the Board and LABZ.
4. Execute Sole Selling Agents agreement and file the same with RoC in e-form 23 following EFORM COMPLIANCE CHART.
5. Obtain the approval of Central Government by filing e-form I/II for sole selling agent or sole buying agents respectively following EFORM COMPLIANCE CHART.
6. File e-form 23 with ROC within 30 days of passing the special resolution and follow E-FORM COMPLIANCE CHART.

APPOINTMENT OF SOLE SELLING AGENT:

Type of Meeting : General Meeting

Approval : Special Resolution + Special Notice

Applicable Law : Section 309(1) & Articles

E - Forms : 23

Remuneration received by a director for acting in the capacity of the director (by way of sitting fees) and remuneration received by director holding office of place of profit (not by way of professional capacity) shall be determined by Articles or by Resolution (if Articles require) passed in the general meeting.

COMMISSION TO NON-EXECUTIVE DIRECTORS:

Type of Meeting : General Meeting

Approval : Special Resolution + Special Notice

Applicable Law : Section 309(4) & Articles

E - Forms : 23

Non-executive directors (other than MD/WTD) can be paid monthly or quarterly or annual REMUNERATION with Central Government approval whereas COMMISSION can be paid only during profits with shareholders approval by way of Special Resolution which can be valid for a period upto 5 years. During loss, commission can be paid only with Central Government approval.

To Whom	% Sub-Ceiling of Remuneration
Directors of Board Managed Company (where there are NO MD/WTD/Manager)	UPTO 3% (Net Profit)
If there is any MD/WTD/Manager in the company, then for other Directors	UPTO 1% (Net Profit)

Note: The said % excludes sitting fees.

But as per clause 49 of Listing Agreement, all the remuneration paid to non-executive directors needs shareholders approval.

TO APPOINT DIRECTOR OR SUCH PERSON IN PLACE OF PROFIT:

Type of Meeting : General Meeting

Approval : Special Resolution & Central Government (if remuneration is more than Rs. 50,000 p.m)

Applicable Law : Section 314

E - Forms : 23, 24B

OFFICE OR PLACE OF PROFIT means

- Director obtaining ANY remuneration OVER & ABOVE the remuneration to which he is ENTITLED as a Director.
- For others, ANYTHING by way of remuneration.

For instance,

- a director or his relative of the company appointed as a company secretary
- a director or related entity appointed as sole selling agent of the company.

Note: Director is a person who does not receive any remuneration OTHER THAN by way of sitting fees from the Company. Director per se means a Non-Executive Director of the Company. The Executive Directors includes Managing Director and Whole-time Directors.

Section 314 is NOT APPLICABLE TO,

- Any Director appointed by Central Government u/s. 408;
- Appointment of Director as MD / WTD if such appointment & terms of remuneration are in compliance of Schedule XIII or as Banker or Debenture Trustees;
- Appointment of relative as MD / WTD / Manager, where Central Government approval is obtained u/s. 269 or as Banker or Debenture Trustees;

↳ Appointment of Director as Solicitor or Advocate BUT not on retainership (regular) basis; i.e., Professional Services are exempted UNLESS it is on Retainership Basis.

SPECIAL RESOLUTION SHOULD BE PASSED EACH TIME: The Special Resolution u/s. 314 is necessary for INITIAL appointment as well as for SUBSEQUENT appointments with Higher Remuneration, if initial appointment is NOT as per approved time scale.

SECTION 314(1)	**SECTION 314(1B)**
Appointment of below mentioned persons only with **Special Resolution** DIRECTORS - without any remuneration limits are covered. FOLLOWING covered if their Total Monthly Remuneration [TMR] is Rs.50,000 or more, 1. Relative of SUCH Director 2. Firm in which SUCH Director is a Partner; 3. Private Company, in which SUCH Director is a Director or Member. EITHER under, • Holding Company • OR its Subsidiary. It shall be sufficient if the Special Resolution is passed at the General Meeting held for the first time after the holding of such office or place of profit.	Appointment of below mentioned persons only with **Previous approval of Central Government & Prior Special Resolution** FOLLOWING covered if their Total Monthly Remuneration [TMR] is Rs.2,50,000 or more, 1. Relative of Director or Manager; 2. Firm in which Director is a Partner; 3. Private Company, in which Director or **RELATIVE** is a Director or Member **Note:** 1. Directors are specifically excluded. 2. Holding or Subsidiary Co is not covered. The prescribed form for obtaining CG approval being **e-Form 24B**.

Where a relative of a director or a firm in which such relative is a partner, is appointed to an office or place of profit under the company or its subsidiary **without the knowledge of Director**, the consent may be obtained either in the General Meeting aforesaid or within 3 months from the date of the appointment.

The selection and appointment of a relative of a director holding office or place of profit in the company shall be approved by adopting the SAME PROCEDURE applicable to NON-RELATIVES. For LISTED PUBLIC COMPANIES, the SELECTION of director holding office or place of profit shall be approved by SELECTION COMMITTEE, the majority of it should have INDEPENDENT directors & an EXPERT in respective FIELD from outside the company. The Selection Committee of UNLISTED public company should have an EXPERT whereas ANY DIRECTOR can be a member in case of Private companies.

Kindly note, the following procedure need not be followed for APPOINTMENT OF DIRECTORS and also appointment of SUCH other persons in Subsidiary company in place of profit they are covered only u/s. 314(1) where only Special Resolution is required and that can be passed even after appointment.

1. Obtaining approval of Central government u/s. 314(1B) in e-form 24B with details in EFORM COMPLIANCE CHART
2. After obtaining approval of Central government hold board meeting to fix the time, date and venue and place of general meeting and approve the draft notice (along with explanatory statement u/s. 173 (2)) of the general meeting for passing special resolution approving the appointment.

3. Issue notice of the general meeting to - Members - Directors - Auditors - Stock Exchanges
4. Hold the General Meeting to pass above resolution.
5. Forward a copy of proceeding to Stock exchange.
6. File e-form 23 with ROC within 30 days of passing the resolution following EFORM COMPLIANCE CHART.

A company wishes to appoint a person, who is a relative of a director of the company, at a very senior position in the company. As a Company Secretary of that company of that company, what steps would you take at the time of such appointment? (2008 - June)

Draft a resolution for appointment of a relative of a director carrying a monthly remuneration of Rs. 60,000 (2009 - June)

Madhav a chartered accountant, is a director in MNL Limited. The company proposes to appoint / engage the firm M & Co in which Madhav is a partner in one or more of the following capacities:

(i) Consultants on regular retainer basis.

(ii) Authorised representatives to appear before tribunals.

Discuss whether the provision of section 314 are attracted in the above situations (2010 - December) Case 1 attracts Section 314 whereas Case 2 is a professional assignment which is exempted.

TO MAKE LIABILITY OF DIRECTOR/MANAGER UNLIMITED:

Type of Meeting : General Meeting

Approval : Special Resolution & Central Government

(if remuneration is more than Rs. 50,000 p.m)

Applicable Law : Section 322 & 323

E - Forms : 23 & EFORM COMPLIANCE CHART

LIABILITY CLAUSE

If limited by shares	The liability of the **member** is limited to the extent money remaining unpaid on the shares held, in the event of winding up.
If limited by Guarantee	The liability of the **member** is limited to the extent agreed upon by them to be paid, in the event of winding up.
If limited by shares &Guarantee	The liability of the **member** is limited to the extent remaining unpaid on the shares held & agreed to be paid, in the event of winding up.

↳ Liability clause cannot be altered to prejudice the interest of the share holders of the company.

↳ Liability of a member cannot be increased without his written consent.

↳ In case of Unlimited liability company, the liability can be made limited by passing a Special resolution and getting a Fresh Certificate of Registration [Section 32]

↳ But as per Section 45, the liability of the members of a limited company **will be unlimited**, if the following conditions are satisfied-:

1. The number of members is reduced below Statutory Minimum [7 in case of Public Company and 2 in case of Private Company]
2. The Company has carried on business for more than 6 months with such reduced number;
3. Person who is a member of the Company after said 6 months, and cognizant of fact that business is carried out such way;
4. Debt contracted after expiry of said 6 months and to pay up such debt, the liability will be unlimited.

Directors & Managers with Unlimited Liability

↳ Articles should authorize such appointment or amend Articles;

↳ Amend Memorandum to render Unlimited Liability of Director or Manager in a Limited Company by way of Special Resolution;

↳ Effective only when the existing or new directors or managers accord their Consent, in writing, that his liability will be unlimited.

TO MAKE LIABILITY OF DIRECTOR/MANAGER UNLIMITED:

Type of Meeting	: General Meeting
Approval	: Special Resolution & Central Government (if remuneration is more than Rs. 50,000 p.m)
Applicable Law	: Section 372A
E - Forms	: 23

Any company,

↳ Making any loan to other Body Corporate directly or indirectly; 9 Giving any guarantee / providing security,

↳ in connection with a loan made by other person to Body Corporate, or

↳ in connection with a loan made **to other person**, by Body Corporate;

↳ Acquiring any securities of the Body Corporate (**BC**) ;

EXCEEDING 60% of Paid-up Capital & Free Reserves; OR 100% of Free Reserves, whichever is more, shall require **prior approval** of shareholders by the way of special resolution and prior approval of Financial Institutions;

Note: For this section, loan" includes debentures or any deposit of money made by one company with another company, not being a banking company.

Within the Prescribed Limits,

↳ Board Resolution (Not by Circular Resolution) - Unanimous Resolution: sanctioned with the consent of ALL director's present at meeting;

↳ PFI - Prior Approval of Financial Institutions, if there is any default in repayment as per the terms & conditions of the loan.

Guarantee Exceeding the Limits, can be given if

↳ Unanimous Board Resolution is passed to give guarantee in accordance with the provisions of this section;

↳ Only in case of emergencies where it is not possible to get the approval of GM by way of Special Resolution;

↳ Special Resolution (SR) to be passed within 12 months OR Immediate AGM (whichever is earlier) confirming the Board Resolution.

Section 372A - NOT Applicable to

↳ Private Company which is NOT a subsidiary of a public company;

↳ Bank / Insurance / Financing Company - in ordinary course of business;

↳ Any company having object of financing industrial enterprises, or of providing infrastructural facilities;

↳ Investment Companies;

↳ Holding Company to its 100% (WoS) subsidiary; (making loan, giving guarantee, providing security or acquisition of securities);

↳ Rights Issue.

Other conditions - Section 372A is **PROHIBITED** to Defaulters of Section 58A (deposits).

Rate of Interests NOT LESS THAN prevailing Prime Lending Rate (PLR) of RBI.

1. Issue notice for Board meeting under Section 286 and hold the board meeting to consider the proposal to give loan/guarantee or provide security/make investment and a. Pass a board resolution with ALL the directors consenting the specified limit of such loan/ guarantee/ investment. and b. If the aggregate amount of proposed loan/guarantee/security/investment exceeds the specified limit under Section 372A then fix time, date and venue for holding general meeting to pass the special resolution thereat in that regard and c. get the notice of the general meeting along with explanatory statement under Section 173(2) approved by the Board
2. Ensure that the notice of the special resolution contains: i Name of BC; ii Nature of Activities; iii Quantum; iv Sources of funding. **NOTE: NO Blanket Approval** is permitted (every loan / investment to be considered on a case-by-case basis)
3. Issue notice of general meeting to members, directors, auditors and stock exchanges.
4. Hold the general meeting and pass the special resolution and Forward the proceedings of the meeting to stock exchanges.

5. File e-form 23 ROC within 30 days of passing Special Resolution as per EFORM COMPLIANCE CHART.
6. Enter the following particulars in register kept for this purpose in chronological order within 7 days of investment/loan/guarantee/security with details as to Name, Amount, Term, Purpose & Date. **Note:** The register should be open for inspection by members; Otherwise fine UPTO Rs.5000 or Rs. 500 PER day.

1. Draft the specimen resolutions along with requisite explanatory statement, wherever necessary, for transacting the following items of business indicating the kind of meeting at which each resolution is to be passed and the type of resolution required for authorizing Board of Directors of Rosy Limited to acquire shares of Lilly Limited (2008 - December)
2. What is the procedure adopted by the Board of Directors at its meeting for making inter - corporate loans, investments, etc.? (2008 - June)
3. Anmol Limited a widely held listed company, had paid up share capital of Rs. 5 crore, Besides this, it had free reserves of Rs. 15 crore. A proposal for an investment of Rs. 14 Crore in the securities of Briju Limited came up for approval before the meeting of the Board of directors. The Board of Directors of the company comprised of 10 directors out of whom 8 directors were present at the meeting. All directors voted in favour of the resolution. State whether the decision of the Board of directors is tenable in view of the provisions of section 372A.

   Would your answer be different if 2 directors out of 8 directors present at the meeting voted against the resolution? (2007 - June)
4. Draft specimen resolutions stating the authority who can pass it and also the type of resolution. Give reasons for passing the requisite resolution referring to the relevant section(s) of the Companies Act, 1956:
   (i) Health Care Limited (HCL) wants to make investment of Rs. 55 crore and loans of Rs. 45 crore in other companies. Balance Sheet as on 31st March, 2009 shows HCL's paid - up capital of Rs. 35 crore and reserves of Rs. 75 crore.
   (ii) Grow India Limited is sanctioned a credit facility of Rs. 25 Crore by the Union Bank of India, Kapurbavdi Branch, Thane, against its inventory and receivables. The company wants to enjoy the sanctioned credit facility. (2009 - December)
5. Draft of following. In case of resolution, give reasons for passing the requisite resolution stating the authority who can pass it and also the type of resolution referring to the relevant section(s) of the Companies Act, 1956:

   Appropriate resolution to make investment of Rs. 15 crore in preference shares of Sona Tractors Limited a company in trade dealing relationship with the investing company. The investing company has a paid - up equity capital of Rs. 20 Crore, a paid - up preference capital of Rs. 5 crore and general reserve of Rs. 4 crore. The company has no other investment or recoverable loan. (2010 - June)

RESOLUTIONS UNDER POSTAL BALLOT [SECTION 192A]

Postal Ballot INCLUDES voting by share holders by postal or electronic mode INSTEAD OF voting personally by presenting for transacting businesses in a general meeting of the company.

"Voting by electronic mode" MEANS a process for recording votes by the members using a computer based machine to display an electronic ballot and to record the vote and also the number of votes polled in favour or against such that the entire voting gets registered and counted in a electronic registry in a CENTRALISED SERVER. Any agency getting a certificate of **Standardisation Testing & Quality Certification** (STQC) from Department of Information & Technology can enable a platform for ELECTRONIC VOTING for shareholders.

1. A listed company MAY and in the case of resolution relating to those business notified by Central Government SHALL get any resolution passed by means of Postal Ballot, INSTEAD of transacting the business in General Meeting. Thus, in general, all resolutions of listed Company apart from resolutions passed at an AGM can be passed by Postal Ballot.
2. The Central Government has framed rules titled as the Companies (Passing of the Resolution by Postal ballot) Rules, 2011.
3. Where a Company has decided to pass resolution by Postal Ballot, it shall send notice to ALL SHAREHOLDERS along with Draft Resolution explaining the reasons and requesting them to send their assent or dissent, in writing, on a Postal Ballot WITHIN 30 days from the date of posting the letter ["Vote Cast"]. Consent after 30 days shall be treated as if reply from the member has NOT BEEN received.
4. This **Notice** shall be sent BOTH by Registered Post Acknowledgement due (OR some secured mode of posting by Department of Posts OR through E-MAIL if advance opportunity is given to update their emails with depositories) AND advertise in the newspapers regarding dispatch of ballot papers with the following details: the date of completion of despatch of notices; commencement & end of voting through postal ballot or by electronic mode; & the members, who have NOT received postal ballot forms may apply for a duplicate.
5. The notice shall clearly indicate the process and manner for voting by **electronic mode** provided by the AGENCY (**or**) the Company shall also send a **prepaid postage envelope** to facilitate the shareholders to communicate their intention. The NOTE shall be made in the notice for understanding of members that the transaction at Si. No. REQUIRES CONSENT of shareholders through postal ballot;
6. The voting right on postal ballot shall be in PROPORTION to the shareholder's share of the paid-up equity share capital of the company. If a resolution is assented by the REQUISITE MAJORITY by means of Postal Ballot, it shall be DEEMED to have duly passed at the General Meeting convened in that behalf.
7. The board of directors shall appoint 1 SCRUTINIZER, who is not in employment of the company, to conduct the postal ballot voting process in a fair and transparent manner and who shall submit his report as soon as possible after the last date of receipt of Postal Ballots.
8. SCRUTINIZER shall be available at the Registered office of the company for the purpose of ascertaining the requisite majority and shall maintain a register in safe custody [till the

chairman considers, approves and signs the minutes of the meeting] entering requisite details

like the consent, name, number of shares, et al, so as to preserve such ballot papers and other related papers/registers safely till the resolution is given EFFECT to.

9. In case of default, a fine UPTO Rs. 50,000 may be levied.

> 1. "Postal ballot system is an unmixed blessing." Comment. (2010 - June)
> 2. Briefly outline the provisions of the Companies Act, 1956 in regard to postal ballot. (2010 - June)

BUSINESSES IN WHICH THE RESOLUTIONS SHALL BE PASSED BY POSTAL BALLOT

The following businesses conducted by a LISTED COMPANY shall be mandatorily done only through postal ballot,

1. Amendment of Object Clause - special resolution [discussed above]
2. Amendment of Situation Clause; i.e., shifting Registered Office outside the State - special resolution with CLB approval [discussed above]
3. Amend Articles to include Section 3(1)(iii) - special resolution with CG approval
4. Buy Back of Shares u/s. 77A [discussed above]
5. Issue of Sweat Equity Shares u/s. 79A - special resolution [discussed above]
6. Issue of Equity Shares with Differential Rights - ordinary resolution [discussed in Reduction & Variation chapter in Corporate Restructuring]
7. Variation of Shareholders rights u/s. 106 - special resolution [discussed in Reduction & Variation chapter in Corporate Restructuring]

8. Sale of whole or substantially the whole of undertaking u/s. 293(1)(a)- ordinary resolution [discussed in Demerger & Hiving off chapter in Corporate Restructuring]
9. Loan / Guarantee / Security in excess of the limit u/s. 372A - special resolution [discussed above]
10. Election of Small Shareholder Directors u/s. 252 - ordinary resolution
11. Mandatory Public Offer of 20% when there is change in control of listed company as per provisio to Regulation 12 of SEBI Takeover Code is not made as approved by shareholders -special resolution [discussed under Takeover Code chapter in Corporate Restructuring]
12. Prior Shareholders approval by way of Special Resolution WITH votes FOR by PUBLIC shareholders is atleast 2 times votes AGAINST by PUBLIC shareholders, through POSTAL BALLOT as per Regulation 8 of SEBI Delisting Regulations, 2009 [discussed in Delisting chapter in Due Diligence]
13. The non-convertible portion of partly convertible debt instruments issued by a listed issuer, the value of which exceeds Rs.50 lakhs, may be rolled over WITHOUT change in the interest rate, subject to compliance of Section 121 of the Companies Act, 1956 and approval of shareholders by Special Resolution as per Regulation 21 of SEBI (ICDR) Regulations, 2009 [discussed in Convertible Debt Security chapter in Due Diligence].

CONVERSION OF PRIVATE OR PUBLIC COMPANY INTO OTHER

How to convert a Private Company into Public Company? Understand the definition of Private and Public Company. According to Section 3 (1) (iii), Private Company means a company with Paid-up Capital (PC) of Rs. 1 Lakh OR more AND by its Articles (AOA) [has following 4 restrictive clauses],

- RESTRICTS transfer of shares
- LIMITS number of members to 50
- PROHIBITS invitation to public to subscribe for shares/debentures
- PROHIBITS- acceptance or invitation of Public Deposits. Exemptions:Deposits from Company's Directors or their Relatives or Members.

According to Section 3(1) (iv), Public Company means a company which

- Is Not a Private Company
- Has a PC of Rs. 5 lakhs OR more
- Is a Private subsidiary of a Public Company.

Then, amend the Articles by passing a special resolution to remove the four restrictive clauses and increase the Paid-up capital, number of members, number of directors, et al. Get the necessary approval for amendment of Memorandum regarding Name Clause, Capital Clause, et al. File Prospectus or Statement in lieu of Prospectus within 30 days of special resolution. Use the same

procedure, when special resolution is passed. Also, convene a statutory meeting within 6 months of conversion. That's it. By now you know how to convert a Public Company into a Private Company. Yes, by inserting the four restrictive clauses u/s. 3(1)(iii) and amend Memorandum & Articles accordingly.

Procedure for Conversion of a public company into a Private Company

1. Convene a Board meeting and pass the following resolutions:
2. To approve the proposal of conversion of the company into a private company and for that purpose alter the articles to insert therein the 4 conditions specified in section 3(1)(iii).
3. To fix the time, date and venue of an extraordinary general meeting and approve the draft notice containing the special resolutions with Explanatory statement.
4. To change the name of the company, so as to insert the word 'Private' in the company's name before the word 'Limited'.
5. To alter the articles so as to bring them in line with the provisions of the Act conferring upon private companies the privileges and exemptions which it can avail of, if its articles so provide.
6.To file Statement in lieu of prospectus.

NAME CLAUSE

The name of the Company shall end with the word Limited or Private Limited unless it is an unlimited or Section 25 Company. A company may amend its name by passing a special resolution. A company may not amend its name but may convert itself into a Private or Public Company, then also it amounts to amendment of name.

Section 21 read with Section 31

Special Resolution (SR) by Shareholders - **In all cases**	Central Government (CG) Approval - **when public Company is converted into private Company**

↳ File e-Form 1A (for new / change of name) with requisite fee;

↳ File e-Form 23 for Special Resolution within 30 days to RoC.

↳ File e-form 1B for CG approval.

7. A general meeting will be convened and following special resolutions are passed thereat by sending the notice and the explanatory statement,
RESOLVED THAT Subject to the approval of the Central Government u/s. 31, the Articles of Association of the Company be and are altered by inserting therein Article No. .. .. so as to convert the Company into a private company. the name of the Company be and is changed by inserting therein the word 'Private' consequent upon the conversion of the Company into a private company and that Clause ... of the memorandum of the Company and Article ... ..of the articles of association of the Company be and are altered by inserting the word 'Private' therein.
Clause ..... of the memorandum of association and Article ..... of the articles of association of the Company be and are altered and the same be substituted by the following: "The Authorised Share Capital of the Company is Rs. 5 lakhs" The articles of the Company be and are altered as follows: (i) Articles ...... be inserted. (ii) Articles .... be altered in the following manner. Resolved Further That the Board of directors be and is authorized to do such other acts, deeds and things as may be necessary to give effect to this resolution.
8. After the special resolution has been passed at the general meeting, e-Form 23 should be filed with RoC within 30 days following EFORM COMPLIANCE CHART.
9. Make an application to the Registrar in e-form 1B together with the original Certificate of Incorporation for exchanging it with a fresh Certificate consequent to the change of name as a result of the conversion of the company, by adding the word "Private".
10. Note alterations made in the memorandum and articles in every copy.

1. Draft specimen resolutions along with necessary explanatory statement, wherever required, for transacting the following items of business indicating the kind of meeting at which each resolution is to be passed and the type of resolution required for:

   (i) Change of name of the company consequent to the conversion into a public company. (2007 - June)

2. Enumerate the procedure for conversion of a public company into a private company (2009 - June) (2010 - December)

3. State the procedure for appointment of "small shareholders' director". (2007 - June)

4. When does a small shareholders' director vacate office? (2008 - June)

SMALL SHAREHOLDER DIRECTOR [SS DIR] u/s. 252

- A public company having Paid-up Capital (PC) of Rs. 5 Crores OR more AND having 100 or more Small Shareholders (Small Shareholders means shareholders holding shares of Nominal Value UPTO Rs. 20,000/-) may have a director appointed by their small shareholders;
- Appointment of small share holders governed through companies (Appointment of small shareholders Directors) Rules, 2001;
- Company can suo motto or on receipt of Notice from not less than 1/10th of small shareholders proposing the name of a person to act as director on their behalf;
- The notice to be submitted by the small share holders atleast 14 days before the General Meeting and shall be signed atleast 100 small shareholders;
- The SS Director cannot be appointed as MD/WTD;
- An individual cannot be small shareholder for more than 2 companies;
- In case of listed companies, the election of small shareholders should be done through postal Ballot;
- Tenure of such director can be UPTO 3 years and can be re-appointed.

ORDINARY RESOLUTIONS

Section 293: Restrictions on powers of Board (remember SRI BC- the first letters)

Following business as given u/s. 293(1) can only be transacted by an ordinary resolution passed at General Meeting,

A. **Sell**, lease or otherwise **dispose** of the whole, or substantially the whole, of the **undertaking** of the company [such resolution may specify the use, disposal or investment of the sale proceeds]

B. **Remit**, or give time for the repayment of, any **debt** due by a **director** [UNLESS its an advance by bank to its director in the ordinary course of business]

C. **nvestment** of the amount of **compensation** received by the company in respect of the **compulsory acquisition** of whole/substantially the whole of **undertaking** / premises / **property** used and without which it cannot be carried on or can be carried on only with difficulty.

D. **Borrowings exceeding** the aggregate of the **paid-up capital** of the company and its **free reserves** (excluding the temporary loans);[onus on the lender to prove that he advanced the loan in good faith and without knowledge that the limit imposed by that clause had been exceeded]

"Temporary Loans" means loans repayable on demand or within six months from the date of the loan but does not include loans raised for the purpose of financing expenditure of a capital nature.

E. Contribution to **charity** (not directly relating to the business of company or employee welfare) in a **financial year exceeding Rs. 50,000 or 5% of average net profit** for preceding 3 financial years (whichever is greater). The resolution must state that it is to be made to the charity. Even otherwise, it won't affect the title of a buyer or person who leases undertaking in good faith and after exercising due care and caution;

For Sections 293(1)(a), 293(1)(d) & 293(1)(e), filing of e-form 23 is mandatory even though it is an Ordinary Resolution. Similarly even Voluntary Winding up of a company by passing Ordinary resolution mandates filing e-form 23.

LIST OF ORDINARY RESOLUTIONS

The following items require sanction by Ordinary resolution,

Rectification of Name: [Section 22]

Central Government will direct rectification of name mostly in case of company which is incorporated with the name which is identical to the name of the company which is already incorporated.

↳ Company may or shall (as per direction of CG) rectify the name by passing Ordinary Resolution and shall file e-form 24A follow EFORM COMPLIANCE CHART.

↳ Company may rectify the name with previous approval of CG within 5 years of registration of name.

Such direction of CG shall be given within 12 months from registration of name.

DEPOSITS ALONG WITH BORRWINGS EXCEEDING Paid Up Capital & Free Reserves u/s. 58A

CONSENTS U/S. 58A

↳ At Board Meeting or at Committee of the Board, if Deposits along with borrowings is within Paid-up Capital & Free Reserves. [< PC+FR]

↳ Ordinary Resolution if Deposits along with other borrowings EXCEEDS Paid-up (PC) PLUS Free Reserves (FR) [> PC + FR]

PRE-REQUISITES FOR DEPOSITS

↳ The Company shall have a net owned fund of Rs. 1 crore or more to invite public deposits;

↳ Joint holding of deposit [not exceeding 3] is allowed;

↳ Public Deposits payable on DEMAND or having maturity period less than 6 months / 3 months or more than 36 months can NOT be accepted.

Most Minimum Period g 3 months, only for Short Term Deposits UPTO 10% (PC+FR) Maximum Period g 36 months	Minimum period g 6 months;

↳ Rate of interest shall not exceed 12 ½ % PA and interest cannot rest for a short term than a month;

↳ Brokerage only to person who solicit deposit on the basis of the agreement with company and Brokerage UPTO 1%, 1.5% or 2% for Deposits UPTO 1 year, 2 years & 3 years respectively;

↳ Company shall furnish a RECEIPT for the amount received to the depositor WITHIN 8 weeks from the date of receipt of money or realisation of cheques with the Particulars of Deposit.

Registers	**Returns**
Register of Deposits at Registered Office and preserve for 8 Calendar Years.	Return of Deposit as on 31st March to RoC and a copy to RBI, duly certified by the auditor of the company on or before 30th June of every year.

Vary terms of contract referred in Prospectus/SLoP [Section 61]

Issuance of shares at discount (Section 79) ↳ The Company can issue shares @ discount ONLY if it is of the same class of the shares which is ALREADY issued; ↳ The Company should have completed 1 year from the Date of Entitlement to Commence business; ↳ To be approved by Shareholders in General Meeting and resolution to specify the rate of discount; ↳ Confirmation of Company Law Board [CLB] is mandatory and the rate of discount shall NOT exceed 10%; ↳ Issue must be made within 12 months from date of CLB order; ↳ Disclosure in the Prospectuss mandatory
Alteration of Authorised Capital, if it is authorized by AoA [Section 94] and increase Nominal Capital of Unlimited company [Section 98]
The company can re-issue the debentures redeemed unless it is prohibited by Articles or terms of issuance of the original debentures or any contract entered into by the company or the company passed a resolution for canceling the redeemed debentures by passing an Ordinary Resolution and it shall be treated as the issue of a new debenture for the purposes of stamp duty [Section 121].
Section 165: Every public company has to adopt Statutory Report by passing a Ordinary resolution and shall be filed with RoC in e-form 22 following EFORM COMPLIANCE CHART and shall be sent along with Notice to Shareholders. Any default as to convening Statutory Meeting within 6 months of commencement of business or filing Statutory Report can lead to COMPULSORY WINDING UP u/s. 433(1)(b).
Adoption Balance Sheet, Profit & Loss Account and reports of Board of Directors or Auditors u/s. 210 or declaring a dividend [as per Table A]
Inspection of Books of Accounts [Section 209A] ↳ By Authorised Officers of Central Government & RoC, without PRIOR notice; 9 By SEBI, with respect to Sections covered u/s. 55A; ↳ By Director, during Business Hours; **Note:** ↳ By Directors through Authorised Representatives, with a Declaration that it will be used for the intended purposes only; ↳ By **Representative of Holding Company** to inspect accounts of Subsidiary Company u/s. 214 mandates approval by way of Ordinary Resolution; ↳ By Members when directed by the Court or subject to Articles. Any default of Section 209A is a Non-Compoundable offence and further such convicted director or officer shall VACATE the office and disqualified from holding such office in ANY company for 5 years
Appointment of auditors, Remove & appoint other member nominated auditor, appointment of auditors after resignation [Section 224]

• Appoint First Directors, regularize Section 260/262 directors, appoint retiring director or other than retiring director u/s. 255, 256 & 257; • Appointment of Section 313 director in the absence of power in Articles; • Any increase or reduction of number of directors within AoA limits as per Section 258; • Also fix the remuneration of the same u/s. 309 unless Articles otherwise requires
Appointment of MD/WTD/Manager and approving the remuneration u/s. 269.
Removal of director before expiry of term and appoint some one else u/s. 284.
Appointment or disapproving the appointment of Sole Selling Agent of a company who paid-up capital is within Rs.50 lakhs u/s. 294.
• Wind up company voluntarily u/s. 484 and to appoint/fix remuneration of liquidator u/s. 490 and to fill vacancy in Liquidators office u/s. 492; • To authorize directors to exercise some powers even after appointment of liquidator u/s. 491; • In case of Creditors voluntary winding up, for nominating liquidator, nominating members of committee of inspection and to consider & pass accounts laid in meeting u/s. 502 & 503.
To register an existing company under Part IX of Companies Act, 1956.

EXPLANATORY STATEMENT

1. The following 4 business at an Annual General Meeting (AGM) is an Ordinary Business (No Explanatory Statement required),
   i the consideration of the accounts, balance sheet and the reports of the Board of directors and auditors;
   ii the declaration of a dividend;
   iii the appointment of directors in the place of those retiring, and
   iv the appointment of and the fixing of the remuneration of the Auditors.
2. Any business OTHER THAN the 4 said business at an AGM is a Special business mandating Explanatory Statement.
3. Any General Meeting OTHER THAN AGM is an Extraordinary General Meeting (EGM).
4. Any Business transacted at an EGM is a Special Business, which mandates Explanatory Statement u/s. 173(2).
   ↳ If Explanatory Statement is NOT annexed to the Resolutions in the Notice, then the Notice becomes INCOMPLETE and all the Proceedings of the Meeting become INVALID.
   ↳ A Private Limited Company may by its Articles prescribe that provisions of Section 173(2) are NOT applicable to Private Company, thereby exempting such Company to annex Explanatory Statement to the Notice for every Resolution.

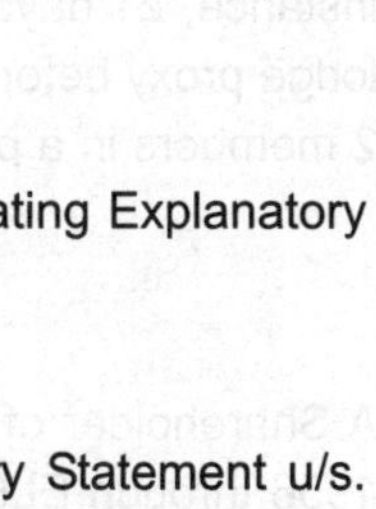

5. Even the above said 4 business are done at an EGM, it becomes a Special Business mandating Explanatory Statement.
6. Thus, all Special Business requires Explanatory Statement.

7. The Explanatory Statement should contain the following:

↳ Material Facts of every Business [with respective number from the Notice]. 'Material Facts' means any important information relating to item of business, that a Member must know, to exercise judgment and to decide the voting on resolution.

↳ Interest of Directors / Manager in the resolution (the extent of share holding interest in that other company if the extent of such shareholding interest is not less than 20% of the paid-up share capital of that other company)

↳ Place where documents are kept for inspection, if any.

8. Besides there are specific particulars which have to incorporated in the explanatory statement in case of buy-back, preferential issue, issue of ESOP etc...

State three things that are required to be covered in any explanatory statement to a resolution. (2008 - December)

As a measure of GREEN INITIATIVE IN THE CORPORATE GOVERNANCE in compliance with Sections 2, 4, 5 and 81 of the Information Technology Act, 2000, the MCA has issued a Circular and clarified that the Company would be in compliance of Section 53 of the Companies Act, 1956 if the SERVICE OF DOCUMENT has been made through ELECTRONIC MODE *(instead of posting)*.

RULES REGARDING GENERAL MEETINGS

[Section 171 to 186]

Section 170: These rules are APPLICABLE to a Private Limited Company, UNLESS Articles PROVIDES otherwise. Meaning, Articles of a Private Limited Company OVERRIDES theseprovisions. For instance, Articles acts differently in case of private and public company. Regards a public company, always Companies Act prevails. When it's a private company, Articles cannot override Companies Act but can enable it conveniently. Say for instance, 21 days notice for General Meeting can be made as less than 21 but not more than 21 days. Also, lodge proxy before 48 hours of General Meeting which cannot be extended but can be relaxed. So as Quorum, 2 members in a private company constitutes quorum, which can be increased but not decreased.

GENERAL MEETINGS THROUGH VIDEO CONFERENCING

A Shareholder of the Company may participate in a general meeting under the provisions of Companies Act, 1956 through ELECTRONIC MODE (ie) video conferencing is allowed to communicate concurrently with each other without an intermediary.

Responsibilities of Chairman & Company Secretary regarding video conferencing:

Prior to the meeting

a. To ensure that the NOTICE should mention necessary information on video conferencing facility and how to access the same.

b. The LISTED COMPANIES shall provide video conferencing connectivity in ATLEAST 5 TOP states based on the no. of shareholders or at places where there are ATLEAST 1000 shareholders as per their registered address with the Depository [Enabling Video conferencing is optional]. Any agency getting a certificate of Standardisation Testing & Quality Certification (STQC) from Department of Information & Technology can enable a platform for ELECTRONIC VOTING for shareholders.

At the meeting

c. To ensure the requisite quorum shall be PERSONALLY present (physically) at the place of the meeting along with the Chairman & Secretary. [AGM should be done at Registered office]

d. To safeguard the integrity & to ensure proper equipments & to ensure none other than authorised participants [i.e. NO OTHER PERSON except shareholder/proxy can] attend the meeting and to repeat or reiterate when there is an interruption in communication channel.

e. To record the Chairman's speech on SUMMARY of decisions taken & the consent/dissent thereof with respect to each agenda item and it shall be preserved for 1 YEAR therefrom.

After the meeting

f. To prepare the minutes considering the PLACE as where Chairman or Secretary sits DURING the meeting and the Statutory Registers shall be DEEMED to have been SIGNED on CONSENT.

g. Circulate DRAFT minutes in SOFT COPY within 7 days of meeting for comments/clarification & then enter in MINUTES BOOK.

Sending financials/annual reports by E-MAIL to members is permitted on satisfying the following conditions:

1. Advance opportunity to be given to member to register & update email id with the company or depository.
2. The companies WEBSITE should display these documents WELL IN ADVANCE & a publication shall be made in newspapers about the same & its availability of it for INSPECTION at the Registered office.
3. If member INSIST on physical copy, then it shall be sent by POST free of COST.

SHORTER NOTICE: Any Notice for a period LESS THAN 21 days is said to be at a 'Shorter Notice'.

↳ Consent of Members mandatory;

↳ Consent to be taken BEFORE the Meeting;

↳ Consent means UNANIMOUS Consent in case of AGM; Meaning, Consent of all the Members and also e-form 23 shall be filed.

↳ Consent means 95% or more of Voting Capital, in case f EGM;

↳ Any consent through Shorter Notice mandates filing of eform 22A with RoC following EFORM COMPLIANCE CHART.

CONTENTS OF NOTICE or DRAFT NOTICE OF AN AGM

Name of the Company → (1)

Registered Office of the Company → (2)

[no.]ANNUAL GENERAL MEETING
of the Company → (3)

HELD
on Day, Date of the Month & Year at the Time &
Venue → (4)

FOR
transacting the following businesses,

Ordinary Business:[As Below] → (5)

1.
2.
3.
4.

Special Business:

Ordinary Resolution
1,2, et al.
Expln. Statement [Sec 173(2)] → (6)

Special Resolution
1,2, et al.
Expln. Statement [Sec 173(2)]

→ (7)

Date: (consider Section 171 & 53)
Place:

Requirement relating to Proxy:

8. Book Closure:

Indicate the period during which the Register of Members and the Share Transfer Registers will remain closed. The books shall NOT be closed for,

- ↳ MORE THAN 30 days AT a time;
- ↳ MORE THAN 45 days PER year.

As per Listing Agreement, every listed company to close their transfer register once a year and 7days advance notice to be given to Stock Exchanges. Book Closure - the date fixed to ascertain the list of shareholders, prior to General Meeting, to find the eligible shareholders for the purpose of issuing notice and distributing corporate benefits.

↳ Record Date - As Listed Companies cannot close their Books for more than once a year, they can fix a Record Date to find the eligible shareholders. Though Record Date is not Book Closure, the 7 days advance notice to be given to Stock Exchanges.

Your assistant has placed before you the following draft notice of forthcoming annual general meeting. Your are required to locate the errors therein, if any, properly re draft the same alongwith explanatory statement wherever required:

ABC LIMITED

Registered Office: 4, Anna Road, Chennai - 600 001.

NOTICE TO ANNUAL GENERAL MEETING
TO THE DIRECTORS:

Notice is hereby given that the 10th General Meeting of the Company will be held at the Admn. Office of the company at 31st Rajaji Road, Chennai at 11.00 PM on Sunday, the 24th September, 2006 to transact the following business:

(i) To finalise the annual report for the year ended 31st March, 2006.

(ii) To confirm the interim dividend already paid and to recommend the final dividend.

(iii) To re - appoint X and Mrs. Y both retire by rotation as directors of the Company.

(iv) To confirm the appoint of Z, who was co - opted as additional director on 26th March, 2006 by the Board.

(v) To appoint auditors.

(vi) To amend the object clause of the memorandum of the company.

I request the members of the Board to make it convenient to attend the meeting.

Thank you

Yours truly,

Chennai (A.B.C.)

17th September 2006 Chief Financial Officer

(2007 - December)

Question yourself with the following:

1. Whether the notice is titled as 10th AGM or not?
2. Whether the Administration Office is within the city?
3. Whether Sunday is a working day?

4. Whether it is held during normal working hours in a day?
5. Whether annual accounts is adopted?
6. Whether the dividend per share to be recommended is mentioned?
7. Whether confirmation of additional director & amendment of object clause is a Special business & what resolution does it require?
8. Whether explanatory statement is enclosed for the Special business?
9. Whether CFO is a director or secretary authorized to issue the notice?

QUORUM [Section 174]

Quorum is the minimum number of Members **PERSONALLY PRESENT** [not by proxy] at the Meeting for the Meeting to be valid.

- Five (5) Members, in case of a Public Limited Company - Quorum.
- Two (2) Members, in case of a Private Limited Company - Quorum.

Articles may prescribe Higher Quorum but NOT less.

1. Article No. 72 of the article of association of the company requires 25 persons to be present personally and / or by proxy to constitute the quorum at a general meeting. The company now wants to have the lowest minimum quorum as provided in the Companies Act, 1956. As the Company Secretary of the Company, how could this be achieved by your company? (amend the articles and fix quorum based on type of company)
2. A complaint has been made to the Registrar of Companies by 5 members asking him to director the Timely Holdings Limited of which they are members to re - convene annual general meeting since they had not received the notice of the company for the annual general meeting held on 30th September, 2008. The Registrar of Companies issues notice as to show cause why such directors should not be issued. What would be your response as the Company Secretary of the aforesaid company? (2009 - December) (An accidental omission to issue notice sans malafide intention and further they have a proof of despatch)

Effect of Quorum, NOT PRESENT within half-an-hour of the Meeting:

1. If it's a Requisitionst Meeting, gets DISSOLVED;
2. Other Meetings gets ADJOURNED, to next week, same date, place & time;
3. If it's a meeting adjourned for want of quorum, then in the adjourned meeting 'Members Present' [even by proxy] will be counted for Quorum. Note, the word Member-s, hence minimum 2 members should be present. When Quorum can be singular, i.e., One Man Quorum,
   - Company Law Board ordered Annual General Meeting;
   - Company Law Board ordered Extraordinary General Meeting;
   - Class Meeting, where there is only one person holding particular class of shares;
   - Creditors Meeting.

PROXY [Section 176]

Proxy = Representative of a Member;

Proxy = Instrument as per Schedule IX.

Requirement relating to Proxy

Every Member who is entitled to 'attend & vote' may appoint a Proxy instead of himself, who is entitled to 'attend & vote' [not by post] AND he/she need not be a Member. The statement to this effect has to be included in the notice for GM.

The Company may adopt Format as per Schedule IX or its Own Format.

The Schedule IX proxy can be rectified whereas not the Own proxy.

REQUIREMENTS OF A VALID PROXY:

↳ "duly signed";

↳ "duly dated",

- later date supercedes
- if both Proxy on same date, both are invalid

↳ duly stamped

↳ duly lodged.

"Duly Lodged" means lodged with the Company BEFORE 48 hours of the General Meeting. Articles can provide a shorter period (requirement of longer time not valid) for submission of Proxies.

INSPECTION OF PROXY REGISTER by a MEMBER

1. 3 days Notice to be given;
2. Inspection to take place BEFORE 24 hours of the General Meeting;
3. No Extracts or Copies to be taken.

NO RIGHTS

Proxy does not have the following rights,
1. Right to Speak at General Meeting;
2. Appointing another Proxy.
3. Right to Vote by Posts;
4. Right to Vote on Show-of-Hands. Meaning, Proxy can demand a Poll before OR on Declaration of Results.

REVOCATION OF PROXY

1. If Member personally attends the Meeting;
2. Shares sold OR Member dies OR Authority revoked AND communicated to the Company.

↳ A company cannot send invitation to member appoint certain person as proxy EXCEPT naming the proxy or list of persons willing to act as proxy, to a member at his request in writing;

↳ A member of a private company shall not be entitled to appoint more than one proxy to attend on the same occasion.

MEMBERS PERSONALLY PRESENT:

The following representatives shall be treated as Members personally present, 9 Representative of a Body Corporate;

↳ Representative of President of India;

↳ Representative of Governor of the State.

VOTING [Section 177]

Voting at the Meeting is by 'show of hands', unless a Poll is demanded.

Show-Off Hands

1 Member - 1 Vote;
Single Vote per Member.

POLL

1 Share - 1 Vote; Number of Votes as many Shares held; Even Proxies are included.

DEMANDING A POLL [Section 179]

When a Poll to be conducted FORTHWITH

↳ Adjournment Motion - i.e., when it relates to adjournment of the General Meeting;

↳ Election of Chairman.

In ALL other cases, the Chairman may conduct a POLL within 48 hours of demand.

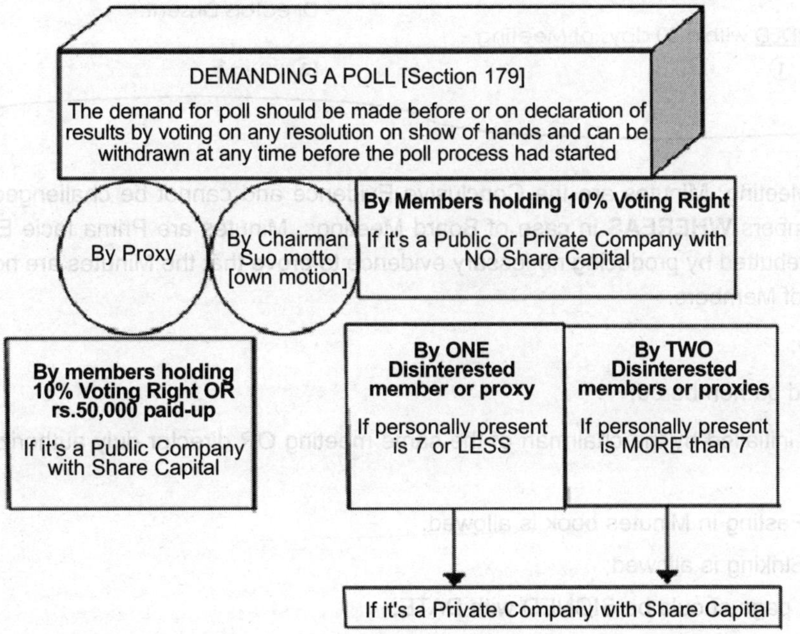

Other provisions relating to POLL:

1. AoA may provide that member shall not exercise VOTING right on shares, when calls are not paid or when co has right of lien.
2. Voting shall not be prohibited by public company when shares not held for period preceding the date on which the vote is taken.
3. Member or proxy may use his votes differently on a poll taken when he is entitled to more than one vote.
4. Chairman shall appoint two scrutineers to scrutinise the votes given on the poll and to report thereon.
5. One scrutineer shall always be a willing member (not being an officer or employee of the company) present at the meeting.
6. The chairman of the meeting shall have power to

   ↳ regulate the manner in which a poll shall be taken;

   ↳ remove a scrutineer, before the result of the poll is declared.
7. The result of the poll shall be deemed to be the decision of the meeting on the resolution on which the poll was taken.

"**MINUTES**" - Recording of fair & correct summary of Proceedings of the Meeting [mandatory statutory register @ the Registered Office]

MINUTES BOOK = CONCLUSIVE EVIDENCE OF THE PROCEEDINGS OF THE MEET

RECORDED within 30 days of Meeting ①

Directors Present:
Directors Dissent: ②

In case of General Meeting, Minutes are the Conclusive Evidence and cannot be challenged & available for INSPECTION of members **WHEREAS** in case of Board Meetings, Minutes are Prima facie Evidence i.e., the presumption can be rebutted by producing necessary evidence to prove that the Minutes are not correct & NOT AVAIL for inspection of Members.

↳ Bounded properly;

↳ Every page should be numbered;

↳ Every page to be initialled by the chairman of the same meeting OR director duly authorized by the Board for the purpose;

↳ No Pasting in Minutes book is allowed;

↳ No Striking is allowed;

↳ Last page should be SIGNED with DATE;

↳ Minutes of Board meeting should also contain,

- the names of the directors present at the meeting; and
- in the case of each resolution passed at the meeting, the names of the directors, if any, dissenting from, or not concurring in, the resolution.

↳ Chairman has the power to ALTER "Minutes" if it's defamatory or irrelevant or immaterial or detrimental to the interest of the Company.

↳ No document purporting to be a report of the proceedings shall be circulated or advertised at the expense of the company, UNLESS it includes the matters required to be contained in the MINUTES of the proceedings of such meeting;

COMMON POINTS TO BE CONSIDERED WHILE DRAFTING MINUTES OF BOARD/GENERAL MEETING

1. Minutes should record essential elements of meeting and should contain the FULL TEXT of resolutions passed along with the type of approval received viz ordinary or special or unanimous.
2. Title to minutes shall be given with the details of the meeting and should state the nature of meeting.
3. Names of persons present should be mentioned. Similarly, if auditor or practicing company secretary is present at the meeting, it should be recorded.
4. Person who acted as a Chairman shall be specified.
5. It shall contain the resolutions passed, name of the proposer & seconder (person who accepts the resolution), whether the resolution was passed or failed should be stated. In case of voting, the details of votes for & against the resolution should be recorded. Minutes may be in narrative form also.

6. Directors dissenting from voting (i.e.) voting against the resolution, shall also be recorded; further statutory provisions may also be recorded such as interested director did not participate as per Section 299. (Minutes of Board Meeting).

7. Any statutory or non-statutory register presented & signed shall also be noted.

8. Meeting generally ends with vote of thanks to chairman which should also be recorded.

SAMPLE MINUTES OF GENERAL MEETING

Minutes of the 9th Annual General Meting of the shareholders of Learn Labz Ltd held at No.5, Ayyapan Temple Street, Chennai at 9 PM on 11th September 2010.

PRESENT - 900 shareholders in person and 100 shareholders by proxy.

Ms. Divya, Partner, M/s. Mittal & Co., Chartered Accountants, Mumbai and Mr. Venkat, Practising Company Secretary were present.

In attendance - Mr. Ashwin, Company Secretary of the company. Mr. Vijay, Chairman of the company took the chair.

1. Chairman declared that quorum is present and welcomed the shareholders. He announced that Proxy register, Register of members and Register of director's shareholding are available for inspection throughout the meeting.
2. With the permission of shareholders, the notice was read and chairman started the Chairman's speech ((it will be about the prospects of the company. Some company publishes the speech in the newspapers as a part of public relations or image building activity. Kindly note, Chairman's speech is not part of statutory agenda of the meeting and hence it cannot be said to be minutes of the meeting)).
3. Mr. Ashwin, the Company Secretary read the auditors report for the year ended 31st March 2010 and the compliance certificate.
4. RESOLUTION NO.1: Consideration of Annual Accounts:

The following ordinary resolution was moved by Chairman and seconded by Ms. Shanti: "Resolved that the audited Balance Sheet of the company as on 31st March 2010 and Profit/Loss account for the year ended 2010, together with Schedules & Notes attached along with the Reports of Directors & Auditors, as circulated to members and laid before the meeting, be and hereby approved & adopted." The Chairman of the meeting invited questions and answered the same. Thereafter the resolution was put to vote and was carried unanimously on show of hands.

5. RESOLUTION 2: Declaration of Dividend: Chairman informed that due to market conditions the company decided to plough back the profits made and has decided not to declare dividend for this year. Shareholders raised queries and were satisfied on justification by the Chairman.
6. RESOLUTION 3: Appointment of retiring director: The following ordinary resolution was moved by Mr. Venkatesh and seconded by Mr. Srinivasan. "Resolved that Mr. Anand, who retires as a Director by rotation and being eligible offers himself for same as a Director, be and is hereby reappointed as a director of the company".

The resolution was put to vote and was carried unanimously.

7. RESOLUTION 4: Appointment of Auditors: The following ordinary resolution was moved by Mr. Bala and seconded by Mr. Subramanian. "Resolved that as per Section 224 of Companies Act, M/s. Mittal & Co., Chartered Accountants, Mumbai, be and hereby appointed as the auditors of the company to hold office from the conclusion of this AGM till the conclusion of next AGM on a remuneration of Rs. 1,00,000 (Rupees One Lakh only) and out of pocket expenses incurred for audit."
8. Mr. Niranjan proposed and Mr. Manoharan seconded a vote of thanks to the chair.

The Chairman thanked all the shareholders present and declared the meeting as concluded.

VIJAY
Chairman
30th September 2010

Draft the minutes of annual general meeting of Happy Limited at which besides adoption of accounts, declaration of dividend, appointment of auditors and the appointment of additional director as regular director featured for consideration and decision. (2009 -June)

There are only 2 sections in Companies Act which allows passing of ***Ordinary resolution with Central Government approval*** if one is unable to pass Special resolution which includes ***Section 81(1A)*** regarding preferential issue and ***Section 149(2A)*** regarding commencing business in Other objects clause. Both of which sections are applicable ***only to a public limited company***. In all other cases, only the concerned approval (i.e.) Special or Ordinary as the case may be is mandatory. By this point, you would be familiar with the basic flow of things whenever a specific kind of resolution is passed. Just remember whensover a question is asked to RE-DRAFT a resolution,

1. First, understand the essence of the thing which they are going to do:
2. then think of the relevant legal provisions and
3. draft a fresh resolution on your own without reading the Resolution which shall be re-drafted,
4. then cross verify what you have written and what they have missed to justify your answer.

By now, you would have understood that while drafting a resolution,

1. Always remember the concerned legal provisions along with sections, if possible. [Resolved that pursuant to Sections ___of Companies Act read with rules & regulations made thereunder]
2. If the resolution mandates approval of general meeting, understand **whether it is a prior approval or post approval**.

- If it is a prior approval, you may start your resolution this way, "Resolved that …… and having obtained the approval of members at general meeting by way of special resolution…".
- If it is a post approval, you may start it this way, "Resolved that …. and subject to the approval of members at general meeting….".

3. Whenever Central Government approval is required along with member's approval, include that too. [Resolved that….having obtained or subject to approval of Central Government…..]
4. The last paragraph of the resolution should contain the e-forms that need to be filed and the authorization given to a person to file the same. [Resolved further that Mr. A, the company secretary of the company be authorized to file e-forms nos. and such other necessary forms as may be required to carry out the said activity".
5. Try remembering all the provisions together.
6. Whenever the question is of a listed company, think whether postal ballot will be attracted? [Any listing agreement provisions to be complied with!]

Further, draft also an explanatory statement whenever the item is normally carried on at an Extraordinary General Meeting or when it is not the 4 Ordinary businesses annual general meeting. Thus, almost every resolution (Special business) apart from adopting accounts, declaring dividend, appointing directors/auditors in the place of those who are retiring will mandate Explanatory Statement. Hence, include that while drafting the resolution.

First, familiarize yourself with the list of items which shall be conducted only At a Board Meeting and not by way of circular resolution. Commit to memory the above mentioned list of items. Other than the said list, all other items can be transacted either at a board meeting or through circular resolution. If any case is not falling under the category of ordinary or special resolution or under list of items which shall be transacted only at a board meeting, then the Company Secretary has a choice to transact the business at a meeting or by circulation.

Board Meeting Resolution

Meeting of Brains = Board Meeting [BM]

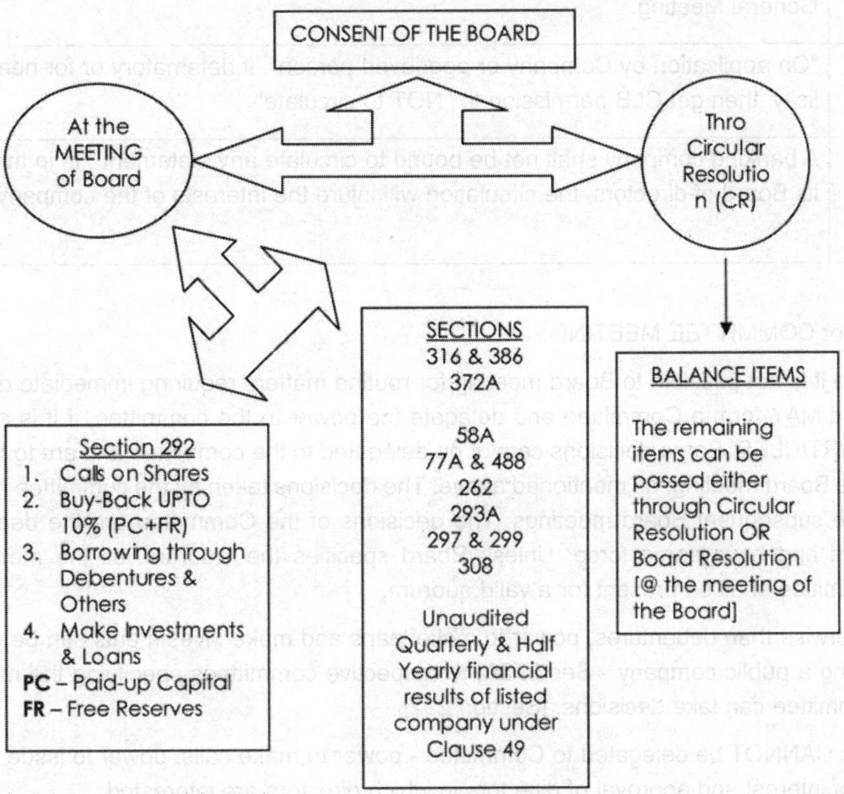

BOARD Meeting RESOLUTION means where one should get Consent of the Board only at the Meeting of the Board of Directors [BoD].

CIRCULAR RESOLUTION can be passed in urgent cases where it is not possible to conduct the Board Meeting or Committee Meeting, the consent can be obtained by circulating the DRAFT resolution to ALL Directors or Committee Members at their usual address in India EXCEPT where it is mandatory to pass resolution on the Board meeting (as mentioned above). Such resolution may be noted in the SUBSEQUENT Board Meeting.

It is necessary that the student understand the difference between the Circular Resolution (Board) u/s. 289 and Circulation of (members) Resolution u/s. 188.

"All resolutions cannot be passed by the Board of directors of a company by circulation." Comment (2008 - June) (2008 - December)

Circulation of Members Resolution [section 188]

On requisition by members representing 1/20th of the voting rights in respect of the resolution to be circulated **OR** by not less than 100 members having the right aforesaid and holding shares in the company on which there has been paid up an aggregate sum of not less than Rs. 1 Lakh,

↳ the company shall give to the members notice [at the expense of requisitionists unless resolved by company otherwise] of any resolution which may properly be moved.

Step 1	The Notice, in writing, shall reach the Company atleast 2 weeks [6 weeks, if it requires notice of Resolution] before the Date of General Meeting [no time limit, if AGM called after deposit of the requisition].
Step 2	Inform forthwith (immediately) the members who are entitled to receive the notice of General Meeting.
Step 3	"On application by Company or aggrieved person", if defamatory or for needless publicity, then get CLB permission to "NOT to circulate".
Step 4	A banking company shall not be bound to circulate any statement , if, in the opinion of its Board of directors, the circulation will injure the interests of the company

Committee of Board or COMMITTEE MEETING:

Since it is not possible to Board meeting for routine matters requiring immediate decisions, the Board MAY form a Committee and delegate the power to the committee, if it is authorised by the ARTICLES. Some decisions cannot be delegated to the committee and are to be taken only in the Board meeting, as mentioned above. The decisions taken by the committee may be noted in the subsequent Board meetings. The decisions of the Committee are the decisions of the Board and have same force. Unless Board specifies the Quorum, all the members of the Committee shall be present for a valid quorum.

Power to borrow otherwise than debentures, power to make loans and make investments can be delegated by the board [of not being a public company - Sec 372A] to respective committees specifying the maximum limit UPTO which the committee can take decisions. [Section 292]

The following powers CANNOT be delegated to Committee - power to make calls, power to issue debentures, notice of disclosure of interest and approval of directors in which directors are interested.

Listed companies have to mandatorily constitute Audit committee and Share holders Grievances committee. One director cannot hold the chairmanship for more than 5 committees of the listed companies and be member of more than 10 such committees. Constitution on remuneration committee is a non-mandatory requirement under clause 49 of the Listing agreement.

Whether the convening the Board meeting through video conferencing is recognised in india ?

Electronic mode of board & committee meetings are permitted (ie) video conferencing is allowed to communicate concurrently with each other without an intermediary. However, every director shall attend atleast 1 MEETING PHYSICALLY every financial year.

Responsibilities of Chairman & Company Secretary regarding video conferencing:

Prior to the meeting

a. To ensure that the NOTICE should mention necessary information on video conferencing facility and request for the confirmation from the director through email or telephone. [Director PRESUMED to attend physically if there is NO confirmation]

At the meeting

b. To ensure the actual presence, a ROLL CALL shall be made where a director needs to state his place, location and then the existence of QUORUM (includes directors participating through video conferencing) may be certified.

c. To safeguard the integrity & to ensure proper equipments & to ensure none other than authorised participants attend the meeting and to repeat or reiterate when there is an interruption

d. To make a ROLL CALL in case of voting by poll & it shall be noted

e. To record the Chairman's speech on SUMMARY of decisions taken & the consent/dissent thereof with respect to each agenda item and it shall be preserved for 1 YEAR therefrom.

f. To ensure presence of QUORUM throughout the meeting, again a ROLL CALL shall be made at the END of meeting.

After the meeting

g. To prepare the minutes considering the PLACE as where Chairman or Secretary sits DURING the meeting and also confirm the MODE OF ATTENDANCE of every director (for last 3 meetings) and the Statutory Registers shall be DEEMED to have been SIGNED on CONSENT.

h. Circulate DRAFT minutes in SOFT COPY within 7 days of meeting for comments/clarification & then enter in MINUTES BOOK.

While drafting the MINUTES of the board meeting where directors attend through video conferencing, the following shall be mentioned:

MINUTES OF THE MEETING OF THE BOARD OF DIRECTORS OF HELD THROUGH VIDEO CONVERENCING (VC) AT 2.00 P.M. AT ____________

Present:

Mr. Raj	Executive Chairman	At Registered Office
Ms. Chand	Company Secretary	At Registered Office
Mr. Matt	Director	through VC from New Delhi
Mrs. Reese	Independent Director	through VC from Amsterdam
Mr. Raut	Independent Director	through VC from South Africa

Attendance of all the Directors of the company during the last 3 meetings are as under:

Sl. No.	Name of the Director	Month, Year	Month, Year	Month, Year
1.		through VC from Hyderabad	attended in person	attended in person
2.		attended in person	attended in person	attended in person
3.		leave of absence	leave of absence	attended in person
4.		leave of absence	attended in person	leave of absence
5.		leave of absence	attended in person	leave of absence
6.		not applicable	not applicable	not applicable
7.		attended in person	attended in person	attended in person
8.		attended in person	attended in person	attended in person

Chairman

Mr. Raj, Chairman occupied the Chair. He made the roll call and confirmed the participation of the Directors and attendance of the Directors during the last 3 meetings. Chairman confirmed the presence of the quorum and conducted the proceedings of the Meeting.

(Then the normal items of the meeting can be included, as per the agenda)

Chairman announced the summary of the decisions taken in the meeting and that all the decisions were approved unanimously by the Directors present at the meeting. Before the conclusion of the Meeting, Chairman made the roll call at the conclusion of the meeting and ensured presence of quorum throughout the meeting.

There being no other business to transact, the Meeting concluded with a vote of thanks to the Chair.

Place: **CHAIRMAN**

Date:

Whether board meeting resolutions or agreements shall be registered with RoC

Section 192 of Companies Act mandates filing of e-form 21 within 30 days to RoC following EFORM COMPLIANCE CHART in case of following,

- Board Resolution for appointment & terms of appointment of Managing Director (MD);
- Board Resolution with copies of terms of appointment of Sole Selling Agent (SSA).

specimen notice of a board meeting

... LIMITED

Mr./Ms. ....

....

Re.: Next Board Meeting

Dear Sir,

The next meeting of the Board of Directors will be held on ...... day, ... 20.........,

at ....am/pm at the registered office of the Company. The agenda of the business to be transacted at the meeting is enclosed/will follow soon.

Please make it convenient to attend the meeting. Please send the enclosed sheet to enable us to make arrangements for your travel and stay.

Yours faithfully,

....

Company Secretary

First Board Meeting

1. Issue notice as per Articles of association of the Company.
2. The first meeting should be convened within 1 month from the date of incorporation. (since auditors have to be appointed within 1 month - Sec.224(5))
3. The following certificates shall be presented before the Board a. Original certificate of incorporation b. Memorandum & Articles of Association c. Designs of common seal, share certificate, letterhead, nameplate, signboard d. Statement of preliminary expenses incurred e. Draft Statement in lieu of prospectus to be submitted before the registrar for obtaining certificate for commencement of business for public companies. f. Pre incorporation agreements g. Attendance registers
4. Place the folders containing agenda, notes to the agenda, draft minutes to agenda, etc on the table before the meeting starts.
5. Obtain the signature of directors before the meeting starts.
6. If quorum is present as required under Section 287, declare the meeting in order.
7. Inform names of directors seeking leave of absence.
8. The directors present may elect one among them as chairman.

9. Help the chairman to conduct meeting.
10. Other items not in agenda can be discussed with the permission of chair.
11. Decide time and place of next board meeting.
12. After the meeting prepare draft minutes reviewed by chairman and other directors for information and comments.
13. Finalise the minutes and enter them into the Minutes Book within 30 days of the meeting. All pages to be consecutively numbered.
14. All pages to be intialed and last page to be dated & signed by the chairman of the meeting or the chairman of the succeeding meeting

Section 291 → General Powers of Board - The Board of directors of a company shall be entitled to exercise all such powers, and to do all such acts and things, as the company is authorised to exercise and do EXCEPT for which the Act , MOA or AOA requires the consent of shareholders or other authority (CG / CLB etc.) No regulation made by the company in general meeting shall invalidate any prior (valid) act of the Board.

ITEMS WHICH SHALL BE DONE ONLY AT BOARD MEETING & NOT BY WAY OF CIRCULAR RESOLUTION

In general the following rules are applicable to board meeting,

- Consent of the Board at the meeting of the Board Meeting for the prescribed cases; in all other cases, even Circular Resolution is permitted.
- Approval by way of Simple Majority.
- Agenda (specific notice) for the Board Meeting is NOT mandatory.

SPECIAL SECTIONS

There are 3 special sections in Board Meeting, which are Sections 316, 386 & 372A which requires,

- Consent of the Board only at the Board Meeting
- Approval of ALL directors present at the meeting (i.e.) Unanimous Approval
- Mandatory AGENDA to be sent to every director in India or at such address in India.

Section 316: Appointment of Managing Director in 2 or more companies A company may appoint or employ a person as its MD,

↳ If such person is MD of 1 company, then with Board Meeting - Unanimous Approval by giving specific notice (Agenda) to all the directors then in India.

↳ If such person is MD of 2 companies, then Central Government may permit such person to appointed, if it is SATISFIED that it is necessary that the companies should for their proper working function as a SINGLE unit and have a COMMON MD.

↳ Further as per Part I(d) of Schedule XIII, the TOTAL REMUNERATION to such MD from ALL the companies shall not exceed the following,

ONE MD or ONE WTD	UPTO 5% (Net Profit)
MORE THAN ONE MD/WTD	UPTO 10% (Net Profit)

Resolution approving the appointment of Managing Directors, notwithstanding that he is already the Managing Director of another company. (2009 & 2010 - December)

Section 386: Appointment of Manager in 2 or more companies

A company may appoint or employ a person as its Manager,

↳ If such person is Manager of 1 company, then with Board Meeting - Unanimous Approval by giving specific notice (Agenda) to all the directors then in India.

↳ If such person is Manager of 2 companies, then Central Government may permit such person to appointed, if it is SATISFIED that it is necessary that the companies should for their proper working function as a SINGLE unit and have a COMMON Manager.

But the SAME may be restricted on COMBINED reading of the following,

- As per Section 387, the remuneration to Manager exceeding 5% requires PRIOR approval of Central Government.
- As per Part I(d) of Schedule XIII, the TOTAL REMUNERATION to such Manager from ALL the companies shall not exceed the following,

ONE MD or ONE WTD or ONE MANAGER	UPTO 5% (NP)
MORE THAN ONE MD/WTD	UPTO 10% (NP)

↳ Thus, an individual may be appointed as MANAGER in ONLY ONE company and not more than one (i.e.) Appointing Manager of 1 company in other company requires Central Government approval to exceed the 5% ceiling of Net Profits.

Section 372A: Inter-corporate Loans & Investments

Any loan or guarantee/security in connection with loan and investments, eXCeeDinG 60% of Paid-up Capital & Free Reserves; OR 100% of Free Reserves, whichever is more, shall require prior approval of shareholders by the way of special resolution and prior approval of Financial Institutions;

Within the Prescribed Limits,

↳ Board Resolution (Not by Circular Resolution) - Unanimous Resolution by giving SPECIFIC NOTICE and shall be sanctioned with the consent of ALL director's present at meeting;

↳ PFI - Prior Approval of Financial Institutions, if there is any default in repayment as per the terms & conditions of the loan.

Guarantee Exceeding the Limits, can be given if

↳ Unanimous Board Resolution is passed to give guarantee in accordance with the provisions of this section;

↳ Only in case of emergencies where it is not possible to get the approval of GM by way of Special Resolution;

↳ Special Resolution (SR) to be passed within 12 months OR Immediate AGM (whichever is earlier) confirming the Board Resolution.

PUBLIC DEPOSITS (Section 58A) & APPROVAL OF ADVERTISEMENT

ACCEPTANCE OF PUBLIC DEPOSITS BY,

↳ Non-Banking Finance Companies (NBFC) is governed by compliance of RBI directions; [i.e, NBFC's need not comply with acceptance of deposit rules notified by MCA].

↳ **Non-Banking non-Finance Companies** is governed by compliance of Section 58A read with Companies (Acceptance of Deposits) Rules, 1975.

S.N	Type of Company	Conditions or Limits for Acceptance of Deposits
1.	**PUBLIC COMPANY after** making a fresh SLoA [R-4A] or advertisement [R-4] in each succeeding financial year, for inviting deposits during that financial year **as per Deposit rules, the date of approval by Board of text of advertisement/sloa has to be specified. Hence, it shall be done only at a Board meeting.**	↳ Deposits invited ONLY as per Rules; ↳ The Company is NOT in default in repayment of Deposits or Interests thereon. Submit copy of **Advertisement** to **RoC** giving Financial Position for 3 preceding years with particulars of deposit, amount overdue, due to small shareholders, max. Amount that can be raised and the amount already raised, along with a **Declaration** that the Company has complied with the Rules & not defaulted u/s. 58A & such deposits shall rank pari passu with unsecured liabilities, is published in English & Vernacular Language Newspaper **OR statement in lieu of Advertisement [SLoA] to RoC**, if such issue is NOT made to Public;  SIGNED by Majority of Directors or agent VALIDITY OF Advertisement or SLoA to accept Public Deposits: Valid till the Latest of, ↳ 6 months from close of Financial Year; ↳ AGM, where Accounts are laid; ↳ AGM should have been held.
2.	PRIVATE COMPANY	Can accept Deposits ONLY from, ↳ its Members ↳ Directors & ↳ Their Reelatives and A Declaration that "it is NOT out of Borrowed Funds" shall be given.
3.	Non-Government Public Company [10%+25%] [Rule 3]	↳ UPTO 10% of Paid-Up Capital PLUS Free Reserves from, ↳ Shareholders & / or ↳ Deposits guaranteed by Directors of the Co. ↳ AND UPTO 25% of Paid-up Capital PLUS Free Reserves from others, including public.
4.	Government Company or Public Sector undertaking	UPTO 35% of Paid-Up Capital PLUS Free Reserves from shareholders, public & others.

(a)	The company must prepare the text of the advertisement containing the particulars laid down in rule 4(2) of the Deposit Rules and also the highlights and major features of the scheme(s) of deposits.
(b)	Place both the texts of the advertisement before the Board at its MEETING and pass a resolution approving the texts. The text in the vernacular language should also be placed before the Board for its approval.
(c)	Arrange for 2 copies of the text to be signed by a MAJORITY of the total number of directors (or by the authorised agents of directors) on the Board, as on the date of the Board meeting at which the text of the advertisement was approved (and not a majority of the directors present at the meeting).
(d)	After the text of the Advertisement has been approved by the Board, arrange to file one copy of each of the texts of the advertisement in English and vernacular language with the RoC.
(e)	Arrange for publication of the advertisement at least once in a leading English newspaper an donce in a vernacular newspaper, circulating in the State in which the registered office of the company is situated. The advertisement in the vernacular newspaper must be in the language of the newspaper.
(f)	A fresh advertisement must be published on or before the date on which the validity period of the previous advertisement has expired; or else, no existing deposit should be renewed and no new deposit should be accepted between the last date of the validity of the previous advertisement and the date of publication of the new advertisement.

DECLARATION OF SOLVENCY SHALL BE DONE ONLY AT BOARD MEETING DECLARATION OF SOLVENCY [DOS] Under Buy Back -

to SEBI, if listed & to RoC [Form 4A]

This DoS is u/s.77A and different from DoS under Winding up

THAT Board has made full enquiry into the affairs of the company AND	are of the opinion that, it is capable of meeting liabilities, AND	WILL NOT be Insolvent WITHIN 1 year (DoS), AND verified by an AFFIDAVIT	SIGNED by 2 OR more Directors, 1 shall be Managing Director, if any

DECLARATION OF SOLVENCY [DOS] Under Winding Up - to RoC

This DoS is u/s. 488 and different from DoS under Buy Back

THAT Board has made full enquiry into he affairs of the Co. AND	And are of the opinion that, no debts, OR that it will be able to pay its debts in FULL	WITHIN such period NOT exceeding 3 years from the COMMENCEMENT of winding up AND verified by an AFFIDAVIT	SIGNED by MAJORITY of Directors

DoS shall be made,

- WITHIN 5 weeks immediately preceding the date of the passing of the Resolution for winding up and filed with RoC before that date
- WITH a copy of the report of the Auditors of the company on the Profit and Loss account and Balance Sheet and Statement of Assets & Liabilities, of the company for the period commencing from the date last such account was prepared till latest practicable date before making such DoS.

PROCEDURE FOR APPOINTING DIRECTOR IN CASUAL VACANCY u/s. 262:

1. Consent and disqualifications: Ensure that proposed directors does not suffer any disqualifications under section 274, 275, 278 and 284 and obtain consent to act as director from the proposed director.
2. Obtain a declaration from the proposed director that he is not disqualified to act as director under Section 274(1)(g) in Form DD-A.
3. Give notice of the BOARD MEETING under section 286, hold the Board meeting and appoint the director by passing a resolution as required under Section 262
4. Such director shall hold office only upto the date up to which the director in whose place he is appointed would have held office if it had not been vacated.
5. File with RoC e-form 32 along within 30 days following EFORM COMPLIANCE CHART.
6. Make necessary entries in registers maintained under section 301, 303 and 307.
7. Inform the concerned stock exchanges.

CALLS ON SHARES

Procedure for making a call [section 91]

1. A call must be made on the authority of the Board of Directors by a resolution passed at its meeting in accordance with ARTICLES and the Board cannot delegate this power. Convene a Board meeting and pass a resolution for making a call. The Board resolution must specify the following details: (a) The number of shares held; (b) The call money payable on each share and the total amount payable; (c) The date, place & manner of payment; interest on delayed payment; (d) Consequences of failure to the call money, i.e., forfeiture of shares. Where the Articles require that the resolution of the directors should indicate the time, amount, place and person to whom the amount of the call should be paid, every requirement is of the same importance and should be STRICTLY complied with.
2. Send the CALL NOTICE to every member who is liable to pay call money specifying the above details, well in advance and strictly in accordance with the provisions of the ARTICLES in all respects.
3. In the case of a listed company as per SEBI Regulations ensure that the calls have been structured in such a manner that the entire subscription money is called within 12 months from the date of allotment.
4. In the case of a listed company as per the Listing Agreement, Call Notice shall be approved by Stock Exchanges and shall be sent to all recognised stock exchanges
5. Make arrangement for COLLECTION OF THE CALL MONEY at select branches of the company's bankers.
6. Despatch by REGISTERED POST the call notice to the concerned shareholder at his registered address. If shares of the company are held jointly by two or more persons, a call notice will be sent to the first-named joint holder but all of them are jointly & severally liable.

7. REMINDERS should be sent to the shareholders who have not paid call money in response to the first notice. It should state that,
   (a) Interest payable on the delayed payment of the call money;
   (b) A warning (atleast 14 days notice) about forfeiture of the shares for non-payment of call money.

8. Make ENTRIES in the Register of Members in respect of call money received. Ask shareholders to send the Share Certificates for necessary ENDORSEMENT. Return the Share Certificates after the endorsement is made and they are initialed/signed by the Company Secretary or other authorised officer and stamped.

9. If the Articles of Association of a company so authorise, the company may accept from any member the whole or a part of the amount remaining unpaid on any shares held by him, although it has not been called up. However the member who has paid any CALL MONEY IN ADVANCE shall not be entitled to any voting rights till it is due and payable.

10. Particulars in respect of amount called up and unpaid call must be disclosed in the BALANCE SHEET as required by Schedule VI

What type of resolution is required for making final call on shares on which 80% money was collected at the time of issue. (2007 - June)

BUY BACK UPTO 10% OF PAID UP CAPITAL & FREE RESERVES u/s. 77A

A company can BUY BACK securities UPTO 25% of Paid up Equity Capital in a Financial Year by spending UPTO 10% of Paid up Equity Capital & Free Reserves by passing a Resolution at the Board Meeting. The detailed procedure is given under FINANCIAL RESTRUCTURING chapter in Corporate Restructuring.

BORROWING THROUGH DEBENTURES & OTHERS

Procedure for BORROWING u/s. 293(1)(d)

The Board of Directors at its Board MEETING can **borrow** UPTO the aggregate of the **paid-up capital** and its **free reserves** (excluding the temporary loans);

"temporary loans" means loans repayable on demand or within six months from the date of the loan but does not include loans raised for the purpose of financing expenditure of a capital nature.

In case the SAID limit is exceeded, approval by shareholders is mandatory. [Onus is on the lender to prove that he advanced the loan in good faith and without knowledge that the limit imposed by that clause had been exceeded]

Debenture is a method of Borrowing,

↳ to be exercised only by a Board of Public Company [read Section 3(1)(iii)]

↳ at a Meeting of the Board [read Section 292]

↳ Total Borrowing including Debentures UPTO [Paid-up Capital + Free Reserves], WITHOUT the consent of Members in General Meeting [read Section 293(1)(d)]

Procedure for allotment of shares/Debentures issued by private placement

Convene a MEETING of the Board/Allotment Committee (if constituted by the Board) by sending notice of the meeting to all the directors/members of the Committee. **Model Board resolution for allotment of shares/debentures** **"RESOLVED THAT** ... (number) equity shares/debentures of the company be and are hereby allotted to the respective applicants in various categories as shown in the Allotment Statement placed on the table, in pursuance of the issue of shares/debentures of the Company by private placement by the circular dated ... .., as per the basis of allotment set out in the Allotment Statement. **FURTHER RESOLVED THAT** 1. The names of the allottees be entered in the Register of Members of the Company. 2. Mr.A, the Company Secretary of the company be authorised to file e-form 2 (for allotment of shares) and e-form 3 (for allotment of debentures) 3. Excess amount of application money received shall be refunded forthwith to them by Refund Orders. 4. In the event of non-payment of allotment money, interest at x% may be charged from the date following the last date fixed for payment of the allotment money to the date of realisation of cheque. 5. X & Y, directors of the company shall sign the share/debenture certificate to be issued to the allottees and Mr.A, Company Secretary is authorised to sign the share certificates as authorised signatory. 6. Common seal be affixed to each share certificate hereby authorised to be issued in the presence of any one director signing the certificate."
2. Pass a resolution for allotment of shares/debentures. If the full value of shares/debentures has not been paid on the application, and any allotment money is payable by the allottee, a resolution in that behalf also would be passed.
3. Send allotment letters to the allottees with requisite stamps affixed as per the Stamp Act of the State in which the Allotment Letters are issued, if the company intends to dispatch share certificates/ debentures
4. Despatch Share Certificates/Debenture Certificates within 3 months from the date of allotment (1 month in the case of a listed company).
5. File RETURN OF ALLOTMENT in e-Form No. 2/3 within 30 days to RoC following the EFORM COMPLIANCE CHART.
6. mmediately after the allotment enter the particulars of the allottees in the REGISTER OF MEMBERS. [Section 150]/Register of debenture holder.
7. Ensure that the provisions in the Articles of Association of the company regarding allotment are duly complied with.

CONTRIBUTION FOR POLITICAL PURPOSE u/s. 293A

Procedure for contributing to charitable, nDF & political purposes

1. Board Meeting approval either by meeting or circular resolution will be enough if contribution for charitable purpose (not directly relating to the business of company or employee welfare) in a financial year does NOT exceed Rs. 50,000 or 5% of average net profit for preceding 3 financial years (whichever is greater); exceeding which shareholders approval u/s. 293(1)(e) is mandatory by filing e-form 23 for ordinary resolution.
2. The contributions to charitable and other funds relating to the business of the company or the welfare of its employees are NOT conditional upon the existence of profits and approval of the company at general meeting.
3. The provisions relating to National Defence Fund (NDF) u/s. 293B are NOT subject to any restrictions; this section OVERRIDES MoA, AoA and the Act.
4. Political contributions are prohibited in case of: • Government companies; and • Companies which are in existence for less than 3 financial years.
5. In other cases, political contributions are permitted by a company in any financial year UPTO 5% of the average net profits (determined in accordance with the provisions of sections 349 and 350) during 3 immediately preceding financial years. [Section 293A] **Note:** Auditors Report will qualify once the Ceiling is exceeded.
6. It covers contribution to any political party or political purpose to any person. Expenditure incurred on advertisements in souvenirs issued by the political parties may on the facts of a particular case amount to political contribution in the guise of advertisement. Thus, Political Contribution by ANY MEANS is covered.
7. It is, therefore, necessary to ensure that the amount paid for each such advertisement should be reasonable and the advertisements are in the interests of the business of the company.
8. Donations in the form of shares will be reckoned in the prescribed ceiling and thus disclosure in the profit and loss account is necessary.

Section 297 - ContraCts in WHiCH DireCtors are intresteD

Not Applicable to

↳ Immovable Property Transactions;

↳ Banking / Insurance Transactions;

↳ Market Price Transactions;

↳ Transactions between 2 PUBLIC LIMITED Companies;

↳ Transactions in ordinary course of business for upto Rs.5000 per year;

↳ Contract of Employment of Director as MD / WTD.

Contracts = P/S/Sy of G/M/S or U/wg of Sh / Deb; Contracts shall be,

↳ Purchase / Sale / Supply of Goods / Materials / Services OR

↳ Underwriting of Shares / Debentures;

Authority

BM - Consent at Board Meeting or Convene BM within 3 months;

PCG - Prior approval of CG, if Paid-up Capital is 1 crore OR more;
File eform 24A for Central Government (CG) approval.

Note- NO blanket consent permissible, meaning, every transaction to be considered separately.

Interested Persons

Director	His Relative	-
Firm	Director or Relative is a Partner	Other Partners of the Firm
Private Company	Director is a Member	Director is a Director

Just 3 Conditions to attract Section 297 [ALL condns mandatory]

↳ Whether it is a Contract, as per this Section;

↳ Check Paid-up Capital to determine the Authority for approval;

↳ Find out whether the Contract is with Interested Persons.

However recently, MCA has decided to approve such CONTRACTS ONLINE if it is approved by Special Resolution to the effect that:

1. Proposed contract is COMPETITIVE @ arm's length WITHOUT CONFLICT of interest & FAVOURABLE as compared to similar contracts.
2. NO default is made in debts or its interest or deposits or filing of financials & returns.
3. The proposed contract is NOT covered under provisions of Managerial personnel or office or place of profit or loans u/s. 295.
4. The company & its directors have complied with Sections 173, 287, 299 - 301 of the Act.

Contravention

"Contract becomes VOIDABLE" @ the option of the BoD, if PC is less than 1 Crore; "629A penalty applies" (ie) Penalty where no specific penalty is provided under the Act. The defaulting company, officer and such other persons shall be imposed fine UPTO Rs.5,000/- & Rs.500 PER day in case of continuing offence.

Note: Director need NOT VACATE u/s. 283.

Sections 299, 300 & 301 - MANDATORY DISCLOSURE OF INTERESTS BY DIRECTOR

Section 299: DISCLOSURE of interest by all Director or Directors of all companies having MORE THAN 2% of Paid-up Capital in OTHER COMPANY & persons covered u/s. 295, 297, 314;

↳ General notice of disclosure (form 24AA) on 12th month of every Financial Year to be given by Director in the Board Meeting;

↳ Notice of Disclosure in the subsequent Board Meeting, as & when the Directors become interested.

CONTRAVENTION → Fine UPTO Rs. 50,000/- [+] vacation of office [+] refund of all remuneration.

Section 300: INTERESTED Director of a Public Limited Company including its Private Subsidiaries,

↳ NOT counted for Quorum;

↳ Not eligible to Vote; not to participate in discussions relating to interested matters; UNLESS OTHERWISE, a CG notification in Official Gazette EXEMPTS.

CONTRAVENTION → Fine Upto rs. 50,000/-

Section 301: **"REGISTER OF CONTRACTS"** for Contracts / Arrangements u/s. 297 / 299 to be updated,

↳ WITHIN 7 days of Board Meeting, where approval is given;

↳ 7 days of receipt @ Registered Office OR 30 days of Contract, whichever is later.

Such Register has to be SIGNED by all Directors & kept at Registered Office & available for inspection on payment of prescribed f ees.

NOT APPLICABLE to,

↳ contract or arrangement for the sale, purchase or supply of any goods, materials or services if the value Rs.1000 or less, in the aggregate in any year;

↳ contract or arrangement by a banking company for the collection of bills or any transaction in the ordinary course of business by banking or insurance company with any of the interested persons u/s. 297;

CONTRAVENTION → Fine UPTO Rs. 5000 per Default.

Model Form No. 24AA for general notice under section 299(3)

To

The Board of Directors,

A Ltd.

I,................, Director of A Ltd., hereby give general notice, pursuant to section 299(3) of the Companies Act, 1956, that I may be regarded as concerned or interested in any contract or arrangement which may, after the date of this notice, be entered into by A Ltd, with any of the following bodies corporate and firms during the financial year ending ....

A. Names of bodies corporate of which i am a Director

B. Names of bodies corporate of which i am a member

Name, No. of Shares held and % of the paid-up capital

C. Names of firms in which I am a member

This notice may please be brought upon and read at the next Board Meeting of the Company.

Date: Signature

Procedure:

Procedure
1. In case of contracts as mentioned in Section 297 any director who is interested has to disclose his interest in Form No. 24AA at the meeting in which contract is approved or if he is not present he has to disclose it in the next meeting.
2. Hold the Board meeting and pass the resolution approving the contract. In case chairman himself is interested a new chairman has to be appointed for the purpose of passing this resolution.
3. In the case of the company having a paid-up share capital of 1 crore or more, obtain previous approval of the Central Government by applying in e-form 24A following EFORM COMPLIANCE CHART. Before making application ensure that general NOTICE is published in newspapers (1 principal language and 1 English) and also sent to members as required under Section 640B.
4. In case of urgent necessity, approval of Board can be obtained within 3 months of entering into the contract.
Maintain a register to enter the details of the above contracts within 7 days of the Board resolution and get it signed by ALL the directors in the next Board Meeting.

NOTICE OF DISCLOSURE OF INTEREST BY DEEMED DIRECTORS [Section 308]

Deemed Director: A 'deemed director' is a person,

- who is NOT appointed as a Director BUT
- the Board of Directors of a Company is ACCUSTOMED TO ACT as per the instructions OR directions of such person.

Note: It includes such body corporate which are accustomed to act as per directions of director OR where director exercises atleast 1/3rd of total voting power.

A person is a 'deemed director' ONLY for following purposes,

- Entry into "Register of Directors" as per Section 303;
- "Register of Directors Shareholding" as per Section 307;
- Disclosure of shareholding / debentureholding in the Company or its Subsidiary or Holding Company;
- Penalty Provisions for 'Officer in Default' as per Section 5
- & no other purposes.

In case of New Company, if Articles do not specify First Directors, the INDIVIDUAL SIGNATORIES to Memorandum are 'deemed to be Directors' as per Section 254.

Any NOTICE of disclosure of interest by a deemed director shall be given IN WRITING, if it is NOT given in a BOARD MEETING, then the person giving the notice shall take steps to bring up and READ at the Board Meeting held next.

By now you would have understood almost the whole of Companies Act and the type of approval required for the same. If any of the items are not included in the list above, it can be done by simply passing a resolution of the board. Just remember, there are only 3 items in Companies Act which require Unanimous approval of the board which are Sections 316, 386 and 372A and all other items require only approval by way of Simple Majority. Also remember provisions regarding appointment of Managing director mandates filing of e-form 23 even if it is a mere board resolution. Again, remember the e-forms to be filed is based on the EFORM COMPLIANCE CHART. Further, also quote whether the directors are interested in the particular resolution. It is advisable to put at the end of drafting resolution that "None of the directors are interested in the resolution" or you could say that "Mr. A, the Managing director of the company is interested in the resolution and has restrained from voting in the resolution".

In this chapter, all the provisions which require the approval of Ministry of Corporate Affairs (Central Government) are summarized. This is one of the most important chapter from exam point of view. Understand the chapter and while answering the questions include the relevant provisions of Board or General meeting if any. Central Government could be Ministry of Corporate Affairs (MCA) unless otherwise the powers under the Act is not delegated to Regional Director or Registrar of Companies.

Application To Central Government

Central Government (CG) has the power of delegating its authority u/s. 637 to Regional Director or Registrar of Companies as the case may be. The following powers & functions CANNOT be delegated - Sections 10, 81, 89(4), 211(3) & (4), 212, 213, 235, 237, 239, 241-245, 247, 250, 259, 268 (& 310, 311,349)), 269, 274(2), 295, 300, 396, 399(4) & (5), 401, 408, 410, 411 (b), 448, 609, 613, 620, 638, 641 & 642. The select procedural requirements are discussed hereunder.

Kindly note, MCA/Central Government has DELEGATED the following powers to Regional Director: Sections 22 [Rectification of name], 224 - (3),(4),(7) & 8(a) [auditors related], 297(1) Proviso [Contracts in which directors are interested], Section 394A [Notice under Compromise or Arrangements], 400 [Notice under Oppression or Mismanagement], Second proviso to 439-(5) and (6) [Petition by RoC for Compulsory winding up], 496(1)(a) & 508(1)(a) [Liquidator to call for General meeting at the end of 1 year from winding up], 551(1) [pending liquidations], 555 - (7)(b) & (9)(a) [unpaid & unclaimed monies], Provisio to 610(1) [inspection of documents] and Section 627 [production of documents].

Further note, MCA/Central Government has DELEGATED the following powers to Registrar of Companies: Sections 21 (Name change), 25 (formation of non-profit organisation), Proviso to 31(1) [alteration of Articles], 108(1D) - revalidation of Share Transfer deed by RoC where there is Registered office of the company or by RoC in the State where Transferee resides and 572 (Change of name of Companies formed under previous Companies Act)

Procedure for modifying requirements of Schedule VI [section 211]

1. Convene a Board meeting to take decision to apply to CG to modify any requirements of Schedule VI as to Balance sheet & Profit/loss account of the company for the purposes of adapting them to the circumstances of the company.

2. File e-form 23AAA following EFORM COMPLIANCE CHART.

   The following information should invariably be furnished with the application in the fields forming part of the eForm:

   - Copies of approvals under Section 211 obtained, if any, during the last three financial years. If the company had been complying with the requirements in the past, reasons as to how the company has been complying in the past.
   - The financial year for which exemption is sought. Precise reasons/justification for seeking exemption. Details of total turnover and exports made by the company during the financial year in respect of which exemption is sought.
   - It should be indicated as to whether the company is maintaining proper purchase/ sales/ stock registers so as to furnish true and fair view of its state of affairs in compliance of Sections 209/211 read with Schedule VI to the Act.

3. Forward a copy to RoC

4. Central Government, on satisfaction may grant the approval.

Procedure for obtaining approval of the Central Government for non-inclusion of certain particulars about subsidiary [section 212]

The Board will consider and approve of the proposal not attaching the accounts of the subsidiary by resolution. It will authorise the secretary to make an application to the Central Government (Regional Director having jurisdiction).
The application will be made in e-form 23AAB following EFORM COMPLIANCE CHART
Finalise the statements relating to the subsidiaries (section 212) after the Central Governments' approval is received. Conditions prescribed in the approval will be complied with. Normally the Government would require the report of the subsidiary and accounts to be sent to the members of the holding company as soon as they are ready.
Provide a copy of the Governments' approval to the auditors of the company.
Forward a copy of the approval to the Registrar while filing the accounts under section 220.

The following information should invariably be furnished with the application (e-form 23AAB) in the fields forming part of the eForm:

- The financial year for which exemption is sought. This year should also be the year mentioned in the accompanying board resolution. Precise reasons/justification for seeking exemption.
- Names of subsidiaries in respect of which exemption is sought. Dates on which the companies became subsidiaries of the applicant company. The financial years of the holding and subsidiary companies under reference.
- Copies of approvals under Section 212 obtained, if any, during the last three financial years.

However, GENERAL EXEMPTION IS GRANTED (without any approval, as mentioned above) to holding company from attaching the particulars of SUBSIDIARIES in its Balance Sheet IF Board of directors give their consent and present consolidated financials (of Holding & All subsidiaries) in Annual Report, the information as to TOTAL capital, reserves, assets & liabilities, turnover, investments, PAT, dividend, etc…duly audited and in strict compliance of Accounting Standards. The Annual Accounts of subsidiaries to be made available for inspection & taking copies by Shareholders at the registered office of the company. So, in order to claim this exemption, even an UNLISTED company has to present CONSOLIDATED FINANCIALS just like a LISTED company.

Procedure for exemption from providing Depreciation out of profits before declaring dividend

1. Convene a Board meeting to take decision to apply to CG for obtaining exemption from providing depreciation out of profits before declaring dividend.
2. File e-form 23AAC following EFORM COMPLIANCE CHART
3. Forward a copy to RoC
4. Central Government, on satisfaction may grant the approval.

Procedure for declaration of Dividend out of reserves of the company not in accordance with Companies (Declaration of Dividend out of reserves) rules, 1975

1. Convene a Board meeting to consider the said proposal.
2. File FORM (e-form) along with certified true copy of MoA, AoA, audited accounts for last 3 years, board resolution and statement indicating amount to be appropriated from reserves for dividend
3. Forward a copy to RoC
4. Central Government, on satisfaction may grant the approval.

COST AUDIT

↳ Statutory Auditor CANNOT be appointed as a Cost Auditor;

↳ SHALL have the same powers and duties as Statutory Auditor;

↳ If subsequent to appointment attracted Disqualifications [same as Statutory Auditor], cease to hold office;

Audit of Cost Records u/s. 233B:

1. Appoint a COST AUDITOR holding valid certificate of PRACTICE under Cost & Works Accountants Act, 1959.
2. The first point of reference regarding the appointment shall be the Audit Committee and it shall ENSURE that such person is FREE from disqualification & does NOT violate the Section 224 limits. Further the Cost Auditor should give a CERTIFICATE of independence & arms length relationship with the Company to the Audit Committee.
3. E-form 23C shall be filed WITHIN 90 days from the date of commencement of every Financial Year and it shall be DEEMED to be approved on EXPIRY of 30 days from filing and the company shall issue a FORMAL letter of appointment to Cost Auditor as approved by the Board and such Cost Auditor shall inform the Central Government about the same WITHIN 30 days of receipt of formal letter.
4. The Report shall be as per Cost Audit (Report) Rules [CARR], 2011.
5. The Annual Report should contain the particulars of Cost Auditor with the DUE date & ACTUAL date of filing Cost Audit Report.
6. In case of contravention by Company or any officer in default, a fine UPTO Rs.50,000/- or UPTO 3 years or both. In case of contravention by Cost Auditor, a find UPTO Rs.5,000/-.

MASTER CIRCULAR ON COST ACCOUNTING RECORDS & COST AUDIT

As per CARR, a Cost auditor is required to comment on the scope and performance of internal audit of cost records. The Cost auditor cannot be the INTERNAL AUDITOR of a company for the period for which he is conducting the cost audit.

The number of companies in respect of which cost audit reports have not been submitted and have become overdue shall also be taken into account for the purposes of ceiling under section 224(1B).

A cost auditor shall be deemed to have concluded his appointment for the relevant financial year as soon as he renders a report to the Central Government in accordance with the Cost Audit Report Rules, as applicable, with a copy to the Company and can be appointed in the OTHER COMPANY thereon.

The duties of the cost accountants appointed to conduct an audit of cost accounts of the company flow directly from the provisions contained under section 233B of the Companies Act, 1956 read with CARR. In any case the report should not be signed by merely affixing the firms name [it should be signed by the Cost Auditor]. Cost audit report for a financial year contains corresponding data for the previous year(s) also.

Section 292A(6) of the Companies Act, 1956 states that the Audit Committee should have discussions with the auditors *[include cost auditors]* periodically about internal control systems, the scope of audit, etc... The presence of the cost auditor in such committees will ensure overall cost management, efficiency in resource utilization, business vertical-wise performance evaluation, proper pricing of inter-unit/inter-company transfers and valuation of inventories. However, the cost auditor, wherever appointed, shall attend and participate at the meetings of the Audit Committee or the Board, as the case may be, but shall neither be a member nor have the right to vote.

Section 295 - LOAN TO DIRECTOR & GUARANTEE, SECURITY in connection with loan to Director

Not Applicable to,

- Private Company;
- Banking Company;
- Transactions from Holding to its Subsidiary company;
- If housing loans provided to Employees are in terms similar to Housing loans provided to other employees. (decision of Madras High Court in MR Electronics Ltd. case)

A company is having a scheme of providing house building loans to its employees / offiers subject to an upper ceiling of Rs. 5 lakh and payment of interest @ 8% per annum. The managing director of the company wants to avail of the house - building loan of Rs. 10 lakh and the Board of Directors passed a resolution for providing him loan of Rs. 10 lakh at an interest rate of 6% per annum. Being secretarial auditor of the company, advise the company as to whether the resolution passed by the Board of directors is valid in view of the provisions of the Companies Act, 1956. If not, what action the company should have taken to provide loan to the managing director? (2007 - June)

Authority - Previous Approval of Central Government is mandatory by filing e-form 24AB following MANDATORY EFORM COMPLIANCE CHART.

The application should be accompanied by the following documents:

1. The rate of interest atleast 4% above prevailing bank rate. The quantum of loan along with other loans taken should be UPTO 25 times of gross salary drawn in the preceeding 6 months prior to making of the application.
2. The proposal should be accompanied with the declaration that the company has not defaulted in making repayments to the investors the amounts as and when they become due to them. The proposal should be approved at the meeting of the Board of Directors and members specific approval to be obtained, wherever required. The loan should not be made out of borrowed funds of the company. No guarantee commission shall be allowed to be paid to anyone in respect of the proposals.
3. Shareholding pattern of the companies (applicant & borrower). List of Directors of the Board of both the companies (applicant & borrower companies wherever applicable) and disclosing inter-se interest, if any. Copy of draft loan agreement. If the loan is backed by any guarantees, then the name and particulars of the guarantors with their consent. Justification for quantum of loan/guarantee or furnishing security by the company.
4. In respect of all proposals, a certificate from the statutory auditors or a company secretary in whole -time practice to the following effect be enclosed stating therein that: -

a. the proposal is in conformity within the provisions of Section 372A of the Companies Act,1956.

b. the company has NOT defaulted in:-

1. the repayment of any fixed deposits accepted by the company under Section 58 A of the Companies Act, 1956 or part thereof or interest thereon
2. Payment of dividend
3. Redemption/repayment of debenture and timely payment of interest thereon
4. Redemption of preference shares and

c. the Company is regular in filing all forms / returns as required to be filed under the Companies Act 1956.

d. the applicant company is NOT in any default on account of undisputed dues of the Central Govt. e.g. Income Tax, Central Excise etc.

5. A NOC/ prior approval of public financial institutions/ banks in case any term loan is subsisting.

Persons Covered

- Director of lending company, or its holding company or any partner or relative of any such director;
- Firm in which any such director or relative is a partner;
- Private company of which any such director is a director or member;
- Body corporate of which 25% or more of the total voting power may be exercised or controlled by any such director, or directors, together;
- Body corporate, the Board of directors, MD or manager whereof is accustomed to act in accordance with the directions or instructions of the Board, or of any director or directors, of the lending company.

MCA CLARIFICATION: When the BENEFICIARY of the loan/guarantee/security is a PUBLIC LIMITED COMPANY, approval of Central Government should ONLY BE SOUGHT if the provisions of Section 295(d) or (e) [dealing with Body Corporate] are attracted.

The following table shall be read from the Lending Companies point of view. Any transaction entered by lending company with persons (other than Directors) in Column 1 who are connected in a way mentioned in Column 2 or 3, shall mandate Central Government approval.

LENDER'S **HOLDING** COMPANY

Director of Holding Company	Or His Partner	Or His Relative
Firm	Where Director is a Partner or	Where Relative of Director is a Partner
Private Company	Where Director is a Member or	Where Director is a Director
Body Corporate	Director holds 25%	-

LENDING COMPANY

Director	Or His Partner	Or His Relative
Firm	Where Director is a Partner or	Where Relative of Director is a Partner
Private Company	Where Director is a Member or	Where Director is a Director
Body Corporate (BC)	Where Director holds 25% or	Where Board/ MD/ Manager of BC is accustomed to act as per Directors

If Prior Approval of Central Government is NOT accorded before giving loan to director or Guarantee / Security in connection with Loan to the Persons Covered in Lending Company & Lender's Holding Company, the 'Director' or 'Director as Partners' or 'Directors as Directors in Private Company' has to VACATE the office u/s. 283. For others, Fine UPTO Rs. 50,000/- OR Imprisonment UPTO 6 months; imprisonment will be reduced proportionately on the basis of payment of Fine. Thus, the offence is COMPOUNDABLE.

OTHER APPLICATIONS TO CENTRAL GOVERNMENT

The appointment of Sole Selling Agent and Office of place of profits also mandates CG approval which is dealt under items requiring SPECIAL RESOLUTONS.

Further, removal of disqualification of Section 274(1)(g) mandates CG approval which is dealt under Disqualification of directors.

INVESTIGATION

Investigation is step after inspection or beyond inspection.

Section 234: Power of RoC [not roving in nature], to call for information / explanation,

↳ arising out of perusal of documents filed (such as Periodical or Casual Returns) under the Act, by way of written orders; OR

↳ if it is represented to the Registrar on materials placed before him by contributory / creditor / interested person after giving the company an opportunity of being heard, by way of written orders;

↳ Report to Central Government for investigation, if it discloses unsatisfactory affair or does not disclose a full and fair statement.

Section 234A gPower to enter, search & seize the documents and keep under custody UPTO 30 days through order of Magistrate of First Class on apprehension that it may be destroyed / mutilated / altered / falsified / secreted and also identification marks may be put.

Section 235	Section 237
Central Government may order investigation on, ↳ Report from RoC u/s. 234.	Central Government sHall order investigation on, ↳ Court Order; ↳ Special Resolution
Central Government sHall order investigation on CLB order, when applications along with evidence and security for the cost for carrying on such investigation, are received from, ↳ Min 200 shareholders holding 1/10th of Voting Capital; ↳ Min 1/5th of Total number of members → for Co not having Share Capital.	Central Government may order investigation if CLB opines, ↳ that business is being carried out to defraud creditors or for fraudulent or unlawful purpose or ↳ that members are not given reasonable information. **Note:** If it is shown that above circumstances do not exist or that they are such that it is impossible for anyone to form an opinion therefrom, the opinion is CHALLENGEABLE on the ground of non-application of mind or perversity or on the ground that it was formed on collateral grounds and was beyond the scope of the statute as decided by Supreme Court in *Barium Chemicals Limited v.* CLB.
Authenticated Inspectors Report to be an Evidence as per Sec 246.	Authenticated Inspectors Report to be Evidence

Investigation may also be initiated u/s. 239 or 247.

Section 239: Investigate into affairs of (other related compaines)

↳ any body corporate which is/was a Holding or Subsidiary or subsidiary of its holding company or vice versa;

↳ any body corporate managed by same MD / Manager;

↳ any body corporate managed by Company / nominee directors of the Company / which is accustomed to act according to the instructions of the company / its directors / MD / Manager / other Company whose directorships is held by employees / nominees of 1st Company.

ONLY after getting prior approval of Central Government [PCG] except in case of holding / subsidiaries companies.

If from any such report as aforesaid, it appears to the Central Government that proceedings ought to be brought in public interest in the name of Company / Body Corporate whose affairs have been investigated,

↳ for recovery of damages for fraud / misfeasance / misconduct in connection with promotion / management of affairs of Company / Body Corporate or

↳ for recovery of any misapplied / wrongful property of Company / Body Corporate.

Investigators has Power to enter, search & seize the documents and keep under custody till the conclusion of Investigation, through order of Magistrate of First Class on apprehension that it may be destroyed / mutilated / altered / falsified / secreted and put identification marks.

Section 247→ Investigation of ownership of Company, CG

↳ may to determine true persons who are financially interested in the success or failure of the company or control or materially influence the policy of the company;

↳ shall for similar purpose as per CLB order.

EXPENSES OF INVESTIGATION [Section 245] – defrayed in first instance by Central Government but reimbursed if,

↳ Prosecuted for criminal liability or for recovery of damages / property;

↳ No prosecution, then the Company / Body Corporate / MD / Manager or applicant;

↳ On recovery of value of property / sums;

IMPOSITION OF RESTRICTION ON SHARES / DEBENTURES [Section 250]

- CLB on,

↳ Suo motto [by itself];

↳ Complaint;

↳ Reference by CG u/s. 247

Has a good reason to find out the relevant fact about any share or debentures, any RESTRICTION has to be imposed UPTO 3 years. Restriction can be on transfer / issue / voting rights / corporate rights and making such acts as VOID unless confirmed by CLB.

For imposition of restriction on voting rights for 3 years or for order that no resolution passed or action taken to effect a change in the composition of the Board of directors before the date of the order shall have effect unless confirmed by the CLB, 3 conditions to be satisfied,

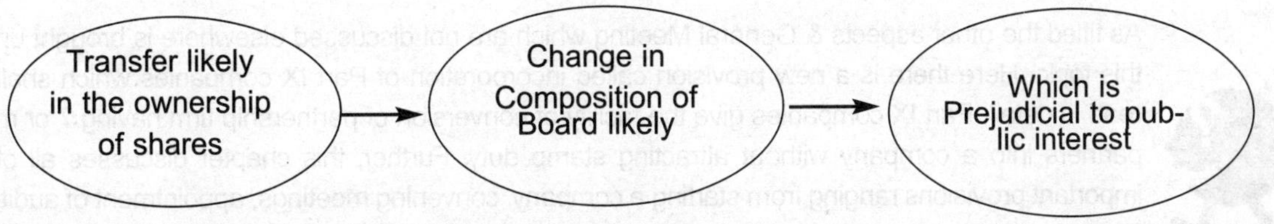

Section 250A → Investigation once commenced, NO stoppage for,

↳ application moved by CIB for relief under section 397 / 398;

↳ Shareholders pass Special Resolution for Voluntary Winding up.

Section 251 → Saving Clause for Legal Advisors / Bankers – NEED NOT communicate any privilege information EXCEPT the name & address of the Client. This is the professional immunity given.

Section 635B → Protection of employees [includes Company Secretary], during 'investigation by inspector' or 'pendency of proceeding u/s. 235 / 237 / 239 / 247' as they can be removed only after prior intimation to CLB of the proposed action to be taken by the company and CLB has to send notice to the company within 30 days, otherwise, the company can remove such employee. The company has an option to appeal CLB order in Court within 30 days.

Only this much mandates the approval of Central Government. Remember you have to understand only the following forms to by heart the whole chapter viz e-form 23AAA, 23AAB & 23AAC, next 23C, then 24AB & 24B, then DD-C, I & II & form for exempting from dividend from reserve rules. Further, else where under the Act, the provisions regarding declaring a company as Nidhi company or opening the branches of Nidhi compay or miscellaneous provisions has mandated filing of e-forms 63, 64 & 65 respectively. Section 295 regarding loan to director and provisions regarding Investigation shall be understood in detail.

As titled the other aspects & General Meeting which are not discussed elsewhere is brought under this topic. Here there is a new provision called incorporation of Part IX companies which shall be read in detail. Part IX companies give the facility of conversion of partnership firm having 7 or more partners into a company without attracting stamp duty. Further, this chapter discusses all other important provisions ranging from starting a company, convening meetings, appointment of auditors, filing of returns, charges etc... which are related to general meetings.

Other Aspects And General Meeting

INCORPORATING A COMPANY

2 persons can start a Private Company
7 persons can start a Public Company

The Company can be,

» Limited by Shares;
» Limited by Guarantee without Share capital;
» Limited by Guarantee with Share Capital;
» Unlimited Company.

Apply in Form DIN-1 for the Directors of the Company to get allotted Directors Identification Number (**DIN**), which is valid throughout the life time & apply for their Digital Signature Certificates

NAME AVAILABILITY & APPROVAL

1. 'Check Company Name' & 'Public Search of Trademark' links in the MCA site will help to identify a name, which is not already registered with RoC or Trademarks Registry;
2. File e-Form 1A with UPTO 6 Name options which shall have a Noun + Verb and end with the word 'Limited' for Public Company &'Private Limited' for Private Company. Eg. Learnlabz KnowledgeSharing Pvt Ltd.
3. If the Name is undesirable, then RoC may reject or ask for re-submission WITHIN 3 days of application and such applicant shall be given ONLY 2 opportunities for such re-submission.
4. RoC to issue 'Name Approval Letter' once the name is neither undesirable nor existing, to the satisfaction of RoC. However, if the Name is certified by Practising CS/CA/CMA, then it shall be approved ONLINE without RoC's consideration.
5. Validity of Name Approval = 60 days. Meaning, within such period file all such forms pertaining to incorporation of the Company. However, even after the EXPIRY of 2 opportunities of re-submission or 60 days as mentioned above, the applicant will be at liberty to file new e-form 1A with prescribed fees of Rs.1000/-.

PREPARATION OF MEMORANDUM & ARTICLES (MoA / AoA)

The MoA shall have Name, Situation, Object, Liability, Capital & Subscription clause. **Both** MoA & AoA shall be stamped, initialed & subscription clause to be signed by each subscriber and atleast 1 witness with details as to Name,

FORMATS AS PER Schedule I

For Company Limited by Shares: Table A for Articles (AoA) Table B for Memorandum (MoA). Public Company can have its own Articles or can adopt Table A.

OTHER FORMATS OF MoA / AoA FOR TYPE OF COMPANIES:

Table C	For Company Limited by Guarantee only
Table D	For Company Limited by Guarantee with Share Capital
Table E	Unlimited Company

e-Form 1

It states that all the provisions regarding incorporation are duly complied. It can be prepared in a plain paper and adequate stamp duty shall be paid online.

Note: It can be signed by Director / Manager / Secretary named in Articles OR PCS / CA / Advocate / Attorney.

Annexures

1. Original Name Availability Letter, which is within Validity period;
2. Memorandum & Articles of Association in plain paper
3. Power of Attorney in stamp paper authorizing a person to make corrections, submit documents & collect the Certificate from RoC;
4. License issued by Regional Director, in case of Section 25 Companies.

Note: Stamp duty for Power of Attorney shall be paid separately and Stamp duty for Memorandum & Articles shall be paid along with the fees for filing forms.

Also, file simultaneously

1. Pre-certified e-Form 18 for Address of Registered Office
2. Pre-certified e-Form 32 for every Director / Secretary of the Company with a consent letter for Public limited company.

CERTIFICATE OF INCORPORATION

RoC issues Certificate of Incorporation on satisfaction, which bears the CIN of the company. The company is said to have been incorporated from the date mentioned in the said Certificate. It is the conclusive evidence as to incorporation of the company.

CERTIFICATE OF COMMENCEMENT OF BUSINESS

RoC issues this Certificate for **Public Company** on satisfaction, after getting prospectus or a statement in lieu of prospectus along with declaration in e-form 19/20. It is the conclusive evidence as to commencement of business and to exercise BORROWING powers.

Note:

1. Only e-form 1 shall be approved by the RoC Office. E-Forms 18 & 32 shall be processed by the system online and taken on record through Straight Through Processing (STP) mode. If e-forms 1, 18, 32 and e-form for Memorandum of Association (MOA) and Articles of Association (AOA) have been certified by the PRACTICING PROFESSIONAL regarding the correctness of the information and declarations given by the subscribers, the application shall be processed electronically and the **DIGITAL CERTIFICATE OF INCORPORATION** shall be issued IMMEDIATELY ONLINE by the Registrar of Companies. if it is found later on that the company ought not to have been registered under provisions of the Companies Act, 1956, the RoC shall take necessary action to put the company in state of SUSPENDED ANIMATION and initiate the process of revocation of the registration (winding up) of the company after giving an opportunity of being HEARD.
2. Thus, average time taken for incorporation of company should be reduced to one (1) day only.
3. In case of e-form 1A (name approval), where it is certified by the professional that it is not an undesirable u/s. 20 of Companies Act, 1956 and Name Availability Guidelines, 2011, it will be approved by the system IMMEDIATELY ONLINE. In other cases, RoC will examine the application and the same may be confirmed. Penal action against the applicant and professional certifying the Name in case of FALSE INFORMATION / CERTIFICATION and in addition to action for professional misconduct will be taken. Further a name, if made available, is liable to be WITHDRAWN any time BEFORE REGISTRATION of the company, if it is founder LATER THAT the same ought not to have been allowed by RoC AFTER giving reasons & an opportunity of being heard.
4. Forms related to establishment of business/branch office in India by Foreign companies like e-forms 37, 39, 44 and 68 will have the highest priority for approval.

Outline the detailed procedure for a public company and also to obtain certificate of commencement of business in the present scenario of e – filing (2007 – December)

Procedure to form and incorporate a company to be licensed under section 25

1. Select atleast 3 names which should indicate the main object of the proposed company. The name should indicate the nature of activities intended to be carried on by the proposed company.
2. An application to Regional Director (RD) in e-Form 24A following EFORM COMPLIANCE CHART requesting for a license to be granted u/s. 25 to a company which is proposed to be incorporated as a company, with limited liability, but without the addition to its name of the word 'Limited' or the words 'Private Limited' as the case may be [Regulation 3 of Companies Regulation, 1956] and file SIMULTANEOUSLY a copy to RoC.
3. Where the application is made by an EXISITNG association, NOT as a company but some other form, in addition to the above documents, documents as per Regulation 4 shall also be attached.
4. Within a WEEK after the submission of the application to the Regional Director, a NOTICE (as per Annexure II of Regulations) of the application should be PUBLISHED (1 English & vernacular newspaper) and a certified copy of the published notice sent to the Regional Director.
5. The Regional Director, being satisfied in all respects, shall then issue the necessary license in the form set out in Annexure III to the Companies Regulations, 1956, and may direct the company to insert in its memorandum or articles or partly in the one and partly in the other, the conditions of the license specified by RD.
6. Arrange to REGISTER the company with RoC, pursuant to the license granted by RD.

Part IX Conversion: comprises of Section 565 to 581.

Registration of Partnership Firm as a Limited Company under part IX of the Companies Act, 1956. It is the best way to convert a firm into a company as there will be no instance of stamp duty.

Check whether partnership firm is having 7 or more partners. If not, increase the number of partners to seven. [Section 565]

Section 566 of the Act defines a joint stock company as 'a company having permanent paid up or nominal share capital of fixed amount divided into shares also of fixed amount or held or transferable as stock, or divided and held partly in one way and partly in the other, and formed on the principle of having for its members the holders of those shares or that stock, and no other persons.

Analyze the existing **partnership deed** and make it in compliance of definition of Joint Stock Company either by way of new deed or supplementary deed.

Check whether the firm is registered with Registrar of Firms. It is advisable to register the firm.

Partners of the firm should meet and decide on the following:

i. The decision to convert the firm into a company.

ii. Identify the outstanding creditors and obtain their consent for the proposed conversion. Check Financial Institutions & Banks regarding negative covenants, if any.

iii. Authorize one or more partners to initiate necessary steps for the proposed conversion and also to sign necessary documents and complete other formalities required in that regard.

iv. Choose the name of the proposed company – similar to existing firm name and to make an application in e-form 1A following EFORM COMPLIANCE CHART to RoC and shall specifically mention that it is a conversion under Part IX.

The partners authorized by the firm shall sign the application and attach with it, the following:

i. Copy of the partnership deed or supplementary partnership deed

ii A letter duly signed by all or majority of the Partners signifying their intention to convert firm into a company.

iii A certified copy of the latest Balance Sheet of the firm, latest Income Tax assessment, if any, and the extract if the resolution passed by the partners of the firm.

Make an application in eform 37/39 following EFORM COMPLIANCE CHART for registration as a limited or unlimited Company.

File e-form 1, 18 & 32 for Incorporation of the company following EFORM COMPLIANCE CHART

When the company makes an application to register itself under part IX of the Act, the list of members and directors required to be delivered to RoC shall be duly verified by the declaration of atleast 2 directors or other principal officers of the company. For this purpose RoC may call for evidence from the company in order to satisfy himself that the company is a joint stock company within the meaning of Section 566.

On satisfying the conditions of this part, RoC shall grant a certificate and on issue of such certificate that the company is a company duly incorporated under this Act.

EFFECT OF REGISTRATION as Part IX:

1. All property at the date of registration shall pass to and VEST (operation of law, hence no stamp duty) in the company as incorporated under the Companies Act, 1956 for all estate and interest of the company therein.

2. The registration of a company in pursuance of Part IX shall not affect its rights or liabilities in respect of any debt or obligation incurred, or any contract into, by to, with or on behalf of the company before registration.

3. All suits and other legal proceedings taken by or against the company, or any public officer or member thereof, which are pending at the time of registration of the company in pursuance of Part IX of the Companies Act, 1956, may be continued in the same manner as if the registration had not taken place.
4. Provisions of Part IX of the Companies Act, 1956 clearly override provisions of the Indian Partnership Act, 1932. On and form such registration of a firm in accordance with the provisions of Part IX of the Act, the partnership Act has no application in so far as that firm is concerned.

INCREASE IN SHARE CAPITAL

Type of Meeting: General Meeting

Approval : Ordinary Resolution, (Special resolution to amend AOA)

E-form : 5, 23

Applicable law : Section 94 of the Act

↳ Memorandum will mention only the AUTHORISED CAPITAL [the maximum limit which Company can raise] of the Company.

↳ Issued [actual offer], Subscribed [accepted offer] & Paid-up Capital [received consideration] may be mentioned only in Balance Sheet [Schedule VI] of the Co.

↳ Authorisation in Articles (AoA) mandatory for amendment of Authorised Capital in the Memorandum (MoA)

↳ Ordinary Resolution for

↳ Consolidation into larger denomination ↳ sub-division into smaller denomination ↳ diminution of share capital [dealt under 'Reduction']	↳ conversion of shares into stock or vice versa ↳ redemption of redeemable preference share ↳ increase in authorized share capital [Section 95]

Note: Ordinary resolution only if it does not require alteration of Articles (AoA), else Special resolution for amendment of Articles to authorize such change in Authorised Share Capital to be passed).

↳ e-Form 5 and e-Form 23 shall be filed with RoC within 30 days of amendment.

Draft the following resolution to give effect to consolidation of shares made by the company in its memorandum of Association. (2010 December)

PROCEDURE

1. The Company has to make sure that ARTICLES contain power to alter the share capital. If there is no such power alter the Articles of Association accordingly u/s. 31.
2. Hold Board meeting for transaction following business: a. Resolution by simple majority for increasing the Authorised share capital of the Company. b. To fix the time, date and venue and place of general meeting and approve the draft notice with explanatory statement for passing i. ordinary resolution for increasing the Authorised share capital by altering Memorandum of association and ii. special resolution to alter the articles of association if it contains details of share capital
3. Issue notice of the general meeting to - Members – Directors – Auditors – Stock Exchanges

4. Hold the General Meeting to pass the following resolution,

RESOLVED THAT

1. pursuant to sections 94, 16 and 31 and other applicable provisions, if any, of the Companies Act, 1956, the authorised share capital of the company be increased from Rs. .... (Rupees ....) divided into .... equity shares of Rs. 10 (Rupees ten) each to Rs. .... (Rupees ....) divided into .... equity shares of Rs. 10 each.
2. clause .... of the memorandum & clause …… of articles be and is hereby altered to read as follows:

"The Share Capital of the Company is Rs. .... (Rupees ....) divided into .... (.......... crores) Equity Shares of Rs. 10 (Rupees ten) each with power to increase or reduce the capital as may be determined by the Directors and to vary, modify or abrogate any such rights, privileges or conditions in such manner as may for the time being be provided by the regulations of the Company, and to consolidate or sub-divide the shares and issue shares of higher or lower denominations."

3. the Board of Directors, be and is authorised to do and perform all such other acts, deeds and things as may be necessary or desirable to give effect to this resolution.

5. Forward a copy of proceeding to Stock exchange.

6. File with RoC within 30 days of resolution following EFORM COMPLIANCE CHART,
   - e-form 5 (for alteration of capital clause)
   - e-form 23 (for passing special resolution)

The same procedure shall be followed for REDEMPTION of preference shares too, the provisions are as under. Kindly note a public company can issue preference shares which shall be REDEEMABLE within 20 years and IRREDEEMABLE preference shares cannot be issued.

REDEEMABLE PREFERENCE SHARES

Section 80

"Redeemable means Repayable"

↳ Applicable only to Public Limited companies;

↳ Articles should authorize such issue;

↳ Only fully paid shares Preference Shares can be redeemed.

Redemption Shall Be Out of

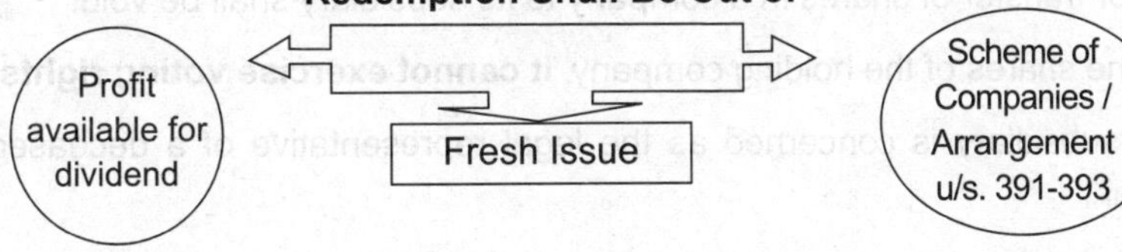

Other Provisions on redemption:

↳ Capital Redemption Reserve (CRR) to be created;

↳ CRR = Nominal Value of Capital to be redeemed;

↳ Premium payable on Preference Shares, if any, can be paid only out of profits of the Company or out of Company's 'Securities Premium Account';

↳ Such CRR can be utilized only for Bonus issue, otherwise it amounts to reduction of capital u/s 100.

Redemption of preference shares is not reduction u/s 100 as authorized capital remains unchanged and also re-issue of the preference shares of same class UPTO redeemed value of preference shares is not increase of authorized capital and no stamp duty is payable, if the old shares are redeemed within one month of the old shares.

"Holding & Subsidiary Company" – Section 4:

A Company is HOLDING of the other, <u>if that Other</u> is its SUBSIDIARY.

Here, Company includes Body Corporate (BC).

Three ways to establish Holding-Subsidiary relationship,

↳ by controlling the Composition of Board of Directors;

↳ by exercising MORE THAN 50% of Total Voting Power or Nominal Value of Equity Shares;

↳ Subsidiary of a Subsidiary is the Subsidiary of the Parent Company. If [s → (S) → H], then [s → H].

The composition of a company's Board of Directors [BoD] shall be deemed to be controlled by another company if, that other company by its discretion, can appoint / remove the holders of all or a majority of the directorships,

↳ Without the approval of the other company;

↳ After his appointment in office / employment in the other Company;

↳ Who are nominees of other Company or its subsidiary.

In determining whether one company is a subsidiary of another:

INCLUDE – any shares held or voting rights by any person as a nominee for that other company / by subsidiary / its nominee.

EXCLUDE – any shares held or power exercisable by

↳ that other Company / its subsidiaries / nominees / in fiduciary capacity;

↳ virtue of provisions of any debentures of the first-mentioned company or of a trust deed for securing issue of such debentures;

↳ way of security by lending Co in ordinary course of business.

As per Section 42, a subsidiary cannot be a member of its holding company and

↳ any allotment or transfer of shares in a company to its subsidiary shall be void.

↳ Even if it has the shares of the holding company, **it cannot exercise voting rights EXCEPT:**

  ↳ where the subsidiary is concerned as the legal representative of a deceased member of the holding company; or

  ↳ where the subsidiary is concerned as trustee, and subsidiary is not beneficially interested under trust and its interest in the shares is only by way of security for the purposes of a transaction entered into by it in the ordinary course of a business which includes the lending of money.

Wholly-owned subsidiary (WoS)

Section 49 of the Act enables a company shall make & hold all investments in its OWN NAME. The exception being that a Holding Company may hold shares in its Subsidiaries in the Name of its Nominee to SATISFY the requirement of STATUTORY minimum (2 for private & 7 for public) under the Act. Thus, if the 'entire' capital of one company is held by another in which case the former becomes what is called 'wholly-owned' or '100%' subsidiary of the latter. But as single person cannot start a company, section 49 can be made applicable to such companies by appointing nominees.

Further u/s. 187C read with Companies (Declaration of Beneficial Interest in Share) Rules, 1975, a person whose name is entered in the Register of Members as the holder of shares but who does NOT hold beneficial interest in such share (like, Nominees) shall file a DECLARATION within 30 days of appointment/change to the company with Name & Particulars and the company shall file the same with RoC in e-form 22B within 30 days of receipt of declaration.

Indian Private Company which is a Subsidiary of Foreign Body Corporate:

Will be treated as a PRIVATE COMPANY, if 100% of the Share Capital of the Private Company is held by the Foreign Company; (ie) if it is a WoS of foreign company.

Will be treated as a Subsidiary of a PUBLIC COMPANY, if less than 100% Foreign Shareholding held by Foreign Body (ies) Corporate. Kindly note that u/s. 3(1) (iv) of the Act, a subsidiary of public company is a public company.

PROCEDURE FOR ACQUISITION OF A SUBSIDIARY

1. Convene a Board meeting to approve the proposal and pass a resolution for acquiring shares in the subsidiary. If section 372A is attracted, then the resolution has to be passed with the consent of ALL the directors present in the meeting. Section 372A deals with Intercorpoate loans & investments.
2. General meeting approval (if section 372A is attracted). Obtain approval of the company by passing a special resolution. Follow the procedure laid down in the section.
3. A Contract for purchase of shares must be executed.
4. Appoint nominees of the holding company to the Board of subsidiary.
5. File forms & maintain register.

MANNER OF AFFIXATION OF SEAL

The mode of affixation of the COMMON SEAL is generally provided by the ARTICLES of a c ompany. Table A mandates Board or Committee resolution needed for affixation of seal and it should be done in the presence of at least 2 directors and of the secretary or person appointed by Board for the purpose; and such persons shall also SIGN every instrument to which the seal of the company is so affixed in their presence. A person having power to manage the affairs has IMPLIED power to affix the seal and directors empowered u/s. 291. Where the articles make special provisions as to the affixing of the seal, these provisions must be STRICTLY followed.

Board Resolution for Adoption of Common Seal

The Company Secretary produced to the meeting a Seal bearing the Company's name, an impression of which Seal appears in the margin against this resolution. The following resolution was unanimously passed.

RESOLVED THAT the Common Seal of the Company, the impression of which Seal appears in the margin against this resolution be and is hereby adopted as the Common Seal of the Company.	Impression of the Common Seal

Board resolution to authorise affixation of common seal

RESOLVED THAT pursuant to regulation .... of the articles of association of the Company, the common seal of the Company be affixed to the instrument submitted to this meeting and expressed to be made between A of the one part and the Company of the other part in the presence of X and Y, two directors and Z, the secretary of the Company who shall sign the instrument

Procedure for having an official seal outside India

1. Check whether the Articles authorise the company to have an official seal for use in any territory, district or place NOT situated in India. Otherwise, alter the Articles suitably.
2: Ensure that the OBJECTS of the company cover the transacting of business outside India. Otherwise it will be necessary to alter the objects clause.
3. Prepare the official seal. It should be a FACSIMILE (*i.e.* exact copy) of the common seal. In ADDITION the name of the territory, district or place where it is to be used shall be engraved thereon.
4. Pass a Board resolution adopting the seal referred to above as the official seal of the company. RECORD and authenticate its impression.
5. The Board will pass a RESOLUTION or POWER of attorney may be executed under common seal AUTHORISING a person in the territory, district or place to affix the official seal to any deed or other documents to which the company is a party in the said area.
6. The person shall, by writing under his hand, CERTIFY on the deed or other document to which the seal is affixed, the date and place at which, it is affixed
7. The given authority may be REVOKED by board resolution or taking back power of attorney and by issuing PUBLIC NOTICE in newspapers.

> Draft Specimen resolutions with requisite explanatory statement, wherever necessary, for transacting the following items of business indicating the kind of meeting at which each resolution is to be passed and the type of resolution required for:
>
> (i) Adoption of common seal of the company. (2008 – June)

PROSPECTUS = Invitation to Offer for Public

Not Applicable to Private Company

OFFER DOCUMENT is dealt in detail under SEBI (Issue of Capital & Disclosure Requirements) Regulations, 2009 under the chapter PUBLIC ISSUE OF EQUITY.

Prospectus is MANDATORY when Invitation is made to PUBLIC for Subscription of Shares / Debentures.

An offer / invitation is treated as NOT made to public when,

- ↳ Offer / invitation NOT being calculated to result in the shares / debentures becoming available for subscription / purchase by persons OTHER THAN those receiving the offer or invitation (not to persons exceeding 49 in number)
- ↳ Offer / invitation made as a domestic concern of the person making and receiving the offer or invitation (not to persons exceeding 49 in number).

Note: Who can apply for the shares in response to the invitation shall be checked to determine offer to public.

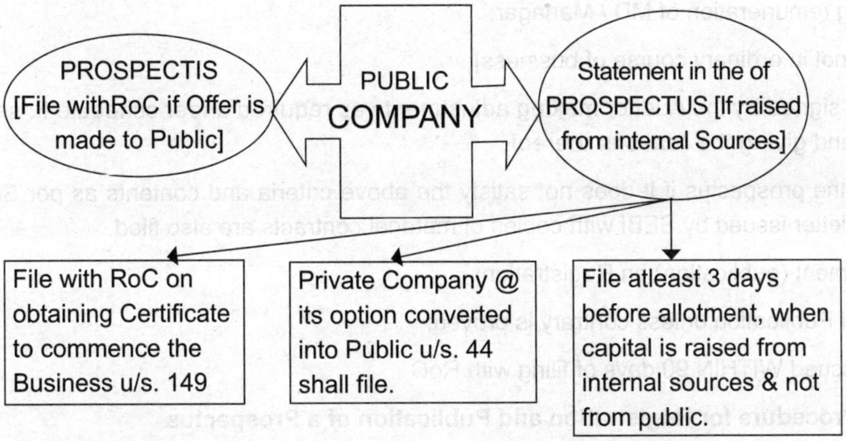

SCHEDULES to Companies Act	PARTICULARS
II	Contents of Prospectus
III	Statement in Lieu of Prospectus
IV	Statement in Lieu of Prospectus u/s. 44 (on conversion into Public Company)

CONTENTS OF PROSPECTUS [Section 56]

Parts of Schedule II	CONTENTS
I → Information to be given	↳ General Information about the issue; ↳ Capital Structure, Terms & Particulars; ↳ Company, Management & Project; ↳ Particulars about issues made during 3 previous years; ↳ Details of outstanding litigations, criminal prosecutions, et al.
II → Reports to be set out	↳ Information about Consent of Directors, Experts, CS, Auditors, etc... ↳ Financial Information about Auditors Report for 5 previous years; by means of this issue, if any; ↳ Negative Covenants in loan agreement; ↳ Statutory information about issues including Minimum Subscription, Underwriting, etc...
III → Explanation about requirement of Part I & II	↳ For Companies which are working for less than 5 years; ↳ Accounting details should be certified by Chartered Accountant; ↳ Documents specified in the Prospectus should be available for Inspection; ↳ A declaration that ALL relevant provisions of Companies Act have been complied with.

DATING, SIGNING & REGISTRATION & ISSUE OF PROSPECTUS

1. Board has to approve by passing a Board Resolution;
2. To be signed by Director & Prospective Directors;
3. To be filed with RoC for registration u/s. 60;
4. Along with the copy to be delivered to the Registrar as aforesaid, the following documents must be filed:
   - ↳ Letters of consent of Experts and Persons named in the prospectus as the auditor, legal adviser, attorney, solicitor, banker / broker to act in that capacity.
   - ↳ Contract entered within 2 years before the date of prospectus,

↳ appointing or fixing remuneration of MD / Manager;

↳ Material contract [not in ordinary course of business].

↳ Written statement signed by the Auditor making adjustments as required under schedule II, setting out the adjustments and giving the reasons thereof.

5 RoC will not register the prospectus if it does not satisfy the above criteria and contents as per Sec 56. In practice, observation letter issued by SEBI with copies of material contracts are also filed.

6. To issue an Advertisement (publication) on Registration;

7. DATE shall be Date of Publication unless contrary is proved;

8. Prospectus shall be issued WITHIN 90 days of filing with RoC.

Procedure for Registration and Publication of a Prospectus

1. A prospectus must be dated and that date unless the contrary is proved, is to be taken as the date of publication of prospectus. [Section 55] It must be registered before publication with the Registrar. [Section 60]
2. No prospectus can be issued more than 90 days after the date on which a copy thereof is delivered for registration; and if a prospectus is to be issued, it shall be deemed a prospectus a copy of which has not been delivered under the section to the Registrar.
3. Pass a resolution to APPROVE the prospectus at the meeting of the BOARD.
4. Pass a board resolution relating to opening of Bank Accounts as regards the issue. [Section 73].
5. A printed copy of the prospectus will be SIGNED by every person named therein as a director or by his agent authorised in writing by way of Power of Attorney.
6. File electronically a copy of the Prospectus with the Registrar as an attachment to e-Form 62 following EFORM COMPLIANCE CHART after incorporating any changes, if any. Only after such filing, it can be issued.
7. A minimum number of copies of application forms and prospectus to be supplied to all the registered members of the stock exchanges, underwriters, managers to the issue.
8. Separate application forms in different colours should be provided for reservation to employees, shareholders of the promoter company and non-resident Indians with all instructions as applicable.
9. Comply with SEBI (Issue of Capital & Disclosure Requirements) Regulations, 2009

PRE-INCORPORATION CONTRACT

Any contract which are entered by Promoters BEFORE incorporation of company and is WARRANTED by the terms of incorporation are called Pre-incorporation contracts. These contracts will be BINDING on the incorporated company ONLY if it is RATIFIED (adopted retrospectively) by the company AFTER incorporation.

AGREEMENT BY COMPANY ADOPTING PRE-INCORPORATION CONTRACT

This agreement is made at Delhi on _________ between Mr.A of the 1st part, Mr. B of the 2nd part and AB Ltd (hereinafter referred as the company) on the 3rd party.

WHEREAS the execution of the contract on _________ (hereinafter referred to as the contract) between Mr. A, the vendor and Mr.B, on behalf of the company and the said company is incorporated under Companies Act, 1956.

Now it is hereby agreed by & between parties hereto as under:

1.The said contract is hereby adopted by the company and shall be binding on Mr. A and the company in the same manner as if the company had been in existence at the date of agreement.

2. Mr. B who actually signed on behalf of the proposed company shall be discharged from all liability under the said contract as the company had adopted & ratified the said contracts.

IN WITNESS WHEREOF the parties put their hands & signature & the company caused its common seal affixed in the presence of Mr. X & Mr. Y, directors of the company who have set their hands on the day, date, month & year above written in terms of Board Resolution at the meeting held on ______.

Signatures/Common seal with Witness (& description)

PROVISIONAL CONTRACT

Any contract entered AFTER incorporation but BEFORE obtaining Certificate of Commencement of business is a provisional contract. Such contract of a public company AUTOMATICALLY gets confirmed on obtaining the certificate of commencement of business.

COMMISSION & BROKERAGE

COMMISSION FOR SUBSCRIPTION OF SHARES [Section 76]

A company may pay a commission to any person in consideration of

↳ subscribing / agreeing to subscribe, shares / debentures OR

↳ his procuring or agreeing to procure subscriptions,

ONLY IF Articles authorises and is UPTO 5% of price for shares & 2.5% for debentures and such shall be disclosed in Prospectus. The company shall file e-Form 4 following EFORM COMPLIANCE CHART to RoC.

Underwriting guarantees subscription for an agreed number of shares whereas Broker does NOT guarantee any subscription. BROKERAGE can be paid ONLY to those who deal in shares and whose business includes procuring of subscribers for shares.

Every Underwriter or Broker shall be registered with SEBI and shall comply with SEBI (Intermediaries) Regulations, 2008 read with respective regulations.

AGREEMENT TO ACT AS BROKER

Name & address of the firm of brokers who agree to act as brokers.

Ref No.___ dated ____

The Board of Directors

(of the company for whose public issue

the firm agrees to act)

Re: Proposed Public Issue of _____ (type of security) of Rs.____ each for cash at par of ___ Ltd.

Dear Sir,

We, the undersigned hereby testify & consent to act as brokers to the said issue captioned above by ___ Ltd and to our name being inserted as brokers in the prospectus which the company intends to issue for the proposed issue and we hereby authorize the said company to deliver this consent to RoC, Chennai pursuant to Section 60 of Companies Act, 1956.

As required u/s. 76, we are agreeable to accept 1.5% on the issue price as brokerage on allotment made in respect of applications bearing rubber stamp as brokers.

Thank you,

Yours faithfully,

For _____

SAMPLE UNDERWRITING CONTRACT

WHEREAS the company is about to offer for public subscription as issue of _____ shares of ____ each in accordance with terms of draft prospectus (copy attached) therein as may be mutually agreed upon between the company and the underwriters. It is hereby agreed as follows,

If the said shares shall on or before the day ___ of 2010 (or such later date mutually agreed upon but not after ___ 2010) be offered by company for subscription by public, the underwriters shall on or before the closing of subscription list shall apply for the said ____ shares.

If on the closing of lists under the said prospectus, if all the shares are allotted to public, then underwriters liability will cease but if it is not allotted, then the difference number of shares shall be allotted to underwriters.

The company shall pay the underwriters in cash within ____ 10 days from the allotment of the said ____ shares a commission at the rate of ___ on the nominal value of shares.

This agreement is to be irrevocable on the part of the underwriters and in case of default, it authorizes the company to CAUSE APPLICATION to be made for such shares in the name & on behalf of the underwriters & authorize directors to allot said shares to underwriters, thereby, the underwriters shall hold the company and said applicants be indemnified in respect of such application.

Returns:

The RETURNS to be filed under the Companies Act are as follows.

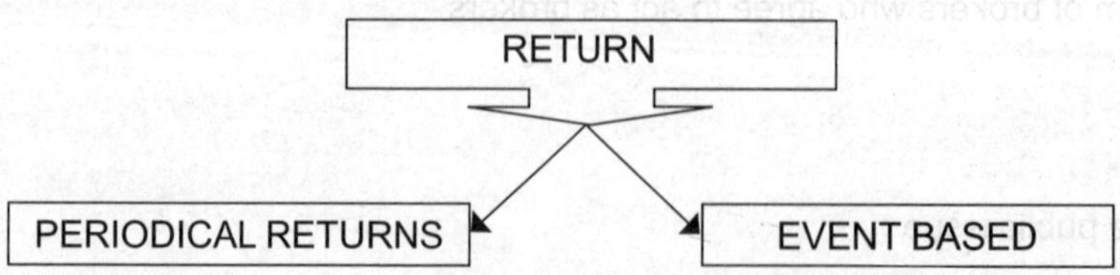

A Periodical Return OR Non-Event based Return is one that is REQUIRED to be filed periodically, WHETHER OR NOT, the even takes place. For instance, Annual Accounts, Annual Returns, Compliance Certificate, et al are Annual Periodic Returns.

A Casual Return or Event based Return is one that is REQUIRED to be filed ONLY on the HAPPENING of a particular Event. For instance, e-Form 23 to be filed for Resolutions requiring registration u/s. 192, including Special Resolution.

FORM & CONTENTS OF ANNUAL ACCOUNTS

The contents of the Accounts should be as per Schedule VI of Companies Act. The Annual Accounts should be in VERTICAL FORM ONLY.

The Parts I, II, III & IV are dispensed with. The NEW FORMATS (as mentioned below) has evolved. Now, it is divided into:

A. General Instructions
B. Part I – Form of Balance Sheet
C. General Instructions for Preparation of Balance Sheet
D. Part II – Form of Statement of Profit and Loss
E. General Instructions for Preparation of Statement of Profit and Loss

Note: The requirements of the Act or Regulatory authorities and/or accounting standards will prevail over the Schedule VI.

The Accounting Standards issued by ICAI may be referred for definition of terms. The rounding off of figures shall be made NEAREST to hundreds or thousands or lakhs or millions or decimals thereof if turnover is LESS THAN Rs.100 crores and to the NEAREST of lakhs or millions or crores or decimals thereof in OTHER CASES.

The NEW FORMATS classifies & defines the CURRENT & NON-CURRENT assets & liabilities (WITHOUT netting off) for the purpose of reporting. It may so happen that the SAME item may be current in one quarter & non-current in next quarter. Each item in the Balance Sheet and profit and loss account to be CROSS-REFERENCED to any related information in the NOTES TO ACCOUNTS. The Notes to provide WHERE REQUIRED (considering important & excessive information):- (a) narrative descriptions or break up of items recognized in those statements and (b) information about items that do not qualify for recognition in those statements. COMPARATIVE AMOUNTS needs to be presented for all items shown in the financial statements including notes.

An asset/liability shall be classified as CURRENT when it satisfies any of the following:

- It is expected to be realized/settled in the company's normal OPERATING CYCLE (the time between the acquisition of assets for processing & their realization in cash or cash equivalents).
- It is held primarily for the purpose of being traded.
- It is expected to be realized/settled within 12 months after the reporting date.

ASSET is cash or cash equivalent unless it is RESTRICTED from being exchanged or used to settle a liability for atleast 12 months AFTER the reporting date. LIABILITY: The Company does not have an unconditional right to defer settlement of the liability for atleast 12 months after the reporting date.

Trade Receivables and Trade Payables are defined as receivables/payables on account of goods sold or services rendered in the normal course of business.

The following has become the NEW FORMAT of Revised Schedule VI as compared by **Mr. MP Vijayakumar, FCA, AICWA, FCS** in his presentation:

BALANCE SHEET:

SCHEDULE VI - OLD

1. EQUITY AND LIABILITIES

(1) Shareholders' funds
- (a) Captal
- (b) Reserves and surplus

(2) Loan funds
- (a) Secured loans
- (b) Unsecured loans

(3) Current liabilities and provisions:
- (a) Liabilities
- (b) Provisions

(4) Profit and Loss Account (both Debit and Creadit)

II. ASSETS

(1) Fixed assets:
- (a) Gross; black
- (b) Less : Depreciation
- (c) Net block
- (d) Capital work-in-progress

(2) Investments

(3) Current assets, loans and advances:
- (a) Inventories
- (b) Sundry debtors
- (c) Cash and bank balances
- (d) Other current assets
- (e) Loans and advances

SCHEDULE VI - REVISED

1. EQUITY AND LIABILITIES

(1) Shareholders' funds
- (a) Share Captal
- (b) Reserves and surplus
- (c) Money received against share warrants

(2) Share application money pending allotment

(3) Non-current liabilities
- (a) Long-term borrowings
- (b) Deferred tax liabilities (Net)
- (c) Other Long term liabilities
- (d) Long-term provisions

(4) Current liabilities
- (a) Short-term borrowings
- (b) Trade payables
- (c) Other current liabilities
- (d) Short-term provisions

II. ASSETS

(1) Non-current assets
- (a) Fixed assets
  - (i) Tangible assets
  - (ii) Intangible assets
  - (iii) Capital work-in-progress
  - (iv) Intangible assets under developments
- (b) Non-current investments
- (c) Deferred tax assets (net)
- (d) Long-term loans and advances
- (e) Other non-current assets

(2) Current assets
- (a) Current investments
- (b) Inventories
- (c) Trade receivables
- (d) Cash and cash equivalents
- (e) Short-term loans and advances
- (f) Other current assets

PROFIT & LOSS ACCOUNT:

Particulars

I. Revenue from operations

II. Other income

III. Total Revenue (I + II)

IV. Expenses:

Cost of materials consumed(A+B)

Purchases of Stock-in-Trade(A)

Changes in inventories of finished goods(B)

work-in-progress and Stock-in-Trade

Employee benefits expense

Finance costs

Depreciation and amortization expense

Other expenses

Total expenses

V. Profit before exceptional and extraordinary items and tax (III-IV)

VI. Exceptional items

VII. Profit before extraordinary items and tax (V - VI)

VIII. Extraordinary Items

IX. Profit before tax (VII- VIII)

X Tax expense:

(1) Current tax

(2) Deferred tax

XI Profit (Loss) for the period from continuing operations (IX-X)

XII Profit/(loss) from discontinuing operations

XIII Tax expense of discontinuing operations

XIV Profit/(loss) from Discontinuing operations (after tax) (XII-XIII)

XV Profit (Loss) for the period (XI + XIV)

XVI Earnings per equity share:

(1) Basic

(2) Diluted

AS-3	For Listed Company, Cash Flow Statement as per Accounting Standard (AS – 3) is mandatory
e-Forms	**Filing** WITHIN 30 days from the date on which the Accounts are LAID before the Members at the Annual General Meeting (AGM)
23 AC	Balance Sheet
23 ACA	Profit & Loss Account; In case of Private Company, Profit & Loss Account to be filed SEPARATELY as they are NOT available for Public Inspection.
If Balance Sheet is NOT adopted in the AGM **or** AGM is adjourned without Adoption **or** AGM not held during the Year.	Statement of that fact and of the reasons shall be annexed to the Balance sheet and to be filed with the ROC.

Changing Financial Year

As per Section 210 the Balance sheet and Profit and loss account has to be laid before the Company in Annual General Meeting.

As per Section 2(17), "financial year" means in relation to any body corporate, the period in respect of which any profit and loss account of the body corporate laid before it in annual general meeting is made up, whether that period is a year or not.

Apply to RoC, if extension of time is required to conduct AGM.
Convene a Board meeting after giving notice of the meeting in writing to every director of the company for the time being in India and at his usual address in India to every other director.
If the financial year is extended beyond a period of 12 calendar months and the company requires more time to finalise the accounts, the company should apply to RoC in e-form 61 following EFORM COMPLIANCE CHART for obtaining extension of time for holding AGM, pursuant to the second proviso to section 166(1).
The consent of the Assessing Officer of the Income Tax department is also required to be obtained by the company.

Gel–Well Limited wants to change the period of its financial year. Can it do so? If yes, then sate the procedure to be followed by the Company. (2008 – December)

AUTHENTICATION OF ACCOUNTS [Section 215]

- In case of Banking Company, Section 29 of Banking Regulation Act will apply;
- In case of any other Company,
  - Manager or Secretary, if any AND
  - By NOT less than 2 Directors, one shall be MD, if any.
- If only one out of the two Directors are PRESENT in India, such Director has to sign stating the reasons for non-compliance of Section 215;
- If the OTHER Director expires, Additional Director to be appointed for authentication of Accounts.

RE-OPENING OF ADOPTED ACCOUNTS:

↳ The Annual Accounts shall be adopted at an AGM, as per Section 210;

↳ Normally, Accounts once adopted SHALL NOT be re-opened;

↳ Adopted Accounts can be re-opened for Tax, Insurance & Law purposes; [MCA Notification]

↳ The re-opened Accounts shall be laid either at the AGM / EGM.

The Company has uploaded older version of annual accounts without making the recent corrections and paid the filing fees. Can they file their annual accounts under section 220 once again (with changes made), resulting into filing/availability of more than one such accounts in the Registry for a particular financial year?

No. A company cannot lay more than one set of annual accounts for a particular financial year unless it has reopened/revised such annual accounts after their adoption in the Annual General Meeting on the grounds specified in Ministry's circular Number 1/2003 (as mentioned above).

CONTENTS OF ANNUAL RETURNS

Every company limited by shares has to file Annual return with ROC apart from filing Annual Report under section 159 with,

1. Contents as **AT** the Date of AGM; Contents are listed in the Table;
2. Prescribed Format is Schedule V for Company Limited by Shares;
3. To be **filed** in e-Form 20B WITHIN 60 days of date of AGM or AGM ought to have taken place.

CONTENTS	PARTICULARS OF
1.	Company
2.	Share Capital or Debentures
3.	Director, Manager, Secretary, BOTH past & present;
4.	Share Transfers between LAST AGM & PRESENT AGM and full LIST of Members for last 5 years [except that of dematerialised shares]
5.	Signed by Secretary & Director OR 2 Directors, including Managing Director, if any.
6.	Pre-Certification by a Practising Professional that, 1. Compliance of Section 3(1)(iii) for Private Company; 2. All the information's are true & correct; 3. Transfer & Allotment of Shares or Debentures are appropriately recorded; 4. Unpaid Dividend unclaimed for 7 years, transferred to Investors Education & Protection Fund. In case of Listed Companies, it should be Certified by a Company Secretary in Whole-time Practice.

Books of Accounts [Section 209]

Particulars as,
- ↳ Receipts & Payments;
- ↳ Sales & Purchases;
- ↳ Assets & Liabilities;
- ↳ Particulars relating to utilisation of Material Cost as CG specify.

- ↳ The Accounts should be prepared so as to give **a true and fair view** of the state of affairs and to explain the transactions of the company in **accrual basis** following **double entry book keeping system.**
- ↳ Comply with the Accounting Standards (AS) prescribed by CG consultation with the National Advisory Committee on Accounting Standards shall be ensured. If AS not followed, the deviation, reason and financial effect shall be disclosed in the P&L.CG on request or with the consent of the Board of directors may modify the requirement of this section. [e-Form 23AAA to be filed]

PRESERVATION OF ACCOUNTS:

The Book Accounts like with the Vouchers in GOOD ORDER for 8 Previous Financial Years.

Board Resolution for Deciding a Place other than the Registered Office to Keep Books of Account

The Board approves the keeping of all or any of the Books of Account of the company at the office of the company at ..... (name of the place) and authorises the Secretary of the Company to send necessary notice to the Registrar of Companies, ...

PROVISIONS AS TO ANNUAL GENERAL MEETING (AGM)

1. AGM can be held on any Working Day, as on the Date of Notice. Thus an AGM cannot be held on Sunday or any Public Holiday, known as on the date of issuing Notice. This restriction is NOT applicable to Section 25 Companies.
2. It shall be held during Business Hours.
3. It shall be held at the Registered Office or at any place where Registered Office is situated.
4. First AGM
   - ↳ WITHIN 18 months from the Date of 'Certificate of Incorporation' OR
   - ↳ WITHIN 9 months from the Close of Financial Year.

Note: Hence there may be a case where the company need not hold AGM in the year of Incorporation and the following year.

5. Subsequent AGM – should be held at the earliest of the following dates,
   - ↳ Held every Calendar Year
   - ↳ WITHIN 15 months from the Date of 'Last AGM' and can be extended for further 3 months with RoC approval for special reasons only. If such extension of Financial Year is granted, there is NO violation even if AGM is NOT held in a Calendar Year
   - ↳ WITHIN 6 months from the Close of Financial Year [Sec. 210]
   - ↳ A public company by its article or resolution passed in AGM may fix time for its AGM and a private company, as agreed by all its members, may fix time and place.
6. Default – If a company fails to hold an AGM or even after receiving an order u/s. 167, then a fine UPTO Rs.50,000 can be imposed and thus a compoundable offence.
7. AGM can be called by CLB

Section 167: If default in holding an AGM, CLB on the application of any member of the company, call, or direct the calling of, a general meeting of the company. CLB may direct that one member of the company present in person or by proxy shall be deemed to constitute a meeting. **(One person GM)**.

PROVISIONS AS TO EGM

EGM may be called by Board of Directors	Board of Directors, *AT the request of Members*, to CALL FOR within 21 days of the Request and to HOLD EGM within 45 days of the Request.	Else the Requisitionists themselves HOLDING 1/10th of Paid up Capital OR Voting Power may CALL FOR an EGM within 3 months of requisition.	Company Law Board u/s. 186 - If impracticable, CLB on its own motion or on application of director / member who would be entitled to vote at the meeting; CLB may direct **One person GM.**

1. EGM may be called by requisition [Section 169] The Board of directors shall has to call an EGM on the requisition of following no. of members-

↳ Company having Share Capital → 1/10th of Paid-up Capital with voting rights;

↳ Company not having Share Capital → 1/10th of Total voting power of all members.

2. The requisition shall set out the matters for the consideration of which the meeting is to be called, shall be signed by the requisitionists, and shall be deposited at the registered office of the company.
3. Board has to call the EGM within 21 days from the date of the deposit of a valid requisition and the meeting should be held within 45 days from the date of the deposit of the requisition. Else the requisitionists themselves call the meeting within 3 months from the date of requisition.
4. Any reasonable expenses incurred by the requisitionists may be defrayed by the company and the company shall recover it by deducting from the remuneration to be paid to the directors.
5. Companies Act is silent regarding the place of holding EGM.

ABC LIMITED

Registered office: ....

Notice to Shareholders of 9th AGM of the Company

NOTICE is hereby given that the ...... [no.] Annual General Meeting of the Company will be held on the .... day of ...., ... at venue .... at .... time A.M/P.M. to transact the business specified in the notice of the meeting already posted individually to the members of the Company.

NOTICE is also hereby given pursuant to section 154 of the Companies Act, 1956 that the register of members and the share transfer books of the Company will remain closed from .... to .... (both days inclusive).

Place: ....

By order of the Board of directors

Date: ....

Company Secretary

Procedure for Voting by Poll

Procedure for Voting by Poll
Every person who desires to vote is given a paper headed "POLLING PAPER" with the following columns: Name of member & proxy; Number & Type of shares held with Folio No. in Register of Members and DP ID & Client ID (for demat shares); Resolution number as per notice of the meeting; Total number of votes; Votes "For" and "Against"; Signature of the member/proxy.
Every such person is advised to FILL the details and SIGN the polling paper. A member/proxy having more than one vote is entitled to use his votes differently all for or against or some for and some against the resolution; he need not use all his votes in the same way [Section 183].
The Chairman to appoint 2 persons to supervise and scrutinize the poll called SCRUTINEERS, out of them, atleast one should be a member & not an officer/employee of the company, who are assisted by the Company Secretary and his staff. [Section 184].
The Chairman requests the members and proxies present at the meeting to cast their VOTES by the Polling Paper. The members/proxies collect the Polling Papers, fill and sign them and then drop them in a box kept for the purpose.
The scrutineers collect the Polling Papers and, after scrutiny, prepare a REPORT and submit it to the Chairman, duly signed and dated, giving the following particulars: Votes for/against the resolution & INVALID votes with reasons By members present in person/by proxies Total votes cast FOR & AGAINST the resolution Majority for the resolution by No. & %
The Chairman will DECLARE the result of voting by poll. The result of the poll shall be deemed to be the decision of the meeting on the resolution on which the poll was taken [Section 185].
The decision as declared by the Chairman will be RECORDED in the minutes of the meeting.

Procedure for Passing Resolutions Requiring Special Notice

BUSINESS REQUIRING **SPECIAL NOTICE** u/s. 190 requiring Ordinary Resolution

↳ Removal of Auditor u/s. 225;

↳ Removal of Director u/s. 284;

↳ Appointment of another Auditor;

↳ Appointment of another Director;

The secretary must satisfy himself that where a special notice has been RECEIVED by the company, it has been given in accordance with the provisions of section 190.

Atleast 14 clear days' notice must have been given to the company before meeting.

In cases where the company itself proposes to make a resolution requiring a special notice there is no question of any special notice being given to the company. Instead, the required special notice may be included in the notice of the meeting itself or 14 days notice afresh to the shareholders as provided under the section.

The special notice must be placed before a meeting of the Board or circulated to the directors.

- If it is possible, the notice of the resolutions will be given to the members INDIVIDUALLY.
- If it is not practicable then the secretary must cause the notice of the resolutions to be PUBLISHED in a newspaper atleast 7 days before the meeting.

When the particular item of business is being considered the chairman must ask the member who gave special notice of the resolution to propose the same which will have to be seconded. After discussion, it must be put to vote and the chairman will then declare the result.

If the resolution is such as is required to be filed with the RoC, it will be so filed within 30 days of passing the resolution.

Enumerate the matters to be passed by resolutions requiring special notice (2008 – June)

ACTIVITY SCHEDULE FOR ANNUAL GENERAL MEETING

BEFORE THE MEETING

1. Issue notice under Section 286, convene a Board meeting, invite the auditors and transact following business
   a. To consider and discuss the report of audit committee on the annual accounts.
   b. To approve the accounts and authorise signing of accounts
   c. To secure auditors report
   d. To approve draft board report under Section 217(include explanation on reservation of audit report and attach compliance certificate from Company Secretary in whole time practice)
   e. To approve date, time and place along with the notice of the annual general meeting. (Notice to contain ordinary business as per Section 173 and special business if any along with explanatory statement for the same. Date of AGM cannot be on a public holiday and place should be registered office or within same city, town or village of the registered office.
   f. To consider closure of register of members and share transfer books of the company in compliance with section 154, authorise company secretary to arrange for publication in newspaper. Inform stock exchange 42 days in advance about the closure.
   g. To consider appointment of auditor from whom 224(1B) statement has been obtained
2. Information within 15 minutes of the Board meeting to stock exchanges about
   a. Details of dividends/cash bonuses
   b. Financial information
   c. Amounts appropriated for reserves, if any
3. Prepare annual report by printing notice of the meeting, balance sheet, profit and loss account, reports of the directors and auditors, etc.
4. Issue notice atleast 21 clear days before meeting excluding the date of posting and date of meeting and hence it shall be 21 days + 2 (for clear) + 2 (for post).
5. Issue notice to members, directors, auditors and stock exchanges.
6. check proxies and authorized representations received
7. Prepare detailed agenda in consultation with chairman.
8. Make arrangements for printing dividend warrant.

AT THE MEETING
1. Obtain attendance of all the members present or alternatively collect attendance slips.
2. If quorum is present read out the notice of meeting if advised by chairman.
3. To read Auditor's Report when item relating adoption of accounts is taken.
4. To help chairman in conducting meeting including taking of poll, etc.
5. To take notes of proceedings of meeting (to prepare Minutes)
6. Keep before the meeting register of directors share holding (Sec 307), Register of Members, Minutes Book, copy of annual report for INSPECTION.
AFTER THE MEETING
1. Prepare minutes and get it initialed in each page and dated and signed in the last page by the Chairman within 30 days of meeting.
2. Deposit Dividend tax rate as applicable and deposit Dividend in a separate bank account within 5 days.
3. Send intimation of appointment to auditors within 7 days of meeting and WITHIN 30 days of intimation, the auditor has to confirm or refuse the appointment by filing e-Form 23B following EFORM COMPLIANCE CHART.
4. File with ROC within 30 days of meeting following EFORM COMPLIANCE CHART, • make payment of dividend (ie) dispatch dividend warrants • e-form 32 for directors or secretaries • e-form 23 for special resolution & specific ordinary resolution • e-form 23AC & 23ACA for balance sheet and profit & loss account • e-form 66 regarding compliance certificate, if applicable
6. In case company has invited deposits, send copy of balance sheet to RBI.
7. File annual return within 60 days as per Schedule V of the Act in e-form 20B/21A as required u/s. 159/160 for company having & not having share capital respectively.

Note: Extraordinary General Meeting Schedule: Similar to Annual General Meeting.

DIVIDENDS

[Sec. 205, 205A, 205C, 206, 206A & 207]

Dividend means the Return on Investment (RoI) in Capital;

Preference shareholders shall be paid with dividend before Equity shareholders. In case of default u/s. 80A of Companies Act regarding default in case of irredeemable preference shares, dividend CANNOT be paid to EQUITY shareholders for ever.

The Payment of dividend is an Ordinary Business (OB) requiring Ordinary Resolution (OR);

FINAL DIVIDEND [at the AGM]	**INTERIM DIVIDEND** [between 2 AGMs]
↳ Recommended by Board [BoD]	• Recommended by Board [BoD]
↳ UPTO BoD's recommendation [if, Table A] may be DECLARED by Shareholders.	• DECLARED by BoD

Dividend shall be paid out of

1. profits;
2. profit for previous Financial Years and
3. amount PROVIDED by the Government for this purpose.

The Company has to provide for the

↳ depreciation for the Previous Financial Years and

↳ Amount of Loss of the Previous Financial Years OR Amount equal to the amount of depreciation whichever is LESS, shall be SETOFF against the Previous Year profit , BEFORE declaring the Dividend.

Model ordinary resolution to be passed at an annual general meeting for the declaration of dividend

THE BOARD RESOLVED THAT the following dividends, namely:

a	At the rate of ....% on the .... Redeemable Cumulative Preference Shares of Rs. 10 each;
b	At the rate of ....% on the .... Equity Shares of Rs. 10 each fully paid up for the full financial year;

as recommended by the Board of directors for payment for the financial year ......, to be paid to the shareholders of the Company whose names will appear on the Register of Members as on indly note, a listed company can declare and disclose the dividend on PER SHARE basis only as per Clause 20A of listing agreement.

Board Resolution to Decide Interim Dividend

The Board approves payment of interim dividend at the rate of Rs ...... (........%) per equity share be paid to the shareholders of the Company whose name will appear on the register of members on the record date, *i.e.*, ------- and the notice of the record date be given to the ------ Stock Exchanges, as required under the Listing Agreement.

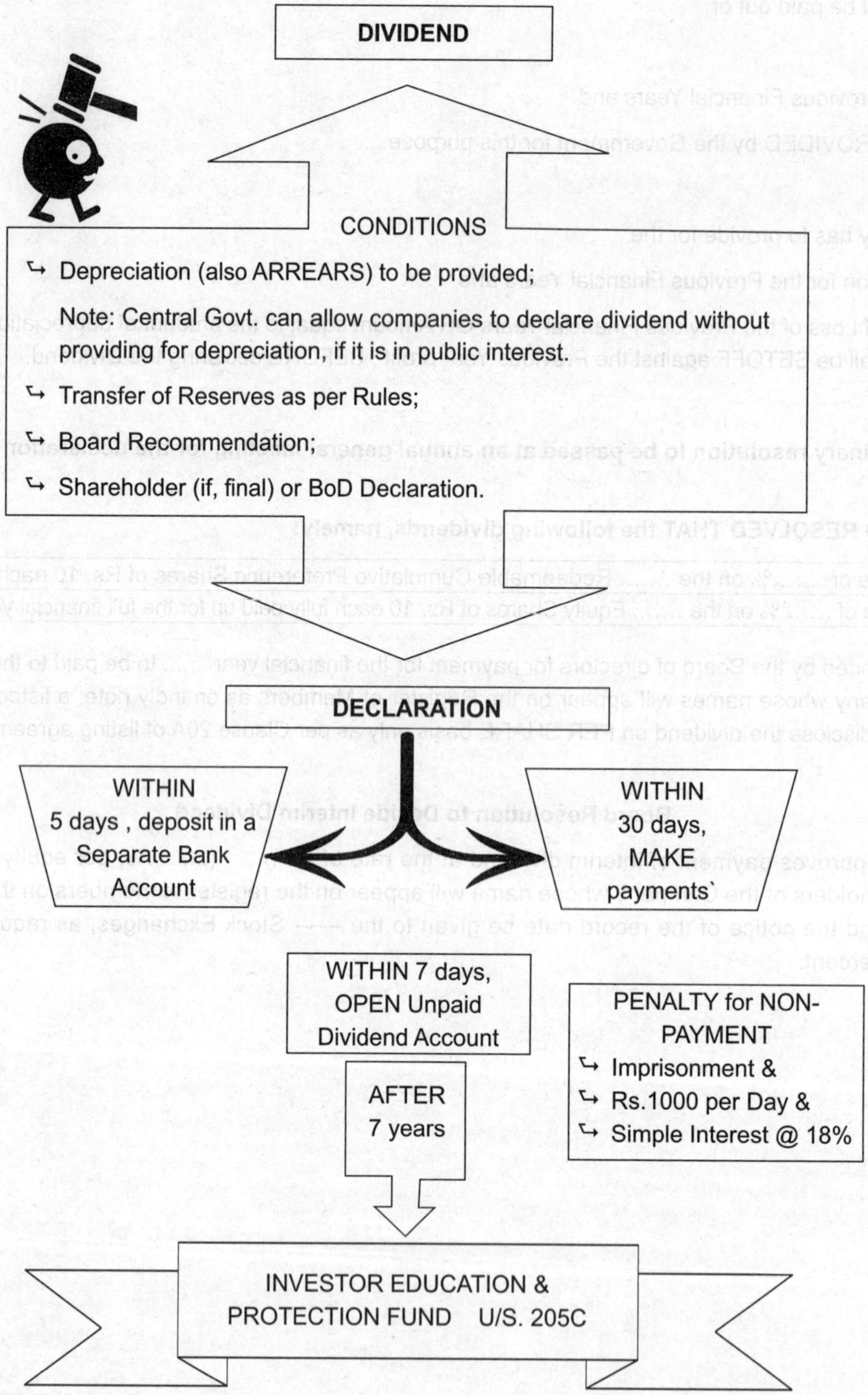
DIVIDEND
CONDITIONS
↳ Depreciation (also ARREARS) to be provided;
Note: Central Govt. can allow companies to declare dividend without providing for depreciation, if it is in public interest.
↳ Transfer of Reserves as per Rules;
↳ Board Recommendation;
↳ Shareholder (if, final) or BoD Declaration.
DECLARATION
WITHIN 5 days , deposit in a Separate Bank Account
WITHIN 30 days, MAKE payments`
WITHIN 7 days, OPEN Unpaid Dividend Account
PENALTY for NON-PAYMENT
↳ Imprisonment &
↳ Rs.1000 per Day &
↳ Simple Interest @ 18%
AFTER 7 years
INVESTOR EDUCATION & PROTECTION FUND U/S. 205C

When a Dividend NEED NOT be paid WITHIN 30 days of Declaration ?

1. By operation of law;
2. Shareholders Directions cannot be complied;
3. Where there is Dispute as to Dividend;
4. Lawfully adjusted against sum due from the Shareholder;
5. Any other reason, NOT due to any default of Company.

Note-

1. **"Declared Dividend is a Debt";**
2. Dividends ONLY to the Names in "Register of Members" OR order OR Banker;
3. Payment in Cash / Cheque / Warrant;
4. Section 206A: If a VALID instrument of TRANSFER is lodged during Book Closure, THEN the Dividend / Rights / Bonus of the underlying shares should be kept in ABEYANCE & TRANSFERRED to the Transferee on lifting the Book Closure period.
5. Dividend u/s. 616(c) of Companies Act for companies generating or supplying electricity under Electricity Act, 2003: As per the Tariff policy of Central Electricity Regulatory Commission (CERC), such electricity companies shout provide depreciation UPTO 90% of cost of asset before distributing dividend, the compliance of which shall be sufficient compliance of Section 205 of Companies Act.

Companies (Transfer of Profits to Reserve) Rules, 1975

1. Transfer to Reserves as per the prescribed Central Government rules;
2. ONLY out of Current Year Profits;
3. The following % to be transferred,

DIVIDEND [%]	TRANSFER [%]
UPTO 10%	-
UPTO 12.5%	2.5%
UPTO 15%	5%
UPTO 20%	7.5%
MORE THAN 20%	10%

4. The above mentioned Transfer % will NOT apply, if kept in credit of Profit & Loss Account;
5. Transfer % could be LESS, if NO dividend is paid in Current Year;
6. Transfer % could be HIGH, if Net Profit after Tax is LOWER by 20% or MORE THAN Average Net Profit of 2 Previous Years; OTHERWISE, it has to comply with following conditions,

↳ Dividend % "GREATER THAN or EQUAL TO" Average % (Dividend) in 3 Previous Years (PY);

↳ If Bonus paid in 3 PY, then Dividend Quantum in monetary terms "GREATER THAN or EQUAL TO" Average Quantum of Dividend in 3 PY.

Companies (Declaration out of Reserve) Rules, 1975

1. If Current Profits are NOT adequate, only then Dividend could be declared out of Reserves after complying with the Central Government rules in this regard.
2. Dividend % is LOWER of 10% or Average % in 5 Previous Years.

3. Amount UPTO 1/10th (PC+FR) can be withdrawn from Reserves, which shall be FIRST utilized to set-off LOSSES in the Current Year and the SURPLUS for Dividend; FR – Free Reserves.
4. Balance in Reserve Account SHALL be 15% or MORE of Paid-up Capital (PC).

INVESTOR EDUCATION & PROTECTION FUND

IEPF - [Section 205C]

↳ Established By Central Government;

↳ For CREDIT of amounts which have remained UNCLAIMED and UNPAID for a period of 7 years from the date they became DUE for payment.

↳ The following are the AMOUNTS to be credited,

1. Amounts in the Unpaid Dividend of the Company;
2. Application moneys received for allotment, DUE for refund;
3. Matured DEPOSITS with the Companies;
4. Matured DEBENTURES with the Companies;
5. Grants & Donations by Central Government, State Governments or others;
6. Interest or other income received out of the INVESTMENT made from the Fund;
7. The IEPF can be utilized for,
   i. Promotion of Investor Awareness;
   ii. Protection of the Interests of Investors.

IN accordance with the Rules.

For which purpose, e-form 1 (IEPF) shall be filed following EFILING COMPLIANCE CHART.

1. Investor Education and Protection Fund (IEPF). (2007 – December)
2. The Board of Directors of your company desires to declare dividend out of reserves. Being the Secretary of the company, give your advice to the Board of directors regarding the conditions and procedure to be followed for declaration of dividend out of reserves? (2007 – June)
3. Draft the specimen resolutions along with requisite explanatory statement, wherever necessary, for transacting the following items of business indicating the kind of meeting at which each resolution is to be passed and the type of resolution required for declaration of Interim dividend. (2007 – December)
4. "No dividend can be recommended by the Board of directors of the company in case the company has incurred losses during the financial year for which dividend is to be recommended." Comment. (2008 – June)
5. Draft the specimen resolutions along with requisite explanatory statement, wherever necessary, for transacting the following items of business indicating the kind of meeting at which each resolution is to be passed and the type of resolution required for recommending payment of dividend on equity shares out of current profits. (2008 – December)
6. Draft of following, In case of resolution, give reasons for passing the requisite resolution stating the authority who can pass it and also the type of resolution referring to the relevant section(s) of the Companies Act, 1956 resolution recommending declaration of dividend to shareholders without providing for depreciation (2010 – June)

7. Resolution for declaring interim dividend. (2010 – December)

8. Anmol Limited has incurred a loss or Rs. 16 crore during the financial year ended 31st March, 2008. The Company had been declaring dividend regularly since last 15 years and had accumulated undistributed profits of Rs. 150 crore. During last five financial years, the company declared dividend on equity share capital of Rs. 50 crore at the rate of 20%, 25%, 30%, 35% and 40% respectively. The Chairman of the company did not want to break the track record of declaration of dividends and wanted to declare dividend @ 40% for the financial year 2007 – 08 also. Being the Company Secretary of Anmol Limited what would be your advice to the Board of directors of the Company? (2008 – December)

APPOINTMENT OF AUDITORS

AUDIT

Ordinary Business

Appointment of Auditor is an Ordinary Business at AGM requiring Ordinary Resolution.

Before Appointment, Company shall obtain written Consent from Auditor to act as such and a certificate that the number of Auditorships is WITHIN limits specified u/s. 224(1B).

[Not applicable to a Private company]

[Limits under Sec 224 (1B) -:

- Companies paid-up capital LESS THAN 25 Lakhs twenty such companies;
- in any other case, 20 companies, out of which not more than 10 shall be companies each of which has a paid-up share capital of Rs.25 lakhs or more.

Ordinary Business requiring Special Resolution ONLY when, [Sec. 224A]

If Company is having 25% or more of Paid-up Capital by,

- Public Financial Institution or Government Company or Central or State Government;
- Financial Institution under State Act WHERE State Government holds 51% or More;
- Nationalized Banks or Insurance Company doing General Insurance business.

Post Appointment,

Companies have to INTIMATE within 7 days to Auditors; Auditors Intimation WITHIN 30 days to ROC (eform 23B).

Disqualification of a Person to act as a Statutory Auditor of the Company, if such person is a

- A Body Corporate;
- An Officer or Employee of the Company;
- a partner, or is in the employment with an officer; or employee of Co.
- a person who is indebted to the company/ given any guarantee or provided any security in connection with the indebtedness of any third person to the company for an amount exceeding Rs.1,000.
- a person holding any security (having voting rights) of that Company;
- disqualified to become auditor of the Subsidiary/Holding/ subsidiary of that Company's holding company.

Statutory Auditor CANNOT act as Internal Auditor as,

- Internal Audit is a part of Management &
- To be commented in CARO

MCA has clarified that LLP of Chartered Accountants will NOT BE TREATED as a Body Corporate for the limited purpose of Section 226(3)(a) of the Companies Act, 1956. This means, a CA's LLP can audit accounts.

Appointment of First Auditor:

1. Obtain Section 224(1B) certificate in writing from the auditor stating that his appointment is within the limits (specified number) prescribed under Section 224. The **specified number** shall be, • 20 public companies – if each has a paid up capital of less than Rs.25 lakhs • 20 public companies – if UPTO 10 companies are with paid up capital of atleast Rs. 25 lakhs. • For firm of auditors, specified number shall be the number of companies specified for every partner who is not in full time employment elsewhere. **Note:** Specified number will apply only to firms & to persons who are in full time employment elsewhere and it is NOT applicable to branch audit or audit of foreign company.
2. Convene a Board meeting within 1 month of incorporation and appoint the Auditor.
3. In case board fails to exercise its power to appoint first auditor, company in general meeting may appoint first auditor. So, hold a board meeting, discuss the matter, finalise first auditor and approve the notice of general meeting.
4. Issue notice of the general meeting to - Members – Directors – Auditors – Stock Exchanges
5. Hold the General Meeting to pass above resolution.
6. Inform the auditor about the appointment along with certified copy of the resolution passed within 7 days of appointment.
7. Within 30 days of intimation by the company, the auditor has to confirm or refuse the appointment by filing e-Form 23B.

Re-appointment of Auditors:

1. Obtain 224(1B) certificate in writing from the auditor stating that his appointment is within the limits prescribed under Section 224.
2. In an annual general meeting appointment of auditor is an ordinary business. Pass an ordinary resolution. If 224A is applicable then pass special resolution.
3. Inform the auditor about the appointment along with certified copy of the resolution passed within 7 days of appointment.
4. File e-form 23 with the RoC within 30 days of passing the special resolution
5. Within 30 days of intimation by the company, the auditor has to confirm or refuse the appointment by filing e-Form 23B.

Kindly note, as per Section 619 the auditors of Government Company (as defined u/s. 617) shall be appointed or re-appointed by the Comptroller and Auditor General (**CAG**) of India provided that limit u/s. 224 shall only apply to such auditor and no other provision of Section 224 will apply. Normally, the person who appoints will fix the remuneration but when appointment of auditor is made by CAG, the remuneration of the auditor so appointed will be fixed by company at its General meeting. Kindly note, CAG audit is also mandatory for such companies in which atleast 51% of paid-up capital is held by CG/SG or Government companies or corporations owned/controlled by CG/SG.

Filling the casual vacancy

A casual vacancy of auditor caused by death can be filled by the BoD by means of a resolution. If there are two auditors or more, other auditors can act even if one or more of them has/have resigned. However casual vacancy caused by resignation can be filled only in general meeting. Other procedures like 224(1B) statement, intimation to auditor and e-form 23B have to be followed.

REMOVAL OF AUDITOR

CASUAL VACANCY (Removal before END of the Term)

The BoD has the AUTHORITY to appoint, if vacancy, • CAUSED by DEATH	**The Shareholder has the AUTHORITY to decide,** • CAUSED by RESIGNATION • AFTER Auditor Approval u/s. 224(1B).

PROVISIONS – REMOVAL BEFORE EXPIRY OF TERM

↳ Previous approval of the Central Government (delegated to Regional Director) EXCEPT first Auditors;

↳ Special Notice to be given to pass a resolution in GM.

Special notice shall be required for a resolution at an AGM appointing as Auditor a person other than a Retiring Auditor, or providing expressly that a Retiring Auditor shall NOT be re-appointed,

- ↳ On receipt of notice of such a resolution, the Company shall forthwith send a copy thereof to the Retiring Auditor.
- ↳ Any representations, in writing made by the Auditor to the Company and requests their notification to members of the Company, the Company shall,
  - ↳ send a copy of the representations to every member of the Company to whom notice of the meeting is sent; OR
  - ↳ the representations shall be read out at the meeting; OR
  - ↳ CG to be satisfied that the rights conferred are being abused to secure needless publicity for defamatory matter, then the representations need not be sent.

↳ Other cases: Sec 225- Provisions as to resolutions for appointing or removing auditors.

Removal of first auditors:

The first auditors can be removed by appointing another auditor in his place in general meeting.

Removal of subsequent auditor: (before expiry of his term)

1. Convene a Board meeting to decide removal of existing auditor setting out the reason therefore and authorise person to apply to Central Government (powers delegated to Regional Director)
2. Apply to the Regional Director in e-form 24A following EFORM COMPLIANCE CHART.
3. On receipt of approval convene a Board meeting to a. Decide appointment of new AUDITOR b. Approve notice of general meeting for passing necessary resolution
4. Obtain Section 224(1B) certificate from auditor that appointment made will be in accordance with Section 224.
5. Hold the general meeting and pass ordinary resolution for appointment of new auditor.
6. Inform the auditor about the appointment along with certified copy of the resolution passed within 7 days of appointment. Also inform the removed auditor about his removal.
7. File e-form 23, if any with the ROC within 30 days of special resolution.
8. Within 30 days of intimation by the company, the auditor has to confirm or refuse the appointment by filing e-Form 23B.

Audit of accounts of branch office of Company

↳ By the Company's Auditor or a member of ICAI [in consultation with Company's auditor] OR if the branch is outside India, any person who are qualified to be appointed as auditors under the laws of that country;

↳ Company's Auditor shall have a right of access at all times to the books and accounts and vouchers of the company maintained at the branch office and in case of Banking companies, the copies of Books of Accounts transmitted to Principal office;

↳ Branch auditor shall prepare a report on the Accounts of the branch office examined by him and forward the same to the Company's Auditor to enable him to prepare the Auditor's report;

↳ Have the SAME powers and duties as Company's Auditors;

↳ CG may relax any of the provisions.

Appointment of Branch Auditor: (Section 228)

1. Convene a Board meeting to aa. ppoint a person who has necessary qualification to be appointed as branch auditor and b. approve the notice of general of meeting to pass resolution appointing the branch auditor.
2. Send notice of the general meeting at least 21 days before the meeting to - Members – auditors – directors – stock exchanges
3. Hold the general meeting and pass the resolution.
4. Intimate stock exchanges and concerned auditor about his appointment.

Appointment of auditors of Government Companies:

As per 619(2) of the Companies Act, 1956, auditors of Government company shall be appointed or re-appointed by the Comptroller and Auditor General of India (CAG).

Other procedures are similar to appointment of auditor.

1. Draft the specimen resolutions along with requisite explanatory statement, wherever necessary, for transacting the following items of business indicating the kind of meeting at which each resolution is to be passed and the type of resolution required for appointment of an auditor, a person other than a retiring auditor. (2007 – June)
2. Outline the procedure for removal of the statutory auditor. (2007 – December)
3. Draft the specimen resolutions along with requisite explanatory statement, wherever necessary, for transacting the following items of business indicating the kind of meeting at which each resolution is to be passed and the type of resolution required for appointment of auditors Shankar & Co in place of Sundar & Co who resigned from the office of auditors. (2008 – June)
4. When is section 228 applicable? Outline the procedure for appointment of branch auditor. (2008 – December)
5. Outline the procedure for removal of the statutory auditor. (2009 – June)
6. Which type of companies are subject to audit by Comptroller and Auditor General of India? Is there any need for having statutory audit by professional auditors? State the legal position in this regard. (2009 – June)
7. Draft specimen resolutions stating the authority who can pass it and also the type of resolution. Given reasons for passing the requisite resolution referring to the relevant sections(s) of the Companies Act, 1956:

   New Biotech (P) Limited wants to appoint the first auditors in the regular course within a fortnight of the registration of the company. (2009 – December)
8. Draft general meeting resolution for appointment of branch auditor. (2010 – December)

AUDITORS REPORT

Sec. 227 – Duties of Directors: The auditor shall make a report to the MEMBERS of the company on the accounts examined by him, and on every balance sheet [as at the end of Financial Year (FY)] and profit and loss account [for its FY] and the report shall state whether, in his opinion and to the best of his INFORMATION and according to the EXPLANATIONS given to him, the said accounts give the information required by this Act in the manner so required and give a TRUE AND FAIRVIEW;

The Auditor shall INQUIRE,

- loans and advances made by the company on the basis of security have been properly secured and the terms not prejudicial to the interests of the company or its members;
- where transactions of the company which are represented merely by book entries are not prejudicial to the interests of the company;
- whether so much of the Assets of the company [Not being Investment or Banking Co] as consist of shares, debentures and other securities have been sold at a price less than that at which they were purchased by the company;
- whether Loans and Advances made by the company have been shown as DEPOSITS;
- whether Personal expenses have been charged to REVENUE account;
- where it is stated in the books and papers of the company that any shares have been allotted for cash, whether cash has actually been received in respect of such allotment;

The Auditor's report shall also STATE,

- whether he has obtained all the INFORMATION and EXPLANATIONS which to the best of his knowledge and belief were necessary for the purposes of his audit;
- whether, in his opinion, proper books of account and proper returns adequate for the purposes of his audit have been received from BRANCHES not visited by him; and report on the accounts of any branch office audited by a person OTHER THAN the company's auditor has been forwarded to him;
- whether the company's B/S and P&L dealt with by the report are in,
  - compliance with Accounting Standards; &
  - agreement with the books of account and returns;
- in THICK type or in ITALICS the observations or comments of the auditors which have any ADVERSE effect on the functioning of the company;
- Whether any Director is disqualified u/s. 274(1)(g)

Note: CG may direct that Additional Matters be included.

INSPECTION OF AUDITORS REPORT

- As per Section 230, the Auditors Report shall be read at the General Meeting and shall be open to Inspection by ANY MEMBER of the Company;
- The Auditors Report is available for inspection DURING business hours;
- AND during & conclusion of Annual General Meeting.

SPECIAL AUDIT

Section 233A

When?

Central Government, is of the Opinion, that,

↳ that AFFAIRS of Company are NOT being managed in accordance with SOUND business principles or PRUDENT commercial practices; or

↳ that Company is being managed in a manner likely to cause SERIOUS injury or damage to the INTERESTS of the trade, industry or business; or

↳ that the financial position of any company is such as to ENDANGER its solvency.

CG may DIRECT,

↳ Special audit of the Company's accounts for such period and

↳ appoint any member of ICAI or the company's auditor to conduct;

↳ Make the report to the CG instead of members;

↳ The Central Government may take such ACTION on the report or send to the Company either a copy of, or relevant extract from, the report with its comments thereon AND require the company either to CIRCULATE that to its members or to have it READ before the company at its next General Meeting.

↳ Expenses of the Special Audit to be PAID by the Company.

CHARGES

CHARGES REQUIRING REGISTRATION as per Sec 125:

The following charges created by the company requires registration,

↳ For Securing Issue of Debentures;

↳ On Book Debts;

↳ On Uncalled Share Capital;

↳ On Calls made BUT not paid;

↳ On Immovable Property OR any interest on Immovable Property;

↳ On Movable Property EXCLUDING Pledge;

↳ On Ship, Goodwill, Patent or License under IPR;

↳ FLOATING CHARGE on Undertaking or any Property of the Company;

↳ Mortgage.

If Property is acquired SUBJECT TO Charge u/s. 125, it is required to be REGISTERED, as per Section 127.

Section 126 – Registration of Charges is the Constructive Notice that the Charge exists;

Section 134 – REGISTRATION OF CREATION / MODIFICATION & TIME LIMIT

It is the duty of the Company to register the charge with RoC but any Interested Person (Charge holder) may also cause a Charge to be registered and recover the cost from the Company.

Every company shall cause a copy of every instrument creating any charge requiring registration and Register of charges to be kept at the registered office of the company for inspection by its members and others.

CREATION / MODIFICATION OF CHARGE	DEBENTURES
e-Form 8 [Registration with RoC] following EFORM COMPLIANCE CHART to be FILED from **WITHIN 30 days** of CREATION or MODIFICATION of Charge with details like-: ↳ the DATE of its creation or the date of the acquisition of the property, if its an existing charge on such acquisition; ↳ the AMOUNT secured by the charge; ↳ short particulars of the PROPERTY charged; ↳ and the persons ENTITLED to the charge.	e-Form 10 to be filed **WITHIN 30 days** of execution of Debenture Trust Deed, with a copy of debenture trust deed with details like, ↳ The total amount secured by the whole series; ↳ the dates of the resolutions authorising the issue and the date of the covering deed, by which the security is created or defined; ↳ a general description of the property charged; ↳ the names of the trustees, if any, for the debenture holders ↳ particulars as to the amount or rate per cent of the commission, discount or allowance so paid or made to person agreeing to subscribe or procure subscriptions.

↳ If delayed, a Further period of 30 days is allowed for Registration,

↳ On showing Sufficient Cause, AND

↳ Payment of Additional Filing Fees as per Schedule X.

↳ If further delayed, the company has to approach **Company Law Board** for Registration, **on elapse of such period of 60 days** from Creation or Modification of Charge. Order of CLB for CONDONATION OF DELAY shall NOT prejudice any rights acquired in respect of property concerned by any third party BEFORE the Charge is ACTUALLY REGISTERED as "whoever is PRIOR in Time is PRIOR in right [law]" [Section 141]

COMPANY	PROPERTY	TIME for REGISTRATION
Incorporated Outside India	Situated Outside India	The Time will start Ticking form the Date when the Documents are RECEIVED in India by Post.
Incorporated in India	Situated Outside India	According to the Laws of the Country in which Charge is Created

1. Satisfaction of Charges (2007 – December)
2. What particulars in respect of each charge are required to be filed with the Registrar of Companies? (2008 – December)
3. 'Charge', 'Mortgage' and 'Pledge'. (2009 – June)
4. A charge for Rs. 3 crore was created and registered by Dada Fims Limited in favour of State Bank of India. The same was fully repaid on 31st August, 2009, but the relevant 'E – Form' for registering the satisfaction of the charge was filed on 10th October, 2009. The Company then realised that it has unintentionally delayed the filing and has attracted penal provision of the Companies Act, 1956 in this regard. The company has approached Chetan, a Practising Company secretary for his advice as regards the possibility of any Condonation of the offence. What would be the advice? (2010 – January)

Section 125 – EFFECT OF NON-REGISTRATION

"it is the SECURITY (Not, Debt) that is DESTROYED" in case of non-registration of charge.

Non-registration of charge does NOT prejudice the 'Unsecured Creditor', except the charge created is VOID as against the Liquidator & Other Creditors of the Company at the time of liquidation.

The CONCESSIONS to Chargee / Creditor on Non-Registration are,

↳ Section 134 – To register charge & RECOVER the money payable

↳ Section 125(3) – Money secured becomes IMMEDIATELY payable.

MEMORANDUM OF SATISFACTION u/s. 138, 139 & 140:

'Payment in FULL' intimation will be given by Debtor on satisfaction of charge (ie) on full repayment of loan.

↳ File e-Form 17 [Registration with RoC] following EFORM COMPLIANCE CHART to be FILED within 30 days of SATISFACTION of Charge;

↳ Verification by RoC, by way of a Show-Cause-Notice to Creditor or Charge holder;

↳ Charge holder should CONFIRM within 14 days to Company;

↳ If further delayed, the company has to approach **Company Law Board** for Registration, **on elapse of such period of 30 days** from satisfaction of Charge.

SECTION 132 – The Certificate of Registration stands as Conclusive Evidence [which cannot be rebutted] of Compliance of Requirements as to Registration and not of facts / figures in the certificate.

Procedure for Registration of Charges:

1. The Company at its general meeting should have authorized its Board of Directors to file charge on the assets and properties of the Company to provide security for repayment of borrowing in favor of lender under Section 293(1)(a).
2. Using such authority given under 293(1)(a) the Board shall sign the loan documents.
3. If the charge falls under any of the specified categories mentioned under Section 125(4), particulars of the charge shall be registered within 30 days of creation of charge with the RoC in e-form 8 (other than debentures) or e-form 10 (debentures) following EFORM COMPLIANCE CHART. **Note:** A charge not registered is void against the liquidator and any other creditor of the Company.
4. In case the charge is created outside India then it can be registered within 30 days from the date it could have been received in India in due course of post.
5. The registrar will register the form and issue a certificate that the charge has been registered to Company and the creditor.

Procedure for Modification of Charge:

Similar to that of registration of charges.

Procedure for Rectification of Register of Charges with RoC:

Earlier, when the companies DOES NOT register the charges, any person interested in charge can make an application to Company Law Board (CLB) for granting extension of time for registering the charge with RoC [u/s. 141]. Recently, this power is shifted to Central Government, which in turn has delegated the same to RoC. The application shall be enclosed with the copy of resolutions passed u/s. 292 or 293 of Companies Act in relation to charges.

Though the basic provisions of Companies Act are also dealt with, it is highly advisable to read the General Meetings portion of Companies Act in detail. You may also follow Only This Much for CS Executive Program for the said purpose. The provisions in this chapter are in addition to the basic provisions learnt at the executive level. Hence if you feel you do not understand some provision, do read again your company law syllabus in Executive level. Again don't forget the mantra of reading again and again, as many times as possible till you get the hang of the subject. As the syllabus of Company law is vast anything can be covered under the subject Company Secretarial Practice. Hence, understand the provisions the right way.

The other aspects & Board Meeting which are not discussed elsewhere are cumulated in this chapter. This chapter goes on the presumption that one understands the basic provisions of Board Meeting dealt at the Executive level of Company Secretary exams. Though it has highlighted the essence of basic provisions, it is highly advisable to refresh the Executive basics again. As said, most of the provisions discussed hereunder can be passed with or without a Board meeting. Further this portion also discusses drafting of Managing Directors agreement, Directors report which shall also be concentrated for the DRAFTING portion in the syllabus.

Other Aspects And Board Meeting

QUALIFICATION TO ACT AS A DIRECTOR

1. An Individual, NOT a Body Corporate;
2. Shall have a Directors Identification Number [DIN];
3. Age – Completed 18 years;
4. Education – Articles may prescribe.
5. Hold Share Qualification, if required by Articles or Table A

SHARE QUALIFICATION

Own Articles
MAY prescribe;
In case of Public Limited Company Section 270 shall be complied with.

Tab A
Minimum 1 Share

Section 270 prescribes,

↳ Qualification shares shall be allotted within 2 months of appointment;
↳ Qualification share shall be one share, if nominal value exceeds Rs.5,000/-
↳ DEFAULT of the above – Vacation u/s. 283.

DISQUALIFICATION OF DIRECTOR

Section 274 On Appointment
(@ the time of appt - Entry)

a) Found to be of unsound mind by court.
b) An undischarged insolvent.
c) Applied to be adjudicated as insolent [called Debtors petition]
d) Convicted in Offence involving Moral Turpitude and Imprisonment for more than 6 months & 5 years not elapsed from such conviction
e) Call money DUE for more than 6 months.
f) Court order u/s. 203* is in force.
g) #

* Section 203: Order for Guilty or convicted of an Offence in promotion, formation, management or winding up.

Note -

↳ Central Government has the power to RELAX point (e) & (f) only;

↳ Validity of acts by directors whose appointment found invalid LATER: **[Section 290]-** Acts done by a person as a director shall be valid, even if it was later discovered that his appointment was invalid by reason of any defect or disqualification or had terminated by virtue of any provision of Act Articles. But after his appointment has been shown to the company to be invalid or to have terminated, the subsequent acts are not valid.

 # Section 274(1)(g)# is Disqualification criteria applicable NOT APPLICABLE for Private Limited Companies. According to which, in case of

DEFAULT in either of the following, [in respect of Public Company, where he is / was a Director]

↳ Filing of Annual Account **and** Annual Returns for continuously 3 years;

↳ Repayment of Deposits or its Interest or Redemption of Debenture on due date or on payment of Dividend and failure continues for 1 year or more;

THEN, such Director is disqualified for a period of 5 years to get appointed as Director of ANY PUBLIC company,

↳ Company to intimate RoC in eform DD-B within 30 days following EFORM COMPLIANCE CHART.

↳ Such Director to intimate in Form DDA on appointment / re-appointment.

The said disqualification can be removed by filing eform DD-C to Central Government following EFORM COMPLIANCE CHART.

> As a Company Secretary, draft a specimen notice of disqualification under Section 274 (1)(g) for a director of your company who is otherwise eligible for re – appointment in the ensuing annual general meeting (2010 – December)

RESIGNATION, VACATION & REMOVAL

RESIGNATION

↳ Director →On tendering Letter of Resignation Unless Otherwise provided by AoA;

↳ If Director is an MD → On Acceptance of such Resignation Letter by BoD as decided in *Achutha Pai Vs. RoC case*.

↳ THEN, Company to file E-Form 32 to RoC.

> How does a director resign from the Board of directors in a private limited company, if the Board fails to accept his resignation? (2010 – December) The board need not accept resignation in case of a private limited company.

In order to avoid such eventualities wherever there is MANAGEMENT DISPUTE, the company is required to **mandatorily file the attachment** relating to **cause of cessation** alongwith e-form 32 with the ROC concerned irrespective of the ground of cessation, viz (a) retirement; (b) disqualification; (c) death; (d) resignation; (e) vacation of office u/s 283 or 313 or 260; (f) removal u/s 284; (g) withdrawal of nomination by appointing authority or (h) absence of re-appointment.

In case, any Director is **aggrieved** with his/her cessation in the company, such person may file complaint in the **Investor Complaint Form** (Form INV). On receipt of complaint, the ROC concerned will examine the complaint and mark the company as having 'MANAGEMENT DISPUTE'. Also, the ROC will issue a letter to the company and the parties to settle the matter amicably or get an order/interim order from a Court or Tribunal of competent jurisdiction. Till such dispute is settled, the documents filed by the company and by the contesting groups of Directors will not be approved/registered/recorded and will thus NOT be available in the registry for PUBLIC VIEWING.

Procedure for removal of a director by the Central Government:

The Central Government shall, by order, remove from office any director concerned in the conduct and management of the affairs of a company, against whom there is a decision of the Company Law Board under Section 388D of the Act (Section 388E).

The decision of the Company Law Board is given on a reference made by the central Government under Section 388B of the Act.

(a) that any person concerned in the conduct and management of the affairs of a company is or has been, in connection therewith, guilty of fraud, misfeasance, persistent negligence or default in carrying out his obligations and functions under the law, or breach of trust; or

(b) the business of a company is not or has been conducted and managed by such person in accordance with sound business principles or prudent commercial practices; or

(c) the business of a company is or has been conducted and managed by such person in a manner which is likely to cause, or has caused, serious injury or damage to the interest of the trade, industry or business to which such company pertains; or

(d) the business of a company is or has been conducted and managed by such person with intent to defraud its creditors, members or any other persons or otherwise for a fraudulent or unlawful purpose or in a manner prejudicial to public interest;

the Central Government may state a case against the person aforesaid and refer the same to the Company Law Board with a request that the Company Law Board may inquire into the case and record a decision as to whether or not such person is a fit and proper person to hold the office of director or other connected with the conduct and management of any company.

VACATION OF DIRECTOR u/s. 283: It is after appointment of directors. A person occupying the position of director, deemed to vacate his position, if

SIX grounds	similar to Disqualification u/s. 274 ↳ Found to be of unsound mind by court ↳ An undischarged insolvent ↳ Applied to be abjudicated as insolvent [called Debtors Petition] ↳ Court Order u/s. 203* in in force ↳ Convicted in Offence involving Moral Turpitude and Imprisonment for more than 6 months & 5 years not elapsed from such conviction ↳ Call money DUE for more than 6 months.

TWO grounds	↳ NOT attended 3 Consecutive Board Meeting OR for 3 months without Leave / Absence. ↳ Not Acquired/failed to retain Qualification Shares (if required as per Articles) within 2 months of Appointment.
TWO grounds	↳ Default u/s. 295 → NA to Private, Bank or Holding to its Subsidiaries; ↳ No Disclosure u/s. 299; [Note Sec. 297 is not covered].
ONE ground	↳ Removal u/s. 284 by members. It is **NA** to Sec. 265 [directors appointed through proportional representation], IDRA Director & director appointed inOffice for Life in a Private Company; Removal can be done by Co/CG/CLB.
ONE ground	↳ Ceasing Employment in case of Employment-Linked Directorships [like, Whole-time Director]
ADDITIONAL grounds	↳ Private Company may prescribe Additional Grounds apart from the above mentioned 12 grounds for Vacation through its **Articles**.

Not Applicable [NA] to,

↳ Central Government Directors u/s. 408, Nominee Directors, Small Shareholder Director and BIFR Director.

A director of the company remained absent, without notice, for 6 meetings during first quarter of 2009.

REMOVAL OF DIRECTOR u/s. 284 – Special Notice

Authority – General Meeting requiring Ordinary Resolution OR by CLB on issues of Oppression / Mismanagement u/s. 397 or 398 OR by CG on defrauding Creditors or fraud, et al.

Process:

Step 1	The Notice, in writing, shall reach the Company atleast 14 days before the Date of General Meeting
Step 2	Inform forthwith (immediately) the Concerned Director with a Copy of the Notice
Step 3	"Director Representation", in writing, to be circulated as Individual Notice to Members or read-out at General Meeting
Step 4	"Director Representation", if defamatory or for needless publicity, then get CLB permission to "NOT to circulate"
Step 5	Director (whether member or not) is given the Opportunity of being HEARD in the General Meeting. This is the only place where a Non-Member can speak at a General Meeting.
Step 6	Consider Section 257 Notice [proposal by Member], if any or proceed with provisions of Section 262 for appointment.

Note:

Compensation only for Section 318 to 320; NO Compensation if removal by CG or CLB & also BAR from Directorships for a period of 5 years.

Section 257: Right of person OTHER than Retiring Director to stand for Directorships on proposal by a Member [quote number of shares with Folio No.] OR by a candidate [not necessarily the Member] by depositing Rs. 500/- atleast 14 days before the date of General Meeting, then Company shall intimate to every Member or publish Advertisement atleast 7 days before the date of General Meeting. The procedure is almost similar to SPECIAL NOTICE procedure. The said deposited will be refunded on appointment, otherwise, it shall stand forfeited.

Notice by a member proposing another member's name for directorship of the company. (D 10)

Procedure for charging a director/officer with the responsibility of compliance

If the Board of directors of any company want to charge any particular director or other officer with the responsibility of complying with any provision of the Act in pursuance of the provision in clause (*f*) of section 5, then the procedure outlined below should be followed:

(*a*) Obtain the consent of such director or officer in Form 1AB.

(*b*) Pass a resolution at a meeting of the Board of directors for charging the director or officer with the responsibility of complying with one or more provisions of the Act, as specified in the resolution.

(*c*) Within 30 days from the Board meeting, file e-form 1AA with RoC following EFORM COMPLIANCE CHART.

(*d*) Whenever the consent given by a director or officer is revoked or withdrawn, file e-Form 1AA again.

(*e*) If the company does not have any of the officers specified in clauses (*a*) to (*c*) of section 5 and in pursuance of the provision in clause (*g*) thereof the Board of directors of the company may charge any director with the responsibility of complying with any provision of the Act by filing e-form 1AA.

Section 252, 258 & 259 deals with Number of Directors to be APPOINTED in the Board,

Private Limited	**Public Limited**
Minimum is 2	Minimum is 3
Maximum is Unlimited	Maximum is 12*

* = In case of Public Limited Company, if the Articles at the time of incorporation is silent regarding the max. no. of directors or provide for less than 12 directors, then if the company want to increase the number of directors beyond 12 ,then it has to pass ordinary resolution and then apply to the Central Government for approval. The increase beyond 12 will be valid only after the Central Government's approval.

Procedure for Increase in Number of Directors

1. Hold the Board Meeting a. To consider the increase in number of director more than 12 b. To issue notice of general meeting along with explanatory statement for passing a special resolution for increasing number of directors subject to the approval of Central Government.
2. Issue notices to - Members – Directors – Auditors – Stock Exchanges.
3. Hold the meeting and pass the special resolution
4. Inform stock exchange the proceedings of the meeting.
5. File e-form 23 with ROC within 30 days of passing Special Resolution following EFORM COMPLIANCE CHART.
6. Publish General notice u/s. 640B and make application to Central Government in e-form 24 following EFORM COMPLIANCE CHART.
7. In a Board meeting appoint additional directors, file e-form 32 along with prescribed fees and make necessary entries in the register of companies as detailed in the case of appointment.

DIRECTORS APPOINTED BY BOARD

Particulars	Section 260	Section 262	Section 313
Provides for Appointment of	Additional Director	Directors in Casual Vacancy	Alternate Directors
Applicability	All companies	Only Public Limited	All companies
When to Appoint?	At the discretion of the Board	If Director appointed by Member dies, resigns, etc…	If Original Director is outside State for more than 3 months
Articles [AoA]	Shall authorize or amend AoA	-	Shall authorize or amend AoA
Authority	Board Resolution or Circular Resolution	Only by way of Board Resolution	Act is Silent [Board Resolution or Circular Resolution]
Term	Till the ensuing AGM or re-appointed by Members in the AGM	Till the term of Director in whose place he is appointed	Till the Original Director returns to the State or Original Director term expires

1. Draft the specimen resolutions along with requisite explanatory statement, wherever necessary, for transacting the following items of business indicating the kind of meeting at which each resolution is to be passed and the type of resolution required for appointment of a person as a director who is an additional director. (2007 – June)

2. The Board of Directors of Swarn Limited had five directors. One of them died and the Board appointed Rajat in his place to fill – up the casual vacancy. However, Rajat resigned from the Board after two months of his appointment. The Board wishes to appoint Bhagat in place of Rajat to full – up the casual vacancy. As a Company Secretary of that company, would be your advice to the Board and why? (2008 – June) As Rajat is not a director appointed by shareholders, the casual vacancy will not arise on his resignation. Bhagat can be appointed as an Additional director only.

DIRECTORS APPOINTED BY SHAREHOLDERS

APPOINTMENT OF DIRECTORS BY SHARE HOLDERS

[Not applicable to Private Company]

TOTAL STRENGTH OF THE BOARD

Non-Rotational

1/3rd of the Total Strength of the Board.

Note: While calculating the number of Directors to retire, the number of following Directors are NOT counted,

- Nominee Directors;
- Government Directors u/s. 408;
- Directors appointed by BIFR.

Rotational

2/3rd of the Total Strength of the Board. [rounded off to next integer]

1/3rd [number nearest to 1/3rd] shall retire @ every AGM, which is an Ordinary Business.

Note: It's a seniority based retirement, if both are appointed on same date, then its based on Lots.

Bal-ance 1/3rd

Rotational Directors are called Non-Permanent Directors and Non-Rotational Directors are Permanent Directors.

Points, when Appointing a Director @ General Meeting

- Appointment of more than one director cannot be approved through a single resolution [called Omnibus Resolution] in the general meeting
- UNLESS a resolution that it shall be so made has first been agreed to by the meeting without any vote being given against it [called Unanimous Approval]
- A resolution moved in contravention shall be void, whether or not objection was taken at the time to its being so moved
- Where a resolution so moved is passed, no provision for the automatic re-appointment of the director retiring by rotation in default of another appointment shall apply

Ammol Limited in its annual general meeting appointed all its directors by passing one single resolution. No objection was made to the resolution by any one present in the meeting. Examine the validity of the appointment and subsequent acts of the Board of directors explaining the relevant provisions of the Companies Act, 1956. Will it make any difference, if ammon Limited is a government company? (2010 – December)

AUTOMATIC RE-APPOINTMENT u/s. 256

- If in the General Meeting,
- the place of the RETIRING DIRECTOR is not so filled up AND

↳ the meeting has not expressly resolved not to fill the vacancy,

↳ then meeting shall stand adjourned till the same day in the next week, at the same time and place (In case of public holidays, next day).

↳ If even in the adjourned meeting,

PROPORTIONAL REPRESENTATION

for "Rotational Director" u/s. 265

[Not Applicable to Private Limited Company]

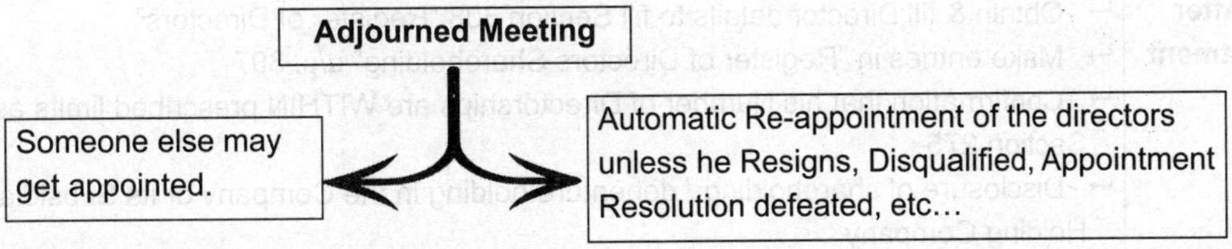

↳ AoA should authorise such Appointment;

↳ Could be mandated by Central Government u/s. 408;

↳ Over-riding Clause [Notwithstanding] (section 284 regarding Vacation, cannot be invoked to remove such Directors)

↳ Min. 2/3rd of Total No. of Dir can be appointed for Term of 3 years;

↳ Appoint provisions as like S-262 re Director in Casual Vacancy;

↳ 2 systems of appoint viz., Single Transferable Vote or Cumulative Voting; (say, if 5 Candidates, then 5 Votes for every shareholder, which can be voted for ONE or DISTRIBUTED among <= 5 candidates)

Write a note on proportional representation and illustrate your answer. (2008 –December)

Assignment of Office by Directors

Section 312 - Assignment of Office of Director is prohibited under the Act. Assignment is VOID. Assignment is appointing one another individual as a Director on his behalf, during the Tenure of Original. The Supreme Court in Oriental Metal Pressing (P) Ltd v. B.K. Thakoor held that an MD holding office for life in private company, appointed a person by will to succeed after death is valid as it's an appointment and not an assignment during life time.

SECRETARIAL PRACTICE FOR APPOINTMENT / CHANGE IN DIRECTORS

Steps	Secretarial Practice
Steps Before Appointment	↳ Submission of DIN ↳ Consent Letter to act as Director u/s. 264 for Public Limited Company, which is a mandatory attachment to e-Form 32 ↳ Declaration by Director of Public Limited Company, in Form DDA prescribed under Companies (Disqualification of Directors u/s. 274(1)(g) of Companies Act, 1956) Rules, 2003 that he is NOT disqualified from ALL such Companies in which he is a Director.
Steps On Appointment / Change	As per Section 303, for any change in Director i.e, appointment, removal, resignation, death, e-Form 32 to be filed WITHIN 30 days of such change following EFORM COMPLIANCE CHART.
Steps After Appointment	↳ Obtain & fill Director details to fill Section 303 "Register of Directors" ↳ Make entries in "Register of Directors Shareholding" u/s. 307 ↳ Confirmation that his Number of Directorships are WITHIN prescribed limits as per Section 275 ↳ Disclosure of shareholding / debenture holding in the Company or its Subsidiary or Holding Company ↳ List of Directorships where he/she should be regarded as INTERESTED u/s. 299 ↳ List of Relatives as per Section 2(41) read with Section 6 & Schedule IA

LIST OF RELATIVES (as given above) are,

- Members of Hindu Undivided Family (HUF)
- Husband & Wife
- Following 22 relatives,

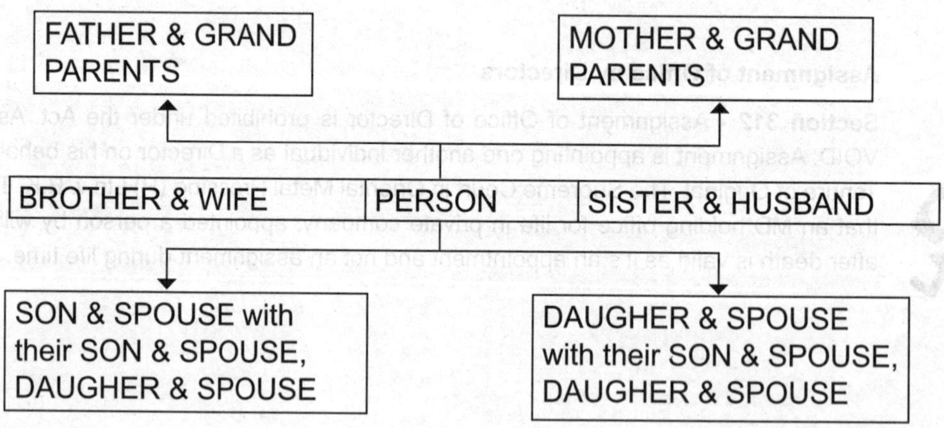

NOMINEE DIRECTOR

Financial Institutions & Banks MAY appoint nominee directors as per their respective loan agreement. Such nominee directors may be appointed even if the total strength of the board exceeds the ceiling and such directors neither need to retire by rotation nor required to hold qualification shares. Further disqualification u/s. 274 will not attract them. For all other purposes, nominee directors are just like any other directors who will be counted for quorum, shall disclose his interest, certify the documents, etc...Nominee directors are protected from legal liability as a director, in respect of anything done by them in GOOD FAITH.

> As a Company Secretary of Smart Enterprises Limited how would you tackle the following situations:
>
> The Union Bank of India has given a loan of ` 25 crore for the company's new project and as per one of the terms of sanction it wants to nominate its Chief Manager, Vijay on the Board. (2010 – June)

Appointment of Nominee Director and Procedure for Varying Terms of Appointment of Non Rotational Directors:

1. Before making the application, formalities as to giving of general notice to the members u/s 640B of the Act, etc. are to be complied with.
2. Alter the Articles if there is no provision for such an appointment by passing a special resolution. Approval of the Central Government u/s 268 of the Companies Act shall have to be obtained in case an amendment of any provision relating to appointment of non-rational director by filing e-form 25B following MANDATORY COMPLIANCE CHART.
3. Copy of the special resolution passed shall be filed along with e-form 23 following EFORM COMPLIANCE CHART with the RoC within 30 days of passing of resolution using the DIN of directors.
4. On receipt of intimation of the nomination of the company, the Board of Directors will take note of the nomination.
5. The nominated director shall give notice to the company u / s 308, 305 of the companies Act, 1956.
6. The particulars of the director shall be entered by the company in the register kept for this purpose under section 303.

Till Directors are appointed the INDIVIDUAL subscribers to the memorandum are deemed to be the Directors.

Board of DIRECTORS REPORT

Section No.	Details
212(3)	Statement of holding company's interest in the subsidiary. It may be given separately or as part of Directors Report
217(1)(a)	State of the Company's affairs
217(1)(b)	Amount proposed to be carried to any Reserves in the Balance Sheet. i.e, appropriation of profits to reserve
217(1)(c)	Amount recommended to be paid to shareholders as Dividend
217(1)(d)	Material Changes and comments, if any, affecting the financial position of the company occurred after the close of Financial Year and date of Report of Board of Directors [called "Events after Balance Sheet"]
217(1)(e)	Conservation of energy, Technology Absorption, Foreign Exchange Earnings & Outgo. These details should be submitted in prescribed form.
217(2)	Changes during Financial Year

217(2A)	Statement giving details of employees whose salaries are beyond prescribed limit – presently, Rs. 5 lakhs per month or Rs. 60 lakhs per annum OR in receipt of remuneration MORE THAN Managerial Personnel AND he along with Dependants HOLD 2% or more.
217(3)	Fullest information & explanation about every reservation, qualification or adverse remarks in the Auditors Report
217(2B)	If company had entered into Buy Back of Shares as per approval of Members and if Buy Back was not completed within specified time, Board should specify reasons for the failure [Sec. 77A]
217(2AA)	Directors Responsibility Statement that, ↳ Accounting Standards (AS) had been followed and explanation relating to Material Departures, if any; ↳ Reasonable & Prudent Accounting Policies followed to give a true & fair view as at the end of period; ↳ Adequate Accounting Records maintained for safeguarding assets and preventing irregularities; ↳ Annual Accounts are prepared on on-going basis.
292A	Reasons for not accepting decision of Audit Committee formed u/s. 292A, if applicable
292A(4)	Composition of Audit Committee – it may be given separately or as part of Directors Report or as part of Corporate Governance Report
383A(1) proviso	Secretarial Compliance Certificate, if applicable, should be attached to the Report of Board. Number of meetings of Board & Committees held during the year and Meetings attended by each Director.
SEBI	Details of Sweat Equity issued, ESOP & ESPS
SEBI	Requirements as per Listing Agreement, in case of Listed Companies, as per SEBI guidelines
Signed	By the Chairman of the Board, if so authorized, Otherwise by such number of Directors who are authorized to AUTHENTICATE the Accounts u/s. 215.

SAMPLE DIRECTORS REPORT

Dear Members

Your Directors have pleasure in presenting the Second Annual Report together with the Audited Accouns for the financial year ended March 31, 2009.

1. Financial Performance

Particular	2007-2008	2008-2009
PBIDT	912.92	778.42
Interest		
Profit after interest	912.92	778.42
Depreciation	112.22	128.22
Profit after Depreciation	800.20	650.22
Provision for taxation	80.20	50.22
Profit after Tax	720.00	600.00

2. Performance for The Financial Year 2008-2009

The company has achieved a turnover of 4612-48 lakhs for the year ended March, 31 2009. The plant adheres to excellent safety norms and conducts periodical audits and training programs.

3. Dividend

The Board has not recommended any dividend for the financial year 2008-09 in view of carry forward of accumulated issues.

4. Disclosure under 217(2A) and 217(1)(e)

Information in accordance with the provision of Section 217(2A) of the Companies Act 1956 read with Companies (Disclosure of Particulars in the Report of Board of Directors) Rules, 1988 is given in Annexure 1 to the Directors Report.

Your company has no activity with regars to conservation of energy. Research & Development on technology absorption. During the year, the Foreign Currency earnings was 634.32 lakhs expenditure was 64.93 lakhs.

5. Public Deposit

The Company has not accepted any public deposit during the year and there was no outstanding deposit anytime during the year.

6. Directors

Mr. Sankaranarayanan and Mr. Ram, Directors, retire by rotation and being eligible offer themselves for re-appointment.

7. Director's Responsibility Statement

Pursuant to the requirement of Section 217(2A) ofthe Companies Act, 1956, the i)...(ii)... (iii)... (iv)...

> **Management Discussion and Analysis** [mandatory for listed companies as per Chause 49 of Listing Agreement]: It is an analysis of financial condition and results of operations; it should provide for discussion on industry structure, opportunities & threats, segment/product wise performance and financial vs. operational performance; it should also disclose the outlook, risks & concerns, internal control system & its adequacy and number of people employed with material developments.

Industry Structure and Developemt:

ABC Ltd is the fastest growing automobile industry in the world. ABC Ltd is manufacturing automobiles with both petrol and diesel variants. The automobiles especially cars running with batteries are getting popular and the company is taking initiative to explore into these areas.

Outlook

The petrol variants were chosen over the diesel variants due to low maintenance cost. But since the companies have started working towards efficiency of diesel vehicles, the demand for diesel variants of the cars is increasing.

Strength [SWOT]

ABC Ltd has turned to be a the market leader of small cars in a very short period.

Weakness

The company being in initial period requires to strengthen its organizational structure.

Opportunities

Rapid economic development throughout Asia continues to increase the demand for automobiles.

Threats

The company faces a stiff competition for high quality automobiles with low prices.

Risk and concerns

The company will be exporting the cars and will be facing currency fluctuating risk. The company is looking to enter into forward contracts to mitigate this risk.

Segment wise/Product wise performance

Particulars	Units	Amount (Rs. In Lakhs)
Turnover on Sale of small cars	1200	4000.00
Turnover on other sales		612.48
Total		4612.48

Internal Control Systems and their adequacy:

ABC Ltd maintains an adequate internal control system that provides effectiveness and efficiency. Our internal auditors are xyz & Co.

Financial Performance with respect to Operational performance:

The company has achieved a turnover of 4612.48 Lakhs for the year ended March 31, 2009.

Human resources

The total number of employees are at 2300 and over 86% are professionally/technically qualified and experienced.

Corporate Governance:

WE believe that Corporation Governance is at the heart of Shareholder value creation. Our governance practice along with the Auditor's Certificate on its compliance are attached hereto as annexure to this report.

Acknowledgements

The Directors take this opportunity to thanks the suppliers, shareholders, bankers and other stakeholders for their faith reposed in the Company and thank the Government of India. State Governments and regulatory authorities and agencies for their assistance and looks forward to their continued support. The Directors place on record their sincere appreciation of the contribution of all employees which enabled the quick progress of the Company.

Discuss the various aspects of 'responsibility and accountability' of the Board in corporate culture. (2010 – June)

Directors' responsibility statement. (2008 and 2010 – December)

Draft the specimen resolutions along with requisite explanatory statement, wherever necessary, for transacting the following items of business indicating the kind of meeting at which each resolution is to be passed and the type of resolution required for adoption of annual of annual report by Divakar Limited for the year ended 31st March 2008. (2008 – June)

State the items that are to be covered under the director's responsibility statement prepared under Section 217 (2AA). (2008 – June) (2009-June)

Enumerate the contents of Management Discussion and Analysis Report (MDAR) which forms part of the Board of directors' report (2009 – December) (2010-June)

MANAGING/WHOLE TIME DIRECTORS (MD/WTD) OR MANAGERS

The appointment of either MD or WTD or Manager is obligatory for a public company having paid-up share capital of Rs. 5 crores or more. MD, Manager & WTD is defined u/s. 2(26), 2(24) and explanation to Section 269 respectively. Such person shall be disqualified u/s. 274, 267 or 385 or under Schedule XIII. The term of office shall be 5 years and can be extended with approvals. Any appointment of MD/WTD or Manager OR any amendment to provision contained in MOA /AOA or Agreement, which in effect increase the remuneration of the director (including MD/WTD) (u/s. 310) and any direct or indirect increase in the remuneration of the said persons has to comply with Schedule XIII or else get CG approval (u/s. 311) by filing e-form 25C/25A.

Sec 267 – Disqualification for MD/WTD	Section 385 – Disqualification for Manager
↳ is an undischarged insolvent, or has **at any time been** adjudged an insolvent; ↳ suspend, or has at any time suspended, payment to his creditors, or makes, or has **at any time** made, a composition with them; ↳ is, or has **at any time** been, convicted by a Court (**India or outside**) of an offence involving moral turpitude. ↳ Central Government **cannot relax**. These disqualifications are in addition to those specified in Sec 274 to directors.	↳ an undischarged insolvent, or has at any time within the **preceding 5 years** been adjudged an insolvent; ↳ suspends, or has at any time within the **preceding 5 years** suspended payment to or made composition with , his creditors; ↳ is, or has at any time within the **preceding 5 years** been, convicted by a **Court in India** of an offence involving moral turpitude ↳ Central Government **may relax** by removing the disqualification either generally or in relation to particular company, by way of a Notification in the Official Gazette.
Court Order u/s. 203 to restrain fraudulent persons from managing the Companies. When a person is Guilty or convicted of an Offence in promotion, formation, management or winding up of the Company.	

FURTHER DISQUALIFICATION UNDER SCHEDULE XIII
For MD / WTD / Manager

↳ Should not have been punished with imprisonment OR Fine EXCEEDING Rs.1000/- for CONVICTION of an offence under
- ↳ Companies Act, SEBI & SCRA;
- ↳ Income Tax, Wealth Tax & Indirect Tax Laws;
- ↳ Foreign Exchange Laws;
- ↳ IDRA, MRTP, SICA & Indian Stamp Act;
- ↳ Essential Commodities & Food Adulteration Act.

↳ Not detained under Conservation of Foreign Exchange and Prevention of Smuggling Activities Act, 1974 [COFEPOSA]

With Central Government Approval, above mentioned persons may be appointed]

↳ Director who has Not Completed 25 years or who has Attained 70 years of Age can be appointed by passing a Special Resolution of the Members;

↳ If Appointed as Managerial Personnel in one or more Company (CG approval) but NOT exceeding the remuneration limits prescribed under the Schedule (not more than 2 Companies);

↳ Person Resident in India or any person Residing in India for past 12 months can be appointed immediately preceding the Appointment and who has come to stay in India for employment or business purpose, can be appointed subject to certain conditions

Compulsory Appointment – MD/WTD/Marger
(Section 269 read with Sch.XIII)
For Public Company having 5 Cores or more of Paid-up Capital

Comply Sch XIII
- ↳ Pass Ordinary Resolution & then appoint or appoint at Board Meeting & pass Ordinary Resolution at 1st General Meeting held next to the appointment
- ↳ File eform 25C within 90 days from Appt. by Shareholders

Encl: Follow MANDATORY EFORM COMPLIANCE CHART.

CG Approval
(Non-Compliance of Sch. XIII)
- ↳ Pass Ordinary Resolution & then appoint or appoint at Board Meeting & pass Ordinary Resolution at 1st General Meeting held next to the appointment
- ↳ Get Central Government approval either before or after the General Meeting
- ↳ Publish Section 640B Notice in 2 Newspapers.
- ↳ File eform 25A within 90 days from Appointment by Shareholders.

Encl: Follow MANDATORY EFORM COMPLIANCE CHART.

Ef = Eform; PCS = Practicising Company Secretary; d = days; yrs = years; Encl = Enclosure.

CONTRAVENTION:
↳ Co. UPTO Rs. 50,000/-
↳ Officers in Default UPTO Rs.1lakh
↳ MD/WTD/Mgr (Vacation) [+](Rs.1lakh) [+] (Refund of all Remuneration received);

An amendment of any provision relating to the appointment or re-appointment of a MD/WTD/Mgr or a Director not liable to retire by rotation, shall not have any effect, unless approved by the Central Government as per Section 268. For approval of CG under this section application in e-Form 25B has to be filed following MANDATORY EFORM COMPLIANCE CHART.

(Section 198) **Remuneration Ceiling MD/WTD/Mgr**
UPTO 11% of Net Profits calculated as per Sec. 349 & 350.

Not Applicable to Private Company

↳ As per Section 309, Non-Executive Directors can be paid REMUNERATION by way of FEE for each meeting of Board OR Committee attended by him, which is termed as SITTING FEES.

↳ Proviso to Section 310 provides that INCREASE in Sitting Fees UPTO prescribed limit will NOT require approval of Central Government and is a part of Managerial Remuneration.

↳ Sitting Fees for MD or WTD ONLY with Prior Approval of Central Government as there is NO provision in Schedule XIII for such payment.

↳ Section 198 specifically provides that the 11% shall be EXCLUSIVE of Sitting Fees, therefore, Sitting Fees can be paid EVEN if there is LOSS.

↳ Prescribed Limits are,

Sitting Fees PER Meeting	**Based on Either [Paid-up Capital + Free Reserves]**	**Or Turnover**
UPTO Rs. 20,000/-	10 crores OR more	50 Crores OR more
UPTO Rs. 10,000/-	LESS THAN 10 crores	LESS THAN 50 crores

Further as per Section 309 the remuneration to single MD/WTD/Manager shall NOT exceed 5% and in case of MD/WTD in more than one company, it shall NOT exceed 10% of Net profits. If MD/WTD is a PROFESSIONAL, then such remuneration can be EXCLUDED from the said ceiling limits on approval of Central Government.

Procedure for Appointment of MD/WTD/Manager:

1. Hold the Board meeting
   a. To consider the appointment of a person as managing director. Such person shall not be disqualified under Section 267 and 274 of the Act or disability under section 316 of the act. (in case of manager Section 385 and 386)
   b. To approve the draft agreement signed and executed by and between the Company and managing director.
   c. Fix the time, date and place and issue the notice to conduct the general meeting to pass necessary resolution as required under schedule XIII of the Act.
2. File e-form 23 for Board Resolution following EFORM COMPLIANCE CHART.
3. Issue notices to - Members – Directors – Auditors – Stock Exchanges.
4. Hold the meeting and pass the necessary resolution
5. Inform stock exchange the proceedings of the meeting.
6. Publish Section 640B general notice in newspapers and send the same to members. If the appointment is not according to Schedule XIII then make an application in e-form 25A within 90 days following MANDATORY EFORM COMPLIANCE CHART to Central Government as per Section 269.
7. Execute the AGREEMENT and file e-form 23 for Agreement following EFORM COMPLIANCE CHART. Obtain notice in Form 24AA as required u/s 305 of the Act.
8. Make necessary entries in registers maintained under section 301, 303 and 307.
9. If the appointment is as per Schedule XIII then file e-form 25C within 90 days to RoC following EFORM COMPLIANCE CHART.
10. Inform stock exchange immediately after appointment of Managing Director.

Procedure for fixation/revision of remuneration to Managing director:

Usually the remuneration paid is given in the agreement entered into while appointment. If not the procedure to be followed is similar to above.

SAMPLE SECTION 640B NOTICE FOR INCREASE IN REMUNERATION

Notice is hereby given u/s. 640B of the Companies Act, 1956 that the company intends to make an application to the Central Government for its approval u/s. 310 of the Act to increase in remuneration payable to Mr…….., the Managing Director of the company.

Address of Registered office — For Labz Limited,

Dated — Company Secretary.

A notice under Section 640B for the Central Government's approval to increase remuneration of the managing director. (J 2009)

SAMPLE Managing Director's Agreement

This Agreement is made at ...... on .... between .... Limited and its Managing Director Mr........

PREAMBLE

(1) ... .Limited ("the Company") is a public company incorporated under the Companies Act, 1956 and has its Registered Office at ....

(2) Mr .... aged years, an Indian resident, currently living at..........

(3) The Board of Directors of the Company appointed Mr ...... as the Managing Director of the Company by a resolution.

This Agreement sets out the terms and conditions governing the appointment of the Managing Director........

DEFINITIONS

1. "Articles" means the Articles of ABC Limited.
2. "Company" means ABC Limited.
3. "Managing Director" means ....
4. "Board" means the Board of directors of ABC Limited.

AGREEMENT

1) The Company appoints Mr................ as its Managing Director and the Mr........... agrees to act as a Managing Director of the Company for 5 years from ....
2) The Managing Director shall work under the superintendence, control and direction of the Company's Board, shall have the powers of general conduct and management of business and affairs of the company in relation to the following functions, namely: (*a*)........, (*b*) ...., (*c*)........, except in the matters which may be specifically required to be done by the Board either by the Act or by the Articles.
3) Without restricting the general powers and authorities as mentioned above, the Managing Director will have the following powers to be exercised on behalf of the Company,

   1.

   2.

   3.
4) The Company or the Managing director may terminate this Agreement before its term is over by giving a notice of the intention to terminate it at least 3 months before the date on which the termination is to come into effect. If such notice is given, the Agreement will come to an end when the 3 months notice period is over.
5) For the services provided, the Company shall pay the Managing Director the remuneration specified in the Schedule below.
6) Subject to the provisions of the Act, the Managing Director will not be liable to retirement by rotation while he continues to hold office of the Managing Director, but his/her office of Managing Director will come to an end if he ceases to hold office of Director for any reason.
7) The Managing Director shall not, while he holds the office of Managing Director or at any time thereafter, reveal to any person or use for his own or somebody else's benefit, or confidential information obtained by him concerning Company's business or affairs or any trade secrets or processes of the Company. The Managing Director shall, while he holds the office of the Managing Director, also use his best effort to prevent any other person from doing so.

8) The Managing Director shall not engage himself in any business which will directly compete with the business of the Company while he holds the office of the Managing Director or at any time thereafter for 5 (five) years.

SIGNING AND SEALING

The authorised officer of the Company and the Managing Director signed, this Agreement on ....

The Common Seal of... Ltd. was affixed to Agreement in accordance with the resolution of the Board, dated in the presence of Mr...... , Director.

Schedule

SALARY

Rs.... (Rupees .... only) per month

PERQUISITES:

In addition to the aforesaid salary, the Managing Director shall be entitled to the following perquisites:

(*a*) Fully furnished residential accommodation.

(*b*) Reimbursement of all medical expenses incurred for self and family.

(*c*) Leave travel assistance for self and family as per Company rules.

(d) A car with driver for official purpose.

(*e*) Telephone and fax facilities at residence.

(*f*) Contribution to provident fund, superannuation fund or annuity fund and gratuity.

Family for the above purpose means wife, dependent children and dependent parents of the Managing Director.

COMMISSION

Commission shall be decided by the Board of Directors based on the net profits of the Company each year subject to the condition that the aggregate remuneration of the Managing Director shall not exceed 5% of the net profits of the Company, in accordance with sections 198, 309 and Schedule XIII to the Companies Act, 1956.

IN WITNESS WHEREOF the company has caused its Common Seat to be hereunto affixed and the Managing Director has hereunto set his hand the day and year first hereinabove written.

The Common Seal of ....Ltd. was hereunto affixed pursuant to a resolution of the Board of directors of the company, dated the ....in the presence of Shri.............. the Director thereof.

Director

SIGNED SEALED AND DELIVERED by the above named Shri..............the Director of the company in the presence of Shri............. Director	SIGNED SEALED AND DELIVERED by the within named Shri................. the Managing Director in the presence of Shri.................. Managing Director

Agreement with Vivek as the Managing Director of Grow Fast Limited for a period of 3 years at a remuneration of Rs. 20 lakh per month with perquisites allowable under Scheduel XIII to the Companies Act, 1956, but with no commission. The company is consistently earning profits and the remuneration will be subject to the provisions of sections 198 and 309. (Only main body of the resolution is to be drafted containing the duties, responsibilities and powers of the appointee) (2010 – June)

NORMAL MINIMUM REMUNERATION (as per Schedule XIII)

In the event of loss of inadequacy of profits in previous financial year, following remuneration shall be paid to Managing Director or WTD or Manager only if the company has not made any default in debts/debenture interest for a continuous period of 30 days in Previous financial year.

Effective Capital (EC) [as on last date of Previous Financial Year of appointment]	**NORMAL MINIMUM Remuneration** [Maximum limits]
LESS THAN 1Crore	Rs. 75000/month
1 Crore to LESS THAN 5 Crores	Rs. 1 lakh/month
5 Crores to LESS THAN 25 Crores	Rs. 1.25 lakhs/month
25 Crores to LESSTHAN 50 Crores	Rs. 1.5 lakhs/month
50 Crores to LESS THAN 100 Crores	Rs. 1.75 lakhs/month
100 Crores OR more	Rs. 2 lakhs/month

"Effective Capital" (EC) is equal to Paid-up Capital (+) Securities Premium (+) LongTerm Loan/Deposits repayable after 1 year (+) Reserves & Surplus (-) Revaluation Reserve (-) Investment in Shares/Securities (-) Accumulated Losses (-) Preliminary Expenses not written off.

Conditions for payment:

↳ Normal Minimum Remuneration is based on Effective Capital (if EC increases, minimum remuneration also increases prospectively) which requires (RCA) Remuneration Committee approval (+) Ordinary Resolution;

↳ [UPTO 2 [X] Normal Minimum remuneration] can be paid with RCA approval (+) Special Resolution (Valid for 3 years) (+) specific details given in notice to shareholders of the meeting in which the said resolution is to be passed.

↳ Any violation of the above terms would require specific PRIOR approval of Central Government for UNLISTED companies. However, in case of LISTED or SUBSIDIARY of a Listed company: [MORE THAN 2 [X] Normal Minimum remuneration] or where there is Negative Effective Capital, it can be paid with RCA approval (+) Special Resolution (Valid for 3 yrs) (+) specific details given in notice to shareholders of the meeting in which the said resolution is to be passed (+) Central Government Approval. Thus, the limit of 2 times of Normal Minimum Remuneration can be EXCEEDED by such listed companies ONLY with prior Central Government approval. Still a subsidiary of a listed company NEED NOT require Central Government approval as mentioned above, if —

i. the Remuneration Committee and Board of Directors of the holding company give their CONSENT for the amount of such remuneration of the applicant and for the said amount to be DEEMED REMUNERATION by the holding company for the purpose of section 198 of the Companies Act, 1956 AND

ii. a special resolution has been passed at the general meeting of the company for payment of remuneration of the applicant AND

iii the remuneration of the applicant is deemed to be remuneration PAID BY HOLDING company AND

iv. all members of the subsidiary are BODIES CORPORATE.

Even further both listed company & its subsidiaries shall NOT require Central Government approval if –

i. the remuneration is fixed by Board of Industrial and Financial Reconstruction (BIFR) or

ii. the managerial person is NOT having any interest in the capital of the company or its holding company, directly or indirectly or through any other statutory structures (any entity which is entitled to hold shares in any company formed under any statute) AND

iii. the managerial person is NOT having any direct or indirect interest or related to the directors or promoters of the company or its holding company at any time during last 2 years on/before date of appointment AND

iv. the managerial person is having a GRADUATE level qualification with EXPERT and specialized knowledge in the field of his profession.

↳ Managerial personnel of SEZ can get remuneration not exceeding Rs. 2,40,00,000 per annum or Rs. 20,00,000 per month, if such SEZ has not come out with any Public Issue in India and has made NO default in debts or debentures or its interest for a continuous period of 30 days in the ANY financial year.

↳ In addition to the perquisites, an expatriate managerial person (including a non resident Indian) shall be eligible to the following perquisites which shall not be included in the computation of the ceiling on remuneration :

- *Children's education allowance* for 2 Children for a maximum of Rs. 5,000 per month per child.
- *Holiday passage for children studying outside India/family staying abroad*: Return holiday passage once in a year by economy class or once in two years by first class to children and to the members of the family from the place of their study or stay abroad to India.
- *Leave travel concession*: where it is proposed that the leave be spent in home country instead of anywhere in India.

↳ 'Remuneration Committee' for listed company means that a committee which consists of at least 3 non-executive independent directors including nominee directors, if any. 'Remuneration Committee' for unlisted or any other company shall be Remuneration Committee of DIRECTORS.

Buoyant Limited a loss incurring company, wants to appoint Jolly as Managing Director w.e.f. 15th March, 2009 on a total remuneration of Rs. 10 lakh per month (all inclusive). Its paid – up capital is Rs. 5 crore, reserves Rs. 3 crore and term loans Rs. 10 crore. The company has accounting year ending on 31st March every year. (D 2009)

There are two executive directors in your company who are technocrats. The company is a public limited company. The company has incurred huge losses in the last two years. The company wants to enhance their remuneration to Rs. 6 lakh per month from existing Rs. 4 lakh. The data from the balance sheet of the last year indicates that the paid – up capital of the company is Rs. 10 crore and accumulated losses of Rs. 1067 crore, term loan and other long – term borrowings are Rs. 5 crore. Besides, the company holds a long – term investment of Rs. 7 crore. The company's remuneration committee has recommended to the proposed and the company is regular in repayment of its debts. As the Company Secretary, how would you deal with the matter? (2010 – June)

DIRECTORS & OFFICERS (D&O) LIABILITY INSURANCE or Management Errors & Omission (E&O) Policy

Directors And Officers Liability Insurance provides FINANCIAL PROTECTION for Directors & officers of the company in the event they are sued in conjunction with performance of their duties as they relate to the company. Since director can be held personally responsible for acts of the company, most directors and officers will demand that they be protected rather than put their personal assets at stake.

D & O coverage comprises two sections,

(a) Damages awarded against D & O including legal cost & defence cost.

(b) Company reimbursement.

Section 201 of the companies Act, 1956 specifically provides that any provisions, whether contained in the AoA or Agreement exempting any director from or indemnifying him against any liability in respect of any negligence, breach of trust or breach of duty shall be VOID. This section does not however prevent a company from taking out an insurance policy; the premium for the insurance policy may be paid by the company.

What is not covered?

- Criminal behavior
- Libel, slander or other defamation
- Fraudulent acts of an insured
- Professional liability (Cover under a professional liability policy),
- Environmental damage or pollution
- Bodily injury or property damage
- Fines, penalties and other penal liability.

Is the policy on a "Claims Made" or an "Occurrence" basis?

The policy is on 'claims made basis' similar to product liability insurance. This will allow only claims made during the period if such claims may be as a result of wrongful acts committed prior to the inception of the policy and would be covered so long as such acts were not thought to give rise to a claim.

What is directors' and officers' liability insurance? (2010 – December)

Thus ends the basic discussion on Companies Act with all provisions concerning board & general meetings. If you feel you have understood or not understood either way, start reading all the provisions again from the beginning now. Once you can remember the EFORM COMPLIANCE CHART given at the end of the first chapter under Company Secretarial Practice, that's when you can be sure that you can enjoy writing exams. Hence it is highly advisable learn by rote the list of e-forms that shall be filed along with the mandatory attachments, signatory authorities and the relevant provisions. Turn to EFORM COMPLIANCE CHART and start reading, recollecting and updating again, again and again.

It is very essential to remember the various group rights that can be enforced by members, signatory requirements for various items and the list of registers which shall be maintained along with the basic provisions.

Group Rights, Signatory And Registers

GROUP RIGHTS UNDER COMPANIES ACT

Section	About	No. of members required
Sec 106	Variation of rights of holders of special classes of shares	↳ Passing a Special Resolution at a Meeting of Holders of that Class of Shares OR ↳ With Consent of 3/4th of Members, in writing;
Sec 107	Rights of Dissentient Shareholders to cancel the Variation u/s. 106	Such Variation can be cancelled WITHIN 21 days from the date of Special Resolution or Consent, on application to Court, by 10% OR more of the shares of that class who did not consent to such Variation.
Sec 169	Calling of extraordinary general meeting [EGM] on requisition	Company having share capital, such number at the date of the deposit of the requisition, holding 1/10th OR more of the paid-up capital of the company; Company NOT having share capital, holding 1/10th OR more of the total voting power at the said date.
Sec 179	Demand for Poll	Public Company with Share Capital, By Disinterested Members holding 10% Voting Right OR Rs.50,000 Paid-up; Private Company with Share Capital, ↳ If personally present is 7 or LESS, then by ONE Disinterested Member or Proxy ↳ If personally present is MORE than 7, then by TWO Disinterested Members or Proxies; Any other Company, By Disinterested Members holding 10% Voting Right;
Sec 188	Circulation of Members Resolution	such number of members as represent 1/20th OR more of the total voting power of all the members having at the date of the requisition a right to vote on the resolution or business to which the requisition relates; **OR** 100 members OR more having the right aforesaid **and** holding shares in the company on which there has been paid-up of aggregate sum of one lakh OR more, of rupees in all;
Sec 235	Investigation of the affairs of a company	Company having a share capital, ↳ an application has been received from 200 members OR more; or ↳ from members holding 1/10th OR more of the total voting power therein Company NOT having share capital, application from 1/5th OR more of Total in Register of Members (RoM)

Sec 252	Appointment of "Small Shareholder Director" by Small Share Holders holding Shares for Nominal Val UPTO Rs. 20,000/-	A public company having Paid-up Capital (PC) of ↳ Rs. 5 Crores OR more AND ↳ having 100 or more Small Share Holders may have a director appointed by their small shareholders;
Sec 287	Quorum for Board Meeting	<u>Quorum – 1st Condition</u> 2 Dir OR 1/3rd of Total Strength, whichever is HIGHER <u>Quorum – 2nd Condition</u> "IF" Interested Dir 2/3rd OR more of Total Strength (TS) "THEN" Balance 1/3rd if 2 Dir or More, constitute a Valid Quorum for the Meeting
Sec 399	Eligibility Criteria for application under Oppression & Mismanagement	<u>Company having share capital</u>, Lesser of ↳ 100 members or ↳ 1/10th of Total Members or ↳ 1/10th of Issued Capital in which all calls are paid <u>Company NOT having share capital</u>, 1/5th OR more of Total number of members in Register.

SIGNATURES UNDER COMPANIES ACT

DOCUMENT	SIGNED BY
Directors Report [Sec 217]	↳ Chairman, if authorized; ↳ If not authorised Manager or Secretary, if any; AND 2 or more Directors, including an MD, if any;
Balance Sheet & Annual Accounts [Sec 215]	↳ In case of Banking Company, Section 29 of Banking Regulation Act will apply; ↳ In case of any other Company, ↳ Manager or Secretary, if any AND ↳ By NOT less than 2 Directors, one shall be MD, if any.
Annual Return [Sec 161]	↳ a director AND by the manager or secretary of the company, OR ↳ where there is no manager or secretary, by two directors of the company, one of whom shall be the managing director where there is one ↳ If listed, Annual Returns shall be certified by Company Secretary in whole-time practice
Auditors Report [Sec 229]	↳ the person appointed as auditor of the company OR ↳ where a firm is so appointed , ONLY a partner in the firm practising in India
Prospectus [Sec 60]	↳ EVERY person who is named therein as a director OR ↳ proposed director of the company or by his agent authorised in writing

Statement in lieu of Prospectus [SLOP]	↳ EVERY person who is named therein as a director OR ↳ proposed director of the company or by his agent authorised in writing
Register of Contracts in which Directors are interested u/s. 301	All Directors PRESENT at the Board Meeting
Advertisement/Statement in lieu of advertisement. Rule 4(4)	↳ majority of the directors on the Board as constituted at the time the Board approved the advertisement, OR ↳ their agents, duly authorised by them in writing
Statutory Report (Sec 165)	certified as correct by 2 OR more directors of the company one of whom shall be a managing director, where there is one.
Solvency Certificate of buy-back (Sec 77A)	at least 2 directors of the company, one of whom shall be the managing director, if any
Solvency Certificate in case of voluntary winding-up(Sec 488)	Two or Majority , whichever is higher
Statement of Affairs (Sec 454)	↳ one or more of the persons who are at the relevant date the directors AND ↳ by the person who is at that date the manager, secretary or other chief officer of the company, OR ↳ such of the persons ↳ officers of the company; Within one year before the relevant date, ↳ taken part in the formation of the company at any time ↳ in the employment of the company & capable of giving the information required ↳ officers of, or in the employment of, a company or officer to which the statement relates as the Official Liquidator require, subject to the direction of the Court.
Share Certificate [Rule 6 of Companies (Issue of Shares Certificates) Rules, 1960]	↳ which shall be affixed in the presence of (i) two directors or persons acting on behalf of the directors under a duly registered power of attorney; and ↳ (ii) the secretary or some other person appointed by the Board for the purpose. ↳ The two directors or their attorneys and the secretary or other person shall sign the share certificate
General Meeting minutes [Sec 193]	↳ the chairman of the same meeting within the aforesaid period of thirty days OR ↳ in the event of the death or inability of that chairman within that period, by a director duly authorised by the Board for the purpose ↳
Committee / Board Meeting Minutes [Sec 193]	↳ the chairman of the said meeting OR ↳ the chairman of the next succeeding meeting

REGISTERS & INSPECTION UNDER COMPANIES ACT - A SNAPSHOT

MEMBERS need not be allowed to INSPECT the following:

↳ Minutes of board & committee meeting (Sec 193)

↳ Register of buy back (Sec 77A)

↳ Register of Directors shareholding ONLY during 14 days before AGM, during AGM & 3 days after that; Open for RoC & CG – at all times & copy to be provided (Sec 307)

↳ Books of Accounts – cannot be inspected unless authorised by GM or for applying u/s. 397-398 (Sec 209)

COPIES NEED NOT BE SUPPLIED for the following:

↳ Register of Investment in securities made by Company, not in Companies' name [S49]

↳ Register of charges

↳ Dividend Register [not statutory]

↳ Books of accounts

↳ Register of Buy back

↳ Register of Directors &

↳ Reg. Of Directors shareholding

↳ Instrument evidencing charge

CAN BE INSPECTED & COPY TO BE PROVIDED of the following

↳ Register of Fixed Deposits

↳ Register & Index of Members

↳ Register & Index of Debenture holders

↳ Foreign Register of Members

↳ General Meeting Minutes

↳ Cost Accounting Records

↳ Register of Renewed Share Certificates

↳ Copy of Annual Return & Annexures

↳ Register of Contracts

STATUTORY BOOKS THAT SHALL BE KEPT AT REGISTERED OFFICE

- Register of Investments not held in companies name
- Register of Fixed Deposits
- Register of Mortgages & Charges
- Register & Index of Members & Debenture holders
- Foreign register & index of Members & Debenture holders
- Annual Return, Minutes Book & Books of Accounts

- Register of Contracts in which directors are interested
- Register of Directors, Managers, etc…
- Register of Directors shareholding in shares, debentures, etc…
- Register of loans, guarantees & investments in other companies
- Register of shares bought back
- Register of renewed & duplicate share certificate
- Books of Accounts
- Annual Return

6. STATISTICAL BOOKS

In addition to the books of accounts and statutory books mentioned earlier, a company usually maintains a number of statisitical books in order to keep complete records of the numerous details connected with the business operations. The keeping of such books has become a necessity although there is no legal compulsion for the same. The following is a list of such important books.

1. Share Application and Allotment Book
2. Share Call Book
3. Share Certificate Book
4. Share Transfer Book
5. Debenture interest Book
6. Director's Attendance Book
7. Agenda Book
8. Dividend Mandate Register
9. Share Warrants Register
10. Register of Certified transfers
11. Register of lost share certificates
12. Register of powers of attorney
13. Register of probates
14. Register of declaration under Section 187C
15. Register of documents sealed
16. Register of Proxies
17. Register of inspection
18. Register of records and documents destroyed
19. Register of investors complaints
20. Register of transmission of shares
21. Register of transfer of debentures
22. Register of transmission of debentures

23. Register of employee stock options
24. Register of Sweat Equity Shares
25. Register of Respect of SEBI (Substantial Acquisition of Shares and Takeovers) Regulations, 1997
26. Register of respect of SEBI (Prohibition of Insider Trading) Regulations, 1992
27. Annual Return.

NON STATUTORY BOOKS

- Directors & Shareholders/Proxies Attendance
- Sealed documents
- Share Application & Allotment
- Share Transfer & Transmission & Nomination
- Dividend & Dividend Mandates
- Power of Attorney & Death Certificates
- Particulars of Bank Account & Fixed Assets.

OTHER BOOKS AS PER SECRETARIAL STANDARD 4 (SS-4)

- Register of postal ballot
- Register of documents executed under common seal
- Register of investors complaints
- Register of employee stock options & sweat equity
- Register under Takeover code & Insider trading.

This chapter is essential to answer most of the questions; especially when asked to list out the Non-statutory books to be maintained. It is advisable to be through with this chapter and apply it according to the releveant requirement. For example, when you are answering a question on employee stock option mention that Register of employee stock option is required to be maintained at the Registered office as recommended under Secretarial Standards.

The items other than those covered above may require approval of Company Law Board (CLB). This chapter lists down the various provisions under Companies Act which requires either approval or confirmation of CLB. CLB will function till National Company Law Tribunal (NCLT) is constituted and given effect. The provisions regarding NCLT are also discussed under Sick Industry chapter in Corporate Restructuring.

Company Law Board (CLB)

Company Law Board (CLB) is a quasi judicial tribunal constituted u/s. 10E of Companies Act, 1956 which in due course will be replaced by National Company Law Tribunal (NCLT). CLB sits as benches to decide a case; it has New Delhi Bench, Chennai Bench, Mumbai Bench and Kolkata Bench. New Delhi Bench & Chennai bench has principal powers over Northern & Southern region respectively. CLB has all the powers of Civil Court and further CLB orders can be enforced as if it was an order of court. CLB orders are appeallable to High Court within 60 days. The proceedings of CLB are governed by Company Law Board Regulations, 1991, according to which,

- Every application or petition filed by petition or authorized representative (as per Form 5) shall have a general heading as per Form 1 consisting of (CAUSE TITLE)
  - BEFORE THE CHENNAI BENCH
  - IN THE MATTER OF SECTION 397 OF COMPANIES ACT
  - IN THE MATTER OF ABC LTD having its registered office at
- The application or petition shall be made in writing in one side of foolscap paper with double space & dated, containing the following particulars,
  - Particulars of company, whether petitioner or not

  - Particulars of Petitioner with Name & Description
  - Particulars of Respondents with Name & Description
  - Jurisdiction of bench & applicability of Limitation
  - Facts of case with all Proofs in the Annexures
  - Declaration that subject matter is not pending with any court/forum
  - List of Relief sought and the last relief shall be "such other order as the Board may deem fit" and Interim orders, if any
  - Particulars of payment of fees & Enclosures as per Annexure 3 of Regulations.

NOTE: Such application/petition shall be drawn on 3rd person.

- Every application/petition (apart from Section 58A & 117C) shall be accompanied by an AFFIDAVIT stating knowledge of deponent, information received, belief, etc.. drawn up in 1st person with Name & Particulars of deponent.
- Serve a copy on all the respondents, RoC, Regional Director, Central Government, as the case may be and attach evidence of service.

LIST OF SECTIONS INVOLVING CLB

The following list of sections involves CLB in Companies Act, 1956,

SECTION	PARTICULARS	CLB
17(2)	Shifting of Registered Office from State to State	CLB confirmation is mandatory
18(4)	If such CLB confirmation order u/s. 17 is NOT filed with RoC within 3 months in e-form 21 	Application to CLB to extend the time for filing
19	If such CLB confirmation order u/s. 17 is NOT filed with RoC within EXTENDED time in e-form 21	Application to CLB to revive the order within further period of 1 month
43	Consequences of Default in Complying with conditions constituting a company Private Company u/s. 3(1)(iii)	Petition to CLB praying relief shall be made
49(10)	Refusal of Inspection of Register of Investments of Company not held in its Own Name	Member or debenture holder can file Petition to CLB to allow immediate inspection of the same
58A(9)	Failure to repay matured Deposits	Application by depositor or CLB itself to order repayment
79(2)	Issue of Shares At a Discount	Petition to CLB to get its sanction
80A(1)	Issue redeemable preference shares in lieu of redemption of Irredeemable Preference Shares	Petition to CLB to get its consent
111	In case of refusal Register Transfer of shares or transmission of shares or debentures of PRIVATE company within 2 months of refusal or 4 months of lodgment, then OR WITHOUT sufficient cause a name is entered or omitted or delayed to enter in RoM	Transferor or Transferee can Appeal to CLB and in the other case, application can be made to CLB to rectify the Register of Members (RoM)
111A(2)	In case of refusal to register transfer of shares of PUBLIC company within 2 months OR if transfer is in violation of SEBI regulations, etc.. 	**Transferee** can appeal to CLB to direct rectification of RoM and in case of violation of law, rectification shall be made after enquiry
113(1)	If Debenture certificates are not delivered or registered within 3 months of allotment or 2 months of transfer. Kindly note, this provision is not applicable to share certificates.	Company can file a petition to CLB to extend a further period of 9 months for delivery.
113(3)	Company on which notice is served to issue certificates as above but has not complied within 10 days	The entitled person can file petition to CLB

117B(4)	If the assets of the company are insufficient or likely to become "Insufficient" to discharge the principal amount as and when it become due.	Debenture trustee may file a Petition to caution CLB & praying to impose restriction
117C(4)	Failure to redeem the debentures on the date of maturity	Debenture holder to apply to CLB to redeem the debentures immediately
118(3)	Default in Furnishing copy of the trust deed within 7 days of request	The entitled can apply to CLB to furnish a copy immediately
141(1)(3)	e-form 8 for creation/modification of charge is not filed within 60 days or e-form 17 is not filed within 30 days or any omission or misstatement of particulars with respect to charge	Company or any interested person can file Petition to CLB to extend or condone the delay or to rectify register of charges
144(4)	Refusal to permit inspection of Company's Register of charges or Inspection of Instruments creating charge	The members or creditors can file a Petition to CLB to direct inspection
163(6)	Refusal to permit inspection or extract of Registers & Returns to member or debenture holder or any other entitled person 	Petition to CLB to compel immediate 'Inspection" of Registers and Returns or to furnish the copies thereof to the person requiring It.
167(1)	In case of default in holding an AGM	CLB to call or direct AGM on application of members
186	In case of impracticability in holding an EGM	CLB on its own or on application by any director or member or entitled person shall call an EGM
188 & 225(3) & 284	Circulation of Members Resolution OR resolutions for appointing or removing auditors OR representations of removed director before expiry of term	Application by company or aggrieved to CLB not to circulate the same if it is to secure needless publicity of defamatory matters
196(4)	Refusal to permit inspection of minute books of general meetings or copy is not supplied within 7 days of request	Members can apply to CLB to compel inspection immediately or to direct supply of copies
219(4)	Refusal of right of Member to obtain copies of Balance sheet and auditors report within 7 days of request	Member or debenture holder or deposit holder can file petition to CLB to supply the same
235	Investigation of the Affairs of the Company on application by 200 members or 1/10th of voting	Petition to CLB to investigate the affairs
250	To retain status quo on transfer, issue or to exercise voting rights on shares or debentures	On reference by CG or on complaint by person, CLB to impose restrictions during transfer or likely transfer.
269(7)	Central Government opines appointment of MD/ WTD/Manager is not as per Section 269 read with Schedule XIII but e-form 25C is filed	On reference by CG, CLB to issue show cause notice to company, such person & other responsible officers
304(2)(b)	Refusal to allow Inspection of register of directors	Members can file petition to CLB to direct immediate inspection

307(9)	Refusal to inspect Register of directors shareholding during 14 days before & 3 days within AGM Note: authorized CG representative or RoC can inspect at any time	Member or debenture holder or can apply to CLB to compel an immediate inspection of Register
388B – 388E	In case of frauds, misfeasance, breach of trust and also of imprudent or unwise practices, conduct of business injurious to trade, industry or business, etc by MD/WTD/Manager/Director/ Officer or an act with intent to defraud its creditors, members or other persons or for a fraudulent or unlawful purpose.	CG can refer to CLB; CLB can pass Interim order restricting such person and may remove the person. Such person will be disqualified to act as director in ANY company for 5 years.
397 to 409	CLB powers are dealt in detail under Oppression & Mismanagement.	
610(2)	Inspection, Production and evidence of documents kept by RoC	Any person can compel RoC with leave of Court/CLB
614(1)	In case default under Companies Act is not made good within 14 notice of notice	Member or Creditor or RoC may apply to CLB to make good default
621A	Dealt separately under the head COMPOSITION OF OFFENCES.	

OPPRESSION & MISMANAGEMENT

[Section 397 & 398]

The management of the Company is based on the majority rule. Even differences among members or any other issue or approval under Companies Act is resolved by a vote of majority. This is said to be a matter of internal management of Company and Court do not usually interfere once the majority of the shareholders approve. This is said to be the rule in *Foss vs. Harbottle or Foss Case*. But in cases of oppression or mismanagement, minority rights will be protected.

Rule in Foss v. Harbottle
OR
Rule of Majority OR
Non-interference by Court

- Compliance of Law;
- Act ratified by Ordinary Resolution;
- Proper Plaintiff is the Company (Not, the individual member)

This is a provision for Convenience & Expediency, to avoid multiplicity of suits.

Exceptions to Foss case
OR
Rule of Minority OR
Interference by Courts OR
Protection of Minority Interest

OPPRESSION & MISMANAGEMENT

- Ultra Vires Act (beyond the powers);
- Fraud on Minority;
- Invasion of Individual Rights;
- Articles amendment for the vested interest of few;
- Special resolution mandated but ordinary resolution is passed with CG approval route is taken, for vested interest of few (for preferential issue or commencement of new business)

Eligibility u/s. 399
[only @ the time of filing petition to CLB – Entry]

Joint Holders are counted as Single Member – Section 3(1)(iii)

For Companies having Share Capital
Lesser of
↳ 100 Members
↳ 1/10 (Toto Members)
↳ 1/10 (Issued Capital in which calls are paid)

For Companies having Share Capital
↳ 1/5 (Total number of members in Register of Members)

Central Government u/s.401
↳ May itself apply
↳ Authorise any person to move CLB

Consent Letter to CLB

I am aggrieved of...
(with Material facts).

I complain...

S/d & dt.

NO blanket consent

Every person should give his consent.

Eligible Persons
↳ Self
↳ Attorney holder
↳ Legal heir of deceased.

Central Government u/s. 400
CLB to give notice & consider views of CG before passing the final order.

OPPRESSION u/s. 397 (curative)	**MISMANAGEMENT u/s. 398** (curative & preventive)
Petition to CLB shall be filed.	Petition to CLB shall be filed.
Satisfaction of Sec 399 Eligibility Criteria for filing the petition by Eligible persons giving their consent.	Satisfaction of Sec 399 Eligibility Criteria for filing the petition by Eligible persons giving their consent.
<u>Complaint</u> – that the affairs of the company are BEING conducted in a manner prejudicial to the public interest or oppressive to Member-s.	<u>Complaint</u> – ↳ that the affairs of the company are BEING conducted or ↳ that a material change in the management or control or ownership or membership of company IN a manner prejudicial to public interest or **prejudicial to the interests of the company**.
Past / isolated act cannot be a subject matter as the word used is "being".	Past / isolated act cannot be a subject matter as the word used is "being".
<u>Apprehensions</u> – NOT a valid ground to make the petition.	<u>Apprehensions</u> (likely to happen) – is a valid ground to make the petition.
CLB has powers to pass INTERIM ORDER from the date of application before passing FINAL ORDER.	

The facts would justify winding up under 'Just & Equitable' clause but CLB is of opinion that to Wind up would unfairly prejudice such member-s and **with a view to** bringing to end the matters complained of, pass an order.	CLB is of the opinion, that it is likely that the affairs of the company will be conducted as aforesaid, and **with a view to** bringing to an end or preventing the matters complained of or apprehended, pass an order.

SPECIAL POWERS OF CLB u/s. 402

↳ Frame Future bye-laws of the Company.

↳ Order to purchase Minority Shares by Majority; Note: Compliance of Sec 77A (Buy Back) is NOT required.

↳ Order for Reduction of Capital; Note: Compliance of Sec 100 (approval of High Court) is NOT required.

↳ To set aside / modify / alter / cancel any agreements with

- ↳ Director / MD / Manager → Then, such person disqualified for a period of 5 years from such company to be appointed as such; further no compensation shall be given for loss of office.
- ↳ Others → Only after due notice & getting the consent of the concerned person.

↳ To cancel / set-aside any transfer [fraudulent preference] / delivery of goods or payment / execution ↳ other act w.r.t property, by / against company WITHIN 3 months before the date of the application.

↳ To provide for any other matter for which in the opinion of the CLB it is just and equitable that ↳ provision should be made.

OTHER POWERS OF CLB

↳ If CLB modified the Memorandum or Articles by order, file with ROC within 30 days; Note: Compliance of other provisions are NOT required; and the company cannot inconsistently alter the MOA / AOA without the LEAVE (permission) of CLB. [Sec 404]

↳ CLB may add (to implead) additional respondents to the petition [Sec 405].

↳ CLB may direct the company to appoint directors by proportional representation (Sec 265) or appoint Additional Directors and any change can take effect only with CONFIRMATION of CLB.

↳ CLB may appoint **<u>Government Directors u/s. 408</u>** and such directors,

↳ Shall be appointed for a period UPTO 3 years (CG may remove them and appoint some other person in their place)

- ↳ On appointment, no change in Board without permission of CG.
- ↳ Will not be counted for the calculating rotational directors;
- ↳ Not liable to retire by rotation;
- ↳ Not required to hold qualification shares;
- ↳ Report to Central Government on affairs of the company.
- ↳ CG may give additional directions including directions to remove an auditor already appointed and to appoint another auditor in his place or to alter the articles of the company.

<u>CLB ORDER</u> [Change in BoD] <u>u/s. 409</u>

NOT applicable to Private Company

Transfer or transfer likely in the ownership of shares → Change in Composition of Board likely → which is Prejudicial to affairs of the Company

On complaint by MD / Manager / Director as aforesaid, the CLB may order that NO resolution / action takes effect UNLESS confirmed by CLB.

Try remembering the time limits given under the items which require either the approval or confirmation of Company Law Board and apply it at the respective places. There are almost 44 places in Companies Act, 1956 which are related with CLB, this chapter aims to summarise that requirements. Any act which is **burdensome, harsh, and wrongful along with a lack of probity & fair dealings to a member** can be oppressive in nature. Try to correlate the above said Section 409 along with Section 250 dealt under investigation.

Transfer of Shares

SHARE CERTIFICATE

Section 84 read with Companies (Issue of Shares Certificates) Rules, 1960

1. Issued under common seal affixed in the presence of
   ↳ two directors or duly authorized persons by directors and
   ↳ the secretary / person appointed by Board for the purpose.
   ↳ The two directors (one should be a person other than MD / WTD) or their attorneys and
   ↳ the secretary or other person shall SIGN the share certificate

   [director may sign by affixing signature by means of machine / equipment / other mechanical means such as engraving in metal / lithography, BUT NOT by means of a rubber stamp].
2. Prima Facie evidence as to title and amount paid-up – VALID unless otherwise disputed.
   ↳ Binds the company
   ↳ Precedents over Register of Members.
3. Issuance of original / duplicate share certificate at a Board of Directors (BoD) or Committee Meeting,
   ↳ If BoD comprises UPTO 6 Directors, Board / Committee meeting should have atleast 2 Directors;
   ↳ If BoD comprises MORE THAN 6 Directors, Board / Committee meeting should have atleast 3 Directors.
   ↳ In case of issue of duplicate share certificate, the following shall be inscribed "Duplicate issued in lieu of Share Certificate No.......".
   ↳ "Register of Renewed and Duplicate Share Certificate" shall be maintained & updated.
4. As per Section 113, Share Certificate to be issued,
   ↳ WITHIN 3 months, in case of Allotment;
   ↳ WITHIN 2 months of Lodgement, in case of Transfer;
   ↳ WITHIN 1 month in case of Transfer by Listed Companies.

Note: In case of Debenture Certificates, the said period of 3 months/2 months for delivery & registration can be extended to further period of 9 months by filing a petition with CLB.

5. Cannot be issued except
   ↳ By a Board resolution;
   ↳ On surrender of allotment letter / letter of acceptance or renunciation (except in case of bonus shares) [in case letter is lost, same conditions as share certificate is lost].

Resolution for issue of original share certificate

"RESOLVED THAT the share certificates numbered .... to ..... for ..... Equity Shares bearing distinctive numbers from ..... to ..... be issued to the persons mentioned in the list placed on the Table duly initialed by the chairman, under the Common Seal of the Company and the same be signed by any two directors of the company and countersigned by the Company Secretary".

Resolution for issue of duplicate share certificates

"RESOLVED THAT the application Nos. ...... to ..... as described in the Register of Renewed and Duplicate Share Certificates, for the issue of duplicate share certificates in lieu of the original certificates reported to have been lost and not traceable be and hereby sanctioned to be issued to the applicants under the Common Seal of the Company and the same be signed by any two directors and countersigned by the Company Secretary".

6. If share certificate is:

↳ Lost / destroyed, share holder has to execute an Indemnity Bond and produce necessary evidence and pay out-of-pocket expenses incurred by a company in investigating evidence;

↳ Mutilated / exhausted, share holder has to surrender the old certificate;

TO GET a fresh share certificate & to make Entry in Register of Members about issue of duplicate / renewal certificate.

EXPULSION OF A MEMBER

Articles of Association of a company authorising the Board of Directors to expel a member is illegal and void [Bajaj Auto Ltd.] as it militates [decisive factor in preventing] against rights of member and powers of CG u/s. 111 and powers of Court u/s. 107, 395 & 397 of the Act.

CESSATION OF MEMBERSHIP

A person may lose his membership of a company and cease to be its member due to any of the following reasons:

↳ Transfer of shares;
↳ Transmission of shares on death;
↳ Co buys back the shares and cancels them;
↳ Co. amalgamated with another Co.;
↳ One Co is member of another when the former Co wind up;
↳ Co is struck-off by RoC u/s. 560;
↳ Rectification of register of members by CLB;
↳ Shares are forfeited / surrendered / lien is exercised;
↳ Shares gifted to any person;
↳ Shares auctioned by order of Court / Statutory authority;
↳ Shares registered in name of bank / financial institution / person who had lent money and shares given as collateral security with Certificate & Transfer form.

STOCK

↳ Set of shares put together in a bundle;
↳ Register of Members should show amount (value) of stock.

Thus, Stock is a set of FULL-PAID share bundled with UNEQUAL amounts, having NO nominal value or distinctive number and TRANSFERABLE in whole numbers or fraction.

Conversion of fully paid shares into stock: Only a public limited company can issue stock if its,

↳ Articles authorize such conversion;
↳ Shareholders approve by way of Ordinary Resolution.
↳ Intimate RoC within 30 days in e-form 5 following EFORM COMPLIANCE CHART.
↳ Issue stocks and Remove the names of the persons from the register of members of the company to whom stock has been issued in exchanges for the shares.
↳ Then, all the provisions of the Act, which are applicable to shares only, shall cease to apply on so much of the shares capital as is converted into stock.

PROCEDURE FOR RE – CONVERSION OF STOCK INTO FULLY PAID SHARES:

Broadly the Procedural steps are same as discussed in conversion of shares into stock.

SHARE TRANSFERS

[Section 108]

- "Proper Instrument" for Transfer [Form 7B – Share Transfer Deed];
- "duly dated"; "duly signed"; "duly stamped"; & "duly executed";
- By Transferor & Transferee;
- With Consideration [however, Gift is permissible];
- Along with relevant Share Certificates or endorsement on share transfer form that Original Certificates has been lodged with Company [Certification of Transfer], when there is a partial transfer.

"Duly Dated" means, a date stamp should be made BEFORE,

- Signature of transferor, AND
- Entry is made, in the Share Transfer Deed.

For date stamp, it has to be presented to the prescribed authority (including RoC), who shall stamp or otherwise.

"Duly Signed" means share transfer deed shall be "signed by Transferor or registered Authorised Representatives or ALL Transferors, in case of Joint Holdings".

"Duly Stamped" means,

- Stamps affixed should be of adequate value, AND
- Adhesive stamps should be cancelled by drawing lines.

"Duly Executed" means,

- when ALL required details are completed by both Transferor and Transferee, AND
- the deed is 'duly stamped' and then 'duly signed'.

Vivek purchased 5,000 equity shares of Prosperous Limited and lodged the same for transfer with the company. The company returned these shares under objection that the share transfer stamps affixed on the transfer deed were not cancelled. Vivek thereafter cancelled the stamps and re – lodged the shares for transfer. At this time, the company affected the transfer and returned the duly transferred shares to Vivek. In the meantime, the market price of the shares went down substantially. Vivek filed a case against the company claiming that, due to unwarranted objection raised by the company, he was deprived of the profits which he could have earned by disposing of the shares at higher price. State with reasons whether the claim of Vivek is tenable. (2008 – June)

In the Section 108, the words "Duly Stamped" are of great importance. Section 12 of the Indian Stamp Act provides that any instrument bearing an adhesive stamp which has not been cancelled so that it cannot be used again, shall, so far as such stamp is concerned, be deemed to be unstamped. The share transfer stamps affixed on the share transfer form are required to be cancelled either before or at the time of execution of the deed. Therefore, the company shall have the right to return the shares under objection, if the stamps are not properly cancelled.

In the given problem, Vivek, the transferee, subsequently (after the company returned), cancelled the stamps and relodged the shares for transfer and the company affected the transfer. In the meantime, the market price of the shares went down and Vivek filed a case against the company claiming that due to unwarranted objection raised by the company, he was deprived of the opportunity to sell the shares at higher price. In Re. Coronation Tea Co.Ltd case, it was held that if the stamp is not cancelled, then the effect is the same as if the instrument is not stamped. In view of the provisions of Section 108(1) read with the provisions of the Indian Stamp Act,1899 the claim of Vivek is not tenable in the Count of law and his case would be dismissed.

An **application** for registration of a transfer of the shares in a company may be made either by the transferor or by the transferee.

Where the application is made by the transferor for partly paid shares, the transfer shall be registered, only AFTER giving notice to transferee and getting No Objection within 2 weeks of Notice.

The Share Transfer Deed (form) after duly executed by transferor and transferee and duly dated to be submitted to Company along with the share certificate for registering the transfer within 12 months from the date of stamping OR date of closure of share transfer register, whichever is later, in case of listed companies and within 2 months from the presentation in case of unlisted companies. Further, SEBI has mandated submission of PAN card copy for registration of physical transfer of shares of a listed company.

Revalidation of Share Transfer Deed is permissible AFTER its expiry date by way of application in Form 7C to RoC for a further period of 1 month, where in the opinion of the Central Government (RoC), it is necessary to avoid hardship.

TRANSFER OF SHARES IN A PRIVATE LIMITED COMPANY: [Section 111]

1. Section 3(1)(iii) RESTRICTS transfer of Shares as specified in the Articles of the Company; Transfer in violation of Articles is VOID;
2. Pre-emption Clause: Shares can be transferred to non-member ONLY if existing member is not willing to buy the shares, that too, at the bonafide and not arbitrary discretion of the Directors;
3. The Board will have to give reasons for refusal to transfer, WITHIN 2 months from the date of lodgment of transfer deed or intimation of transfer, as per Section 111;
4. APPEAL against refusal WITHIN 2 months from the date of receipt of Refusal or WITHIN 4 months from the date of lodgment to CLB by TRANSFEROR or TRANSFEREE or person intimating transmission;
5. APPLICATION to CLB for rectification of Register of Members shall be made by the Company or member or aggrieved person if name of any person is, without sufficient cause, entered / removed or unnecessary delay is caused;
6. The CLB order shall be complied within 10 days.
7. CLB may prohibit transfer u/s. 250, during Investigation.

TRANSFER OF SHARES IN A PUBLIC LIMITED COMPANY: [Section 111A]

1. Shares in a Public Limited Company are FREELY transferable irrespective of any provision in its Articles UNLESS such transfer is in Contravention of SEBI Act, SICA, FEMA or any other law as per Section 111A; In Maruti Udyog Ltd v. Pentamedia Graphics, it was held that a Public Limited Company cannot refuse to register transfer of shares on any grounds whatsoever, except those specified in Section 111A;
2. The Board will have to give reasons for refusal to transfer, WITHIN 2 months from the date of lodgment of transfer deed or intimation of transfer, as per Section 111A; On refusal to Transfer, ALL the Corporate Benefits accruing to Transferor should be kept in abeyance, as per Section 206A;
3. APPEAL to CLB against refusal WITHIN 2 months from the date on which instrument of transfer is delivered to the company by the TRANSFEREE;
4. APPLICATION to CLB within 2 months for rectification of Register of Members can be made by Company or depositor or investor or SEBI, if transfer is in contravention of said Acts;
5. The CLB order shall be complied within 10 days.
6. CLB may RESTRICT voting rights ONLY u/s. 250, during Investigation, as Section 111A has an overriding effect.

TRANSFER OF SHARES IN CASE OF DEMAT HOLDINGS:

In case of electronic shares, ONLY name of the Depositories are entered in the Register of Members and transfer will take place online. There is no requirement of Stamp Duty during such transfer. The requirement in case of Transfer of Shares applies only to Physical Shares.

FORGED TRANSFERS - *Null & Void*
When the signatures of the transferor not matched with the specimen signature of the transferor, then intimate the transferor regarding the lodgement of the transfer deed and require him to convey his objection, if any, within specified period of time.

Where a company acts in good faith and registers a transfer produced by the transferee and issues fresh certificate to him but later it is found that the transfer was forged and the company is compelled to restore the shares, the transferee is liable to indemnify the company against its liability. [Sh Cert is a prima facie evidence]

TRANSPOSITION OF JOINT NAMES
- ↳ Joint shareholders may want to alter or re-arrange the order of their names in the register of members of the company.
- ↳ It does not involve transfer of shares by the holder to another person and a simple letter [no transfer deed required] signed by all the joint holders in this regard is enough.
- ↳ Share Transfer Deed to be executed only for,
- ↳ Transposition in respect of part holding;
- ↳ Addition / deletion / substitution of one / more names;
- ↳ Splitting Joint Holding in names of each / some of Joint Holders.

TRANSMISSION OF SHARES

An act by operation of law [VESTING], takes place,
- ↳ On death of Member OR on death of last surviving Member, in case of Joint holdings;
- ↳ On adjudication as Insolvent;
- ↳ On becoming lunatic;
- ↳ On Amalgamation / Merger / Liquidation;
- ↳ When Minor becomes Major.

Transmission is an involuntary act by operation of law, while transfer is a voluntary act. Hence, transmission **cannot be refused** by the Company, even on the grounds on which a transfer [Sec 111 / 111A] may be declined.

As per Table A [Articles]:
- ↳ Legal Representative is the Entitled Person AND should produce evidence to the satisfaction of the Board;
- ↳ The entitled person may register himself OR transfer the shares to another, as if transfer by Original Member; Otherwise, Company may issue a notice to act on the same;
- ↳ "Shareholder" – A person entitled to shares is entitled to ALL Corporate Benefits. "Member" – However he can attend General Meetings AND vote only after his name is registered as a Member.

Procedure for registration of transmission of shares
(1) The provisions in the articles of association of the company regarding transmission of shares and the evidence required to be produced by the legal heir/representative of the deceased shareholder should be checked.
(2) If articles do not contain any provision on the subject, check whether there is any resolution passed by the Board in this regard.
(3) Generally, the documents required to be submitted include the following:
  (a) An application for transmission of shares;

(b) Certificate of death (original with one photocopy or a certified true copy);
(c) Succession certificate where the deceased has not left a will;
(d) Probate or Letters of Administration where the deceased has left a will;
(e) An affidavit regarding confirmation as to the legal heir(s) of the deceased;
(f) Indemnity Bond with or without surety;
(g) Guarantee by one/two person/s as required by the company.

(4) On being satisfied about the claim for transmission of the shares, place the application before the Board or the Transfer Committee for approval.

(5) After it is approved, register the transmission in the Register of Members and make necessary endorsement in the Share Certificate and dispatch the same to the concerned member.

TRANSMISSION OF SHARES IN CASE OF DEMAT HOLDINGS:

The Depository has no authority to transmit the securities. The Company is the sole authority in case of transmission. However, in case of Nomination made with the Depository Participant, the transmission can be made to the Nominee on production of death Certificate to such Depository Participant.

NOMINATION OF SHARES

"Nominee" – entitled to ALL rights to the EXCLUSION of all other persons.

↳ A shareholder can nominate a person in the prescribed manner. The shares will VEST in the nominee in case of death of Nominator as per Section 109A.
↳ Form 2B is the prescribed form for Nomination, to be signed by the Nominator or ALL Nominators, in case of Joint Holdings.
↳ The Nomination OVERRRIDES any provision in respect of transmission by operation of law or will.
↳ The nominee may register himself OR transfer the shares to another, as if transfer by Original Member as per Section 109B. Otherwise, Company may issue a notice to act on the same.
↳ No stamp duty on transfer by way of Nomination.

In case of physical shares, the nominee can be one or more. In case of demat shares, the Depository Participant permit only one Nominee per Account.

Procedure for registration of transmission in the case of nomination

(1) On the death of the nominator, the nominee will have the option, either
(a) To get himself registered as holder of the share or debenture; or
(b) To transfer the share or debenture.

(2) If the nominee elects to get himself registered as a member or debenture holder of the company, he should send to the company:
(a) a notice in writing signed by him stating that he so elects; and
(b) the death certificate of the deceased shareholder or debenture holder, as the case may be.

(3) Usually companies would require the following documents:
(a) Certified true copy of death certificate of shareholder.
(b) Proof of date of birth of the nominee.
(c) An affidavit/declaration by the nominee declaring his rights.
(d) The original share certificate.

(5) On receiving the documents mentioned above, the company will verify the authenticity and, if satisfied, register the nominee as a member in its Register of Members/Register of Debenture Holders and give intimation thereof to the nominee.

(6) In the case of transmission of shares or debentures to the nominee of shareholder/debenture holder by operation of law by virtue of a statutory provision contained in section 109B of the Companies Act. This transmission will not require share transfer form. Hence, it will not require payment of stamp duty.

RETURN OF ALLOTMENT

- ↪ For shares allotted in cash, file e-Form 2 within 30 days from allotment following EFORM COMPLIANCE CHART with RoC but RoC can extend the time limit;
- ↪ For bonus shares, a return stating details of shares with particulars of with copy of resolution authorising the issue shall be filed;
- ↪ For shares issued at discount, copy of the CLB order filed along with the return;
- ↪ For shares (not being bonus shares) allotted otherwise than in cash, a contract in writing as to title with duly stamped contract of sale shall be filed with RoC in e-Form 3 following EFORM COMPLIANCE CHART;
- ↪ For re-issue of forfeited shares, no return is required.

Compliance Certificate under Companies Act, 1956 ENSURES that legal & procedural requirements are duly complied with and also instills professional DISCIPLINE in the working of the company, thus building up the necessary CONFIDENCE in the state of affairs of the company. It shall be issued by a Practising Company Secretary (PCS).

Compliance Certificate

Section 383A read with Companies (Compliance Certificate) Rules, 2001

A member of the Institute shall be deemed "to be in practice" (PCS) when, individually / in partnership with members of ICSI / ICAI / ICWAI,

- ↳ Engages himself in the practice of the profession of Company Secretaries to, or in relation to, any company; or
- ↳ Offers to perform or performs services in relation to the promotion, forming, incorporation, amalgamation, reconstruction, reorganization or winding up of companies; or
- ↳ Offers to perform or performs such services as may be performed by an authorised representative of a company with respect to filing, registering, presenting, attesting or verifying any documents (including forms, applications and returns) by or on behalf of the company, OR RTA or Issue house or Share & Stock Broker or Secretarial auditor or consultant or adviser to company including legal or procedural matter under Companies Act, SEBI, SCRA, MRTP, FEMA & IDRA, or issuing certificates on behalf.
- ↳ Holds himself out to the public as a Company Secretary in practice;
- ↳ Renders professional services or assistance with respect to matters of principle or detail relating to the practice of the profession of Company Secretaries.
- ↳ Renders such other services as, in the opinion of the Council, are or may be rendered by a Company Secretary in practice;

Putting CS / CA / CMA before the name is permitted. Advertisement (as per the guidelines) through a write up of his services AND his firms services is permissible.

Professional misconduct in relation to members of the Institute is broadly structured as under:

- ↳ Professional misconduct in relation to members of the Institute in practice. (Part I of Schedule I, containing 12 clauses)
- ↳ Professional misconduct in relation to members of the Institute in service. (Part II of Schedule I, containing 3 clauses).
- ↳ Professional misconduct in relation to members of the Institute generally. (Part III of Schedule I, containing 4 clauses).
- ↳ Professional misconduct in relation to members of the Institute in practice requiring action by a High Court (Part I of Schedule II, containing 10 clauses)

↳ Professional misconduct in relation to members of the Institute generally requiring action by a High Court (Part II of Schedule II, containing 2 clauses).

PROVISIONS – Section 383A

↳ Requirement relating to appointment of Company Secretary is mandatory for all companies having a minimum PC of Rs. 5 crores.

↳ All companies having a PC of Rs.2 crores but not exceeding Rs.5 crores shall either obtain a compulsory Compliance Certificate from a Practising Company Secretary (PCS) or mandatorily appoint a Company Secretary.

↳ All companies having a PC of Rs.10 lakhs but not exceeding Rs.2 crores shall obtain a compulsory Compliance Certificate from a Practising Company Secretary (PCS), which shall be addressed to shareholders.

↳ Optional Compliance Certificate for those companies having a PC less than Rs.10 lakhs or more than Rs.5 crores, in which case it shall addressed to Board of Directors.

↳ Default of which will entail a penalty UPTO Rs.500/- per day.

↳ **Where the Board of directors of any such company comprises only 2 directors, neither of them shall be appointed as company secretary of the company.**

Total Paid-up Capital of the Company	Compliance Certificate (CC)	Company Secretary (CS)
5 crores or more	Optional	mandatory
2 crores to 5 crores	Optional, if CS is appointed	optional, if CC is obtained
10 lakhs to 2 crores	Mandatory	optional
Less than 10 lakhs	Optional	optional

Note: PC = Paid-up Capital which includes all money flows for which shares are allotted, thereby consider Equity, Preference & also partly paid-up to the extent of paid-up.

In the proposed Companies Bill, 2011, the position of Company Secretary is more strengthened because of introduction of a new definition called **Key Managerial Personnel (KMP)** [Clause 203]

Every company belonging to such class or classes of companies as may be prescribed shall have the following whole-time key managerial personnel,—

(i) Managing director, or Chief Executive Officer or manager and in their absence, a whole-time director; and

(ii) Company Secretary.

Unless the articles of a company provide otherwise, an individual shall not be the chairperson of the company as well as the managing director or Chief Executive Officer of the company at the same time.

Every Company Secretary being a KMP shall be appointed by a resolution of the Board which shall contain the terms and conditions of appointment including the remuneration. If any vacancy in the office of KMP is created, the same shall be filled up by the Board at a meeting of the Board within a period of six months from the date of such vacancy.

If a company does not appoint a Company Secretary, the penalty proposed is : On company – one lakh rupees which may extend to five lakh rupees; On every director and KMP who is in default – 50,000 rupees and 1,000 rupees per day if contravention continues.

Functions of Company Secretary (Clause 205):

(a) to report to the Board about compliance with the provisions of this Act, the rules made thereunder and other laws applicable to the company;

(b) to ensure that the company complies with the applicable secretarial standards;

(c) to discharge such other duties as may be prescribed.

APPOINTMENT OF CS & Compliance Certificate

- Law is silent can be appointed in BM but, it is advisable to be appointed by shareholders at AGM & will have the office till the conclusion of next AGM.
- Attach Compliance Certificate to Directors Report which in turn is attached with Accounts & circulated to shareholders as per S-219.
- Certifies only the compliance relating to Company Law & it is for every Financial year.
- File with RoC in e-Form 66 within 30 days of AGM, if NO AGM within 30 days of AGM ought to have taken place u/s.166, if AGM ADJOURNED within 30 days of such adjournment.

FORMAT OF COMPLIANCE CERTIFICATE

QUALIFICATION / RESERVATION / ADVERSE REMARKS may be given at relevant places; The following things shall be certified based on the best of information & according to the examination carried out and explanation furnished.

1) Maintenance of List of Registers & that all entries are recorded.
2) Filing of List of Forms & Returns to RoC, RD, CG or other authorities.
3) If Private company, then compliance of Section 3(1)(iii).

4) Number of meetings of Board & whether Minutes recorded.
5) Details of closure of Register of members or debenture holders.
6) Date of AGM & EGM, whether held after giving due Notice & whether Minutes are duly recorded.
7) Advances to Director & compliance with Sections 295, 297, 301 & 314.
8) Board or Committee approval for Issue of duplicate share certificate and the company has delivered all the certificates on allotment/transfer/transmission of securities.
9) Company has complied with payment of dividend, transfer to unpaid dividend a/c, subsequent credit of amount lying for 7 years to IEPF and requirements of Section 217.
10) Appointment of Director on Board is duly made in compliance of Sections 260, 262 & 313 & whether proper appointment of MD is complaint of Section 269 read with Schedule XIII or whether CG approval is obtained and appointment of SSA was made in compliance of Sections 294, 294A & 294AA.
11) Whether necessary approvals of RD, RoC, CLB & MCA were obtained as required?
12) The directors have disclosed their interest to the Board as per Section 299.
13) Issue of shares/debentures/securities, Buy back u/s. 77A, Redemption of Preference shares □ whether made as per the provisions.
14) Compliance with requirements of S-58A & 58AA as to invitation/acceptance/repayment of deposits and whether the company has filed advertisement or statement in lieu of advertisement and Return of deposits.

15) Borrowings, loans & guarantees made/issued by the company whether satisfy the provisions of Section 293(1)(d) & 372A and necessary entries are made in the registers.

16) If the company has changed its Registered office from one state to another, then, whether it has made alteration of MoA/AoA accordingly.

17) List of Prosecutions/SCN for alleged offences; list of penalties imposed shall be prepared.

18) Compliance with Section 417 as to Deposit from employees & Section 418 as to Deposit of Provident Fund.

It is highly advisable to read the quoted sections from COMPANY SECRETARIAL PRACTICE.

PENALTY FOR FALSE STATEMENTS – Section 628

If in any return, report, certificate, balance sheet, pro¬spectus, statement or other document required by or for the purposes of any of the provisions of this Act, any person makes a statement—

- which is false in any material particular, knowing it to be false;
- OR which omits any material fact, knowing it to be materi¬al;

he shall, save as otherwise expressly provided in this Act, be punishable with imprisonment for a term which may extend to two years, and shall also be liable to fine.

CERTIFICATION FEES FOR COMPLIANCE CERTIFICATE

Certification fees charged by a PCS shall be NOT less than Rs. 5000/- in a Financial year per Compliance Certificate per Company. The following are the conditions,

Paid up Capital of the Company	MINIMUM Certification fees
LESS THAN Rs. 50 lakhs	Rs. 5,000/-
Rs.50 lakhs to Rs. 1 crore	Rs. 7,500/-
Rs.1 crore & above	Rs.10,000/-

CEILING ON NUMBER OF COMPLIANCE CERTIFICATE TO BE ISSUED

PCS can ISSUE Compliance Certifica te &/or SIGN Annual Return UPTO 80 companies, in aggregate, in a CALENDAR YEAR. In case of PCS firm, the limit would apply to each partner. Any non-compliance of this provision will amount to PROFESSIONAL MISCONDUCT under Part II of Schedule II to Company Secretaries Act, 1980.

OTHER PROVISIONS

- To verify all available records, if not practicable, obtain "Letter of Representation" from the company.
- On new appointment/change, communicate the earlier incumbent by Registered Post.

A company Secretary is appointed in addition to Directors, so if a company has only 2 directors, none of them **shall** be appointed as CS. Every company having a paid-up capital of 5 crores or more, **shall** have a whole-time CS and every company having a paid-up capital of 10 lakhs but not exceeding 5 crores, shall obtain Compliance Certificate from a CS in whole-time practice (PCS). Basically the compliance certificate certifies the compliance of Company Law for a particular financial year and has to be filed in e-Form 66, when filing annual financials of the company.

REDUCTION OF SHARE CAPITAL

Section 100 to 104

Ways of Reduction:

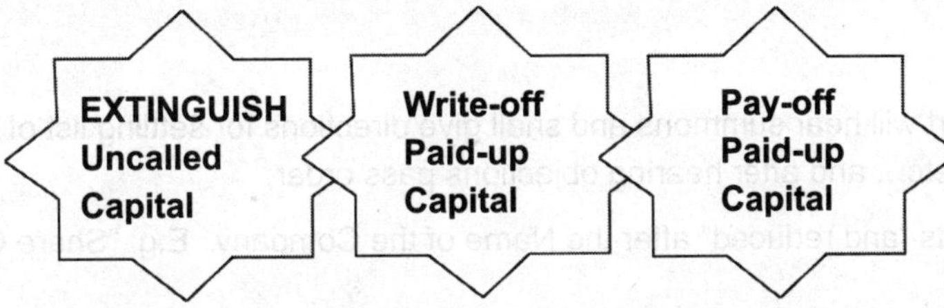

1. Reduce Liability - **Extinguish** Share Capital Not Paid-up;
2. **Cancel** Paid-up Capital → Lost / Unrepresented by Available Assets;
3. **Pay off** Paid-up Capital, not required by Company OR Pay off but on a condition that it may be called up when necessary.

Conditions for Reduction:

↳ Company should be "Limited by Shares";

↳ Articles of Association should authorize such Reduction of Capital;

↳ Special Resolution to be passed;

↳ Court Confirmation to protect the interests of Creditors, Shareholders and Public. Creditors need to be paid or secured or consented for such Reduction.

PROCEDURE FOR REDUCTION OF CAPITAL

Special Resolution	Convene a General Meeting to get the approval of shareholders by way of Special Resolution for the Reduction
Court	File a petition to Court to get its confirmation for proposed Reduction
Creditors	Court to protect the INTEREST of creditors by settling the list of creditors: ↳ The company has to prepare 'List of Creditors' ↳ keep a copy at the registered office for inspection ↳ dispatch the copy of the list to all the creditors ↳ make an advertisement to that effect and ↳ file the copy of the same (advertisement and copy of the list) in the court; ↳ Court to give an opportunity to object in specified cases or as per Court's direction; ↳ On objection, Company has to make payment or to fully secure the creditors

Court Order	On reduction.
ROC	Minutes approved by court to be filed with ROC along with e-form 21 within 30 days for the order to take effect.

Court Order on Reduction:

↳ File petition to Court; Court will hear summons and shall give directions for settling list of creditors, dispatch of notice, advertisement, etc… and after hearing objections pass order;

↳ May order to add the words "and reduced" after the Name of the Company. E.g. "Share Capital Limited and Reduced"

↳ May declare Reasons for Reduction of Share Capital which shall be published and circulated to the Members.

↳ File copy of Court Order in e-Form 21 within 30 days of Order.

↳ The Capital Clause in Memorandum of Association shall be suitably amended by substituting the Minutes.

When a Court Order is Not Required on Reduction ?

1. Reduction of Capital as per the Order of Company Law Board consequent to Oppression and Mismanagement.
2. In case of scheme of Compromise or Arrangement u/s. 391 to 394 and such Reduction is in connection with the Scheme.
3. The Company purchasing its own securities u/s. 77A.
4. Redemption of preference shares is not reduction u/s 100 as authorized capital remains unchanged and also re-issue upto redeemed value of preference shares is not increase of authorized capital.
5. **Diminution of Issued Capital** means canceling the Shares Issued but Not applied for. This reduces 'Issued Capital' as shown in the Balance Sheet. It's canceling Unalloted shares by passing a Ordinary Resolution if Articles authorizes and a return (e-Form 5) to be filed with Registrar within 30 days of Cancellation [Sec 95].
6. Forfeiture of Shares as per Articles of the Company, if Call Money is not paid. Such Forfeiture does not vest the property in respect of forfeited shares in the company and hence does not require Court Approval;

↳ Forfeiture should be done in good faith and Articles to mention the Rights & Liabilities after Forfeiture.

↳ "Unless every condition in Articles is strictly and literally complied with, it could be fatal for forfeiture" as decided in Public Passenger Services Ltd v. M A Khader.

↳ "Re-issue of Forfeited share is NOT an allotment but it's a SALE".

7. **Surrender of Shares** to the Nominee of the Company, as per Articles is permissible, ONLY if it is used merely to avoid the formalities of forfeiture and NOT otherwise. Further, Company cannot make any payment to Shareholder who surrenders the shares and it does not require Court Approval.

Forfeiture	Surrender	Lien
Can be made only in respect of amount unpaid on the Shares.	Is a Voluntary Forfeiture but not a device for relieving the Shareholders from Liability	Extends even to, any other Amount receivable, as per Articles.
Lien: "Right to retain some property for SOME DEBT". Note: In case of Listed Company, there is no difference between Forfeiture & Lien, as Listed Company cannot have lien on fully paid shares.		

VARIATION OF SHAREHOLDERS RIGHTS

Sec 106 & 107

PROPORTION

Voting Right is normally proportional to the Share of Member in the Paid-up Capital of the Company, unless Equity Shares with DIFFERENTIAL VOTING RIGHTS are issued.

<u>VARIATION</u>

Rights of any Class of Shareholders may be varied,

↳ Passing a Special Resolution at a Meeting of Holders of that Class of Shares OR

↳ With Consent of 3/4th of Members, in writing;

<u>AUTHORISATION</u>

↳ Such Variation should be authorized by Memorandum or Articles of the Company OR

↳ Such Variation should not be prohibited by the Terms of Issue of that Class of Shares;

<u>CANCELLATION</u>

↳ Such Variation can be cancelled WITHIN 21 days from the date of Special Resolution or Consent, on application to Court, by 10% OR more of the shares of that class who did not consent to such Variation.

<u>CONFIRMATION</u>

↳ Court on satisfaction that such variation would UNFARILY prejudice the holders of that class of shares, then may CANCEL the Variation;

↳ File copy of Court Order in e-Form 21 within 30 days of such Order and then a Physical Copy of such Order need also be submitted.

BUY BACK PROVISIONS

BUY BACK BY AN UNLISTED COMPANY

↳ Comply Section 77A, 77AA & 77B of Companies Act, 1956 AND

↳ Comply 'Private Limited Company & Unlisted Public Limited Company (Buy Back of Securities) Rules, 1999'.

BUY BACK BY A LISTED COMPANY

↳ Comply Section 77A, 77AA & 77B of Companies Act, 1956 AND

↳ Comply 'SEBI (Buy Back of Securities) Regulations, 1998' AND

↳ Listing Agreement.

BUY BACK UNDER COMPANIES ACT

S- 77B [>] 77A [>] Companies Act

Section 77A OVERRIDES all other provisions of Companies Act, as it starts with the words "Notwithstanding anything contained in the Act" but is SUBJECT to Section 77B of Companies Act. Though Capital is reduced under Buy Back, the provisions of Section 100 of Companies Act, requiring Court Approval is NOT REQUIRED as Section 77A overrides all other (Sec.100) provisions of Companies Act. Thus, only sections 77A, 77AA & 77B to be complied with.

77B – PROHIBITION OF BUY BACK

Through Subsidiary (-ies)	Through Investment Company (ies)	**Default** in deposit or loan or its interest, dividend, redemption of preference / debt	**Non-compliance** of S-159=Annual Return; S-207= Dividend; S211-=Annual Accounts

77A – BUY BACK

SOURCES

Free Reserves as per latest audited Balance Sheet, free for distribution as Dividend	Securities Premium Account	Proceeds of shares / specified securities, NOT of the same kind issued earlier

77AA – the "Nominal Value of Shares purchased" to be TRANSFERRED to Capital Redemption Reserve (CRR) Account, if shares bought back using Free Reserves.

CONDITIONS

ARTICLES of Association of the Company should AUTHORISE	Shares / Specified Securities to be FULLY PAID-UP	Debt:Equity after Buy Back UPTO 2:1 OR as per Central Government

BUY UPTO 25% of **Paid-Up Equity** in a Financial Year

Board Meeting (NOT, Circular Resolution) SPEND UPTO 10% of **Paid-Up Equity & Free Reserves and** no buy back can be made within next 365 days

General Meeting (Special Resolution) SPEND UPTO 25% of **Paid-Up Capital & Free Reserves**

NO FURTHER BUY BACK WITHIN 365 DAYS FROM THE DATE OF OFFER

COMPLETION OF BUY BACK

↳ WITHIN 12 months from the date of BOARD / SPECIAL RESOLUTION;

↳ OTHERWISE, Reasons for non-completion of Buy Back, to be given in DIRECTORS REPORT u/s. 217 **UNLESS** approved by shareholders through Special Resolution.

FULL DISCLOSURE IN EXPLANATORY STATEMENT, as to

Material Facts Necessity of Buy back Class of Securities	Amount to be spent Time limit for completion

MODES OF BUY BACK

from EXISTING SHAREHOLDERS on proportionate basis	From OPEN MARKET	from ODD LOTS [means, LOT less than Marketable lot]	from ESOP / Sweat Equity Holders

DECLARATION OF SOLVENCY [DoS] – to SEBI, if listed & to RoC [Form 4A]

THAT Board has made full enquiry into the affairs of the company AND	are of the opinion that, it is capable of meeting liabilities, AND	WILL NOT be Insolvent WITHIN 1 year (DoS), AND verified by an AFFIDAVIT	SIGNED by 2 OR more Directors, 1 shall be Managing Director, if any

RESTRICTION ON FURTHER ISSUE of same kind of shares / securities, INCLUDING rights issue UPTO 6 months from the Completion of Buy Back

EXCEPTIONS

(meaning, the following can be done during the 6 months)

↳ Bonus Issue;

↳ Discharge of subsisting (existing) obligations,

- ↳ Conversion of Warrants / Stock options / Sweat Equity;
- ↳ Conversion of Preference / Debentures INTO Equity.

EXTINGUISH & physically Destroy securities bought, WITHIN 7 days of Completion	Maintain Statutory Register of details of Shares Bought in Form 4B	RETURN of Buy Back WITHIN 30 days of Completion in Form 4C	DEFAULT OF SECTION UPTO Rs. 50,000 or UPTO 2 years or Both

ICDR Provisions Summary

ICDR stands for SEBI (Issue of Capital & Disclosure Requirements) Regulations, 2009 The company has three options to make public issue which are called eligibility criteria. One being Profitability route where company having 3 crores of net tangible assets, 1 crore of networth and track record of distributable profits can go. Failing which, book building is permitted when QIB's assure to invest atleast 50% OR when project is appraised and invested by Financial Institutions or Scheduled Commercial Banks. If it's an existing listed company coming with a public issue then the issue size not to exceed 5 times of pre-issue networth, failing which, it has to take book building route as said above. IPO Grading is mandatory for IPO's.

The promoter shall contribute atleast 20% of post issue capital and shall be locked-in for a period of 3 years. The price of public issue may be predetermined by demand & supply in the market. In case of book building issue, price band may be given, where public bid at various rates in the price band and finally, the company along with the Merchant Banker in consultation with Stock exchange determine the cut-off price.

IPO under book building route can have a green shoe option if it is mentioned in the prospectus which is a post listing price stabilization mechanism when the issue is over subscribed.

Rights issue shall be governed by Section 81(1) and if it is for a value of 50 lakhs or more, then ICDR regulations also be complied with.

Bonus issue can be made only when all the shares are fully paid and cannot be made out of revaluation reserves.

A preferential issue by a listed company shall in addition to compliance of Section 81(1A) of Companies Act, also comply with Chapter VII of ICDR Regulations and fix a price higher of 26 weeks & 2 weeks high & low preceding the relevant date. If preferential allotment is made only to QIB's, then it can also come under Chapter VII of ICDR Regulations titled as QIP, which is priced at an average weekly high & low of 2 weeks preceding the relevant date.

ESOP is a benefit or right given to employees of a listed company under a scheme which shall be compliant of ESOP guidelines. The vesting of ESOP shall take place only after an year of granting, then it can be exercised at the option of the employees.

Refer Module IV book for detailed provisions.

Equity Listing Agreement Summary

The Summary of Equity Listing Agreement Compliances as per NSE Compliance Calendar:

QUARTERLY COMPLIANCES

• Clause 35 - Shareholding Pattern	**Within 21 days from quarter end**
• Clause 41 - Financial Results	**Within 45 days from quarter end**
• Clause 49 - Corporate Governance	**Within 15 days from quarter end**
• Reconciliation of Share Capital Audit	**Within 30 days from quarter end**

OTHER COMPLIANCE REQUIREMENTS

Compliance Clauses/Regulations

- **Clause 16 – Notice for Corporate Action**

↳ The Company is required to close its transfer books at least once a year at the time of the Annual General Meeting if they have not been otherwise closed at any time during the year.

↳ The Company must ensure that there is a gap of at least 30 days between 2 book closure and/or record date.

↳ The Company shall give an advance notice of at least 7 working days (Excluding the date of the intimation and record date/book closure start date) to the Stock Exchange for corporate actions (Book closure/Record date) fixed for the purpose of corporate benefits like mergers, de-mergers, split , bonus, dividend, rights etc.

- **Clause 19 – Notice for Board Meeting to consider the prescribed matters**

↳ The Company shall give an advance notice of at least 2 working days (Excluding the date of the intimation and date of the meeting) to Stock Exchange, of board meeting fixed for recommendation or declaration of a dividend or convertible debentures or of debentures carrying a right to subscribe to equity shares or the passing over of the dividend or the issue of right or proposal for buy back of securities is to be considered. Further, the company will recommend or declare all dividend and / or cash bonuses at least five days before commencement of the book-closure or record date fixed for the purpose.

- **Clause 20 – Outcome of Board Meeting held under Clause 19**

↳ The Company has to intimate the outcome of the board meeting (as intimated under clause 19)immediately on the day of board meeting once concluded.

↳ Further, the company shall intimate to the Exchange the date on which dividend shall be paid/dispatched.

- **Clause 20A – Declaration of Dividend**

↳ The Company has to declare and disclose the dividend on per share basis only.

- **Clause 22 – Credit of Bonus Shares**

↳ The company shall intimate to the Exchange the date on which bonus shares, declared, if any, would be credited/dispatched.

- **Clause 30 – Change in Directors/Auditors**

↳ The company has to intimate to the Stock Exchange:

a. of any change in the Issuer's directorate by death, resignation, removal or otherwise;

b. of any change of Managing Director, Managing Agents or Secretaries and Treasurers;

c. of any change of Auditors appointed to audit the books and accounts of the Issuer.

- **Clause 31 – Submission of copies of Annual Report/Proceedings of AGM/EGM**

↳ The Company has to submit to the Stock Exchange :

a. six copies of the Statutory and Directors' Annual Reports, Balance Sheets and Profits & Loss Accounts and of all periodical and special reports as soon as they are issued and one copy each to all the recognized Stock Exchanges in India.

b. copy of the proceedings at all Annual and Extraordinary General Meetings.

- **Clause 32 – Disclosures in Annual Report/Change of name**

↳ The Company is required to make the following disclosures in the Annual Report :

↳ To publish Consolidated Financial Statements in the annual report in addition to the individual financial statements. Further, Audit of Consolidated Financial Statements by the statutory auditors of the company and the filing of Consolidated Financial Statements audited by the statutory auditors of the company with the stock exchanges shall be mandatory.

↳ Disclosures in compliance with the Accounting Standard on "Related Party Disclosures".

↳ Cash flow statement along with the Balance Sheet and Profit and Loss Account.

↳ All listed companies which decide to change their names shall be required to comply with the following conditions:

a. A time period of at least 1 year should have elapsed from the last name change.

b. At least 50% of its total revenue in the preceding 1 year period should have been accounted for by the new activity suggested by the new name.

- **Clause 33 – Amendment in Memorandum of Association and Articles of Association**

↳ The Company is required to submit to the Stock Exchange certified copy of amended Memorandum and Articles of Association of the company

- **Clause 36 – Disclosure of Price-Sensitive Information**

↳ The Company has to intimate to the Stock Exchange about the material events which will have a bearing on the performance / operations of the company as well as price sensitive information both at the time of occurrence of the event and subsequently after the cessation of the event.

- **Clause 38 – Listing Fees**

↳ The Company is required to pay Annual Listing Fee on or before April 30 computed on the basis of the capital of the Issuer as on March 31.

- **Clause 41 – Notice for Board Meeting and other submissions w.r.t Financial Results**

↳ The Company shall give an advance notice of at least 7 clear calendar days (Excluding the date of the intimation and date of the meeting) to the Stock Exchange, of board meeting fixed to consider financial results.

↳ In case of unaudited financial results, the company is required to submit Limited Review Report within 45 days from the end of the quarter.

Note:

- The gap between previous Book Closure/Record Date (BC/RD) and current BC/RD should not be less than 30 days
- The company will recommend or declare all dividend and / or cash bonuses at least 5 days before commencement of the book-closure or record date fixed for the purpose
- Saturdays, Sundays and Stock Exchange Holidays ignored for calculating no. of days

Particulars on Corporate Governance provisions	Clause of Listing agreement	Compliance Status Yes/ No	Remarks
I. Board of Directors	49(I)		
(A) Composition of Board	49 (IA)		
(B) Non-executive Directors' compensation & disclosures	49 (IB)		
(C) Other provisions as to Board and Committees	49 (IC)		
(D) Code of Conduct	49 (ID)		
II. Audit Committee	49 (II)		
(A) Qualified & Independent Audit Committee	49 (IIA)		
(B) Meeting of Audit Committee	49 (IIB)		
(C) Powers of Audit Committee	49 (IIC)		
(D) Role of Audit Committee	49 II(D)		
(E) Review of Information by Audit Committee	49 (IIE)		
III. Subsidiary Companies	49 (III)		
IV. Disclosures	49 (IV)		

(A) Basis of related party transactions	49 (IV A)		
(B) Disclosure of Accounting Treatment	49 (IV B)		
(C) Board Disclosures	49 (IV C)		
(D) Proceeds from public issues, rights issues, preferential issues etc.	49 (IV D)		
(E) Remuneration of Directors	49 (IV E)		
(F) Management	49 (IV F)		
(G) Shareholders	49 (IV G)		
V. CEO/CFO Certification	49 (V)		
VI. Report on Corporate Governance	49 (VI)		
VII. Compliance	49 (VII)		

FOREIGN COMPANIES/COMPANIES INCORPORATED OUTSIDE INDIA

(Part XI of Companies Act: Sections 592 – 602)

This is for Companies which are incorporated in foreign countries but have offices and places of business in India are described as foreign companies. Say for instance, the branch office & liaison office as discussed under Foreign Direct Investments. For foreign companies, Global Location Number (GLN) is allotted. The Directors of foreign companies NEED NOT have DIN and the Authorised representative NEED NOT register DSC.

However, if 50% or more of the paid-up share capital of a foreign company having an established place of business in India is held by one or more citizens of India or bodies corporate incorporated in India, whether singly or in the aggregate, THEN such company shall comply with such of the provisions of the Act, AS IF IT WERE a company incorporated in India.

Documents to be delivered to the Registrar by Foreign Companies in e-form 44 (has a prioritised approval):

(a) a certified copy of the charter, statutes or memorandum and articles of the company or other instruments constituting or defining the constitution of the company, and if the instrument is not in English language certified translation thereof; (b) the full address of the registered or principal office of the company; (c) a list of the directors and secretary of the company with complete particulars;
If above things are altered, file a RETURN in e-form 49 on/before 31st January of the Year
(d) the name and address or the names and addresses of some one or more persons resident in India authorised to accept on behalf of the company service of process and any notices or other documents required to be served on the company, and (e) the full address of the office of the company in India, which is to be deemed its principal place of business in India.
If above things are altered, file a RETURN in e-form 52 within 1 month of alteration

Accounts of Foreign Company (with its subsidiaries) to be laid in General meeting & given to RoC.

Obligation to State Name of Foreign Company in Name Boards & Stationeries in English & Local language along with the Country of Incorporation of the company

Service on Foreign Company: To the name and address of a person resident in India OR if it has not been given to RoC or if at any time all the persons whose names and addresses have been so delivered are dead or have ceased to reside or refuse to accept services on behalf of the foreign company, then the document may be served on the company itself by leaving it at or sending it by post to, any place of business established by the company in India.

Effect of Company's Failure to Comply with the Provisions of Part XI of the Companies Act,1956 :

Under Section 599 if a foreign company fails to comply with any of the foregoing provisions of Part XI, such a failure will not affect the validity of any contract, dealing or transaction entered into by the company, it will be liable to be sued in respect thereof. But it cannot bring any suit, claim any set off, make any counter-claim or institute any legal proceeding in respect of any such contract, dealing or transaction until it has complied with the provisions of that Part.

Others:

The provision of Sections 124 to 145, 159, 209, 234 to 246, 397 to 399 & winding up shall apply mutatis mutandis (as such with necessary changes) to Companies Incorporate Outside India. It shall also file the Form Annual Return u/s. 600 of Companies Act.

It is one of the most important chapters from the exam point of view. Insider is a person who has inside information of company. This SEBI regulation imposes restrictions on using inside information outside affecting others. Insider trading regulations are applicable only to a listed company. This regulation shall be read in detail. Further it is important for the Governance portion in Governance, Business Ethics & Sustainability also.

Insider Trading

SEBI (Prohibition of Insider Trading) Regulations, 1992

Regulation 2(c) - Connected Person: (connected 6 months prior to insider trading)

Any person who is a DIRECTOR or DEEMED DIRECTOR (accustomed to act) OR Occupies the position of OFFICER or EMPLOYEE or POSITION having professional or business relationship with the company and who may REASONABLY EXPECTED to have access to unpublished price sensitive information (UPSI).

Regulation 2(e) – Insider:

- Any person who is/was CONNECTED with company or is person DEEMED TO BE CONNECTED with company AND who is reasonably expected to have access to UPSI of securities OR
- Any person who has received or had access to such UPSI.

Regulation 2(h) - Person deemed to be connected:

- Companies under the same management within the meaning of section 370(1B) or 372(11) of Companies Act OR Section 2(g) of the MRTP Act, 1969.
- Intermediary u/s. 12 of SEBI Act read with Regulations
- Employees of Intermediary or member/employee of Trustees or AMC of MF who have a FIDUCIARY relationship with company
- Member/employee of Board of Public Financial Institutions
- Official/employee of self regulatory organization recognized (SRO)
- Relative of ABOVE or CONNECTED person/their relative or Banker of company OR an association in which SUCH persons hold MORE THAN 10%.

Regulation 2(ha) - Price Sensitive Information (PSI):

INFORMATION directly or indirectly related to a company and IF PUBLISHED is likely to MATERIALLY affect the price of the securities of the company.

The following are DEEMED to be PSIs:

- Periodical financial results of the company or intended declaration of dividend
- Issue or buy back of securities or Major expansion plans
- Amalgamations, merger, takeovers
- Disposal of the whole or substantial part of the undertaking
- significant changes in policies, plans or operations of the company.

Regulation 2(k) - UNPUBLISHED:

Information not published by the company or its agents and is NOT SPECIFIC in nature.

PROHIBITION ON DEALING, COMMUNICATING OR COUNSELING

- An insider shall NOT deal in securities of a company listed on a stock exchange when in possession of UPSI.
- An insider shall NOT communicate, counsel or procure any UPSI to any person while in possession of UPSI deal in securities.
- No Company shall deal in securities of ANOTHER company or ASSOCIATE of that other company while in possession of UPSI. In such cases, the following DEFENCES can be taken to prove otherwise,

1. The decision to enter into such transaction made by a person OTHER THAN officer/employee of company.
2. The company has systems and procedures (like Chinese Wall) or arrangements in place that DEMARCATE the activities in such a way that the person who entered into the transaction cannot have access to information in possession of the officer or employee of the company.
3. No such information was communicated and no such advice was given.
4. Acquisition of shares of listed company as per SEBI Takeover Code.

Insider on contravention of above (Prohibition on dealing or communicating or counselling) shall be GUILTY of insider trading and a penalty of 25 crores OR 3 times, the Profits made out of the same whichever is HIGHER may be levied.

INVESTIGATION

SEBI may make inquiries and appoint Investigating Authorities or Qualified Auditors to inspect books, records of insider/other person based on complaint or on its own motion after giving a reasonable notice and it shall be the DUTY of every director, proprietor, partner, officer & employee to give reasonable ASSISTANCE during investigation.

The Investigating Authority will submit a REPORT to SEBI; then SEBI will communicate FINDINGS; such person shall reply WITHIN 21 days.

Then SEBI may initiate CRIMINAL prosecutions or issue directions as per Regulation 11.

Regulation 13 – Disclosure of Number of Shares/Voting Rights:

Director or Officer or Substantial Shareholders	→→→→→→→→→→→→→ In Form A, B, C, D (as per Schedule III) within 2 working days of allotment or acquisition or becoming director/officer or or promoter/promoter group as the case may be	Submit to Listed Companies	→→→→→→→→→→ In Form A, B, C, D (as per Schedule III) within 2 working days of receipt of information	Intimate to Stock Exchange

Types of Disclosures:

INITIAL DISCLOSURE	CONTINUAL DISCLOSURE
Form A: by any person holding atleast 5%	**Form C:** by any person holding atleast 5% or change in holding/ voting exceeding 2%
Form B: by any director/officer or dependants or promoter/promoter group [as per SEBI Takeover Code] disclosing shares or voting rights or position taken in derivatives by director/officer or dependants	**Form D:** by any director/officer or dependants or or promoter/ promoter group when change is MORE THAN, lowest of • Rs.5 lakhs • 25,000 shares • 1% of holding or voting.

In a case, Shri. Dilip Pendse was the Managing Director of Tata Finance Ltd (TFL) and the Director of Nishkalp Investment and Trading Co Ltd (a wholly owned subsidiary of TFL). The unpublished price sensitive information was the loss of Rs.79.37 crores suffered by Nishkalp, which was published on 30th April 2001. But by then Smt. Anuradha Pendse (relative of Shri Pendse) & her company Nalini Properties and Dr. Anjali Beke (a close friend & associate of Shri Pendse) & her company Anjudi Properties has sold 40,000 and 2,30,000 shares respectively. It was alleged that on account of the sale, unjust profit accrued to the entites and SEBI barred those persons from accessing securities market for 5 years.

SEBI's allegation of Insider trading against Hindustan UniLever (HUL) [which it escaped] for purchasing eight lakh shares of Brooke Bond Lipton India (BBLIL) from Unit Trust of India a month before the merger of the two companies. HLL was a deemed connected person and also had price sensitive information which would have affected the market price of shares. However, the information was published (prior to acquisition through media), even though not confirmed or authenticated by the company. Hence, SAT ruled SEBI had not established in its order the gravity of the case, so as to merit prosecution!!!

Raj Rajaratnam and Insider Trading

In October 2009, the Justice Department charged Raj Rajaratnam, a New York hedge fund manager, with 14 counts of securities fraud and conspiracy. Rajaratnam, who was found guilty on all 14 counts on May 11, 2011, had allegedly cultivated a network of executives at, among others, Intel, McKinsey, IBM, and Goldman Sachs. These insiders provided him with material nonpublic information. Preet Bharara, the Government's attorney, argued in the case that Raj Rajaratnam had made approximately $60 million in illicit profits from inside information. Raj Rajaratnam was the 35th person to be convicted of insider trading of 47 people charged since 2010. This effort to prosecute insider trading has been marked by more aggressive tactics such as wiretapping to prosecute insider-trading cases, which might otherwise be difficult to prove.

Raj Rajaratnam was the Sri-Lankan manager of the hedge fund Galleon Group, which managed $6.5 billion at its height. Rajat Gupta is a former director at Goldman Sachs and head of McKinsey consulting. He also served on the board of Procter & Gamble. Warren Buffet is the CEO of Berkshire Hathaway, an investment company.

On September 23, 2008, Warren Buffet agreed to pay $5 billion for preferred shares of Goldman Sachs and this information was not announced until 6 PM but before then Raj Rajaratnam bought 175,000 shares of Goldman Sachs and when the information came to knowledge, Rajaratnam sold his shares, for a profit of $900,000.

Rajat Gupta had called Rajaratnam immediately after the board meeting at which Warren Buffet's infusion had been announced, and told him of the money Goldman expected to receive. This information was material to the price of Goldman stock, thus inciting Rajaratnam to make the trade, something he would otherwise not have done.

POLICY ON DISCLOSURES AND INTERNAL PROCEDURE FOR PREVENTION OF INSIDER TRADING

All listed companies and organizations (including intermediaries, SROs, recognized stock exchanges, public financial institution, professional firms assisting listed companies) associated with the securities market shall frame & comply with CODE OF INTERNAL PROCEDURE (as per Schedule I) and abide by CODE OF CORPORATE DISCLOSURE PRACTICES (as per Schedule II) and adopt appropriate mechanism & procedures (like, Whistle Blower policy) to ENFORCE it.

CODE OF INTERNAL PROCEDURE (SCHEDULE I): Every listed company and intermediaries (for their & clients securities) shall comply with this 2 parts,

- Part A: Model Code of Conduct for Prevention of Insider Trading for Listed Companies
- Part B: Model Code of Conduct for Prevention of Insider Trading for Other Entities.

It also encompasses the following,

1. COMPLIANCE OFFICER: A SENIOR LEVEL EMPLOYEE may be appointed as compliance officer to report to MD/CEO and such person shall be responsible for policies & procedures to preserve PSI, pre-clearance & monitoring of trades, implementation of code of conduct under supervision of board; also maintain LIST of designated employees & declarations from directors or employees for 3 years and clarify regarding Insider Trading Regulations & Code of Conduct.

   DESIGNATED EMPLOYEE includes officers comprising top 3 tiers of management or designated employees to whom trading restrictions shall be applicable.

2. TRADING WINDOW: It is the trading period. It shall be CLOSED for employees or directors or designated employees at the time of considering items which are "DEEMED to be PSIs"; it shall be OPENED after 24 hours. When trading window is closed, the said persons shall NOT deal with company's securities, EXCEPT for exercising options under ESOPs.

3. **PRE-CLEARANCE OF TRADE:** This is a case where the said persons & their DEPENDANTS can get a PRIOR permission of company to deal with securities by following PRE-CLEARANCE procedure (i.e) by making an APPLICATION to Compliance Officer intimating his INTENTION to deal with details and executing an UNDERTAKING that,

   - Said persons does NOT have access or has NOT received any PSI **till** signing this undertaking
   - If such person receive PSI **after** signing undertaking but before dealing, then dealing shall be made only after such information becomes PUBLIC
   - Has complied with Code of Conduct & has made full & true disclosure.

   Pre-cleared transaction shall be executed WITHIN 1 week, else fresh clearance is required.

4. RESTRICTIONS: All directors or officers or designated employees shall NOT buy the securities sold or sell the securities bought in secondary market WITHIN 6 months and also NOT to enter into derivative transactions of company's shares. In case of IPO to said persons, the holding period shall be 30 days, unless waived by Compliance Officer.

5. NEED TO KNOW basis: PSI is to be handled on "need to know" basis, i.e., UPSI should be disclosed only to those within the company who NEED the information to discharge their duty.

6. **CHINESE WALL:** to SEPARATE areas of organization & SEGREGATE employees,

OVER THE WALL is permitted (i.e., confidential information may be given) in exc eptional cases on NEED TO KNOW basis after intimating Compliance Officer

7. **RESTRICTED/GREY LIST:** This is a LIST of transactions maintained by Compliance Officer which is HIGHLY CONFIDENTIAL in nature, where TRADING is restricted to MONITOR the Chinese Wall. The list may contain the following,

- Trading in client securities by Intermediaries
- Securities dealt on behalf of clients or MFs
- Securities of listed companies, when an organization handles assignment or makes project appraisal or credit rating of listed company

Kindly note, securities in this LIST will be BLOCKED for dealing by designated employees/directors/partners at the time of PRE-CLEARANCE itself.

1. There is an alleged act of insider trading on the part of Harsh who was the Finance Manager of Master Mind Limited a listed company. However, he left the company 100 days prior to the alleged act of insider trading. It is contended that in the instant case, Harsh cannot be treated as a ' connected person' as he had left the organisation prior to the act of insider trading. Do you agree? Answer with reasons. (2008 – June)

   See Regulation 2(c) above. Further, Section 2(30) of the Act , 1956 provides inclusive definition of the term officer' according to which "officer" includes any director , manager or secretary or any other person in accordance with whose directors or instructions the board of directors or any one or more of the directors is or are accustomed to act

   In the given case , harsh , finance manager comes within the purview of section 2(30) i.e. officers left the company 100 days prior to the alleges act insider trading since he was finance manager [being 'officer'in accordance with section 2(30)] in the company 100 days before happening of alleged act of insider trading i.e. within the time limit of six months as specified in Act , he can be treated as connected person

2. Explain the external reporting requirements by Compliance Officer as laid down under the SEBI (Prohibition of Insider Trading) Regulations, 1992. (2009 June)

CODE OF CORPORATE DISCLOSURE PRACTICES FOR PREVENTION OF INSIDER TRADING (Schedule II)

It is a policy to ensure timely & adequate disclosure of PSIs which shall be overseen by a SENIOR OFFICER of listed company such as Compliance Officer; such person is responsible to ensure COMPLIANCE of this regulation, disclosure of PSIs to stock exchanges, analysts, shareholders, media & educating staff on disclosure policies and procedure. The following points may be considered,

- Designate a person to give approval before disclosure of information who shall also decide whether Public Announcement is necessary for verifying/denying rumours.
- There shall be timely & adequate disclosure of shareholdings or ownership and changes in ownership.
- Only PUBLIC INFORMATION shall be given to analyst or brokers or research persons or large investors like institutions; instead simultaneously make the information public; such information may be made before 2 company's official and preferably be RECORDED.
- UNANTICIPATED QUESTIONS may be taken on notice and a considered response given later after Public Announcement.
- All the information which is disseminated as above shall be made available in WEBSITE of the company and Stock Exchange should also ensure immediate display of INSTANT information in the WEBSITE of the stock exchange.

The various types of CODES given under this chapter are much relevant for the portion on Governance. The compliances which shall be made under this chapter by filing forms are relevant for the Due Diligence portion also. The concepts like Chinese walls, inside areas, trading windows shall also be understood in detail for Company Secretarial practice.

This chapter summarises the basic provisions of Limited Liability Partnerships (LLP) which is a new form of entity which can be started in India. It gives the protection of a Body Corporate.

Higlights of Limited Liability Partnership (LLP) Act, 2008

LIMITED LIABILITY PARTNERSHIP (LLP) ACT, 2008

LLP is a form of organization or a business vehicle which blends the advantages of Partnership and Company SANS its disadvantages. A comparison chart can make one understand better,

PARTICULARS	PARTNERSHIP	COMPANY	LLP
Governing law	The Indian Partnership Act, 1932	The Companies Act, 1956	Limited Liability Partnership Act, 2008
Formation, Registration, periodical compliances & dissolution	Immediate formation & registration is optional. No periodically compliances except audit for Income tax purpose. Non-statutory formalities for dissolution.	Lengthy prescribed procedure for formation, compliances & dissolution to be followed & registration is mandatory	Simple prescribed procedure for formation, compliances & dissolution to be followed & registration is mandatory
Body Corporate having perpetual succession & can own/dispose property	NO	Yes	Yes
Assets & Liabilities	Assets are owned jointly by partners whereas liability is unlimited	Assets are owned by company & liability is limited unless it is an unlimited company	Assets are owned by LLPs & liability is limited EXCEPT where fraud stands proved
Maximum number of partners/members	10 in case of banking & 20 for others	50 members in case of Private company & No limit for public company	No limit
Public shareholding & Public deposit	Not permitted	Only a public company can accept	Not permitted
Key Managerial Personnel	Not applicable	Shall appoint Managing Director & Company Secretary if the Paid-up capital is 5 crores or more	Should appoint & to have at all times 2 or more DESIGNATED partners, out of whom atleast 1 shall be resident in India

Resignation	Retirement of partner provisions of the Act will apply which is cumbersome	Directors can resign subject to Articles of Association	Act has enabled quicker resignation & has provided what the resigning partners will get.

Describe the basic features of limited liability partnership (LLP) and distinguish it from normal partnership (2009 – June)

The unique features of LLPs are as follows,

1. LLP Act has 81 sections divided into 14 chapters & 4 schedules and LLP Rules consists of 40 rules with 29 forms and another 310 rules for winding up. The Act got the assent of President on 7th January 2009.
2. Designated Partners (DP) are responsible for all acts, matters and things as are required to be complied as per the LLP Act, LLP Rules and LLP Agreement including filing of documents, returns etc. and any vacancy in such office shall be filled within 30 days. If in any case such vacancy is not filled and there are NO two DPs, then EACH partner shall be deemed as DP. Every DP has to obtain a Designated Partner Identification Number (DPIN). If a person has been allotted DPIN, the said DPIN shall also be used as DIN for all purposes under Limited Liability Partnership Act, 2008 and VICE VERSA. If a person has been allotted both DIN and DPIN, his DPIN will stand cancelled and his DIN hereon will be sued for both purposes.

3. The mutual rights and duties of Partners will be decided by LLP Agreement or Schedule I to the Act.
4. **A standard LLP agreement** should provide for the following,

a. Induction of partners;

b. Responsibility for day-to-day affairs & operation of bank account

c. Acquisition or disposal of assets

d. Specify the category of partner (whether working partner or not), provide name of working partners, their duties & responsibilities, tenure of appointment and components of remuneration

e. Contribution to capital, remuneration & share of profit to partners; also specify whether capital of partners carries any interest

f. Matters or transactions requiring absolute majority of partners

g. Liability of partner acting WITHOUT consent of LLP or acting in competition with LLP or acting in fraud

h. Removal of partners

i. Dispute Resolution.

5. Existing partnership firms, private limited companies and unlisted public limited companies can be CONVERTED into LLPs according to Schedule II, III & IV. Further LLPs has the facility of merger, demerger, compromise & arrangements.
6. Every partner of LLP is an agent of LLP and NOT of other partners. A partner of LLP would be personally liable for his (& not any other partners) wrongful act or omission.
7. **WHISTLE BLOWING:** A partner/employee who willingly cooperates and provides useful information during investigation or helps in conviction of partner/employee will subject to REDUCED PENALTY or even WAIVER of penalty.
8. Audit of LLP will be mandatory only if the turnover exceeds Rs.40 lakhs in a Financial Year or contribution exceeds Rs. 25 lakhs.

9. Every LLP has to file STATEMENT OF ACCOUNTS & SOLVENCY to Registrar within 30 days of the close of 6 months from Financial Year; replace 30 with 60 days for filing of ANNUAL RETURNS.

10. Partnership Act will have NO application under this law whereas Central Government may by notification make Companies Act applicable to LLPs.

11. Reserve name of LLP in Form 1, file incorporation document in Form 2, file LLP agreement in Form 3 and file partnership details to Registrar in Form 4.

12. LLP has a centralized Registrar of LLP and it is governed by Ministry of Corporate Affairs.

13. Company Law Board (CLB) has the power to direct an LLP or its Designated Partners or its Partners to make good any default in complying with the provisions of this Act or to request the Registrar to amend & resubmit a document.

14. CLB on its own or on application by 1/5th of total partners can declare that investigation ought to be conducted and then Central Government shall order investigation.

15. Any orders of refusal to convert into an LLP passed by Registrar are appealable to CLB.

TAXATION OF LLP

With regards to taxation, LLPs are treated as Partnerships BUT LLPs cannot enjoy the benefit of DEEMING TAXATION u/s. 44AD of Income Tax under Profits & Gains from business/profession. The Return of Income shall be signed by Designated Partner. In case of any taxes DUE in previous year which CANNOT be recovered, then NOTWITHSTANDING LLP Act, every LLP partner in previous year is JOINTLY & SEVERALLY liable UNLESS he proves that non-recovery cannot be attributed to any gross neglect, misfeasance or breach of duty on his part in relation to the affairs of LLP. Kindly notes, share of profits of partners are NOT liable to Dividend Tax & also Minimum Alternate Tax is NOT applicable to LLPs.

LLPs for PROFESSIONALS of ICSI

The Company Secretaries Regulation, 1982 permits the Practising Company Secretary (PCS) to become PASSIVE PARTNER (means cannot be Designated Partner or take part in Management) of LLP, the objects of which include carrying out NON-ATTESTATION SERVICES (which are not attestation services) whether or not the PCS holds substantial interest (means 25% of profits) in that LLP.

"ATTESTATION SERVICES" include services which require signing any certificate, document, report or any other statements relating thereto on behalf of a Company Secretary in Practice or a firm of such Company Secretaries in his or its professional capacity or which require signing anything that is required to be signed by a Company Secretary in practice.

If such LLP is engaged in ANY OTHER BUSINESS then he can become PASSIVE PARTNER WITHOUT holding substantial interest in the same.

Drafting LLP agreement also gains significance for the Drafting portion of your syllabus. Hence remember the basic provisions under this Act while drafting. LLP provisions are almost similar to Companies Act but it is simpler & faster.

The Institute of Company Secretaries of India (ICSI) has set up Secretarial Standards which are currently recommendatory in nature and once it's recognized it would become mandatory. Even Companies Bill, 2009 recognises the same. These standards lay down a set of principles which companies are expected to adopt and adhere to, in discharging their responsibilities. The Secretarial Standards Board (SSB) of ICSI issues the said standards and its functions are clarifying issues arising out of the Secretarial standards, issuing guidance notes and reviewing/ updating at periodic intervals. Guidance notes are issued to facilitate the corporate sector to comply with Secretarial Standards.

Higlights of Secretarial Standards

Secretarial Standards are the policy documents related to various aspects of secretarial practices in the corporate sector. These standards lay down the set of principles which companies are expected to adopt and adhere to in discharging their responsibilities. It is supplement to existing laws and regulations and not a substitute as such

PROCEDURE FOR ISSUING SECRETARIAL STANDARDS

The procedure as depicted in the following flowchart is adopted for formulating and issuing Secretarial Standards:

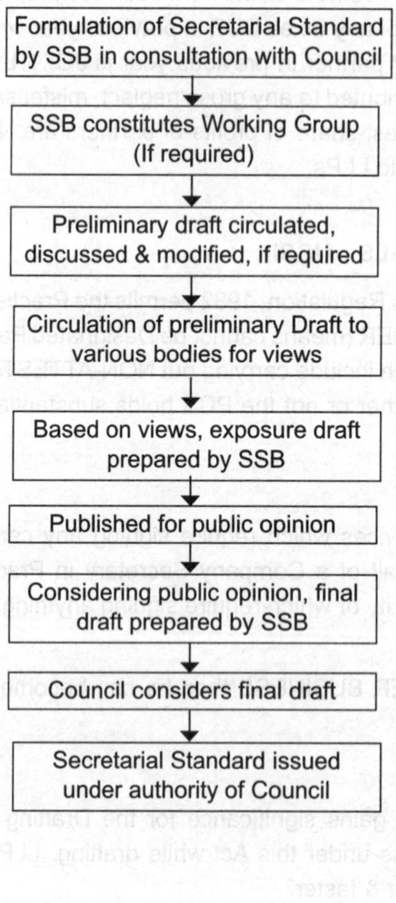

VARIOUS SECRETARIAL STANDARDS:

The Institute of Company Secretaries of India, acknowledging this need has issued ten Secretarial Standards on topics namely:

- Meetings of the Board of Directors (SS-1)
- General Meetings (SS-2)
- Dividend (SS-3)
- Registers and Records (SS-4)
- Minutes (SS-5)
- Transmission of Shares and Debentures (SS-6)
- Passing Resolutions by Circulation (SS-7)
- Affixing of Common Seal (SS-8)
- Forfeiture of Shares (SS-9)
- Board of Directors Report (SS-10)

Secretarial Standards (as per Clause 118 of Companies Bill, 2011)

The much awaited recognition to the Secretarial Standards has been given in the Bill. The Companies Bill makes it mandatory for every company to comply with such Secretarial Standards as may be prescribed with respect to General Meetings and Board Meetings. This is a landmark turning point in respect of standardization and harmonization of Secretarial Standards.

In this chapter, only the very basic essence of the standard is given. While answering the question, remember to club the following points with the provisions of Companies Act, 1956.

SS-1 Board Meeting

Notice with day, date, time & venue to be given to every director	• Notice at least 15 days before the date of meeting by hand or post or facsimile or email. • Agenda to be sent atleast 7 days before meeting
Time gap between meetings	maximum interval of 120 days between two meetings
Attendance Register	It shall be maintained carrying signature of directors attending the meeting.
Preservation	Notice/Agenda to be preserved for 10 years.

SS-2 General Meeting

Notice shall be in writing at the address in India/abroad	• To be given to every Members, Directors, Auditors, the Practising Company Secretary who has given the Compliance Certificate and Debenture Trustees, if any • should be sent at least 25 days in advance of the Meeting.
Chairman	• Should explain the objective and implications of each Resolution before the Resolution is put to vote. • Shall chair only the disinterested business (disinterested business to be chaired by Vice Chairman).
Rescinding of resolutions	Resolutions should not be rescinded other than by a Resolution passed at a subsequent Meeting.

Reading of reports	Auditors report & Compliance certificate shall be read at the meeting.
Distribution of gifts	No gifts, gift coupons, or cash in lieu of gifts should be distributed.
Preservation	• Minutes to be preserved permanently • Notice should be preserved for 3 years.

SS-3 Dividends

Dividends	• should not be declared out of the Securities Premium Account or the Capital Redemption Reserve Account or Revaluation Reserve or Amalgamation Reserve or out of profit on re-issue of forfeited shares or out of profit earned prior to the incorporation of the company. • Should be paid in cash, not in kind. • Calls in arrears and any other sum due from a Member may be adjusted against Dividend payable to the Member.
Preservation	Dividend warrants returned by the Bank, after payment thereof, and the Dividend Registers should be preserved for a period of 8 years.
Annual Report	• should disclose the total amount lying in the Unpaid Dividend Account of the company in respect of the last seven years. • Disclose the amount transferred to IEPF.

SS-4 Registers & records

It discusses the maintenance, closure, inspection, authentication and preservation of the prescribed (given under the Chapter called Registers & Inspection) registers for the smooth, efficient and systematic functioning of the company. The Information Technology Act, 2000 permits maintenance of registers & records in electronic mode but it should be done in accordance with Companies Act, 1956.

SS-5 Minutes

Minutes of Board Meeting	• Mention the invitees, if any. • Record the directors dissent • Record that interested director did not participate or vote. • The date of entering the Minutes in Minutes book should be specified. • Extracts of the Minutes should be given only after the Minutes have been duly signed. Within 15 days from the date of the Meeting the draft Minutes should be circulated to all the members of the Board or the Committee, for their comments, which should be sent within 7 days of receipt of draft minutes.
Preservation of minutes of Board meeting & General meeting	• Minute book should be preserved permanently • In case of merger, amalgamation, etc transferee company to preserve minutes of transferor company permanently.
Minutes of General Meeting	• should be written in third person and in past tense. • Should state that quorum is present and number of persons attended on their own or by proxy. • The date of entering the Minutes in Minutes book should be specified. • Extracts of the Minutes should be given only after the Minutes have been duly signed.

SS-6 Transmission

- The word "transmission" means devolution of title to Shares otherwise than by transfer.
- On transmission of Shares, the person to whom the Shares are transmitted becomes the registered shareholder of the company and is entitled to all rights and subject to all liabilities attached to the Shares.
- In case the deceased held Shares in more than one company, the legal heir(s)/Nominee has to correspond with each of the companies by submitting relevant documents, alongwith the share certificates to effect transmission of Shares.

SS-7 Circular Resolution

- A Draft Resolution should be sent with the necessary papers to ALL **(including interested & in abroad)** Directors by hand, or post or by facsimile or by email or by any other electronic mode.
- Circulation Resolutions shall be passed only for urgent matters.
- The Resolution should be deemed to have been passed on the date on which it is signed and dated as approved by all the Directors then in India, being not less than the Quorum, or on the date on which it is approved by the majority of the Directors entitled to vote on the Resolution, whichever is earlier.
- Such Resolutions to be noted in next Board Meeting and recorded in Minutes.

SS-8 Common Seal

- It shall be kept under custody of officers authorized by Board.
- A new official seal in place of an existing official seal should be adopted by a resolution of the Board for use outside India and the impression of which shall be recorded in the Minutes.
- The person affixing the official seal shall sign and write on the deed or other instrument, the date and place at which it is affixed.

SS-9 Forfeiture of shares

- Date of forfeiture not being earlier than the expiry of 21 days from the date of posting the notice of forfeiture.
- The date of approval by the Board is the date of forfeiture.
- The declaration by official authorized by the board shall be conclusive evidence of forfeiture as against all persons claiming to be entitled to the shares of the company which have been forfeited.
- There should be a reference to the forfeiture of shares in the report of the directors and in the Register of Members.
- The Board can annul (cancel) the forfeiture by passing a resolution before the reissue of forfeited shares.

SS-10 Board of Directors Report

As a good corporate practice, the Directors Report should also contain disclosures with regard to:

i. the names of directors retiring by rotation and whether or not they other themselves for reappointment;

ii. casual vacancies occurred during the period by reason of death or resignation, and names of directors who filled such vacancies.

iii. appointment of additional directors/alternate directory

iv. nominations and withdrawal of nominees;

v. name of the director, if any, nominated by small shareholders;

vi. name of retiring Auditors and /or Practising Company Secretary and whether or not they are eligible and willing for reappointment;

vii. name of Auditors and/or Practising Company Secretary, if any, who resigned during the year;

viii. change in auditor during the year;

ix. appointment of relatives of directors to an office or place of profit;

x. reasons for delay, if any, in holding Annual General Meeting.

GUIDANCE NOTES ISSUED by ICSI:

To facilitate the corporate sector to comply with the Secretarial Standards, the SSB also formulates Guidance Notes. The Institute has issued Guidance Notes on:

– Meetings of the Board of Directors

– General Meetings

– Passing of the Resolution by Postal Ballot

– Dividend

– Buy-Back of Securities

– Board's Report

– Corporate Governance Certificate (Clause 49 of the Listing Agreement)

– Preferential Issue of Shares

– Related Party transactions – Listing of Corporate debt.

SSB has also brought out a Consultative Paper on Meetings of the Board of Directors through tele/video-conferencing.

1. Mention the scope and main functions of the Secretarial Standards Board. (2007 – June)

2. Name the secretarial standards issued by the Institute of Company Secretaries of India (2008 – June)

3. Bring out the salient aspects of Secretarial Standard – 3 on dividends in respect of (i) interim dividend; and (ii) unpaid / unclaimed dividend. (2009 – June)

4. Answer the following with reference to Secretarial Standard – 7 on passing of Board resolution by circulation process:

(i) Who is authorised to decide that certain resolutions (other than those specified in section 292) are to be taken up for consideration by circulation as against in a meeting? (2010 – June)

(ii) What procedure is to be followed for passing a resolution by circulation? Are interested directors eligible to receive the proposed resolution and related papers?

(iii) How is a proposed (circulated) resolution considered approved or not?

Secretarial Standards by the corporate sector will lead to good corporate governance practices, making them comparable with best practices in the world. There is a need to realize this importance of Secretarial Standards and implement it for good corporate governance practices for the survival of corporations and therefore the entire economy. There are many corporates who publish their Annual Reports and conducts their corporates in compliance of Secretarial Standards. Do intimate ICSI, if you follow secretarial standards in your company!!!

Highlights of Companies Bill, 2011

(relevant extracts from ICSI Summary)

- The Bill has 470 clauses and 7 schedules as against 658 Sections and 15 schedules in the existing Companies Act, 1956.
- The entire bill has been divided into 29 chapters.
- Following chapters have been introduced, viz.
  - Registered Valuers (ch.17);
  - Government companies (ch. 23);
  - Companies to furnish information or statistics (ch. 25);
  - Nidhis (ch. 26);
  - National Company Law Tribunal & Appellate Tribunal (ch. 27);
  - Special Courts (ch. 28)
- The Bill empowers Central Government to make rules, etc. through delegated legislation after having detailed consultative process (clause 470 and others).
- The Bill provides for self-regulatory process and stringent compliance regime.

The salient features of the Bill:

1. Classification and Registration

- **Concept of One Person Company (OPC limited)** [Clause 2(62)].
- **Small companies have been defined** (maximum paid-up share capital not exceeding Rs. 50 Lakhs) and have been subjected to a less stringent regulatory framework [Clause 2(85)].
- **Entrenchment Provision** has been proposed in the Bill [clause 5(3)].
- **Conversion of Companies already registered** has been introduced [Clause 18].
- A declaration to the effect that all the requirements of the Act in respect of registration and matters precedent or incidental thereto have been complied with. Company Secretaries continue to be recognized for the purpose of giving this declaration [Clause 7(1)(b)].

2 Duties of directors [Clause 166]

For the first time duties of directors have been defined in the Bill. A director of a company shall:

- act in accordance with the articles of the company.
- act in good faith in order to promote the objects of the company for the benefit of its members as a whole, and in the best interests of the company, its employees, the shareholders, the community and for the protection of environment.
- exercise his duties with due and reasonable care, skill and diligence and shall exercise independent judgment.
- not involve in a situation in which he may have a direct or indirect interest that conflicts, or possibly may conflict, with the interest of the company.
- not achieve or attempt to achieve any undue gain or advantage either to himself or to his relatives, partners, or associates and if such director is found guilty of making any undue gain under sub-section (7), he shall be liable to pay an amount equal to that gain to the company.
- not assign his office and any assignment so made shall be void.

Penalty: If a director of the company contravenes the provisions of this section such director shall be punishable with fine which shall not be less than one lakh rupees but which may extend to five lakh rupees.

3. Certain Insurance Premium not to be treated as part of remuneration [Clause 197 (13)]:

The premium paid on any insurance taken by a company on behalf of its managing director, whole-time director, manager, Chief Executive Officer, Chief Financial Officer or **Company Secretary** for indemnifying any of them against any liability in respect of any negligence, default, misfeasance, breach of duty or breach of trust for which they may be guilty in relation to the company, **shall not be treated as part of the remuneration** payable to any such personnel.

4. Board Meetings (Clause 173)

➢ **Notice**

At least seven days' notice is required to be given for a Board meeting. The notice may be sent by electronic means to every director at his address registered with the company [Clause 173(3)].

A Board Meeting may be called at **shorter notice** subject to the condition that **at least one independent director,** if any, shall be present at the meeting. However, in the absence of any independent director from such a meeting, the decisions taken at such meeting shall be final only on ratification thereof by at least one independent director [1st & 2nd Proviso to clause 173].

5. Investor Protection Measures

➢ **Issue and transfer** of securities and non-payment of dividend by listed companies, has to be administered by SEBI by making regulations.(Clause 24)

➢ An **act of fraudulent inducement** of persons to invest money is **punishable with imprisonment** for a term which may extend to ten years and with fine which shall not be less than the amount involved in fraud, but which may extend to three times the amount involved (Clause 36 & 447).

➢ **A suit may be filed by a person who is affected by any misleading statement** or the inclusion or omission of any matter in the Prospectus or who has invested money by fraudulent inducement (Clause 37).

6. Annual Return [Clause 92]

➢ Every company shall prepare a return (hereinafter referred to as the annual return) in the prescribed form containing the particulars as they stood on the close of the financial year regarding;

(i) its registered office, principal business activities, particulars of its holding, subsidiary and associate companies;

(ii) its shares, debentures and other securities and shareholding pattern;

(iii) its indebtedness;

(iv) its members and debenture-holders along with changes therein since the close of the previous financial year;

(v) its promoters, directors, key managerial personnel along with changes therein since the close of the last financial year;

(vi) meetings of members or a class thereof, Board and its various committees along with attendance details;

(vii) remuneration of directors and key managerial personnel;

(viii) penalties imposed on the company, its directors or officers and details of compounding of offences;

(ix) **matters related to certification of compliances, disclosures as may be prescribed;**

(x) details in respect of shares held by foreign institutional investors; and

(xi) such other matters as may be prescribed.

The prescribed disclosures under the Annual Return shows significant transformation in non financial annual disclosures and reporting by companies as compared to the existing format.

Similar to the existing compliance certificate as stipulated under section 383A of Companies Act, 1956 certification of compliances has been prescribed under clause 92(1)(ix).

➢ **Annual Return is required to be signed by:**

(i) A director and the **Company Secretary**, or where there is no Company Secretary, by a Company Secretary in whole-time practice.

It means that now in respect of all the companies, whether private or public, listed or unlisted, if no Company Secretary is appointed by the company, the Annual Return is compulsorily required to be signed by the Company Secretary in practice.

(ii) A **Company Secretary** in whole-time practice in respect of:

(a) a company having such paid-up capital and turnover as may be prescribed, and

(b) a company whose shares are listed on a recognized stock exchange.

The **Practicing Company Secretary** has to certify that the annual return states the facts correctly and adequately and that the Company has complied with all the provisions of the Act.

It means, in case of a listed company, even if the Annual Return is signed by the Company Secretary in employment of the Company, it is further required to be signed by the Company Secretary in Whole time practice. Also, in case of a company having such paid up capital and turnover as may be prescribed and even if the company is not listed, the Annual Return is required to be signed by the Company Secretary in whole time practice in addition to the Company Secretary in employment.

(iii) In relation to a One Person Company and Small Company, the annual return is required to be signed by the **Company Secretary**, or where there is no Company Secretary, by one director of the company.

➢ ***Certification regarding compliances***

By signing the return, a Company Secretary certifies that the annual return states the facts correctly and adequately and that the company has complied with all the provisions of the Act. In addition, the adequacy of disclosures made is required to be certified by the Company Secretary in the Annual Return. It is a great opportunity as well as a challenge for the Company Secretaries.

- **In case a Company Secretary in whole-time practice certifies the annual return otherwise than in conformity with the requirements of this section or the rules made there under, such Company Secretary shall be punishable with fine which shall not be less than fifty thousand rupees but which may extend to five lakh rupees.**

7. Related Party Transactions

➢ **Every contract or arrangement entered into with a related party shall be referred to in the Board's Report along with the justification for entering into such contract or arrangement** [Clause 188(2)].

➢ Any arrangement between a company and its directors in respect of acquisition of assets for consideration other than cash shall require prior approval by a resolution in general meeting and if the director or connected person is a director of its holding company, approval is required to be obtained by passing a resolution in general meeting of the holding company [Clause 192].

➢ Where a one person company limited by shares or by guarantee enters into a contract with the sole member of the company who is also its director, the company shall, unless the contract is in writing, ensure that the terms of the contract or offer are contained in the memorandum or are recorded in the minutes of the first Board meeting held after entering into the contract. The company shall inform the Registrar about every contract entered into by the company and recorded in the minutes (Clause 193).

➢ **Directors and the key managerial personnel of a company are prohibited from forward dealings in securities of the company** (Clause 194).

The terms multinational and transnational company broadly cover any company which carries on directly. or indirectly business in more than one country.

Higlights Of Global Developments In Company Law

with specific reference to UK, US & Singapore

TYPES OF COMPANY IN UNITED KINGDOM (UK)

- Private company limited by shares ("Ltd") – the members' liability is limited to the amount unpaid on shares they hold and such shares may not be offered to the general public.
- Public company limited by shares ("PLC") – the company's shares are offered for sale to the general public through a stock exchange and the members' liability is limited to the amount unpaid on shares held by them.
- European public limited company -

  Further, European Union legislation allows overseas companies to establish a European public limited company (also known as a "SE"). An SE can be registered in any member state of the EU, and the registration can be easily transferred to another member state.

  Several ways of forming an SE

  - By merger
  - As a holding company
  - As a subsidiary
  - By a PLC transforming into an SE

COMPANIES ACT, 2006 - under phased implementation in UK

Most of the new provisions in the UK Companies Act, 2006 are made applicable as till October 2008. The last trench of phased implementation of remaining provisions of the Act will be applicable from 1st October 2009, which include,

- Company – introduction, formation & constitution
- Company – name, registered office & members
- Buy back of shares by Limited Company
- Annual Returns & Charges
- Overseas Companies
- Registrar of Companies.

The basic method of forming a company under the Companies Act 2006 remains largely unchanged from the 1985 Act, there are a few fundamental changes –

- Subscribers forming a company shall become its members.
- If company has share capital, Subscribers also agree to take at least one share.

- The memorandum of association will be a purely historical document and will *only* contain details of the subscribers.
- All other information presently contained in the memorandum will instead be captured through the application process and not be possible to amend or update the memorandum after registration.
- A company's articles, therefore, become the main working constitutional document for a company.

On compliance of UK Corporate laws, one can meet most of the legal requirements of European Union, that being the significance of understanding UK Companies Act.

PROCEDURE FOR INCORPORATION

- One or more person can form a Private Limited Company.

  Note: Even one person can form a Public Company from 1st October 2009.

2. Name Check to get the Unique Name:

   Briefly, the restrictions are that:

   - one cannot register the same name as another company;
   - the use of certain words is restricted; and

   Names likely to cause offence are not allowed.

3. Prepare the following documents,

   - A memorandum of ass ociation - The form of the memorandum is set out in a set of tables, the Companies (Table A to F) Regulations or Forms are also available free of charge from the Companies House website.
   - Articles of association (except where Table A is adopted without modification) - Forms must be signed by at least one secretary and one director, who cannot be the same person. The statement must also contain consent by each of the persons named as director, as secretary or as one of joint secretaries, to act in the relevant capacity.
   - Form 10 regarding details of the first director(s), secretary and the intended address of the registered office.
   - Form 12 regarding compliance with all the legal requirements relating to the incorporation of a company in the presence of a notary public.

4. Filing of incorporation documents with the Registrar of Companies.
5. The standard registration fee is higher for same day incorporation. The Registration Certificate issued is the Conclusive evidence as to Incorporation.

OTHER REQUIREMENTS

Company Secretary: Since 6th April 2008, companies have not been obliged to appoint a company secretary, although they may choose to do so if they wish.

Annual General Meeting: Under the Companies Act 2006, private companies are no longer required to hold an AGM unless they positively opt to do so. Shareholders can demand an AGM if at least 10% wish to hold one. In such circumstances, private companies will need to give 14 days' notice.

Other Meetings: For limited companies the notice period is 14 days. For unlimited companies, it is 7 days to be given for other meetings of the Company. When important decisions have been taken at meetings, Companies House has to be notified within 15 days.

Filing yearly accounts and the company's annual return with Companies House

irectors are personally responsible for submitting yearly accounts and the company's annual return to the Registrar of Companies. It can be done either online or offline.

Penalties for late returns and informing Companies House

- Penalties are severe and Directors may be prosecuted.

If no return or accounts are filed at all, Companies House may also strike the company off the register.

Procedure for Formation of Limited Liability Company (LLC) in United States of America (USA)

The following procedure for formation of an LLC is almost similar in most of the States and the approval authority differs according to the State as there is NO unified company law. But Internal Revenue Service (IRS) – the US Department of Treasury for taxation purpose is a unified Central authority. Even there is a centralized securities agency called Securities Exchange Commission (SEC), which is one of the most powerful administrative agencies in the world.

Other Requirements

- LLC agreement shall be executed.
- There is no minimum capital requirement to form an LLC.
- Even single person can form an LLC.
- Appointment of Company Secretary is not mandatory.
- Accounts shall be maintained and need not be audited.

Annual Returns shall be filed every two years. If an LLC is formed prior to June 16 in any given year, its first Two-Year Report is due June 16 that same year. Its next Two-Year Report will not be due for another 2 years. If an LLC is formed after June 16 in a given year, its first Two-Year Report will be due June 16 the following year. Again, its next Two-Year Report will not be due for another 2 years.

Kindly note, an LLC can later be converted into a CORPORATION at any time. From a tax angle, an LLC can elect to be taxed as a C-Corporation or an S-Corporation. In general an LLC is the preferred entity of choice. It is more flexible for U.S. and foreign owners, has fewer formalities than a corporation and just as much liability protection.

BASIC REQUIREMENTS TO INCORPORATE A SINGAPORE COMPANY

- Anyone (a local or a foreign person) can register a new Singapore company.
- 100% foreign ownership allowed
- Minimum paid up capital of 1 USD only
- Concept of authorized capital no longer exists
- Minimum of 1 director and 1 shareholder required (shareholder need not be resident of Singapore)
- At least one director must be a local resident director (Singapore citizen, permanent resident, or Employment Pass /Dependent Pass holder) & all other directors can be foreign directors
- Must have a local registered address
- Must have a local qualified company secretary

1. Briefly state how the UK White paper, 2005 envisages to reform the role of directors (2007 – June)
2. How is election of directors dealt with by the Canadian Company Law? (2007 – December)
3. Discuss directors' remuneration report in the light of Companies Act, 2006 of the United Kingdom. (2009 – December)
4. State the requirement for audit of the financial accounting statements under the UK Companies Act, 2006 (2010 – June)

This chapter discusses only the basic highlights of provisions of Company law in other countries. It is highly advisable to supplement reading of ICSI's study material for this topic to understand the developments of company laws in various other countries.

Are you Correct/Incorrect with reasons?

1. A listed company cannot issue sweat equity shares to its promoters.
2. Since a producer company is an innovation , it does not need the words 'limited' at ete end of its name
3. E-form relates to registration of charges
4. A company declared defunct u/s 560 can never be included again in the register of the companies maimtained by the registrar of companies
5. The insider trading regulations promulgated by SEBI excludes the auditor of the company from the scope of the regulations
6. Under UK companies Act, 2006 a director of a public company can be removed before expiry of his term only by a special resolution
7. A fresh notice of every adjourned meeting is necessary
8. A proxy shall not be entitled to vote on show of hands in the general meeting
9. In terms of clause 49 of the listing agreement not less than 40% of directors shall consist of independent directors
10. Resignation of a whole time director shall take effect once resignation is tendered
11. Povisions of section 372A do not apply in the case of loan/guarantee by a company to another company in which it is holding 90% of the paid –up capital
12. As s private company, by virtue of becoming a subsidiary of a public company, gains the legal status of a public company, it is necessary that such a private company has to amend its articles of association to remove the basic features of a private company as given in section3(1)(iii)
13. It is not always necessary that a company must hold majority of nominal value of equity share capital of another of another company to make the latter company its subsidiary
14. The central government's power under the Companies act 1956 go beyond the role of a merger regulator, but stretch to become the ultimate dispute resolution authority for a company
15. An order for conducting investigation of a company having one Lakh equity shares (issued and paid up)

cannot be made by the company law board on the application of just 750 members of that company

16. It is incumbent on the statutory auditor of a company to fully incorporate the report of the branch auditor of that company when the accounts of the branch have been audited by another auditor.
17. In a situation where the winding-up order for a company has been made by the court and the liquidator has been appointed, it is still permissible to propose a scheme of compromise under under section 391.
18. The board of directors of a company can apply to the court for winding up without obtaining member's approval
19. 'one person company' can be registered as a company under the Companies act, 1956
20. The term 'insider' in the context of the insider trading means a person who is or was connected with the company or deemed to have been connected with the company and who is reasonably expected to have access to unpublished price sensitive information in respect of securities of a company. The expression 'person' appearing above is restricted to natural person and juridical person like a company, but excludes firm and other association of persons
21. When the company law board seized of a petition between the parties involving oppression and mismanagement, the winding up proceeding in respect of the company concerned can be entertained by the court and continued
22. A public limited company can have equity share capital alone , but it cannot have preference share capital alone
23. a company is not bound to close its register of members even for a single day
24. Interim dividend can be declared out of reserves by a company which has even incurred a loss
25. The annual general meeting of a company for the current year as also for the previous year can be held on the same day
26. A group of 44 members of a company limited by shares holding in aggregate 2% of the issued share capital of the company cannot under any circumstances apply to the company law board alleging mismanagement of the company the company has 55 members
27. The expression 'free reserves' for the purpose of section 372A dose not include the balance of the credit of 'securities premium account'
28. An article in the article of association can be amended by the members of the company by passing a special resolution
29. A company may get exemption from the provisions of section 212
30. The eligibility criteria to apply for seeking relief under section 397 etc inter alia provide for holding not less than 20% of the issued share capital of the company
31. No stamp duty on transfer of shares in electronic form (demat mode) is payable
32. It is mandatory to constitute audit committee in all public limited companies

ANSWERS

1. INCORRECT- As per section 79A (1) (d) of the companies Act of 1956 , the sweat equity shares of a company whose equity shares are listed on a recognized stock exchange , are to be issued in accordance with the regulations made by the securties & exchannge board of India in this behalf . Under

regulations 6 of SEBI (issue of sweat equity) Regulations , 2002 , a listed company can issue sweat equity shares to its promoters

2. INCORRECT- Section 581C of the companies Act , 1956 mandates the use of the word 'limited' after the the name of the producer company

3. CORRECT-E-form 10 relates to registration of charges ariseing of issue of denbuters

4. INCORRECT- The company , or any number of creditors by way of an application to the court can request fot the restoration of the company's name before the expiry of twenty years from the date the company has been declared defunct in the official gazette.

5. INCORRECT- As per regulation 2(g) of the SEBI ([Prohibition of insider trading) Regulation, 1992 , an 'auditor' is included within the definition of 'officer' of a company '

6. INCORRECT- Section 168 of the UK companies Act of 2006 , allows removal of director of any company before the expiry of his term by passing a ordinary resolution

7. INCORRECT- An adjourned meting is merely the continuation of the original meeting & unless the articles of association of the company provides otherwise , a fresh notice of the adjourned meeting is not necessary , if however , the meeting is adjourned sine die , a fresh notice must be given

8. CORRECT- A proxy shall not be entitled to vote on show of hands in the general meeting unless the articles of association of the company provides otherwise ,a proxy is entitled to vote on a poll , future , a proxy does not have any right to speak at the meeting (vide section 176)

9. INCORRECT-As per clause 49 I (A) of the listing agreement where the chairman of the board is a non-executive director , atleast one-third of the board should comprise of independent directors & in case he is an executive director, atleast half of the board should comprise of independent directors

10. INCORRECT- Resignation of a whole time director before the expire of his terms of office becomes effective only when it is accepted by the company as he is bound by the terms & conditions of his appointments

11. INCORRECT- section 372A(8)(c) of the Companies Act ,1956 , specifically provides that nothing contained in Section 372A shall apply to any loan made by a holding company to its wholly owned subsidiary . Further , sub-section 7(d) of section 372A of the Act provides that nothing contained in the section shall apply to any guarantee given or any security provided by a holding company in respect of loan made to its wholly owned subs dairy . therefore , the provisions of section section 372A of the companies Act, 1956 will apply in the case of loan/guaranteed by a company to another company in which he is holding 90% of the paid-up capital.

12. Correct - There is a provision in the companies act requiring the alteration of the basic characteristics of a company when incorporated as a private company. The terming of a private company as a public company when it become a subsidiary of a public company is only for regulatory/monitoring purposes. The definition of a public company given in the section 3(i)(iv) of a companies act does not contemplate any change in the basic characteristics of a private company.

13. Correct - It is always necessary that a company must hold majority of the nominal value of equity share capital any other company to make the latter company subsidiary.

A company also become a subsidiary of another company when that company controls the composition of the board of directors of the first company vide section 4(1) (a) of the companies act 1956

14. Incorrect - The central government is not the ultimate dispute resolution authority for a company. The company law board and the court bodies recognized under the companies act for dispute resolution.

15. Correct - In the case of a company having a share capital, section235(2) enables 'not less than 200 members' to make application to the company law board irrespective of the total number of members or total voting right in the company.
16. Correct - Section228(3)((c) inter alia, require the branch auditor to prepare his report and forward the same to the statutory auditor and the statutory auditor has been empowered therein to deal with the branch audit report in such manner as he deems necessary. Section227 (3)(bb) of the act corroborates this power but requires the statutory auditor this power but require the statutory auditor to state hoe he has dealt with the branch audit report
17. Correct - Section 391(3)(1) of the act explicitly allow the liquidator of a company in liquidation to make application for compromise or arrangement. In other words, when a company is being wound up, only the liquidator has the authority to propose a scheme of compromise under section 391.
18. Section 433 of the act provides that a company may be wound up by the court, inter alia, if the company has passed a special resolution of its being wound up by the court. Ordinarily, directors are not entitled to present a winding up petition in the name of the company without the authority of the general meeting. however, a winding up petition has indeed been presented by the directors. On this basis, it appears that if after submission of their application, the directors get a special resolution at general meeting ratify the action of the directors, the application will be allowed.
19. Incorrect - The companies' act 1956 still does not recognise the registration of a one person company. Dr.j.j. Irani Expert committee on new company law has recognized the concept. The committee has recommended that to bring professionalism, formation of one person companies be permitted to be registered and incorporated under the companies act.
20. Correct - The term 'person' as defined in clause(e) of regulation 2 of SEBI (Prohibition of insider training) regulation, 1992, when read together with clause 2(h)(ix) includes firms or association of person is a concern, firm, trust, Hindu Undivided family, company or association of persons wherein any of the director or deemed director or relative or banker of the company have more than 10 percent of the holding or interest. Also, the general clauses act 1997 while defining 'person' includes firm and association of persons, besides others.
21. Correct - The supreme court of India in worldwide Agencies(p) Ltd v Mrs.Margarest T Desor (1990) 67 comp.cas 607 has held that there is no inherent conflict in pursing sections 397/398 and section 433. The j&k High court in A.K.puri v. Devi Das Gopal kishanlal Ltd. [1995]67 CLA 1 has observed that there is no statutory prohibition in the companies act which requires stay of winding up proceeding while company Law Board is seized of a petition under 397
22. CORRECT-By the very definition of 'preference share capital' in section 85 , preference shareholders have certain preferential rights over the equity shareholders . so , in the absence of equity share holders , there cannot be preference share capital
23. CORRECT- Section 154 of the Companies act , has not made the closure of the register mandatory .As per secretarial standards 4 (cl.4.2.1) issued by ICSI a company is not bound to close its register even for a day , a company choose to close its register so as to update it for reckoning entitlements to dividend , right bonus etc , such closure may be for a period or periods not exceeding in aggregate 45 days in a year , but not exceeding 30 days at any one time
24. INCORRECT-Though section 205(1A) has empowered the board to declare interim dividend , but such dividend cannot be declared out of reserves . according to secretarial standard 3 issued by ICSI (cl 1.2.2) , while final dividend may be paid out of free reserves subject to compliance of the rules , no interim dividend should be paid , in the event of a loss or inadequacy of profits , by transfers out of any reserves

25. CORRECT-section 166 of Companies Act , 1956 provides as under

1. In every calendar year there must be 1(one) AGM held
2. The time gap between two consecutive AGM must not be more than 15 months , however, the ROC is authorized to extends this by 3 (three) months for a valid reasons
3. Form the closure of the accounting year AGM must be held within 6 months u/s 210

However , there is no provision in the Act prohibiting the holding of two AGM's on the same day .The situations where two AGMs may be held on the same day:

1.The first & second AGM may be held on same day

2. When the company changes financial year two AGMs may be held on the same day

There should , however , be separate notices for each meeting ,& they should be held at different

Timings on the same day after the conclusion of the 1st AGM

26. INCORRECT- The central government section 399(4) of the companies act , 1956 may authorize such application alleging mismanagement , if it is satisfied that circumstances justify allowing such application

27. INCORRECT- section 372(A) of the companies act , 1956 , while explaining the term 'free reserves'

Has specifically included securities premium account balance in the term 'free reserves' 'free reserves' means those reserve which , as per the latest audited balance sheet of the company, are free for distribution as dividend & shall include balance to the credit of the securities premium account but shall not include share application money

28. CORRECT- Vide section 31 of the companies Act . 1956 , an article in the articles of association can be amended by the members of the company by passing a special resolution

29. CORRECT-Under section 212(8) of the companies Act , 1956 , a company may get exemption from the compliance of the provisions of section 212 at the Act directing that in relation to any subsidiary section 212 shall not apply or shall not apply to the extend as directed

30. INCORRECT-The eligibility criteria to apply for seeking relief u/s 397 etc inter alia provides for holding not less than 10% of the issued shares capital of the company

31. CORRECT- No stamp duty on transfer of shares in electronic form (demat mode) is payable [vide depositories Act , 1996]

32. INCORRECT- It is not mandatory to constitute audit committee in all public limited companies.It is mandatory for those public companies having paid-up capital of 5 cores or more [vide section 292A(1)] . future , all listed companies are mandatorily required under clause 49 of the listing agreement to constitute an audit committee

FILL YOUR BLANKS

1. ------------------ is the conclusive evidence in ease of a company that the statutory requirements have been complied with

2. In case of minimum subscription is not received or refund is delayed ------ % interest to be paid by a company
3. --------- is a new form of legal entity recognized in India directly
4. Buy – back securities should be physically destroyed within -------- days
5. A user can check the status of transactions by entering the -------- on website of MCA-21
6. The Companies Act , 1956 allows a company to convert its fully paid-up shares into -----------
7. A ------ is allotted at a time of registration of charge
8. The directors appointed by the principle of ---- hold office for -------- & cannot be removed by the company in general meeting u/s 284
9. Causal vacancy in the board may arise from death ,------- & ----------- (mention any two reasons)
10. The declaration of bonus issue in lieu of --------- is not permitted
11. Form 23AA relating to keeping of books of accounts at a place other than the registered office is required to be filed within --------- days with registrar of companies
12. Approval of the ------ is required to be taken for changing the name of the company u/s 21
13. A copy of the order passed by the company law board is required to be filed with registrar of the companies in e-form no. ---------
14. it is the situation of the ----- of the company that decides the jurisdiction of the of the court in that company's matters
15. ------------- policy adopted by a company it is to prevent the misuse of confidential information in the context of insider trading
16. Alteration to articles of associations requires a ------ resolution u/s ----of the companies Act ,1956
17. Allotment of equity shares requires e-form -------- whereas increase in authorised capital needs e-form --------
18. Once dividend is declared it has to be paid within -------- but unpaid account balance needs to be transferred within 7 years to ----------

ANSWERS

1. Certificate of incorporation
2. 6%
3. Limited liability partnership
4. Seven days
5. Service request number
6. Stock
7. Charge identification number
8. Proportional representation , three years
9. Resignation
10. Dividend
11. 7

12. Central government

13. 21

14. Registered office

15. Chinese wall

16. Special , 31

17. 2 & 5

18. 30 days & Investors education & protection fund

CHOOSE THE CORRECT ANSWER

1. A notice of disclosure of interest at the board meeting is the require of section

a) 295

b) 269

c) 297

d) 299

2. A director appointed by board to hold the office until the conclusion of next annual general meeting is known as

a) Additional director

b) Nominee director

c) Alternative Director

d) Director retireing by rotation

3. As per the provisions of the companies Act , 1956 the form of the proxy must be deposited with the company atleast

a) 24 hours before the time of the annual general meeting

b) 36 hours before the time of the annual general meeting

c) 48 hours before the time of the annual general meeting

d) 72 hours before the time of the annual general meeting

4. The applicant for availbility of name of the purposed company can have option to give maximum

a) 3 alternative names

b) 4 alternative names

c) 5 alternative names

d) 6 alternative names

5. A person who is a company secretary & director of a company is

a) Employee director

b) Non –executive director

c) Exeuctive director

d) Independent director

6. A company in which 50.25% of shares are held by one state goverment while the rest of the shares are held by private sector companies & by retail holders i.e. members of public is a

a) Goverment company

b) public sector company

c) Corporation

d) Private sector company

7. The minimum number of directors of the audit committee in the case of a listed company With 12 directors shall be

1. 2 directors

2. 3 directors

3. 4 directors

4. 5 directors

8. The central government may exempt any class of companies from complying with the provisions of schedule VI of the Companies Act , 1956 if it is necessary to grant such exemption in the

a) National interest

b) Public interest

c) Social interest

d) Company's interest

9. In a listed company with 11 directors , what is the quorum for the board meeting

a) 2 Directors

b) 3 Directors

c) 4 Directors

d) 5 Directors

10. A causal vacancy arising out of resignation of company's auditor can be filled by

a) Company in general meeting in ordinary resolution

b) Company in general meeting in special resolution

c) Board of directors

d) Audit committee

11. Which one of the following sections of the Act specifies that the provisions of the companies Act , 1956 override the provisions in the memorandum of association

a) Section 2

b) section 4

c) Section 9

d) Section 13

12. On incorporation of a company , the registrar of companies in addition to certification of incorporation issues a unique identification number called

a) Unique corporate number

b) Corporate identification number

c) Company identification number

d) Unique identification number

13. The appointment of a statutory auditor u/s 224 A is with reference of 25% of

a) Paid- up capital

b) Issued capital

c) Subscribed capital

d) Only equity capital

14. Non –executive director of a public limited company may get remuneration on quarterly basis if such basis of payment is approved by/under

a) Articles of association of the company

b) General meeting of the company

c) Central government

d) Schedule XIII of the Companies Act , 1956

15. Annual return of a company having share capital is to filed with the registrar of companies im e-form

a) 20A

b) 20B

c) 25A

d) 25B

16. On striking of the name of a company considered defunct , the registrar of companies is required to

a) Publish notice in the official gazette

b) Inform state government

c) Inform central government

d) Inform ministry of corporate affairs

17. A member of ICSI in practice deemed to be guilty of professional misconduct if he issues compliances certificates/signs annual returns in aggregate in a calendar year for more than

a) 20 companies

b) 50 companies

c) 80 companies

d) 100 companies

ANSWERS

1. 299
2. Additional director
3. 48 hours

4. 5 alternative names
5. Executive director
6. Public sector company
7. 3 directors
8. Public interest
9. 4 Directors
10. Company in general meeting in ordinary resolution
11. Section 9
12. Corporate identification number
13. Subscribed capital
14. Central government
15. 20B
16. Publish notice in the official gazette
17. 80 companies

POWER OF RoC TO STRIKE DEFUNCT COMPANIES OFF THE REGISTER

[Section 560]

This is one of the easiest ways to close a non-running business or a business where all assets and liabilities are disposed off. It may happen when business is discontinued, main person died, registered office might be sold off or for such other reason. RoC may issue a letter to the Company at its Registered office or to director or manager or persons at their last known address or at the address mentioned in subscriber clause of Memorandum (MoA). Then send a Show Cause Notice within 14 days after the elapse of 1 month asking "why not the name of your company be published in the Official Gazette to strike its name off the Registrar". Meaning, the company has to satisfy RoC, if it has to remain functioning as a Company, otherwise, RoC will take actions to dissolve the company without winding up.

If the Company is being Wound Up and,

↳ NO Liquidator is appointed OR

↳ NO returns by Liquidator for 6 months OR more,

THEN, after giving notice to the Liquidator at last known address, the name of the Company is published in the Official Gazette to strike its name off the Register on completion of the period of 3 months.

DEFUNCT COMPANIES: It means a company which has nil asset and liability and

(i) has not commenced any business activity or operation since incorporation; or

(ii) is not carrying over any business activity or operation for last one year before making application under Form FTE (Fast Track Exit Scheme).

Kindly note, the following companies are NOT eligible to apply u/s. 560 EVEN THOUGH they are not having any business activities and also not having any assets or liabilities,

1. Non Banking Financial Company (NBFC) registered with RBI but has NOT obtained No Objection Certificate to avail the exit option OR an Unregistered NBFC.
2. Collective Investment Management Company (CIMC) registered with SEBI but has NOT obtained No Objection Certificate to avail the exit option OR an Unregistered CIMC.
3. Government Companies WITHOUT approval letter from the concerned Ministry.
4. Company registered u/s. 25 of Companies Act, 1956.
5. Company having dues PENDING with any banks, financial institutions, taxation authorities, Government departments or any other local authorities.
6. Company on which any prosecution for NON-COMPOUNDABLE offence is pending before any competent authority.
7. Listed Companies or companies delisted for violation of listing agreement
8. Vanishing Companies: Companies which directors & registered office is NOT traceable & has NOT filed returns for consecutive 2 years.

PROCEDURE INVOLVED IN STRIKING OFF

1. RoC can strike off the name of a company on its OWN MOTION by following the procedure given in the chart below.
2. RoC can strike off the name from Register on receiving an APPLICATION from the company that it is a defunct company (i.e.) it is not carrying on business on operation along with,
   a. Board Resolution
   b. Affidavit by atleast 2 directors to the effect that the company has no assets or liabilities and that it has not been carrying on any business on operation with latest balance sheet.
   c. Indemnity bond by 2 directors to the effect that liabilities of the company, if any, will be met by them even after striking off the name.
3. RoC if satisfied with the compliance of Section 560 read with MCA guidelines made thereunder may proceed to strike the name off the Register and publish a notification in the Official Gazette.

ROC ON ITS OWN MOTION

If Register (RoC) has a REASON TO CAUSE TO BELIEVE that Company is NOT in business or Operation, then RoC will send a "Letter" in this regard

Within 14 days AFTER the elapse of 1 month from the Letter by RoC

Letter by Registered Post referring FIRST letter and stating that it will be published in the Official Gazette to strike its name

AFTER 1 month

Unless cause is SHOWN to the CONTRARY, publication in the Official Gazette, to strike the name OFF the Register

AFTER 3 months

The Name of the Company is STRUCK OFF from the Register by RoC and the Company SHALL STAND dissolved.

NOTE: On an application by Company or Member or Creditor WITHIN 20 years from the date of such Dissolution, the defunct company may be restored. This is called RESTORATION which is different from Revival u/s. 559. The restoration order shall be filed with RoC in e-form 21and then the company shall be deemed to have continued in existence AS IF the name was never struck off.

ROC ON RECEIVING APPLICATION FROM DEFUNCT COMPANY

MCA has released Fast Track Exit (FTE) scheme for this purpose. A brief summary of the same is under:

1. An application to be made in forms FTE with fees of Rs. 5,000/- as certified by Practicing Professional. In case, the application in Form FTE, is not being digitally signed by any of the Director or Manager or Secretary, a physical copy of the Form duly filled in, shall be signed manually by a director authorised by the Board of Directors of the company and shall be attached with the application Form at the time of its filing electronically; Similarly if such Directors name is not available in the online database, the practising professional shall certify the LIST OF PRESENT DIRECTORS of the company.

2. The Application shall be accompanied by an AFFIDAVIT of directors to the effect that the company has not carried on business or discontinued the business with effect from the date; an INDEMNITY BOND to the effect that any losses, claim and liabilities on the company, will be met in full by every director individually or collectively even after striking off; these shall be stamped, notarised and duly executed; and a Statement of Accounts annexed prepared as on date NOT PRIOR to more than 1 month preceding the date of filing Form FTE, duly certified by a statutory auditor or PCA.

3. The company shall disclose pending litigations if any, involving the company while applying under FTE; If the pending prosecutions are only for non-filing of Annual Returns under section 159 and Balance Sheet under section 220 of the Companies Act, 1956, such application may be accepted provided the applicants have already filed the compounding application. However, steps for final strike of the name of the company will be taken only after disposal of compounding application by the competent authority.

Objectives for Revision

1. The following are treated as Body Corporate under Companies Act, 1956
   a) Public Financial Institutions
   b) Municipal Corporations
   c) Co-operative Societies
   d) All the above
   e) None of the above
2. The following foreign company shall comply with Companies Act,
   a) 50% of Authorised Capital is held by Indian Citizens or Company
   b) 50% of Paid-up Capital is held by Indian Citizens or Company
   c) 51% of Paid-up capital is held by Indian Citizens or Company
   d) 60% of Paid-up capital is held by Indian Citizens or Company
3. What is the company in which 51% of paid-up share capital is held by Central or State Government,
   a) Public Sector Undertaking
   b) Public Company
   c) Government Company
   d) Section 25 Company
4. A private company in which a foreign body corporate holds 90% is treated as,
   a) Private Company
   b) Public Company
   c) Foreign Company
   d) Any of the above
5. A private company in which a foreign body corporate holds 100% is treated as,
   a) Private Company
   b) Public Company
   c) Foreign Company
   d) Any of the above
6. A company can be treated as subsidiary of other, if that other,
   a) controls the composition of its Board of Directors
   b) exercises 50% of total voting power
   c) exercises 50% of nominal value of equity shares
   d) All the above
   e) None of the above
7. The following can be done without having an internet connection,
   a) Check Form

b) Pre-scrutiny

c) Both

d) None

8. The signing of e-form by a practicing professional in addition to Director or Secretary of the Company is called,

a) Pre-scrutiny

b) Pre-certification

c) Both

d) None

9. The process of registering Digital Signature of Director or Secretary with MCA Site is called,

a) Pre-certification

b) Role Check

c) Creation of Login ID

d) None

10. The minimum number of directors in a public company is,

a) 2

b) 3

c) 5

d) 7

11. A public company can be started by

a) 2 persons

b) 3 persons

c) 5 persons

d) 7 persons

12. The name approved by RoC is valid for,

a) 30 days

b) 60 days

c) 3 months

d) 6 months

13. The following forms to be filed at the time of incorporation of a company,

a) e-Form 1A

b) e-Form 1

c) e-Form 23

d) All the above

e) None of the above

14. The company limited by shares and guarantee can adopt Articles as per,

a) Table A

b) Table B

c) Table C

d) Table D

e) Table E

15. The Contracts entered by Company before getting Certificate of Incorporation are called,

a) Pre-incorporation Contract

b) Provisional Contract

c) Contract in lieu of Incorporation

d) Contract in lieu of Commencement

16. The Contracts entered by Company before getting Certificate of Commencement of business are called,

a) Pre-incorporation Contract

b) Provisional Contract

c) Contract in lieu of Incorporation

d) Contract in lieu of Commencement

17. Partnership or Association more than 7 members are treated as Unregistered Company.

18. Company includes a Company incorporated outside India.

19. Company includes Body Corporate.

20. Producer Company is a Private Company

21. Government Company is government.

22. Subsidiary Company can exercise voting rights of its shares in holding company.

23. Subsidiary company can exercise voting rights of its shares in holding company as a legal representative of deceased member of holding company.

24. The document of any company filed online is available for inspection to any one.

25. DIN is mandatory to apply for name of the company.

26. The address of the company is mentioned in the Memorandum of the Company.

27. All forms filed during incorporation require pre-certification by a Professional.

28. The provisional contracts are binding on the company from the date it has entered the contract.

29. Every company is bound by pre-incorporation contracts.

30. The following e-Forms to be filed for change of name,

a) Form 23

b) Form 1A

c) Both

d) None

31. What approval to be sought to shift the registered office of the company from RoC to RoC within state,

a) Board Resolution

b) Special Resolution

c) Special Resolution and Approval of Regional Director

d) Special Resolution and Approval of Company Law Board

32. What approval to be sought by a private company to start an activity mentioned in the other objects of the company,

a) Board Resolution

b) Special Resolution

c) Special Resolution and Approval of Regional Director

d) Special Resolution and Approval of Company Law Board

33. The following form to be filed for statutory declaration of compliance by a public company which has issued prospectus,

a) e-form 19

b) e-form 20

c) e-form 21

d) All the above

34. For the purpose of incorporation, registration fee has to be paid to RoC based on,

a) Number of Subscribers to MoA

b) Number of Directors in the Company

c) Place where registered office is situated

d) Authorised Capital of the company

35. Company can rectify the name after approval.

36. Whether the liability of a members be increased.

37. RoC issues Certificate of Incorporation for a Public Company with 5 subscribers, by mistake. Whether provisions of Companies Act are complied?

38. A Certificate of Incorporation can legalise any illegal objects mentioned in MoA.

39. A public company can get Certificate of Commencement of business anytime after getting the Certificate of Incorporation.

40. The public company can be converted into private company with the approval of _______.

41. The private company can be converted into public company with the approval of _______.

42. A public company can start an activity mentioned in the other object clause of MoA by____ passing a _______.

43. The only clause in the MoA which can amended by way of ordinary resolution is _______, provided if Articles authorizes.

44. If Articles provide that a cheque must be signed atleast by 2 directors, the outsider dealing with the company must ensure that it is so signed, otherwise he cannot claim it.

45. Doctrine of Indoor Management can protect an outsider who is cheated up on a forged document.

46. The directors shall be personally liable for the entire ultra vires act done by them on behalf of the company.

47. The transaction which is ultra vires the AoA can be ratified by shareholders by way of special resolution.

48. If all the shares of the company is held in demat mode then,

a) An electronic Register of Members can be maintained

b) Physical Register to be maintained with names of all shareholders

c) Physical Register to be maintained with names of depositories

d) Register of Members need not be maintained

49. Issue made to existing shareholders where share are issued as fully paid is called,

a) Public Issue

b) Rights Issue

c) Bonus Issue

d) Preferential Issue

50. Share Certificate can be issued only at the Board Meeting where,

a) 2 or more directors are present, if the Board has up to 6 directors

b) 3 or more directors are present, if the Board has more than 6 directors

c) Both the above

d) None of the above

51. The Share Transfer Deed after duly executed by transferor and transferee and duly dated to be submitted to Co along with the share certificate for registering the transfer

a) within 2 months of stamping by RoC in case of listed company

b) within 2 months of stamping by RoC in case of unlisted company

c) within 12 months of stamping by RoC in case of listed company

d) None of the above

52. Share transfer deed has to be duly executed for the following,

a) Transfer of shares

b) Transposition in respect of part holding

c) Altering one or more names

d) All of the above

e) None of the above

53. Share transfer deed need not be executed for the following,

a) Transmission of shares

b) Transposition (altering order of names)

c) Nominee to get shares under Nomination

d) All the above

e) None of the above

54. Register of Members need not be maintained, if all the shares of the company are held in demat mode.

55. Partnership firm can become a shareholder of the company.

56. Equity Shares with DVR can be issued by all companies.

57. A Company convicted under the provisions of FEMA can issue Equity Shares with DVR.

58. Can Board of Directors expel a member of the Company.

59. A Company which failed to redeem the irredeemable preference share cannot declare dividend on preference shares forever.

60. Sweat equity shares can be issued for a value of 10 crores by passing a special resolution.

61. Every issue made to public shall be listed in stock exchanges.

62. Unsecured debentures are treated as deposits.

63. Debenture holder can file winding up petition.

64. Share Transfer Deed shall be executed for transmission of shares and necessary stamp duty to be paid.

65. ________ reserve to be created when redeemable preference shares are redeemed out of profits of the Company.

66. Sweat equity shares issued to managerial personnel for consideration otherwise than cash shall form part of ___________ .

67. Sweat equity shares are subject to lock in of _______ from the date of allotment.

68. The offer to existing shareholders as rights issue shall be kept open for a minimum period of ______ .

69. The public company shall make preferential allotment within___________of receipt of application money.

70. Total borrowings of the company along with debentures exceeding Paid-up capital and Free Reserves of the Company shall be done only at __________.

71. When a member signs & transfers the share transfer deed without filling name of transferee and date, then it is ___________ .

72. The process of returning the certified instrument of transfer to transferor (in case of partial transfer) with the words "Certificate Lodged" is called ________ .

73. ____________ is issued when securities are issued in stages over a period of time within a year.

    a) Deemed Prospectus
    b) Shelf Prospectus
    c) Red herring Prospectus
    d) Information Memorandum

74. The shelf prospectus shall be valid for

    a) 1 year from the date of opening of first issue of securities
    b) 1 year from the date of first allotment of securities
    c) 6 months from the date of allotment of securities
    d) 3 months after the first issue of securities

75. ____________ is a prospectus which does not have complete particulars on price & quantum of securities offered.

    a) Deemed Prospectus
    b) Shelf Prospectus
    c) Red herring Prospectus
    d) Information Memorandum

76. The company may pay commission to any person for subscription,

    a) up to 5% of price for shares

b) up to 2.5% of price for debentures

c) Any of the above

d) up to 5% of price for any security

77. The following is an untrue statement in prospectus,

a) non-disclosure in prospectus

b) wrong disclosure in prospectus

c) half disclosure in prospectus

d) all the above

78. The following statement is correct,

a) Share application money should be refunded within 10 days of 120 days from the date of issuance of prospectus

b) Excess subscription money received shall be repaid within 8 days of due

c) Stock Exchange to grant permission to list within 10 weeks from the date of closure of issue

d) All the above

79. There are two information memorandums under Companies Act.

80. Re-issue of forfeited shares is an allotment.

81. A Managing Director or Company Secretary can allot shares.

82. A private company shall file prospectus with RoC.

83. The Schedule II of the Companies Act lists the contents of ________.

84. The Schedule III of the Companies Act lists the contents of ________.

85. The prospectus shall be issued within ________ of its registration by RoC.

86. ________ is an application made to company for acquiring or subscribing shares in a fictitious name and is prohibited.

87. ________ is a memorandum containing the salient features of prospectus.

88. ________ means a prospectus issued by financial institution or bank for one or more issues of securities specified.

89. The terms of contract referred to in the prospectus can be varied only by passing ________.

90. The return of allotment in ________ shall be filed for allotting shares within 30 days to RoC.

91. A company cannot accept or renew the following deposit,

a) Repayable on demand

b) Repayable within 6 months

c) Repayable more than 36 months

d) Any of the above

92. A non-government public company may accept ______% of paid-up share capital & free reserves as deposits,

a) 10% from shareholders or deposits guaranteed by directors

b) 25% from others

c) Both the above

d) 35% from shareholders & others

93. A government company may accept _____% of paid-up share capital & free reserves as deposits,

a) 10% from shareholders or deposits guaranteed by directors

b) 25% from others

c) Both the above

d) 35% from shareholders & others

94. The following are not treated as free reserves for the purpose of deposits,

a) Capital Redemption Reserve & Debenture Redemption Reserve

b) General Reserve & Securities Premium Account

c) Reserve for bad debts & revaluation reserve for assets

d) All the above

95. The Company can pay only the following brokerage on deposits,

a) 1%, 1.5% & 2% for deposits up to 1 year, 2 year & 3 years respectively

b) 0.5%, 1% & 2% for deposits up to 1 year, 2 year & 3 years respectively

c) 1% for all deposits

d) 2% for all deposits

96. The advertisement or SLoA with respect to deposits is valid till latest of,

a) 3 months from close of Financial Year or Annual General Meeting

b) 6 months from holding Annual General Meeting

c) 6 months from adoption of annual accounts

d) 6 months from close of Financial Year or Annual General Meeting

97. The following is the penal interest for default made to small depositors,

a) 20% compoundable on annual basis for small depositors

b) 18% compoundable on annual basis for other depositors

c) Both the above

d) 20% for all depositors

98. All public limited company can accept public deposits.

99. A private company can accept deposits from members, directors & relatives.

100. The company accepting deposits are required to deposit _______ maturing during the year by 30th April of each year in liquid assets.

101. Company shall furnish a receipt for the amount received to the depositor _______ from the date of receipt of money or realisation of cheques with the Particulars of Deposit.

102. The register of deposits shall be preserved for a period of __________ .

103. The company must deduct a rate of interest of ________ of deposits as penalty in case of premature repayment.

104. Even company has to intimate CLB on monthly basis within _______of default made to small depositors.

105. Where a company fails to repay deposits, deposit holder can make an application to _____ .

106. The return of deposits as on 31st March of every year shall be filed within _____ of every year.

107. The following forms to be filed for creation & modification of charge,

a) e-Form 8 within 30 days to RoC

b) e-Form 8 & 17 within 30 days to RoC

c) e-Form 17 within 30 days to RoC

d) None of the above

108. If company is situated outside India & property on which charge is created is also outside India,

a) it shall be registered with RoC within 30 days of receiving documents by post

b) it need not be registered with RoC

c) it shall be registered according to the laws of the other country

d) None of the above

109. The charge is void against liquidator in case of non-registration means, _____

a) On liquidation, debt is void

b) On liquidation, chargeholder assumes the status of secured creditor

c) On liquidation, chargeholder assumes the status of unsecured creditor

d) None of the above

110. The process of conversion of floating charge into fixed charge for the purpose of its enforcement is called _____________ .

111. ________ is ambulatory and shifting in nature and cannot be enforced until certain event occurs.

112. The _______________ of charge stands as conclusive evidence as to compliance of requirements of registration.

113. Mortgage shall be registered as charge u/s. 125 of Companies Act.

114. Only the company can register the charge with RoC.

115. The copies of Register of charge can be taken be member or creditor.

116. If charge is not registered with RoC, the debt gets destroyed.

117. If last AGM was held on 30.10.2007 and the annual accounts is closed on 31.3.2007, then the next AGM shall be held on

a) 31.12.2008 i.e, every calendar year shall have an AGM

b) 31.1.2009 i.e, gap between last & next AGM shall be within 15 months

c) 30.9.2007 i.e, within 6 months from the close of financial year

d) Latest of the above dates

118. The following are ordinary business, if held at an AGM,

a) Consideration of annual accounts with annexures

b) Declaration of dividend

c) Appointment of directors in place of those retiring by rotation

d) Appointment & fixing of remuneration of auditors

e) All the above

119. The following business requires special notice to be given,

a) Removal of auditor

b) Appointment of another auditor

c) Removal of director

d) Appointment of another director

e) All the above

120. The following is a special business and mandates explanatory statement,

a) Declaration of dividend in AGM

b) Declaration of dividend in EGM

c) Both

d) None

121. The members holding __________ may requisition the board of directors to convene an EGM.

a) 10% of Issued Capital

b) 20% of Issued Capital

c) 1/10th of Paid-up capital or Voting power

d) 1/20th of Paid-up capital or Voting power

122. EGM may be called by the requisition of shareholders holding prescribed value by depositing the requisition at,

a) Corporate Office of the company

b) Registered Office of the company

c) Head Office of the company

d) Any of the above

123. General Meeting can be conducted by giving shorter notice to members,

a) with the consent of all members in case of AGM

b) with the consent of 95% of voting capital in case of EGM

c) Any of the above

d) None of the above

124. The following statement with respect to length of notice with respect to general meeting is correct,

a) Articles of private company can prescribe 10 days notice & is valid

b) Articles of public company can prescribe 10 days notice & is valid

c) Articles of private company can prescribe 30 days notice & is valid

d) None of the above

125. The following statements are correct with respect to book closure,

a) Register of members can be closed for 30 days at a time

b) Register of members can be closed for 45 days per year

c) Both the above

d) None of the above

126. The following is a special resolution,

a) when vote for the resolution is greater than the vote cast against

b) when vote for the resolution are not less than 3 times the votes cast against

c) when all vote for the resolution

d) when all vote against the resolution

127. The following resolution shall be passed only through postal ballot in case of listed companies,

a) amendment of object clause

b) buy back of shares

c) loan or guarantee or security in excess of limits prescribed u/s. 372A

d) all the above

128. The minimum quorum for adjourned meeting of a public company if meeting is adjourned for want of quorum is,

a) 5

b) 3

c) 2

d) 1

129. Chairman shall have the power of casting vote,

a) In case of equality of votes

b) In case of equality of votes, only when articles authorize

c) In case of special resolution

d) All the above

130. The following proxy is valid and such proxy can attend the general meeting,

a) proxy dated earlier but lodged later

b) proxy dated earlier & lodged earlier

c) proxy dated later & lodged earlier or later

d) None of the above

131. In case of voting by show off hands,

a) every member has one vote

b) every share has one vote

c) proxies are counted

d) All the above

132. When a poll demanded shall be conducted forthwith (immediately)?

a) adjournment of general meeting

b) election of chairman

c) Both the cases

d) None of the above

133. The following members or proxy can demand a poll,

a) Members holding 10% voting right or Rs.50,000 paid-up in case of public company

b) One member or proxy if 7 or less members of private company are personally present

c) Two members or proxies if more than 7 members of private company are personally present

d) Any of the above

134. The following resolutions to be registered with RoC by filing e-form 23,

a) all special resolution

b) ordinary resolution for appointing sole selling agent

c) ordinary resolution for voluntary winding up

d) all the above resolutions

135. The statutory report shall contain an abstract of receipts & payments since incorporation ________ atleast upto ____________ from the date of statutory report.

136. ___________ is a notice given 14 days in advance to the meeting.

137. The board of directors has to call for an EGM requisitioned by members within ______ of the request and hold the meeting within _______ of the request or members themselves hold the meeting _______ within of the request.

138. ________ exclude the date of service of notice and the date of meeting.

139. If business to be transacted relates to any other company and if director owns ________ of the paid-up capital of that other company, then it shall be given in explanatory statement.

140. _________ enables the members to vote at the meeting without physically attending the meeting.

141. _________ is appointed by the board to conduct the postal ballot voting process.

142. The assent or dissent in case of postal ballot shall be send by the members within ________.

143. ______ is the minimum number of members personally present at the meeting for the meeting to be valid.

144. ________ is the statutory register which stands as a conclusive evidence of the proceeding of general meeting.

145. Minutes of the general meeting must be recorded within _______ of the meeting.

146. Minutes of the general meeting are available for ______ of members.

147. ________ gives the instrument of proxy.

148. The poll demanded for other than adjournment or election of chairman, may be taken within ______ .

149. Chairman shall appoint ________ to scrutinize the votes given on the poll.

150. A requisition requiring notice of a resolution to be given to the members of the company must be deposited at the registered office _____ before the date of the meeting at which it is intended to move the resolution.

151. A requisition requiring only circulation of a resolution to the members of the company must be deposited at the registered office _____ before the date of the meeting at which it is intended to move the resolution.

152. Members at statutory meeting can discuss any matter and pass resolutions, whether given in notice or not.

153. AGM shall be held on a working day.

154. AGM shall be held at registered office of the company.

155. Can AGM be held within statutory time limit & then adjourn the meeting beyond statutory date for consideration of accounts.

156. One person AGM is possible.

157. Ordinary business & ordinary resolution are one & the same.

158. All business requiring special notice mandates ordinary resolution.

159. All special resolution mandates explanatory statement.

160. Explanatory statement shall be annexed with every resolution, when it's a special business.

161. CLB can call for an EGM.

162. A private company shall annex explanatory statement to every special business.

163. Notice of general meetings shall be given to all joint holders.

164. A member who has not received the notice can invalidate the proceedings of the meeting.

165. Book closure & record date are one & the same.

166. Advance notice of record date & book closure shall be given to stock exchange by a listed company.

167. Postal ballot includes voting by electronic means.

168. The listed company shall conduct the prescribed business only through postal ballot.

169. Scrutinizer appointed in case of postal ballot can be an employee of the company.

170. Proxies will be counted for quorum.

171. Person authorized by resolution of Company will be treated as a member personally present for the purpose of quorum.

172. Minutes of the general meeting can be signed by the director duly authorized by the board.

173. Chairman can alter the minutes if it is defamatory or detrimental to the interest of the company.

174. Chairman can exercise the power of casting vote in case of special resolution.

175. Proxy can be appointed for all the meetings.

176. The proxy lodged for the original meeting is also valid for adjourned meeting.

177. The authorized representative of President of India or Governor of the state can appoint a proxy.

178. Proxy can vote on show of hands.

179. Proxy is valid even after transfer or transmission by member.

180. Can a member attend the meeting after appointing proxy?

181. Even e-Form 23 has to be filed for certain board resolutions.

182. Can a Chairman remove the scrutinizer at a poll?

183. Dividend shall be paid out of,

a) Current year profits

b) Profits for previous financial years

c) Amount provided by Government for dividend

d) Any of the above

184. The following statement is correct,

a) Final Dividend is declared by Board of Directors

b) Interim Dividend is declared by Board of Directors

c) Final Dividend is recommended by Shareholders

d) Interim Dividend is recommended by Shareholders

185. If Board recommends 10% as final dividend, following statement holds good,

(Assume Table A is adopted as Articles of the Company)

a) Shareholders can declare 10% or less as dividend

b) Shareholders can declare more than 10% as dividend

c) Shareholders cannot declare dividend

d) None of the above

186. Dividend need not be paid within 30 days of declaration, when

a) Dividend is not transferred to a bank account

b) Board recommends to hold dividend for want of funds

c) It is legally adjusted against sum due from shareholder

d) Any of the above

187. The following action shall be taken when dividend is declared,

a) Within 5 days, deposit in a separate bank account

b) Within 7 days, deposit in unpaid dividend account

c) Within 30 days of deposit in bank account, make payments

d) All the above

188. When a dividend shall be credited to Investor Education & Protection Fund?

a) After 7 years of declaration of dividend, if remains unpaid

b) After 7 years of depositing in bank account, if remains unpaid

c) After 7 years of opening unpaid dividend account, if remains unpaid

d) After 30 days of making payments to shareholders, if remains unpaid

189. The following penalty can be imposed for non-payment of dividend,

a) Imprisonment & Fine of Rs.1000/- per day

b) Simple Interest @ 18%

c) Any of the above

d) All the above

190. The following dividend can be declared out of reserves after complying with the CG rules,

a) 10%

b) Average% in 5 previous years

c) Higher of the above

d) Lower of the above

191. The following amount can be withdrawn from reserves for payment of dividend, after complying with the CG

rules,

a) 10% of Paid-up capital & Free reserves

b) Reserves equivalent to profits

c) Reserves maintained for last 5 years

d) All the above

192. The following amounts which is due beyond prescribed period shall be credited to IEPF,

a) Matured deposits with the companies

b) Matured debentures with the companies

c) Application money due for refund

d) All the above

193. Interest can be paid out of capital with the approval of Central Government,

a) up to 10%

b) up to 12%

c) up to 15%

d) At any %

194. Interest out of capital can be paid for a period,

a) not exceeding the close of the half year during which work has completed

b) not exceeding the close of the half year next after the half year during which work has completed

c) not exceeding a period of 10 years

d) not exceeding a period of 12 years

195. Reduction of capital mandates the following approvals,

a) Shareholders approval by way of ordinary resolution

b) Confirmation by Court

c) Confirmation by Company Law Board

d) All the above

196. Whether the following amounts to reduction of capital if Rs.100/- is the nominal value per share?

a) Rs.75/- which is already paid-up is declared as the nominal value per share

b) Rs.75/- becomes nominal value by returning back Rs.25/- per share

c) Rs. 100/- remains as nominal value but by returning back Rs.25/- per share which may be called up in future

d) All the above

197. The Court may direct the company which has reduced its share capital to add the following words to the name of the company for prescribed period after reduction,

a) "and altered"

b) "and amended"

c) "and reduced"

d) "and paid"

198. The following shall not amount to reduction of capital requiring Court approval,
   a) Reduction as per CLB order on oppression & mismanagement
   b) Reduction as per Scheme of arrangement u/s. 391-394
   c) Reduction by buying back the securities u/s. 77A
   d) Reduction by redemption of preference shares
   e) All the above

199. The following requires Ordinary Resolution and filing of e-Form 5,
   a) Dimunition of Issued capital
   b) Reduction of Share capital
   c) Buyback of Share capital
   d) Forfeiture of shares
   e) All the above

200. Which of the following has to be paid first in the event of winding up of the company?
   a) Preference Shareholders
   b) Equity Shareholders
   c) Shareholders paid Calls-in-advance
   d) Directors

201. The rights of any class of shareholders may be varied,
   a) By passing special resolution or getting consent of 3/4th members, in writing
   b) By passing ordinary resolution
   c) By passing extraordinary resolution
   d) Not applicable

202. Variation of class of shareholders can be cancelled by 10% of that class by applying to Court,
   a) Within 60 days from the date of the concerned special resolution
   b) Within 30 days from the date of the concerned special resolution
   c) Within 21 days from the date of the concerned special resolution
   d) Cannot be cancelled once approved by way of special resolution

203. An individual can be appointed as director in,
   a) 12 Public & Private Companies
   b) 15 Public & Private Companies
   c) 12 Public Companies
   d) 15 Public Companies

204. The following statement is correct,
   a) Maximum 12 directors in a Public or Private Company
   b) Maximum 15 directors in a Public or Private Company
   c) Maximum 12 directors in a Public Company

d) Maximum 12 directors in a Private Company

205. Whether a director has to be a member of the company?

a) Hold atleast 1 share if Table A is adopted as Articles

b) If own Articles of Private Limited Company mandates director to be a member

c) If own Articles of Public Limited Company mandates to acquire qualification shares within 2 months

d) All the above

206. The following will attract disqualification of a director in a public limited company u/s. 274(1)(g)

a) Non filing of annual accounts beyond 1 financial year

b) Non filing of annual returns for any 3 continuous financial years

c) Non filing of annual accounts and returns for any 3 continuous financial years

d) Non filing of annual returns beyond 3 continuous financial years

207. The term period of additional director shall be,

a) till the term of director in whose term he is appointed

b) till the date of ensuing AGM or ought to have been held

c) till the original returns to the State

d) till the original director term expires

208. For the purpose of calculating 2/3rd of directors who shall retire by rotation, the following are excluded,

a) Additional Director

b) Central Government Director u/s. 408

c) Small Shareholder Director u/s. 252

d) Nominee Directors

e) All of the above

209. The following director will hold office only upto the last day on which the AGM should have been held,

a) Rotational Director

b) Additional Director

c) Both the above

d) None of the above

210. The notice to appoint small shareholder director shall comply with the following,

a) Given atleast 14 days before the meeting

b) Given by atleast 1/10th of small shareholders

c) Signed by atleast 100 small shareholders

d) All the above

211. The following does not attract vacation of office by director u/s. 283

a) Accepting loan, guarantee or security in contravention of Sec 295

b) Entering into contracts which he is interested without complying Sec 297

c) Failure to disclose his interest in the contract u/s. 299

d) None of the above

212. What are the approvals required if a public company is giving loan to a private company which is having common directors?
   a) CG approval u/s. 295
   b) Approval u/s. 372A
   c) Both of the above
   d) None of the above
213. The loan to following persons are covered u/s. 295 requiring CG approval,
   a) A private company in which relative of director is a director
   b) A private company in which relative of director is a member
   c) A private company in which director is a director or member
   d) All of the above
214. Sec 297 regarding the contracts in which directors are interested is not applicable to,
   a) Transactions between 2 public limited companies
   b) Transactions between 2 private limited companies
   c) Transaction by a private limited company
   d) Transaction by a public limited company
215. When the approval of Central Government is necessary for contracts in which directors, etc… are interested u/s. 297
   a) if it is a contract for purchase/sale/supply of goods/materials/services
   b) if it is a contract with directors or such other interested person
   c) if it is a contract by company having paid-up capital of Rs. 1 crore or more
   d) if it is a contract by public limited company
216. The following professional services will not attract provisions of Sec 314 regarding holding of office or place of profit:
   a) Services rendered in professional capacity by advocate or practicing CS/CA, etc...
   b) Services rendered in professional capacity in regular retainership basis
   c) Services rendered in professional capacity with the post of solicitor, technician, etc…
   d) All of the above
217. Determine whether the following transaction is valid u/s. 372A regarding intercorporate loans & investments,
   a) Loan within 60% of Paid-up Capital & Free Reserves with Simple Majority approval of Board
   b) Loan within 100% of Free Reserves with Unanimous approval of Board
   c) Loan exceeding 60% of Paid-up Capital & Free Reserves or 100% of Free Reserves, whichever is less with shareholders approval
   d) None of the above
218. Every public company shall have 3 directors and every other company shall have atleast ___ directors.
219. The nominal value of the qualification shares for a director shall be exceed _____ or the _____ nominal of where it exceeds Rs. 5000/-.

220. means the directors who assume the office of director from the date of incorporation.

221. The total number of directors and the additional directors appointed by the board shall _____ not exceed the _____ as prescribed by the Articles.

222. The casual vacancy will arise only in the case of directors appointed by _________.

223. The directors appointed in casual vacancy are not directors who _______ as his term expires with the term of original director.

224. The alternate director is appointed by the ________ in during the absence of director for a period of atleast from the State.

225. The alternate director shall vacate the office when original director ________ where Board Meetings are ordinarily held.

226. Atleast _______ of total number of directors of public company shall retire by rotation.

227. If the place of retiring director is not filled up in AGM and in its adjournment, also the meetings have not expressly resolved not to fill up the vacancy then, _________ of retiring director takes place.

228. The provisions regarding rotation of directors shall not apply to _________ unless Articles otherwise provides.

229. A small shareholder means a shareholder holding shares of nominal value of _________.

230. The public limited company having a paid-up capital of ______ and having ________ small shareholders may appoint a small shareholder director.

231. A small shareholder cannot be appointed as small shareholder director for more than ________.

232. The term of small shareholder director shall not exceed ________ without re-appointment.

233. In case of a public limited company, _________ shall be a mandatory attachment when filing e-Form 32 for appointment of such director.

234. u/s. 190 is required for removal of a director before expiry of his term u/s. 284.

235. The contravention of Section 295 in cases of loan to a director not only attracts penalty or imprisonment but also _________ by the concerned director.

236. Section 299 will not apply to contract entered between 2 companies and the directors shareholding interest is _________.

237. The interested directors presence shall not be counted for ________ or ________ at the time of dealing the interested discussion.

238. Director obtaining any remuneration over & above the remuneration to which he is entitled as a director shall be deemed to be an _________.

239. A director is appointed in the office or place of profit for a total monthly remuneration of Rs. 50,000 or more mandates approval ____________.

240. A relative of a director is appointed in the office or place of profit for a total monthly remuneration of Rs. 50,000 or more mandates approval ____________.

241. Where any person is covered u/s. 314 is proposed to be paid a higher remuneration, ____________ it will require a _______ unless it is a mere re-appointment with same remuneration.

242. The director contravening Sec 314 shall be liable to ________ on & from the next date following the General Meeting held next after appointment.

243. A company which has made default regarding _______ cannot make any loan to body corporate u/s. 372A till the default subsists.

244. Can a private company have more than 12 directors in its Board?

245. Can a company increase or decrease the number of directors in the office by passing an ordinary resolution?

246. Can a director call for a meeting if minimum number of members in the Board reduced below the quorum requirements?

247. Can a company go directorless and still function with members?

248. Can shareholders agreement prohibit appointment of new directors?

249. Can any person become a director?

250. Can an individual be a director in 15 public limited companies, one private limited company, one unlimited company and one Section 25 company?

251. A public limited company has not filed annual accounts and annual returns for 3 continuous financial years, whether the director of the company is disqualified to become a director of any other private limited company.

252. Can an undischarged insolvent be appointed as director of the company with the permission of Central Government?

253. Can a director who has become insolvent subsequently after his appointment is disqualified u/s. 274?

254. Can there be a director without Directors Identification Number (DIN)?

255. If there is a provision in Articles of Private Limited company to obtain qualification shares by Director, whether it has to be obtained within 2 months as per Sec 270?

256. Whether a director of a public limited company which mandates share qualification by its Articles should acquire the shares within 2 months.

257. Can a director assign his office as a director?

258. All subscribers to Memorandum will become the directors of the company.

259. Whether additional director appointed u/s. 260 has to retire by rotation.

260. Can additional director be appointed as Managing Director of the company?

261. Can additional director continue in office after AGM?

262. Can alternate director be appointed as Managing Director of the company?

263. Can a member appoint a director at the General Meeting who is not a retiring director?

264. Whether a small shareholder director retires by rotation and can he be appointed as MD/WTD?

265. Can Managing Director resign his office by merely tendering a letter of resignation?

266. Whether compensation can be paid to director vacating office u/s. 283.

267. Can Articles provide for removal of director only by a Special Resolution?

268. Whether salary advance given to Managing Director's wife who was employed in the company amount to loan u/s. 295 requiring CG approval.

269. Whether contracts' concerning sale or purchase of immovable property requires approval u/s. 297 if Directors are interested.

270. Whether failure to disclosure interest u/s. 299 by a director will invalidate the contract.

271. Whether prior approval by way of special resolution to mandatory to make loans or guarantee exceeding the limits u/s. 372A,

272. The company has to convene a general meeting to exceed the limits prescribed u/s. 372A for the purposes of inter-corporate loans & investments.

273. The consent of the Board can be sought either at a _________ or through a _________ .

274. The board meeting shall be held atleast once in every ________ and there shall be atleast ___________ .

275. The notice of board meeting shall be given, in writing, to _______ and at ____________ his _______ to every other director.

276. The non-receipt of ______ can invalidate the proceedings of board meeting.

277. means a director whose presence cannot be considered for the purpose of quorum.

278. If the number of directors falls below the quorum, then the remaining directors may act only for the purpose of _______ or _____________ .

279. The quorum shall be present _________ in case of board meeting unless the Articles provide otherwise.

280. The chairman shall be present ____ from the appointed time of board meeting; otherwise, directors willing may chair the meeting.

281. can be exercised by the Chairman when the other votes are equally divided.

282. The minute's book of the board meeting is the ______ evidence of the proceedings of the meeting and is for inspection of members.

283. is a remuneration paid to non-executive director for attending the meeting.

284. The restriction on powers of board u/s. 293 which shall be exercised only at a general meeting shall not be applicable to ________ .

285. The total money's borrowed in aggregate by a public company exceeding the _________ of the company mandates approval of shareholders in general meeting.

286. The ____________ in the directors report u/s. 217 shall state that accounting standards & policies are followed and accounting records & accounts are prepared on ongoing basis.

287. The number of board meetings held during the year and meetings attended by each director shall be given in the _______ .

288. Whether business transacted through a resolution by circulation can be considered as a board meeting for u/s. 285.

289. Can a board meeting be called for & convened by a Manager or Secretary of the company?

290. Whether board meetings has to be held only at the registered office of the company.

291. Can a board meeting be held anywhere if statutory registers are involved?

292. Can a board meeting take place on a public holiday?

293. Whether notice to be given to interested directors for a board meeting?

294. Whether notice to be given to original director outside India when an alternate director is appointed u/s. 313.

295. Whether interested directors are counted for the purpose of quorum.

296. Whether proxy is counted for the quorum of board meeting.

297. Can there be one director quorum?

298. Whether sitting fees can be paid for Managing Director or Whole-time Director.

299. Whether directors' report has to be signed only by the chairman of the board.

300. Every company has to mandatorily appoint managerial personnel.
301. Any individual can be appointed as a Managing Director.
302. Can MD be a rotational or non-rotational director?
303. Can additional director be appointed as MD?
304. Can a private company appoint a MD or WTD?
305. Is there any limit for private companies in which an individual can be an MD or Manager?
306. Can an individual be appointed as MD who has not completed 25 years or attained 70 years of age?
307. Can sitting fees be paid remuneration when there are no profits or inadequate profits?
308. Can non-executive directors be paid remuneration other than sitting fees, when there are no profits or inadequate profits?
309. Can managerial remuneration be paid to MD/WTD/Mgr when there are no profits or inadequate profits?
310. Can MD/WTD receive commission from his company and its subsidiary company?
311. Whether the net profits for calculation of managerial remuneration means net profits as shown by the Profit & Loss account.
312. Can remuneration to an MD/WTD/Mgr be paid by way of monthly payment?
313. Whether directors are eligible for sitting fees in the adjourned board meeting for want of quorum.
314. Can directors be paid traveling expense, hotel expenses or other expenses in addition to the sitting fees for attending board meetings?
315. Can a company appoint Manager & a Managing Director?
316. Can disqualification of MD u/s. 267 or disqualification of Manager u/s. 385 be condoned by CG?
317. Whether Managing Director is an employee of the company.
318. A Company Secretary in practice can certify upto a maximum of _____ of Annual Returns in a year,
    a) 30 unlisted Companies
    b) 30 listed Companies
    c) 20 Public Companies
    d) 20 listed Companies
319. How many Compliance Certificates can be given by a Company Secretary in practice?
    a) 30 certificates in a financial year
    b) 30 certificates in a calendar year
    c) 50 certificates in a financial year
    d) 50 certificates in a calendar year
320. A company having a paid-up capital of Rs. 3 crores have the following options,
    a) Shall appoint a Company Secretary
    b) Shall obtain Compliance Certificate from practicing Company Secretary
    c) Either of the above
    d) Both the above

321. The following may be appointed as sole selling agent of the company,

a) Individual

b) Firm

c) Body Corporate

d) Any of the above

322. The term of appointment of sole selling agent of the company,

a) Every year

b) upto 3 years

c) upto 5 years

d) No period is prescribed

323. The substantial interest for the purpose of appointment of sole selling agent is reckoned as under:

a) 50 lakhs of paid-up capital

b) 2% of shareholding

c) 5% of paid-up capital or Rs. 5 lakhs whichever is less

d) 20% of voting power

324. The following companies are not eligible to make political contributions,

a) Government Companies

b) Banking Companies

c) Non-Banking Finance Companies

d) All the above

325. The following statement is correct,

a) Political contribution can be approved through Circular Resolution

b) Contribution to National Defence Fund can be approved by Circular Resolution

c) Contribution to National Defence Fund need not be disclosed in Annual Accounts

d) All of the above

326. The appointment of sole selling agent for a company having a paid-up capital of ______ can be approved by way of ordinary resolution.

327. The compensation on termination of sole selling agency shall be lesser of commission for______ or______.

328. The contribution for political purpose can be made for an amount not exceeding __________ during preceding

329. The company which contravenes the provisions of political contribution shall be punished with a fine which may extend to ________.

330. Any amount of expenditure by way of publication by or on behalf of political party shall be ________.

331. The company can extend financial year of the company beyond 12 months,

a) upto 15 months with Board Resolution

b) upto 18 months with Board Resolution & prior approval of RoC

c) Any of the above

d) None of the above

332. The following has the right to demand unabridged annual accounts of the company without any fee or charge,

a) member of the company

b) debenture-holder of the company

c) depositor of a company

d) All of the above

333. The following forms to be filed once the accounts are adopted at the AGM,

a) e-Form 23AC for Balance Sheet within 30 days of AGM

b) e-Form 23ACA for profit & loss account within 30 days of AGM

c) e-Form 66 for Compliance Certificate within 30 days of AGM, if applicable

d) e-Form 20B for Annual Return within 60 days of AGM

e) All of the above

334. The books of accounts & other books and papers of every company are open to inspection without giving notice to the following persons,

a) Registrar of Companies

b) Officer of Government

c) Officer of SEBI

d) Any of the above

335. The following statement is incorrect regarding fixing remuneration of an auditor,

a) If auditor is appointed by Board, then by Board

b) If auditor is appointed by Central Government, then by CG

c) If auditor is appointed by C&AG, then by C&AG

d) By Members in General meeting, in other cases

336. Can a company maintain its books of accounts at its branch office?

337. Can books of accounts be maintained at a place other than registered office by the company?

338. Can director inspect books of accounts of the company?

339. Can annual accounts be re-opened for revision after its adoption by shareholders at AGM?

340. Whether preference shareholders are entitled to notices of general meetings, annual accounts, etc...

341. Whether the copies of profit & loss account filed by private limited companies are available for inspection.

342. Auditor can be removed before expiry of term by the company in general meeting only with the previous approval of Central Government.

343. Whether auditor can hold his office if AGM is not conducted or adjourned.

344. All the ordinary business at an AGM requires only ordinary resolution.

345. Can an auditor of the company attend general meeting?

346. Whether an auditor can access books of accounts only after closure of accounts.

347. Whether branch auditor has to be the statutory auditor of the company.

348. Can a cost auditor be appointed by the board of directors for cost audit?

349. The following members of the company may apply to CLB for oppression:

a) Lesser of 100 members or 10% of total members

b) Holding 10% of Issued Capital

c) Any of the above

d) 1000 members or 20% of total members

350. The following are the instances of oppression,

a) Non-declaration of dividend

b) Depriving a member of the right to dividend after it is declared

c) Drawing of remuneration by a director to which he is not legally entitled

d) Denial of inspection of books to a shareholder

e) Non-holding of meeting of the directors

351. The following acts are not held to be oppressive

a) Passing of a resolution by the directors of private company without disclosing nature of their interest

b) Issue of further shares benefiting a section of the shareholders

c) Passing a resolution to allot further shares to non-members

d) Refusal to register transmission under will

e) Registration of transfers in violation of Articles

352. The following are the instances of mismanagement,

a) Bonafide decision of the Board not to recommend dividend & to accumulate profits

b) Building up of reserves & thereafter non-declaration of dividend

c) Continuation of managing directors in office after the expiry of their term

d) Removal of secretary by majority decision of board not prejudicially affecting the interest of the company or the public interest

e) Mere making of loss

353. The following are the instances of not involving mismanagement,

a) Diversion of funds to benefit the majority

b) Mere allegation that assets of the company have not been applied properly

c) Advance loans without execution of document

d) Operation of bank account by unauthorized person

e) Illegal constitution of board of directors

354. The Government Directors appointed u/s. 408 by CLB

a) Will not be counted for the calculating rotational directors

b) Not liable to retire by rotation

c) Not required to hold qualification shares

d) All of the above

355. The basic principle of majority rule is laid down in ____________

356. The act can be said to be ________ if it is continuous, burdensome, harsh & wrongful.

357. The specified members can apply to CLB for oppression alleging that the affairs of the company are being conducted in a manner ____________ or in a manner ____________.

358. The specified members can apply to CLB for mismanagement alleging that the affairs of the company are being conducted in a manner____________ or in a manner ____________.

359. The Central Government directors appointed u/s. 402 for oppression or mismanagement by CLB for a period not exceeding _______ ,

360. If some members who consented to the application for oppression ceased to be members by selling shares or withdrawn their consent, whether the application is still maintainable.

361. Can a preference shareholding make an application to CLB for oppression?

362. Whether compliance of Sec 77A regarding buy back or Sec 100 regards reduction of capital is mandatory when CLB orders purchase of shares.

363. Can minority shareholders not satisfying the eligibility criteria u/s. 399 apply for oppression or mismanagement?

364. Can CLB order that no resolution of the company shall take effect unless confirmed by CLB?

365. The exchange ratio for the purpose of merger of amalgamation is arrived based on,

a) Effective Date

b) Appointed Date

c) Completion of procedures date

d) Any of the dates

366. The following can approve the scheme of merger or amalgamation or demerger:

a) By majority of members representing 3/4th in value

b) By way of an ordinary resolution

c) By way of special resolution

d) Any of the above

367. The order for winding up of transferor company can be passed only after ____________that, the affairs of the Company are not prejudicial to the interest of its Members or Public Interest.

a) Report of Official Liquidator

b) Report of RoC

c) Report of Regional Director

d) Report of CLB

368. The order for dissolution of transferor company can be passed only after __________that, the affairs of the Company are not prejudicial to the interest of its Members or Public Interest.

a) Report of Official Liquidator

b) Report of RoC

c) Report of Regional Director

d) Report of CLB

369. The following is the effective date for the purpose of merger or amalgamation,

a) the date determined by Transferor & Transferee Company

b) the date on which exchange ratio is fixed

c) the date of order of High Court

d) the date of filing of the Order of the High Court with RoC

370. If transferee holds more than 10% of shares to which the offer relates, then following approval is required for the purpose of Sec 395,

a) Offer is accepted by shareholders holding atleast 90% of value of shares

b) Offer is accepted by atleast 3/4th in number of holders

c) Both the above

d) None of the above

371. Mergers & amalgamations are _________ & not a compromise.

372. The Transferor Company gets ________ on Amalgamation.

373. The Assets & Liabilities as on the __________ will be transferred & vested with the transferee only on the __________ .

374. The date on which the Scheme gets approved and the Order of Court is filed with RoC is called _______ .

375. The appropriate authority for approval of scheme of mergers or amalgamation in______ .

376. The transferee company must get acceptance of __________ before the expiry of offer u/s. 395.

377. A person aggrieved by amalgamation order of CG u/s. 396, he may appeal to CLB _________ of date of publication in official gazette.

378. Can a foreign body corporate merge with Indian company?

379. Can an Indian company merge with a foreign body corporate?

380. Whether the objects of transferor & transferee company be the same.

381. Can court wind up the company in compromise & arrangement?

382. The books & papers of amalgamated company can be disposed after merger.

ANSWERS:

1. a) Public Financial Institutions
2. b) 50% of Paid-up Capital is held by Indian Citizens or Company
3. c) Government Company
4. b) Public Company
5. a) Private Company
6. a) controls the composition of its Board of Directors
7. a) Check Form
8. b) Pre-certification
9. b) Role Check
10. b) 3
11. d) 7 persons

12. b) 60 days
13. b) e-Form 1
14. d) Table D
15. a) Pre-incorporation Contract
16. b) Provisional Contract
17. No, such associations more than 7 members may only be wound up under Companies Act as unregistered company and not treated as Unregistered Company for any other purpose.
18. No, only Body Corporate includes Company incorporated outside India.
19. No, as body corporate includes company and Company incorporated outside India.
20. No, Producer Company is neither a private nor a public company but however for the purpose of administration, it is treated as deemed private company.
21. No, company under Companies Act, is a separate legal entity from the members constituting it.
22. No, subsidiary company cannot hold shares in holding company and even if it holds, it cannot exercise the voting rights
23. Yes, it is permitted and further if subsidiary is a trustee by way of transaction entered in the course of business, then also it can exercise voting rights and for no other purpose.
24. Yes, on payment prescribed fee through MCA site.
25. Yes, only persons with DIN can apply for the name of the company.
26. No, the situation clause of Memorandum mentions only the state in which the Company is situated and not the address
27. No, only e-from 18 and 32 requires pre-certification whereas e-Form 1 can be signed by Director or Secretary of the company
28. No, provisional contracts are binding only from the date of commencement of business by a public company
29. No, a company is bound by pre-incorporation contracts only if it enters new contract after incorporation.
30. C) Both
31. c) Special Resolution and Approval of Regional Director
32. a) Board Resolution
33. a) e-form 19
34. d) Authorised Capital of the company
35. Yes, company can rectify the name but only with the prior approval of Central Government or as per the directions of Central Government and not on its own.
36. No, the liability of a member cannot be increased without his written consent.
37. Yes, Certificate of Incorporation is conclusive evidence as to incorporation and the validity of which cannot be questioned after the issue. Further, all requirements of the Act pertaining to incorporation is deemed to be complied with.
38. No, as the Certificate of Incorporation is only a conclusive evidence for the purpose of incorporation.
39. No, as if the public company does not commence business within 1 year from the date of incorporation, it is enough ground to file winding-up petition against the company.

40. Central Government

41. shareholders by special resolution.

42. special resolution

43. capital clause

44. Yes, it is based on the doctrine of constructive notice which protects the company against the outsider.

45. No, the company cannot be held liable, as forgery is nullity in law.

46. Yes, it is based on the doctrine of lifting the Corporate Veil when the transactions are beyond the scope of MoA of the company.

47. shareholders by way of special resolution.

48. c) Physical Register to be maintained with names of depositories

49. c) Bonus Issue

50. c) Both the above

51. c) within 12 months of stamping by RoC in case of listed company

52. d) All of the above

53. d) All the above.

54. No, RoM is a mandatory statutory register to be maintained under Companies Act and if all shares are in demat mode, then the name of depositories will be entered in RoM.

55. No, as a partnership firm is not separate legal entity but it can hold the shares in the name of partners. Note, a firm can be a member of Section 25 company.

56. No, it can be issued by only such companies with distributable profits in 3 preceeding previous years and satisfy prescribed conditions.

57. No, the Company should not be convicted under SEBI, SCRA & FEMA to issue equity shares with DVR.

58. No, the power by the Board to expel a member shall be illegal and void.

59. No, the company that has made default u/s. 80A, then the company cannot declare dividend on equity shares forever.

60. No, sweat equity cannot be issued for more than 5 crores or more than 15% of paid-up capital unless CG approval is obtained.

61. Yes, Companies Act mandates every issue made to public to make an application for listing to stock exchanges after complying with SEBI ICDR Regulations.

62. Yes, unsecured debentures are treated at par with deposits and have to comply with Section 58A.

63. Yes, both secured & unsecured debenture holder may file a winding up petition as creditor to the company.

64. No, in case of transmission of shares no share transfer deed be lodged and therefore no consideration or stamp duty is involved.

65. Capital Redemption

66. managerial remuneration.

67. 3 years

68. 15 days.

69. 60 days

70. General Meeting.
71. blank transfer
72. certification of transfer.
73. b) Shelf Prospectus
74. a) 1 year from the date of opening of first issue of securities
75. c) Red herring Prospectus
76. c) Any of the above
77. d) all the above
78. d) All the above
79. Yes, one is filed for subsequent issues with shelf prospectus and other is issued to elicit demand before issuing Red herring prospectus.
80. No, re-issue of forfeited shares is sale and not allotment; hence no returns are filed.
81. No, board of directors or board authorized committee can only allot shares.
82. No, a private company by definition cannot offer shares to public and further prospectus is applicable only to public company.
83. prospectus.
84. statement in lieu of prospectus.
85. 90 days
86. Impersonation
87. Impersonation
88. Shelf Prospectus
89. ordinary resolution.
90. e-form 2
91. d) Any of the above
92. c) Both the above
93. d) 35% from shareholders & others
94. c) Reserve for bad debts & revaluation reserve for assets
95. a) 1%, 1.5% & 2% for deposits up to 1 year, 2 year & 3 years respectively
96. d) 6 months from close of Financial Year or Annual General Meeting
97. c) Both the above
98. No, only public companies having net owned fund of Rs. 1 crore may accept deposit.
99. Yes, provided they give a declaration that it is not out of borrowed funds.
100. 15% of amount of deposits
101. within 8 weeks
102. 8 calendar years.
103. 1% for the unexpired period
104. 60 days

105. Company law board.

106. 30th June.

107. a) e-Form 8 within 30 days to RoC

108. a) it shall be registered with RoC within 30 days of receiving documents by post

109. c) On liquidation, chargeholder assumes the status of unsecured creditor

110. crystallization of floating charge.

111. Floating charge

112. certificate of registration.

113. Yes, as Charge includes Mortgage as per Companies Act.

114. No, in addition to the company, the interested person (chargeholder) can also register the charge with RoC

115. No, Register of charge is only open for inspection by member or creditor and copies are not allowed to be taken

116. No, its only the security that is destroyed in case of non-registration and not the debt. In fact, money becomes payable immediately due to non-registration.

117. c) 30.9.2007 i.e, within 6 months from the close of financial year

118. e) All the above

119. e) All the above

120. b) Declaration of dividend in EGM

121. c) 1/10th of Paid-up capital or Voting power

122. b) Registered Office of the company

123. c) Any of the above

124. a) Articles of private company can prescribe 10 days notice & is valid

125. c) Both the above

126. b) when vote for the resolution are not less than 3 times the votes cast against

127. d) all the above

128. c) 2

129. b) In case of equality of votes, only when articles authorize

130. c) proxy dated later & lodged earlier or later

131. a) every member has one vote

132. c) Both the cases

133. d) Any of the above

134. d) all the above resolutions

135. 7 days

136. Special Notice

137. Extraordinary General Meeting (EGM).

138. 21 days , 45 days , 3 months

139. 20% or more

140. Postal ballot
141. Scrutinizer
142. 30 days
143. Quorum
144. Minutes Book
145. 30 days
146. inspection
147. Schedule IX
148. 48 hours of demand.
149. 2 scrutineers
150. atleast 6 weeks
151. atleast 2 weeks
152. No, though members are at absolute liberty to discuss any matter arising out of statutory report, resolutions shall be passed only for the contents in the notice.
153. Yes, it shall be a working day as on the date of issuing notice.
154. Yes, AGM may be held at registered office or at any place within the postal limits & the local limits of the city.
155. No, though the company can adjourn AGM, the adjourned AGM must also be held within the statutory period.
156. Yes, in case of default of AGM or impracticability of EGM & CLB convenes an AGM / EGM, it may direct that one member present in person or proxy shall be deemed to constitute a meeting.
157. No, the prescribed 4 business if done at an AGM is an ordinary business and all other business are special whereas members approval by way of ordinary resolution is prescribed for cases where special resolution is not mandated.
158. Yes, all business requiring special notice u/s. 190 mandates ordinary resolution.
159. No, all special business including where special resolution is required mandates explanatory statement.
160. Yes, otherwise the notice of meeting becomes incomplete and proceedings become invalid.
161. Yes, in case of impracticability of holding EGM, CLB on its own motion or on application of director or member can call for an EGM.
162. Yes, unless the articles of private company is amended to exclude the applicability of Sec 173(2) pertaining to explanatory statement.
163. No, notice of general meeting is required to be served only on the first named joint holders.
164. Yes, however accidental omission will not invalidate the proceedings of the meeting.
165. No, book closure is closing the share transfer books to ascertain eligible shareholders on a particular date whereas record date is ascertaining eligible holders without closing the books.
166. Yes, 42 days notice for physical shares, 30 days notice for demat shares & 7 working days notice for rights issue shall be given to stock exchanges.
167. Yes, Postal ballot includes voting by members by postal or electronic mode instead of voting by being present personally for transacting business in general meeting.

168. Yes, the list of business given in the Companies Rules, 2001 shall be made by listed company only through postal ballot.

169. No, scrutinizer who is appointed by board for postal ballot voting process shall not be in employment of the company.

170. No, only members present in person and not by proxies shall be counted for quorum.

171. Yes, such situation will arise, if company is a member of the other.

172. Yes, but only in case of inability of the chairman of the meeting.

173. Yes, the discretion of the chairman with regard to the inclusion or exclusion of any matter is absolute & unfettered.

174. No, chairman can put the casting or second vote only in case of tie (ordinary resolution).

175. No, proxies can be appointed only in case of general meeting & not board meeting.

176. Yes, also fresh proxies can be lodged for adjourned meetings.

177. Yes, such authorized representatives are treated as members personally present and hence has the right to appoint proxy.

178. No, proxy can vote only on poll and has the right to demand poll.

179. Yes, unless the transfer or transmission intimation was received by the company before voting on the resolution.

180. Yes, in such case the proxy stands revoked.

181. Yes, board resolution regarding appointment or re-appointment or amendment or variation in terms of Managing director shall be registered with RoC.

182. Yes, the chairman can remove any scrutinizer before declaration of result of the poll.

183. d) Any of the above

184. b) Interim Dividend is declared by Board of Directors

185. a) Shareholders can declare 10% or less as dividend

186. c) It is legally adjusted against sum due from shareholder

187. a) Within 5 days, deposit in a separate bank account

188. c) After 7 years of opening unpaid dividend account, if remains unpaid

189. d) All the above

190. d) Lower of the above

191. a) 10% of Paid-up capital & Free reserves

192. d) All the above

193. b) up to 12%

194. b) not exceeding the close of the half year next after the half year during which work has completed

195. b) Confirmation by Court

196. d) All the above

197. c) "and reduced"

198. e) All the above

199. a) Dimunition of Issued capital

200. c) Shareholders paid Calls-in-advance
201. a) By passing special resolution or getting consent of 3/4th members, in writing
202. c) Within 21 days from the date of the concerned special resolution
203. a) 15 Public Companies
204. c) Maximum 12 directors in a Public Company
205. d) All of the above
206. c) Non filing of annual accounts and returns for any 3 continuous financial years
207. b) till the date of ensuing AGM or ought to have been held
208. e) All of the above
209. c) Both the above
210. d) All the above
211. b) Entering into contracts which he is interested without complying Sec 297
212. c) Both of the above
213. c) A private company in which director is a director or member
214. a) Transactions between 2 public limited companies
215. c) if it is a contract by company having paid-up capital of Rs. 1 crore or more
216. a) Services rendered in professional capacity by advocate or practicing CS/CA, etc...
217. b) Loan within 100% of Free Reserves with Unanimous approval of Board
218. 2
219. Rs. 5,000/-, one share
220. First Directors
221. maximum number of directors
222. Company in General Meeting
223. retire by rotation
224. board of directors , 3 months
225. returns to the State
226. 2/3rd
227. automatic reappointment
228. private limited company
229. Rs. 20,000 or less
230. Rs. 5 crores or more , 1000 or more
231. 2 companies
232. 3 years
233. consent to act as director
234. Special Notice
235. vacation of office

236. less than 2%.

237. quorum , voting

238. office or place of profit

239. by way of special resolution u/s. 314(1).

240. of Central Government and approval by way of special resolution u/s. 314(1B).

241. fresh special resolution

242. vacate office

243. deposits u/s. 58A

244. Yes, as there is no approval required even if directors of private company exceed 12.

245. Yes, if it's within the maximum limit of directors prescribed in the Articles.

246. Yes, but only for the purpose of increasing the quorum or of summoning a general meeting of the company.

247. Yes, members can either make application to CLB or convene & hold EGM to get the directors appointed thereat.

248. No, shareholders cannot dictate terms to directors except by amendment of AoA or by removal of directors as decided in Rolta India Ltd v. Venire Industries Ltd.

249. No, as per Sec. 253, no body corporate or firm or association becomes a director. So, only an individual can be appointed as director.

250. Yes, as Section 275 mandates that an individual shall not hold office in more than 15 public limited companies only.

251. No, as per Section 274(1)(g) if the Company has made any default, then all such directors shall not be eligible to be appointed as director of any other PUBLIC limited company for a period of 5 years from the default.

252. No, as per Section 274, CG has the power to remove disqualifications only in the cases of conviction or call money due.

253. No, as disqualification u/s. 274 occurs when an individual is proposed to be appointed as a director but such director shall vacate office automatically u/s. 283.

254. No, as per the provisio to Section 253, no company shall appoint or reappoint a person as director unless DIN has been allotted to him.

255. No, as Section 270 regarding qualification of shares is applicable only to public limited company which has prescribed share qualification in its Articles

256. Yes, but more specifically the directors name should appear in the Register of Members within 2 months from his appointment.

257. No, as per Sec 312, no director shall assign his office during his life time.

258. No, if First Directors were not named in the Articles, then subscribers to Memorandum, who are individuals, shall be deemed to be the directors.

259. No, additional director is excluded in determining the number of directors retiring by rotation for the purpose of Sec 255.

260. Yes, additional director is a director for all purposes and can be appointed as MD/WTD on compliance of provisions of the Act.

261. No, unless he is regularized as a director by members.

262. Yes, alternate director can be appointed as MD even if the original director was not so but not vice versa.

263. Yes, as per Sec 257, a member who intends to appoint a director shall give a 14 days notice before General Meeting with a deposit of Rs.500/-

264. No, though a small share holder director is a director for all the purposes of the Act he shall neither retire by rotation nor be appointed as MD/WTD.

265. No, MD can resign his office only when the resignation is accepted by the Board of Directors as decided in Achutha Pai v. RoC.

266. No, as per Sec 318, no compensation shall be paid to a director who vacates office u/s. 283.

267. No, any director can be removed by ordinary resolution in General Meeting u/s. 284 and thus Articles cannot provide remove only by Special Resolution.

268. No, as per the decision in M.R. Electronic Components Ltd v. Assitant RoC, though the salary advance was similar to loan, if the person receiving it is as per the terms of the agreement then Sec 295 will not attract.

269. No, as contract should be concerned with purchase or sale or supply of goods or materials or services only to attract Sec 297.

270. No, only the concerned director shall be levied with a penalty and shall be deemed to have vacated his office u/s. 283

271. Yes, but there is a special case when guarantee is given exceeding the limits in case of emergency, then special resolution can be passed subsequently.

272. Yes, but a listed public company has to get the approval only through postal ballot.

273. Board Meeting , Circular Resolution

274. 3 calendar months ,

275. every director in India , usual address in India

276. notice

277. Interested director

278. increasing the number of directors , summoning a general meeting

279. within 15 minutes

280. within 5 minutes

281. Casting or Second or Deciding vote

282. prima facie , not available

283. Sitting fees

284. private limited company.

285. paid-up capital and free reserves

286. directors responsibility statement

287. directors' report.

288. No, Sec 285 mandates that board meeting shall be held once in every 3 calendar months and not by way of circulation.

289. No, board meeting may or convened by a director or a Manager/Secretary shall convene a board meeting at the instance of director.

290. No, as the Act is silent, board meetings can be held anywhere.

291. Yes, provided an inspection time of statutory register is prescribed in the Articles for atleast 2 hours per day, and then statutory registers can be taken away during other times.

292. Yes, a board meeting can be held on a public holiday but an adjourned board meeting for the want of quorum cannot be held on a public holiday.

293. Yes, notice must be given to a director even if he is precluded from voting in a particular meeting.

294. Yes, notice has to given to original director also at his usual address in India even when an alternate director is appointed.

295. As per Sec 300, interested directors are not counted for the purpose of quorum unless otherwise it is a private limited company, for which Sec 300 does not apply.

296. No, as there is no provision for directors to appoint a proxy in the board meeting.

297. Yes, it may be in extreme cases where there were only 2 directors and one director died, and then such single director can call for general meeting to appoint directors.

298. Yes, but only with the approval of CG, sitting fees can be paid to MD/WTD as there is no provision in Schedule XIII for such payment.

299. Yes, the chairman has to sign the directors report, authorized, otherwise, it has to be signed by manager or secretary and by not less than 2 directors.

300. No, only a public limited company having paid-up capital of Rs. 5 crores or more has to mandatorily appoint managerial personnel.

301. No, as per Sec 2(26) of the Act only a director who is an individual can be appointed as an MD whereas a Manager can be an individual as per Sec 2(24).

302. Yes, if an MD is a rotational director his term of office as MD will come to an end if shareholders has not re-appointed as director in the AGM.

303. Yes, such additional director's office as MD will also come to an end in the ensuing AGM unless regularized as a director in the same AGM.

304. Yes, a private company can appoint MD or WTD without the approval of CG and also it need not limit the term of appointment to 5 years.

305. No, a person can hold the office of MD or Manager in any number of private companies.

306. Yes, but only with the approval of shareholders by way of special resolution.

307. Yes, sitting fees can be paid irrespective of profits; as such fees payable to director shall not be covered within the specified limit of 11%.

308. No, in case of no profit or inadequate profit, no further payment can be made to non-executive directors.

309. Yes, in case of no profits or inadequate profits, remuneration to managerial personnel may be paid within the limits prescribed under Schedule XIII without CG approval.

310. No, a director who is in receipt of commission from the company & who is either in whole-time employment or MD shall not be entitled to receive any commission or other remuneration from any subsidiary of such company.

311. No, net profits here means net profits of the company for any financial year computed in the manner laid down in Sec 349 & 350 of the Act.

312. Yes, remuneration to managerial personnel may be paid either by way of monthly payment &/or specified % of net profits.

313. Yes, sitting fees is a remuneration paid to directors present at the meeting and hence it has to be paid even if board meeting was adjourned for want of quorum or otherwise.

314. Yes, provided the Articles of Association should authorize such payment.

315. No, as per Sec 197A, a company cannot employ both MD & Manager but can simultaneously have WTD & Manager.

316. No, disqualification of MD u/s 267 cannot be condoned by CG whereas disqualification u/s. 385 for Manager can be condoned by CG.

317. Yes, MD is an employee of the company as Schedule XIII provides for payment of Gratuity & Provident Fund to MD.

318. b) 30 listed Companies

319. d) 50 certificates in a calendar year

320. c) Either of the above

321. d) Any of the above

322. c) upto 5 years

323. c) 5% of paid-up capital or Rs. 5 lakhs whichever is less

324. a) Government Companies

325. b) Contribution to National Defence Fund can be approved by Circular Resolution

326. less than 50 lakhs

327. 3 years , average commission for 3 years multiplied by unexpired period.

328. 5% of average net profits , 3 financial years

329. 3 times the amount contributed

330. deemed to be a political contribution.

331. c) Any of the above

332. d) Any of the above

333. e) Any of the above

334. d) Any of the above

335. c) If auditor is appointed by C&AG, then by C&AG

336. Yes, where a company has branch office, books of accounts may be kept at branch and summarized returns should be sent to registered office at intervals not more than 3 months.

337. Yes, it can be maintained anywhere in India provided it is approved by Board & intimated to RoC within 7 days of change.

338. Yes, director has a statutory right to inspect books of accounts of the company during business hours but has no right to make copies of it.

339. No, normally accounts once adopted shall not be re-opened unless for tax, insurance & law purposes and such accounts to be laid at subsequent AGM/EGM.

340. Yes, though preference shareholders are not entitled to vote at general meetings, they are still entitled to receive notices of general meetings, annual accounts, etc…

341. No, profit & loss account of a private company is not available for inspection to any person other than a member of the concerned company.

342. Yes, but first auditors are an exception who can be removed without CG approval.

343. Yes, auditor shall continue to hold office until the conclusion of adjourned AGM or till AGM is held & conducted.

344. Yes, but there is an exception to this rule, when auditor is appointed by a company in which 25% or more of subscribed capital is held by Government, Public Financial Banks, Nationalised banks, etc…in which case, special resolution is mandatory.

345. Yes, an auditor is entitled to attend all General Meetings of the company u/s. 231 and shall be given an opportunity of being heard on part of business which concerns him.

346. No, auditor has the right to access books at all times during the period he acts as an auditor.

347. No, though branch auditor may be the statutory auditor, the company in general meeting authorizes board to appoint any other qualified CA in consultation with statutory auditor.

348. Yes, but only with the prior approval of Central Government, Cost Auditor can be appointed by the Board.

349. c) Any of the above

350. b) Depriving a member of the right to dividend after it is declared

351. c) Passing a resolution to allot further shares to non-members

352. c) Continuation of managing directors in office after the expiry of their term

353. b) Mere allegation that assets of the company have not been applied properly

354.

355. Foss v. Harbottle.

356. oppression

357. prejudicial to public interest , oppressive to any members

358. prejudicial to public interest , prejudicial to the interest of the company

359. 3 years

360. Yes, the requirements as to minimum holding are to be satisfied only at the time of filing of the application.

361. Yes, the application should be made by requisite number of members, thus a preference shareholder is also entitled to make an application to CLB.

362. No, CLB has special powers u/s. 402 to order buy back and in case of purchase, the consequent reduction of capital does not require compliance of 77A & 100.

363. Yes, Central Government has the power to authorize any person to move CLB u/s. 401.

364. Yes, in case of public company, on application by MD or Director regarding likely change in composition of board prejudicially can pass such order u/s. 409.

365. b) Appointed Date

366. a) By majority of members representing 3/4th in value

367. b) Report of RoC

368. a) Report of Official Liquidator

369. d) the date of filing of the Order of the High Court with RoC

370. c) Both the above

371. arrangements

372. dissolved

373. Appointed date , effective date.

374. effective date.

375. High Court.

376. 90% of shareholders in value

377. within 30 days

378. Yes, the Transferor Company can be a Body Corporate but the Transferee Company shall be a Company registered under Companies Act, 1956.

379. No, as the Transferor Company can be a Body Corporate but the Transferee Company shall be a Company registered under Companies Act, 1956.

380. No, the objects of both the transferor company and the transferee company need not be same as object clause can be amended

381. Yes, court has powers u/s. 392 to wind up the company if it feels that the scheme of compromise or arrangement cannot be worked out satisfactorily.

382. No, the books and papers of all such company can be disposed off only with the prior permission of the Central Government

Drafting, Appearances & Pleadings (DAP)

- Company Secretarial Practice (CSP)

In general, any secretarial practice to a law comes with the law itself. For instance, Foreign Trade Policy gives the law whereas Handbook of Procedures gives the procedures for implementing the law. Drafting is however, different and here, drafting by itself means the Legal Drafting. There is no specific enactment governing Drafting but it has evolved over the years and is imbibed in every law. Thus, drafting is a crystallization (pooling of thoughts/facts with clarity) and expression (making it in writing) of a legal right, privilege, function, duty, or status in a definitive/structured form.

The SAMPLE DEEDS given in this material are based on the teachings of our GURU Shri K S Anantharaman. Shri K S Anantharaman is an Advocate and Professor who has authored many books including Lectures on Company Law, General and Commercial laws.

Laws Governing Drafting, Appearances & Pleadings

ACT	YEAR
Indian Contract Act	1872
Indian Evidence Act	1872
Transfer of Property Act	1882
Powers of Attorney Act	1882
Indian Trust Act	1882
Indian Easement Act	1882
General Clauses Act	1897
Indian Stamp Act	1899
Registration Act	1908
Code of Civil Procedure	1908
Indian Succession Act	1925
Sale of Goods Act	1930
Indian Partnership Act	1932
The Notaries Act	1952
The Companies Act	1956
Copyrights Act	1957
Income Tax Act	1961
Limitation Act	1963
Patents Act	1970
Contempt of Courts Act	1971
Hire Purchase Act	1972
Benami Transactions (Prohibitions) Act	1988
Securities & Exchange Board of India (SEBI) Act	1992
Arbitration and Conciliation Act	1996
Trade Marks Act	1999
Foreign Exchange Management Act	1999
The Competition Act	2002
The Limited Liability Partnership Act	2008

All the Acts shall be read with Rules, Regulations and Notifications as amended on date along with the relevant cases. Further provisions regarding appeals, revisions, etc… under various Direct & Indirect Tax Laws; Tribunals, compounding and consent order provisions under Securities laws are also covered.

The relevant provisions of the said Acts are dealt at appropriate places. Subsequent to drafting and its finalisation, the formalities of authenticating the deed or instrument must be performed. These formalities could include attestation, registration, or stamping or all or any of these, depending on the relevant law regulating such deed or instrument. In this chapter the essence of the basic legislations governing the formalities of Registration & Stamping are covered.

Choose your best:

1. Arbitration & Conciliation Act, was passed in year:
   a) 1998
   b) 1988
   c) 1996
   d) 1995

2. The documents required compulsory registration are
   a) Instruments of gifts of immovable property.
   b) Lease of immovable property from year to year or for any term exceeding one year or
   c) reserving a yearly rent
   d) Instruments which create or extinguish any right or title to or in an immovable property of a value of more than one hundred rupees.
   e) All of above.

3. A document which requires registration but not registered within a period of 4 months then the parties can apply for registration with a subsequent period of
   a) 3 months.
   b) 15 days.
   c) 4 months.
   d) 8 months

4. The following Act is passed in the year 1882 is
   a) Transfer of Property Act
   b) Indian Trust Act
   c) Power of Attorney Act
   d) All of the above
   e) None of the above

5. Which of the Act is passed in the 1897:
   a) Indian Contract Act
   b) Indian Evidence Act
   c) General Clauses Act
   d) Indian Trust Act

6. Where the document should be presented for registration under Registration Act?
   a) Sub-registrar of assurances
   b) Registrar of company
   c) Court.

Ans:

1. C)
2. D)
3. C)
4. D)
5. C)
6. A)

Fill your blanks:

1. Section 17 of the Registration Act, 1908 lays down different categories of documents for which registration is ____________.
2. The Indian succession Act was passed in _____.

Ans:

1. Compulsory
2. 1925

Give your reasons:

1. As per Section 2(6) of registration act 1908 the term immovable property includes standing timber, growing crops.
2. Every document requires compulsory registration.
3. A document which is required to be registered but not registered can count as evidence in a court.
4. Contempt of Courts Act 1971 governs pleadings.
5. Witness is not required for registration.

Ans:

1. Incorrect, because it does not include standing timber, growing crops.
2. Incorrect, because there are few documents which are optional for registration as given in Section 18 of the Registration Act.
3. Incorrect, because as per Section 49(c) of the Act, if a document, of which registration is compulsory u/s 17 of Registration Act has not been registered, it CANNOT be produce as evidence in a court.
4. Correct
5. Incorrect as for registration at least 2 witnesses are required.

REGISTRATION ACT, 1908

Registration MEANS recording of the contents of a document with a Registering Officer and preservation of copies of the original document. Registration provides safety and security to transactions relating to immovable property, even if the document is lost or destroyed. It gives publicity and public exposure to documents thereby preventing forgeries and frauds in regard to transactions and execution of documents.

The Registration Act, 1908, was enacted with the intention of providing orderliness, discipline and public notice in regard to transactions relating to immovable property and protection from fraud and forgery of documents of transfer. This is achieved by requiring compulsory registration of certain types of documents and providing for consequences of non-registration.

COMPULSORY REGISTRATION

Section 17 of the Registration Act, 1908 lays down different categories of documents for which registration is compulsory. The documents relating to the following transactions of IMMOVABLE PROPERTIES are required to be compulsorily registered:

a) Instruments of gift of immovable property.

b) Lease of immovable property from year to year or for any term exceeding one year or reserving a yearly rent.

c) Instruments which create or extinguish any right or title to or in an immovable property of a value of more than one hundred rupees.

Under section 2(6) of the Registration Act, 1908 the term "Immovable property" INCLUDES "Land, buildings, hereditary allowances, rights to ways, lights, fisheries or any other benefit to arise out of land, and things attached to the earth, or permanently fastened to any thing which is attached to the earth, but not standing timber, growing crops or grass."

NOTE: Any "Agreement of Sale" or "Agreement of Lease" NEED NOT be registered as it DOES NOT involve transfer of possession of immovable property.

OPTIONAL REGISTRATION

Section 18 of the Act lays down the instruments of which registration is optional. Some of these instruments are listed as under:-

a) Instruments (other than instruments of gifts and wills) relating to the transfer of an immovable property, the value of which is less than Rs. 100/-

b) Instruments acknowledging the receipt or payment of any consideration.

c) Lease of an immovable property for a term not exceeding 1 year.

d) Instruments transferring any decree or order of a court where the subject matter of such decree or order is an immovable property, the value of which is less than Rs. 100/-.

e) Wills (may be attested under Indian Succession Act).

NON REGISTRATION, NOT EVIDENCE

According to Section 49(c) of the Act, if a document, of which registration is COMPULSORY under Section 17 of Registration Act, has not been registered, it CANNOT be produced as evidence in a court of law.

DELAY IN REGISTRATION (4 + 4 months)

As per the provisions of Section 25 of Registration Act, 1908 if a document is not presented for registration within 4 months of execution (signing) [or its arrival in India], then the parties to the agreement can apply to the Registrar WITHIN a subsequent period of 4 months, who may direct that on payment of a fine UPTO 10 times the proper registration fees, such a document should be admitted for registration.

PROCEDURE FOR REGISTRATION

For registration of any instrument,

- the original document should be typed/printed on one side only
- along with 2 photocopies of the original have to be submitted
- in the presence of 2 witnesses and
- on payment of the appropriate registration fees to the Registrar.

A power of attorney holder may REGISTER a document, if the Power of Attorney is EXECUTED & AUTHENTICATED before the Registrar or Magistrate or where the Principal granting power of attorney is OUTSIDE India, then by a notary or Judge or Magistrate or representative of Central Government.

The landmark judgment on *Suraj Lamp & Industries Pvt. Ltd. v. State of Haryana & Anr.* by Hon'ble Supreme Court of India lays down following principles as to validity & legality of Sale/transfer by General Power of Attorney Sales (for short `GPA Sales') or Sale Agreement/General Power of Attorney/Will transfers (for short `SA/GPA/WILL' transfers) [without making a registered sale deed] to a series of prospective real estate dealers by avoiding multiple stamp duties/registration fees so as to increase their profit margin:

- Immovable property can be legally and lawfully transferred / conveyed only by a registered deed of conveyance/ Sale deed. Similarly, a lease can be validly transferred only under a registered Assignment of Lease.
- GPA Sales or `SA/GPA/WILL' transfers do not convey any title nor create any interest in an immovable property EXCEPT to the limited extent as provided in Section 53A of the Transfer of Property Act.
- Section 53A: If the prospective buyer is put in POSSESSION of the property in pursuance to a sale agreement, the owner of the property CANNOT disturb the possession by the prospective buyer, however the legal ownership remains with the OWNER UNTIL a registered Sale Deed is duly executed.
- However, there is NO BAR in carrying out genuine transactions involving registration of sale deed by an agent holding a registered power of attorney and acting for the owner of the property as mentioned above.

DESCRIPTION OF PROPERTY IN SCHEDULE

Section 21 of the Act deals with the provisions relating to the description of an immovable property along with maps or plans to IDENTIFY the property involved BY the Registering Authority. The description should mention whether House & Building, Land & Building or Vacant site along with,

- the area of the property,
- the number of the property,
- the boundaries of the property,
- the streets on which it is situated, along with name of the village, taluk or district
- the city Survey Number [if not mentioned is a ground for REFUSAL to registration]

It is the discretion of the registering officer to refuse to accept a document if the description of the immovable property is not sufficient to identify the property correctly.

PLACE OF REGISTRATION

As per Section 28 and 29 of the Registration Act the document should be presented for registration at the office of the SUB-REGISTRAR OF ASSURANCES within whose sub district the whole or some portion of the property to which such document relates is situated or in the office of the Sub-Registrar situated at Mumbai, Delhi, Madras or Calcutta.

NO ENCUMBRANCES or TITLE VERIFICATION

In order to find out if the title of the seller is clear and marketable, one has to take search of the property at the offices of the relevant Sub-Registrars. The objections pertaining to the title of the property can be easily verified after taking the search, for example: if the party has mortgaged and registered the documents with the Sub Registrar of Assurances then it can be known only after taking the search of the property.

Title Report is the report of search in the ownership of the property of the person which shall be done at Tehsildar office, Registrar office, Municipal taxes office and Civil courts for pending proceedings.

INDIAN STAMP ACT, 1899

Stamp Duty prescribed in Indian Stamp Act, 1899 is applicable ONLY in respect of few documents such as bill of exchange, cheques, promissory notes, bill of lading, letter of credit, policy of insurance, transfer of share, debentures, proxies and receipts (**under Union List**). In all other documents, rates prescribed by State Government prevail (**under State List**). However 'Stamp duties' OTHER THAN powers to decide rates of stamp duty such as principles of valuation, mode of payment, adjudication, allowances for stamps, penalty and prosecution (**under Concurrent List**), state law CANNOT be contrary to the central law UNLESS prior assent of President was obtained.

According to Section 3, 17 & 18 of the Act, an INSTRUMENT chargeable with duty and executed by ANY person in INDIA shall be stamped BEFORE or AT THE TIME OF execution (signing), if it is mentioned in the SCHEDULE I to this Act. If it is executed OUT OF INDIA, then it may be stamped WITHIN 3 MONTHS of its RECEIPT in India.

DULY STAMPED

'Duly Stamped' MEANS that the instrument bears a IMPRESSED or ADHESIVE stamp NOT LESS THAN proper amount AND that such stamp has been USED or AFFIXED in accordance with law. Impressed or Adhesive stamp shall be used in such a way that it cannot be used again, for instance, adhesive stamp to be effectively cancelled. [Sec 2(11)]

NON STAMPING, NOT EVIDENCE

According to Section 35 of the Act, an INSTRUMENT not chargeable to duty or NOT stamped,

- shall NOT be admitted as evidence [may be IMPOUNDED by person having authority to receive evidence for levy of duty & penalty by Collector]
- shall NOT be registered.

Supreme Court in case of *Avinash Kumar Chauhan v. Vijay Krishna Mishra* held that as Section 35 of the Indian Stamp Act, 1899 categorically provides that sale agreement (of land) which is not stamped shall not be admitted FOR ANY PURPOSE WHATSOEVER. If all purposes for which document is sought to be brought in evidence are excluded, the document would not be admissible for COLLATERAL PURPOSES.

EXPIRY OF STAMP PAPER

Indian Stamp Act, 1899 nowhere prescribes any expiry date for use of a stamp paper. Section 54 merely provides that a person possessing a stamp paper for which he has NO IMMEDIATE USE (which is not spoiled or rendered unfit or useless), can seek REFUND of the value thereof by SURRENDERING such stamp paper to the Collector PROVIDED IT was purchased WITHIN 6 MONTHS next preceding the date on which it was so surrendered. The stipulation of the period of 6 months prescribed in Section 54 is only for the purpose of seeking refund of the value of the unused stamp paper, and NOT FOR USE of the stamp paper.

According to Supreme Court judgement dated 19/02/2008 in the case of *Thiruvengada Pillai Vs. Navaneethammal and another*, **THE STAMP PAPERS DO NOT HAVE ANY EXPIRY PERIOD**. However, the said ruling WOULD NOT apply to the State of Maharashtra, as it is matter falling under CONCURRENT LIST where Section 52B(b) of the Bombay Stamp Act [State Law] specifically provides that stamps which have NOT BEEN USED WITHIN 6 months from the date of purchase, shall be rendered INVALID.

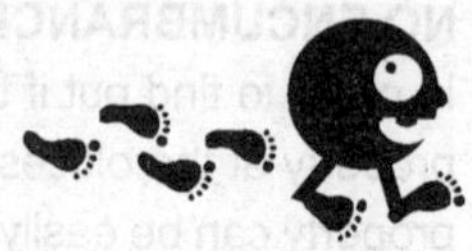

VALUATION OF STAMP DUTY UNDER SALE REGISTRATION

The Supreme Court in a recent case under the bench comprising Justices A K Mathur and Markandey Katju held that if a property is in litigation for a long time and during the pendency, if prices of the property have shot up, the buyer shall have to pay stamp duty at the enhanced market value of the property and further NOTED that " it is true that no one should suffer on account of the pendency of the matter, but this consideration does NOT affect the principles of interpretation of a taxing statute. If a TAXING STATUTE has to be construed **STRICTLY**, then the plea that the incumbent took a long time to get a decree for execution against the vendor cannot weigh with the court for interpreting the provisions of taxing statutes.

Hence, the Supreme Court has held that **THE STAMP DUTY ON PROPERTY HAS TO BE PAID ACCORDING TO ITS MARKET VALUE ON THE DATE OF REGISTRATION OF THE SALE DEED.**

Kindly note, the principles of VALUATION falls under the Concurrent List, where state law with prior assent of President can OVERRIDE central law.

Broadly these are the laws governing drafting in India. It is highly advisable to remember the full name of the Act along with the Year in which it is passed, which can help one to quote at appropriate places and that is the significance of this chapter. Further, the provisions of Registration Act and Stamp Act shall be kept in mind for drafting any type of deed. Registration of documents makes the process of verification and certification of title easier and simpler. In general, the instruments which normally attract stamp duty are transfer, sale, lease, mortgage, gift or any other such commercial transactions.

NEED FOR KNOWLEDGE ABOUT DRAFTING & CONVEYANCING TO CORPORATE EXECUTIVES:

1. To seek legal advice from legal experts
2. To carry out documentation departmentally
3. To study & interpret the documents.

General Principles Of Drafting

DOCUMENTATION

Documentation refers to Drafting & Conveyancing. It is the ACTIVITY which symbolizes PREPARATION of documents, including FINALISATION & EXECUTION thereof.

DRAFTING

Drafting may be defined as the SYNTHESIS (combination) of LAW and FACT in a LANGUAGE form. Thus, the important elements in drafting are,

1. The Law
2. The Facts
3. The Language.

Drafting means presenting of COMMERCIAL TRANSACTION in its legal and its facts, in a SYSTEMATIC MANNER. It involves THINKING & COMPOSING.

Drafting in legal sense means an act (or an art) of preparing the legal documents like agreements, contracts, deeds, etc.

CONVEYANCING

Conveyancing connotes a DEED whereby TITLE to a PROPERTY is transferred from one person to another, but does NOT include acquisition by INHERITANCE.

For instance, a document of immovable property once COMPLETED & REGISTERED becomes a conveyance.

Thus, Conveyancing is the art of drafting deeds and documents whereby property is transferred by one person to another. Also, read the head "DOCUMENTS" below.

Section 2(10) of Indian Stamp Act, 1899 defines as conveyance INCLUDES a conveyance on sale and every instrument by which property, whether movable or immovable is transferred during one's LIFETIME. Thus the transfer shall be INTER VIVOS (between living persons).

Section 5 of Transfer of Property Act defines Transfer of Property as "transfer of property" means an act by which a living person CONVEYS property, in present or in future, to one or more other living persons, or to himself, or to himself and one or more other living persons; and "to transfer property" is to perform such act. In the definition the word CONVEYS shall be read with "present or in future" and PROPERTY shall be in existence at the time of transfer.

DRAFTING	CONVEYANCING
Preparation of DOCUMENTS for TRANSFER of property & others covered by General clauses Act, 1897 & OTHER laws	• DOCUMENTATION of transfer of property, where the equitable title passes • FINALISATION, where the legal title passes focusing more on Registration Act & Stamp laws

S.No	CONVEYANCING	CONTRACT
1.	Governed by Transfer of property Act, 1882	Governed by Indian Contract Act, 1872
2.	DOCUMENTATION of transfer of property	It remains to be PERFORMED & also demands SPECIFIC PERFORMANCE
3.	It ALTERS ownership of existing right (i.e.) No right of action is created	It may/may not create a RIGHT of action.

GENERAL PRINCIPLES FOR DRAFTING or PRECAUTIONS WHILE DRAFTING

The duty of a draftsman is to express the intention of the parties CLEARLY & CONCISELY in a technical language.

- To understand the FACTS of the case
- Ascertain the Name, Description & Addresses of the parties
- To understand LEGAL Provisions & Formalities on the subject matter
- Divided into Paragraph & every para should not be more than 5 lines
- Use Simple words & Avoid repetition of words
- Use of active voice
- Description of property to be given in SCHEDULE
- Document to be serially NUMBERED
- The words shall be used in ORDINARY SENSE
- Use CONSISTENT TERMS for recurring words.

1. Drafting of petitions, deeds and documents is an art. Even acquiring working knowledge in this demands application of skills of higher order? Discuss pinpointing the skills and tasks involved in such an exercise (D'10)
2. Explain in detail the general principles of drafting & conveyancing & other writings (J'09)
3. In the present litigational corporate scenario, what are the role expectations from a Company Secretary with regard to drafting and conveyancing? (2010 – December)

IMPORTANT PRINCIPLES OF DRAFTING THE DOCUMENTS

1) **Fowlers' FIVE rules of drafting:** Every writer should endeavour to be 1) direct 2) simple 3) brief 4) vigorous and 5) lucid (clear). In short, the preference should be given to familiar, concrete, simple, short & saxon word with active voice in drafting.
2) **Sketch or scheme of the draft document is advisable before taking up the drafting:** The writer must write down the points, issues involved, facts of the case, etc…
3) **Skeleton draft and its self-appraisal:** The writer should prepare the documents with the help of the sketch of the document & do self appraisal. This requires noting down the important points to be incorporated in the document.
4) **Special attention to be given to certain documents:** The writer should be familiar with the laws & rules and should ensure that proper title is conveyed while preparing the document.
5) **Expert's opinion:** The writer should consult the experts. The document should be vetted for suitability & legal fitness.

To sum up, the document should be self-explanatory, clear to any person who has competent knowledge in the subject and must be readily intelligible to lay man.

Particulars	DO's ON DRAFTING	DON'Ts ON DRAFTING
WORDS	Reduce GROUP of words to a single word	Use of words of same/confusing sounds/ spellings
SENTENCES	Write SHORTER sentences & fewer RIGHT words with more ideas	Unnumbered paragraphs & large sentences
CONSTRUCTION	AVOID round-about construction & repetition	Successive negative phrases & words with multiple meanings while constructing a sentence
FLOW OF THOUGHTS	Know your meaning & read your written draft as a READER	Mixture of present & past tenses, mistake in spellings leading to change in meaning of words and irregular flow of meaning

RULE OF REASONABLE EXPECTATION

This rule shall be applied in case of INTERPRETATION of INFORMAL AGREEMENTS. The agreement is to be interpreted in the sense in which the party who used the words in question should reasonably have apprehended that the other party may apprehend them.

RULES UNDER FORMAL AGREEMENTS

1. Section 91 of Indian Evidence Act, 1872 THE DOCUMENT ITSELF is the best evidence. In cases where secondary evidence is admissible, it may be given.
2. Section 92 of Indian Evidence Act, 1872 deals with EXCLUSION of evidence or ORAL AGREEMENT when DOCUMENT is proved as per Section 91 subject to certain provisions of Section 92.

3. CLEAR & UNAMBIGUOUS WORDS prevail over any hypothetical considerations or supposed intentions (i.e.) ONLY the normal or natural & primary meanings of the said WORDS should be considered as a means of LIBERAL CONSTRUCTION unless otherwise contract gives a different meaning.
4. AMBIGUOUS WORDS – Then, consider the INTENTION OF PARTIES.
5. EXECUTED CONTRACT prevails over the Executory Contract.
6. EARLIER CLAUSE PREVAILS: An obligation created by a clause CANNOT be made repugnant (contradicted) by a latter clause.
7. HANDWRITING PREVAILS: If something is ADDED in handwriting or by a typewriter to a PRINTED FORM, such addition should prevail over the language in print.
8. DEED VOID PROSPECTIVELY: If a MATERIAL ALTERATION by erasure, interlineations, or otherwise is made in a material part of a deed after its execution WITHOUT the consent of all parties liable thereunder, the deed is thereby made void with prospective effect.

CERTAIN TERMS

INSTRUMENT

Instrument INCLUDES every document by which any right or liability IS or PURPORTS to be created, transferred, modified, limited, extended, extinguished or recorded. [Section 2(14) of Indian Stamp Act, 1899]

DOCUMENT

Document MEANS any matter expressed or described upon any substance by means of letters, figures or marks, or by more than one of those means, intended to be used, or which may be used, for the purpose of recording that matter. [Section 3 of Indian Evidence Act, 1872]

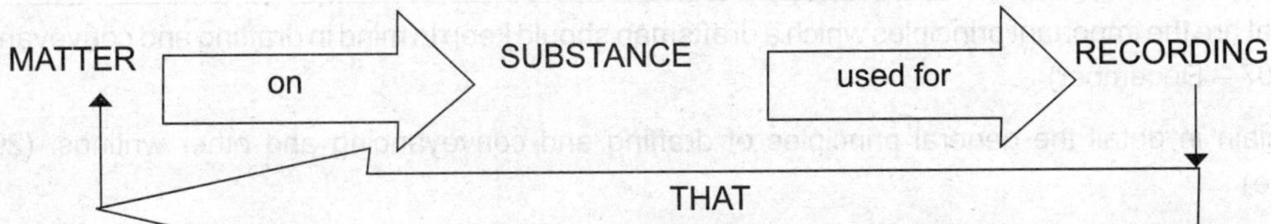

'Document' shall include any matter written, expressed or described upon any substance by means of letters, figures or marks, or by more by than one of those means which is intended to be used, or which may be used, for the purpose of recording this matter. [Section 3(18) of General Clauses Act, 1897]

DEED

A Deed is an instrument by which two or more persons agree to EFFECT any right or liability (legal disposition). It is a non-testamentary instrument. For eg, Sale Deed, Partnership Deed, Bonds, etc.

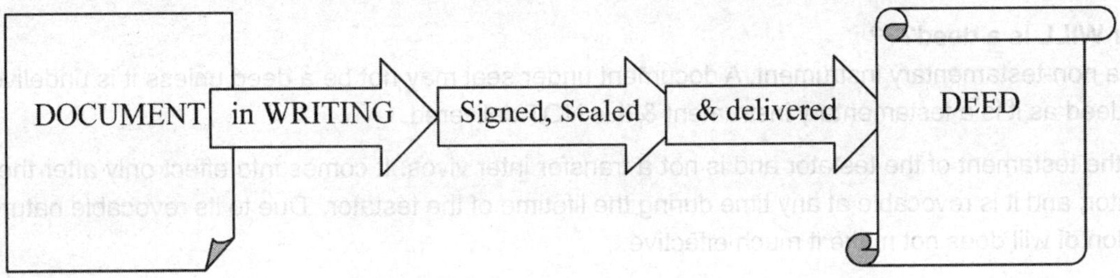

Deeds are in writing, signed, sealed and delivered. Deeds are instruments, but all instruments are not deeds.

Thus,

- All deeds ARE documents or instruments & not otherwise.
- All deeds & documents ARE instruments & not otherwise.

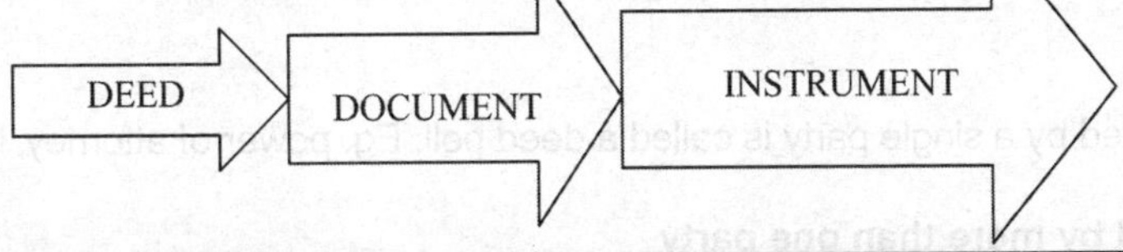

1. Deed & instrument (dec 07, j 09)
2. Drafting & conveyance (dec 08)
3. 'Conveyance' and 'Contract' (D' 12)
4. Document & deed (dec 09)
5. Define 'document'. Explain various kinds of deeds (2009 – June)
6. Explain the following:
   - (a) Deed Pool (2010 – June)
   - (b) Deed Poll (2010 – June)
   - (c) Indenture (2010 – June & 2007 - June)
   - (d) Cyrographum (2010 – June)
   - (e) Deed Escrow (2010 – June, 2010 – December & 2007 - June)

7. What are the important principles which a draftsman should keep in mind in drafting and conveyancing? (2007 – December)

8. Explain in detail the general principles of drafting and conveyancing and other writings. (2009 – June)

9. What are the do's and don'ts which should be considered while drafting documents? (2010 – June)

10. "Drafting of petitions, deeds and documents is an art. Even acquiring working knowledge in this demands application of skills of higher order." Discuss pin – pointing the skills and tasks involved in such an exercise.

11. Whether an unburnt fresh hard disk in a computer is a 'document' within the meaning of section 3 read with section 65B of the Indian Evidence Act, 1872? Discuss with reference to case Law. (2010 – December). Clue: Yes, a hard disc that is once written upon or subjected to any change is itself an electronic record even if it DOES NOT at present contain any accessible information as decided in the Dharamvir case.

Whether WILL is a deed???

Deed is a non-testamentary instrument. A document under seal may not be a deed unless it is undelivered. Will is not a deed as it is a testamentary instrument & it is NOT delivered.

A will is the testament of the testator and is not a transfer inter vivos. It comes into effect only after the death of the testator; and it is revocable at any time during the lifetime of the testator. Due to its revocable nature, even a registration of will does not make it much effective.

KINDS OF DEED: good or lawful deed (conveys good/lawful title), good & sufficient/marketable deed, inclusive deed, latent deed (for 20 years or more, kept in a strong box), pretended deed (prima facie valid), voluntary deed (without any valuable consideration), warranty deed and special warranty deed like limited warranty (not carries notice of title defects) or warrant titles only against the claimers.

DEED POOL – photocopies

A deed between two or more parties where as many copies are made as there are parties, so that each may be in a possession of a copy. This arrangement is known as deed pool.

DEED POLL

A deed made and executed by a single party is called a deed poll. Eg. power of attorney, license.

INDENTURE - executed by more than one party

Indenture are those deeds in which there are two or more parties. It was written in duplicate upon one piece of material and two parts were severed so as to leave a vary edge. By this forgery of documents is very difficult. The other way of indenture is by WRITING & TEARING the word **CYROGRAPHUM**, so that it becomes difficult to tear exactly that way.

DEED ESCROW

A deed SIGNED by one party will be delivered to ANOTHER as an 'escrow'. The deed will operate from the date when the other party to the transaction also signs it (i.e.) till it is last signed. Eg. A circular resolution passed by the Board of Directors is considered to be passed when all the directors sign the same.

ENGROSSMENT & STAMPING – The document after approval is engrossed (i.e.) COPIED fair on non-judicial STAMP paper of appropriate value as per Indian Stamp Act, 1899. Kindly note that, if the document is not properly stamped, it will be rendered inadmissible in evidence nor it will be registered.

WHERE IS THE LAND???					
ADJACENT – land lying nearby other land	ADJOINING – land touching each other	ABUT – land to touch at one end of the land	CONTIGUOUS – land lying in close proximity to other land	VICINITY (on) – the state of being near a land	NEAR (at) – land lying close by other land
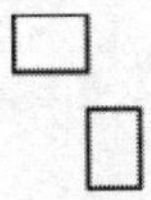	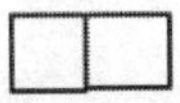	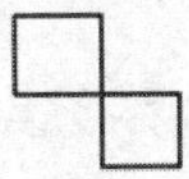	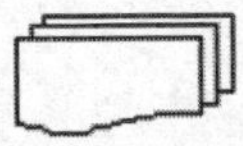	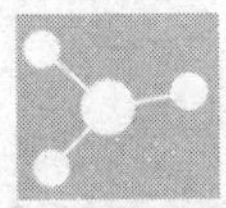	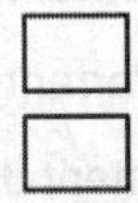

The respective pictorial views of the land are as above:

Choose your best

1. Conveyancing means –
   a) Preparation of documents from transfer of property & others covered by General Clauses Act 1897.
   b) Documentation of transfer of property.
   c) It remains to be performed & also demand specific performance.

2. Instrument includes-
   a) Every Document
   b) Documents by which any right is or purports to be created, transferred, modified, limited extended, extinguished or recorded.
   c) Both of the above.
   d) None of the above.

3. Which of the following are Deeds:
   a) Marketable deed.
   b) Will
   c) None of above.

4. Land lying near by other land is called:
   a) Adjacent
   b) Adjoining
   c) Contiguous
   d) Vicinity

5. The format of deed includes:
   a) Recitals.

b) Name & description of parties

c) Signature

d) All of above.

6. A deed kept for twenty years or more in man's escritoire or strong box is called

a) Pretended deed

b) Lawful deed

c) Warranty deed

d) Latent deed

Ans

1. B)
2. C)
3. A)
4. A)
5. D)
6. D)

Fill your blanks

1. Documentation is the activity which symbolizes preparation of documents, including ____________ thereof.
2. Drafting may be defined as the synthesis (combination) of ________ in a language form.
3. Conveyancing does not include acquisition by way of ____________.
4. A deed kept in box for more than 20 years is ___________ deed.
5. A deed executed by more than one party is ____________.
6. A deed made & executed by single party is called a ___________.
7. A deed between two or more parties where as many copies are made as there are parties, so that each may be in possession of a copy. This arrangement is known as ___________.
8. Deed signed by one Party will be delivered to another as an __________.
9. ___________ word is used to define land touching each other.

Ans

1. finalization & execution
2. law & fact
3. inheritance
4. latent
5. indenture

6. Deed Poll
7. Deed pool
8. Escrow
9. Adjoining

Explain your reasons

1. All deeds are documents & vice-versa i.e, all documents are deed.
2. Will is a Deed.
3. The state of being near a land is described as NEAR.
4. Drafting is first thinking & second composing
5. If a document is not properly stamped , it is rendered indamissable in evidence
6. Agreements not creating an interest in immovable property are not compulsorily registrable

Ans:

1. Incorrect, because all documents are not deed.
2. Incorrect, because will is a testamentary instrument & it is undelivered, where as Deed is a non testamentary instrument & it is delivered.
3. Incorrect, because it is called VICINITY & NEAR means land lying close by other land.
4. Correct
5. Correct
6. Correct

How to start drafting in simple steps?

Step 1: Plan it well

1. Take instructions from the client
2. Analyse the instruction & compartmentalize as to Facts & Law
3. Ascertain the purpose & objective behind this drafting
4. Research the relevant up-to-date law and find appropriate forms or precedents

Step 2: Put it in Writing

1. Prepare a Skeleton draft
2. Ensure that all the content conceived during the Planning stage has been incorporated in the draft

Step 3: Revise it again & again

1. Re-analyse the instruction received, re-write the draft, re-organise & edit the material
2. Also, concentrate on spelling & grammar

As said there is a conventional practice of drafting in some specific formats. Here, a simple sale deed is taken for illustration. While reading understand the words used & stressed as those are very essential to call a deed as a deed, though not mandated by law. Further, while drafting such deeds the concerned legal provisions shall always be kept in mind. The deeds are given in the form of (scientific) diagrams by marking Numbers at appropriate places, which are then, explained below with details. Now, start reading, drafting, reading, drafting, reading, drafting again and again to master the subject.

Deed Sample With Sale Deed Provisions

SAMPLE DEED

SALE DEED BY A COMPANY → 1

THIS SALE DEED is entered into at KOLKATA, this, the 25th day of August, 2012 → 2

BY

Labz Limited, a limited liability company registered under the Companies Act, 1956 under the Certificate of Incorporation number 99-1234 of 2000 and Corporate Identification Number (CIN) UL1234555991234/2003 in the office of the Registrar of Companies, Maharashtra at Mumbai having its Registered Office at No. 13, Jolly Maker Chambers, Mumbai – 400021 through its ATTORNEY Mr. Shiva appointed under the Power of Attorney dated 25th August 2012 given under the common seal of the company hereinafter referred to as the VENDOR ON THE ONE PART. → 3A

IN FAVOUR OF

Mr. Mani S/O. Mr. Ravi, Hindu, aged 25 years residing at 9, Veeraperumal Koil Street, Chennai – 600004 hereinafter referred to as the PURCHASER which term shall mean & include his legal heirs, representatives, administrators, nominees and assigns ON THE OTHER PART. → 3B

WHEREAS the VENDOR is the absolute owner of the house & ground bearing No.3A, Ahiripukur, Kolkata - 700019, hereinafter referred to as PROPERTY, more fully described in the SCHEDULE, he having purchased it from Mr. Ram on 25th day of February 2005 through a sale deed registered as document number 5959 of 2005 in the sub-registrar office at Kolkata. → 4A

AND WHEREAS the PURCHASER has offered to buy the aforesaid PROPERTY for a sum of Rs. 10,00,00,000 [RUPEES TEN CRORES ONLY] in pursuance of which an agreement dated 1st August 2012 was entered into between the VENDOR and the PURCHASER. → 4B

NOW THIS AGREEMENT WITNESSESS AS FOLLOWS: → 5

THAT in consideration of a sum of Rs. 10,00,00,000 [RUPEES TEN CRORES] to be paid by the PURCHASER to the VENDOR in the manner set forth below: → 6

1. An advance of Rs. 5,00,00,000 [RUPEES FIVE CRORE] was paid on 12th June 2012 towards the agreement of sale dated 10th June 2012.
2. Payment of Rs. 1,00,00,000 [RUPEES ONE CRORE] by way of cash to the VENDOR.
3. Payment of balance Rs. 4,00,00,000 [RUPEES TEN CRORES] by way of Cheque drawn on AXIS BANK, Kolkata dated 20th August 2012, bearing Cheque No. 287129, the receipt of which the VENDOR hereby acknowledges. → 7

The VENDOR transfers to the PURCHASER BY WAY OF SALE, the house & ground bearing → 8
No.3A, Ahiripukur, Kolkata - 700019, hereinafter referred to as PROPERTY more particularly → 9
described in the SCHEDULE hereunder TO HAVE AND TO HOLD THE SAME ABSOLUTELY AND FOR EVER. → 10

The VENDOR and the PURCHASER HEREBY MUTUALLY covenants as follows: → 13

1. The VENDOR is the absolute owner in possession of the PROPERTY. There are no encumbrances, → 14
lien or charge over the said PROPERTY.

2. The VENDOR covenants that he has paid the corporation tax, water tax, sewerage tax and electricity bills up to the date of sale and the PURCHASER shall be liable to pay corporation tax, water tax, sewerage tax and electricity bills from the date of sale.

3. The VENDOR covenants with the PURCHASER to deliver possession of the PROPERTY on the execution and registration of the sale deed.

IN WITNESS WHEREOF THE PARTIES HAVE SIGNED THIS DEED ON THE DATE, MONTH, YEAR ABOVE WRITTEN. → 17

VENDOR → 18

Labz Limited through its ATTORNEY under Power of Attorney dated 25th day of August 2012.

PURCHASER.

WITNESS 1: (Name & Description) → 19

WITNESS 2:

SCHEDULE → 22

All that house and ground bearing No.3A, Ahiripukur, Kolkata – 700019 under Town Survey (TS) No. 5599 in the sub-district of Ahiripukur in Kolkata measuring 10 grounds bounded,

ON THE NORTH BY: House & ground bearing No.1, Ahiripukur, Kolkata.

ON THE SOUTH BY: House & ground bearing No.5, Ahiripukur, Kolkata.

ON THE WEST BY: House & ground bearing No.2, Ahiripukur, Kolkata.

ON THE EAST BY: 1st Lane, Ahiripukur Road, Kolkata.

COMPONENTS OF SALE DEED

1. **Deed Title –** It should be in capital letters, bold & centered. It describes the nature of the deed. (eg) THIS DEED OF SALE…

2. **Place and Date of execution –** It should be written in words & figures. It is to reckon limitation period, stamp duty, jurisdiction, etc…A deed will NOT be invalid if a deed does not bear any date, or bears an impossible date, and evidence will be admissible to ascertain the true date of the deed.

3. **Name and Description of Parties –** The transferor should be mentioned first, then confirming party, if any, and then, the transferee, including inter-parties. The full description includes, Name, Age, S/o or D/o., Nationality, Address, relation to document, and includes his/her legal heirs, successors, assigns and legal representatives. In case either of the party is the Company, then also describe the nature of the company along with its Corporate Identification Number (CIN), the registrar office of registration and the place where Registered Office of the company is situated. Further, also to state the authorized

Attorney as empowered to enter the deed on behalf of the company. One shall ensure that the transferor is a person COMPETENT to contract.

4. **Recitals** – It contains the short story of (past events of) property UPTO it's vesting into its transferors. Simply put, recitals are statements that lead to the operative part of the deed. It is of two types A) Narrative Recitals (past events) and B) Inductory Recitals (motive/intention behind execution). Narrative Recitals are followed with Inductory Recitals. It starts with the words "WHEREAS" & AND WHEREAS.

Whether Recitals act as Estoppel???

Yes, recitals helps in INTERPRETING operative clause, ONLY WHEN the terms of the deed are not clear or are ambiguous. (Estoppel means stopped from denying)

Whether Recitals are Evidence???

No, recitals are not generally taken into evidence, but are open for interpretation for the courts. To put it more clear, ambiguity in operative part may be cleared with recitals whereas ambiguity in recitals has no importance. If both the recitals and operative part are CLEAR, but they are INCONSISTENT with each other, the operative part is to be PREFERRED.

5. **Testatum** – It is the WITNESSING clause, containing the INTENTION of the parties. It refers to the Inductory Recitals of the agreement. It states that whatever declared is true to their knowledge and belief. It also states Consideration and acknowledgement of Receipt. It usually begins with the words "NOW THIS DEED WITNESSES …."

OPERATIVE CLAUSES

6. **Consideration** – To ascertain the Stamp Duty.
7. **Receipt** – It is the acknowledgement of Consideration.
8. **Operative Clause** – (eg) Transfer by way of…
9. **Description of Property** – The property should be FULLY described for making the location of the property easier. Normally, it will be given in the SCHEDULE. It is for the purpose of Registration Act, 1908.
10. **Premises and Habendum** – Habendum states the INTEREST, the purchaser is to take in the property. It mentions to what extent the right is transferred or vested. It mentions the ENCUMBERANCES, if any. It starts with the words "TO HAVE AND TO HOLD".
11. **Parcels Clause** – This is a methodical (technical) description of the property transferred. It will be accompanied by true copies of maps, plans, etc…It usually starts with the words "ALL THE PIECE & PARCEL OF….." It has become redundant because of Section 8 of Transfer of Property Act, 1882 which enables the transfer FORTHWITH of ALL interest which the transferor is then capable of passing in the property and in the legal incidents thereof.
12. **Exceptions and Reservations** – The rights to be enjoyed by the Transferor as agreed by Transferee. It uses the words "SUBJECT TO". Kindly note, Section 8 of Transfer of Property Act, 1882 mandates transfer of ALL interest and Section 10 of the Act stipulates any condition restraining transferee to dispose of his interest in the property is VOID.
13. **Covenants** (agreement of conditions) – It means conditions/stipulations accepted by the promisor either to do or refrain from doing an act. It may be expressed or implied. Covenant is defined as an agreement under seal, whereby parties stipulates for the truth of certain facts. The transferor's covenants & transferee's covenants may be mentioned separately. For instance, "THAT the transferor is the OWNER of the property & has a right to transfer"; "THAT the transferee shall have the property conveyed to him". covenant clause may include undertakings also.

14. Undertakings – (eg) The Parties HERE to HEREBY MUTUALLY AGREE…

15. Force Majeure – excuses for non-performance. It safeguards the parties from those acts whose happening is beyond control. (eg) Acts of God, change of law, natural calamity, etc…

16. Arbitration Clause – The parties to the contract may agree that in the event of any dispute or difference or opinion, the matter shall be settled by an arbitrator.

17. Testimonium Clause – It is a DECLARATION by the parties subscribing the signature in the presence of WITNESS on the day mentioned in the deed. It starts with the words "IN WITNESS WHEREOF THE PARTIES HERETO SET THEIR HANDS ON THIS DATE, MONTH AND YEAR MENTIONED ABOVE"

18. Signature

19. Witness – to attest the deed; there shall be atleast 2 witnesses to sign along with their Name & address.

20. Attestation – "Attestation" is EVIDENCING of EXECUTION. It is mandatory for Mortgage deed, Gift deed & Wills. It shall satisfy the following conditions:

a) Must have seen the EXECUTANT sign the deed

b) Must have received a PERSONAL ACKNOWLEDGEMENT of signature

c) Must SIGN the deed in the presence of Executants. It may be done by 2 witnesses, as mentioned above or by a Notary Public.

21. Endorsements and supplemental Deeds – It means to write on the back or on the face of a document to give legal significance to a particular document with reference to NEW FACTS to be added in it. It may be done either by Endorsement or by way of Supplemental Deed. A supplemental deed is executed to give effect to the new facts in the deed. It shall be STAMPED according to the nature of transaction which they evidence.

22. Annexures or Schedules – The Schedule of Property to be given as per the requirements of Registration Act, 1908.

23. Reservation and Exceptions, if any: A reseveration clause can be RESERVING THE EASEMENT RIGHT (to a common way) to someone while conveying the property. An exception clause can be a RIGHT TO RETAIN the MINING right in a property (without ENDANGERING the surface of the land), while conveying the property.

AGREEMENT TO SELL	SALE (Contract for Sale)
It is an agreement that sale is to take place in future	It is a transfer of ownership (i.e.) sale of immovable property
Ownership remains with the seller/vendor	The ownership is VESTED in the purchaser/buyer
It is an executory contract	It is an executed contract
It does NOT convey any title to the purchaser	It passes (CONFERS) absolute title to the purchaser.

POINTS SPECIFIC TO DIFFERENTIATION BETWEEN "AGREEMENT OF SALE" & "SALE DEED"

Meaning, unless specifically mentioned, all other points remains the same. There may be special deed or agreement with more clauses as per the parties requirement.

CLAUSE	AGREEMENT OF SALE	SALE DEED
DEED TITLE	This AGREEMENT OF SALE	This SALE DEED
PARTIES	BETWEEN Party 1 AND Party 2	BY Party 1 IN FAVOUR OF Party 2

INDUCTORY RECITALS	Offer and Acceptance of Offer	Quote the Agreement of Sale with Date
CONSIDERATION	The PURCHASER agrees to pay the BALANCE within prescribed period from the date of this agreement	The payment of BALANCE and acknowledgment of its receipt
OPERATIVE CLAUSE	The VENDOR agrees that on receipt of the BALANCE amount, he has to EXECUTE the Sale Deed	The VENDOR transfers the property to the PURCHASER BY WAY OF SALE TO HAVE & TO HOLD the same absolutely and FOR EVER
COVENANTS	The VENDOR agrees to PRESENT the deed for registration and further agrees that he shall DELIVER the document of TITLE to the PURCHASER	The VENDOR covenants with the PURCHASER to deliver the PROPERTY on the execution and registration of the Sale Deed.

AGREEMENT OF SALE OF A HOUSE PROPERTY

THIS AGREEMENT is entered into at KOLKATA, this, the 25th day of August, 2007

BETWEEN

Mr. Jain S/O. Mr. Raj, Hindu, aged 23 years residing at 22, Lodi Road, New Delhi – 110003 hereinafter referred to as the VENDOR which term shall mean & include his legal heirs, representatives, administrators, nominees and assigns ON THE ONE PART.

AND

Mr. Mani S/O. Mr. Ravi, Hindu, aged 25 years residing at 9, Mosque Street, Chennai – 600034 hereinafter referred to as the PURCHASER which term shall mean & include his legal heirs, representatives, administrators, nominees and assigns ON THE OTHER PART.

WHEREAS the VENDOR is the absolute owner of the *house & ground* bearing No.3A, Ahiripukur, Kolkata - 700019, hereinafter referred to as PROPERTY, he having purchased it from Mr. Ram on 25th day of February 2005 through a sale deed registered as document number 5959 of 2005 in the sub-registrar office at Kolkata.

AND WHEREAS the PURCHASER has offered to buy the aforesaid PROPERTY for a sum of Rs. 10,00,00,000 [RUPEES TEN CRORES ONLY] the offer having been accepted by the VENDOR.

NOW THIS AGREEMENT WITNESSESS AS FOLLOWS:
THAT in consideration of a sum of Rs. 1,00,00,000 [RUPEES ONE CRORE ONLY] paid by the PURCHASER to the VENDOR hereby acknowledges, the parties agree as follows:

1. The VENDOR agrees to sell and the PURCHASER agrees to buy the house & ground bearing No.3A, Ahiripukur, Kolkata - 700019, hereinafter referred to as PROPERTY, more fully described in the SCHEDULE hereunder.

2. The parties have agreed that the PURCHASER shall pay to the VENDOR, a sum of Rs. 10,00,00,000 [RUPEES TEN CRORES ONLY] towards the price of the PROPERTY on which an advance of Rs. 1,00,00,000 [RUPEES ONE CRORE ONLY] has been paid to the VENDOR as stated above.

3. The PURCHASER agrees to pay the balance of Rs. 9,00,00,000 [RUPEES NINE CRORES ONLY] within 6 months from the date of this agreement.

4. The VENDOR agrees that on receipt of the balance amount as stated above, the VENDOR shall execute a sale deed in respect of the PROPERTY in favour of the PURCHASER.

5. The VENDOR further agrees on the execution of the sale deed, he shall present the deed for registration.
6. The VENDOR agrees that he shall deliver the possession of the property to the PURCHASER on the execution of the sale deed and also deliver the document of title relating to the PROPERTY in his possession to the PURCHASER.
7. The VENDOR declares that the sale is free from any encumbrances, *lis pen dens.*
8. The parties agree that the taxes in respect of the property up to the date of sale will be paid by the VENDOR and after the sale the PURCHASER shall be liable for the payment of taxes in respect of the PROPERTY.

1. Explain Habendum. What does a Habendum clause signify in a document (2009 – December, 2007 – June & 2010 December)
2. What is meant by 'recitals' as a component in a deed? What is its evidentiary value? (2010 – December)
3. Define the term 'deed'. Explain any seven usual clauses in a deed. (D'10 & 2009)
4. Testimonium Clause (2007 – June & 2010 – December)
5. Convenants & Undertakings (D'10, J'09 & J'08)
6. Draft an agreement of sale of immovable property (2007 – June)
7. Draft a specimen of deed of sale by liquidator of a company in voluntary liquidation (2008 – December) – Just like the normal sale deed with Liquidator as Seller.
8. Mention important aspects which should be kept in mind while drafting a sale deed of an immovable property by a limited company. (2010 – June) – Clue: Concentrate on description of Company & Power of Attorney to executants.

Try understanding the terms used. Every deed will state the name & description of parties. Kindly observe how to describe if one of the parties is an individual or a company or a firm. Further, there are some standard words like WHEREAS which are put in capital letters to highlight. You can use the same way (capital letters) in exams too, it differentiates the provisions and the formats. Drafting deed is like FILL IN THE BLANKS where one should understand both the question & answer. The question in the FILL UPS will be the format of a deed (which differs from deed to deed) and the answer of the FILL UPS depends on the specific questions or situations for the given case (which can be built up by oneself).

The basic provisions regarding all types of charges are covered in this chapter along with the legal & drafting provisions. It is advisable to make thorough with legal provisions before studying the format of the concerned deeds.

Deeds Of Mortgages, Charges, Hypothecations, Leases & Licenses

CONCEPTS & LEGAL PROVISIONS:

MORTGAGE

A MORTGAGE is a TRANSFER OF INTEREST in a specific IMMOVABLE PROPERTY for the purpose of securing,

- Monetary transaction (LOAN); OR
- Creditor – Debtor relationship (DEBT); OR
- Performance of Contractual Obligation (ACKNOWLEDGEMENT).

Section 58 of the Transfer of Property Act, 1882 deals with definition and various kinds of mortgages whereas Sections 60 to 66 dealing with the rights and liabilities of mortgagor.

Kindly note, TRANSFER OF INTEREST (by creating a charge) in a specific MOVABLE PROPERTY is a HYPOTHECATION. For instance, mortgage of plant & machinery, stock-in-trade, etc... without delivery of possession is hypothecation.

TERMS

- Transferor is the MORTGAGOR (borrower)
- Transferee is the MORTGAGEE
- Principal Money & Interest is the MORTGAGE MONEY
- Instrument effecting transfer is the MORTGAGE DEED.

TYPES OF MORTGAGE

TYPE & FEATURE	DELIVERY of Property	REMEDY on Default
SIMPLE MORTGAGE binds mortgagor to pay mortgage money & gives the "right to cause the property sold" to mortgagee in case of default.	NO delivery of possession	Sale through Court or u/s. 69 of Transfer of Property Act, 1882
ENGLISH MORTGAGE transfers the ownership ABSOLUTELY with a PROVISIO to re-transfer on payment of mortgage money.	Delivery of possession	Sale through Court or implied right u/s. 69 of Transfer of Property Act, 1882
MORTGAGE BY CONDITIONAL SALE (i.e.) there will be an Ostensible sale; which becomes VOID on repayment or becomes ABSOLUTE on default.	Delivery of possession	Suit for foreclosure by mortgagor. Foreclosure means to take legal measures to TERMINATE mortgage and to TAKE possession.

 USUFRUCTUARY MORTGAGE transfers the POSSESSION of property and to receive rents/ profit IN LIEU OF interest or mortgage money; hence right of REDEMPTION is available to mortgagor. Usufruct means to enjoy others property without prejudice to it. Redemption means the 'RIGHT TO TAKE BACK' by repaying the mortgage money. Restricting the right to redemption is known as CLOG ON REDEMPTION and it shall be VOID.	Delivery of possession	Suit for possession by mortgagor
EQUITABLE MORTGAGE or DEPOSIT OF TITLE DEEDS only in Notified towns; No stamp duty; The steps include, • Execute Promissory Note; • Deposit Title Deeds (with an intention to create security); • Get Memorandum to such effect. The registration is not compulsory for Mortgage by deposit of title deeds.	No delivery of possession	Sale through Court
ANOMALOUS MORTGAGE or Customary Mortgage is the combination of any of the above OR other than those set out above.		

Kindly note, REGISTRATION is mandatory for all types of mortgage and also REGISTRATION shall be done on RELEASE/REcONVEYANcE of the mortgaged property EXcEPT for Mortgage by Deposit of Title Deeds. Kindly note, mortgage by deposit of title deeds to secure any loan or advances granted by banks and financial institutions is to be registered in the CENTRAL REGISTRY under Securitisation and Reconstruction of Financial Assets and Enforcement of Security Interest (SARFAESI) Act, 2002 through www.cersai.org.in.

Section 69 of Transfer of Property Act, 1882 deals with Simple Mortgage and PRIVATE SALE [sale without intervention of court], which shall be **incorporated** or expressly conferred [specific clause shall be included] in the Mortgage Deed. It is applicable only for Property in Metros and Notified towns OR where Mortgagee is a Government. The mortgagee before exercising the right of private sale shall give 3 MONTHS notice, in WRITING, to the Mortgagor UNLESS OTHERWISE atleast Rs.500/- is in arrears towards interest for more than 3 MONTHS.

Section 69 of Transfer of Property Act, 1882 also deals with English Mortgage and Suo Motto PRIVATE SALE [sale without intervention of court] which is inherent [implied right without any clause in the deed] IF neither the Mortgagor nor the Mortgagee is a Hindu/Mohammedan/Buddhist. This section is taken advantage of by CORPORATE bodies (not being Bank or Financial institution) who are NOT natural persons since such bodies are NOT deemed to belong to any religion. Bank/FI has a specific power of Private Sale granted under SARFAESI Act, 2002 [dealt under Corporate Restructuring].

In case of Company entering into mortgage transaction, it shall have power in its OBJECT CLAUSE with a Board Resolution and as approved by Shareholders u/s. 293(1)(a) of Companies Act, 1956 to sell, lease or OTHERWISE (includes mortgage) dispose the whole or substantially the whole of the undertaking of the Company.

CHARGE

Where immovable property of one person is

- by act of parties or operation of law
- made SECURITY for the payment of money to another and

- the transaction does NOT amount to mortgage, then it is called Charge and
- all provisions which apply to a simple mortgage shall apply.

Sections 100 and 101 of The Transfer of Property Act, 1882 lay down the provisions relating to Charges.

The basic difference between a mortgage and a charge is that Charge only gives a RIGHT TO PAYMENT out of a particular property, without transferring any interest in the property. But in mortgage, the essence is a transfer of interest in specific property. Every mortgage there is a charge, but every charge is not a mortgage **[Mortgage > Charge].**

SNO.	MORTGAGE	CHARGE
1.	Transfer of Interest;	No such transfer;
2.	ONLY by act of parties;	By act of parties or by operation of Law;
3.	Pre-supposes debt;	Not necessarily;
4.	There can be a security as well as personal liability;	The remedy of the charge holder is against the property (security) only;
5.	Creates Jus-in-rem (right against world);	Creates Jus-ad-rem;
6.	Can be enforced against transferee with or without Notice;	Can be enforced ONLY with Notice.
7.	The Mortgage deed shall be executed and registered & attested by two witnesses	The Instrument of Charge may be executed and need not be attested or registered.

Floating charge is one which is created on the movable goods, including stock-in-trade. The two main elements of floating charge are – 1) the non-performance of a property and its constant change 2) it does not itself fasten and settle down until the happening of a particular event.

FLOATING CHARGES – These are 'shifting in nature'. The ELEMENTS includes,

↳ Freedom to deal with;

↳ Having Elements of Fluctuation;

↳ Free from ENCUMBERANCES.

CRYSTALLISATION – Floating charge becoming Fixed charge for the purpose of enforcement, when,

↳ Cease to carry on Business;

↳ Company on Liquidation;

↳ Appointment of Receiver;

↳ Chargee's suit for Recovery [Intervention by Chargeholder].

FIXED CHARGE	FLOATING CHARGE
Fastens on Ascertained & Defined Property	'Shifting in Nature' or Non-permanence of Property
Company can deal with the property ONLY with the Consent of the Chargeholder	Company carries on the business normally.

PARTITION: separation of right already vested

Partition is NOT a transfer whereas it is an ADJUSTMENT in the EXISTING right and does NOT create any new right.

HYPOTHECATION: Transfer of Property in GOODS.

Hypothecation agreement is a document by which the LEGAL PROPERTY (ownership) in goods passes to the person who LENDS money on them, but the POSSESSION does not pass. The parties are Hypothecator and Hypothecatee.

A pledge is a BAILMENT of the goods as SECURITY for payment of a debt or performance of a promise. The parties are PAWNOR & PAWNEE.

HYPOTHECATION	PLEDGE
An extended form of pledge	-
Not governed by any laws but governed by principles of equity and justice	Governed by Sections 172 to 176 of Indian Contract Act, 1872
The rights of the lender and the borrower are strictly governed by the terms and conditions of the hypothecation agreement executed by the parties	The rights of the lender and the borrower are governed by Section 176 of Indian Contract Act, 1872
The movable assets REMAIN in the possession of the borrower and he has ABSOLUTE right to convert, sell and deal with them in any manner in the course of business whereas the legal TITLE VESTS in the lending institution by virtue of the agreement	Pledge cannot exist without bailment or transfer of possession.

LEASE: "Transfer of right to enjoy property"

Lease involves the right to USE an asset (equipment or real property) for CONSIDERATION without ASSUMING or intending to assume, ownership.

Sections 105 to 117 under Chapter V of Transfer of Property Act, 1882 deals with leases.

The covenants (i.e.) terms & conditions of lease agreement are found in Section 108 of Transfer of Property Act, 1882 which are as follows:

Lessor's rights & liabilities:

- To disclose any defect in the property
- To put the lessee in possession of the property
- To allow lessee in peaceful possession on payment of rent and performance of contractual obligation.

Lessee's rights & liabilities:

- To void the lease, if property is destroyed or rendered unfit
- To give notice to lessor to get repairs done or adjust expenses from rent
- To transfer the property absolutely or by way of mortgage or sub lease
- To disclose any interest which increases the value of property
- To put lessor in possession of property on determination of lease.

Section 111 of Transfer of Property Act, 1882 deals with DETERMINATION or TERMINATION of lease: Kindly note 'surrender of lease' is not a transfer.

• By efflux of time	• By termination of lessor's interest
• By happening of an event	• By express surrender
• By merger (i.e.) where rights of both lessor & lessee are vested with same person	• By implied surrender
	• By forfeiture on breach of condition or denial of lessor's title or insolvency of lessee.

Section 106 & 107 of Transfer of Property Act, 1882 read with Section 17(1)(d) of the Registration Act, 1908 mandates registration of all leases from year to year, or for a term exceeding a year, or reserving a yearly rent must be registered. Meaning, leases renewable from month to month or less than 1 year may be delivered by possession.

The STAMPING of lease is mandatory for all leases including under-lease, sub-lease or agreement to let or sub-let. A SUB LEASE is a DEMISE by a lessee for LESSER term than he himself has and demise BEYOND the term amounts to ASSIGNMENT. A sub lessee is entitled to RELIEF against forfeiture u/s. 114.

FORFEITURE of lease takes place u/s. 114 ONLY if lessee does NOT pay the RENT or breaches any COVENANT in the terms of lease after giving notice of breach. Forfeiture means to AVOID the lease and to ENTER into possession by lessor.

LICENSE: Governed under Chapter VI of Indian Easements Act, 1882: Sections 52-64

LICENSE: "Right to do something on grantor's land". For instance, A sells the trees growing on his land to B, B is entitled to go on the land and take away the trees.

Section 52 of Indian Easements Act, 1882 – LICENSE –

- where one person grants to another, OR to a definite number of other persons,
- a RIGHT to **do**, or CONTINUE to **do**, in or upon the IMMOVABLE PROPERTY of the grantor,
- something which would, in the ABSENCE of such right, be UNLAWFUL **and**
- such right does NOT amount to an easement or an interest in the property.

SNO	LEASE	LICENSE
	A POSITIVE RIGHT	
1.	Governed by Transfer of Property Act, 1882	Governed by Indian Easement Act, 1882
2.	TRANSFER of right to enjoy property (Instrument creating right)	No such transfer; (Instrument granting right to do something on grantor's land)
3.	The lessee is entitled to DELIVERY of possession;	Not entitled;
4.	The Consideration is paid by way of RENT;	The Consideration is paid by way of FEE;
5.	The lessee may SUE trespassers in his OWN name	The licensee may SUE trespassers BUT in the name of GRANTOR
6.	The lessee may SUB-LET;	The licensee cannot assign UNLESS it is a license to attend a place of public entertainment which may be transferred by licencee;
7.	The lessor may TERMINATE the lease – only with Notice	Licensor may revoke WITHOUT Notice UNLESS, it is coupled with Transfer of Property Licensee has executed a work of permanent nature
8.	Remedy for breach is specially enforceable	Remedy for breach is DAMAGES;
9.	As it is an instrument CREATING right, registration is mandatory	As it is an instrument GRANTING right, registration is optional
10.	The lessee is Liable for rent and public nuisance	The licensee Not liable for rent and public nuisance.

1. Draft important clauses of an agreement on behalf of a firm to hypothecate goods to execute fixed loan from Reliable Bank Limited. (2008 – June)
2. Define:
   (i) Hypothecation agreement
   (ii) Lease
   (iii) Licence (2009 – June)
3. Usufructuary mortgage (2009 – June)
4. Necessary clauses in a sub – lease deed (2010 – December)
5. What are the principal tests to determine whether a charge is a fixed charge or a floating charge? (2008 – December)
6. Comment on 'Habendum' and 'reddendum' mean the same thing in a lease agreement. (2008 – December)
7. Attempt the following:
   (a) Define – Mortgage
   (b) Draft a specimen of memorandum of mortgage by deposit of title deeds (2009 – June)
8. Explain any two types of mortgage. (2010 – June)
9. What is the difference between 'mortgage' and 'lease' from the point of view of drafting of an agreement? (2010 – December) – Clue: Pay attention to special clauses like Reddundum
10. Draft a specimen deed for surrender of lease. (2007 – December)
11. "All licences are revocable at the will of the licensor." Comment (2008 – June)
12. Draft a specimen of equitable mortgage by a limited company in favour of a bank for securing the amount due on cash credit. (2008 – June)
13. Fixed charge & floating charge (j 07)
14. English mortgage & simple mortgage (dec 09)

OPERATIVE CLAUSE in License Deed: "License and authorizes to do" OR "grants liberty and licence to do", etc...

Registration Act, 1908 (Section 17) – License has to be registered, ONLY if it creates any right, title or interest in immovable property.

Indian Stamp Act, 1899 (Article 5, Schedule I) – The license deed shall be stamped ONLY if it is a separate deed.

LEAVE & LICENSE AGREEMENT: 'Leave' means permission. Thus a leave & license agreement does NOT create any interest in the premises in favour of the licensee but gives the licensee the mere right to USE & OCCUPY the premises for a temporary period.

Juridical Possession → with Licensor

Constructive Possession → with Licensee

The liability to pay Income Tax falls upon the owner and the Municipal Taxes may be levied by the authorities.

Fill Your Best Answer

1. A __________is a transfer of interest in a specific immovable property for the purpose of securing loans, debt, and acknowledgement.
2. The mortgagee before exercising the right of private sale u/s. 69 of Transfer of Property Act shall give________ notice, in writing, to the mortgagee unless otherwise agreed upon.
3. Separation of right already vested is called_______.
4. ___________is one which is created on the movable goods, including stock in trade.
5. ____________mortgage is a combination of all forms of mortgage.
6. The mortgagee advances further sums of money to the mortgagor on the same condition. The deed executed to secure the advance of further sums of money is called ________________.

Choose Your Best Answer

1. Difference between mortgage & charge

a) Mortgage can be made only by act of parties, whereas charge can be created only by operation of law.

b) Both can be enforced against transferee with or without notice.

c) The mortgage deed shall be executed & registered & attested by two witnesses whereas the instrument of charge may be executed and need not be attested or registered.

d) In mortgage there is no transfer of interest where as in charge there is transfer of interest.

2. Company can deal with the property only with the consent of charge holder in case of

a) Fixed charge

b) Floating charge

c) In both fixed & floating charge

d) None of above.

3. A mortgage binds himself to repay the mortgaged money on certain date and transfers the mortgaged property absolutely to the mortgagee subject to the proviso that he will re-transfer it to the mortgagor upon payment of the mortgage money as agreed is called :

a) English mortgage

b) Mortgage by conditional sale

c) Simple mortgage

d) Usufructuary mortgage

4. Transfer of right to enjoy property means :

a) License

b) Lease

c) Mortgage

d) Leave & license

5. The provisions regarding license is governed by :

a) Transfer of Property Act.

b) Indian Easement Act.

c) Indian Contract Act.

d) None of the above.

6. In leave & license agreement, the juridical possession is with :

a) Licensor.

b) Licensee.

c) Both a & b

d) None of the above.

7. A clause which states that whatever is declared is true to the knowledge & belief is called:

a) Testatum

b) Recitals

c) Reddendum clause

d) None of the above.

8. A clause which states the period of lease is called:

a) Testatum

b) Recitals

c) Reddendum clause

d) None of the above.

9. In case of company , mortgage of the property should be duly authorised

a) By object clause of memorandum of association & approval by resolution of the board

b) Only by the object clause of the memorandum of association

c) By the resolution passed in the meeting of the Shareholders

d) By articles of association

Find Your Best Answer

1. Will there be a delivery of possession in case of Simple Mortgage?
2. Registration of mortgage is not compulsory.
3. All the provision of simple mortgage will apply to charge.

4. Every charge is a mortgage but every mortgage is not a charge.
5. Partition is a transfer.
6. Hypothecation and pledge is the same.

Answers:

1. Mortgage
2. 3 Months
3. Partition
4. Floating charge
5. Anomalous
6. "Deed of further charge"

1. C
2. A
3. A
4. B
5. B
6. A
7. A
8. C
9. A

1. Incorrect, as there will NOT be any delivery of possession in case of Simple Mortgage
2. Incorrect, because registration is mandatory for all mortgages. However, Mortgage by Deposit of Title deeds is permitted in notified towns without registration.
3. Correct
4. Incorrect, The basic difference between a mortgage & charge is that charge only gives the right to payment out of particular property, without transferring any interest in the property .In mortgage, the essence is a transfer of interest in specific property. Thus, every mortgage is a charge but every charge is not mortgage.
5. Incorrect, partition is not a transfer but a mere division of properties among existing co-owners.
6. Incorrect, both are different. In hypothecation the movable assets remains in the possession of the borrower & the legal title vests with lending institution by virtue of agreement whereas in pledge the possession of the movable assets of the borrower are transferred.

SAMPLE DEEDS

MORTGAGE DEED 1

THIS SIMPLE MORTGAGE DEED is executed at Chennai, this, the 25th day of August 2012. 2

By

Labz Limited, a limited liability company registered under the Companies Act, 1956 under the 3
Certificate of Incorporation number 99-1234 of 2000 and Corporate Identification Number (CIN) UL123455591234/2003 in the office of the Registrar of Companies, Maharashtra at Mumbai having its Registered Office at No. 13, Jolly Maker Chambers, Mumbai –400021 through its ATTORNEY Mr. Shiva appointed under the Power of Attorney dated 25th August 2012 given under the common seal of the company hereinafter referred to as the MORTGAGOR.

In the favour of

AXIS BANK, a private bank having its office at 9, Wheatcrofts Road Chennai – 600034 hereinafter referred to as the MORTGAGEE.

WHEREAS the MORTGAGOR is the absolute owner of the house & ground bearing No.3A, Ahiripukur, Kolkata -700019, hereinafter referred to as PROPERTY, more particularly described in the SCHEDULE hereunder; 4

AND WHEREAS the MORTGAGOR requires a sum of Rs. 10,00,00,000 [RUPEES TEN CRORES ONLY] for its working capital;

AND WHEREAS the MORTGAGEE has agreed to lend a sum of Rs. 10,00,00,000 [RUPEES TEN CRORES ONLY] to MORTGAGOR on the security of the PROPERTY;

NOW THIS DEED WITNESSESS AS FOLLOWS: 5

6
That in consideration of a sum of Rs. 10,00,00,000 [RUPEES TEN CRORES ONLY] given by the MORTGAGEE by Cheque drawn on AXIS BANK, Kolkata dated 20th August 2012, bearing Cheque No. 287129, the receipt of which the MORTGAGOR hereby acknowledges, the 7
MORTGAGOR transfers by way of SIMPLE MORTGAGE all that house & ground bearing No.3A, 8
Ahiripukur, Kolkata -700019, hereinafter referred to as PROPERTY, more particularly described in 9
the SCHEDULE hereunder.

THE PARTIES COVENANT AS FOLLOWS: 10

1. The parties agree that the loan is for a period of 10 years from the date of the execution of this deed.
2. The MORTGAGOR shall pay to the MORTGAGEE, a simple interest @ 9% which shall be due and payable on the 5thday of English Calendar Month.
3. The MORTGAGOR declares that there are no other encumbrances, charges, lien or lis pendens over the said PROPERTY hereby mortgaged.
4. The MORTGAGOR agrees that in case the MORTGAGOR commits any default in the repayment of the loan, the MORTGAGEE shall have the RIGHT TO CAUSE THE PROPERTY to be sold through the Court.
5. The MORTGAGOR expressly confers upon the MORTGAGEE, the right to sell the PROPERTY privately [that is to say without the intervention of the Court] under Section 69 of the Transfer of

Property Act, 1882. However, before exercising the right of private sale, the MORTGAGEE shall give 3 MONTHS NOTICE in writing to the MORTGAGOR of its intention to sell.

IN WITNESS WHEREOF THE PARTIES HAVE SIGNED THIS DEED ON THE DATE, MONTH, YEAR ABOVE WRITTEN. → 11

→ 12

MORTGAGOR

Labz Limited through its ATTORNEY under Power of Attorney dated 25th day of August 2007.

WITNESSES → 13

1. V. Vijay,

   145, Cyber Apartments,

   Kolkata.

2. X. Rakesh,

   595, Milky way lane,

   Kolkata.

MORTGAGEE.

SCHEDULE → 13

COMPONENTS OF MORTGAGE DEED

1. **Deed Title** – It should be in capital letters, bold & centered. It describes the nature of the deed. (eg) THIS DEED OF SIMPLE MORTGAGE or any other type of mortgage.
2. **Place and Date of execution** – It should be written in words & figures. It is to reckon limitation period, stamp duty, jurisdiction, etc…
3. **Name and Description of Parties** – The transferor should be mentioned first, then confirming party, if any, and then, the transferee, including inter-parties. The full description includes, Name, Age, S/o or D/o., Nationality, Address, relation to document, and includes his/her legal heirs, successors, assigns and legal representatives. In case either of the party is the Company, then also describe the nature of the company along with its Corporate Identification Number (CIN), the registrar office of registration and the place where Registered Office of the company is situated. Further, also to state the authorized Attorney as empowered to enter the deed on behalf of the Company.
4. **Recitals** – It contains the short story of (past events of) property UPTO it's vesting into its transferors. It is of two types A) Narrative Recitals (past events) and B) Inductory Recitals (intention behind execution). Narrative Recitals are followed with Inductory Recitals. It starts with the words "WHEREAS" & AND WHEREAS.
5. **Testatum** – It is the WITNESSING clause. It refers to the Inductory Recitals of the agreement. It states that whatever declared is true to their knowledge and belief. It also states Consideration and acknowledgement of Receipt. It usually begins with the words "NOW THIS DEED WITNESSES …."

OPERATIVE CLAUSES

6. **Consideration** – To ascertain the Stamp Duty.
7. **Receipt** – It is the acknowledgement of Consideration.
8. **Operative Clause** – (eg) Transfer by way of...
9. **Description of Property** – The property should be FULLY described for making the location of the property easier. Normally, it will be given in the SCHEDULE. It is for the purpose of Registration Act, 1908.
10. **Covenants** (agreement of conditions) – It means conditions accepted by the promisor either to do or refrain from doing an act. It may be expressed or implied.

A. Covenants by Mortgagor

- To repair the mortgaged property
- To insure the mortgaged property in the name of the mortgagee
- Not to grant leases exceeding 1 YEAR OR accept surrender of existing lease thereof, without written permission of mortgagee [Section 65A of Transfer of Property Act, 1882 deals power to mortgagor to lease the mortgaged property UPTO 3 years with condition to re-entry on default]
- To pay outgoings like rates, taxes, duties, etc...

B. Other Important Covenants

- Period fixed for mortgage (i.e.) the period upto which mortgagor is debarred from redeeming the security and mortgagee not to call his money.
- Power of sale of mortgaged property to recover dues
- Power to appoint Receiver u/s. 69A of Transfer of Property Act, 1882 if interest is in arrears for 2 or more months to exercise the Private Sale u/s. 69 and such receiver is the agent of mortgagor.
- Proviso for Redemption u/s. 60A of Transfer of Property Act, 1882 (i.e.) re-transfer of mortgaged property on payment of dues

11. **Testimonium Clause** – It is a DECLARATION by the parties subscribing the signature in the presence of WITNESS on the day mentioned in the deed. It starts with the words "IN WITNESS WHEREOF THE PARTIES HERETO SET THEIR HANDS ON THIS DATE, MONTH AND YEAR MENTIONED ABOVE"
12. Signature
13. Witness – Atleast 2 witnesses shall attest the deed as per Section 59 of Transfer of Property Act, 1882.
14. **Attestation** – By the notary public, if required.
15. **Annexures or Schedules** – The Schedule of Property to be given as per the requirements of Registration Act, 1908.

MEMORANDUM FOR DEPOSIT OF TITLE DEEDS

This MEMORANDUM entered into at Chennai, this, the 25th day of August, 2012,

of

Mr. Raj (Mortgagor) as BENEFICIAL OWNER has deposited

With

Mr. Vijay (Mortgagee),

The Original Title Deeds comprised in Schedule A hereto, relating to the PREMISES belonging to the said Mr. Raj and situated at Mylapore, more fully described in Schedule B with INTENT to create a charge thereon for securing repayment to the said Mr. Vijay of the sum of Rs. 1,00,000 (Rupees One lakh only) this day lent and advanced by the said Mr. Vijay to the said Mr. Raj on demand on interest for the same from this date at the rate of 10% per annum.

The said Mr. Raj do hereby undertake as and when required by the said Mr. Vijay to execute and register at the costs of the said Mr. Raj a legal mortgage in such form and containing such covenants and provisions as he may reasonably require.

Signed on the day, date, month and year above written.

MORTGAGOR

SCHEDULE A

Description of the Title Deeds deposited.

SCHEDULE B

Description of the Property.

DEED OF REDEMPTION OR RECONVEYANCE OF MORTGAGED PROPERTY BY THE MORTGAGEE IN FAVOUR OF THE MORTGAGOR

THIS DEED is made at 25th day of August 2012

between

Mr. Mani S/O. Mr. Ravi, Hindu, aged 25 years residing at 9, Veeraperumal Koil Street, Chennai – 600004 hereinafter referred to as the MORTGAGEE which term shall mean & include his legal heirs, representatives, administrators, nominees and assigns ON THE OTHER PART.

And

Mr. Sakti S/O. Mr. Shiv, Hindu, aged 25 years residing at 9, Veeraperumal Koil Street, Chennai – 600004 hereinafter referred to as the MORTGAGOR which term shall mean & include his legal heirs, representatives, administrators, nominees and assigns ON THE OTHER PART.

WHEREBY by a mortgage deed dated 25th day of August 2007, the property mentioned in that deed was mortgaged by the said Mr. Sakti in favour of the said Mr. Mani to secure payment of the amount of Rs. 10,00,000 (Rupees Ten lakhs only) with interest 10% per annum.

NOW THIS DEED OF RECONVEYANCE WITNESSES AS FOLLOWS:

That is consideration of all principal moneys and interest secured by the said mortgage deed dated 25th day of August 2007. Having been paid, the receipt whereof the said Mr. Main hereby acknowledges.

The said Mr. Mani as mortgagee hereby REDEEMS or RECONVEYS unto the said Mr. Sakti all the property comprised in the said mortgage deed to **hold** the same upto and to the **use** of the said Mr. Sakti as ABSOLUTE owner DISCHARGED from all principal money and interest secured by and from all claims and demands under the aforesaid mortgage deed.

INSTRUMENT OF CHARGE

THIS INSTRUMENT OF CHARGE is executed at Chennai, this, the 25th of August 2012.

By

Labz Limited, a limited liability company registered under the Companies Act, 1956 under the Certificate of Incorporation number 99-1234 of 2000 and Corporate Identification Number (CIN) UL123455591234/2003 in the office of the Registrar of Companies, Maharashtra at Mumbai having its Registered Office at No. 13, Jolly Maker Chambers, Mumbai – 400021 through its ATTORNEY Mr. Shiva appointed under the Power of

Attorney dated 25th August 2009 given under the common seal of the company hereinafter referred to as the BORROWER.

In the favour of

AXIS BANK, a private bank having its office at 9, Wheatcrofts Road Chennai – 600034 hereinafter referred to as the CHARGEE or HOLDER OF CHARGE.

WHEREAS the BORROWER is the absolute owner of the *house & ground* bearing No.3A, Ahiripukur, Kolkata - 700019, hereinafter referred to as PROPERTY, more particularly described in the SCHEDULE hereunder.

AND WHEREAS the BORROWER **requires a sum** of Rs. 20,00,000 (Rupees Twenty Lakhs only) for its working capital.

NOW THIS INSTRUMENT OF CHARGE WITNESSES AS FOLLOWS:

That in consideration of a sum of Rs. 20,00,000 (Rupees Twenty Lakhs only) received from the CHARGEE, the BORROWER company CREATES A CHARGE in favour of CHARGEE on the PROPERTY, more particularly described in the SCHEDULE hereunder.

The parties covenant as follows:

IN WITNESS WHEREOF THE BORROWER has signed this instrument, on the date, month and year above written.

BORROWER

Through its Power of Attorney dated 10th July 2012.

HYPOTHECATION AGREEMENT to secure fixed loan

The Manager,

Axis Bank,

Mylapore Branch,

Chennai – 600 004.

Sir/Madam,

In consideration of your Bank advancing to me/us a loan for the sum of Rs. 10,00,000 (Rupees Ten Lakhs only), I/We hereby

Agree to

Hypothecate and **hold** under **lien** to the Bank as security for the repayment as per Schedule hereto of the principal amount of loan and interest on demand at 10% per annum subject to a maximum of 5% per annum above Bank rate.

I/We agree as follows:

1. The goods so held under lien are declared to be our absolute property and to be stored in my/our godowns at MIDC Industrial Area and Mylapore.

2. To furnish full and correct statement of particulars of all goods so held under lien with the market value thereof respectively at the close of business on the last day of each English Calendar month so long as money remains due in respect of the said loan.

3. To keep goods under lien and my/our possession, separately, and no moneys shall be borrowed by me/us on the security of such goods to impair or affect goods under lien.

4. The goods under lien can be dealt in the ordinary course of business but shall not reduce the value below the amount of the said debt plus the margin of 10%, default of which, the proceeds of such sale to be paid into the bank as a part satisfaction of the loan.

5. To empower you to enter godowns for the purpose of inspection and taking an account of the said goods.

6. To empower you to take possession of any goods under lien under this agreement and to exercise full rights of a pawnee under Indian Contract Act, failing payment of the amount under this loan on or before 30th September 2012 without any notice.

7. To insure all the goods under lien against fire to their full value and to deposit the policies with Bank.

It is understood that the bank's lien on the goods, so held under this agreement shall extend to any other sum for which I/we either separately or jointly become indebted or liable to the bank on any account.

HYPOTHECATEE

SCHEDULE OF GOODS

LEASE DEED → 1

THIS LEASE DEED is executed at Kolkata, this, the 25thday of August 2012 → 2

By

Mr. Mani S/O. Mr. Ravi, Hindu, aged 25 years residing at 9, Wheatcrofts Road Chennai – 600034 hereinafter referred to as the LESSOR which term shall mean & include his legal heirs, representatives, administrators, nominees and assigns ON THE ONE PART → 3

In the favour of

Labz Limited, a limited liability company registered under the Companies Act, 1956 under the Certificate of Incorporation number 99-1234 of 2000 and Corporate Identification Number(CIN) UL1234555991234/2003 in the office of the Registrar of Companies, Maharashtra at Mumbai having its Registered Office at No. 13, Jolly Maker Chambers, Mumbai –400021 through its ATTORNEY Mr. Shiva appointed under the Power of Attorney dated 25th August 2012 given under the common seal of the company hereinafter referred to as the LESSEE ON THE OTHER PART.

WHEREAS the LESSOR is the sole and absolute owner of the house & ground bearing No.3A, Ahiripukur, Kolkata -700019, hereinafter referred to as PROPERTY, more particularly described in the SCHEDULE hereunder; → 4

AND WHEREAS the LESSOR has agreed to transfer BY WAY OF LEASE the PROPERTY, to the LESSEE;

NOW THIS LEASE DEED WITNESSES AS FOLLOWS: 5

1. The LESSOR transfers by way of LEASE, all that house & ground bearing No.3A, Ahiripukur, Kolkata -700019, hereinafter referred to as PROPERTY, more particularly described in the SCHEDULE hereunder to the LESSEE. 6 7

2. The LEASE shall commence from 25th August 2012.

3. The LESSEE shall pay to the LESSOR a sum of Rs. 1,00,000 [RUPEES ONE LAKH ONLY] towards RENT which shall be payable on or before the 5th day of succeeding English Calendar Month. 9

4. The LESSEE has deposited to the LESSOR a sum of Rs. 1,00,00,000 [RUPEES ONE CRORE ONLY] as a Security Deposit; This deposit shall be refunded by the LESSOR to the LESSEE on the termination of the LEASE and the LESSEE surrendering the vacant possession of the PROPERTY to the LESSOR.

THE PARTIES COVENANT AS FOLLOWS: 8

5. The duration of the LEASE shall be 5 years [FIVE YEARS ONLY] from the commencement of the LEASE.

6. The LEASE may be terminated either by the LESSOR or the LESSEE by giving THREE MONTHS notice in writing to the party of his intention to terminate the LEASE. However, the THREE MONTHS notice is not required if the LESSEE terminates the LEASE and pays to the LESSOR THREE MONTHS rent in lieu of the notice.

7. The LESSOR shall deliver the vacant possession of the PROPERTY to the LESSEE on and from the commencement of the LEASE.

8. The LESSEE agrees not to sublet the PROPERTY.

9. The LESSEE agrees not to make any permanent construction of superstructure upon the premises hereby leased. However any temporary constructions or superstructures may be made with the consent in writing of the LESSOR. Such super structure of additions shall be removed by the LESSEE on the termination of the LEASE and at the cost of the LESSEE.

10. The LESSOR shall pay the PROPERTY tax to the Corporation; The Electricity bills shall be paid by the LESSEE in the name of the LESSOR.

11. The LESSEE agrees to keep the PROPERTY in a good condition.

IN WITNESS WHEREOF THE LESSOR HAS SIGNED THIS DEED UNDER HIS HAND AND THE LESSEE HAS SIGNED THIS DEED THROUGH ITS ATTORNEY ON THE DAY, MONTH, YEAR ABOVE WRITTEN. 10

LESSOR 11

WITNESSES 12

LESSEE

Labz Limited through its ATTORNEY under Power of Attorney dated 25th day of August 2012.

SCHEDULE 14

All that *house and ground* bearing No.3A, Ahiripukur, Kolkata –700019 under Town Survey (TS) No.

5599 in the sub-district of Ahiripukur in Kolkata measuring 10 AFFIgrounds bounded,

ON THE NORTH BY: House & ground bearing No.1, Ahiripukur, Kolkata.

ON THE SOUTH BY: House & ground bearing No.5, Ahiripukur, Kolkata.

ON THE WEST BY: House & ground bearing No.2, Ahiripukur, Kolkata.

ON THE EAST BY: 1st Lane, Ahiripukur Road, Kolkata.

COMPONENTS OF LEASE DEED

1. **Deed Title** – It should be in capital letters, bold & centered. It describes the nature of the deed. (eg) THIS LEASE DEED…
2. **Place and Date of execution** – It should be written in words & figures. It is to reckon limitation period, stamp duty, jurisdiction, etc…
3. **Name and Description of Parties** – The transferor should be mentioned first, then confirming party, if any, and then, the transferee, including inter-parties. The full description includes, Name, Age, S/o or D/o., Nationality, Address, relation to document, and includes his/her legal heirs, successors, assigns and legal representatives. In case either of the party is the Company, then also describe the nature of the company along with its Corporate Identification Number (CIN), the registrar office of registration and the place where Registered Office of the company is situated. Further, also to state the authorized Attorney as empowered to enter the deed on behalf of the Company.
4. **Recitals** – It contains the short story of (past events of) property UPTO it's vesting into its transferors. It is of two types A) Narrative Recitals (past events) and B) Inductory Recitals (intention behind execution). Narrative Recitals are followed with Inductory Recitals. It starts with the words "WHEREAS" & AND WHEREAS.
5. **Testatum** – It is the WITNESSING clause. It refers to the Inductory Recitals of the agreement. It states that whatever declared is true to their knowledge and belief. It also states Consideration and acknowledgement of Receipt. It usually begins with the words "NOW THIS DEED WITNESSES …."

OPERATIVE CLAUSES

6. **Operative Clause** – (eg) Transfer by way of…
7. **Description of Property** – The property should be FULLY described for making the location of the property easier. Normally, it will be given in the SCHEDULE. It is for the purpose of Registration Act, 1908.
8. **Covenants** (agreement of conditions) – It means conditions accepted by the promisor either to do or refrain from doing an act. It may be expressed or implied. Kindly refer Section 108 above.

9. **REDDENDUM CLAUSE** – The mode and time fixed for payment shall be mentioned. The rent is payable during the term of the lease.
10. **Testimonium Clause** – It is a DECLARATION by the parties subscribing the signature in the presence of WITNESS on the day mentioned in the deed. It starts with the words "IN WITNESS WHEREOF THE PARTIES HERETO SET THEIR HANDS ON THIS DATE, MONTH AND YEAR MENTIONED ABOVE"
11. **Signature**
12. **Witness**
13. **Attestation** – By the notary public, if required.

14. **Annexures or Schedules** – The Schedule of Property to be given as per the requirements of Registration Act, 1908.

COVENANT FOR RENEWAL IN LEASE:

"That if the LESSEE pay the rent punctually and regularly **and** duly observe **and** perform the covenants herein contained and apply in **writing** to the LANDLORD not less than 1 month **prior** to the expiration of the term herein RESERVED for renewal of the lease, then LESSOR may grant a NEW LEASE of the said land for a further period of 2 years on the same terms and conditions except the covenant for renewal and subject to such variations as may be mutually agreed."

All the said deeds shall not be reproduced as such but it is advisable to stick with the same formats for easy remembrance and study. The legal provisions are like formulas in the mathematical problems. Meaning, on reading a question from question paper, immediately start writing the formulas (legal provisions) either on your mind or in the margins of the answer paper. Now think of the Structure of the deed. Then, using the structure and applying the formula, enjoy drafting the deed.

This chapter deals with provisions and formats of Hire purchase and Trade related agreements. While studying the following, never forget the principle of studying drafting (i.e.) "start reading, drafting, reading, drafting, reading, drafting and again to master the subject."

Hire Purchase & Trade Related Agreements

Hire Purchase agreement is an agreement wherein goods are sold by one person to another person, the consideration of which is payable inn installments.

Laws involved:

1. Indian Contract Act, 1872
2. Sale of Goods Act, 1930
3. Hire purchase Act, 1972
4. Indian Stamp Act, 1899
5. Central Sales Tax Act, 1956 (Value Added Tax)

Can goods be re-possessed if Hire Purchase agreement provides for the same in case of default of payment of installment dues?

Yes, if the agreement permits financiers to take possession of the financed vehicles, there is NO legal impedime nt on such possession being taken as decided by Supreme Court in the case of *Orix Auto Finance (India) Ltd v. Jagmander Singh*. Hirer can still avail any statutory remedy as may be available.

Note: These are matters of contract & unless the party shows that contract is unconscionable or opposed to public policy, writ petitions cannot be filed.

POINTS TO BE CONSIDERED WHILE DRAFTING THE HIRE PURCHASE AGREEMENT:

1. Minimum of two parties.
2. Subject matter must be goods, as defined under the Sale of Goods Act, 1930.
3. Date of Execution
4. Place of Execution
5. Description of the goods must be stated.
6. Cost of the goods – to be stated.
7. Indigenous or imported.
8. Amount of installments payable and the total number of installments
9. Rights → Owner / → Hirer
10. Obligation → Owner / → Hirer

11. Rights → Owner
→ Hirer to terminate & damages on breach.

12. Rights of hirer on payment off last installment.

HIRE PURCHASE INSTALLMENT AGREEMENT

THIS DEED OF HIRE PURCHASE AGREEMENT executed at Chennai on this 6th day of June 2012

BETWEEN

M/s.ABC & CO., a firm registered under the Partnership Act, 1932 and having their principal office at 132, P.J. Towers, Nariman Point, Mumbai represented by its managing partner, Mr.A, herein after referred as OWNER (which term shall include his successors, assigns and legal representatives), being PARTY OF THE FIRST PART.

AND

Mr. Y, Son of Mr. P, aged 25 years, residing at 10, Jeejeboy Towers, Thane herein after referred as HIRER (which term shall include his successors, assigns and legal representatives), being PARTY OF THE SECOND PART.

WHEREAS the OWNER is the dealer of various is the dealer of various Consumer Electronic goods like Television, Washing Machine, and Refrigerator.

WHEREAS the HIRER expressed his desire to buy a washing machine from the Owner under the Hire purchase Scheme.

WHEREAS the OWNER agrees to sell the goods and the hirer agrees to buy on Hire purchase installment basis.

NOW THIS DEED WITNESSES AS FOLLOWS:

1. The owner shall sell and deliver a washing machine more fully described in the Schedule, to the hirer at his place.
2. The cost of the goods is Rs. 30000 inclusive of all taxes.
3. The hirer paid a sum of Rs. 7500 as initial / down payment being 25% of the cost of goods and the same is acknowledged by the owner.
4. The Hirer agrees to pay Rs.3000 per month for 10 installments commencing from 7th June, 2012.
5. The ownership of the goods shall continue to be vested in last installment is paid.
6. The owner or his Agent has right to visit and the inspect goods in time by giving sufficient notice.
7. Hirer shall take the necessary steps in maintenance of the goods and also protect it from the damages.
8. Hirer has the right to buy the goods either upon full payment of consideration or on payment of last installment.
9. Hirer undertakes to pay all the insurance charges, taxes and duties.
10. Both the parties deserve the right to terminate the Agreement by giving 3 months notice on each other.
11. In the event of default of payment by the hirer, the owner has the right to take back the goods and claim damages and interest at 24% on defaulted payment.
12. The owner is responsible and liable for any defect in the goods and ensures the maintenance during the warranty period.

13. In case of breach of Agreement by the Owner, the Hirer has a right to call for replacement of goods or claim damages or return of installments paid, along with 18% interest.

14. The disputes or differences shall be settled within the jurisdiction of Chennai and at its courts.

IN WITNESS WHERE OF BOTH PARTIES SET THEIR HANDS ON THIS DAY, MONTH AND YEAR MENTIONED ABOVE.

HIRER — OWNER

Witness — Witness

1. Agreement wherein goods are sold by one person to another person, the consideration of which is payable in installment is called as:

a) Trade related agreement.

b) Lease agreement.

c) Hire purchase agreement.

d) Sale deed agreement.

2. Parties involveD in trade related agreement are:

a) Manufacturer & dealer

b) Manufacturer & wholesaler

c) Manufacturer & Agent

d) Manufacturer& retailer

e) All of above

f) None of above

3. Dealership agreement is a form of:

a) Trade related agreement

b) Hire purchase agreement

c) Both of above

d) None of above

4. Points to be consider while drafting a hire-purchase agreement:

a) Minimum two parties

b) Rights of owner or hirer

c) Obligation of owner or hirer

d) All of above

e) b & c

5. An agent for the seller to sell the property at public auction is called :

a) Auctioneer

b) Factor

c) Broker

d) Del credere agent

6. Agency + guarantee is known as:

a) Broker

b) Factor

c) Del credere agent

d) None of the above

ANS

1. C
2. E
3. A
4. D
5. A
6. C

TRADE RELATED AGREEMENTS

These are agreements involving two parties –

- Manufacturer and
- Dealer/Wholesaler/Agent /Retailer.

TYPES OF TRADE RELATED AGREEMENTS:

1. Dealership Agreement
2. Distributorship agreement.
3. Agency Agreement.
4. Marketing Arrangement Agreement.
5. Export Agreement

FEATURES OF TRADE RELATED AGREEMENTS:

1. Types of goods – Movable goods. Goods are defined under Sales of Goods Act, 1930.
2. Parties – Two parties.
3. Description of the goods to be specified.
4. Consideration must be stated.
5. Schedule of delivery.

6. Inspection of goods and period upto which the rejections may be accepted.
7. Mode of Payment.
8. Allowance of rebate, discount, etc.,
9. Cost of transportation, insurance and other service charges [C.i.f] – who shall bear.
10. Central Excise Duty, Sales Tax, etc., shall be at the rate as applicable at the time of clearance of goods.
11. Term / period of Agreement
12. Renewal provisions
13. In case of termination, procedure for the same.
14. Arbitration clause.
15. Force Majure clause.

APPLICABLE LAWS:

- Indian Contract Act, 1872
- Sale of Goods Act, 1930
- The Companies Act, 1956
- The Competition Act, 2002

AGENCY AGREEMENT:

The essential ingredients of Commercial Agency Agreements are,

1. Date of commencement and termination of agency
2. goods or products to be covered by agency
3. the contractual territory
4. Nature of agency (eg) Sole or exclusive agency
5. For the acts of agent, the principal is liable unless the principal has exceeded his authority
6. Consideration is not required to create an agency
7. The rate and basis of commission payable to the agent
8. Conditions regarding reimbursement of expenses incurred by the agent
9. Payment of commission on orders received directly by the principal from the agents territory
10. When the commission will accrue and payable and currency of payment
11. Circumstances when Principal refuse validity to accept orders

It is governed by Chapter X covering Sections 182 to 238 of the Indian Contract Act, 1872. Also, the provisions of Companies Act, 1956 dealing with Sole Selling or Buying Agents u/s. 294, 294A and 294AA shall be complied with.

KINDS OF AGENT

- Auctioneer – An agent for the seller to sell the property at public auction
- Factor – An agent (having POSSESSION) to whom goods are CONSIGNED for the purpose of sale
- Broker – An agent employed to NEGOTIATE a contract between his Principal and a third person

• **Del Credere Agent** – An agent employed for SALE with EXTRA remuneration (del credere commission) to collect PAYMENT from buyer. Thus, it is AGENCY + GUARANTEE (solvency & performance of contract). The commission paid to an agent in a contract of agency coupled with interest is known as del credere. Kindly note Section 202 of Indian Contract Act, 1872, states that where the agency is coupled with interest (such as del credere) CANNOT be revoked PREJUDICIAL to the interest of the Agent.

1. Del Credere Agency (2009 – June and 2010 – December)

DEALERSHIP AGREEMENT

THIS DEED OF DEALERSHIP AGREEMENT entered into at Chennai on this 8th day of June, 2012

BETWEEN

Labz Limited, a limited liability company registered under the Companies Act, 1956 under the Certificate of Incorporation number 99-1234 of 2000 and Corporate Identification Number (CIN) UL1234555991234/2003 in the office of the Registrar of Companies, Maharashtra at Mumbai having its Registered Office at No. 13, Jolly Maker Chambers, Mumbai – 400021 through its ATTORNEY Mr. Shiva appointed under the Power of Attorney dated 25th August 2012 given under the common seal of the company hereinafter referred to as the MANUFACTURER ON THE FIRST PART.

AND

M/s Learn Labz & Co., a firm registered under the Partnership Act, 1932 and having their Principal Office at 128, Veeraperumal Koil Street, Mylapore, Chennai represented by its Partner, Mr. Ram, herein after referred as "DEALER", which term shall mean and include its successors and assigns, of the SECOND PART.

WHEREAS the MANUFACTURER is having all infrastructure facilities at No. 10, Industrial Area, Padi, Chennai to manufacture educational toolkits and corporate stationeries such as e-learning tools, headphones, compact disks & e-pads under Brand name "LABZ"

AND WHEREAS,

1. the DEALER is already in the business of e-learning solutions for professional courses and has a network throughout the Southern parts of the country.
2. the DEALER approached the MANUFACTURER and expressed the desire to act as the DEALER for the goods of the MANUFACTURER.
3. the MANUFACTURER accepted to appoint the DEALER and both the parties agreed to the following terms and conditions.

NOW THIS DEED WITNESSES AS FOLLOWS:

1. The MANUFACTURER **undertakes to manufacture the goods** more fully described in the SCHEDULE.
2. The DEALER **undertakes to act as DEALER and sell the goods** of the MANUFACTURER.
3. The DEALER shall deposit a sum of Rs.5,00,000/- [Rupees Five Lakhs Only] as Security Deposit, which shall not carry any interest. It shall be refunded upon termination of agreement or adjusted / forfeited as per the Clauses of the Agreement.
4. The DEALER shall well in advance inform the MANUFACTURER, giving the details and description of the goods and place an order.
5. The MANUFACTURER shall confirm the order within 3 days.

6. The MANUFACTURER shall manufacture the goods as per the description of the order and maintain quality, conduct test before dispatch.
7. The DEALER shall honour and pay the amount within 14 days through normal banking channels.
8. The DEALER undertakes to place order and lift the minimum quantity as per schedule B.
9. The MANUFACTURER shall allow an additional discount of 5%, in the event of immediate cash payment or if order exceeds by 50% of the committed quantity.
10. The DEALER has the right to appoint sub-dealers, sub-agents, retailers and other market intermediaries to sell the goods, without prejudicial to the interests of the manufacturer.
11. This agreement may be terminated by either party by giving 30 days notice on each other, subject to the execution of orders already placed.
12. Both the parties shall be governed under Force Majeure for non-performance of act beyond their control.
13. In the event of any disputes or differences, the same shall be settled under the Arbitration and Conciliation Act and Rules.

IN WITNESS WHERE OF THE PARTIES THERETO HAVE SET THEIR ON THIS DAY, MONTH AND YEAR MENTIONED ABOVE.

DEALER	MANUFACTURER
WITNESS	WITNESS

These are agreements made during the sale of movable properties. Understand the basic provisions and its implications before advising the provisions regarding the nature of the agreement. These are just standard formats and such of the formats shall be amended to suit the requirements of the questions asked.

The basic legal provisions of foreign collaborations will be governed under FEMA, FIPB and RBI which are dealt in detail under the ALLIANCES portion of Strategic Management & International Trade subject. Keep in mind the said provisions while drafting the agreement.

Foreign Collaboration & Outsourcing Agreement

Foreign Collaboration Agreements mean when two or more parties (one Indian party and the other foreign party) join hands for exchange of technical know-how, etc. for business transactions.

1. Mention important guidelines for entering into foreign collaboration agreements. (2007 & 2009 – June)
2. Ultra Vision Textiles Limited is entering into a foreign collaboration with Omega Inc., USA for technical know – how and assistance for the proposed textile machinery manufacturing project. Draft a suitable foreign collaboration agreement. (2010 – June)

The Regulators

1. Government of India through Notifications & Rules by publishing in Official Gazette
2. Ministry of Commerce (has Department of Industrial Policy & Promotion which specifies Sectoral Caps through FDI Policy – released on April 2012 & will be revised on April 2013)
3. Reserve Bank of India (through Regulations & Master Circulars gives procedures on Foreign Investments, released on July every year)
4. Ministry of Finance (has Foreign Investment Promotion Board for Government approvals & Directorate of Enforcement for investigations)

Consideration in Foreign Collaborations & Technology Transfer Agreements:

The Consideration plays a crucial role in determining the type of investment into India. The Foreign Joint Venture party has two options:

1. Lumpsum Payment vs. Royalty: The Indian Joint Venture Company may in lieu of technology transfer agree for a lumpsum consideration to be paid or a payment of royalty as a % of units sold. As per the extant FEMA Regulations, the royalty or lumpsum payment can freely remitted out of India **WITHOUT ANY CEILING LIMITS** subject to withholding of taxes, if any.

Note: The Current FDI Policy of India also permit conversion of royalty or lumpsum fees into equity shares of the Indian company subject to approvals & intimations, if any.

2. Dividend on Investments: In case of investments made into the equity of the company by the Foreign Joint Venture partner, such person will be able to repatriate DIVIDEND out of India, which is again a CURRENT ACCOUNT TRANSACTION under FEMA which is freely permitted subject to taxes, if any.

Note: The Current FDI policy also permits allotment of shares for non-cash consideration like import of new machinery, conversion of External Commercial Borrowings, reimbursement of preliminary expenses subject to approvals & intimations, if any.

GUIDELINES:

1. **Investment** – In case of equity participation, FEMA reporting arrangements regarding Foreign Direct Investment to be complied with by allotting shares within 180 days of receipt of money.
2. **Royalty, Lumpsum payment & Remittances** – Appropriate Technology Agreement to be entered into and shall comply with provisions regarding Current Account Transactions and approval of Ministry of Commerce & Industry, if any. Royalty should be calculated on the basis of net ex-factory selling price of the product less excise duties and cost of imported components. The remittances are allowed only on the basis of prevailing exchange rates.
3. **Duration of agreement & its renewal –** In case of Government Approval route, specific time period will be provided in the approval itself. Normally, it may range from 5 years to 10 years. It may have a clause for renewal or extension of agreement on merit.
4. **Sub-licensing** – Subject to Central Government approval, there will not be any restriction on sub-licensing of the technical know-how to other Indian parties.
5. **Exports** – Subject to Licensing arrangements of Foreign Collaborator, there will not be any restriction on the free export to all countries.
6. **Procurement of capital goods, spares, raw materials, etc...** without any restriction and Indian Collaborator should have control over PRICING facility & SELLING arrangements.
7. **Technicians** deputed are either sides are subject to approval of RBI or **training** of Indian technicians should be incorporated as a clause in the agreement.
8. **Exploitation of Indian Patents** until its expiry can be used with compensation by Foreign Collaborator and on expiry it shall revert to Indian company.
9. **Consultancy** should be obtained from Indian Company as a prime consultant as much as possible.
10. **Indian Laws** – All collaboration agreements shall be subject to Indian laws.

SAMPLE FOREIGN COLLABORATION AGREEMENT

THIS FOREIGN COLLABORATION AGREEMENT executed this 1st day of February 2012 between Zillion Labz LLC, a foreign company incorporated in the United States and having its registered office at No. 10, Labz lane, Delaware 7666, Hereinafter called the **U.S. COMPANY OF THE ONE PART.**

AND

Labz Limited, a limited liability company registered under the Companies Act, 1956 under the Certificate of Incorporation number 99-1234 of 2000 and Corporate Identification Number (CIN) UL1234555991234/2003 in the office of the Registrar of Companies, Maharashtra at Mumbai having its Registered Office at No. 13, Jolly Maker Chambers, Mumbai – 400021, Hereinafter called the **INDIAN COMPANY OF THE SECOND PART.**

WHEREAS the INDIAN COMPANY has been incorporated having for its object as the manufacture and production of ROBOTICS EQUIPMENTS. WHEREAS the INDIAN COMPANY has already factory buildings, installed plant and machinery and commenced its manufacture and production of ROBOTICS EQUIPMENTS.

AND WHEREAS

1. the INDIAN COMPANY is desirous of procuring the latest technique and know – how relates to the manufacture of the above said equipments;
2. the INDIAN COMPANY therefore approached the U.S company who have considerable experience in the said field and requested them to extend to them necessary technical assistance in that behalf ;
3. the U.S COMPANY has agreed to extend technical assistance and to furnish to the INDIAN COMPANY for improvement of their business the requisite know – how and also to supply technicians or training to successfully handle and exploit the technical know – how subject to the terms and conditions set out hereunder.

NOW THIS AGREEMENT WITNESS AS FOLLOWS:

1. In consideration of the remuneration paid by the INDIAN COMPANY to the U.S COMPANY, it shall supply to the INDIAN COMPANY:

   A. Technical advice and know – how for the purpose of improving the existing factories for the manufacture of ROBOTICS EQUIPMENTS;

   B. renders advice in the matter of purchase of the further plants and machinery suitable and necessary for the factory;

   C. lend the services of the technicians to assists the INDIAN COMPANY in carrying out the improvement to the factories;

   D. impart technical training to Indian personnel at their works in America to enable them to operate machinery and to exploit the technical know-how to the best advantage;

2. for technical know-how and data supplied by the U.S COMPANY to the INDIAN COMPANY as above, the Indian company shall make a lump sum payment of USD 2,00,000 [UNITED STATES DOLLAR TWO LAKHS ONLY] to the U.S COMPANY phased as follows:

   a. one-third on execution of agreement;

   b. one-third, on the U.S COMPANY supplying the INDIAN COMPANY necessary know-how, which shall be done within 15 days from its execution thereof;

   c. The balance one-third thereafter after commencement of production.

3. This agreement shall be in force for a period of 5 years at the first instance, subject to extension for a further period of 5 years by mutual agreement.

4. There shall be no restriction on the Indian company exporting their products to foreign countries.

5. Technicians who may be deputed by the U.S COMPANY to the INDIAN COMPANY to advice and assist the Indian company under this agreement shall be paid their salary,

Traveling expenses and boarding and lodging by the Indian company.

6. The parties hereto mutually agree that they will each inform the other of any new development during the continuance of this agreement.

7. The INDIAN COMPANY shall maintain the utmost secrecy in connection with any technical data supplied by the U.S COMPANY under this agreement and in particular shall keep all data concerned with manufacturing process under lock and key.

8. On the expiry of the period prescribed herein or of extended period provided in clause 3 (supra) or upon the termination of this agreement for any reason the INDIAN COMPANY shall return to the U.S COMPANY all copies of information data or material under this agreement and then in its possession and shall expressly refrain from communicating any such information, technical data or material received by it hereunder to any person, firm or company whatsoever.

IN WITNESS WHEREOF THE PARTIES HERETO HAVE SIGNED THIS AGREEMENT THIS DAY, MONTH & YEAR ABOVE WRITTEN IN THE PRESENCE OF THE FOLLOWING WITNESSES:

OUTSOURCING AGREEMENT

Outsourcing is the CONTRACTING OUT of Company's non-core, non-revenue producing activities to SPECIALISTS. It is a STRATEGIC MANAGEMENT TOOL to restructure the organization around what it does BEST (i.e.) based on Core Competencies. It can be,

- Information Technology Outsourcing
- Business Process Outsourcing – human resource, finance & other administrative functions

- Knowledge Process Outsourcing – legal, paralegal & other highly skilled activities.

The factors to be considered while drafting an outsourcing agreement include,

1. Duties & Obligations of Outsourcer & Service provider
2. Security, Confidentiality & Non-compete
3. NEGATIVE COVENANT – one party agrees NOT to do something (specific performance);
4. Fees & payment terms
5. Term of agreement
6. Events of Defaults
7. Dispute resolution mechanism
8. Arbitration Clause
9. Appeal & Enforcement
10. Legal Provisions and Compliances.

SAMPLE OUTSOURCING TERMS FOR AGREEMENT

TERMS & CONDITIONS FOR CONVERTING HARD COPIES OF BOOK IN A BLUE RAY DISC

1. M/s. Knowledge World Publishers Pvt. Ltd. would perform the job of digitization (of the relevant portions marked for digitization) of the book including Data punching/Scanning, OCR Validation, proof-reading (at an accuracy level of 99.9 %).Tagging according to search parameters, Linking, Indexing etc.
2. The copyright of the contents of the CD, marketing rights and all other rights pertaining to the said CD would solely vest with the Learn Labz Pvt Ltd
3. M/s Knowledge World Publishers Pvt Ltd undertakes to complete the assignment within a period of 100 days from the date of execution of this agreement.
4. The total project cost to be paid to M/s Knowledge World Publishers Pvt Ltd would be as follows.
5. All other covenants including Arbitration, Force Majeure, etc… may be included.

Thus about foreign collaboration and outsourcing agreements. All the deeds given here are in its simplest form with most mandatory requirements. Students can add more points to the same based on your understanding of the subject for the purpose of exams.

Arbitration

Arbitration & Conciliation Act, 1996 is a self contained code and Code of Civil Procedure, 1908 or Indian Evidence Act, 1872 is NOT applicable unless specifically made applicable. However, Limitation Act, 1963 is applicable.

ARBITRATION AGREEMENT

An agreement by the parties to SUBMIT to arbitration ALL or CERTAIN disputes which MAY have arisen or MAY arise IN respect of a defined legal RELATIONSHIP which may be CONTRACTUAL or NOT.

METHODS

Either at the time of ENTERING into the Contract OR after the dispute has ARISEN.

It may be in the form of,

- An arbitration CLAUSE in a Contract – which shall be in WRITING & forms part of the contract. Kindly note, even if the whole contract is NULL & VOID, it will NOT INVALIDATE the Arbitration Clause as it is independent of the OTHER terms of Contract.
- A SEPARATE agreement by itself – which shall be in WRITING with DOCUMENTS signed by parties OR any other RECORD such as telegrams, letters OR by an EXCHANGE of statements of claim & defence.

ARBITRATION CLAUSE:

ALL DISPUTES, CLAIMS AND DIFFERENCE WHATSOEVER ARISING BETWEEN THE PARTIES OUT OF OR RELATING TO THE CONSTRUCTION, MEANING AND OPERATION OR EFFECT OF THIS CONTRACT OR BREACH, TERMINATION OR INVALIDITY THEREOF, WILL BE SETTLED IN ACCORDANCE WITH PROVISIONS OF ARBITRATION AND CONCILIATION ACT, 1996 AND THE AWARD MADE IN PURSUANCE THEREOF SHALL BE BINDING UPON THE PARTIES.

AGREEMENT:

It should provide for,

1. Mode of appointment of Arbitrators
2. Number of Arbitrators
3. Qualifications of Arbitrators
4. Venue of Arbitration
5. Language of Arbitration
6. Cost of Arbitration
7. Time limit for commencement of Arbitration
8. Hearing
9. Arbitration Procedure and the applicable law
10. Interim relief, if any

(a) What are the pre – requisites of 'arbitration'? Draft the specimen of an arbitration agreement to refer dispute to an arbitral tribunal. (J'09)

(b) Arbitration award (2010 – December)

(c) Draft a specimen arbitration agreement to refer a dispute to two arbitrators. (2010 – June)

SAMPLE ARBITRATION AGREEMENT

THIS ARBITRATION AGREEMENT IS ENTERED INTO AT CHENNAI, THIS, THE 25TH DAY OF AUGUST 2012

BETWEEN

R.Mani S/O. Mr. Ravi, Hindu, aged 25 years residing at No. 144, Palaniandavar Colony, Sivakasi – 4000219 hereinafter referred to as the FIRST PARTNER

AND

S. Anand S/O. Mr. Senthil, Hindu, aged 24 years residing at No. 99, Lake Area, Chennai – 600025 hereinafter referred to as the SECOND PARTNER

All the partners are collectively referred to as the PARTNERS.

WHEREAS the PARTNERS have entered into an AGREEMENT on 25th day of August 2012 which shall be read as part and parcel of this AGREEMENT;

AND WHEREAS a dispute has arisen between the PARTNERS in respect of the performance of the CONTRACT;

NOW THE PARTNERS AGREE TO REFER THE DISPUTE TO ARBITRATION:

1. That the following POINTS OF DISPUTE arisen between the parties are hereby referred to Mr. Ram, the ARBITRATOR for his decision and award
2. The POINTS OF DISPUTE are:
   a. Whether the SECOND PARTNER ....
   b. Whether the FIRST PARTNER ....
   c. ....
3. The said ARBITRATOR shall allow the parties to file their respective claims and contentions and to file documents relied upon by them within such reasonable time as the ARBITRATOR may direct.
4. The said ARBITRATOR shall make his AWARD within a period of 2 months (TWO MONTHS) from the date of service of a copy of this agreement, which may be extended with the consent of both the PARTNERS.
5. The AWARD given by the ARBITRATOR will be binding on the PARTNERS and the ARBITRATOR has the full power to award or not to award payment of cost to this ARBITRATION by one party to other as he deems fit.
6. The ARBITRATION shall be subject to the provisions of the ARBITRATION & CONCILIATION ACT 1996.

IN WITNESSES WHEREOF THE PARTNERS HAVE SIGNED THIS DEED ON THE DAY, MONTH, YEAR ABOVE WRITTEN.

1. FIRST PARTNER

2. SECOND PARTNER

LEGAL PROVISIONS

INTERVENTION BY COURT

OVERRIDING all other laws, Court can intervene ONLY as provided under this Arbitration & Conciliation Act, 1996 and NOT under any other Act,

- Power to refer matter to Arbitration
- Interim measures of protection
- Appointment of Arbitrator in certain cases
- Termination of Mandate of Arbitrator
- Assistance in taking Evidence

- Setting aside the Award
- Enforcement of an Award by way of Decree
- Appeal from certain orders of Court
- Reference of dispute to Arbitration in Insolvency proceedings.

COURT SHALL REFER TO ARBITRATION

If any party approaches the court DESPITE the Arbitration Agreement, the OTHER PARTY has to raise the OBJECTION BEFORE submitting his FIRST statement on the substance of dispute, then Court SHALL refer the dispute to Arbitration. However, WINDING UP of a company cannot be referred to Arbitration. Kindly note, CONSUMER FORUM can entertain complaint irrespective of Arbitration.

ARBITRAL TRIBUNAL

The parties are FREE to determine the NUMBER of Arbitrators and their NATIONALITY OR there will be SOLE Arbitrator but in any case there shall NOT be an EVEN number of Arbitrators.

In the ABSENCE of any agreement to APPOINT Arbitrators, EACH party shall appoint one Arbitrator WITHIN 30 days of REQUEST and the APPOINTED Arbitrator shall appoint the THIRD or PRESIDING Arbitrator WITHIN 30 days of APPOINTMENT, **default of which**, ON REQUEST, the appointment shall be made by the CHIEF JUSTICE or any person or Institution designated by him (& their decision is FINAL).

An Arbitrator so appointed may be CHALLENGED after passing AWARD only,

- When circumstances give rise to JUSTIFIABLE doubts as to his independence or impartiality
- When he does NOT possess the QUALIFICATION as agreed to by the parties
- & such other reasons which parties became aware AFTER appointment.

Further, the parties are FREE to agree upon the Rules of Arbitration, its Place, Language, etc...

ARBITRAL AWARD – the decision of Arbitral Tribunal

- It shall be in writing
- Signed by the members of Arbitral Tribunal & delivered to EACH party
- Shall state the reasons UNLESS other wise agreed
- Shall state the date & place of Arbitration

STAMPING of Arbitral Award is mandatory under Indian Stamp Act, 1899 and once signed, it cannot be re-written on a Stamp Paper.

REGISTRATION of Indian Arbitral Award under Registration Act, 1908 is mandatory if it purports to operate or create or declare or assign or limit any RIGHT OF IMMOVABLE PROPERTY.

Thus, any arbitration award which merely declares the pre-existing facts/rights need NOT be registered. Meaning, in such cases, even an unregistered award can be made a rule of court as per the decision of Supreme Court in *N Khosala v. Rajlaxmi & others.*

Note: FOREIGN ARBITRAL AWARD does not require any registration.

VIDEOCON INDUSTRIES LIMITED v. UNION OF INDIA & ANR

There was a Production Sharing Contract (PSC) between Government of India and a consortium of 4 Oil & Natural Gas Companies across different Countries for resources within the area of India's territorial waters and exclusive economic zones. Though Kuala Lumpur was decided as the venue for Arbitration, due to outbreak of epidemic SARS, it was shifted to London. However, there is NO change in the juridical seat of Arbitrator as there was NO written agreement enabling this shift but it is a mere physical relocation. Further, Hon'ble Supreme Court of India held that as the Arbitration agreement specifically mentions that it shall be governed by laws of England, the Indian Courts do not have any jurisdiction over this matter.

An Arbitral award may be SET ASIDE by the COURT on application made by the parties WITHIN 3 months (extendable-30 days) of AWARD **ONLY** u/s. 34 grounds,

1. INCAPACITY of parties
2. INVALIDITY of Arbitration agreement
3. NO proper notice is given for appointment of Arbitrator or Arbitral Proceedings
4. UNABLE to present his case
5. Award deals with DISPUTES NOT CONTEMPLATED or CONTAINS DECISIONS beyond the SUBMISSION to Arbitration
6. COMPOSITION of Tribunal was NOT with agreement of parties.
7. SUBJECT MATTER is NOT capable of settlement by Arbitration or Award is in CONFLICT with Public Policy of India [fraud/corruption].

The Arbitral Award becomes FINAL & BINDING when time for making application to Court for setting aside the order is over and it can be ENFORCED as if it is a DECREE OF COURT and is NOT necessary to submit a copy of it to Court for its SANCTION.

APPEAL & WRITS

As per Section 37, an APPEAL lies ONLY against the ORDERS granting or refusing to grant any INTERIM measure by Court, setting aside or refusing to SET ASIDE an arbitral award and order of Arbitral Tribunal accepting the challenge to its JURISDICTION or relating to interim measure. However, REVISION PETITION (discussed under Pleadings) lies in High Court against Civil Court orders.

NO SECOND APPEAL (discussed under Pleadings) shall lie from an order passed in appeal u/s. 37 without affecting the right to appeal to Supreme Court.

NO WRIT or REVISION to High Court against order of Arbitrator can be exercised as **Arbitrator is NOT a tribunal or court**. However, Writ Jurisdiction of High Court and Special Lea ve Petition under Supreme Court remain unaffected.

NO INTERNATIONAL ARBITRATION BY TWO INDIAN COMPANIES

In the case of *TDM Infrastructure Private Limited vs. UE Development India Pvt. Ltd.*, Supreme Court clarified that in case of any domestic arbitration, the arbitration tribunals shall determine the dispute in accordance with the substantive law of India in force at that time and restricts them from using the law of any other country. The Court held that the incorporation in India was sufficient to determine the nationality of the Company. The intention of the legislature appears to be clear that Indian nationals should not be permitted to derogate from Indian law. This is part of the public policy of the country.

1. State with reference to case law whether a foreign arbitration award can be executed by an Indian Court. (2008 – December)

2. What are the requisites of an 'award' under the Arbitration and Conciliation Act, 1996? (2009 – December)

Kindly refer the case laws given under the head "PRACTICE CASE LAWS MADE FROM EXAM POINT OF VIEW" at the end of this book.

CAN ARBITRATION CLAUSE BE EVOKED AFTER FULL & FINAL DISCHARGE

The Supreme Court in the case of *National Insurance Company Ltd v. Boghara Polyfab (P) Ltd* held that,

- If a full & final discharge OR No due Certificate is issued confirming satisfaction of claim by either of the parties to the agreement **AND**
- Such discharge or certificate is obtained by fraud or undue influence or coercion

Then, it will be ignored; the other party will be examined on merits to decide the matter. That means if the Chief Justice concludes the full discharge is due to fraud, the agreement will NOT be discharged, consequently the dispute be referred to arbitration. Thus, in case of RECESSION of contract by mutual agreement or NOVATION of contract by substituting with new contract, the arbitration clause in the old contract also ceases to exist unless otherwise it is by fraud or coercion.

Note: Novation is the substitution of existing contract for a new contract whereas Memorandum of Understanding (MoU) is less formal than a contract.

SAMPLE ARBITRAL AWARD

IN THE MATTER OF THE ARBITRATION & CONCILIATION ACT, 1996

AND

IN THE MATTER OF ARBITRATION AGREEMENT DATED
10TH DAY OF SEPTEMBER 2012

BETWEEN

A.N.S. VIJAY → → → → PARTY ON THE FIRST PART

AND

Labz Limited → → → → PARTY ON THE SECOND PART

a limited liability company registered under the Companies Act, 1956 under the Certificate of Incorporation number 99-1234 of 2000 and Corporate Identification Number L123456642003 in the office of the Registrar of Companies, Maharashtra at Mumbai having its Registered Office at No. 13, Jolly Maker Chambers, Mumbai – 400021 through its ATTORNEY Mr. Shiva appointed under the Power of Attorney dated 25th August 2012 given under the common seal of the company.

ARBITRAL AWARD

1. This AWARD is given relating to a DISPUTE which arose on 26th day of December 2012 between the above mentioned parties in respect of the defect in the machinery supplied by the PARTY ON THE FIRST PART to the PARTY ON THE SECOND PART.
2. The CONTENTION of the PARTY ON THE SECOND PART is that it placed an order with the PARTY ON THE FIRST PART on 25th day of August 2012 SPECIFYING THE PURPOSE for which it is required.
3. The PARY ON THE FIRST PART supplied the machinery on 31st day of August 2012; However when the machinery was put into use, it was found that the machinery did not meet the requirements FOR WHICH it was ordered.
4. The PARTY ON THE FIRST PART CONTENDS that he is the manufacturer of the machinery meant for the purpose required by the PARTY ON THE SECOND PART; Such machinery was supplied to the PARTY ON THE SECOND PART; It is ONLY AFTER *THREE MONTHS* after the date of supply, the PARTY ON THE SECOND PART complained about this to the PARTY ON THE FIRST PART.

The ARBITRATOR HEARD THE DEPOSITION of both the parties and perused the documents filed by both the parties. Further as agreed to by both the parties, a Mechanical Engineer Mr. Ravi was APPOINTED TO CHECK AND FIND OUT WHETHER IT WAS FIT FOR THE PURPOSE required by the PARTY ON THE SECOND PART. The Engineer has in his report dated 5th day of September 2012 stated that the machinery was not fit for the purpose for which it was required.

With the result the ARBITRATOR gives the following award:

1. The PARTY ON THE SECOND PART shall *return* the machinery to the PARTY ON THE FIRST PART who shall *receive* the same.
2. The PARTY ON THE FIRST PART shall *refund* the price paid for the machinery together with an *interest @ 9% p.a.* from the date of sale till the refund of the above price.

Signed & Dated

ARBITRATOR.

1. An agreement by the parties to submit to arbitration all or certain disputes which may have arisen or may arise in respect of a defined legal relationship which may be contractual or not is called:

a) Joint venture agreement

b) Arbitration agreement

c) Gift agreement

d) Pre-nap agreement

Ans: b

2. Arbitration agreement includes:

a) Mode of appointment

b) Number of arbitrators

c) Language of arbitration

d) All of above.

Ans: d

3. In Arbitral award the decision of arbitral tribunal should be in :

a) Written

b) Oral

c) In any form oral or written.

Ans: a

4. Court shall refer the matter to arbitration when there is:

a) Arbitration agreement

b) Plaintiff dies

c) Plaintiff & defendant are in two different places

d) Petition is not valid

Ans: a

5. Consumer forum can entertain a complaint:

a) When there is one party

b) When there is no arbitration agreement

c) When there are more than 3 arbitrators

d) Irrespective of arbitration

Ans: d

6. In the absence of agreement to appoint arbitrators who can appoint the arbitrator:

a) The first party

b) The second party

c) Public prosecutor

d) Chief justice or any person or institution designated by chief justice

Ans: d

7. Is an arbitration award final :

a) Yes

b) No

c) Yes but on the circumstance giving rise to doubts of independence or impartiality

d) None of the above

Ans: c

8. Registration of Indian Arbitral Award comes under :

a) Arbitration & Conciliation Act

b) Transfer Of Property Act

c) Immovable Property Act

d) Registration Act

Ans: d

9. Arbitral award can be set aside under:

a) Section 62a Arbitration & Conciliation Act

b) Section 44 Arbitration & Conciliation Act

c) Section 72 Arbitration & Conciliation Act

d) Section 34 Arbitration & Conciliation Act

Ans: Section 34 Arbitration & Conciliation Act

10. International Arbitration cannot take place between:

a) Two Indian Companies

b) Two foreign Companies

c) Indian & Foreign Company

d) None of the above

Ans: a

This chapter provides you with the legal provisions, concepts and formats of agreements related to guarantees and service agreements. Here, the concepts are very important to be understood in the right manner. The chapter also deals with the provisions regarding apprentices.

Guarantees & Service Agreements

LEGAL PROVISION

Section 126 of Indian Contract Act, 1872 defines contract of guarantee. The Contract of Guarantee is when,

- The SURETY agrees with the CREDITOR
- to discharge the liability of the PRINICPAL DEBTOR, in case of default.

According to Section 127, the CONSIDERATION shall be "anything done or any promise made by the CREDITOR to the PRINCIPAL DEBTOR at the desire of the SURETY."

The TERMS of guarantee shall be STRICTLY construed.

SURETY'S LIABILITY: [Section 128] – liable to CREDITOR irrespective of anything.

Subject to a contract to the contrary,

- The liability of surety is CO-EXTENSIVE with that of principal debtor.
- The liability of principal debtor is PRIMARY whereas surety is SECONDARY, though arises simultaneously.
- The mere fact that the contract between the creditor and the principal debtor is VOID **or** INSOLVENCY of principal debtor DOES NOT discharge a surety.

SUBROGATION: [Section 140]

When the PRINCIPAL DEBTOR commits default and the SURETY performs the obligation, the SURETY is invested with all the rights which the CREDITOR has against the PRINCIPAL DEBTOR.

CONTINUING GUARANTEE: [Section 129-131]

The continuing guarantee,

- Extends to a SERIES OF TRANSACTIONS.
- A FRESH LIABILITY shall accrue from time to time (like rent payment)
- The surety,
  - May REVOKE in respect of FUTURE transactions, by giving NOTICE to the creditor.
  - On death, gets REVOKED regards FUTURE transactions.

OTHER TYPES OF GUARANTEE

1. **FIDELITY GUARANTEE** is a guarantee GUARANTEEING an employer against the MISCONDUCT of an employee or to ANSWER for the debt or default of another. The SURETY will be discharged if an employee is retained after proving DISHONESTY, WITHOUT giving notice to GUARANTOR.
2. **COUNTER GUARANTEE** is a guarantee given by the PRINCIPAL DEBTOR to the SURETY providing him CONTINUING INDEMNITY against any loss or damage that SURETY may suffer on account of DEFAULT on the part of PRINCIPAL DEBTOR.

3. **PERFORMANCE GUARANTEE** is a guarantee which ENSURES the contracted performance and surety UNDERTAKES to compensate the person in WHOSE FAVOUR the guarantee is given [in the event of FAILURE] against the person on WHOSE BEHALF the guarantee is given.

4. **BANK GUARANTEE** is a guarantee given by the bank on behalf of its CLIENT to ANOTHER PERSON with whom the client has entered into a CONTRACT to perform some job, CONTINGENCY of which, it may be ENFORCED.

1. Explain the following types of guarantee:

(i) Contract of guarantee

(ii) Continuing guarantee

(iii) Bank guarantee (2010 – June)

2. Briefly explain the contents of a service contract. Draft a specimen agreement of employment of manager of a business concern. (2009 – December)

3. Counter guarantee & fidelity guarantee (dec 09)

4. Alpha Industries Limited wishes to appoint Ram Avtar & Co., Advocates as their legal consultant on an annual retainership basis. Draft a suitable agreement assuming facts, wherever necessary. (2010 – June) Clue: Key Clauses are under:

a) The retainership shall be from dd/mm/yy to dd/mm/yy. It will automatically expire on dd/mm/yy unless extended in writing. During the retainership period, either side can terminate the agreement by giving ... months notice or retaineship charges for the notice perios, without assigning any reasons.

b) You shall interact with Mrs/Miss/Mr....... of our company during your retainership for all decisions/ queries.

c) you shall be given....no pf persons for your assignment.

d) Your assignment shall be as follows......

e) Your retainership fees would be Rs...... per month. You would raise inoice on .....th of every month. Your invoice will become payable by....pf every month. You may levy service tax/you retainership fees is inclusive of service tax.

f) You shall be paid conveyance for official purpose.

g) Any outstation travel and boarding shall be billed extra to the company/firm. Limits on travelling and boarding expenses are as follows...

SERVICE AGREEMENTS

Service agreements are the agreements between employer and employee defining clearly and expressly the terms of employment. In case of Government Service or Statutory Corporations, such 'terms of employment' is governed by Government order and Statutory rules, instead of separate service agreement.

The contents of a service contract,

1. The time or period of employment

2. The remuneration and other perquisites

3. Duties of the employee
4. Powers of the employer
5. Leave and the terms on which it will be granted with provisions as to paid leave
6. Modes and termination (determination) grounds of employment during the term
7. Restrictive covenants and kindly note, agreements in restraint of trade is void u/s. 27 of Indian Contract Act, 1872
8. Central & State level LABOUR LEGISLATIONS and its applicable provisions.

> The renewal of term of service of an employee may include a clause,
>
> "THE TERMS & CONDITIONS OF THIS RENEWAL AGREEMENT SHALL BE THE SAME AS ARE CONTAINED IN THE SERVICE AGREEMENT DATED 1ST FEBRUARY 2012 IN SO FAR AS THEY MAY BE APPLICABLE TO THE EMPLOYMENT UNDER THIS AGREEMENT AND ALL THE TERMS & CONDITIONS CONTAINED IN THE SAID SERVICE AGREEMENT SHALL BE DEEMED TO HAVE BEEN INCORPORATED IN THIS AGREEMENT".

ENQUIRY & INVESTIGATION

Investigation is the process of ascertainment of facts. Investigation constitutes the following steps under Criminal Procedure Code,

1. Proceeding to the spot.
2. Ascertainment of the facts & circumstances of the case.
3. Discovery & arrest of established offender.
4. Collection of evidence relating to commission of offence.
5. Examining persons & recording their statements in writing.
6. Seizure of things considered necessary in the investigation.
7. To present the offender before the magistrate court for trial.

INVESTIGATION REPORT should cover wide areas ranging from investigation of title to ownership to investigation of criminal act and shall be prepared by the person carrying on the investigation.

> ENQUIRY & INVESTIGATION (j 07)

Enquiry is the stage that follows investigation. Enquiry means every enquiry other than a trial under Criminal procedure by Magistrate or court. For proper conduct of enquiry,

1. Employee should be informed of charges;
2. Witnesses should be examined;
3. Employee should be given fair opportunity to cross examine the witness.
4. The enquiry officer (a quasi judicial body) should record his findings with reasons by way of ENQUIRY REPORT. All the contents should be based upon records. The officer should give only the findings within the scope of his charge and give specific findings on each charge.

5. Copy of the enquiry report shall be given to the workman.

Note: In case of enquiry, employee cannot engage a lawyer to defend his case.

Further note that, the enquiry report is not final or conclusive. A Disciplinary authority not below the rank/grade of Appointing authority can overturn the same by giving a fresh hearing. Even a subordinate authority can issue a CHARGE SHEET but only appointing authority is competent to terminate the services.

HIRE & FIRE CLAUSE: A clause in an agreement for removal of employee from service by giving 3 months notice is a hire & fire clause. It is violative of Section 23 of Indian Contract Act, 1872 as it is against public policy.

SUSPENSION

Suspension is NOT a termination from service. It is an executive action whereby an employee is kept out of duty temporarily PENDING action against him for any misconduct. Such suspension can be made only after giving an opportunity of being heard. The period should not be unduly long and whatever disciplinary action (charge sheet) is contemplated should be commenced after suspension.

SAMPLE SUSPENSION ORDER

WHEREAS disciplinary proceedings against Mr. _______, Production Manager are contemplated for the following alleged misconduct,

DESCRIPTION OF MISCONDUCT

Now, therefore the undersigned in terms of Rule No. ____ of the approved standing orders for executive managers of the company, hereby place the said Mr. ______ under suspension with immediate effect with a subsistence allowance as per Standing orders..

Mr. _______ shall make himself available for inquiry or disciplinary proceedings whenever required so.

S/d-

Name & Designation of the Suspending Authority.

DISCHARGE, REMOVAL & DISMISSAL

- Discharge mean removal from service without any stigma.
- In cases of grave & serious misconduct, it may become necessary to initiate action for dismissal/removal of an employee from service.
- Dismissal means termination from employment as a penalty. It shall be done only after giving an opportunity of being heard. Any termination without following the principles of natural justice is violative of Article 21 of Constitution. In case of Government, dismissal may create a disqualification for future employment too with Government.

- Removal is also a type of dismissal but in case of Government, it does not create a disqualification for future employment with them.

SAMPLE ORDER OF DISMISSAL

Shri Vijay
S/o. Ajay at Delhi.

Dear Sir,

Your explanation was celled for vide our letter no. _____ dated ______on the various charges specified therein. The explanation furnished by you vide your letter dated ________ was not found to be satisfactory and an enquiry was ordered.

You were informed of the enquiry vide letter No. _____ dated _____. The Enquiry officer conducted the enquiry and submitted the report, by which the officer has found you to be guilty of gross negligence constituting a grave & serious misconduct.

Now it has been decided that you should be dismissed from service and accordingly you are dismissed with effect from ________.

You can collect your dues from _______ branch/department on any working day during the normal working hours.

Yours faithfully,

S/d-

APPRENTICES ACT, 1961

The main purpose of the Act is to provide practical training to technically qualified persons who should be of minimum 14 years, in various trades for a period ranging between 6 months to 4 years. The employer has to make arrangements for practical training. Employer will pay stipend to apprentice at prescribed rates. Apprentice should maintain a work diary in prescribed form. A CONTRACT OF APPRENTICESHIP shall be executed and registered with Apprenticeship Advisor. An apprentice is entitled to a casual leave of 12 days, medical leave of 15 days & extraordinary leave of 10 days in a year. Only the provisions of Factories Act regarding health, safety & welfare and Workmen's Compensation Act for compensation regarding employment injury will be applicable to him. The Act has prescribed the minimum stipend payable. On completion of training, every apprentice has to appear for a test conducted by National Council to get the Certificate of proficiency. These are the points which shall be kept in mind will drafting a contract of apprenticeship.

Thus, when appointing an employee, the said points shall be kept in mind to reduce legal cases and issues. Hope you remember the concepts, provisions and formats.

This chapter shall be understood in detail to understand the provisions dealt under the part of Appearances & Pleadings. Keep updating the formats in your mind slots. Repeated reading is mandatory.

Deeds Drawn In First Person

[Affidavit & Power of Attorney]

Deeds can be classified into two:

1. Deeds drawn in first person
2. Deeds drawn in third person

Affidavit and power of attorney are drawn in first person.

AFFIDAVIT:

An Affidavit is a sworn statement. Every fact stated shall be true. A false affidavit will attract penal liability. An affidavit cannot be amended. However the Court may permit the deponent to file a BETTER affidavit.

Affidavit may be,

- An affidavit supporting a petition or
- An affidavit verifying the facts given in a petition

Both the affidavits shall start with the CAUSE TITLE (name of the body before whom the affidavit is filed) of the petition shall be given. If it is an affidavit, given before a company, the name and description of the company shall be given.

SAMPLE AFFIDAVIT TO PASSPORT OFFICE

I, Vijay S/o. Mr. Shankar, Hindu, aged 55 years and residing at No.10, Pandurang Budhkar Marg, Parel, Mumbai – 400034 do SOLEMNLY AND SINCERELY AFFIRM and state as follows:-

Note: A Christian shall not swear. Hence, the wording will be "MAKE OATH AND STATE AS FOLLOWS".

Now, state the facts. **Enumerate them.**

a) I am the applicant in this matter

b) I was born on DATE MONTH, YEAR, in CITY, STATE, INDIA. I am a native and citizen of INDIA. My address in INDIA is No.10, Pandurang Budhkar Marg, Parel, Mumbai - 400034.

c) That the names of my parents and spouse are as follows: Mr. Shankar, Mrs. Shankar, Mrs. Vijay

d) That no proceedings in respect of any criminal offence alleged to have been committed by me are pending before any criminal court in India;

e) That I will not engage outside India in activities prejudicial to the sovereignty and integrity of India.

f) I make the statements contained in this affidavit conscientiously, knowing the same to be true.

At the end, conclude by the following words.

Solemnly affirmed before me.

Date and place | Deponent

About Attestation:

As per Section 558 of Companies Act, 1956, an affidavit shall be sworn before any Court or Tribunal or Judge or persons lawfully authorized to take & receive affidavits in India or any other country (even before Indian Consul) for them to take judicial notice. Apart from company matters attestation may be by a notary public. In civil court an advocate (other than advocate on record) may attest an affidavit. For deeds under the Transfer of Property Act, 1882 attestation shall be done by two or more witnesses who have seen the executants sign the document or received a personal acknowledgement from the executants that he has signed the document.

Every exhibit annexed to an affidavit shall be marked with the number of the proceeding to which it relates, and shall be initialed and dated by the authority before whom it is sworn as per Company Court Rules, 1959.

By virtue of Order VI, Rule 15(4) of the Civil Procedure Code, all PLEADINGS require to be filed along with an AFFIDAVIT. Any affidavit has to be necessarily ATTESTED by an Oath Commissioner or a Notary Public.

POWER OF ATTORNEY

Section 1A of the Power of attorney Act, 1882 defines Power of Attorney to INCLUDE any instrument empowering a specified person TO ACT FOR AND IN THE NAME of the persons executing it.

Section 2(21) of Indian Stamp Act, 1899 defines Power of Attorney, to INCLUDE any instrument (not chargeable with a fee under the law relating to court fee for the time being in force) empowering a specified persons to act for and in the name of the person executing it.

Section 48 of the Companies Act, 1956 read with Articles of Association provides for EXECUTION of deeds. The company **may** empower any person as its ATTORNEY, in writing under its common seal, which then be BINDING the company for the acts of the attorney. The use of common seal requires a Board Resolution. UNLESS OTHERWISE Articles or Board Resolution otherwise provide, non-putting of seal on an agreement may not invalidate the agreement, if it has otherwise been properly EXECUTED.

Though Power of Attorney holder is similar to AGENT, an agent is not empowered to use the name of the principal [u/s. 182 of Indian Contract Act, 1872] whereas the attorney can use the principal's name [u/s. 1A of Power of Attorney Act, 1882] in the transaction entered into him".

A power of attorney in regard to a SINGLE TRANSACTION is known as a **special power of attorney** (or particular power of attorney), whereas when the attorney is empowered to act generally or in MORE THAN ONE TRANSACTION, it is known as **general power of attorney**. A power of attorney is in the nature of DEED POLL (i.e.) deed made & executed by one party.

A power of attorney can always be REVOKED at the discretion of donor. But u/s. 202 of Indian Contract Act, 1872, if the agency is coupled with interest then it CANNOT be revoked PREJUDICIAL to the interest of the Agent [even if the instrument does not state specifically that it is irrevocable]. **Irrevocable Power of Attorney** is normally executed in favour of financial institutions by a company who offer financial assistance which needs to be registered.

1. Draft a power of attorney to execute a deed of sale. (2009 – December)
2. Power of attorney and letter of authority (2009 – June)
3. What are the ingredients that are necessary to prepare a Power of Attorney (2009 – December)
4. Projects Construction Engineering Co., (PCEC) had been awarded four project works by Karnataka Medical Supplies Corporation Limited (KMSCL) for Rs. 500 Lakh each. They have sought financial assistance from a commercial bank who agrees to provide the loan but wants a power of attorney from

KMSCL to recover dues on the above contracts on behalf of PCEC, including right to sue for realizing dues from KMSCL. Prepare a power of attorney (2008 – December)

5. Attempt the following:

   (a) Draft an affidavit of creditor in proof of his debt in proceeding for the liquidation of a company (J'09)

6. Affidavit (2009 – June)

7. Define 'affidavit'. What rules and guiding principles should be followed while drawing up an affidavit? (2009 – December)

As per Section 32(c) read with Section 33 of Registration Act, 1908 every Special Power of attorney which gives authority to PRESENT a document for registration (of immovable property) must be EXECUTED before and AUTHENTICATED by the Registrar or Sub-registrar. Thus, a general power of attorney even though it deals with immovable property need NOT be registered. Also, irrevocable power of attorney to be registered with Registration authorities but it will not be reflected in the Encumbrance Certificate.

Every power of attorney is liable to stamp duty under Indian Stamp Act, 1899, also a power of attorney executed in a foreign country should be stamped within 3 months of its being received in India. Take for instance, **PROXY** u/s. 176 of Companies Act, 1956 is a power of attorney which is liable to stamp duty of 30 paise. Kindly note, such Power of Attorney shall be stamped as that of SALE/CONVEYANCE.

A perusal of Section 85 of Indian Evidence Act, 1872, shows that the court must presume that a Power of Attorney as duly authenticated by a Public Notary or any court or by Indian Consul or representative of the Central Government was validly executed and authenticated.

Section 3 of Power of Attorney Act, 1882 provides that all acts or payments performed or paid by the attorney AFTER the revocation BY death, unsoundness or insolvency of the DONOR of power BUT BEFORE the attorney comes to know about the termination, shall be VALID & BINDING upon the third party as well as donor and his legal representatives.

Give Your Reasons:

Power of attorney is an instrument of transfer in regard to any right, title or interest in an immovable property

Answers:

Incorrect, as power of attorney is creation of an agency whereby the grantor authorizes the grantee to do the acts specified therein, on behalf of grantor, which when executed will be binding on the grantor as if done by him. Even an irrevocable attorney does not have the effect of transferring title to the grantee. AN ATTORNEY HOLDER MAY HOWEVER EXECUTE A DEED OF CONVEYANCE IN EXERCISE OF THE POWER GRANTED UNDER THE POWER OF ATTORNEY AND CONVEY TITLE ON BEHALF OF THE GRANTOR as decided by Hon'ble Supreme Court in .

MODEL POWER OF ATTORNEY

KNOW ALL MEN BY THESE PRESENTS THAT I Jain S/O. Mr. Raj, Hindu, aged 23 years residing at 22, Lodi Road, New Delhi – 110003 do hereby constitute and appoint Mr. Mani S/O. Mr. Ravi, Hindu, aged 25 years residing at 9, Veeraperumal Koil Street, Chennai – 600034, as my ATTORNEY to do the following acts, deeds & things:

[LIST OUT THE ACTS FOR WHICH POWER IS GIVEN]

1. To negotiate for the sale of *house & ground* bearing No.3A, Ahiripukur, Kolkata – 700019.
2. To enter into agreement to sell the above said property.
3. To receive consideration in respect of the agreement and acknowledge receipt.
4. To execute a sale deed on my behalf in favour of the purchaser.
5. To receive the price and acknowledge the receipt of the same.
6. To present the sale deed for registration.
7. To do all other acts, deeds and things necessary in respect of the sale.

I DECLARE that all the acts, deeds and things done by my ATTORNEY shall be my acts, deeds and things. I AGREE to ratify all acts, deeds and things done by my ATTORNEY on my behalf.

DATED at New Delhi this the 25th August, 2007.

RAJ.

In cases where the Company is giving a Power of Attorney, COMMON SEAL shall be AFFIXED along with the Board Resolution for the same.

"RESOLVED THAT the common seal of the Company be and hereby affixed to the Power of Attorney dated 25th August, 2012 in the presence of Mr. Shyam & Ms. Ananya, the Director & Company Secretary of the company shall sign the same as a token thereof ".

IRREVOCABLE POWER OF ATTORNEY

THIS IRREVOCABLE POWER OF ATTORNEY given by the COMPANY MORTGAGOR to empower the BANK MORTGAGEE to sell the MORTGAGED PROPERTY under the MORTGAGE DEED dated 25th August, 2005 registered as document no. 55/2005 in case the COMPANY commits DEFAULT in the repayment of mortgaged debt.

THIS POWER OF ATTORNEY shall not be revoked by the COMPANY to the prejudice of the BANK. In other words, THIS POWER OF ATTORNEY may be revoked only on the COMPANY redeeming the mortgage under the MORTGAGE DEED dated 25th August 2005.

Whenever you answer any question regarding drafting of deeds, try quoting the laws applicable for the same with full name and the year. The first page of Drafting book also gives the list of Acts applicable along with years in chronological order, keep reading.

Indian Partnership Act, 1932 is highly advisable to be read before reading this chapter. Though the chapter has cumulated the most essential provision, reading the Act can give a better understanding.

Partnership Deeds

LEGAL PROVISIONS

Partnership is a RELATIONSHIP created by an AGREEMENT governed by Indian Partnership Act, 1932.

Section 4 of the Act defines 'partnership' as a RELATION between PERSONS who have AGREED (agreement) to share PROFITS of business carried on by ALL or ANY ONE (mutual agency) of them acting for all. The partners are SELF-EMPLOYED and participate IN the business. The relationship between among partners and firm is that of Principal and Agent INTER SE.

The Partnership is created by AGREEMENT and not by registration, though registration is OPTIONAL, it is highly advisable as an UNREGSITERED partnership form or its Partners CANNOT take the assistance of CIVIL COURT to enforce any right arising out of a contract or conferred by Indian Partnership Act, 1932. However, a partner of an UNREGISTERED partnership firm may file a suit for,

- Dissolution of the firm
- For accounts when the firm is already dissolved
- For his share in the assets of the dissolved firm.

Note: A partner of an unregistered firm may apply to Court for reference to ARBITRATION.

WHO CAN BE PARTNERS?

1. ONLY natural & legal persons.
2. A partnership FIRM or Hindu Undivided Family (HUF) cannot become a Partner as they are not legal persons. However, Partnership Firm may be a member of Section 25 company.

   NOTE: As per Benami Transactions (Prohibitions) Act, 1988 a Firm cannot be a Benami partner in another Firm. Even in representative capacity, a partner of a sub partnership CANNOT be joined in a MAIN partnership as representing the sub partnership. However, he can join in his INDIVIDUAL capacity.
3. Company being a legal person can enter into partnership PROVIDED the Articles of Association empowers the same.
4. Minor can become a partner with the consent of ALL partners ONLY for the BENEFITS of partnership. Minor has to take a decision whether to become a partner or not WITHIN 6 months of attaining majority or on knowledge of admission.

NUMBER OF PARTNERS

Section 11 of Companies Act, 1956 deals with Prohibition of associations and PARTNERSHIPS exceeding 10 **numbers** in case of Banking and 20 **numbers** for any other business; they are held to be **"ILLEGAL ASSOCIATIONS".**

If the various individual members of one or more joint Hindu families (aka HUF) form an Agreement of Partnership among themselves, then each individual male & female member [NOT being a Minor] must be reckoned as a person for the purpose of calculating **numbers** under this section. HUF by itself is not an Illegal Association but if it enters into Partnership with other HUF, then the total individual members of both the HUF shall not exceed the limit prescribed under section 11 of Companies Act, 1956.

PARTNERSHIP AT WILL – If there is NO provision in the Partnership Agreement for the DURATION or for the (DE)TERMINATION of the partnership, then such partnership is AT WILL.

ACTIONS IN PARTNESHIP FIRM:

1. **Introduction of a Partner** [Section 31] – Unless the Partnership Agreement otherwise provides, the consent of ALL the existing partners is required to introduce a person as PARTNER in a FIRM. The partnership deed shall be entered and shall be executed, attested & registered as below.
2. **Retirement of a Partner** [Section 32] – By CONSENT of all other partners or By an EXPRESS agreement. In case of Partnership At Will, notice of retirement shall be given in WRITING to all the other partners. The execution of Retirement Deed results in RECONSTITUTION of the firm. Thus, a FRESH reconstitution deed shall be executed and all formalities applicable to Partnership Deed shall be complied with.
3. **Power to Expel of a Partner** [Section 33] – Only by EXPRESS agreement of MAJORITY of the partners and to be used in a BONA FIDE manner for the Firm's BENEFIT after giving an opportunity of being HEARD.

DISSOLUTION OF A PARTNERSHIP FIRM:

DISSOLUTION OF PARTNERSHIP happens when SOME partners continue the business of the firm whereas the DISSOLUTION OF THE PARTNERSHIP FIRM happens on dissolution of partnership between ALL the partners of the firm and shall be executed on a stamp paper of appropriate value and filed with Registrar. (i.e.) When JURAL relation between all the partners INTER SE is SNAPPED, this constitutes dissolution of partnership FIRM. The dissolution becomes effective on PUBLIC NOTICE. The modes of dissolution are,

1. Mutual Consent of ALL partners as per the Partnership Agreement u/s. 40
2. Compulsory Dissolution u/s. 41 if BUSINESS or partnership WAY to carry on the business becomes UNLAWFUL; Or by ADJUDICATION of ALL the partners or ALL except one partner.

   NOTE: The NOMINATION of successor is NOT effective in case where firm consist of 2 partners only as it stands DISSOLVED on the death of a partner.
3. Contingency u/s. 42 subject to Partnership Agreement on death or insolvency of a partner or on expiry of period or on completion of adventure.
4. Duration at WILL u/s. 43 in case of Partnership At Will by giving notice in WRITING to all other partners of the intention to DISSOLVE.
5. Dissolution by Court u/s. 44 on account of insanity or permanent incapacity or misconduct or willful/persistent breach of agreement or impracticability or transfer of whole interest (by sale or attachment) or loss or on any other JUST & EQUITABLE ground.

NOTE: If dissolution involves TRANSFER of immovable property to any person OTHER THAN the original partners then Indian Stamp Act, 1899 prescribes the same duty as "CONVEYANCE" and profits/gains arising from transfer or capital asset by way of distribution of capital assets on dissolution will attract Section 45(4) of Income Tax Act, 1961 dealing with Capital Gains.

INSOLVENCY/DEATH OF A PARTNER u/s. 34 & 35

Where a partner in a firm is DEAD or ADJUDICATED as an insolvent, he CEASES to be a partner from the date of the DEATH or ORDER of adjudication. The dissolution of firm consequently depends on Partnership Agreement (u/s. 42) WHEREAS if the firm is NOT dissolved,

- the ESTATE of the INSOLVENT partner is NOT liable for any act of the FIRM
- the FIRM is NOT liable for any act of INSOLVENT.

PURCHASE OF BUSINES BY A PARTNER or WINDING UP u/s. 46

On DISSOLUTION of a Firm, every Partner or his REPRESENTATIVE is entitled as against ALL THE OTHERS,

- to have the PROPERTY of the Firm applied in payment of the DEBTS & LIABILITIES of the firm.
- to have the SURPLUS distributed among the partners or their representatives according to their RIGHTS.

EXECUTION & ATTESTATION & REGISTRATION

Partnership/Dissolution Deed is liable for Stamp Duty under Indian Stamp Act, 1899. Partnership/Dissolution Deed must be executed and attested as a BOND on a non-judicial stamp paper of PROPER VALUE. The copy of the PARTNERSHIP DEED must be sent to the REGISTRAR OF PARTNERSHIP FIRMS along with the prescribed form duly completed for issue of ACKNOWLEDGEMENT of firm. All subsequent CHANGES shall also be notified to the Registrar.

The REGISTRATION of such deeds is OPTIONAL under Registration Act, 1908, HOWEVER if there is a TRANSFER OF IMMOVABLE PROPERTY worth Rs. 100/- or more in case of Dissolution of Partnership, the registration is MANDATORY.

Can Partnership Deed be executed earlier than date of Stamp paper?

Normally, date cannot be earlier than the date of stamp paper. An oral partnership could thereafter be reduced to writing BUT EVEN IN SUCH CASES the deed must be drawn up WITHIN the accounting year. In case where the operation is RETROSPECTIVE it shall be indicated in the RECITALS. Kindly note, Section 40(b)(v) of Income Tax Act, 1961 mandates remuneration to working partners shall relate to any period falling AFTER the date of executing partnership deed.

SAMPLE PARTNERSHIP DEED

THIS PARTNERSHIP DEED is executed at Mumbai, this, the 25th day of August 2012

AMONG

R.Mani S/O. Mr. Ravi, Hindu, aged 25 years residing at No. 144, Palaniandavar Colony, Sivakasi – 4000219 hereinafter referred to as the FIRST PARTNER

AND

S. Anand S/O. Mr. Senthil, Hindu, aged 24 years residing at No. 99, Lake Area, Chennai – 600025 hereinafter referred to as the SECOND PARTNER

All the partners are collectively referred to as the PARTNERS.

WHEREAS the PARTNERS have been carrying on jointly the business of rendering Professional services of legal nature with regard to Individuals, Partnerships, Foreign citizens and Corporates without any formal agreement;

AND WHEREAS the partners have decided to enter into a PARTNERSHIP AGREEMENT to continue and carry on the business already carried on;

NOW THIS PARTNERSHIP DEED WITNESSES AS FOLLOWS:

1. NAME : The name of the partnership firm, hereinafter referred to as the FIRM shall be Secretarial Partners;
2. COMMENCEMENT : The FIRM shall be deemed to have come into existence as and from 25th August 2012 retrospectively;
3. PLACE OF BUSINESS : The FIRM shall be situated at No. 9, Wheatcrofts Road, Nungambakkam, Chennai – 600034. The branch office may be situated at such other places which the partners may determine from time to time;

4. BUSINESS : The business of the FIRM shall be rendering Professional services of legal nature with regard to Individuals, Partnerships, Foreign citizens, Corporates and any other business as the partners may decide from time to time.

5. CAPITAL : The capital of the FIRM shall be contributed by the PARTNERS in the manner set forth below:

1. FIRST PARTNER → Rs. 1,00,00,000 [RUPEES ONE CRORE ONLY];

2. SECOND PARTNER → Rs. 1,00,00,000 [RUPEES ONE CRORE ONLY];

6. SHARING OF PROFITS : The partners shall share the net profits in the RATIO OF CAPITAL; The partners shall bear the losses, if any, EQUALLY.

7. ADVANCES : Any partner may if so required with the consent of all the partners make advances to the FIRM; Such advance shall carry an interest @ 9% per annum; However the FIRM shall not retain such advance if the purpose for which the advance so given is achieved; The advance so given shall be refunded to the PARTNERS.

8. BANK ACCOUNT : The FIRM shall open a current account with the AXIS BANK, Nungambakkam branch, Chennai in the name of the FIRM; Cheques shall be drawn, endorsed by the First Partner in the name and on behalf of the FIRM.

9. Any other negotiable instruments, other than cheque may be drawn, endorsed, accepted by any of the PARTNERS on behalf of the FIRM.

10. DURATION : The duration of the FIRM shall be at the WILL of the PARTNERS.

11. DEATH & INSOLVENCY : The death or insolvency of any partner shall not have the effect of dissolving the FIRM.

12. DISPUTE : Any dispute touching the business of the FIRM shall be referred to ARBITRATION; The provisions of Arbitration & Conciliation Act, 1996 shall apply.

13. RESIDUAL :For matters not expressly provided in this DEED, the provisions of the PARTNERSHIP ACT, 1932 shall apply.

IN WITNESSES WHEREOF THE PARTNERS HAVE SIGNED THIS DEED ON THE DAY, MONTH, YEAR ABOVE WRITTEN.

1. FIRST PARTNER

2. SECOND PARTNER

DEED OF DISSOLUTION OF PARTNERSHIP

THIS DEED OF DISSOLUTION is executed at Mumbai, this, the 25th day of August 2012

AMONG

R.Mani S/O. Mr. Ravi, Hindu, aged 25 years residing at No. 144, Palaniandavar Colony, Sivakasi – 4000219 hereinafter referred to as the RETIRING PARTNER

AND

S. Anand S/O. Mr. Senthil, Hindu, aged 24 years residing at No. 99, Lake Area, Chennai – 600025 hereinafter referred to as the CONTINUING PARTNER

All the partners are collectively referred to as the PARTNERS.

WHEREAS the PARTNERS have been carrying on business of DEALING IN BOARDS under the name and style of VIJAYSRE ENTERPRISES in partnership UNDER AND BY virtue of a deed of partnership executed by them on 1st day of January 2000.

AND WHEREAS the PARTNERS have mutually agreed to DISSOLVE the said partnership firm in the manner as below:

NOW THEREFORE THIS DEED WITNESSES AS FOLLOWS:

1. That the said partnership is HEREBY DISSOLVED with effect from the date of this deed.
2. That the parties HERETO shall NOTIFY the dissolution of the said partnership to the Registrar of Firms within 30 days from the date of this deed.
3. That the ACCOUNTS of the assets and liabilities of the said partnership have been taken and the final balance sheet has been prepared and SIGNED by the PARTNERS.
4. That in consideration of Rs. 1,00,00,000 [RUPEES ONE CRORE ONLY] paid by the CONTINUING PARTNER to the RETIRING PARTNER (the receipt whereof the CONTINUING PARTNER hereby acknowledges) the RETIRING PARTNER hereby releases, relinquishes, grants, assigns and conveys all that his share in the said partnership business and properties including goodwill to hold the same to CONTINUING PARTNERS absolutely.
5. That the CONTINUING PARTNER shall hereinafter be ENTITLED to continue and carry on the said business ALONE or in PARTNERSHIP WITH OTHERS in and under the same name and style.
6. That the RETIRING PARTNER and CONTINUING PARTNER shall, and are meant to, include their respective heirs, representatives, successors and assigns.

IN THE WITNESS WHEREOF THE PARTNERS HERETO HAVE AFFIXED THEIR HANDS TO THIS DEED AT MUMBAI IN PRESENCE OF THE WITNESSES ON THE DATE AND YEAR ABOVE WRITTEN.

WITNESS 1 RETIRING PARTNER

WITNESS 2: CONTINUING PARTNER

NOTICE TO DISSOLUTION OF PARTNERSHIP FOR INSERTION IN NEWSPAPER

NOTICE IS HEREBY GIVEN THAT PARTNERSHIP subsisting between us the undersigned VIJAY AND MEERA carrying on business as at MUMBAI under the style or firm of VIJAYSRE ENTERPRISES and has this day been dissolved by MUTUAL CONSENT (or by effluxion of time). All debts due to and owing by the said late firm will be received and paid by the said Vijay, who will continue to carry on the said business under the same style and firm.

Dated Signed

1. Retirement and expulsion of partners (2009 – June)
2. Draft a specimen preamble and any three essential clause in a deed of dissolution of partnership by which one partner sells his share in partnership property to the other partner. (2008 – December)
3. Draft a deed of agreement of admission of a new partner into a partnership firm (2009 – December)
4. Draft a specimen notices (i) to determine partnership at will; and (ii) to dissolve partnership. (2008 – June)
5. Three partners, Aman, Bhuvan and Chaman, decided to dissolve their firm name ABC & Co by mutual consent. However, Aman agreed to continue the business in his own name, as a sole proprietor, and all the other partners agreed to this. Draft a notice of dissolution of ABC & Co. for insertion in a national newspaper. (2010 – December)

Kindly note that the concept of Limited Liability Partnership (LLP) will not clash with the nature of general partnership. Drafting of LLP agreements are dealt under the chapter called Highlights of LLP Act under Company Secretarial Practice. Thus, about partnership provisions.

It is advisable to start this chapter after understanding the basic provisions of Indian Trusts Act though the appropriate provisions are given at respective places. Further this chapter deals with the gifting provisions.

Instrument Of Trust & Gift Deeds

LEGAL PROVISIONS

As per Section 3 of the Indian Trusts Act, 1882, Trust is an OBLIGATION annexed to the OWNERSHIP of a property and arising out of a confidence REPOSED in and ACCEPTED by the owner OR declared/ accepted by him for the BENEFIT of another or of another & the owner.

CLASSIFICATION OF TRUST BASED ON PURPOSE

The object of a **PUBLIC TRUST** OR Charitable Trust is to carry out a purpose BENEFICIAL to the society at LARGE or the members of an UNCERTAIN or fluctuating body WHEREAS the object of a **PRIVATE TRUST** is to benefit either ONE person or certain DEFINITE person.

CREATION OF TRUST

The person creating the trust must be legally COMPETENT to contract and a trust may be created on behalf of a MINOR with the leave (permission) of the Civil Court of Original Jurisdiction. A person can be appointed as TRUSTEE if he is CAPABLE of holding property.

1. CERTAINITY AS TO INTENTION – The intention to create a trust must be UNMISTAKENLY construed from the expression which the SETTLOR has used.
2. CERTAINITY AS TO PURPOSE & OBJECT OF TRUST
   a. Beneficiaries should be identifiable with CERTAINITY
   b. The INTEREST beneficiary take should be DISCOVERABLE.
3. CERTAINITY ABOUT TRUST PROPERTY – The property to be SPECIFICALLY ascertained and TRANSFERRED by settlor to the trustee UNLESS it is a TRUST BY WILL or Author of trust himself becomes the trustee.

EXECUTION OF TRUST

The duty of the TRUSTEE is to execute the trust and,

1. Bound to fulfill the PURPOSE of the trust
2. Obey the DIRECTIONS of the author of the trust EXCEPT as modified by consent of ALL beneficiaries (including minor, by Principal Civil Court of original jurisdiction)
3. NOT bound to obey direction which would be IMPRACTICABLE, illegal or manifestly INJURIOUS to beneficiaries.

EXTINCTION OF TRUST

1. When purpose is completely FULFILLED or becomes UNLAWFUL
2. When fulfillment of purpose becomes IMPOSSIBLE by destruction of trust property
3. When trust being revocable is EXPRESSLY REVOKED
4. When trust is created by will, REVOKED at the PLEASURE of testator.

REVOCATION OF TRUST

1. With the CONSENT of ALL beneficiaries COMPETENT to contract
2. By EXPRESSLY RESERVED power of author of trust if trust is declared by way of Non-Testamentary instrument or Word of Mouth
3. At the PLEASURE of the author of trust if it is for the payment of DEBT of the author of trust and has NOT been communicated to creditors.

REGISTRATION & STAMPING

As per Section 5 of the Act, TRUST OF IMMOVABLE PROPERTY can be created only by NON-TESTAMENTARY instrument signed by the Author of the Trust and is REGISTERED (under Registration Act, 1908) or by Will of Author. Thus, 'WILL' need NOT be registered even if it pertains to immovable property. The Trust declared OTHER than Will, is liable for Stamp Duty under Indian Stamp Act, 1899.

TRUST AMONG HINDUS & MUSLIMS

Hindu Religious, Charitable endowments and Muslim 'Wakfs', though PAR TAKE the character of Trust, Indian Trusts Act, 1899 will NOT apply for such case. The deeds of the same must be REGISTERED under Registration Act, 1908 if they relate to IMMOVABLE property worth Rs. 100/- or above.

1. Draft a specimen trust deed for creating a superannuation fund. (2007 – December)
2. Discuss the contents of a trust deed. (2010 – June)
3. Author of the trust – Explain (2010 – December)
4. What are the ingredients that are necessary to prepare an Instrument of trust (2009 – December)

DRAFTING INSTRUMENT OF TRUST

Instrument of Trust is the INSTRUMENT by which trust is DECLARED. It should contain the details about,

1. **Author of the Trust or Testator** – a person who REPOSES or DECLARES the confidence
2. **Trustee** – a person who ACCEPTS the confidence
3. **Beneficiary or Cestui-qui-Trust** – a person for whose BENEFIT the confidence is accepted
4. **Trust Property or Trust Money** – the SUBJECT MATTER of the trust
5. **Intention & purpose to create trust**
6. **Transfer of legal ownership of property**: If trustee is a STRANGER the property is transferable to him "UPON TRUST" [Operative Clause] UNLESS author himself is the Trustee.
7. **Declaration of Trust:** If AUTHOR himself is the trustee and the deed require a mere declaration of trust, it is drafted as a DEED POLL. It has to be declared as that he "DEDICATES" or "SETS APART" the property in trust [Operative Clause].
8. **Duties, rights & liability** of Settlor, Trustee and Beneficiary.

DEBENTURE TRUST DEED

The provisions regarding Debentures are governed under Sections 117 to 123 of Companies Act, 1956. Debenture is a method of BORROWING,

- To be exercised only by a Board of Public Company [Section 3(1)(iii)]
- At a Meeting of the Board [Section 292]

- Total Borrowing including Debentures UPTO [Paid-up Capita + Free Reserves] WITHOUT the consent of Members in General Meeting [Section 293(1)(d)]

Section 117A defines "Debenture Trust Deed" as Trust Deed for SECURING issue of debentures and shall be in such FORM and shall be EXECUTED within prescribed period which shall be,

- Open for inspection to share/debenture holders
- Copies can be obtained on payment of prescribed fees.

PROVISIONS ON DEBENTURES:

1. Section 2(12) – Debentures INCLUDE "debenture stock", "bonds", and any other "securities" of a Company, whether constituting a Charge on the assets of the Company OR not.
   ↳ Secured Debentures may be issued;
   ↳ Unsecured Debentures = Deposits u/s. 58A.
2. Section 117 PROHIBITS Debentures carrying Voting Rights.
3. "Debenture Trustee" to be appointed as per Section 117B and the name of such trustee should be included in the prospectus with its consent.

↳ A person is NOT eligible to be appointed as a Debenture Trustee, if he / she,
↳ Beneficially HOLDS shares in the Company;
↳ Is beneficially ENTITLED to money which are to be paid by the Company by the Debenture Trustee;
↳ Has entered into GUARANTEE in respect of principal debts secured by the debentures or interest thereon;
↳ The duties of Debenture Trustees are follows,
↳ To protect interest of debenture holders;
↳ To redress grievances of the debenture holders;
↳ To ensure securities are created within prescribed time;
↳ To ensure adequacy of assets and ensure the terms & conditions of issue given in Prospectus vis-à-vis Debenture Trust Deed & Debenture Certificate are not inconsistent;
↳ To ensure that the company does not commit any breach of covenants and provisions of the trust deed;
↳ To take such reasonable steps to remedy any breach of the covenants of the trust deed or the terms of issue;
↳ May file a petition before CLB, if the secured assets are not sufficient to meet the debts and CLB may impose restriction for incurring further liabilities.
↳ To convene Debenture Holders Meeting, as & when required.

4. Any provision contained in a trust deed or in contract with debenture holders, exempting a trustee from, or indemnifying him against, liability for breach of trust, where he fails to show the degree of care and diligence required, shall be void.
5. "Debenture Redemption Reserve" to be created u/s. 117C and adequate amounts to be credited from the profits of every year TILL redemption of debentures.
6. "Secured Debenture Holders" shall rank in PRIORITY over all other claims during Winding Up.
7. A contract with a company to take up and pay for any debentures of the company may be enforced by a decree for specific performance.
8. The company can re-issue the debentures redeemed unless it is prohibited by Articles or terms of issuance of the original debentures or any contract entered into by the company or the company passed a resolution for canceling the redeemed debentures and it shall be treated as the issue of a new debenture for the purposes of stamp duty [Section 121].

POINTS SPECIFIC TO DEBENTURE TRUST DEED

1. The Debenture Trust Deed gives a LEGAL MORTGAGE on block capital and a FLOATING SECURITY on the other assets of the company in FAVOUR of Debenture Trustee on behalf of Debenture Holders.
2. It shall give details of the CONDITIONS under which loan is ADVANCED.
3. It should specify the details of REMUNERATION PAYABLE to the Trustee, their DUTIES & RESPONSIBILITIES in relation to a Trust Property.
4. Any provision contained in the DEBENTURE TRUST DEED or in contract with debenture holders, EXEMPTING a Debenture Trustee from, or indemnifying him against, liability for breach of trust shall be VOID. [Section 119]
5. It also gives the details of RIGHTS of Debenture Holders to be exercised through Debenture Trustee in case of DEFAULT by the company in payment of interest and principal as agreed upon.

REGISTRATION & STAMPING

The issue of 'debenture' shall be stamped as per Indian Stamp Act, 1899 BUT if a 'debenture trust deed' ACCOMPANYING a series of debentures is DULY STAMPED, NO stamp is necessary to be affixed on the issue of 'debentures'. Hence, there are 2 parts, ONE is a Mortgage Deed which sets out the terms & conditions subject to which debentures are issued and OTHER is a Debenture which provides for transfer of debenture as a marketable security. The debenture trust deed is REGISTRABLE and can be registered with the REGISTRAR.

TRUST DEEDS CONSTITUTING PROVIDENT FUND, SUPERANNUATION FUND, PENSION FUND, GRATUITY FUND ETC…

The Companies create Provident, Superannuation, Pension & Gratuity Fund, etc… through DECLARATION OF TRUST for the benefit of their employees. Take for instance, Employees Provident Funds and Miscellaneous Provisions Act, 1952 enables EMPLOYER to maintain their OWN PROVIDENT FUND ACCOUNT, only if,

- It is a Large Establishment [having 100 or more employees]
- No default in payment OR No offence under the Act for 3 previous years

Hence, such Employer's who have got the said exemption OR for those employees who are NOT governed the said Act can create a PROVIDENT FUND TRUST.

Even Gratuity Act, 1972 has a similar provision. The said deeds shall be IRREVOCABLE and provisions of Income Tax Act, 1961 read with the provisions of Income Tax Rules, 1962 shall be complied with, in addition to the provision of the respective Act read with the Scheme, as applicable.

Then, Company has to make APPLICATION TO THE COMMISSIONER OF INCOME TAX for recognition of the respective fund, ONLY then deductions will be allowed.

SAMPLE DEBENTURE TRUST DEED

THIS DEBENTURE TRUST DEED is executed at Kolkata, this, the 25th day of August 2012

BY

Labz Limited, a limited liability company registered under the Companies Act, 1956 under the Certificate of Incorporation number 99-1234 of 2000 and Corporate Identification Number (CIN) UL12345692003 in the office of the Registrar of Companies, Maharashtra at Mumbai having its Registered Office at No. 13, Jolly Maker Chambers, Mumbai – 400021 through its ATTORNEY Mr. Shiva appointed under the Power of Attorney dated 25th August 2012 given under the common seal of the company hereinafter referred to as the COMPANY

IN THE FAVOUR OF

Mr. Mani S/O. Mr. Ravi, Hindu, aged 25 years residing at 9, Wheatcrofts Road Chennai – 600034 hereinafter referred to as the LESSOR which term shall mean & include his legal heirs, representatives, administrators, nominees and assigns ON THE ONE PART

AND

Mr. Jain S/O. Mr. Raj, Hindu, aged 23 years residing at 22, Lodi Road, New Delhi – 110003 hereinafter referred to as the TRUSTEES.

WHEREAS the COMPANY has issued a series of 1,00,000 DEBENTURES of Rs. 1000 each aggregating to Rs. 10,00,00,000 [RUPEES TEN CRORES];

AND WHEREAS it is necessary to appoint DEBENTURE TRUSTEE under Section 117B of the Companies Act, 1956;

NOW THE COMPANY APPOINTS THE TRUSTEES FOR THE BENEFIT OF THE DEBENTURE HOLDERS:

1. The TRUSTEES shall *not beneficially hold shares* in the COMPANY.
2. The TRUSTEES shall *not be beneficially entitled* to monies which are to be paid by the COMPANY to the DEBENTURE TRUSTEE.
3. The TRUSTEES have *not entered into guarantee* in respect of the Principal Debts secured by the debentures or interest thereon.

THE TRUSTEES AGREE THAT:

1. They will *protect the interest* of the holder of debentures.
2. They will ensure that the securities will be *created within* the stipulated time.
3. They will *redress the grievance* of the holders of debentures effectively.

THE TRUSTEES ARE ENTITILED TO TAKE THE FOLLOWING STEPS TO PROTECT THE DEBENTURE HOLDERS

1. They shall ensure the assets of the COMPANY (issuing debentures) and each of the Guarantors are *sufficient to discharge* the principal amount *at all times.*
2. They shall satisfy themselves that the Prospectus or the Letter of Offer does not contain any matter which is *inconsistent* with the terms of the debenture or with the trust deed.
3. They shall ensure that the COMPANY does *not commit any breach* of covenant of the TRUST DEED or the *terms* of issue of DEBENTURES.
4. They shall take such reasonable steps to *remedy any breach* of covenant of the TRUST DEED or the *terms* of issue of DEBENTURES.
5. They shall take steps to *call a meeting* of the holders of DEBENTURES as and when such a meeting is *required* to be held.

IF AT ANY TIME, the TRUSTEES come to a conclusion that the assets of the COMPANY are *not sufficient* or is likely to become *insufficient* to discharge the Principal amount as and when becomes due, the TRUSTEE shall file a *petition before the* Central Government.

IN WITNESS WHEREOF THE PARTIES HAVE SIGNED THIS DEED ON THE DATE, MONTH, YEAR ABOVE WRITTEN.

Labz Limited through its ATTORNEY under Power of Attorney dated 25th day of August 2012.

R. MANI.

GIFT DEED

Section 122 of Transfer of Property Act, 1882 defines 'GIFT as the TRANSFER of certain existing movable or immovable PROPERTY made VOLUNTARILY and WITHOUT CONSIDERATION by one person to another, and the same is ACCEPTED by the later. It creates Donor – Donee relationship. The REGISTRATION of gift of immovable property is mandatory and optional for movable property. Revocation of GIFT shall not depend on the will of donor. The provisions of Indian Succession Act, 1925 shall also be complied with.

It may be,

OUT OF NATURAL LOVE & AFFECTION →if among relatives;

IN consideration of ESTEEM & REGARDS →otherwise (i.e.) with other persons;

The 2 conditions to be satisfied by Donor in case of gift:

- To be made during the during lifetime of Donor;
- While having the Capability to Contract.

The condition to be satisfied by Donee in case of gift:

- To be ALIVE on the date of receipt.

MODEL GIFT DEED

THIS DEED OF GIFT executed at Chennai on this 6th day of June 2012

BETWEEN

Mr. X, son of Mr. Y, aged 45 years residing at XYZ herein after referred as "Donor"(which term shall include his successors, assigns and legal representatives), being PARTY OF THE FIRST PART.

AND

Mr. Y, Son of Z, aged 34 years residing at ABC herein after referred as "Donee" (which term shall include his successors, assigns and legal representatives), being PARTY OF THE SECOND PART.

WHEREAS the Donor is the owner of the property, more fully described in the Schedule.

WHEREAS the Donor acquired the property out of his income vide Sale deed registered at the Sub–Registrar office, Central on 16th April, 1980.

AND WHEREAS the Donor OUT OF LOVE AND AFFECTION decided to gift the Scheduled property to the Donee and The Donee agreed to accept the Gift.

NOW THIS DEED WITNESSES AS FOLLOWS:

1. That the Donor does, hereby, OUT OF NATURAL LOVE AND AFFECTION, grant, convey and TRANSFER BY WAY OF GIFT to the donee, of the properties more fully described in the Schedule.
2. That the Donor CONFIRMS that this Deed of Gift is Executed, without any force, compulsion, threat or undue influence.
3. That the Donor acquired the property out of his own income and the present value of the property is Rs. 10,00,000 [RUPEES TEN LAKHS ONLY]
4. That the Donee ACCEPTS the Gift and takes the Delivery of the possession of the entire property mentioned in the SCHEDULE.

IN WITNESS THE PARTIES HERETO HAVE SET THEIR HANDS AND SIGNATURES HERETO THE DAY, THE MONTH AND THE YEAR FIRST ABOVE WRITTEN.

I ACCEPT THE GIFT.

DONEE　　　　　　　　　　　　　　　　　　　　　　　　　　　　　　DONOR

WITNESS　　　　　　　　　　　　　　　　　　　　　　　　　　　　　WITNESS

Also read debenture provisions from Company Secretarial Practice and debt provisions from Due Diligence & Corporate Compliance management to understand the SEBI & Company law aspects.

Intellectual Property Laws is an area of practice which require high legal & technical skills. Here, the ownership value is very high and hence demand proper regulations. Some aspects of international obligations on Intellectual Property is also dealt under the portion of International Trade.

Assignment Under Intellectual Property Laws & Debts

= Transfer of Ownership

PATENT

According to Patents Act, 1970 read with Patents (Amendment) Act, 2005, patent MEANS patent FOR ANY INVENTION granted under this Act FOR article/process of making an article BY applying idea/principle.

Patentee can assign, license, mortgage or create other interest in his rights in favour of any other person. Section 68 of the Act mandates that the same shall be IN WRITING and the AGREEMENT between the parties concerned to be reduced in the form of a DOCUMENT embodying all the TERMS & CONDITIONS governing their rights and obligation and shall be duly EXECUTED.

Section 69 of the Act provides for REGISTRATION OF TITLE if person becomes entitled to a Patent by ASSIGNMENT, TRANSMISSION or by operation of LAW. It is mandatory to be admitted as EVIDENCE of the tile of any person. Hence, registration though optional is highly advisable for ASSIGNEE of the patent.

COPYRIGHT

According to Copyrights Act, 1957, copyright means the right to REPRODUCE for the purpose of DISTRIBUTION of original literary, dramatic, music, artistic work, cinematograph films and sound recording.

Copyright is a BUNDLE of rights. According to Section 18 of the Act, the owner of copyright can ASSIGN the copyright to a work which can be PARTIAL or FULL subject to limitations and for LIMITED or FULL term. On assignment, the assignee gets the RIGHTS ASSIGNED and balance rights REMAIN with the assignor.

The assignment,

- Shall be in writing, duly signed by assignor or his authorized agent
- Shall specify the details of work being assigned and rights assigned
- The Duration unless otherwise specified, shall be 5 years
- The territorial extent of assignment unless otherwise specified, shall be India
- Shall specify the amount of royalty

If the ASSIGNEE does not make USE of rights assigned WITHIN a period of 1 year from the date of assignment, it will be DEEMED to have elapsed.

The assignment shall be stamped and is based on payment of LUMPSUM while licenses are based on ROYALTY per copy sold.

TRADEMARK

According to Trademarks Act, 1999, Trademark is one which is capable of being REPRESENTED graphically and capable in DISTINGUISHING the goods or services of one person FROM those of others.

According to Section 37, 38 & 39 of the Act, REGISTERED & UNREGISTERED Trademark can be ASSIGNED or TRANSMITTED with or without GOODWILL of business, by registered proprietor to another and to give effectual

RECEIPTS for any consideration for such assignment. It shall be REGISTERED at any time with Registrar u/s. 45, to be accepted as EVIDENCE.

The following assignment or transmission is NOT permitted u/s. 40, 41 & 42 if,

1. Likely to cause confusion – where exclusive rights are CREATED IN MORE THAN one person in respect of same/associated goods/services.

2. One person in One part & Other person in Other part of India – where exclusive rights are CREATED TERRITORIALLY IN MORE than one person in respect of same/associated goods/services.

3. Assignment WITHOUT good will – where NO application is made to Registrar WITHIN 6 months for directions for issue of advertisement of assignment.

CERTIFICATION Trademark is one which is used IN ADDITION to users own Trademark such as BIS, AGMARK. It shall be assigned/transmitted ONLY with the CONSENT of Registrar.

ASSOCIATED Trademark is one which is IDENTICAL with another registered Trademark of same proprietor such as Britannia Milkbikis and Britannia Bourbon. It shall be assigned/transmitted ONLY as WHOLE.

1. Draft a specimen deed of assignment of a registered trade mark. (2007 – December)
2. Draft a specimen of the deed of assignment of a patent. (2008 – June)
3. What is 'deed of assignment'? Draft a specimen deed of assignment of copyright of a novel. (2009 – December)
4. Draft a specimen of deed of assignment of shares in a company (2008 – December)

ASSIGNMENT OF COPYRIGHT

THIS AGREEMENT is entered into at CHENNAI, this, the 25th day of August, 2012

BETWEEN

Mr. Jain S/O. Mr. Raj, Hindu, aged 23 years residing at 6, Patti Street, Sivakasi - 626189 hereinafter referred to as the COPYRIGHT OWNER or the ASSIGNOR ON THE ONE PART.

AND

Mr. Mani, the owner of Big Entertainment residing at 9, Sterling Road Chennai – 600034 hereinafter referred to as ASSIGNEE ON THE OTHER PART.

WHEREAS the ASSIGNOR is the author of the Sound Recording titled MP3SLRFM, he being the owner of the Copyright;

AND WHEREAS the ASSIGNEE has offered a sum of Rs. 1,00,000 [RUPEES ONE LAKH ONLY] as a Royalty for the assignment of the copyright in respect of such work;

NOW THIS AGREEMENT WITNESSES AS FOLLOWS:

1. The ASSIGNOR who is the owner of the COPYRIGHT in the existing Sound Recording titled MP3SLRFM assigns in favour of the ASSIGNEE, the COPYRIGHT in respect of the COPYRIGHT.
2. The ASSIGNEE shall publish the work and before the release of the first copy shall pay a sum of Rs. 1,00,000 [RUPEES ONE LAKH ONLY] as Royalty for every edition of the Sound Recording.
3. The ASSIGNMENT is for a period of FIVE YEARS from the date of ASSIGNMENT.
4. The ASSIGNMENT shall extend to the territory of India.
5. If the ASSIGNEE does not exercise the rights assigned to him within a period of ONE YEAR from the date of assignment shall be deemed to have been lapsed after the expiry of the said period of ONE YEAR.
6. The ASSIGNOR undertakes to revise and carry out any amendments made to the Act as and when necessary or on the publication of the First Edition as the case may be.
7. The ASSIGNEE agrees to publish the work in the style and manner given by the ASSIGNOR in the floppy disk containing the ASSIGNMENT.
8. The ASSIGNEE further agrees not to make any changes or distort the work written by the ASSIGNOR which is the subject matter of this ASSIGNMENT.

IN WITNESSES WHEREOF THE PARTIES HAVE SIGNED THIS AGREEMENT ACT AT CHENNAI ON THE DATE, MONTH, YEAR ABOVE WRITTEN.

ASSIGNOR ASSIGNEE

ASSIGNMENT OF PATENT

THIS DEED OF ASSIGNMENT OF Patent made this 1st day of August 2010 at Bengaloolru

BETWEEN _

(Assignor's name), at (Department at IISc), Indian Institute of Science, Bengalorru – 560012, Karnataka State, India hereinafter referred to as the ASSIGNOR of the one part;

AND

M/S. INDIAN INSTITUTE OF SCIENCE, at Bengalooru – 560 012, Karnataka State, India hereinafter referred to as the ASSIGNEE of the other part.

WHEREAS, the ASSIGNEE has engaged (Assignor's name), S/o __________, aged 45 years, residing at (Address of Assignor), the ASSIGNOR as a research student in the (Dept. at IISc) for carrying out research in the field of (Subject of Research).

AND WHEREAS, it is agreed by and between the ASSIGNEE and the ASSIGNOR that whatever inventions / discoveries / ideas / theories and concepts developed and / or enunciated by the ASSIGNOR during the period of his tenure with the ASSIGNEE shall be the exclusive property of the ASSIGNEE.

NOW THIS DEED WITNESSETH it is hereby agreed by and between the parties as follows:

In consideration of his employment, the ASSIGNOR hereby agrees with the ASSIGNEE that all the PATENT RIGHTS arising out of the research or developmental work carried out by him shall accrue to the ASSIGNEE and all inventions / discoveries / ideas / theories and concepts so developed or enunciated by the EMPLOYEE/ STUDENT shall be the sole and absolute property of the ASSIGNEE and it shall be lawful to deal with such discoveries / ideas / theories and concepts in any manner whatsoever as the ASSIGNEE may deem fit.

The ASSIGNOR hereby agrees and undertakes with the ASSIGNEE that he shall, if and whenever required by the ASSIGNEE join with the Institute in applying for registration for patent or patents in respect of such inventions / discoveries / ideas / theories and concepts or other similar production, both in India and any other part of the world, for the said inventions and shall on request by and at the cost of the Institute execute and do all the instruments and things necessary to vest the property in the said inventions / discoveries / ideas / theories and concepts and any application for registration pf patent or patents thereof or other similar production as aforesaid, that may be obtained in respect thereof, by the Institute or any person or persons or company appointed by the Institute, together with rights which may belong or accrue thereto.

IN WITNESS WHEREOF, the ASSIGNEE and the ASSIGNOR has superscribed their respective hands to this DEED OF ASSIGNMENT in Bengalooru on the day, month and year first above written.

SIGNED AND DELIVERED BY THE
SAID (Assignor's Name)
ASSIGNOR OF THE ABOVE NAMED

SIGNED AND DELIVERED BY THE
SAID (Registrar's Name)
ON BEHALF OF THE ASSIGNEE

WITNESSES:

ACTIONABLE CLAIM

Section 3 of Transfer of Property Act, 1882, defines Actionable Claim as,

- Claim to any debt OTHER THAN
- Mortgage of immovable property
- Hypothecation or Pledge of movable property

- Claim to any BENEFICIAL INTEREST in movable property NOT in possession, either actual or constructive of the claimant
- WHICH civil courts recognize as affording grounds for RELIEF
- WHETHER such debt or beneficial interest be existent/accruing/conditional/contingent.

Thus, actionable claim is any UNSECURED debt or interest in MOVABLE property not in possession of the claimant.

The TRANSFER (assignment) of actionable claim **with or without** CONSIDERATION,

1. Shall be effected only by execution of instrument IN WRITING
2. Shall be SIGNED by the transferor or his duly authorized agent
3. Shall be COMPLETE & effectual upon the EXECUTION of such instrument.

THEREUPON,

- All the rights & remedies of the TRANSFEROR whether by way of damages or otherwise,
- Shall vest in the TRANSFEREE,
- Whether the NOTICE of transfer is given or not.

A **BUSINESS DEBT** is a property. Debt is an EXISTING obligation to pay a sum of money now or in FUTURE such as book debts, provident fund, arrears of rent, wages due, etc... Thus, debt is an ACTIONABLE CLAIM and is heritable and assignable and it is treated as property under Transfer of Property Act, 1882.

The **WARRANTY OF SOLVENCY OF DEBTOR** given u/s. 133 of Transfer of Property Act, 1882 applies ONLY at the time of transfer and is LIMITED only to the value of CONSIDERATION.

ASSIGNMENT OF RIGHTS UNDER FIRE INSURANCE POLICY u/s. 135 of Transfer of Property Act, 1882 (i.e.) the assignee in WHOM the property INSURED shall be ABSOLUTELY vested at the date of assignment shall have TRANSFERRED & VESTED in him ALL rights of SUIT as if the 'Contract in the Policy' had been made with himself.

1. Draft a specimen deed of sale of a business and assignment of goodwill. (2010 – December)

SAMPLE ASSIGNMENTOF BUSINESS DEBTS

THIS DEED OF ASSIGNMENT OF BUSINESS DEBTS made at CHENNAI, this, the 25th day of August, 2012

BETWEEN

Mr. Jain the owner of VIJAYSRE ENTERPRISES residing at 6, Patti Street, Sivakasi - 626189 hereinafter referred to as the ASSIGNOR ON THE ONE PART.

AND

Mr. Mani, S/o. Mr. Raj, Hindu, aged 25 years residing at 9, Sterling Road Chennai – 600034 hereinafter referred to as ASSIGNEE ON THE OTHER PART.

WHEREAS the assignor has, for some time been carrying on the business of dealing in Papers & Boards in the course whereof the several persons whose names, addresses and occupations are mentioned in the SCHEDULE appended hereto, have become LAWFULLY DEBTORS TO HIM and so for the several sums of money set opposite to their respective names;

AND WHEREAS the assignor has contracted with the assignee for the absolute sale to him of the said business debts at VIJAYSRE ENTERPRISES and for the sum of Rs. 1,00,00,000/- (RUPEES ONE CRORE ONLY)

NOW THIS DEED WITNESSES that in consideration of the sum of Rs. 1,00,00,000/- (RUPEES ONE CRORE ONLY) now paid to the ASSIGNOR by the ASSIGNEE (the receipt whereof the assignor hereby acknowledges), the said ASSIGNOR, as beneficial owner, does hereby transfer, sell and assign unto and to the use of the said assignee, all the several said debts, and sums of money specified in the SCHEDULE which are now due and owing to the assignor TO HAVE AND TO RECEIVE THEM FOR HIS ABSOLUTE USE AND BENEFIT WITH ABSOLUTE POWER, AUTHORITY AND LIBERTY to enforce payment thereof by suit or otherwise and that the ASSIGNOR does hereby covenant with the ASSIGNEE that all the several debts are lawfully due to him and the parties by whom they are payable are alive, and further that he has not entered into any arrangement with any of them and that the ASSIGNOR shall at all times hereafter do, execute and perform all such and other acts, deeds, things, or writings as may be reasonably required for realization of the said debts, and further and better and more effectively transferring and/or assuring them or any of them in favour of the ASSIGNEE.

IN WITNESS WHEREOF THE ASSIGNOR AND THE ASSIGNEE DO HERETO AFFIX THEIR SIGNATURES ON THE DAY, MONTH AND THE YEAR ABOVE MENTIONED.

Witness: Assignor)

Witness: (Assignor)

Also read the provisions of audit of Intellectual property under Due Diligence part of the book. This being the last chapter in drafting, hope you kept drafting and mastered the subjects. The reason for stressing it repeatedly is because unless otherwise you draft practically it becomes time consuming and very tough during exams. Enjoy drafting.

It is a stage after drafting. Simple, once court papers are prepared, it shall be presented in the Court and this chapter deals with how to present in the court and the relevant provisions for the same. It is highly advisable to read appeal provisions of Company Law Board, Securities Appellate Tribunal and such other related things while reading this chapter. Writs are very important from practical & examination point of view. Before venturing into the chapter, read Code of Civil Procedure and Constitutional provisions regarding writs.

Appearances & Pleadings

A practicing Company Secretary (PCS) can appear as authorized representative before following:

1. Company Law Board or proposed National Company Law Tribunal (NCLT)
2. Securities Appellate Tribunal (SAT) u/s. 15V of SEBI Act, 1992, Section 23C of Depositories Act, 1996 and Section 22C of Securities Contract Regulation Act, 1956
3. Erstwhile Monopolies Restrictive Trade Practice Commission (MRTPC) or existing Competition Commission of India (CCI) u/s. 35 and 53S of Competition Act, 2002, as amended
4. Consumer Forums under Consumer Protection Act, 1986
5. Central Electricity Regulatory Commission (CERC) under Clause 6 of Central Electricity Commission order, 1999
6. Telecom Regulatory Authority of India (TRAI) u/s. 17 of TRAI Act, 1997, as amended
7. Income Tax authorities including Income Tax Appellate Tribunal (ITAT)
8. Central Excise, Service Tax and Customs authorities including CESTAT (Tribunal)

GUIDELINES FOR PROFESSIONAL DRESS OF COMPANY SECRETARIES

To enhance the visibility and brand building of the profession and ensuring uniformity, while appearing before judicial/quasi-judicial bodies and tribunals:

1. The professional dress for male members of ICSI will be NAVY BLUE SUIT and WHITE SHIRT with a TIE (preferably of the ICSI) or NAVY BLUE BUTTONED UP COAT over a pant or a NAVY BLUE SAFARI SUIT.
2. The professional dress for female members of ICSI will be saree or any other dress of a sober colour with a NAVY BLUE JACKET.
3. Members in employment may wear the dress/uniform as specified by the EMPLOYER for all employees or if allowed the aforesaid professional dress.

PROFESSIONAL ETIQUETTES & COURT CRAFTS

Etiquette is the fine art of BEHAVING in FRONT of OTHERS. It is a set of practices and form which are followed in wide variety of situations such as dressing, handshake, communication, invitation, dining, etc...

Court Craft is the art of ADVOCACY for EFFECTIVE DELIVERY of results to the clients when one act as an authorized representative before Tribunal or quasi judicial body. However a good advocacy or NEGOTIATING skills will NOT compensate the lack of appropriate knowledge in LAW. The principles of advocacy include,

1. To act in the best interest of client
2. To keep the client properly informed

3. To carry out instructions with diligence and competence
4. To act impartially and offer frank, independent advice
5. To maintain client confidentiality.

CONDUCT & ETIQUETTE OF COMPANY SECRETARY

1. DUTY TO COURT
   i. To conduct himself with dignity and self respect
   ii. To maintain a respective attitude towards judicial office (court/tribunal)
   iii. Not to influence the decision of a court by illegal or improper means
   iv. To restrain and prevent his client from resorting to sharp and unfair practices
   v. Should not act or plead in any matter in which he is himself PECUNIARILY INTERESTED.
2. DUTY TO CLIENT
   i. Shall not ordinarily withdraw from engagement once accepted without suffice cause and unless sufficient notice is given to client
   ii. Shall make full and frank disclosures to the client relating to any interest which is likely affect client's judgment in continuing the engagement
   iii. Shall defend accused of crime regardless of personal opinion bearing in mind that law requires no man should be convicted without adequate evidence
   iv. Shall not do anything taking advantage on the confidence reposed by client.
3. DUTY TO OPPONENT
   i. Shall communicate or negotiate upon the subject matter of controversy ONLY with the respective Advocate handling the case
   ii. Shall do his best to carry out the legitimate promise made to the opposite party.

ADVOCACY TIPS

While pleading, a Judge in the pleading looks for,

1. Clarity as his time is limited
2. Credibility in the argument (i.e.) true and on the right side by understanding the Judge's PSYCHOLOGY to prefer your version of truth
3. Be likeable – atleast be more likeable than your opponent and learn to LISTEN
4. Demeanor & Eye Contact – the physical appearance and pleadings
5. Voice modulation – To emphasize on points that have to be emphasized. Use anger strategically and always be in control of it.
6. Entertain your Judge – humour will often bail you out of tough spot.

DRAFTING WRITTEN PLEADINGS

While drafting written pleadings,

1. Quote relevant provisions in the petition and excerpts of observations made by the court relevant to the point by highlighting material facts, decisions, etc…
2. Draft innocuous (harmless) prayers in a manner to satisfy your requirements
3. Do not suppress facts

4. File your reply at earliest opportunity to each paragraph of the petition

5. File rejoinder immediately on receiving reply with specific points in affidavit.

[Relevant legal provisions regarding pleadings are discussed in the next chapter]

Thus, Company Secretaries should be able to formulate and present a coherent submission based on facts, general principles and legal authority in a structured, concise and persuasive manner. They should understand the crucial importance of preparation and the best way to undertake it.

1. "Practising of good professional etiquettes is necessary for professional success in the emerging business scenario." Discuss (2009 – June and 2010 - December)
2. "In presenting a case before the tribunal / quasi – judicial body, a Company secretary owes duty to the court, to the client and to the opponent." Describe these duties of the Company Secretary. (2009 – December)
3. What is meant by 'etiquette'? What are the invitation etiquettes to be observed by a Company Secretary? (2010 – June)
4. What are the advocacy tips to be borne in mind by Practising Company Secretary while appearing before a tribunal? (2010 – June)
5. Communication etiquettes (2009 – December)
6. Advocacy tips to professionals (2009 – December)

PLEADINGS

In India, 'pleadings' are governed by Civil Procedure Code, 1902 read with Indian Evidence Act, 1872.

PLEADINGS = PLAINT + WRITTEN STATEMENT

Suit will commence on PRESENTATION of **plaint** with,

- Cause Title
- Name, Description & Address of Plaintiff and Defendant
- Material Facts (NOT the law or evidence) of the case with reasons for entitlement of right
- Jurisdiction of Court
- Prayer – the specific relief sought.
- Verification, Annexure of Documents filed, Documentary evidences, etc…

The **written statement** (or reply or replication or rejoinder) is the DEFENCE filed by the defendant with,

- Cause Title
- Address to which the service of summons, process and notice to be effected
- Facts, admitting or denying the allegations (averments) made by the plaintiff (which will become the FACT IN ISSUE)

It may be different for different & conflicting defences OR joint defence, in case of same defence to claim.

The preferable sequential order of defence to several pleas in the written statement,

1. All admissions & denials of acts alleged in the plaint (including additional facts, if any)

2. Plead defences which are applicable to the whole case.

3. Plead defences which apply only to a part of claim. It should be prefaced like,

   - As to the profits claimed by plaintiff, defendant contends that…
   - As to the price of books purchased by defendant, defendant contends that…

IMPORTANT CONSIDERATIONS

1. Every averment (allegation) of the plaint or petition which are incorrect or false, to be SPECIFICALLY denied in the written statement, otherwise, it is presumed to have been admitted [Order 8 Rule 5 – O8R5 of CPC]. On denial, the onus to prove the same will fall upon the complainant.
2. The written statement shall be signed and filed by constituted attorney or duly authorized person.
3. It shall be verified by an AFFIDAVIT duly drawn, sworn and notarized.
4. File all supporting papers, documentary evidence, annual accounts, registers, invoices and other relevant papers duly page numbered.
5. No pleadings, No evidence – hence, plead/deny every point unless the burden of PROOF lies on the other side.
6. Prayer should claim all possible relief, otherwise such relief will not be allowed.

FORMS OF DEFENCE

1. TRAVERSE means to deny the plaint totally and categorically
2. SPECIAL DEFENCE or 'Confession & Avoidance' means to admit allegations but destroying its effect (eg) in suit based on contract, defendant may admit that he made the contract, but may avoid the effect of admission by pleading performance, fraud or limitation, etc…
3. DEMURRER or 'Objection in point of law' (i.e.) even if the facts are true, they are insufficient to entitle to relief. (eg) facts do not state a cause of action or that the special damages claimed are too remote.

4. DILATORY PLEA or Dilatory Trail tactics to put off a decision by way of "Preliminary Objections" or by a separation application filed at the earliest opportunity. (eg) suit has not been properly framed, mis-joinder or non-joinder or defects in cause of action and the case cannot be decided until those defects are removed. For instance, if unregistered contract forms the basis of a claim, which requires mandatory registration u/s. 17 of Registration Act, 1908, then it should be pointed out that the same could not be looked into as it is not an evidence.
5. PEREMPTORY PLEAS or 'Pleas in the bar' which are imperative and goes to the root of the case unlike dilatory pleas.

The defences can be taken either jointly or alternatively, even if such defences are inconsistent unless otherwise there is contradiction of facts. Also, all such defences relate to question of fact should be taken in the first instance, otherwise he may not be allowed to advance it at a later stage.

LEGAL SUBMISSIONS/PLEADINGS or Preliminary Objections

It is an essential **dilatory plea** which should be exercised at earlier possible opportunity by finding whether there were compliances of all legal provisions in every plea filed by petitioners and to find the consequences of non-compliances. **Special defences** can be used in this regard to question the effectiveness of suit filed by the petitioner.

COUNTER AFFIDAVIT	REPLY	REJOINDER (or Replication or Subsequent Pleadings)
Pleadings (written statement) filed by a defendant or respondent in ANSWER to the claims SET OUT by plaintiff or petitioner in the form of affidavit.	Pleadings filed by either plaintiff/petitioner or defendant/ respondent in ANSWER to claims raised by other party and confined to miscellaneous or interim applications.	Written statement or reply of plaintiff or petitioner by way of DEFENCE to pleases raised in Counter Affidavit or written statement from defendant or respondent

AFFIDAVIT-IN-EVIDENCE

It is a deposition, meaning, a PRETRIAL discovery device by which one party questions the other party for the other party. It shall be tendered with ORIGINALS or CARBON copies (not only photocopies) of all supporting documents by the person PERSONALLY INVOLVED in the whole transaction or by such other person who has joined in his place.

1. Governed by Sections 101-103, 106 & 109-111 of Indian Evidence Act, 1872.
2. No extraneous evidence can be looked into in absence of specific pleadings.
3. Every allegations or charges or grounds relating to **facts** shall be reproduced duly supported by documentary evidence. Kindly note, the **legal** provisions though not reproduced herewith can be introduced while arguing the case.
4. File documentary evidence to demolish the defence or case set up by the opposite party. One can also bring expert witness or outside witness in support of case if the facts and circumstances warrants and permitted by Court/Tribunal.

RULE OF ADVERSE INFERENCE

The Court will be justified in drawing an adverse inference against a party,

- As it is INCUMBENT on such party to produce the BEST evidence in possession on the issue involved.
- As it is equally INCUMBENT on such party to produce EXPERT evidence in complex issues pertaining to engineering, medical, technology or sciences as Court is not the expert body in such case.

PRELIMINARY SUBMISSIONS

The preliminary submissions should (confine to) state the TRUE & CORRECT **facts** regarding ISSUES suppressed OR not disclosed by other side in the pleadings. In addition, **Legal** provisions or objections relevant to be mentioned SO AS TO demonstrate that RELIEF claimed by opponent is not eligible or by the party should be allowed.

ARGUMENTS ON MERITS = Arguments related to FACTS pleaded by parties

The lawyer or authorised representative should,

- Point out the pleadings of parties and the relevant evidence in support thereof lead by the parties. If there is no evidence, it should be specifically pointed out.
- Ensure that all contradictions in the pleadings are duly pointed out in submissions.
- Ensure proof of service of notice of the case.
- Highlight facts or contradictions extracted from the opponent during Cross Examination or such other factual issues involved.

APPEAL

Appeal is the application by a party to an appellate court, asking it to set aside or revise a decision of a subordinate court. If the defendant (plaintiff) files an appeal he is known as 'APPELLANT/Defendant (plaintiff) whereas the other party who has to answer is called RESPONDENT/Plaintiff (defendant).

Appeal & Non-appealable Orders:

- An appeal lies from any DECREE (including ex parte decree) passed by any court exercising original jurisdiction.
- No appeal lies from ex parte dismissal and from a decree passed by the consent of parties.
- Non-appealable orders may be filed as Revision Petition before High Court.

Concepts:

- Ex parte decree may be passed when defendant or his counsel is NOT present on the date of hearing. In such cases, the defendant has the option to appeal or make interlocutory application within 30 days to set aside the same and to restore & hear the case on merits.
- Ex parte dismissal is when plaintiff or his counsel is NOT present on the date of hearing. In such cases, only Interlocutory application may be filed within 30 days to set aside the same and to restore & hear the case on merits as it is not appealable.
- The decree passed by consent of parties is called Compromise Decree. For instance, Consent Order under SEBI Act is not appealable before SAT.
- Interlocutory means BETWEEN. Interlocutory application may be made for temporary injunction or attachment or application for stay, etc... BEFORE judgment. Interlocutory order is an order passed by the Court during the PENDENCY of the suit.

Types:

Appeals from Original Decrees – appeal preferred from every decree passed by any court exercising original jurisdiction on points of LAW or FACTS.

- Second Appeals – such appeal lie to High Court from every decree passed by any subordinate Court ONLY on points of SUBSTANTIAL question of LAW.
- Appeals from Orders – such appeal would lie only from prescribed orders on grounds of DEFECTS or IRREGULARITY of law such as order allowing special cost, refusing leave to institute a suit, for compensation, imposing fine or directing detention or such other appealable orders.

- Appeals to Supreme Court, are discussed in detail.

Appeals to Supreme Court:

Section 109 of CPC, 1908 prescribes 2 conditions for an appeal to lie before Supreme Court,

- There should be any judgment, decree or final order in a CIVIL PROCEEDING of a HIGH COURT
- High Court to CERTIFY that case involves substantial question of LAW of general importance **and** in its OPINION it needs to be decided by Supreme Court.

ORDINARY APPEALS TO SUPREME COURT [Articles 132-135 of Constitution]

1. Appeals in **constitutional** cases irrespective of whether civil, criminal or otherwise, where High Court CERTIFIES that substantial question of law as to INTERPRETATION of Constitution is involved.
2. Appeals in **civil** cases when Section 109 (of CPC, 1908) CONDITIONS are satisfied, as above.

3. Appeals in **criminal** cases in EXCEPTIONAL circumstances where the demand of JUSTICE requires interference by Supreme Court either WITH or WITHOUT the Certificate (of Fitness) of High Court or by way of Special Leave petition (SLP).

If Public Authority to whom Respondent is made, is situated within Mumbai city than Bombay High Court (BHC) has ORIGINAL JURISDICTION and if it is situated outside Mumbai city, then BHC has APPELLATE JURISDICTION. If Respondents are situated BOTH in Mumbai and outside Mumbai, than the Court will have ORIGINAL JURISDICTION.

1. What is meant by 'pleadings'? Explain the fundamental rules of pleadings. (2010 – December)
2. Rule of adverse inference (2010 – June)
3. Representative suit (2010 – June)
4. Define – Rejoinder (2009 – June)
5. "It is incumbent upon the defendant to file his defence in writing, else the court may pronounce judgment against him or make such order as it deems fit". Examine the statement and enumerate important points while drafting the reply or a written statement. (2010 – June)
6. Mention the important considerations while drafting an affidavit in evidence. (2010 – June)
7. Explain the Counter affidavit (2010 – December)
8. 'Revision' under the Code of Civil Procedure, 1908 (2008 – June)
9. Explain what is 'appeal' in the context of the Code of Civil Procedure, 1908. What are the different kinds of appeals under the code of Civil Procedure, 1908? (2007 – June)
10. What are the important factors that you will bear in mind while drafting an appeal? (2008 – December)
11. Define the following : Appeal (J'09)

SPECIAL LEAVE PETITION (SLP) [Article 136 of Constitution read with Section 112 of CPC]

Where High Court refused to issue the required CERTIFICATE as above, to enable the aggrieved party to APPEAL to the Supreme Court, then appeal for special leave u/A 136 to **SUPREME COURT** may be filed from judgment, decree or order passed or made by ANY court or tribunal in the TERRITORY of India OTHER THAN the court or tribunal under any law relating to ARMED FORCES. If the Petition is filed against the Judgment of the High Court, the time limit is 90 DAYS from the date of Judgment/Order and if the Petition is filed against the Order of High Court refusing to grant Certificate of Fitness for Appeal, the time limit is 60 days from the date of Order refusing to grant Certificate.

{the first page of the petition is called CAUSE TITLE}

IN THE SUPREME COURT OF INDIA

CIVIL APPELLATE JURISDICTION

{Order XVI Rules 4(1) (a)}

(Under Article 136 of the Constitution of India)

SPECIAL LEAVE PETITION (CIVIL) NO.____ OF 2010

[Arising out of the Impugned Final Judgment and Order dated 25.05.2010 passed by the High Court of Delhi at New Delhi in W.P. (C) No. 3522/2010]

IN THE MATTER OF:

Centre for Public Interest Litigation through its General Secretary, 43, Lawyer's Chambers, Supreme Court of India, New Delhi-110001

... PETITIONER

The Union of India through its Secretary, Department of Telecommunications, Sanchar Bhawan, 20, Ashoka Road, New Delhi 110 001

... RESPONDENT

1. That the PETITIONER is challenging by way of this SPECIAL LEAVE PETITION the order of High court dated 25.05.2010, whereby the High Court dismissed the Petition filed by the PETITIONERS.
2. That the QUESTIONS OF LAW involved in this matter are,
3. Whether,

   • Whether the High Court erred in not taking into account the nature and the scale of the 2G spectrum scam that has defrauded and swindled the national exchequer an amount to the tune of tens of thousands of crores?

   • Whether the High Court erred in dismissing the case without appreciating the right to live in an environment free of corruption is part of right to life guaranteed under Article 21 of the Constitution of India?
4. Hon'ble High court has fallen into error in taking the view that:

   • That the PETITIONERS' petition was to seek a thorough court monitored investigation into the 2G spectrum allocation scam that has caused the national exchequer an estimated Rs. 70,000 crores and huge national outrage.

   • This petition into such a serious scam should not have been summarily dismissed considering the nature and extent of the scam and the shocking facts of this case
5. That the RESPONDENT had filed a petition....which was CONTESTED by PETITIONER on the grounds that....[List the grounds]
6. That High Court after hearing the parties, holding sufficient grounds, dismissed the Petition filed by the PETITIONERS.
7. That the PETITIONER has not filed any appeal or other proceeding relating to this matter in this HON'BLE cOURT or any other court.

PETITIONER ACCORDINGLY PRAYS THAT THIS HON'BLE COURT TO ALLOW THE APPEAL, SET ASIDE THE IMPUGNED ORDER PASSED BY HIGH COURT AND DISMISS THE PETITION FILED BY RESPONDENT IN HIGH cOURT & TO PASS SUCH OTHER AND FURTHER ORDER OR ORDERS AS THIS HON'BLE COURT MAY DEEM FIT AND PROPER IN THE FACTS AND CIRCUMSTANCES OF THE CASE.

PETITIONERS' AFFIDAVIT

{Put the CAUSE TITLE}

I, ________, the Petitioner above named, aged about ...do hereby beg to state on solemn affirmation as under:

1. The PETITIONERS have filed the present petition inter-alia for various reliefs as more particularly set out in the petition. I repeat, reiterate and adopt the statements made in the petition as if the same are incorporated herein and form part of the present AFFIDAVIT. I crave leave to refer to and rely upon the papers and proceedings in the petition when produced. I state that there is urgency in the matter.

2. In the said circumstances, I say and submit that the petitioners are entitled for the reliefs as prayed for and if the same are not granted, irreparable loss and harm would be caused to the petitioners. I say and submit that this petition be made absolute with cost.

Solemnly affirmed at Mumbai

This day of . 2010

(signed)

PETITIONER

Additional Evidence in Appeal:

The parties to an appeal are NOT entitled to produce additional evidence, but the Appellate Court has DISCRETION to allow additional evidence after RECORDING the reasons when,

- Lower Court refuse to admit evidence which ought to have been admitted
- Party establishes that evidence was not submitted, without his fault
- Appellate Court requires document or witness to pronounce judgment
- Other substantial cause.

Contents of Appellate Judgment:

1. the points of determination
2. the decision thereon
3. the reasons for the decision &
4. where the decree appealed from is REVERSED or varied, the relief to which the appellant is ENTITLED to.

CONTENTS OF APPEAL:

A Memorandum of Appeal must SET FORTH concisely and under distinct heads the GROUNDS of objection to the DECREE appealed from WITHOUT any argument or narrative, which should be NUMBERED consequently. The contents of appeal includes,

FORMAL PART – Memorandum of Appeal

1. Name of Appellate Court
2. Appeal in Suit Number from

3. Appeal Number (to be kept blank)
4. Name & Description of the parties
5. Describe the Suit Number of the Court and the Date of decree, or final order against which appeal is preferred

MATERIAL PART – Grounds of Appeal

6. State the grounds of objection on which it is preferred

PRAYER

7. Relief sought for.

ANNEXURES

8. Copy of the decree and the judgment, or order appealed
9. Power of Attorney or Vakalatnama

SAMPLE CIVIL APPEAL

IN THE HIGH COURT OF JUDICATURE: TAMIL NADU: AT CHENNAI
CIVIL APPELLATE JURISDICTION

REGULAR CIVIL APPEAL NO. 10 OF 2012

BETWEEN

CAUSE TITLE

Subash,

Aged 25 years

Doctor

128, VP Street, Vellore..APPELLANT/PLAINTIFF

AND

LABZ LIMITED

33, Appar Street, Vellore

Represented by its Company Secretary Mr. Best.........RESPONDENT/DEFENDANT

The ADDRESS FOR SERVICE of all notices, process, summons, etc... on the above named APPELLANTS is that of their Counsel M/s. Axe, Advocates, High Court of Chennai.

The above named APPELLANT begs to present this MEMORANDUM OF APPEAL against the Decree and Judgment dated 25th day of February 2012 passed in (Original Suit) O.S. No. 9 of 2012 on the file of Senior Civil Judge Mr. Honstha, Chennai for the following:

GROUNDS

1. The Decree and Judgment of Trial Court is contrary to law
2. The trial court ERRED in dismissing the suit
3. The trial court OUGHT TO HAVE held that appellant is not liable to pay development charges
4. The trial court OUGHT TO HAVE seen the demand for Rs. 1000 per sq.mt is unreasonable and not guided by any policy of Government
5. The trial court OUGHT TO HAVE....

For the above grounds and other grounds to be URGED at the time of hearing, the **HON'BLE COURT** may be pleased to SET ASIDE Decree and Judgment dated 25th day of February 2012 passed in O.S. No. 9 of 2012 and pass such other ORDER or orders as this **HON'BLE COURT** may deem fit and proper in the circumstances of the case.

VALUE OF THE APPEAL

Value of Appeal is Rs. 1,00,000/- . Court Fee paid is Rs. 10,000/- (Kindly note, if the suit is INCAPABLE of valuation, then Court fee shall be Rs. 400/-)

Place **COUNSEL FOR THE APPELLANT**

Date

REVIEW [Section 114 of CPC]	**REVISION** [Section 115 of CPC]	**REFERENCE**
By the person aggrieved or SAME COURT which passed the decree or order for which there is NO appeal or no appeal preferred	By HIGH COURT calling for any record of any case decided by sub-ordinate court for which there is NO appeal	By ANY COURT for the opinion of High Court suo motto or on application by parties to proceedings
The grounds include, • Discovery of new & important matter as evidence after decree • Any apparent mistake or error on the face of record • Other Sufficient reasons	The grounds include, Exercising jurisdiction, • NOT vested by law • Illegally or with material irregularity Or Failing to exercise jurisdiction vested by law	The conditions include, • Question of law • Reasonable doubt on question of law • Facts & points on which doubt is entertained

SAMPLE CIVIL REVISION PETITION

IN THE HIGH COURT OF JUDICATURE: ANDHRA PRADESH: AT HYDERABAD

CIVIL APPELLATE JURISDICTION

CIVIL REVISION PETITION NO. 10 OF 2012

CAUSE TITLE

BETWEEN

Subash,

Aged 25 years

Doctor

128, VP Street, Tirupati……………………………………PETITIONER/DEFENDANT

AND

LABZ LIMITED

33, Appar Street, Tirupati

Represented by its Company Secretary Mr. Wow.........RESPONDENT/PLAINTIFF

The ADDRESS FOR SERVICE of all notices, process, summons, etc... on the above named PETITIONER is that of their Counsel M/s. Axe, Advocates, High Court of Hyderabad.

The above named PETITIONER humbly present this MEMORANDUM OF GROUNDS OF CIVIL REVISION PETITION to this HON'BLE COURT against the Order dated 25th day of February 2012 passed in O.S. No. 9 of 2012 on the file of Senior Civil Judge Mr. Yashwa, Hyderabad for the following:

GROUNDS

1. The orders passed by the lower court are contrary to law and liable to be set aside.
2. The lower court OUGHT TO HAVE allowed the PETITIONER to cross examine Mr. Yes, as he is crucial and important witness.
3. The lower court OUGHT TO HAVE....
4. The lower court FAILED TO HONOUR the principles of natural justice. Right to cross examination is one such principle.
5. The lower court FAILED TO FOLLOW the well established principle that justice should not only be done but it must also appear to have been done.

It is therefore PRAYED that this HON'BLE COURT may be pleased to SET ASIDE the order dated 25th day of February 2012 passed in O.S. No. 9 of 2012 PENDING and ALLOW the PETITIONER to cross examine Mr. Yes and pass such other ORDER or orders as this HON'BLE COURT may deem fit and proper in the circumstances of the case.

Place **COUNSEL FOR THE PETITIONER**

Date

WRITS

Article 32 and 226 of Constitution of India CONFERS writ jurisdiction on Supreme Court (for Fundamental Rights & others under Constitution) and High Court (for Fundamental Rights & any other purpose) respectively. Any interim order (for instance, stay of a G.O or cancellation of license pending disposal of the main petition) shall be through a Writ Miscellaneous Petition (W.M.P).

Writ is an INSTRUMENT or ORDER of the Court by which the Court DIRECTS an individual or official or authority TO DO an Act or ABSTINENCE.

1. **CERTIORARI** – "WE CERTIFY" [ONLY after decision]

(This is to CHALLENGE the interim/final ILLEGAL order of a Court/Tribunal.)

By High Court to Inferior Court/Tribunal/Legal Authority;

Grounds – Want to exercise / exercise EXCESS of Jurisdiction; or violation of procedure or disregard to principles of NATURAL JUSTICE.

SAMPLE WRIT PETITION

IN THE HIGH COURT OF JUDICATURE OF MAHARASHTRA AT MUMBAI

(Writ Petition) W.P. No. 48888 OF 2012

BETWEEN

CAUSE TITLE

Labz Limited

Elipinston,

Mumbai.

Represented by its Managing Director...**PETITIONER**

AND

Superintendent of Customs & Central Excise, Parel

Additional Commissioner of Customs & Central Excise, Parel

Commissioner of Customs & Excise, Parel ....**RESPONDENTS**

PETITION UNDER ARTICLE 226 OF CONSTITUTION OF INDIA

AFFIDAVIT OF VIJAY TEMBE

I, Vijay Tembe, S/o. Shankar Tembe, HINDU, aged 25, residing at No.5, Parle Lane, Elipinston, Mumbai – 400009 do SOLEMNLY and SINCERELY affirm and state as follows:

1. I state that I am the Managing Director of the Company herein situated at Mumbai.
2. It is submitted that PETITIONER has An SEZ at Navi Mumbai engaged in farming and hatching of prawns.
3. I state that PETITIONER is registered under Central Excise Act and is approved by Ministry of Commerce & Industry for the said purpose.
4. I state that the FIRST RESPONDENT on inspection of goods imported without payment of duty on 15th August 2012 were found missing and a show cause notice was issued to PETITIONER demanding amount of Rs. 10 crores of Central Excise & Customs Duty on 20th August 2012.
5. I stated that the PETITIONER has submitted an elaborated reply to the said show cause notice by a letter dated 25th August 2012.
6. I state that without taking into consideration the reply to show cause notice, the SECOND RESPONDENT has passed orders confirming demand made in show cause notice and also passed an order imposing penalty under Central Excise & Customs rules.
7. Aggrieved by the orders of the SECOND RESPONDENT the PETITIONER filed an appeal before the THIRD RESPONDENT which was dismissed without taking into consideration the dispensation of duty by an order dated 30th August 2012.
8. I state that the learned Commissioner neither gave an opportunity of being heard NOR had applied his mind before passing the said order sought to be quashed by this petition.

I humbly submit that the **HON'BLE COURT** may be pleased to issue a WRIT OF CERTIORARI or any other appropriate writ or order or direction QUASHING the order no. 10 of 2012 dated 30th August 2012 and pass such other order or orders as this **HON'BLE COURT** may DEEM fit and proper in the circumstance of the case.

ATTESTATION **DEPONENT**

Verification Statement

I, Vijay Tembe, Managing Director, S/o. Shankar Tembe of the PETITIONER acquainted with the facts do hereby verify and state that the CONTENTS of the AFFIDAVIT filed in support of the WRIT PETITION are true to my personal knowledge, those of points 1 to 5 & 7 are facts true to MY KNOWLEDGE based on information and those are true to my knowledge based on records and believed to be correct and those of point 6 is based on LEGAL ADVICE believed to be CORRECT.

VERIFIED AT MUMBAI on this 15th day of July 2012.

ADVOCATE **DEPONENT**

MEMORANDUM OF WRIT PETITION
(SPECIAL ORIGINAL JURISDICTION)
UNDER ARTICLE 226 OF THE CONSTITUTION OF INDIA
IN THE COURT OF JUDICATURE OF TAMILNADU AT CHENNAI
W.P. NO. 59999 OF 2012

BETWEEN

Labz Limited

Elipinston,

Mumbai.

Represented by its Managing Director...**PETITIONER**

AND

1. Superintend of Customs & Central Excise, Parle
2. Additional Commissioner of Customs & Central Excise, Parle
3. Commissioner of Customs & Excise, Parel ....**RESPONDENTS**

Address for service on the above named PETITIONERS is that of their Counsel M/s. Axe, Advocates, High Court of Mumbai.

NOTE: The following Prayer lines differs in case of writ petition viz. Certiorari, prohibition, mandamus, quo warranto and habeous corpus.

FOR THE REASONS CONTAINED IN THE ACCOMPANYING AFFIDAVIT, the PETITIONER prays that **HON'BLE COURT** may be pleased to issue a **WRIT OF CERTIORARI** or any other appropriate writ or order or direction QUASHING the order no. 10 of 2012 dated 30th August 2012 and pass such other order or orders as this **HON'BLE COURT** may DEEM fit and proper in the circumstance of the case.

Place: Mumbai **COUNSEL FOR PETITIONER**
Date:

CERTIFICATE

To,
The Registrar General
The Hon'ble Madras High Court
Chennai - 600003

The Present Petition is filed to issue a WRIT OF CERTIORARI quashing the order no. 10 of 2012 dated 30th August 2012 (a very brief note why this writ petition is filed).

Therefore this WRIT PETITION is filed for which this Court has Jurisdiction and therefore be placed before the concerned bench as per High Court Rules.

Dated this day of . 2012

(signed)
PETITIONER
In Person.

GENERAL CONTENT OF WRIT PETITION:
Every filing papers in a Writ Petition shall have a CAUSE TITLE for the reference.

INDEX
Sr.NO. DATE PARTICULARS PAGE NO.

1. CAUSE TITLE
2. SYNOPSIS
3. POINTS, AUTHORITIES & ACTS
4. THE PETITION
5. VERIFICATION
6. MEMORANDUM OF APPEARANCE (called Power of Attorney or Vakalatnama)
7. MEMORANDUM OF REGISTERED ADDRESS
8. LIST OF DOCUMENTS
9. EXHIBIT 'A'
10. EXHIBIT 'B'
11. EXHIBIT 'C'
12. EXHIBIT 'D'
13. EXHIBIT 'E'
14. EXHIBIT 'F'
15. AFFIDAVIT IN SUPPORT OF EVIDENCE.
16. CERTIFICATE

(This is the first page of the Petition).
The LAST PAGE of the Petition is called the Docket.

FORMAT OF WRIT PETITION:
{CAUSE TITLE}

To

Hon'ble The Chief Justice of India and His Lordship's companion Justices of the Supreme Court of India. The Humble petition of the Petitioner abovenamed,

MOST RESPECTFULLY SHOWETH:

1. Facts of the case

2. Question(s) of Law

3. Grounds

4. Averment:-

That the present petitioner has not filed any other petition in any High Court or the Supreme Court of India on the subject matter of the present petition.

PRAYER
{AS SPECIFIC TO THE WRIT}
GENERAL POINTS AS TO WRIT PETITITON:

1. In every Writ Petition, if it involves any agency of the State Government, than the Chief Secretary of respective State Government must be made as one of the Respondents. If the matter involves any Central Government public Authority, then Union of India (Government of India) must be made as one of the Respondents.
2. Petition has to be made on ledger paper (green colored foolscap sized) in TWO sets.
3. Judicial Stamp fee is to be affixed for Rs.250/- for petition & Judicial Stamp fee of Rs.5/- to be affixed on Affidavit.
4. All Exhibits (attachments) on both sets are to be put stamp of "True copy" (at the bottom on the last page of every exhibit) and to be signed by the Petitioner who is going for Affirmation / Notarized.

2. **PROHIBITION – ON TAKING UP THE MATTER**
(This is when grievance is against any Government / Statutory / Municipal authority / any public authority / public officer TO enforce their legal obligations)

It commands Legal Authority to REFRAIN from doing something (BEFORE the decision is passed).

It is an appropriate writ 'to RESTRAIN a Tribunal which THREATENS to assume or assumes a jurisdiction NOT vested in it, SO LONG AS there is something in the proceedings LEFT TO PROHIBIT.'

Note: the following PRAYER lines differs in case of writ petition viz. certiorari, prohibition, mandamus, quo warranto and habeous corpus.

"FOR THE REASONS CONTAINED IN THE ACCOMPANYING AFFIDAVIT, it is most respectfully prayed that a writ direction or order in the nature of prohibition be issued RESTRAINING THE RESPONDENT FROM PROCEEDING TO TAKE FURTHER ACTION AGAINST THE PETITIONER IN THE APPEAL PENDING BEFORE RESPONDENT and also in accordance with cOnstitUtiOn Of india and pass such other Order or Orders as this HON'BLE COURT may deem fit and proper in the circumstances of the case."

3. MANDAMUS – "WE COMMAND"

(This is to seek compensation, for the INACTION of the Public authority / Police officer has resulted in frustration / deprivation of "life and liberty" of any person)

It is also known as 'Writ of Justice'. It will NOT be issued when ALTERNATE remedy by way of appeal or any other remedy under any other statute is available.

- A Judicial remedy;
- In the form of an ORDER from superior court to Government or Court or Corporation or Public authority [all administrative actions];
- Order to DO/FORBEAR from doing some specific ACT;
- Such ACT which the body is OBLIGED to do/refrain from doing;
- In the nature of Public Duty.

The LOCUS STANDI (who can file a petition) is on the petitioner to PROVE that he has a right to ENFORCE public duty in his FAVOUR.

Note: the following PRAYER lines differs in case of writ petition viz. certiorari, prohibition, mandamus, quo warranto and habeous corpus.

"FOR THE REASONS STATED IN THE ACCOMPANYING AFFIDAVIT, it is prayed that this HON'BLE COURT may be pleased to issue a WRIT OF MANDAMUS or any other appropriate writ or order or direction to the RESPONDENT to ABSORB the petitioner as a regular employee in the office of SECOND RESPONDENT in accordance with the notification issued by the FIRST RESPONDENT (Government) dated 27th August 2012 and also in accordance with CONSTITUTION OF INDIA and pass such other Order or Orders as this HON'BLE COURT may deem fit and proper in the circumstances of the case."

4. QUO WARRANTO – holding office under "WHAT AUTHORITY"

(This is for REMOVAL of Public Officer holding public office without authority)

- There should a PUBLIC OFFICE;
- The person should HOLD the same WITHOUT Legal Authority;
- INQUIRY as to whether the appointment as per law.

A petition may lie against the Speaker or Chairman or the Parliament of State Legislatures or any other statutory or local bodies. If the opposite party fails to support his claim, he will be OUSTED (vacated) from the office, and may be ordered to pay fine and costs of the petition.

Note: the following PRAYER lines differs in case of writ petition viz. certiorari, prohibition, mandamus, quo warranto and habeous corpus.

"FOR THE REASONS CONTAINED IN THE ACCOMPANYING AFFIDAVIT .....IS NOT ENTITLED TO HOLD OFFICE OF....AND TO DIRECT HIM NOT TO EXERCISE OR USE THE POSERES, DUITIES, PRIVILEGES, ETC... IN RESPECT OF THE SAID OFFICE..."

5. HABEAS CORPUS – "PRODUCE THE BODY"

(This is to seek immediate release of the person ILLEGALLY arrested.)

It is also called 'Freedom Writ'. It is a writ of RIGHT, not discretionary like other writs.

An effective means of IMMEDIATE RELEASE from unlawful DETENTION (whether in prison or in control & custody);

- When confinement is WITHOUT legal jurisdiction;
- High Court order to BRING such person before court;
- Court TO KNOW the grounds for confinement.

The locus standi is on the DETAINED PERSON or by his friends/relatives on his behalf.

Note: the following PRAYER lines differs in case of writ petition viz. certiorari, prohibition, mandamus, quo warranto and habeous corpus.

"FOR THE REASONS STATED IN THE ACCOMPANYING AFFIDAVIT, it is prayed that this HON'BLE COURT may be pleased to issue a WRIT OF HABEAS CORPUS or any other appropriate writ or order or direction to the RESPONDENT to FORTHWITH (immediately) set the PETITIONER at LIBERTY who has been illegally DETAINED by the RESPONDENTS and pass such other Order or Orders as this HON'BLE COURT may deem fit and proper in the circumstances of the case."

Explain the following:
(a) Habeas corpus
(b) Mandamus. (2010 – June)

As a company Secretary, it is essential to be well versed with the said aspects and equip oneself to act as the general counsel for the clients. The object of the pleading is twofold. First is to afford the other side intimation regarding the particular facts of the case so that they may be met by the other side. Second is to enable the court to determine what really the issue between the parties is. Furthermore it is mandated that all the material particulars must be provided so that the other party knows fully well what all it has to counter. The most important particulars of a plaint are the parties to the suit, the cause of action, the jurisdiction of the court, valuation of the suit and any limitations that might be there apart from the relief sought. Here again, 400 repeated reading, will only serve the purpose.

Composition or compounding provisions are dealt under various laws including Companies Act, SEBI, Criminal Procedure Code and under Foreign Exchange Management Act.

Composition Of Offences

COMPOUNDING under Section 621A of Companies Act, 1956

COMPOUNDING: It means,

- the defaulting person agrees to pay a sum [UPTO Max Fine]
- to credit of Government and
- Government agrees NOT to institute prosecution or to withdraw the prosecution.

On Compounding, the person will not be convicted by RoC, shareholder or any person authorized by Central Government and in cases where prosecutions were instituted, the company or its officer in relation shall be DISCHARGED for the compounded offence. Further compounding does not amount to conviction.

ROC FILING FEES – According to Section 611 of Companies Act, 1956, fees in Schedule X to be paid and in case of delayed filing, an additional fee NOT exceeding 10 times the said fees may be levied by Registrar of Companies. Kindly note, the Compounding SUM shall not exceed the filing fees together with additional filing fee, if any.

COMPOUNDABLE OFFENCES: The following offences (penal actions) can be compounded. The imposition of,

- Fine only
- Fine or Imprisonment or both.

NON-COMPOUNDABLE OFFENCES: The following offences (penal actions) cannot be compounded. The imposition of,

- Imprisonment only
- Fine and Imprisonment.

COMPOUNDING AUTHORITY: A joint application by the defaulting person (accused) & complainant to be made to RoC (e-form 61) along with Board resolution, Power of attorney (Form 5 – CLB Regulations), Affidavit, General profile of the company, Facts of case, Compliance made, Prayer for compounding, & detailed application as per CLB Regulations, which shall be forwarded accordingly,

- Offences punishable with fine up to Rs. 50,000/- be compounded with RD.
- All other prescribed offences including fine more than Rs. 50,000/- be compounded with CLB.

COMPOUNDING OF OFFENCES:

- Similar Offences cannot be compounded within 3 years of first compounding;
- Different Offences may be compoundable.

COMPOUNDING ORDER:

- To file or register with such return, account or other document with fees to RoC in e-Form 21 within 7 days of Compounding Order.
- Intimation by RoC to Court if offence is compounded pending prosecution.

Any officer or employee, who fails to comply the same, shall be punishable with imprisonment UPTO 6 months or find UPTO Rs. 50,000/- or both.

INSTANCES OF NON-COMPOUNDABLE OFFENCES:
Sections 58A, 58AA, 209A, 269, 293A and 446A, 540, 541, 628, 629, etc...

In the case of *Amadhi Investments Ltd*, it was held even the Board of Directors of the company can file compounding application, in case the directors on whom the Show Cause Notice (SCN) is issued by RoC has resigned the company.

COMPOUNDING UNDER FEMA

[Section 15 of FEMA read with Foreign Exchange (Compounding Proceedings) Rules, 2000]

Any contravention can be compounded under FEMA if person who has committed contravention, makes an application. Compounding will be done within 180 days by officers authorized by Central Government.

COMPOUNDABLE OFFENCE

- There should be a civil offence imposing fine only OR imprisonment or fine
- Such offence may be pending before Adjudicating Authority
- Such offence should not have been compounded in last 3 years

NON-COMPOUNDABLE OFFENCE

- When adjudication is complete
- When appeal against adjudication is filed
- Where contraventions are NOT quantifiable
- Where requisite approvals are not obtained from Government/Statutory authority
- Offence had been compounded in last 3 years

COMPOUNDING AUTHORITY

Officer of Enforcement Directorate (not below the rank of Deputy Director)	For offence u/s. 3(a) of FEMA dealing with hawala transactions
Officer of RBI (not below the rank of AGM)	For contravention of all other Sections, provisions, rules, regulations, notifications, directions issued under FEMA

COMPOUNDING PROCEDURE

1. Application in a prescribed form along with the nature of contravention & its reasons, undertaking that they are not under investigation of any agency such as Enforcement Directorate, CBI, etc., a copy of the Memorandum of Association and latest audited balance sheet to RBI, Mumbai (certain cases like DELAY in reporting inward remittance, filing FC-GPR & issue of shares beyond 180 days are delegated to Regional offices of RBI).
2. Application fees is Rs. 5,000/-
3. When Compounding Authority called for additional information or document, it shall be submitted within 30 days or as prescribed.

4. Compounding Authority will hear the applicant
5. Compounding order will be passed within 180 days of application
6. Compounding sum shall be paid within 15 days of the order
7. If complaint was filed already, then further proceedings before Adjudicating Authority will be dropped on paying the Compounding Sum.
8. The Compounded offence cannot be compounded within 3 years (i.e.) the compounding order is applicable for 3 years and thereafter, such offence will be deemed as fresh contravention to be compounded.
9. The following details shall be provided along with the application for compounding:
   - FOR FDI Violations: Applicant NAME, Incorporation DATE & PARTICULARS of foreign entity with date stamped COPIES of all FIRC's & FC-GPR's till date from incorporation.
   - For ECB Violations: Applicant NAME, Incorporation DATE & PARTICULARS of foreign lender, terms of loan agreement, COPIES of all LRN, ECB-2 returns & list of violations.
   - For ODI Violations: Applicant NAME, Incorporation DATE & PARTICULARS of overseas entity, details of investment & remittances, COPIES of UIN's, Share certificates & APR's filed till date.
   - For Violations on Liaison/Branch Offices in India: Applicant NAME, Incorporation DATE & PARTICULARS of incomes & expenses, COPIES of approvals & Annual activity certificates.

FEMA PENALTY:
Section 13 of FEMA imposes penalty UPTO thrice the SUM contravened, if quantifiable or UPTO Rs. 2,00,000/-

SEBI ACT – CONSENT/COMPOUNDING

CONSENT ORDER	COMPOUNDING
Sec 15T of SEBI Act	Sec 24A of SEBI Act
For administrative / civil proceedings	For criminal prosecutions; NOT being an offence punishable with imprisonment only OR imprisonment & fine
BY SEBI	BY SAT
Application at any stage where probable cause of violation has been found	Application before / after institution of proceedings
To appropriate sanction, remedy & deterrence WITHOUT resorting to litigation, lengthy proceedings & consequential delays	To avoid lengthy process, which would save cost, time, mental, agony, etc…in return for payment of compounding charges

Both the consent and compounding matters are to be placed before a High Powered Advisory Committee (HPAC) for appropriate recommendations.

CONSENT ORDER:
Consent orders can be passed either,

- Admitting the guilt
- Without admitting or denying guilt.

CONSENT PROCEDURE:
1. The application for Proposal of Settlement to be made in prescribed form with prescribed fees to SEBI.

2. The proposal will be examined by high powered committee headed by a retired High Court judge and two other external experts.
3. The committee may ask the party to revise the consent terms.
4. The committee will submit its views/recommendations before Competent Authority where proceedings are pending.
5. If the matter is pending with SAT/Court, the draft consent terms recommended by Committee and approved by Competent Authority will be filed with SAT/Court for its determination. In such case, the party is also liable to pay legal expenses incurred by SEBI.
6. The amount payable by the party will be decided depending upon the facts and circumstances of the case, gravity of alleged violation, interest of investors and the securities market and deterrent affect.
7. The consent order will be published through press release and would be put up on SEBI website.
8. Where a matter is pending before SAT/Court, the same consent process will be undertaken and the draft consent terms

Recommended will be filed before the SAT/Court to enable it to pass orders as it deems fit with the consent terms.

COMPOUNDING:

The procedure is almost similar to procedure for consent order, as given above. However, the authority here is Securities Appellate Tribunal (SAT). The orders of SEBI or of Adjudicating Officers are APPEALABLE ORDERS whereas the orders passed with the consent of both the parties (CONSENT ORDERS) are NOT an APPEALABLE ORDER.

Kindly note, there are no provisions in SEBI Act that similar offence cannot be compounded within 3 years unlike Companies Act and FEMA.

The factors which may be taken into account by SAT/Court for the purpose of compounding include,

1. Whether violation is intentional or of circumstances beyond control
2. Party conduct during investigation and history of non-compliance
3. Gravity of charge or is it a violation of technical nature
4. Consideration of Investors harm vis-à-vis Parties gain
5. Compliance schedule proposed by the party.

Failure to obey consent orders would invite appropriate action, including for VIOLATING SEBI orders, besides REVIVAL of the pending action. In this context any proceeding which had been kept in ABEYANCE pending the consent process will BEGIN from such stage at which it was SUSPENDED.

Similarly, if the consent/compounding proposal is NOT acceptable to the high-powered Committee, then it shall inform the parties to WITHDRAW the offer for settlement. In such cases, SEBI and the Entity will be free to resort to legal recourse as may be available to them under law and the proceedings under ABEYANCE will BEGIN from such stage at which it was SUSPENDED.

COMPOUNDING UNDER CRIMINAL PROCEDURE CODE, 1973

Section 320 of Criminal Procedure Code, 1973 provides for compounding of various offences under Indian Penal Code which is of PRIVATE nature & relatively not quite serious and some others as compoundable only with the permission of court to prevent or cure prosecution in such a manner that it is just, fair, and reasonable to both parties. There are certain offences which can be compounded only WITH & WITHOUT the PERMISSION of the Court. On Compounding, the accused will stand ACQUITTED (verdict of NOT GUILTY).

INTERESTING DATA ON SEBI CONSENT ORDERS

The following are the settlement actions agreed by the companies/intermediaries under Consent orders:

- PAID SETTLEMENT AMOUNT
- AGREED VOLUNTARILY NOT TO BUY/SELL/ DEAL IN SECURITIES/ SPECIFIED SCRIPS DIRECTLY/INDIRECTLY
- AGREED VOLUNTARILY TO BE SUSPENDED FROM REGISTRATION AS STOCK BROKER
- AGREED VOLUNTARILY NOT TO BE ASSOCIATED WITH /ACCESSING CAPITAL MARKET /INTERMEDIARIES
- DIRECTED NOT TO INVEST IN LISTED SECURITIES (OTHER THAN MUTUAL FUND)
- AGREED VOLUNTARILY NOT TO BUY/SELL/ DEAL IN SECURITIES/ SPECIFIED SCRIPS OR ACCESS SECURITIES MARKET DIRECTLY/INDIRECTLY IN PROPRIETARY ACCOUNT
- AGREED VOLUNTARILY NOT TO HOLD DIRECTORSHIP IN ANY LISTED COMPANY
- DIRECTED TO IMPLEMENT A POLICY OF ROTATION OF STATUTORY AUDITORS
- AGREED VOLUNTARILY NOT TO REGISTER NEW CLIENTS FOR A PERIOD OF 45 DAYS
- AGREED VOLUNTARILY TO SPEND A SUM OF RS.1 CRORE ON INVESTOR EDUCATION AND AWARENESS PROGRAMME AND ON DEVELOPMENT OF METERIALS FOCUSING ON MAKING INVESTORS MORE AWARE OF THEIR RIGHTS IN CONNECTION WITH INTERNET BASED TRADING IN SECURITIES MARKET WITHIN 6 MONTHS FROM DATE OF RECEIPT OF THIS CONSENT ORDER
- AGREED VOLUNTARILY FOR LOCK-IN OF ONE YEAR ON FIVE LAC SHARES ALLOTTED PURSUANT TO CONVERSION OF WARRANTS ALLOTTED ON PREFERENTIAL BASIS
- AGREED VOLUNTARILY NOT TO ACTIVATE CERTIFICATE OF REGISTRATION AS STOCK BROKER

As per www.watchoutinvestors.com, these are the statistics as on date & increasing at a faster pace:

SNAPSHOT OF CONSENT ORDERS	
NO.OF CONSENT ORDERS PASSED	924
FIRST CONSENT ORDER PASSED ON	30/10/2007
TOTAL NO.OF UNIQUE ENTITIES/PERSONS	1371
TOTAL CONSENT ORDER AMOUNT (RS.)	204,66,02,562
HIGHEST CONSENT ORDER AMOUNT (RS.)	50,00,00,000
LOWEST CONSENT ORDER AMOUNT (RS.)	2,000

Compounding under FCRA, 2010

Section 41 of Foreign Contribution Regulation Act (FCRA), 2010 read with Rule 21 of FCRR deals with composition of offences by Trusts & Non Profit organisations. The provisions are similar to Companies Act. Same offence cannot be compounded within 3 years of the first offence. Secretary, Ministry of Home Affairs, New Delhi being the Compounding Authority; an application on a plain paper as accompanied by a fee of Rs.1000/- (One Thousand only) in the form of a DD/Cheque payable to be made to the Ministry of Home Affairs for composition of offences.

The Act requires an individual or association or its officer or any other employee to obtain permission or file or register with, or deliver or send to, the Central Government or any prescribed authority any return, account or other document, may, direct, by order, if he or it thinks fit to do so, any individual or association or its officer or other employee to file or register with, such return, account or other document within such time as may be specified in the order.

1. What is 'compounding of offences'? Who are vested with such powers under the Companies Act, 1956? What amount of fines can be levied against the Companies? (2007 – December)
2. List out any eight situations in which the drawal of foreign exchange is prohibited under the Foreign Exchange Management (Current Account Transactions) Rules, 2000. (2008 – December)
3. What is 'compounding of offences'? How does compounding of offences take place under the Code of Criminal Procedure, 1973? (2009 – June)
4. What is meant by a 'consent order'? What remedies are available with the Securities and Exchange Board of India if the consent order is violated by a party? 2009 – June)
5. What is 'compounding of offences'? How does compounding of offences take place under the Securities and Exchange Board of India Act, 1992? (2009 – December)
6. What is meaning of the term 'compounding'? What factors are to be taken into consideration for the purpose of compounding of offences under the respective statutes? (2010 – June)
7. Consent order – Explain. (2010 – December)
8. Mention the orders against which no appeal lies to the Securities Appellate Tribunal (SAT) 2009 – December)
9. What are the statutory provisions for appeals to the Securities Appellate Tribunal (SAT) under the Securities and Exchange Board of India Act, 1992? (2010 – June)

Thus about compounding under various Acts. Governance can be built over a period of time by initiatives such as this, thus enforcing the compliances in future.

The provisions of this chapter shall be kept in mind while drafting agreements, especially trade related agreements. Further, the mergers provision of this chapter shall also be read along with the provisions in corporate restructuring.

Competition Act, 2002

OBJECTIVES of Competition Act – considering the economic development,

↳ To prevent adverse effect on competition;

↳ To promote & sustain competition;

↳ To protect interest of consumers;

↳ To ensure freedom of trade carried on by other participants in Indian market;

↳ incidental & connected matters;

and are achieved through appointing Competition Commission of India [CCI].

Except for Combinations (i.e.) Mergers, Amalgamations, Acquisitions & Takeovers in Competition Act, 2002, all other provisions are notified. Hence, as a Company Secretary it is very essential to keep in mind the provisions of the Act before drafting any agreement.

4 ANCHORS OF COMPETITION ACT

The anchors can be classified as Behaviour-oriented (like ACA & AD) which deals with the past agreements between businesses and Structure-oriented (like MAAT) which deals with the future. The behavioural anchors are prohibited whereas structural anchors are regulated. Anti-competitive agreements are similar to Restrictive Trade Practices under MRTP whereas abuse of dominance is similar to Monopolistic Trade Practice.

ACA | **AD** | **MAAT** | **CA**

↳ Prohibition of Anti-Competitive Agreements [ACA]
↳ Prohibition of Abuse of Dominance position [AD]
↳ Regulation of Combination – Mergers & Amalgamations, Acquisitions & Takeovers [MAAT]
↳ Competition Advocacy [CA].

ANTI-COMPETITIVE AGREEMENTS [ACA] – The First Anchor

ACA + AAA = Anti-competitive [Sec 3]

An 'agreement' INCLUDES any arrangement, understanding / concerted action entered into between parties. It need not be, in writing, or formal or intended to be enforceable in law.

Agreement ***by*** enterprise / association of enterprises OR person / association of persons ***in respect of*** production / supply / distribution / storage / control of goods / provision of services, ***which is*** likely to cause Adverse Appreciable Affect [**AAA**] on competition *within* India, is VOID.

ACA

On Presumption Basis	On Affecting Competition
i.e, Rule of Law	i.e, Rule of Reasons
Applicable for Horizontal Agreements, where burden on Defendant to prove.	Applicable for Vertical Agreements, where burden on Defendant to prove.
INCLUDES the following, • Determining Trade prices; • Limits / controls markets / investments, services; • Share Maket / Services; • Bid Rigging / Collusive Bid.	INCLUDES the following, • Tie-in arrangement; • Exclusive Supply / Distribution Agreement; • Refusal to deal; • Resale Price Maintenance [RPM].
Effect: such agreements are actionable per se.	Effect: agreements are actionable only if it creates AAA on competition.

Notes:

↳ Horizontal Agreements are agreements between sellers.

↳ Vertical Agreements are agreements between sellers & buyers.

↳ In MRTP, only the restrictive clauses are VOID, here the whole agreement stands void.

NOT ANTI-COMPETITIVE: [ACA – Exemptions]

↳ Agreements permitted by Laws, like Intellectual Property Laws;

↳ Right for exclusive export.

ABUSE OF DOMINANCE [AD] – The Second Anchor

AD + AAA = Anti-competitive

Agreement **by** enterprise / group **abusing** its 'dominant position' is prohibited.

Dominant Position: 'position of strength' in relevant market, in India, enabling,

_ to operate independently of prevailing competitive forces;

_ affect, in its favour, the competitor / consumer / relevant market / relevant product / relevant geographic market, as per CCI.

Abuse can be,

↳ Exploitative – i.e., as a result of practice, consumers are exploited; or

↳ Exclusionary – i.e., as a result of practice, other competitors are excluded.

Abuse of dominance can be,

↳ Unfair / discriminatory condition in purchase / sale of goods / services [like, full-line forcing].

↳ Unfair / discriminatory price* in purchase / sale of goods / services [not includes discriminatory condition / price].

↳ Limiting / restricting production of goods/provision of services.

↳ Limiting / restricting technical or scientific development relating to goods, services to the prejudice of consumers.

↳ Using dominant position in order to enter another market.

↳ Indulgences in any practices resulting in denial of market access.

↳ Imposing supplementary obligations in contract which have no connection with the subject of such contracts.

REGULATION OF COMBINATIONS [MAAT] – The Third Anchor [Sec. 6]

Mergers, Amalgamations, Acquisitions & Takeovers (MAAT) are covered.

↳ Acquisition of Enterprise(-s) by person(-s) or

↳ Merger / amalgamation of enterprises.

MAAT + AAA = Anti-competitive

Enterprise: [Sec. 2(h)]

Enterprise means a person or a department of the Government, who or which is,

_ engaged in any activity, relating to production, control of goods or articles or provision of services, of any kind, or

_ in investment, or in the business of acquiring, holding, underwriting or dealing with shares, debentures or other securities

_ whether such unit or division or subsidiary is located at the same place where the enterprise is located or at different place(s).

BUT DOES NOT INCLUDE activities related to sovereign functions of Government or activities by Government department dealing with atomic energy, currency, defence and space.

Group: two or more enterprise directly or indirectly in a position to,

_ exercise 26% or more voting rights in other; or

_ appoint more than 50% of board of directors in other; or

_ control the management or affairs of other.

The following Schedule-I items will be exempted from filing with CCI as mentioned in the Chart below:

1. Acquisition entitling UPTO 25% or SUBSTANTIAL assets/business operations for investment purpose or in ordinary course of business, not leading to control.
2. Acquisition where acquirer already has 50% & there is NO change from joint control to SOLE control.
3. An acquisition of assets NOT directly related to the business activity of acquirer or made as an INVESTMENT or in the ordinary course of business, NOT leading to control of the Target enterprise except where the assets being acquired represent SUBSTANTIAL BUSINESS OPERATIONS in a particular location or product or service of the enterprise, of which assets are being acquired, irrespective of whether it is of a separate legal entity or not.
4. Amended or renewed tender offer where notice has been filed by the party making the offer prior to such amendment or renewal of offer. Provided that prior intimation of such change has been duly made;
5. Acquisition of stock-in-trade, raw materials, stores and spares in the ordinary course of business;
6. Acquisition of shares or voting rights pursuant to a bonus issue or stock-splits or consolidation of face value of shares or subscription to rights issue (to extent of entitlement), not leading to acquisition of control;
7. Acquisition of shares or voting rights by a securities underwriter or a registered stock broker on behalf of clients, in the ordinary course of their respective businesses;
8. Acquisition of control, shares, voting rights or assets by one person or enterprise of another person or enterprise within the same group;
9. A merger or amalgamation involving a holding company and its WoS belonging to the same group and/ or mergers or amalgamations involving WoS belonging to the same group.
10. Acquisition of current assets (i.e. interest accrued on investments, stores and spare parts, loose tools, stock-in-trade, works-in-progress, sundry debtors, cash balance on hand and bank balance) in the ordinary course of business;
11. Combinations taking place entirely outside India with insignificant local nexus and effect on markets in India

Note:

1. Any ENTERPRISE being acquired has assets UPTO Rs.250 crores or turnover UPTO Rs.750 crores is exempt from provisions of Section 5.

2. Any GROUP exercising LESS THAN 50% of voting right in other enterprise is exempt from provisions of Section 5.

3. Combination only regulated - no registration required - no prior approval – CCI will only examine whether it creates AAA on competition if it exceeds belowmentioned limits.

N	Particulars u/s.5 of Competition Act	Where	Assets	Turnover
1	↳ Acquisition [Single Acquirer] [Different Goods & Services] ↳ Acquisition of Control over an Enterprise engaged in SIMILAR / Identical goods & services DIRECTLY or INDIRECTLY ↳ Merger or Amalgamation of TWO enterprises.	In India cr-crore; mn-million bn-billion	Rs. 1500 cr	Rs. 4500 cr
		In or outside India, in aggregate	USD 750 cr including Rs. 750 cr in India	USD 2250 cr including Rs. 2250 cr in India
2	↳ Acquisition by Group [Dissimilar Goods & Services] ↳ Acquisition by a Group engaged in SIMILAR / Identical goods & services DIRECTLY or INDIRECTLY ↳ Merger or Amalgamation in a Group	In India	Rs. 6000 cr	Rs. 18000 cr
		In or Outside India, in aggregate	USD 3 bn including Rs. 750 cr in India	USD 9 bn including Rs.2250 cr in India

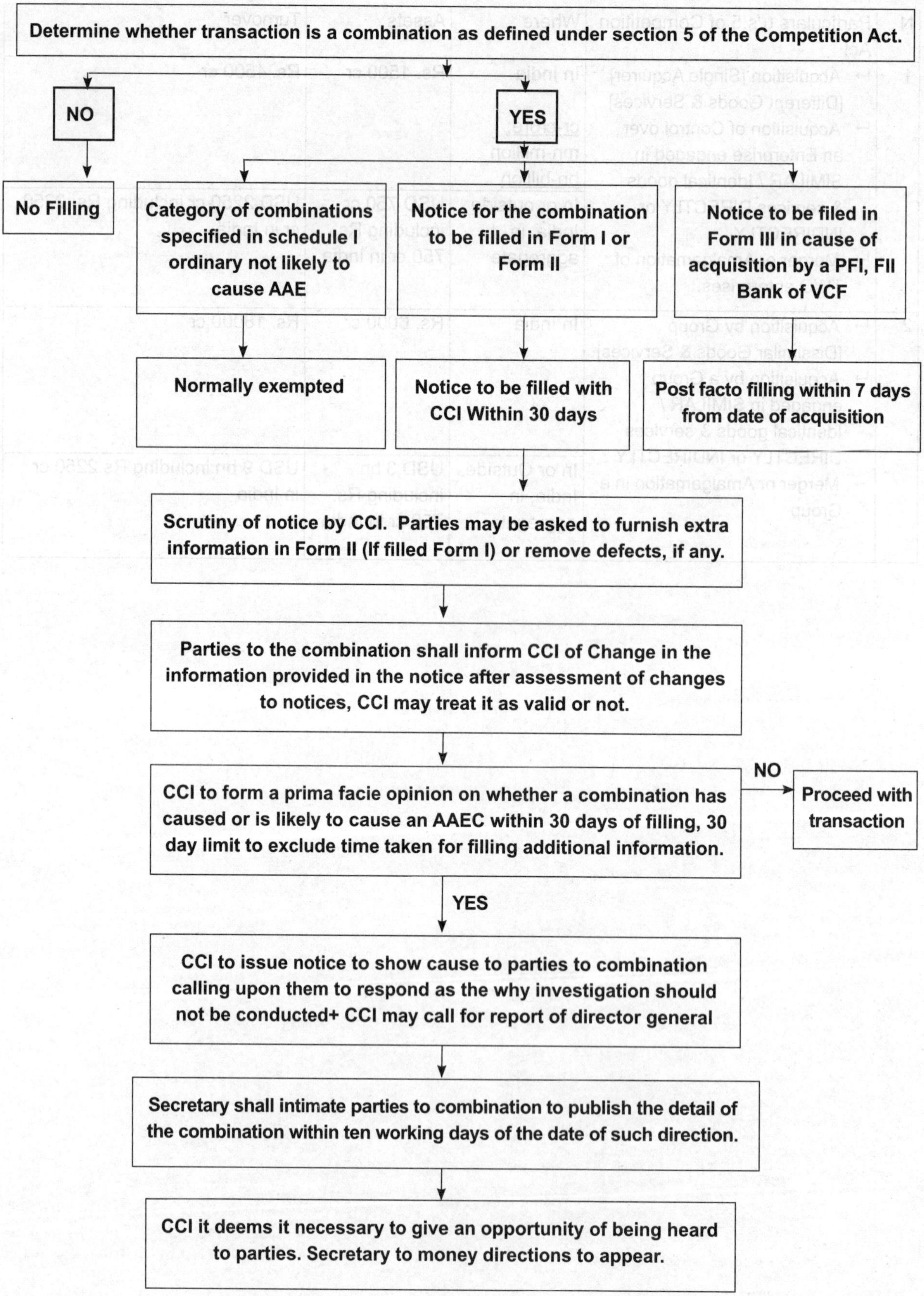
Determine whether transaction is a combination as defined under section 5 of the Competition Act.
NO
YES
No Filling
Category of combinations specified in schedule I ordinary not likely to cause AAE
Notice for the combination to be filled in Form I or Form II
Notice to be filed in Form III in cause of acquisition by a PFI, FII Bank of VCF
Normally exempted
Notice to be filled with CCI Within 30 days
Post facto filling within 7 days from date of acquisition
Scrutiny of notice by CCI. Parties may be asked to furnish extra information in Form II (If filled Form I) or remove defects, if any.
Parties to the combination shall inform CCI of Change in the information provided in the notice after assessment of changes to notices, CCI may treat it as valid or not.
CCI to form a prima facie opinion on whether a combination has caused or is likely to cause an AAEC within 30 days of filling, 30 day limit to exclude time taken for filling additional information.
NO
Proceed with transaction
YES
CCI to issue notice to show cause to parties to combination calling upon them to respond as the why investigation should not be conducted+ CCI may call for report of director general
Secretary shall intimate parties to combination to publish the detail of the combination within ten working days of the date of such direction.
CCI it deems it necessary to give an opportunity of being heard to parties. Secretary to money directions to appear.

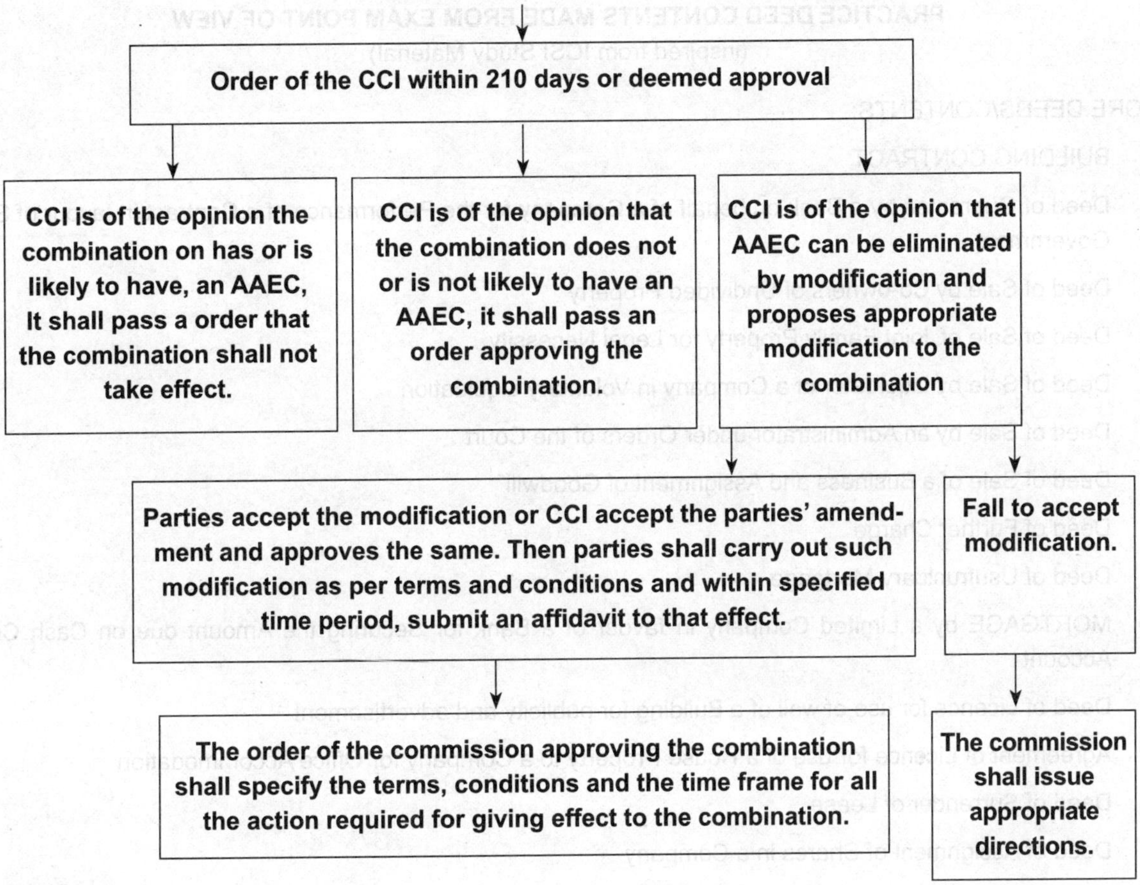

Source: http://www.nishithdesai.com

CCI - Section 19: Commission (CCI) may inquire into alleged contravention of section 3 / section 4 on

i) receipt of information from person / consumer/ trade association with fees.

ii) reference by central / state government or statutory body.

↳ **ACA** – while determining agreement has AAA on competition consider factor like creation of barrier, driving existing competition, improvements in production, consumer benefit, etc.,

↳ **AD** – whether enterprise enjoys dominant position factors into consideration-market share, size of enterprises / competitors, economic power, consumer dependence, entry barriers countervailing buying power, etc.,

↳ **MAAT** - while determining combination shall have AAA on competition factors considered.

(a) actual and potential level competition, (b) extent of barriers, (c) level of combination, (d) extent of market share, (e) possibility of business being failed, (f) effective competition likely to sustain.

Appeal can be made to Competition Appellate Tribunal (CAT) within 60 days of CCI order, thereafter to Supreme Court within 60 days of CAT order.

As Monopolies Restrictive Trade Practices Act, 1969 is repealed and Competition Act is made effective, the said provisions also shall be kept in mind while drafting agreements and the merger schemes.

PRACTICE DEED CONTENTS MADE FROM EXAM POINT OF VIEW

(inspired from ICSI Study Material)

MORE DEEDS/CONTENTS:

1. BUILDING CONTRACT
2. Deed of Guarantee by a Bank on behalf of a Company for the Performance of a Contract in favour of State Government
3. Deed of Sale by Co-owners of Undivided Property
4. Deed of Sale of Joint Family Property for Legal Necessity
5. Deed of Sale by Liquidator of a Company in Voluntary Liquidation
6. Deed of Sale by an Administrator under Orders of the Court
7. Deed of Sale of a Business and Assignment of Goodwill
8. Deed of Further Charge
9. Deed of Usufructuary Mortgage
10. MORTGAGE by a Limited Company in favour of a Bank for Securing the Amount due on Cash Credit Account
11. Deed of Licence for use of wall of a Building for publicity and advertisement
12. Agreement of Licence for use of a House Property to a Company for Office Accommodation
13. Deed of Surrender of Lease
14. Deed of Assignment of Shares in a Company
15. Deed of Assignment of Policy of Life Assurance
16. Deed extending Period of a Partnership
17. Receipt executed by Retiring Partner acknowledging to have received the amount due to him on account of his share in the Partnership Property
18. Notice to Determine Partnership at Will
19. Deed of Revocation of a Trust
20. SPECIAL POWER-OF-ATTORNEY FILED WITH THE REGISTRAR AT THE TIME OF INCORPORATION OF A COMPANY
21. Power-of-Attorney to Advocate for Court Case In the Court of etc.
22. Underwriting Contract
23. Petition for Scheme of Merger or Amalgamation
24. NOTICE OF FORFEITURE
25. A Specimen of the Letter of Offer to the Prospective Company Secretary
26. SPECIMEN FORM OF REVISION PETITION Affidavit of Creditor in proof of his debt in Proceeding for the
27. Liquidation of a Company
28. Lease Agreement with Lessor, Lessee and Bank as Financing Party
29. DRAFT LOAN AGREEMENT
30. Memorandum of Association

31. Articles of Association

32. Letter to Director for passing a resolution by circulation along with draft resolution

33. Notice of disqualification under Section 274(1)(g)

34. NOTICE FOR BOOK CLOSURE

35. Resolution approving transfer of Shares

36. Refer Company Secretarial Practice portions for more drafting under Company Laws & LLP

1. BUILDING CONTRACT

Now this AGREEMENT is reduced into writing and respective parts thereof shall be performed by the OWNER and the BUILDER in accordance with the following terms and conditions:

1. The builder will build and complete the bungalow within 6 months from the date of execution.

2. Subject to the conditions hereinafter contained, the owner will pay to the builder a sum of Rs. 1 crore as an all-inclusive rate in the following manner:

(a) Construction up to plinth level – 10% of the total contract amount.

(b) Completion of walls up to roof level – 15% of the total contract amount.

(c) Completion of roof slab of the entire structure of the bungalow – 30% of the total contract amount.

(d) Fixing of shutters of doors, windows, completion of wooden almirahs, pelmets and all other wood work – 20% of the total contract amount.

(e) Finishing of the entire construction and fixing of electrical and sanitary fittings – 15% of the total contract amount.

(f) After receipt of Completion Certificate from the Municipal authorities - Balance amount of the contract money.

3. It is expressly, agreed between the owner and the builder that in respect of the aforesaid payments and in respect of the construction of the bungalow, time is the essence of this agreement.

4. The builder will permit the owner, his representatives and his architect to have access to the works while the same are under construction and to inspect the same so as to make sure that the construction work is being done according to sanctioned plan and materials are being used as per specifications given by the architect.

5. The owner will not be entitled to take possession of the bungalow until the entire amount is paid within the time stipulated hereinabove.

6. If the owner requires any additional or extra items of work to be carried on by the builder in the bungalow, other than the above specified works, the builder should be informed by the owner in advance and the cost and/ or difference of cost for such items of work as per rates mutually agreed upon should be paid by the owner to the builder in advance.

2. Deed of Guarantee by a Bank on behalf of a Company for the

Performance of a Contract in favour of State Government

NOW THIS DEED WITNESSES AS FOLLOWS:

1. In consideration of the State of Madhya Pradesh having agreed to advance a sum of Rs. 5 crores to the Company, through the Bank, for the purpose hereinafter indicated, the bank, does hereby guarantee that in case the Company shall fail and/or neglect to supply the State, the plant, machinery and equipment of the value of Rs.20 crores in accordance with the tender, when made, the bank shall repay to the State such amount or amounts as the bank may be called upon to pay subject to the maximum limit of Rs.15 crores.

2. This guarantee of the Bank shall be effective immediately upon receipt of the sum of Rs. 5 crores from the State for and on behalf of the Company and shall continue in force until the supply of plant, machinery and equipment of the value aforesaid is fully effected.

3. The guarantee hereinbefore contained shall not be affected by any change in the constitution of the bank or of the Company nor in the event of any winding up being made against the Company.

3. Deed of Sale by Co-owners of Undivided Property

WHEREAS

1. one PQ late of, etc. who was a Hindu governed by the Dayabhaga or Bengal School of Hindu Law died on the................ day of................ intestate, leaving his surviving only two sons viz., the said AB and CD as his heirs and legal representatives under the said school.

2. The said AB and CD are in joint possession and enjoyment of the property hereinafter described as co-owners in equal shares without effecting any partition or division thereof.

3. The said AB and CD have agreed to sell the said properties free from encumbrances, to the said EF for the sum of _...............

NOW THIS DEED WITNESSES that in pursuance of the said agreement and in consideration of the sum of Rupees................, paid to the said AB and CD by the said EF at or immediately before execution of these presents the receipts whereof the said AB and CD hereby admit, acknowledge and confirm, they, the said AB and CD and each as beneficial owner of one equal undivided kinship thereof, do hereby and HEREUNDER GRANT, CONVEY, SELL, TRANSFER, ASSIGN AND ASSURE unto and to the use the said EF ALL THAT, etc. (parcel, etc., as in a conveyance); TO HAVE and TO HOLD

the same unto and to the use of the said EF, his heirs, executors, administrators, representatives and assigns absolutely and for ever.

(follow with Vendor's usual covenants as in a Sale Deed)

4. Deed of Sale of Joint Family Property for Legal Necessity

NOW THIS, INDENTURE WITNESSETH that in pursuance of the said agreement and in consideration of the sum of Rs........................... paid by the said CD to the said AB simultaneously with the execution of these presents he, the said AB doth hereby and hereunder for self and as Karta for and representing all other coparceners of the said joint family do hereby grant, sell, convey, transfer, assign and assure the said property together with all houses, buildings, fixtures etc. to the use of the said CD absolutely and forever.

(follow with Vendor's usual covenants as in a Sale Deed)

Deed of Sale by Liquidator of a Company in Voluntary Liquidation

5. Deed of Sale by Liquidator of a Company in Voluntary Liquidation

WHEREAS

1. by a special resolution passed by the shareholders at an Extraordinary General Meeting held on the 25th day of August 2013, of which notice is duly given, and it was resolved that the company be wound up voluntarily;

2. The said vendor was appointed its voluntary liquidator on 28th day of August 2013.

NOW THIS DEED OF SALE WITNESSES AND IT IS HEREBY AGREED AND DECLARED AS FOLLOWS:

That pursuant to the agreement dated...................... aforementioned and in consideration of the sum of Rs...................... paid by the purchaser before the Sub-Registrar, ... on presentation of this Deed of sale for registration thereof (the receipt whereof the vendor hereby acknowledges) the vendor hereby transfers by way of sale and conveys on behalf of the said company all those items of the property mentioned more particularly in the Schedule attached hereto, unto the said purchaser, his heirs and assigns to have and to hold the same absolutely and forever.

The powers and functions of the RECEIVER have been set out in the Section 69A of Transfer of Property Act and the Receiver is required to apply all money received by him as follows:

(i) in discharge of all rents, taxes, land revenue, rates and outgoings whatever affecting the mortgaged property;

(ii) in keeping down all annual sums or other payments, and the interest on all principals sums, having priority to the mortgage in right whereof he is Receiver;

(iii) in payment of his commission, and of the premiums on fire, life or other insurances, if any, properly payable under the mortgage deed or under this Act, and the cost of executing necessary or proper repairs directed in writing by the mortgagee;

(iv) in payment of the interest falling due under the mortgage;

(v) in or towards discharge of the principal money, if so directed in writing by the mortgagee.

6. Deed of Sale by an Administrator under Orders of the Court

WHEREAS an Administrator, Mr. Takecare is appointed by the Court for the administration of the properties of a deceased person who has made a will and probate is granted by the Court in favour of a person, Mr. Enjoy who claims the right to succession to the properties of the deceased, Mr. Happymemories.

NOW THIS DEED OF SALE WITNESSES AND IT IS HEREBY AGREED BETWEEN THE PARTIES AFOREMENTIONED AND DECLARED AS UNDER:

That in consideration of the receipt of Rs...................... (Rupees....................) paid by the purchaser to the vendor along with the tender dated......................... (the receipt whereof the vendor hereby acknowledges) and on payment by the purchaser to the vendor of the sum of Rs...................... (Rupees.......................) before the Sub-Registrar, ...at the time of presentation of this Deed of Sale for registration (the receipt whereof the vendor hereby acknowledges), the vendor hereby transfers by way of sale and conveys unto the said purchaser, all that property originally belonging to the said...................... mentioned in the item No...................... in the Schedule I attached hereto unto the purchaser, his heirs and assigns to have and to hold the same as an absolute owner

thereof for ever. The possession of the said property conveyed under this Deed has been delivered to the purchaser on the date of the presentation of this Deed for registration before the Sub-Registrar, ...together with title-deed relating to the said item No...................... with a stipulation that the vendor shall at all reasonable times allow inspection of the other documents of title, viz., PARTITION DEED between......................, father of D, and...................... dated........................

along with the deed of reconveyance by the mortgage dated………………… relating to the item No……………….. mentioned in the Schedule I attached hereto as well as item Nos. 2, 4 and 7 mentioned in the Schedule and to produce the said documents of title so retained by the vendor when required by the purchaser at his expense before any Court or arbitrator or authorities.

(Add more terms, if any)

7. Deed of Sale of a Business and Assignment of Goodwill

NOW THIS DEED OF SALE WITNESSES that in pursuance of the said agreement and in consideration of the sum of Rupees………………….. paid by the said CD to the said AB (the receipt whereof the said AB hereby admits and acknowledges), and also in consideration of the covenants and conditions thereunder contained to be observed and performed on the part of the said CD the said AB do hereby and hereunder grant, convey, sell, transfer, assign and assure unto and to the use of the said CD all that the trade or business carried under the name and style of…………….. at premises No………….. with:

1. ALL beneficial interest and goodwill of the said AB and also all the books and
2. other debts now due and owing to him on account of the said trade and the business and
3. all contracts and engagements and benefits and advantages thereof which have been entered into with the said AB and
4. all the stock-in-trade goods, fixtures, articles and things which, at the date of this deed, belong to the said AB on account of the said trade and business, and
5. all the rights, title and interest of the said AB to and in the said premises;

TO HAVE AND TO HOLD the same to the said CD absolutely.

AND THAT THE SAID AB does hereby covenant with the said CD that he, the said AB, will not at any time hereafter, either by himself or in collaboration with any other person or persons, or as a partner or as a director of any limited company carry on the said trade and business of, etc., within a radius of……………… miles of, etc.

AND furthermore that the said AB has good right, full power, absolute authority and title to grant, convey, sell, transfer, assign and assure the trade or business of "….." unto and to the use of the said CD in the manner hereunder indicated together with the benefit of the tenancy according to the nature and tenure of the contract.

AND THIS INDENTURE ALSO WITNESSES that in pursuance of the said agreement in this behalf and in consideration of the premises, the said CD do hereby agree with the said AB that he, the said CD, shall and will from time to time save harmless, indemnify and keep indemnified the said AB and his estate and effects against all losses, claims, demands, costs, charges and expenses as against the several sums of money which by the said books appear to be DUE AND OWING from the said AB in respect or the said trade and business, and also from and against the contracts and engagements to which by the said books the said AB APPEARS TO BE NOW LIABLE and or performance or non-performance thereof.

AND THIS INDENTURE ALSO WITNESSES that the said AB do hereby IRREVOCABLY NOMINATE, APPOINT AND CONSTITUTE the said CD as his attorney for him and in his name to do, execute and perform all acts, deeds, and things as shall be necessary or requisite to carry on the said business as his successor and for that purpose to represent him before all appropriate authorities and in all courts of law and to sue for, recover, realise and to give good valid discharges for all moneys due and payable to him on account of or in connection with the said trade or business hereby assigned and appropriate the same for his use and purposes.

8. Deed of Further Charge

NOW THIS DEED WITNESSETH that in pursuance of the said agreement and in consideration of the sum of Rs............. now paid by the mortgagee to the borrower the receipt whereof the borrower hereby acknowledges:

1. The borrower hereby covenants with the mortgagee to pay to the mortgagee on the............. day of............. 2012 next the sum of............. principal amount with interest at the rate of............. per cent per annum, and if the said moneys are not paid on the aforesaid date, to pay interest at the said rate until payment.

2. The borrower as beneficial owner hereby declares that all and singular the property mortgaged under the aforesaid deed dated............. and more particularly described in the schedule attached hereto shall be security, and stand charged with the payment to the mortgagee of the sum of Rs............. the present advance with interest at the rate of............. per cent per annum, from the date of execution of these presents as well as the sum of Rs............. due on the recited mortgage together with interest thereon and shall not be redeemable until on payment to the mortgage deed

dated............. and the present deed.

3. It is further agreed and declared that the provisions contained in the mortgage deed dated............. shall operate and take effect in like manner for securing payment or the money hereby secured as if the same had formed part of the money secured by the said recited mortgage.

9. Deed of Usufructuary Mortgage

WITNESSES that on consideration of the sum of _............. now paid to the Mortgagor by the Mortgagee (the receipt whereof the Mortgagor does hereby acknowledge), the said 'AB' hereby conveys to the said 'CD'. All that etc. (describe the property): from this day AND THAT the Mortgagee

shall be in possession of the mortgaged property under the terms of the deed for securing payment on the............. day of............. 2012, of the principal sum secured, with the interest thereon at _............. per cent per annum, which mortgage money will be set off against the usufruct of the mortgaged property, and the Mortgagee does hereby promise to keep clear accounts thereof.

THE MORTGAGOR hereby agrees that the Mortgagee shall RETAIN POSSESSION of the mortgaged property until the principal sum together with the interest due be paid off out of the proceeds of the property and on payment of the aforesaid sum, the Mortgagee shall EXECUTE AND REGISTER A RELEASE of the mortgaged property in favour of the Mortgagor, AND THAT the Mortgagee also shall not to, execute, perform nor suffer to the contrary any act deed or thing whereby or by reason or means whereof the value of the said property in his possession may be diminished or the same may

otherwise be prejudiced in title or estate.

THE MORTGAGOR does also agree to pay the Government revenue and the municipal tax of the said property regularly and in case he fails to make such payment, the Mortgagee shall be at liberty to pay such revenue and taxes, and such sum paid shall be considered an additional principal sum advanced to the Mortgagor, and shall carry interest at the rate stipulated above.

AND LASTLY, the Mortgagor also agrees that if he, the Mortgagor, does not pay the principal sum with the interest then due on the stipulated date, this CONVEYANCE WILL BECOME ABSOLUTE and the Mortgagee will be entitled to foreclose the mortgaged property, and thereafter the Mortgagor, his heirs, executors, administrators or assigns shall be absolutely DEBARRED of all the rights to redeem the same.

10. MORTGAGE by a Limited Company in favour of a Bank for Securing the Amount due on Cash Credit Account

1. The BORROWERS hereby covenant with the MORTGAGEES that the borrowers will ON DEMAND pay to the mortgagees the balance which shall be owing on the said cash credit account or any other account or for bills or drafts ACCEPTED, PAID OR DISCOUNTED or advances made for the accommodation of the borrowers upto the limit of Rs............. together with interest at the rate of............. % p.a from the date of the said load or advance until payment.

2. The borrowers as beneficial owners hereby mortgage their property known as............. Printing Press, situated at............. together with all the machinery, engine, etc., and buildings, land attached and appurtenant thereto, and more particularly described in the schedule attached hereto as security for payment of the mortgagees of all principal moneys and interest at the aforesaid rate and other moneys hereby secured.

3. The borrowers further covenant with the mortgagees that all accessories to the mortgaged property shall be liable for the amount due under this Deed from the borrowers to the mortgagees.

4. The borrowers hereby further covenant with the mortgagees that the borrowers will during the continuance of this security keep the mortgaged property in GOOD AND SUBSTANTIAL REPAIRS AND INSURED against loss or damage by fire for Rs....................... in General Insurance Corporation of India in the name of the mortgagees, and will duly and punctually pay all premiums and other moneys necessary for effecting and keeping up such insurance.

5. The borrowers further covenant with the mortgagees that the borrowers shall not lease the mortgaged property for any term exceeding one year or accept, surrender of any existing lease without the previous consent in writing of the mortgagees.

6. And it is hereby further agreed and declared that if the borrowers fail to pay the mortgage money with interest as agreed upon, the mortgagees shall be entitled to realise their dues by sale of the mortgaged property and, if the sale proceeds thereof are insufficient to satisfy the mortgagees' dues, to recover the balance from the person and other property of the mortgagors.

7. Provided always that if the borrowers shall pay to the mortgagees the sum of Rs............. or the amount due on said account with interest thereon from the date hereof at the stipulate rate, the mortgagees will at any time thereafter at the request and cost of the borrowers execute a receipt of the mortgage amount or a DEED OF REDEMPTION AND SURRENDER the premises before mortgaged to the borrowers.

9. By a Resolution of the Board of Directors of the 'AB' Company Limited dated............. Mr............. one of the Directors has been authorised to execute this Deed on behalf of the Company.

11. Deed of Licence for use of wall of a Building for publicity and advertisement for goods, etc.

WHEREAS the said CD has applied to AB for the use of the eastern outside wall of his building being premises No........... for the purposes of utilising the same for publicity and advertisement of his goods, a specimen copy whereof with type and design shall be delivered to the licensor, for a period of 2 years.

The following terms and conditions:

1. That the said CD shall be entitled to use the said outer wall of premises No.............. for the purpose of advertisement of his goods by coloured signs, marks, letters or other representations for 2 years from the date, in dimensions measuring.............. and not contrary to any regulations of the

Municipality or other public body or authority.

2. That the said CD shall pay Rs.............. as such advertisement charges per month in advance within the 5th day of every current month.

3. That in the event the said outer wall or the plaster thereof is damaged on account of any act, default or negligence or omission on the part of CD, he shall forthwith execute all the necessary repairs thereto or in the alternative pay adequate compensation to AB on that account.

4. That the said CD shall pay for all taxes and impositions on account of such advertisement.

5. That the said AB shall be entitled to revoke this licence within the said period of two years only on failure to pay regularly the fees or taxes or impositions as aforesaid.

6. That the said CD shall not be entitled to affix on the said wall any representation of other goods nor have any interest in the said wall and further shall indemnify the said AB against any damage suffered in case such display or advertisement is found to be in breach of statutory rules or authoritative order.

12. Agreement of Licence for use of a House Property to a Company for Office Accommodation

Now, it is hereby expressly agreed and declared by and between the parties on the basis of leave

and licence only (which will stand ipso facto revoked on the expiry of the said term) as follows:

1. This writing shall never be construed as any tenancy agreement or lease nor otherwise creating any other right or interest in the property in favour of the OCCUPIERS which is not at all the intention of the parties but on the contrary merely a temporary agreement or arrangement simply to allow the occupiers to use and occupy portion of the premises for their office accommodation under the control and supervision of the OWNER for which purpose the owner shall retain rooms mentioned in the SCEHEDULE. The owner shall have his own staff in the said rooms for the care and supervision and maintenance of and services to the property.

2. The occupiers shall, in consideration of such accommodation as hereunder provided, pay to the owner a fixed sum of _ ..... as charges for such temporary occupation for the period of .... months which sum will be paid at the rate of .... per month on the .... of every current

month without delay or default and a further sum of _ .... for service charges and also use of fittings and fixtures making thus a sum total of _........... per month.

3. The occupiers have as security deposit for such payments and observance of the covenants hereunder contained, kept with the owner a sum of _............. to be repaid without interest on revocation of licence and surrender and deliver the possession of the said portion of the property subject to such deductions as the owner shall be entitled as against the occupiers.

4. The occupiers shall on expiry of the period of 4 years and licence hereunder granted or earlier revocation thereof, surrender the property and deliver the same to the owner when and in such an event he will be entitled to the refund of _................... subject to deductions.

5. The occupiers shall have no right to make any addition or alteration to the property except temporary removable walls by way of adjustments but shall be entitled to make interior decorations only by temporary wooden partitions which they shall remove at their own costs at the time of surrender of the said portion of the property on expiry of the term of the licence hereby granted or earlier revocation thereof and repairs all the damages, if any caused to the property.

13. Deed of Surrender of Lease

NOW THE DEED WITNESSES that in pursuance of the said agreement and in consideration of a sum of Rs.............. being the token consideration paid by the said CD to AB, the said AB as beneficial user of the said property do hereby give up and relinquish all his leasehold estate and interest in and surrender and deliver possession to the said CD of the premises (or, etc.) comprised in and by the said deed of lease TO HOLD the same as before execution of the lease by the said CD TO HOLD THE INTENT and object that the same shall stand determined to all intents and purposes and that the residue of the said term of.............. years created by the said deed of lease, and all other rights and interests of the said AB in the said premises (or, etc.) BY VIRTUE OF THE SAID DEED shall stand extinguished and merged in the reversion freehold and inheritance of the premises with immediate

effect as if the said lease was never granted nor intended.

AND THIS INDENTURE further witnesses that in consideration of the surrender of the lease which is accepted by the lessor he the said CD do hereby release and discharge the lessee AB, his successor and estate from all claims, demands and liabilities on account of future rent and or arising out of performance or non-performance or hereinbefore recited Indenture of lease.

14. Deed of Assignment of Shares in a Company

That in consideration of the sum of Rs.................... (Rupees....................) paid by the assignee to the assignor, the receipt whereof the assignor hereby acknowledges, the said AB hereby assigns, sells and transfers to the said CD.................... Equity Shares of Rs.................... each, fully paid up, bearing

consecutive Nos................. to.................... (inclusive), which stand in the name of the assignor in the Register of Members of........................ Co. Ltd. TO HOLD the same to the assignee absolutely, subject nevertheless to the conditions on which the assignor held the same up to date AND the assignee hereby agrees to take the said Equity Shares subject to such conditions.

15. Deed of Assignment of Policy of Life Assurance

AND WHEREAS the said AB has agreed to transfer and assign to the said CD the said policy of assurance of a sum of Rs......................... (Rupees..................);

THIS DEED WITNESSES that in consideration of the sum of Rs........................ (Rupees........................) the receipt whereof the said AB hereby acknowledges, the said AB as beneficial owner, hereby transfers and assigns unto and to the use and for the benefit of CD the hereinbefore recited policy of assurance, and the sum of Rs........................ (Rupees........................) hereby assured and all the other

moneys, benefits and advantages to be had, recovered or obtained under or by virtue of the said policy: TO HOLD the same unto and to the use of the said CD absolutely, subject to the conditions as to payment of future premiums and otherwise to be henceforth observed in receipt of the said policy: AND the said AB hereby covenants with the said CD that he, the said AB, shall not do, or knowingly suffer anything to be done, whereby the said policy may be rendered void or voidable or the said CD or his heirs, executors, administrators or assigns may be prevented from receiving the said sum of Rs............................ (Rupees..............................) or any benefit thereunder.

16. Deed extending Period of a Partnership

That the said A.B., C.D. and E.F. will remain and continue partners together in the said trade or business of................................ for the further term of................................ years to be counted from the................................ day of................................ 2012 the day on which the original deed of partnership shall expire, upon such and the same terms and conditions, and with, under and subject to such and the same covenants, provisions and agreements as are expressed and contained in the said original deed of partnership to which this agreement is appended, and to which the said partners hereto, their respective legal representatives would have been subject or liable, if the said deed of partnership and the partnership thereby created, and the several covenants, declarations, provisions and agreements therein mentioned and contained had been made or entered into for the term of ten years instead of the term of 5 years.

17.Receipt executed by Retiring Partner acknowledging to have received the amount due to him on account of his share in the Partnership Property

I, A of..................... aged..................... S/o..................... (the retiring partner) hereby acknowledge to have received from B of..................... (the continuing partner) the sum of Rs..................... being the full amount of all moneys due or owing to me in respect of my share as partner in the business of..................... carried on under the name of..................... by me in partnership with the said B up to day of..................... under the Deed of Partnership Dated.....................

18. Notice to Determine Partnership at Will

To

Messrs C and D of.....................

I hereby give you notice that I intend to dissolve the partnership, substituting between us under the Articles of Partnership dated..................... from the day of.......................

Sd/-

19. Deed of Revocation of a Trust

WHEREAS

1. by a deed of trust dated........................ the SETTLOR transferred him property to the TRUSTEE upon trust to sell the same and with the proceeds of the sale to pay the debts due from the Settlor to the several creditors named in the said deed;

2. trust created as aforesaid has NOT YET BEEN COMMUNICATED to any of the aforesaid creditors;

NOW THIS DEED WITNESSES that the Settlor hereby revokes the trust created by the aforesaid deed of trust.

20. SPECIAL POWER-OF-ATTORNEY FILED WITH THE REGISTRAR AT THE TIME OF INCORPORATION OF A COMPANY

Shri....................., Secretary, ... to represent us before the Registrar of Companies in connection with the incorporation of our Company under the name of..................... He is authorised to make any modification, alteration, correction, additions, in the Memorandum and Articles of Association and other documents filed with the Registrar of Companies for the registration of the Company. He is also authorised to collect the certificate of incorporation (now online though!!!).

Station:

Date:

Acceptance by Directors & Signature of confirmation by Secretary

21. Power-of-Attorney to Advocate for Court Case In the Court of etc.

["CAUSE TITLE"]

BY THIS POWER OF ATTORNEY, I, CD, defendant (or, etc.), in the above suit (or case), do hereby nominate, constitute and appoint EF, advocate etc., my attorney, for me, in my name and on my behalf to appear, act and plead in the said case, to make or present written statements, applications or petitions to the court, to withdraw and receive documents and any money from the court or from the opposite party, either in execution of the decree or otherwise, and on receipt thereof, to sign and deliver for me proper receipts and discharges for the same, and to do all other lawful acts, deeds and things in connection with the case as effectually as I could do the same, if I were personally present; to engage and appoint any other advocate or advocates whenever my said advocate thinks proper to do so.

Provided, however, that, if any part of the advocate's fee remains unpaid before the first hearing of the case (or, etc.), or if any hearing of the case be fixed beyond the limits of this town, then and in such an event my said advocate shall not be bound to appear before the court; Provided ALSO that if the case be dismissed by default, or if it be proceeded ex parte, the said advocate shall not be held responsible for the same except in case of gross negligence, wilful default. And all whatever my said

advocate shall lawfully do, I do hereby agree to and shall in future ratify and confirm.

Accepted, subject to the aforesaid conditions.

EF, Advocate.

22. Underwriting Contract

An agreement made the........... day of........... 20...... between.............. of........... (hereinafter called the underwriters) of the one part, and ....Ltd. whose registered office is situate at.............. (hereinafter called the 'the company') of the other part:

Whereas the company is about to offer for public subscription as issue of................. shares of................. each in accordance with the terms of the draft prospectus a copy of which is annexed hereto, or with such modifications therein as may be mutually agreed upon between the company and the underwriters: Now it Is hereby agreed as follows:

1. If the said................. shares shall on or before the................. day of................. 20.......... (or such latter date as shall be mutually agreed upon by the parties hereto not after than the................. day of................. 20.........) be offered by the company for subscription by the public at par on the terms of such prospectus as aforesaid, the underwriters shall on or before the closing of the subscription list apply at par for the said................. shares.

2. If on the closing of the lists under the said prospectus the said................. shares shall be allotted in respect of applications from the public the responsibility of the underwriters is to cease and no allotment is to be made under this agreement but if the said................. shares shall not be allotted to the public but any smaller number of such shares is so allotted, the undertaking of the underwriters is to stand for the difference between the said................. shares and the number of the shares allotted to the public.

3. The company shall pay to the underwriters in cash within...... days from the allotment of the said................. shares a commission at the rate of p.c. on the nominal value of the shares.

4. This agreement is to be IRREVOCABLE on the part of the underwriters and is to be sufficient in itself to authorise the company in the event of the underwriters not applying for the said................. shares to cause application to be made for such shares or any part thereof in the name and on behalf of the underwriters in accordance with the terms of the said prospectus and authorise the directors of the company to allot the said................. shares to the underwriters.

23. Petition for Scheme of Merger or Amalgamation

In case any question is asked as to "Draft a Petition" to be filed with High Court. The following could be the points:

[insert CAUSE TITLE]

1. The object of the petition is to sanction the scheme of merger.
2. The company was incorporated in ____with details of the company.
3. The main objects of the company are: [list the objectives]
4. The terms of the scheme are: [list the terms of the scheme]
5. The company has made an application to court in Form 33 and Court has given directions in Form 35.
6. The Notice as per Form 36 is issued with Proxy and advertised as per the courts directions [copy of all the proofs is enclosed].
7. The meeting was duly convened and the requisite majority has given its approval.
8. Further the court appointed Chairman has submitted his report in Form 39.

Now, the petitioner humbly prays before the Honourable Court,

1. That the said scheme to be sanctioned so as to be binding on the said class of members or creditors of the company.
2. Or pass such other order as the court may deem fit.

(The said petition shall be verified by an affidavit in Form 25.)

24. NOTICE OF FORFEITURE

.... Limited

Regd Office ....

Date ....

Dear Member,

Sub.: Non-payment of allotment money

You were allotted .... equity shares in the company on ...... The allotment money of Rs. ...... in respect of these shares, which was payable by you on or before .... pursuant to our allotment advice dated .... has not so far been paid by you in spite of 3 reminder notices sent to you earlier.

In exercise of the power conferred by Article ..... of the Articles of Association of the Company, the Board of Directors of the company by its resolution passed on .... has decided to give you final opportunity to pay the unpaid allotment money to avoid the forfeiture of your shares in terms of article ...... of the Articles of Association of the company to pay the allotment money on or before .... together with interest thereon at .... per annum for the period from ..... till the date of payment.

Please note that failure to pay the allotment money including interest thereon within the period stipulated above will lead to forfeiture of your shares.

You are aware that we have already given you three notices with a view to avoiding forfeiture of your shares.

In case you have already paid the allotment money, please ignore this notice.

By order of the Board of Directors

For .... Limited

Company Secretary

25. A Specimen of the Letter of Offer to the Prospective Company Secretary

Name and Address of the company.

Ref. No. Date:

Mr……………………..

………….…………..

Dear Sir,

I have been directed to advise you that the Board of Directors of the company have decided to appoint you as Secretary of the company and the said assignment is hereby offered to you. You are requested to join the service of the company on or before………….. and contact the undersigned so that you may be introduced to the concerned persons before you start functioning.

1. You will be considered to have been appointed with effect from the day you actually join duty.

2. The company shall pay to you a monthly basic salary of Rs……. in the time scale of pay of Rs……………………… with other allowances as are applicable to other employees of the company in the same time scale of pay.

3. You will enjoy other benefits like the medical expenses reimbursement, leave travel allowance, bonus etc. as may be permissible under the company's service rules.

4. You shall be allowed casual leave/sick leave/festival holidays, weekly off days and earned leave as per rules of the company.

5. The company may terminate your service without giving you any notice if you are found by the Board of Directors of the company not performing your assigned duties and your statutory duties properly and to the satisfaction of the Board.

6. As Company Secretary you shall be exclusively responsible: (a) for complying with all the provisions of the Companies Act and the various Rules framed thereunder; (b) maintaining all the statutory and non-statutory essential registers, books, files, records, papers etc.; (c) preparing and filing with the Registrar of Companies and other concerned authorities the required reports, returns, documents, papers etc. complete in all respects and within the prescribed periods of time; and (d) for carrying out the instructions, directions and advice of the Board of Directors of the company given to you from time to time.

7. You shall devote your whole time and attention to the work of the company during your tenure as Company Secretary and shall work with due diligence and using your abilities to your best. You shall obey the orders of the Board of Directors of the company. You shall do your best to promote the interest of the company and shall faithfully serve the company.

8. Please convey your acceptance of the offer and the terms and conditions attached thereto by signing the carbon copy of this letter and returning the same to the company within 7 days from the receipt hereof.

Thanking you.

Yours truly

For………….Ltd.

(………..…………….)

Managing Director

I accept the above offer of the post of Company Secretary with all the terms and

conditions attached thereto and shall join on…………..

(………..…………….)

Company Secretary

26. SPECIMEN FORM OF REVISION PETITION

CAUSE TITLE

[the following is the cause title]

In the High Court of……………………

Civil Appellate Jurisdiction

Civil Revision No…………………… of 20…

IN THE MATTER OF:

ABC S/o…………………… R/o……………………………………

…Petitioner

Versus

XYZ S/o…………………… R/o……………………………………

…Respondent

AND

IN THE MATTER OF:

CIVIL REVISION AGAINST THE ORDER DATED…………………… PASSED BY THE LEARNED SUB-JUDGE, IST CLASS…………………… IN THE SUIT ENTITLED ABC -VS.- XYZ (CIVIL SUIT NO. …………………… OF 20….)

May it please the Hon'ble Chief Justice, High Court of…………………… and his companion Justices.

The petitioner MOST RESPECTFULLY SHOWETH:

A. That the petitioner named above has filed a suit against the respondents for the recovery of possession of a house situated in……………………, fully described in the plaint. The suit is pending in the court of Sub-Judge Ist Class…………………… and the next date of hearing is……………………

B. That on being summoned the respondent appeared before the court below and filed his written statement wherein he denied the petitioner's title set up in the suit property.

C. That the trial court framed issues on……………… and directed the petitioner (plaintiff) to produce evidence, upon which the petitioner promptly furnished to the court below a list of witnesses and also deposited their diet expenses etc., making a request that the witness be summoned by that Court.

D. That the date of hearing is……………………, 201.., none of the witnesses of the petitioner had appeared.

In the facts and circumstances discussed above the petitioner prays that this Hon'ble Court be pleased to quash and set aside the order under revision and direct the court below to provide assistance of the court for summoning the plaintiff witnesses.

PETITIONER

[Affidavit to be filed in support of the fact that the contents of the accompanying revision petition are true and correct to the best of the deponent's knowledge and that nothing has been kept back or concealed].

27. Affidavit of Creditor in proof of his debt in Proceeding for the Liquidation of a Company

[INSERT CAUSE TITLE]

I, A.B., aged........... years, son of Shri.............. resident of......................., do hereby on oath (or on solemn affirmation) state as follows:

1. That the abovenamed company was on the.............. day of................., 20...., the date of the order for winding up the same, and still is justly and truly indebted to me in the sum of Rupees.......................... (Rs........................) only in account of (describe briefly the nature of the debt).

2. That in proof of the aforesaid debt I attach hereto the documents marked A, B and C.

3. That I have not, nor have any person or persons by my order or to my knowledge or belief for my use, received the aforesaid sum of Rupees................. or any part thereof, or any security or satisfaction for the same or any part thereof except the sum or security (state the exact amount of security).

4. That this my affidavit is true, that it conceals nothing and no part of it is false.

Sd/- A.B.

Dated....................... 20... Deponent

Verification

I, the above named deponent, verify that the contents of paragraphs 1 to 4 of this affidavit are true to my personal knowledge.

Sd/- A.B.

Dated.......................

I, ... s/o.. r/o.................................. .... declare, from a perusal of the papers produced by the deponent before me that I am satisfied that he is Shri A.B.

Sd/-.......................

Solemnly affirmed before me on this....................... day of....................... 20....... of....................... (time) by the deponent.

Sd/-.......................
(Oath Commissioner)

28. Lease Agreement with Lessor, Lessee and Bank as Financing Party

THIS **TRIPARTITE** (*involving 3 parties*) AGREEMENT this............................ day of............. (month) .... (year in words) .... BETWEEN.............. an existing Company within the meaning of the Companies Act, 1956 and having its registered office at.............. (hereinafter called "the Lessor Company" which expression shall unless excluded by or repugnant to the context be deemed to include its successors and assigns) of the first part, ...a Company incorporated under the Companies Act, 1956 and having its registered office at.............. (hereinafter called "the Lessee Company" which expression shall unless excluded by or repugnant to the context be deemed to include its successors and assigns) of the second Part

AND.............. a nationalised Bank carrying on business amongst other places in India at.............. (hereinafter called "the Bank" which expression shall unless excluded by or repugnant to the context be deemed to include its successors and assigns) of the third part;

WHEREAS

1. under an Agreement for Hypothecation dated.............. executed by the Lessor Company in favour of the Bank, the Bank granted to the Lessor Company a sum of Rs.............. as and by way of advance in current account to enable the Borrower to purchase.............. (hereinafter referred to as "the said equipment") for the purpose of leasing out the said equipment to the Lessee Company, inter alia, secured by hypothecation of the said equipment upon the terms and conditions therein contained;

2. the Lessor Company has entered into an Agreement for Lease with the Lessee Company on the...... day of...... for leasing out the said equipment to the Lessee Company subject to the payment of rent/hire charges thereby reserved and also subject to the other terms and conditions therein contained;

3. in terms of the sanction of the Bank, the Bank will allow the Lessor Company to grant lease of the said equipment to the Lessee Company, inter alia, upon the following conditions:

(a) that the lease of the said equipment is to be granted by the Lessor Company to the Lessee Company with the consent of the Bank and the Lessee Company should confirm that the said equipment is subject to the Bank's charge under the said Agreement for Hypothecation dated..............;

(b) that the Lessee Company should directly pay to the Bank the rent/hire charges and interest payable by the Lessee Company to the Lessor Company in terms of the said Agreement for Lease dated..............;

(c) the Bank through its officers, agent and nominee be entitled to inspect the said equipment at such time as the Bank may think fit;

(d) that the Lessor Company shall execute a Deed of Assignment in favour of the Bank IRREVOCABLY authorising the Bank to collect rent/hire charges to be paid by the Lessee Company to the Lessor Company towards liquidation of the moneys advanced by the Bank to the Lessor Company and all interest accrued thereon.

NOW THIS AGREEMENT WITNESSETH and it is hereby agreed and declared by and between the parties hereto as follows:

1. The lessee Company hereby confirms that the said equipment is subject to the hypothecation/charges created by the Lessor Company in favour of the Bank under the Agreement for Hypothecation dated..............

2. The Lessee Company hereby undertakes the Bank not to deal with the said equipment which will prejudice the interest of Bank and not to assign or transfer the benefit of the said Agreement of Lease dated..............

3. The Lessee Company hereby undertakes the Bank that the Lessee Company shall not have any claim on the moneys to be realised under the insurance policies to be taken out in respect of the said equipment.

4. That the Lessor Company hereby Irrevocably and unconditionally authorises the Lessee Company to pay all

DRAFTING, APPEARANCES & PLEADINGS

the rent/hire charges payable by the Lessee Company to the Lessor Company in terms of which the Lessee Company hereby confirms and acknowledges.

5. The Lessee Company hereby irrevocably and unconditionally agrees, confirms and declares that irrespective of any disputes between the Lessor Company and the Lessee Company as regards terms, conditions and covenants contained in the Agreement for Lease dated.............., the Lessee Company shall directly pay to the Bank rent/hire charges and interest thereon payable by the Lessee Company to the Lessor Company in terms of the Agreement for Lease dated..............

6. The Lessor Company and the Lessee Company hereby jointly declare and confirm that the Bank through its officers, agent and nominees will be entitled to inspect the said equipment which will be in the possession of the Lessee Company in terms of the Agreement of Lease dated.............. and to take possession thereof if the Bank so thinks fit.

7. The Lessee Company hereby also confirms and declares that if the Lessee Company fails to pay the rent/hire charge to the Bank in terms of these presents, the Bank will be at liberty to take possession of the said equipment if the bank so desires to protect the interest of the Bank.

8. The Lessee Company hereby agrees that the said equipment will bear the seal "hypothecated............................ Bank".

NOW THIS AGREEMENT FURTHER WITNESSETH as follows:

(a) That in pursuance of the said agreement and in consideration of the premises aforesaid, the Lessor Company as beneficial owner hereby TRANSFERS AND ASSIGNS UP to the Bank all the rent/hire charges payable to the Lessor Company by the Lessee Company under the Agreement for

the Lease dated.............. together with power for the Bank to sue, call up or recover and give effectual discharge for the same in the name of the Lessor Company or otherwise.

(b) That the Lessee Company hereby agrees to pay duly and punctually all rents/hire charges payable by the Lessee Company to the Bank under the said Agreement for Lease dated.............. and upon such payment to the Bank the Lessee Company shall be fully discharged from its obligation for payment of the rents/hire charges to the Lessor Company under the said Agreement for Lease dated..............

(c) That the Bank upon receipt of the rents/hire charges mentioned above shall be at liberty to adjust and appropriate the said rents/hire charges in liquidation of the amounts due and payable for principal and interests for the loan granted under the said Agreement for Hypothecation dated..............

(d) That the Lessor Company hereby covenants with the Bank that the Lessor Company has not received any rent/hire charges in advance nor any deposit or advance or premium from the Lessee Company adjustable against the said rents/hire charges.

IN WITNESS WHEREOF the parties hereto have executed these presents on the day, month and year first above written.

SIGNED AND DELIVERED for and on behalf of.............. by Mr.............. Constituted Attorney under the Power of Attorney dated.............. in the presence of..............

29. DRAFT LOAN AGREEMENT

This Loan Agreement ("Agreement") is made on this 11th day of April 2012

BY

Labz Public Company Limited, a company incorporated under the laws of Thailand, having its registered office at 294 - 300, Kingston Road, Bangkapi, Huaykwang, Bangkok 10320, Thailand (hereinafter referred to as the "Lender 1"); &

Comfy office furnishing & General Trading, a partnership having its office at P.O. Box No. 14662, Qualcom, Arabia (hereinafter referred to as the "Lender 2")

AND BETWEEN

Labz Furniture India Private Limited, a private company incorporated under the laws of India, having its registered office at No. 546, 1st Floor. Wales Road, Kolkata - 560 03 (hereinafter referred to as the "Borrower").

WHEREAS THE LENDERS are the shareholders of the Borrower company holding 40% and 30% of shareholding in the Borrower company.

IT IS AGREED as follows:

1. **Loan Amount:** The loan amount under this agreement shall be Rs. 10,00,00,000/- (RUPEES Ten Crores only) (hereinafter referred to as the "Loan Amount").

The currency of account under this Agreement is RUPEES.

2. **Drawdown:** Subject to the terms and conditions hereof, the Lender shall make such advances of credit in Rs. to the Borrower as the Borrower may from time to time make a drawdown request ("Advance") by notice to the Lender, provided that the aggregate of all Advances outstanding and requested at any time shall not exceed the Loan Amount.

3. **Requests for Advances:** Each drawdown request for an Advance under Clause 2 shall be in writing or by electronic mail and executed by an authorised representative of the Borrower, specifying the amount of that Advance.

4. **Interest :** Interest on the outstanding principal amount and other outstanding amounts under this agreement will be calculated and payable in arrears by the Borrower to Lenders on each Interest Payment Date at a fixed rate of simple interest equal to 10% per annum.

5. **Use of Proceeds:** Except as the Lender may otherwise agree in writing, the proceeds of the Advances shall be used by the Borrower for the purpose of acquiring capital goods/new project and expansion of the project.

6. **Payment and repayment and cancellation:** Maturity Date for each Advance shall be the date falling 3 years after the date of last Advance under this Agreement or such later date as the parties may agree in writing.

7. **Rank of Obligations:** All indebtedness under this Agreement is a direct and unsecured obligation of the Borrower and will at all times rank at least equally.

8. **Representations and warranties:** The Borrower represents, warrants and undertakes, as at the date of this Agreement and will be deemed to represent, warrant and undertake as at the date of the Security Document and each Advance , that the Borrower is a company duly incorporated, organized and validly existing under the laws of India and the terms of this agreement.

9. **Covenants:** The Borrower agrees to

(a) Pay all sums of money when due hereunder;

(b) Promptly notify Lender of the occurrence of any Event of Default.

(c) Use the proceeds of the Advance only for the purpose set out in this Agreement.

10. Taxes and deductions: All amounts payable by the Borrower under this Agreement shall be made in Rs. into such bank account as shall be indicated by the Lender. All such amounts shall be paid in full except for any present or future deductions of any nature (except to the extent required by law or regulation).

11. Events of Default: Any one of the following events shall constitute an event of default (each, an "Event of Default") under this Agreement: the non-payment when due of any sum payable hereunder beyond a period of 180 days from the date of receipt of notice of such non-payment and where the representation or warranty made by or on behalf of the Borrower in any documents was incorrect or false when made or deemed to be made.

12. Notices: Any notice under this Agreement shall be in writing or from e-mail id registered with the company.

13. Amendments: This Agreement, or any provision hereof, can only be amended in writing signed by each of the parties.

14. Costs: Each of the parties shall bear its own normal costs in connection with this Agreement.

15. Governing Law: This Agreement shall be governed by and construed under the laws of The India.

16. Jurisdiction: The parties to this Agreement hereby submit in respect of any suit, action or proceeding arising out of this Agreement to the jurisdiction of the courts of Kolkata.

IN WITNESS WHEREOF, the Borrower and the Lender have entered into this Agreement on the date set forth at the beginning of this Agreement.

For and on behalf of

Labz Public Company Limited, Bangkok

By: ………………………………… By: …………………………………

Name: Name:

Title: Director Title: Director

For and on behalf of

Comfy office furnishing & General Trading , Arabia

By: …………………………………

Name: Title: Partner

30. THE COMPANIES ACT 1956

COMPANY LIMITED BY SHARES

MEMORANDUM OF ASSOCIATION (MoA)

OF

LEARN LABZ KNOWLEDGE SHARING PRIVATE LIMITED

I. The name of the Company shall be **LEARN LABZ KNOWLEDGE SHARING PRIVATE LIMITED.**

II. The Registered Office of the Company shall be situated in the State of Tamil Nadu.

III. The Objects for which the Company is established are:

A. The main objects for which the Company is incorporated are to make learning an interesting experience through various means and modes of education, as & when made available through the latest technologies and ancient wisdom.

B. The objects incidental or ancillary to attainment of the above main objects are to acquire spaces, rent equipments, execute agreements as required to promote the main objects of the company.

C. The Other Objects of the company not included in (A) and (B) are to do advertising and indulge in creating designs, animation and enter into the world of graphics.

IV. The liability of the Members is limited.

V. The authorized Share Capital of the Company is Rs. 100,000/- (Rupees One Lakh Only) divided into 1,000 (One thousand) equity shares of Rs. 100 (Rupees One Hundred Only) each.

VI. We, the several persons whose names, addresses and descriptions are subscribed hereunto are desirous of being formed into a Company pursuant of this company Memorandum of Association and we respectively agree to take the number of shares in the Capital of the Company set opposite our respective names.

Sl. No	Signature, Name, Address, description and Occupation of subscribers	Number of Equity Shares taken by each subscribers	Witness with name, address, occupation and description

31. THE COMPANIES ACT 1956

COMPANY LIMITED BY SHARES

ARTICLES OF ASSOCIATION (AoA)

OF

LEARN LABZ KNOWLEDGE SHARING PRIVATE LIMITED

Table 'A' applicable with modification

1. The Regulations contained in Table A in Schedule I to the Companies Act, 1956, so far as the same may be applicable to a Private Company as defined in the Act, shall except otherwise and to the extent provided in these Articles, apply to this Company, in the same manner as if all such regulations of Table A are specifically contained in these Articles.

PRIVATE COMPANY

2. The company is a Private Company within the meaning of Section 3(1)(iii) of the Act, and accordingly the paid up capital of the company is not less than Rs.1,00,000 or such other higher sum as may be prescribed by the Central Government from time to time.

SHARE CAPITAL

3. The authorised capital of the company is as mentioned in the capital clause of Memorandum of Association as amended from time to time.

TRANSFER OF SHARES

4. The Directors may in their absolute and uncontrolled discretion and without assigning any reason decline to register or acknowledge any transfer of shares.

DIRECTORS

5. Subject to section 259 of the Act, the Company may from time to time in General Meeting increase or reduce the number of Directors.

SHARE QUALIFICATION

6. It shall be necessary for a Director to hold atleast One Qualification share in the Company.

RETIREMENT BY ROTATION

7. At every Annual General Meeting of the Company, one-third of the Directors for the time being as are liable to retire by rotation, or if their number is not three or a multiple of three, then the number nearest to one-third shall retire from office.

APPOINTMENT OF DIRECTORS BY TYE BOARD

8. The Board of directors shall have the power to appoint directors under Casual Vacancy or as Additional directors or Alternate director as per the provisions of Companies Act or such other law as applicable.

REMOVAL OF A DIRECTOR

9. Subject to Section 284, the company may by ordinary resolution remove any Director and may by ordinary resolution appoint another person in his or her stead.

GENERAL MEETINGS

10. A general meeting of the Company may be called by giving not less than seven days notice.

SEAL

11. The Company shall have a Common Seal and the Board shall provide for the safe custody thereof.

SIGNATURES

Sl. No	Signature, Name, Address, description and Occupation of subscribers	Witness with name, address, occupation and description

32. Letter to Director for passing a resolution by circulation along with draft resolution

To

Mr.-------------------

Address in India only

Dear Sir,

We are stating hereunder following resolution which is intended to be passed as a resolution by circulation as provided in Section 289 of the Companies Act,1956 for your kind consideration.

"RESOLVED that pursuant to the provisions of Section 313 of the Companies Act, 1956,read with those of Article.......... Of the Articles of Association of the companies, Shri.........be and is hereby appointed as alternate director to Shri.............. during the latter's absence for a period of not less than three months form the state of .... and that the alternate director shall vacate his office as and when Shri.............returns to the said State."

You are requested to return the duly signed duplicate copy of this letter at the registered office of the company within .... Days of this, mentioning your assent/dissent

Yours truly

For -----------------

Company Secretary

33. Notice of disqualification under Section 274(1)(g)

Elantro Ltd.

Registered office ....

To

Shri ....

....

We regret to write to you that since M/s.ABC Co.Ltd. (address..............................) of which you are a director has not filed annual accounts and annual report for a continuous period of three financial years form ------------ to ---------- under section 274(1) (g) of the Companies Act.1956, you are not eligible for being appointed as as director or the company in its ensuing AGM where you due to retire by rotation.

You may kindly note that by virtue of this disqualification. You shall not be eligible to be appointed as director of our company for a period of five years.

Yours truly,

(signed)

Company Secretary

34. NOTICE FOR BOOK CLOSURE

Name of Company: ....

Registered office: ....

Notice

Pursuant to Section 154 of the Companies Act, 1956 and the applicable clauses of the Listing Agreement, notice is hereby given that the register of members and the share transfer register of the company will remain closed, for the purpose of payment of final dividend, from the............ day of................. (Month)............2012 to the .... day of 2012 (both days inclusive).

Members of the company are requested to intimate to the company at its registered office above, their latest postal addresses, where the final dividend warrants may be sent by the company.

Place :...........................

Date: ....

For ....Limited

(.......................................)

Company Secretary

DRAFTING, APPEARANCES & PLEADINGS

35. Resolution approving transfer of Shares

Kind of Meeting : Board or Committee of Board

Type of Resolution : Board Resolution

"RESOLVED THAT the share transfer application(s) as described in the Share Transfer Register being Transfer Nos.............to.......... for the transfer of ....Equity preference Shares in the company be and are hereby approved and that the transferees mentioned therein be registered as members of the company in the place of the respective Transferors in respect of the shares so transferred in the Register of Members of the company.

Refer Company Secretarial Practice portions for more drafting under Company Laws & LLP

PRACTICE CASE LAWS MADE FROM EXAM POINT OF VIEW

1. In an arbitration award, the arbitral tribunal awarded interest pendent lite except in relation to Claim No. 4. The petitioner in whose favour the award was made challenged it on the ground that interest was not awarded in Claim No. 4. Decide with reference to case law.

In a case of C.L.Gupta v. Delhi Development Authority, the Supreme court referred to the case of Secretary, Irrigation Department of Orissa v. GC Roy, where the legal principle qua awarding interest had been laid down as follows: Where the agreement between the parties does not prohibit grant of interest and 'where a party claims interest and that dispute along with the claim (for principal amount or independently) is referred to the arbitrator, he shall have the power to award interest pendente lite [pending litigation]. However, the Supreme Court dismissed the petition stating that the above mentioned principle itself makes it clear that it is not necessary that in every case the arbitration should necessarily award interest pendente lite.

2. Ahmed & co., appellant, and Vijay Engineering Limited respondent, were party to a contract, which did not provide for escalation. However, while deciding the dispute, the arbitral tribunal allowed escalation of price to the respondent. This was challenged unsuccessfully before the High Court by the appellant, who ultimately approached the Supreme Court. Discuss in the light of a decided case whether the petition will be allowed. (2007 – December)

In the case of Food corporation of India v. M/S.A.M.Ahmed & Co., the Supreme Court has held that arbitrator can allow reasonable escalation. The Apex Court Observed: Escalation in our view, is normal and routine incident arising out of gap of time in this inflationary age in performing any contract of any type. In this case, the arbitrator found that there was escalation by way of statutory wage revision and thereway of statutory wage of revision therefore, he came to the conclusion that it was reasonable to allow escalation under the claim. Therefore , the arbitrator in our opinion,had jurisdiction to go into this question. In our opinion , having considered the totality of the circumstances , we feel that it would be just and proper to award interest @9% p.a. throughout instead of 12% as awarded by the arbitrator for the period in question. The impugned order of the High court is modified accordingly.

3. Gujarat Transports Limited entered into an agreement with Raja Textiles Limited which provided for settlement of disputes in terms of the rules of Indian Council of Arbitration. When the dispute arose, Gujarat Transports Limited approached the civil court for appointing an arbitral tribunal and the court appointed a retired judge as the arbitral tribunal. Raja Textiles Limited appealed to the High Court and the appeal was dismissed. The company wants to prefer an appeal to the Supreme Court. Advise (2008 – June)

In the case Tata Iron Steel Co.Ltd.v.Tiwari Road Lines, the Supreme Court allowed the appeal and held as follows : The legislative scheme of section 11 is very clear. If the parties have agreed on a procedure for appointing the arbitrator or arbitrators as contemplated by sub section (2) thereof, then the dispute between the parties has to be decided in accordance with the said procedure (as in the given case). In the matter of settlement of dispute by arbitration, the agreement executed by the parties has to be given great importance and an agreed procedure for appointing arbitrators has been placed on high pedestal and has to be given preferenceto any other mode for securing appointment of an arbitrator.

4. An Indian company invited bids for the supply of equipments from a foreign company. The Indian company issued general conditions which were several times revised. The Indian company placed letter of intent which stated that supply should be made once purchase order is placed. No purchase order was placed for the supply. The Indian company decided not to purchase from the foreign company. The foreign company commenced arbitration proceedings before Indian Council of Arbitration. Decide whether there was an arbitration agreement.

In the case of Rand SA v.Bindalagro chem. Ltd & Anr, K.G.Khosla compressors Ltd., the Apex court held that the parties AGREEING UPON the terms subject to which a contract will be governed, when made is NOT THE SAME as entering into the contract itself. "General does not condition of purchase nor the arbitration clause in the "General conditions of purchase" became effective and enforceable Therefore, initialing of revision NO.4 by DR and BINDAL containing the modifications to "general conditions of purchase" did not bring into existence any arbitration agreement to settle disputes between the parties.

5. The government of a particular State and Sriram Holdings (P) Limited went to arbitration and the arbitrator passed an award on 12th October, 2003 against the appellant, copy of which was received by appellant on 23rd October, 2003. Review was sought on 2nd April, 2004, after 6 months from the date of award. Objections to the award were filed after 10 months from the date of the award. Will the appellant be entitled to file objections under the Arbitration and Conciliation Act, 1996? Support your answer with case law. (2009 – December)

In the case of State of Arunachal Pradesh V.M/s. Daman Construction Co., the Supreme Court held that it was absolutely thoughtlessness on the part of the appellant to have written a letter after six months i.e., on 02.04.2004 seeking review of the interim award. Therefore, the reply given by the arbitrator does not give rise to any cause of action to the appellant so as to move an application under Section 34(3) of the Act. Hence the appeal is dismissed.

6. Management issues an appointment letter to a probationer and the relevant para of his appointment letter reads as follows:

"Clause (I) – You are hereby appointed as a Salesman…. You will serve a probationary period of six months; this period of probation may be extended by a further period of three months or more in suitable cases in the absolute discretion of the company. The company has the right to terminate your services during the period of probation or extended period of probation or before confirmation in writing without notice and without assigning any reason whatsoever.'

Do you think what management did is correct? What are the remedies available to the probationer? (2009 – December)

What management did is not correct as the service is terminated without any reason and wrongfull. In the case of Brooke bond of India (p) Ltd v. YK.Gautam, the industrial tribunal directed the reinstatement of probationer and later the Supreme court upheld the award of the Tribunal. In a service contract the terms of employement should be definitely fixed and clearly expressed. The grounds on which the employement may be determined during the term are generally misconduct, negligence or want of medical fitness should be clearly defined.

7. Koncept Limited was under liquidation. The official liquidator sod 4.68 acres of its land to Affluent Limited by auction. Possession of the land was handed over to Affluent Limited but without any conveyance deed in their favour. Affluent Limited served legal notice on the office liquidator demanding conveyance deed, but in vain. After the expiry of the period prescribed under section 80 of the Code of Civil Procedure, 1908, Affluent Limited instituted a civil suit seeking a decree of specific performance. After due hearings, the civil court decreed the suit and directed defendant official liquidator to convey 4.68 acres of land to plaintiff Affluent Limited after considering any objections in response to a notice to be published in newspapers.

The official liquidator complied with the decree and published notices in newspapers. No objections were received. Still the official liquidator did not execute conveyance deed, on the pretext that along with Koncept Limited Kite Co was also under liquidation and had common boundary wall with Affluent Limited Kite Co.'s land had already been sold. Therefore, the official liquidator was willing to execute conveyance for 3.16 acres of land only and not 4.68 acres of land as claimed by Affluent Limited the judgment creditor. This plea was not pressed in written statement or hearings in the court of civil judge. Decide the official liquidator's liability to execute conveyance deed for the entire area. Cite case law, if any (2010 – December)

In the case of Shivarpan Engineering (P) Ltd. v. Official Liquidator, the point to be decided in the case was whether the Official Liquidator is required to execute conveyance deed for the disputed area of the land. The Official Liquidator was bound to give effect to the earlier orders by conveying 4.68acres of land in favour of the applicant. In the event, the Official Liquidator was unable to deliver 4.68 acres, he was at liberty to execute the conveyance for the area that he could convey and was to refund the sum accordingly to the applicant.

8. Desire Limited proposed to increase its share capital. A notice calling for general meeting for considering and approving increase in share capital was issued to the shareholders. Questioning the validity of the notice, a shareholder objected that the amount of proposed increase was not specified in the notice. Is this objection legally valid? Justify your answer. (2010 – December)

Section 173 of the Companies Act, 1956 requires every company to annex at explanatory statement for every special business to be transacted in the meeting on shareholders. The explanatory statement is to bring to the notice of the members a material facts concerning each item of special business. Therefore, the objection of the shareholder is valid since the details on the item to be considered are lacking. The notice is not a valid notice.

9. Yuvi Limited in a litigation, was levied a penalty by the Company Law Board on 1st February, 2009. It submitted an appeal to the High Court impugning the penalty order but after the stipulated period. Can the High Court condone the delay and allow the appeal? Cite case law, if any. (2010 – December)

In the case of Hetal Alpesh Muchhala v.Adityesh Educational Institute, the court negatively held that u/s. 10F of the Companies Act , 1956 a party is allowed to file an appeal to the High Court within 60 days from the date of communication of the decision or order of CLB. As per the proviso to the section 10F this period may be extended for a further period "not exceeding"60 days if the high court is satisfied that the appellant was prevented by "sufficient cause" from filling the appeal within the initial period of 60 days. The words used in the proviso to section 10F of the act are not exceeding 60 days thereby clearly prescribing the time limit of only 60 days. The "not exceeding" cannot be given any other meaning except "not more than" or "not beyond" or "not thereafter". The proviso clearly shows that the power vested in the court to condone the delay of sufficient cause being shown is directory and subject to the discretion of the court. The court held that the legislature has consciously restricted the right of appeal under the section 10F of the act only to questions of law so as to ensure that there is as far as possible an early finality to the issues and consequent redressal of grievances. All the decisions on questions of fact as decided by the Company Law Board are final and conclusive.

10. The Hon'ble Supreme Court (SC) in a recent judgment in the case of "Trimex International FZE Limited, Dubai vs. Vedanta Aluminium Limited, India", the Hon'ble Supreme Court has accepted the unconditional acceptance through emails and held the same to be a valid contract which satisfies the requirements of Section 4 and 7 of the Contract Act 1872 and further it satisfies Section 2(1)(b), 7 of the Arbitration and Conciliation Act 1996. In the absence of a signed agreement inference can be from documents approved and signed by the parties in the form of exchange emails, letters, telegrams which come within Section 10 and 2(e) of the Contract Act 1972.

As per Section 4: The communication of a proposal is complete when it becomes to the knowledge of the person to whom it is made.

As per Section 7: In order to convert a proposal into a promise the acceptance must - be absolute and unqualified; and be expressed in some usual and reasonable manner, unless the proposal prescribes the manner in which it is to be accepted.

If respondent accepts the offer of petitioner following a very strict time schedule, he cannot escape from the obligations that flowed from such an action -

- Arbitration clause can be **inferred** from various documents duly approved and signed by the parties in *the form of exchange of e-mails, letter, telex, telegrams and other means of tele-communication even in the absence of signed agreement* -
- If no inference can be drawn from the facts that the parties intended to be bound only when a formal agreement had been executed, the validity of the agreement *would not be affected by its lack of formality* -
- On facts, the Commercial Offer carried *no clause making the conclusion of the contract* incumbent upon the Purchase Order -Therefore, the moment commercial offer was *accepted by the respondent, the contract came into existence* - Since the contract contained arbitration clause, petitioner made out case for appointment of arbitrator - Arbitration.

Thus, Once a contract is concluded orally or in writing, the mere fact that a formal contract has to be prepared and initialed by the parties would not affect either the acceptance of the contract so entered into or implementation thereof, even if the formal contract has never been initialed. The Court reiterated its stand that one of the main objectives of the Act is to

minimize the supervisory role of the courts. In holding this, the Court observed that if a number of extra requirements such as seals and originals, stamps etc. are added in considering an arbitration agreement, it would amount to increasing the role of courts and not minimizing it. Relying upon UNCITRAL Model Law, the Court concluded it would be improper and undesirable for the courts to add a number of extra formalities not envisaged

by the legislation. The court's objective should be to achieve the legislative intent. Accordingly, the Court held in favor of the Petitioner and appointed a former judge to arbitrate the matter. Thus, no more stamp papers, franking & its execution of contracts just for the purpose of enforceability!!!

11. **Amendment of grounds in application for challenging arbitral awards** [Hindustan Construction Company Ltd case read with others]

The Supreme Court of India has earlier stated that the procedural law is intended to facilitate, not to obstruct, the course of substantive justice. Now the question here is: What principles govern the amendment of an application for setting aside an award under the Arbitration and Conciliation Act 1996 or an appeal under Section 37 of the Act? The crucial difference in the Section lies in the words "not thereafter" as set out in Section 34(3) of the Act, which thus puts a limit on the time for the court to entertain an application to set aside the award. Under Section 5 of the Limitation Act, there is no such bar where it is merely mentioned that any appeal or any application, other than an application under any of the provisions of Order XXI of the Code of Civil Procedure, 1908 (5 of 1908), may be admitted after the prescribed period if the appellant or the applicant satisfies the court that he had sufficient cause for not preferring the appeal or making the application within such period. Thus, under Arbitration Act, as far as application for setting aside the award is concerned, the period of limitation prescribed is three months which can be extended by another period of 30 days, on sufficient cause being shown to the satisfaction of the Court."

Therefore, the court has the power to allow an amendment where an application under Section 34 of the Act has been made within the prescribed limits, if the peculiar circumstance of the case so warrant and it is so required in the interest of justice. However, if the proposed amendment introduces a fresh claim, which would be barred by limitation on the date of application, such amendment cannot be allowed. Although not every amendment in an application to set aside an arbitral award will be taken as a fresh application, no new grounds can be inserted by way of an amendment after the prescribed period of limitation under the act.

12. Court rules on choice of CURIAL law (ie, the law governing the conduct of the arbitral procedure) **in international commercial arbitrations**

In the case of Yograj Infrastructure Limited v Sang Yong Engineering and Construction Co Ltd, the Supreme Court held that there is an implied exclusion of Part I of the Arbitration and Conciliation Act 1996 if the parties have expressly chosen foreign law as the curial law to govern the arbitration procedure.

In India, the Arbitration act is divided into four parts:

- Part I deals with arbitration;
- Part II deals with the enforcement of certain foreign awards;
- Part III deals with conciliation; and
- Part IV provides for certain supplementary provisions.

In a earlier decision in Bhatia International v Bulk Trading SA, the Supreme Court held that Part I of the act is also applicable to international commercial arbitrations, unless the parties either expressly or impliedly exclude all or any of its provisions. However, such decision would have no application once the parties had agreed to a foreign law for the conduct of arbitration proceedings.

The court held that by choosing a foreign curial law as the law of the seat of arbitration, it would be deemed that it was the intent of parties to exclude Part I of the act. The court therefore dismissed the appeal filed by the appellant, affirming that Indian courts had no jurisdiction as Part I of the act was excluded by express agreement between the parties. Thus, in an international commercial arbitration, the governing law of the agreement is Indian, simply choosing institutional rules will not be enough to exclude the applicability of Part I of the Indian act, unless the rules themselves provide for an alternative law to govern the arbitration agreement. Therefore, as a cautionary approach, where parties intend not to be governed by the act's provisions, it is best specifically to provide for the law governing the arbitration agreement separately and specifically to exclude the applicability of Part I of the act.

13. Supreme Court rules on dragging non-parties to arbitration

It happens in many cases where party A claims that a valid agreement exists and the matter should be referred to arbitration, while party B contends that it has not entered into such an agreement and hence ought not to be subjected to arbitration. However, in two of the recent Supreme Court judgments where, due to the peculiar facts of the case, NON-PARTIES TO THE ARBITRATION AGREEMENT WERE JOINED in the arbitration proceedings. These two judgments deal with the practical aspects of resolution of disputes through arbitration. While it may be that a dispute between two parties to an arbitration agreement presents a scenario in which it is **deemed expedient by one of the parties to enjoin non-parties as parties** to such arbitration proceedings, the position in law (as explained by the Supreme Court) amply clarifies the position and leaves no room for ambiguity. It is clear that a party that is NOT A SIGNATORY to an arbitration agreement cannot be dragged into and made party to the arbitration proceedings for deciding a dispute that may have ARISEN BETWEEN THE SIGNATORIES to the arbitration agreement. Furthermore, if a non-party to the arbitration agreement is IMPLEADED as a party in a petition u/s. 11 of the act, the court should either delete such party from the array of parties or, while appointing an arbitrator, make it clear that the arbitrator is appointed only to decide the dispute between the parties to the arbitration agreement.

In *Deutsche Post bank Home Finance Ltd v Taduri Sridhar*, a developer entered into a development agreement with a land owner for the construction of independent houses and multi-story apartments. Under the agreement,

1. the owner agreed to sell an undivided share of the entire property and the developer agreed to construct a residential apartment for the third party.

2. the financier paid the entire sale price to the developer.

The developer and the third party subsequently entered into a construction agreement whereby the third party entrusted the construction of the flat to the developer. Following a delay in construction and delivery of the apartment, the third party issued notice to the developer invoking arbitration (in terms of the construction agreement), and sought reference of the disputes between the developer and the third party to arbitration. The petitioner (ie, the third party) [who has filed a petition to court to appoint Arbitrator] also sought to bring the financier into the dispute by impleading it as a respondent along with the developer. Since only the third party and the developer were parties to the construction agreement containing the arbitration clause, the financier could not be dragged into the dispute between them by being made a party to the petition under Section 11 of the act.

After examining the facts and its previous judgments, the Supreme Court ruled that the two conditions required for appointment of an arbitrator under Section 11 of the act are:

- the existence of an arbitration agreement between the parties to the petition under Section 11 of the act; and
- the existence of disputes to be referred to arbitration.

Thus, the financier cannot be impleaded as a party while invoking the arbitration clause in an agreement between the developer & third party. However, had there been an arbitration clause in the tripartite agreement, financier could also be made as a party.

In *SN Prasad v Monnet Finance Ltd*, the Hon'ble Supreme court observed that, in view of the definitions of arbitration agreement & parties, there could be reference to arbitration only if there were an agreement between the parties. The court further observed that the act makes clear that an arbitrator can be appointed under the act at the instance of a party to the arbitration agreement only in respect of disputes with another party to the arbitration agreement. If there was a dispute between the party to an arbitration agreement with other parties to the agreement and non-parties to the agreement, reference to arbitration or appointment of arbitrator could be only with respect to the parties to the arbitration agreement, and not to the non-parties.

14. Exercise of writ jurisdiction not absolute bar in case of arbitration clause

In its latest judgment the Supreme Court in the case of Union of India v Tantia Construction Pvt Ltd has justified entertaining a writ petition despite the existence of an arbitration clause on the grounds that there was clear injustice warranting the exercise of discretion by the court and allowing the writ petition under Article 226 of the Constitution.

In the given case, East Central Railway (petitioner) awarded a project for the construction of a rail overbridge to the respondent, pursuant to which an agreement was entered into between the parties. Due to an alteration of the layout and plan for construction, the respondent was instructed by the petitioner to execute additional work at the originally agreed contractual price instead of a revised appreciated price. For which the respondent has filed writ of certiorari to be issued quashing the petitioner's order through which it had rejected the respondent's claim for additional costs and further asking that a writ of mandamus be issued directing the petitioner to allow the respondent to complete only the original work and not carry out any additional work. Justifying the possibility of writ, Supreme Court held it was not obligatory for the courts to direct the parties to pursue the alternative remedy of arbitration when injustice was clear from the facts of the case.

The point to be considered here is the ruling in the case of Harbanslal Sahnia v Indian Oil Corporation Ltd where the Supreme Court summarised the exemptions to the above-settled law that no writ would be competent to enforce contractual obligation. At the discretion of the court, an exemption would occur in the following cases:

- where the writ petitioner seeks enforcement of any fundamental rights;
- where there is a failure of principles of natural justice;
- where proceedings are totally without jurisdiction; or

- where an act or its provisions are challenged.

Therefore, although the general rule appears to be that in cases where an alternative forum is available, which may include the resolution of disputes through the arbitration process, the high court will not generally exercise its writ jurisdiction under Article 226 of the Constitution, this is not an inflexible rule or an absolute bar on the high court from exercising its writ jurisdiction. One such exception, as in the latest judgment, is to curb injustice and uphold the rule of law.

15. Supreme Court affirms limited scope of Section 11 of Arbitration and Conciliation Act

Section 11 of the Arbitration and Conciliation Act 1996 deals with the procedure for the appointment of arbitrators. Before going into the case, the following is worth noting as decided in National Insurance Co Ltd v Boghara Polyfab (P) Ltd, the Supreme Court categorised the issues examined and decided in such petitions under Section 11 into 3:

First, the Chief justice or his or her designate must decide whether:

- the party making the application has approached the appropriate court (ie, the court with jurisdiction to consider the application); and
- an arbitration agreement exists between the parties and, if so, whether the party that has applied under Section 11 of the act is a party to the agreement.

Second, the Chief justice or his or her designate must choose either to decide or to leave to the arbitral tribunal the issues of whether:

- the claim is a dead (ie, time-barred) claim or a live claim; and
- the parties have concluded the contract or transaction by recording the satisfaction of their mutual rights and obligations or by receiving final payment without objection.

Finally, the Chief justice or his or her designate must leave exclusively to the arbitral tribunal the issues of whether:

- the claim falls within the scope of the arbitration clause; and
- the claim in question has merit.

In the case of in Indian Oil Corporation v SPS Engineering, the appellant, Indian Oil Corporation, had entered into a contract with the respondent for the execution of certain works at its refinery within a stipulated timeframe. The appellant has invoked the arbitration clause first and got a final award. Then later, the appellant invoked again. The question was whether the chief justice or his or her designate, in exercising his or her power under Section 11 of the act, can examine the tenability of a claim - in particular, whether the claim is barred by res judicata and whether the application was misconceived or made in bad faith. The chief justice or his or her designate is NOT expected to consider the merits of the claim or examine its tenability WHEREAS a mere limited inquiry should be undertaken to determine whether a claim is a dead claim (ie, whether it is evidently time-barred) and NOT beyond that. Thus, the court has discouraged the filing of MERIT-BASED SUBSTANTIVE LEGAL CLAIMS that are raised by parties at the threshold stage of a Section 11 petition, when such claims properly fall within the DOMAIN OF THE ARBITRAL TRIBUNAL and not the chief justice or his or her designate.

16. Is the appointment of a company employee as sole arbitrator bad per se?

The Supreme Court in its recent judgment in Denel (Pty) Limited v Bharat Electronics Limited came out with a decision on appointment of employee as a arbitrator. The legal proposition that emerges from this judgment is that a clause nominating one of the parties' employees as the sole arbitrator in a dispute cannot be treated as bad per se on the grounds of bias or lack of independence. However, if it can be proved that such arbitrator is guilty of misconduct, fraud or is otherwise disqualified, his or her appointment may be considered as bad in law. Care should be taken while drafting such clauses to ensure that the person nominated is not connected with the subject matter (ie, preferably, he or she is from another department within the same organisation).

17. IN KHALIL AHMED BASHIR AHMED V. TUFELHUSSEIN SAMASBHAI SARANGPURWALA, 1988 SCC 155, THE SUPREME COURT HAS HELD:

"In order to determine whether a document created a licence or a lease the real test is to ascertain the intention of the parties i.e whether they intended to create a license or a lease. If the document creates an interest in the property entitling the transferee to enjoyment, then it is a lease; but if it only permits another to make use of the property without exclusive possession, then it is a licence."

18. LATIF ESTATE LINE INDIA LTD & ORS v. MRS. HADEEJA AMMAL & ORS

Registration Act - Sections 17, 18, 32(A) - Sale of immovable property under registered sale deed - Unilateral cancellation of the sale deed and registering the same with the Registrar (contending that consideration was not received) - Whether such unilateral cancellation and registration is valid - **Held, No** and the following decision was taken:

(i) A deed of cancellation of a sale unilaterally executed by the transferor does not create, assign, limit or extinguish any right, title or interest in the property and is of no effect. Such a document does not create any encumbrance in the property already transferred. Hence such a deed of cancellation cannot be accepted for registration.

(ii) Once title to the property is vested in the transferee by the sale of the property, it cannot be divested unto the transferor by execution and registration of a deed of cancellation even with the consent of the parties. The proper course would be to re-convey the property by a deed of conveyance by the transferee in favour of the transferor.

(iii) Where a transfer is effected by way of sale with the condition that title will pass on payment of consideration, and such intention is clear from the recital in the deed, then such instrument or sale can be cancelled by a deed of cancellation with the consent of both the parties on the ground of non-payment of consideration. The reason is that in such a sale deed, admittedly, the title remained with the transferor.

(iv) In other cases, a complete and absolute sale can be cancelled at the instance of the transferor only by taking recourse to the Civil Court by obtaining a decree of cancellation of sale deed on the ground inter alia of fraud or any other valid reasons.

19. BHARAT RASIKLAL ASHRA v. GAUTAM RASIKLAL ASHRA & ANR [SC]

Arbitration and Conciliation Act, 1996 - Section 11-Arbitrator appointed under partnership deed (of a family partnership) of 1998 in the first arbitration application-Application for appointment of arbitrator under the partnership deed 2000 was objected to on the ground of fabrication of deed- Court appoints the arbitrator of 1998 deed to decide the issue of the validity of the 2000 partnership deed- Whether valid-Held, No.

It is clear that the question whether there is an arbitration agreement has to be decided only by the Chief Justice or his designate and should not be left to the decision of the arbitral tribunal. This is because the question whether there is arbitration agreement is a jurisdictional issue and unless there is a valid arbitration agreement, the application under section 11 of the Act will not be maintainable and the Chief Justice or his designate will have no jurisdiction to appoint an arbitrator under section 11 of the Act. This Court also made it clear that only in regard to the issues shown in the second category, the Chief Justice or his designate has the choice of either deciding them or leaving them to the decision of the arbitral tribunal. Even in regard to the issues falling under the second category, this court made it clear that where allegations of forgery or fabrication are made in regard to the documents, it would be appropriate for the Chief Justice or his designate to decide the issue.

It is well settled that an arbitrator can be appointed only if there is an arbitration agreement in regard to the contract in question. If there is an arbitration agreement in regard to contract A and no arbitration agreement in regard to contract B, obviously a dispute relating to contract B cannot be referred to arbitration on the ground that contract A has an arbitration agreement. Therefore, where there is an arbitration agreement in the partnership deed dated 12.6.1988, but the dispute is raised and an appointment of arbitrator is sought not with reference to the said partnership deed, but with reference to another partnership deed dated 19.5.2000, unless the party filing the application under section 11 of the Act is able to make out that there is a valid arbitration clause as per the contract dated 19.5.2000, there can be no appointment of an arbitrator.

PRACTICE OBJECTIVES MADE FROM EXAM POINT OF VIEW

1. Drafting may be defined as the synthesis of law and fact in a language form. Who said this?
2. The process of drafting operates in two planes: ___________ and the verbal.
3. ______________ is an act of conveyancing or transferring any property whether movable or immovable from one person to another permitted by customs, conventions and law within the legal structure of the country.
4. ________________ include summons, notices, requisitions, order, other legal process, and registers, whether issued, sent or kept in pursuance of this or any other Act, or otherwise as per Companies Act.
5. Once the document transferring immovable property has been completed and registered as required by law, the transaction becomes______________.
6. ____________ should be filled in or elaborated as he proceeds with his work.
7. The main function of the _________ is to provide supplementary test to the document with clarity and convenience.
8. __________ includes an order made by the President in the exercise of his constitutional powers.
9. Instrument includes Acts of Parliament. Comment.
10. A common corner will make two tracts of land __________.
11. In a conveyance of fractional part of a __________; it refers to that portion of the premises set aside for private use, and hence does not include the right to occupancy of any part of a street on which it abuts.
12. When used with reference to the quantity of land conveyed, the words "estimated" and "about" are synonymous with the phrase __________.
13. The words "Easterly", "Westerly" when used alone in the description of land, will be construed to mean _____________ unless other words are used to qualify their meaning.
14. Where, however, the land is described as being the _______ of a city lot and a North to South line will divide the lot almost diagonally, it has been held that parol evidence can be introduced on the theory that such evidence neither enlarges nor diminishes the grant, but merely identifies the land.
15. In interpretation of informal agreements, the rule to be applied is that of___________.
16. A _________constitutes the primary evidence of the terms of a contract, or of a grant, or of any other disposition of property.
17. The __________ should contain all the terms and conditions, preceded by recital of all relevant and material facts.
18. It is the ____________ of the document as disclosed from its whole tenor, that must guide the construction of its contents.
19. Sometimes a contract is completed in two parts. Comment.
20. _________ is a paper or other material thing affording information, proof or evidence of anything.
21. The following are documents:
    a. Words printed, lithographed or photographed
    b. A map or plan

c. An inscription on a metal plate or stone

d. A caricature

e. All of the above

22. An __________ is one which contains within the designated boundaries lands which are expected from the operation of the deed.

23. __________ was polled or cut level at the top and had a polled or clean cut edge.

24. The word __________ was written between two or more copies of the document and the parchment was cut in a jugged line through this word.

25. The ________ determines the territorial and legal jurisdiction of a document as to its registration and for claiming legal remedies for breaches committed by either parties to the document and also for stamping the document, as the stamp duty payable on document differs from State to State.

26. Name the clause which gives excuses for non-performance.

27. Proper Law of Contract

28. What if common seal is not affixed in the contracts executed by the company?

29. Quote some sections of Companies Act which requires certain clauses to be included or not to be included in agreements entered into by the companies.

30. There must be reciprocity of interest between the person who wants to enforce the agreement and the person against whom it is sought to be enforced. Comment.

31. Draft a CLAUSE for Services of Communication in an agreement.

32. Where registration is desired the agreement should be attested by __________.

33. __________is a special type of agency, which combines agency with guarantee.

34. A __________ is the premium or price given by the principal to the agent for guarantee, which presupposes a guarantee.

35. The contract of guarantee in that sense is a contract to indemnify. Comment.

36. Whether fidelity guarantee can be enforced against surety if the guarantor continues to employ even after the employee is proved dishonest?

37. Whether past benefit to the principal debtor can be good consideration for a bond of guarantee. Comment.

38. __________ is a document by which legal property in goods passes to the person who lends money on them, but the possession does not pass.

39. The form of transfer by way of hypothecation is regulated in India by __________

a. Indian Contract Act

b. Transfer of Property Act

c. Sale of Goods Act

d. Hypothecation of Goods Act

e. Principles of Equity & Natural justice

40. Alongwith the hypothecation agreements, the loaning institutions including banks have a plethora of other documents executed by the borrowing companies. Name some.

41. In a leave and licence agreement, the owner is deemed to be in _________ possession of the premises and the licensee is in _______ possession of the premises and hence owner is liable to pay Income tax.

42. Transfer in the case of tangible immovable property or in the case of a reversion or other intangible thing can be made only by a _____________.

43. A ___________of immovable property is a contract that a sale of such property shall take place on terms settled between the parties.

44. ____________ is required to be obtained under Section 230A of the Income-tax Act, 1961 by the seller in all cases where the sale consideration of immovable property exceeds Rs.5,00,000/- as a pre-requisite for registration of the Sale Deed with the Sub-Registrar of Assurances under the Registration Act, 1908.

45. In all cases where the consideration money of the property (in Metros) exceeds Rs.10 lakhs, it is obligatory for the parties to enter into an agreement in writing, at least ______ before the intended date of transfer and submit u/s. 269UC of the Income-tax Act a statement in duplicate and in Form 37-I giving such particulars as required therein to the Appropriate Authority within ________ of such agreement.

46. ________ of the Transfer of Property Act prescribes the rights and liabilities of buyer and seller which can be modified by the parties to a contract by mutual consent and contract to the contrary of these provisions.

47. The Transfer of Property Act, 1882 deals with the mortgage of immovable property alone.

48. The mortgagee will take the ______ in lieu of the interest or part payment of the principal or partly in payment of interest or partly in part payment of the principal.

49. ________ is an oral transaction and no documents like Deed of Mortgage is required to be executed and is a cut short method and skips many formalities like compliance of Section 230A of Income-tax Act, 1961, and 293(1)(a) of the Companies Act.

50. Equitable mortgage or Mortgage by deposit of title deeds can be executed only if the property is located in Mumbai, Chennai and Kolkata and other specified towns.

51. For creation of a mortgage, the Financial Institutions usually insist on a resolution of the shareholders under ________ of the Companies Act, 1956.

52. The mortgage recitals are of two kinds. Comment.

53. In case of __________, the property is charged and assured as security for repayment of mortgage debt.

54. In _______, it is absolutely sold to the mortgagee, subject to the covenants as to re-conveyance upon repayment of debt with interest.

55. The mortgagor shall not grant leases of mortgaged property for a period exceeding ________ without the written permission of the mortgagee or accept surrender of existing leases without like permission.

56. Proviso for redemption clause under Mortgage.

57. In________, the mortgagee has a right to take possession of the property whereas in _________, the possession of the property is given to the mortgagee.

58. The deed executed to secure the advance of further sums of money is called________.

59. Under Section 69A of the Transfer of Property Act, a mortgagee having the right to exercise the

DRAFTING, APPEARANCES & PLEADINGS

power to sell is entitled to appoint by writing signed by him or on his behalf a ________ of the income of the mortgaged property or any part thereof.

60. In the absence of the contract or special law or usage to the contrary, a lease of immovable property for agricultural or manufacturing purpose shall be deemed to be a lease from ______, terminable on the part of either lessor or lessee by _______ notice expiring with the end of a year of the tenancy and the lease of immovable property for any other purpose shall be deemed to be lease from _________, terminable on the part of either lessor or lessee, by ________ notice expiring with the end of a month of the tenancy.

61. The lessor or leasing company, in addition to the lease agreement and the guarantee or in substitution of guarantee, may also accept ____________ of the promoters of the business.

62. In case of _________, provision of non-cancellability should invariably be set forth in the lease agreement whereas in _______ the provision of cancellability is provided with responsibility of the lessor for repairs and maintenance, technology transfer and change of know-how and providing knowledge of running the equipment leased out to lessee.

63. ____________ is a power of attorney executed on a plain paper and are usually issued for collecting some documents or papers, dividend interest etc. on behalf of another.

ANSWERS:

1. T Stanley Robinson in "Drafting Its Application to Conveyancing and Commercial Documents" (1980).
2. the conceptual
3. conveyance
4. document
5. conveyance
6. skeleton draft
7. schedule
8. Instrument
9. No. "Instrument" does not include Acts of Parliament unless there is a statutory definition to that effect in any Act.
10. Contiguous
11. designated LOT
12. more or less
13. "due East", "due West"
14. West half of the emand
15. reasonable expectation
16. deed
17. document
18. dominant intention
19. Yes. At first an executory contract is executed and later on an executed contract. In case of any

difference between the preliminary contract and final contract the terms of the latter must prevail.

20. Document

21. E

22. inclusive deed

23. Deed poll

24. Cyrographum

25. Place

26. Force Majeure

27. In international contracts, the parties are subject to different legal systems and, therefore, they have to choose a legal system which will govern the rights and duties of the parties.

28. Non putting of seal or an agreement may not invalidate the agreement if it has otherwise been properly executed. However, if a document purported to be sealed or signed on behalf of the company is proved to be forged, it does not bind the company.

29. Section 119(1): clauses in Trust deed exempting a trustee against liability for breach of trust, where he fails to show the degree of care and diligence required of him as trustee is VOID. Section 294(2): Sole Selling Agent contract executed by Board is not valid if it is does not have a clause that it is subject to approval by the company in the first general meeting held after the date on which the appointment is made.

30. A stranger to the agreement has no enforceable claim and as such no court shall entertain his claim for specific performance. However, specific performance may be enforced not only against a party to the contract but also against a person claiming title under it.

31. "Any notice may be sent through the post to the last known place of abode or business of the party to whom it is given, and if so sent under a registered post shall be taken to be sufficient service thereof."

32. two witnesses

33. Del Credere Agency

34. commission del credere

35. Yes. The primary idea of a guarantee or suretyship is, an undertaking to indemnify the creditors in case the principal debtor does not fulfil his promise.

36. If the employer of a servant whose fidelity has been guaranteed continues to employ him even after a proved act of dishonesty without notice to the guarantor, the surety is discharged.

37. Consideration between the principal debtor and the creditor is good consideration for guarantee given by surety. It is not necessary that the thing done or the promise made for the benefit of the principal debtor should be at the desire of the surety. The word "done" in the above definition shows that past benefit to the principal debtor can be good consideration for a bond of guarantee.

38. Hypothecation agreement

39. E

40. demand promissory note, collateral personal guarantees of managing directors, directors and other persons having substantial interest in the borrowing entities, second charge on fixed assets like land and building and plant and machinery permanently attached to land by legal or equitable mortgage.

41. legal or judicial & in constructive
42. registered instrument
43. contract for the sale
44. Clearance certificate from the Income-tax Officer
45. 3 months & 15 days
46. Section 55
47. Yes. However, mortgage of movables, such as plant and machinery, stock in trade, policy is perfectly a valid transaction even though the possession is not delivered and the mortgage is only a hypothecation.
48. usufruct
49. Equitable mortgage or Mortgage by deposit of title deeds
50. No. It is not necessary for creation of mortgage that the property be located in the specified town or the company making deposit should have its registered office in that town. It is only that the delivery of title deeds should happen in such specified towns.
51. Section 293(1)(a)
52. Firstly, recital as to the title of the Mortgagor and the second form of recital is as to the agreement for loan
53. simple mortgage
54. an English mortgage
55. one year
56. The mortgagee covenants and declares that on payment of his dues, he shall re-transfer the mortgaged property to the mortgagor or his nominee at his expense.
57. English mortgage & usufractuary mortgage
58. Deed of Further Charge
59. Receiver
60. Year-to-year, 6 months, Month-to-month, 15 days
61. pledge of the shares or assignment of insurance policies
62. finance lease, operating lease
63. Letter of Authority